# Atlas of
# WORLD
# HISTORY

# *Atlas of* WORLD HISTORY

**John Haywood,** Ph. D.

*Honarary Teaching Fellow, University of Lancaster, UK*

with

**Brian Catchpole,** M.A. • **Simon Hall,** M.A.

**Edward Barratt,** M.A.

| | |
|---|---|
| **Project director** | Peter Furtado |
| **Cartographic manager** | Richard Watts |
| **Advisory editors** | Jeremy Black<br>*Professor of History, University of Exeter, UK* |
| | K.M. Chaudhuri<br>*Vasco da Gama Professor of European Exploration, European University Institute, Florence, Italy* |
| | Barry Cunliffe<br>*Professor of European Archaeology, University of Oxford, UK* |
| | Brian M. Fagan<br>*Professor of Anthropology, University of California, Santa Barbara, USA* |
| | J.E. Spence<br>*Associate Fellow, Royal Institute of International Affairs, UK* |
| **Academic advisors** | J.I. Catto<br>*Oriel College, University of Oxford, UK* |
| | Professor Robin Cohen<br>*University of Warwick, UK* |
| | Professor J.H. Elliott<br>*Regius Professor of Modern History, University of Oxford, UK* |
| | Professor Harold James<br>*Princeton University, New Jersey, USA* |
| | Professor Maldwyn A. Jones<br>*University of London, UK* |
| | Dr Stewart Lone<br>*Australian Defence Force Academy* |
| | Dr Oswyn Murray<br>*Balliol College, University of Oxford, UK* |
| | Professor A.J.S. Reid<br>*The Australian National University* |
| | Professor Francis Robinson<br>*Royal Holloway, University of London, UK* |
| | Dr Kate Spence<br>*Christ's College, University of Cambridge, UK* |
| | Professor John K. Thornton<br>*Millersville University, Pennsylvania, USA* |

*This page:*
Ottoman janissaries, c.AD 1820

*Opposite above:*
Chinese bronze horse, c.AD 200

*Opposite below:*
Mughal Indian rug design, c.1550

*Following page:*
*Above:* French revolutionary caricature, c.1789
*Below:* Russian revolutionary poster, c.1920

| | |
|---|---|
| *Art director* | Ayala Kingsley |
| *Art editor* | Martin Anderson |
| *Cartographic editor* | Tim Williams |
| *Editors* | Susan Kennedy |
| | Peter Lewis |
| *Cartographer* | Nathalie Johns |
| *Picture research* | Claire Turner |
| *Production* | Clive Sparling |
| *Editorial assistance* | Marian Dreier |
| *Typesetter* | Brian Blackmore |
| *Illustrations* | Charles Raymond |
| *Proof reader* | Lynne Elson |
| *Index* | Ann Barrett |

AN ANDROMEDA BOOK

Produced and prepared by
Andromeda Oxford Ltd
11–13 The Vineyard
Abingdon
Oxfordshire OX14 3PX

© Andromeda Oxford Ltd 1999

This edition produced in 1999
for Prospero Books, a division of
Chapters Inc., 90 Ronson Drive,
Etobicoke, Ontario M9W 1C1

Exclusive to Chapters in Canada
ISBN 1–55267–307–3

# Contents

## Part 1
## The Ancient World
## (4,000,000 – 500 BC)

**Map no.**

1 Human origins • 4,000,000–100,000 years ago
2 Peopling the Earth • 100,000–10,000 years ago
3 Upper Paleolithic Europe • 35,000 years ago–5000 BC
4 The rise of agriculture • 10,000–500 BC
5 The first cities of Mesopotamia • 4300–2334 BC
6 The foundation of ancient Egypt • 6000–2040 BC
7 Neolithic Europe • 5000–2000 BC
8 The first civilizations of east Asia • 6000–500 BC
9 The world • 2000 BC
10 Middle and New Kingdom Egypt • 2040–332 BC
11 The first civilizations of the Mediterranean • 2000–1100 BC
12 Bronze Age Europe • 2000–500 BC
13 The world • 1000 BC
14 The Assyrian and Babylonian empires • 1000–539 BC
15 The Bible lands • 1000–587 BC
16 The emergence of the Greek city-states • 1100–500 BC
17 The first civilizations of the Americas • 4000–500 BC
18 The Achemenid empire of Persia • 559–480 BC
19 The world • 500 BC

## Part 2
## The Classical World
## (500 BC – AD 600)

20 The Persian wars and 5th-century Greece • 499–435 BC
21 The conquests of Alexander the Great • 336–300 BC
22 The world • 323 BC
23 Early Rome and the Punic wars • 509–201 BC
24 The world • 200 BC
25 The Celts • 500 BC – AD 600
26 China from warring states to first empires • 480 BC – AD 220
27 The growth of the world religions • 600
28 The world • 1 BC
29 The growth of the Roman empire • 201 BC – AD 117
30 Crisis and recovery of the Roman empire • AD 117–376
31 Kushan and Gupta India • AD 50–570
32 The world • AD 400

33 The fall of the western Roman empire • AD 376–480
34 Justinian and the origins of the Byzantine empire • AD 480–629
35 Early states of Africa • 500 BC – AD 600
36 The world • AD 600

## Part 3
## The Medieval World
## (AD 600 – 1492)

37 The great Arab conquests • 632–750
38 The rise of the Carolingian empire • 600–814
39 The ancient Maya • 300 BC – AD 800
40 The world • AD 800
41 Viking Age Europe • 793–1050
42 Native cultures of North America • 600–1500
43 Sui and Tang China • 589–907
44 The spread of the world religions • AD 600–1500
45 The world • AD 1000
46 Feudal Europe • 1050–1300
47 The medieval Turkish empires • 1038–1492
48 The Crusades • 1096–1291
49 The creation of the Mongol empire • 1204–1260
50 Medieval Japan and Korea • 600–1500
51 The world • AD 1279
52 War, revolt and plague in 14th-century Europe • 1300–1400
53 The economy of medieval Europe • 1000–1500
54 Renaissance Europe • 1400–1492
55 Toltecs and Aztecs • 800–1520
56 The Andean civilizations to the fall of the Incas • 700–1533
57 The world • AD 1492

## Part 4
## The Early Modern World
## (1492 – 1783)

**58** Reformation Europe • 1492–1560
**59** The rise of the Ottoman empire • 1492–1640
**60** The world • AD 1530
**61** The rise of Mughal India • 1500–1707
**62** The Spanish–American empire • 1492–1783
**63** Japan and the Tokugawa shogunate • 1500–1800
**64** The world • AD 1600
**65** Europe in the age of the Thirty Years War • 1600–1648
**66** European economic development • 1492–1783
**67** The world • AD 1650
**68** Europe in the age of Louis XIV • 1648–1715
**69** The rise of Manchu China • 1644–1783
**70** European exploration of North America • 1500–1783
**71** The world • AD 1715
**72** Sub-Saharan Africa • 1500–1800
**73** Colonial North America •1650–1763
**74** World trade • AD 1492–1783
**75** The American revolution •1763–1783
**76** The world • AD 1783

## Part 5
## The Nineteenth-Century World
## (1783 – 1914)

**77** Europe in the age of revolution • 1783–1800
**78** Napoleonic Europe • 1800–1815
**79** The world • AD 1812
**80** The growth of nationalism in Europe • 1815–1871
**81** Latin America • 1783–1914
**82** The world • AD 1848
**83** Britain and India • 1783–1914
**84** The expansion of the North America • 1783–1890
**85** The American Civil War • 1850–1865
**86** The world • AD 1880
**87** Population and economy of the United States • 1865–1914
**88** The Russian empire • 1783–1917
**89** Africa and the European empires • 1880–1914
**90** The industrial revolution in Europe • 1783–1914

**91** World trade • AD 1830–1914
**92** World population and migration • AD 1830–1914
**93** Japan in the 19th century • 1800–1914
**94** The decline of Manchu China • 1783–1912
**95** Colonialism in southeast Asia • 1783–1914
**96** The European alliance system • 1871–1914
**97** The world • AD 1914

## Part 6
## The Modern World
## (1914 – PRESENT)

**98** World War I • 1914–1918
**99** The world • AD 1920
**100** The making of the Soviet Union • 1917–1941
**101** Europe between the wars • 1918–1939
**102** The Americas • 1914–1945
**103** Japan and the Asian empires • 1914–1941
**104** The Middle East and north Africa • 1914–1948
**105** World War II in Europe • 1939–1942
**106** The world • AD 1942
**107** World War II in Europe • 1942–1945
**108** World War II in Asia • 1941–1945
**109** The world • AD 1950
**110** Europe divided • 1945–1989
**111** The Americas • 1945–Present
**112** Central America and the Caribbean • 1945–Present
**113** East Asia • 1945–1976
**114** The Indo-China wars • 1954–1976
**115** Arab–Israeli conflict • 1948–1977
**116** The world • AD 1974
**117** Decolonization and nationalism in Africa • 1945–Present
**118** The Middle East • 1977–Present
**119** Europe after the Cold War • 1989–Present
**120** The rise of the Pacific rim • 1976–Present
**121** The world • AD 1999

## ACKNOWLEDGMENTS

## INDEX

# USING THIS ATLAS

This book has a consistent organization and, wherever possible, a standard presentation, to help the reader understand the information shown on each map, and to trace a particular story from region to region, or from period to period. The book is arranged in six chronological parts, each with a brief introduction by a leading historian or archeologist.

## WORLD MAPS AND REGIONAL MAPS

The detailed regional maps are arranged in an approximate chronological order, interspersed with unique world maps, each of which shows the world at a key moment in history.

**World map** spreads show the level of political or social complexity in standard categories from earliest times to the present. States and empires are shown in capital letters, dependencies or territories in upper-and-lower case. Societies or peoples which have not yet developed into states are shown in bold upper-and-lower-case type; the colors indicate their level of social organization.

World map spreads carry timecharts which are organized region by region. The text on these spreads includes many crossreferences to relevant spreads elsewhere in the Atlas.

**Regional map** spreads provide a survey of a part of the world between the dates shown in the map title.

Maps are shown in true cartographic projections, each one chosen for the best presentation of the information on the map. North is generally at the top of the page. Some degree of distortion may be found in the case of some maps, such as those of the whole of Asia, which cover a very large section of the world. Where necessary location maps have been included.

Regional map spreads include standard features. The maps use the typographical conventions of the world maps; thick gray lines indicate major borders, thin lines internal borders.

---

### TYPOGRAPHICAL CONVENTIONS

**World maps**

| | |
|---|---|
| FRANCE | state or empire |
| Belgian Congo | dependency or territory |
| Mongols | tribe, chiefdom or people |
| *Anasazi culture* | cultural group |

**Regional maps**

| | |
|---|---|
| HUNGARY | state or empire |
| Bohemia | dependency or territory |
| Slavs | tribe, chiefdom or people |
| ANATOLIA | geographical region |
| ✕ | battle |
| • | site or town |

---

Campaigns or journeys are indicated by lines with arrowheads; thicker gray arrows are used for migrations or movements of large numbers of people. Trade routes are thinner lines, with arrowheads when the trade is specifically one-way.

Each item shown in the map key is referred to in the text at some point on the spread. The main text on each spread explains and amplifies the information drawn on the map.

The spread also carries a timeline, arranged in geographical or thematic sections. Extended events such as wars or dynasties are shown with colored bands; historical periods (such as "Bronze Age") are indicated with gray bands. Every regional map also carries between five and nine numbered "pointers". These refer to the captions elsewhere on the page, which offer additional historical detail about the places indicated.

Cross-references are provided in the panel on the bottom right; these list the numbers of other maps with related information, together with a suggestion of the relevant themes.

The volume index provides detailed references to the people, places, events and concepts covered in the text, timelines, numbered captions and map keys. For reasons of space it has not been possible to index every town or city shown on the maps, but the states and provinces on the maps are indexed, as are battles, sieges, peoples and journeys, exploration routes and so on.

## Part 1

# THE ANCIENT

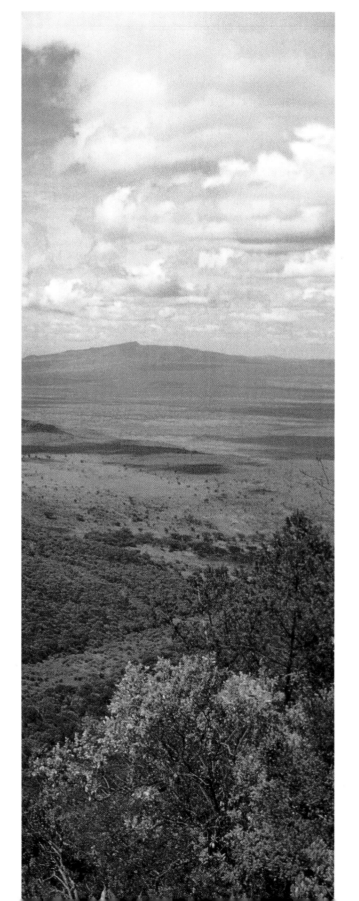

F our million years of biological and cultural evolution are covered in this story of the development of humankind from its origins on the African savanna to the appearance of the literate civilizations and classical empires. The story is the product of research in many disciplines, but the central thread comes from thousands of archeological excavations, of inconspicuous scatters of stone tools and animal bones, hunting camps and farming villages as well as towns and spectacular cities.

Archeologists study and explain changes in societies, indeed in humanity itself, over immensely long periods of time. Why, for example, did some societies acquire farming skills? And how and why did humans cross from Siberia into Alaska and colonize the Americas? The archeologist tries to account for such developments in terms of social organization as well as technology and environmental change.

The key intellectual framework for our most distant past derives from the evolutionary theories of Charles Darwin, formulated in 1859. The theory of evolution by natural selection made it possible to imagine a vast antiquity, a blank timescape for human evolution to unfold over hundreds of thousands, if not millions, of years. Darwin and his contemporaries could only guess at the evolution of humanity. Today, study of the DNA in our body cells tells us that the hominid line – of which *Homo sapiens sapiens* is the culmination – separated from the other apes between four and five million years ago. Today, archeology tells us that human ancestors appeared in Africa and moved out to populate the rest of the world almost two million years ago, and that modern humanity may also have originated in Africa. With its help, we can not only wonder at the art of 30,000 years

THE AFRICAN RIFT VALLEY was the birthplace of humankind.

# WORLD

ago, but also build up chronologies based on scientific analysis as well as on techniques of stylistic comparison. From archeology we know that literate civilizations developed in many places independently throughout the world. Historians using written sources, and archeologists using material remains, can then collaborate in piecing together a narrative of these civilizations.

Modern scholars think of evolution like the branches of a tree, with new species emerging as the endlessly proliferating limbs and twigs, which derive from a trunk of remote common ancestors. Human societies have evolved in many ways; but there are similarities, especially in social and political organization and in the ways in which people make their livings. A flexible classification of human societies into "prestate societies" and "state-organized societies" was made by the American anthropologist Elman Service.

The simplest prestate societies were small family bands, egalitarian groups with communal leadership based on experience. Usually hunters and gatherers of plant foods, band societies prevailed for an immensely long time, until the beginnings of farming. Some survived to modern times.

Early farmers lived in permanent villages, and needed new social institutions to settle quarrels and establish land ownership. Many village societies were "tribes", egalitarian groups with kin-based organization to regulate land ownership and undertake communal tasks. "Chiefdoms" were a development of tribes; power lay in the hands of a few people who controlled trade and accumulated wealth. "State-organized societies" or civilizations operated on a larger scale than chiefdoms. They involved cities and saw the development of a writing system. Early civilizations were centralized, with power concentrated in the hands of a supreme ruler at the pinnacle of a socially stratified society.

Four major themes dominate the long early chapter of our history: the origins of humanity, the evolution and spread of humans, the beginnings of agriculture, and the emergence of civilizations. All of these are bound up with the ways in which food has been secured. For 99 percent of all human history, people lived by hunting and gathering. Our earliest ancestors probably used fleetness of foot and opportunism to scavenge their meat from lion and leopard kills. Hunting may have begun at the same time as modern humans appeared. Stone-tipped spears, then barbed antler projectiles and spearthrowers allowed hunters to shoot game from a safe distance. When the bow-and-arrow came into use some 10,000 years ago, humans could hunt animals of every size and birds on the wing. And as the ice sheets retreated, people intensified the quest for food and permanent settlements began to emerge at some favored sites.

Hunting is often seen as the glamorous part of foraging, but edible plant foods formed the essential diet of humanity for four million years. Our ancestors knew which plants to eat as staples, and which to fall back on in lean times. It was only when populations rose at the en
d of the Ice Age that people began to plant wild grasses and tubers deliberately to extend the range of wild forms that had been gathered for millennia. And, in a remarkably short time – perhaps three thousand years – the growing of crops and the domestication of animals spread very widely.

Farming accelerated the pace of cultural change. At first, civilizations like those of the Egyptians, the Shang and the Sumerians were independent entities. Gradually, though, states became reliant on each other. By 500 BC, empires, much larger entities, played a leading role. But the first four million years had created human biological and cultural diversity and laid the foundations of our own world ■

Human evolution began as the Earth's climate started to cool during the Miocene epoch (25–5 million years ago), and culminated about one million years ago in the Pleistocene Ice Age. During the early Miocene the global climate was warmer than today. Widespread tropical forests in Africa and Eurasia supported diverse populations of early hominoid apes, including a common ancestor of gorillas, chimpanzees and humans.

By the end of the Miocene ice caps had formed at the Poles, and drier conditions in Africa caused tropical forests to shrink. In east Africa, probably the birthplace of the hominids, this was exacerbated by geological movements that led to the uplift of the East African plateau and the formation of the Rift Valley. The ancestral hominids were confined to shrinking "islands" of forest surrounded by open woodland and savanna. As a result they learned to walk on two legs, allowing them to cover long distances on the ground.

The oldest known hominid, 4.4-million-year-old *Ardepithecus ramidus*, was probably bipedal, and the slightly later species *Australopithecus afarensis* certainly was, although (like later australopithecines) it retained a good tree-climbing ability. By 3 million years ago the australopithecines had evolved into two types, known as robusts and graciles. The robusts (named for their massive jaws and teeth) were not human ancestors. The gracile *Australopithecus africanus* had smaller teeth and jaws, and lived on plant foods and meat scavenged from the carcasses of the savanna's herd animals. The first hominid to be considered human, *Homo habilis*, appeared about 2.4 million years ago. This lived in a similar way to the gracile australopithecines, but had a larger brain – almost half the size of a modern human's, compared with a third, for australopithecines and chimpanzees. Whereas the australopithecines used simple tools such as stones and sticks, *Homo habilis* made sharp flakes and chipped pebble tools for butchering large animals. This simple toolmaking culture is known as the Oldowan, for the early hominid fossil site of Olduvai Gorge in the Rift Valley.

About 1.9 million years ago *Homo habilis* was replaced by *Homo erectus*, with a brain size about two-thirds that of modern humans. Over the next million years this proportion grew to three-quarters, the brain evolving rapidly as the climate fluctuated from dry glacial periods to moister, warmer inter-glacial periods. There was little time to adapt physically to new conditions, and intelligent animals that could cope by modifying their

0    600 km
0    400 mi

Hadar
Aa
Bodo
He
Middle
Awash
Ar
Melka
Kunture
Gadeb
Omo
Ra, other
Ra
West Turkana
He
Ileret
Ra, Hh, He
Koobi Fora
Ra, Hh, He
Chesowanja
Ra
Olorgasailie
Peninj
Ra
Ndutu
other
Olduvai Gorge
Ra, Hh, He.
Laetoli
Aa, other
Kalambo Falls
Kabwe
other

**TIMELINE**

**1,600,000** Earliest evidence of the use of fire, at Chesowanja, Kenya and Swartkrans (South Africa)

**1,800,000** Populations of *Homo erectus* reach south and southeast Asia

**c.3,500,000** "Lucy", the most complete *Australopithecus afarensis* found, lives at Hadar, Ethiopia

**c.2,000,000** Stone choppers, from Olduvai Gorge, Tanzania, initiate the Oldowan culture

**c.3,600,000** Hominid bipedal footsteps from this date have been found at Laetoli, Tanzania

**c.2,400,000** Date of the oldest known stone tools, from Hadar, Ethiopia and the start of the African Lower Paleolithic

**1,000,000** Beginning of the modern (Pleistocene) Ice Age

**1,000,000** *Homo erectus* reaches Europe and Asia

| 4,000,000 years ago (ya) | 3,000,000 ya | 2,000,000 ya | 1,500,000 ya | 1,000,000 ya |
|---|---|---|---|---|

Homo habilis
Homo erectus
Australopithecus africanus
*Ardepithecus ramidus*
*Australopithecus afarensis*
Robust Australopithecines
Oldowan culture

LOWER PALEOLITHIC

PLIOCENE EPOCH

TERTIARY PERIOD

**Legend:**

- probable range of early hominids
- probable range of *Homo erectus*, c.500,000 years ago
- range of Neanderthals, c.100,000 ya
- Mousterian culture, c.100,000 ya
- southeast Asian chopper–flake technology
- fossil site
- fossil site with finds of uncertain species

**tool cultures**

- Oldowan, 2-1.2 million years ago (mya)
- Acheulian, 1.5 mya-150,000 ya

**major species found at fossil site**

Ar   *Ardepithecus ramidus*
Aa   *Australopithecus afarensis*
Aaf   *Australopithecus africanus*
Ra   *Australopithecus robustus*
Hh   *Homo habilis*
He   *Homo erectus*
Hsn   *Homo sapiens neanderthalensis*
other   other forms of archaic *Homo sapiens*

- evidence of Neanderthal ritual burial
- use of fire by *Homo erectus*
- conjectural spread of *Homo erectus*
- ancient coastline, in glacial periods
- Pliocene rainforest in Africa

**Timeline (chart):**

100,000 Modern humans begin their migration out of Africa

135,000 Date of the earliest anatomically modern human fossils, from Omo, Ethiopia

300,000 Possibly the oldest known human structure; a hut is found at Terra Amata, France

400,000 The earliest surviving wooden tool, a spear (found in Schöningen, Germany)

500,000 ya     250,000 ya

H. s. sapiens
Archaic *Homo sapiens*
H. s. neanderthalensis

Acheulian culture
Mousterian culture
MID PALEOLITHIC

PLEISTOCENE EPOCH
QUATERNARY PERIOD

behavior had evolutionary advantages. *Homo erectus* mastered the use of fire, and was a more able toolmaker than *Homo habilis*, using the symmetrical hand-ax (a butchery tool) of the Acheulian culture.

*Homo erectus* was the first hominid to live outside Africa. Perhaps as early as 1.8 million years ago it had spread through tropical south and southeast Asia and colonized temperate areas of Europe and northern China before one million years ago. *Homo erectus*, however, did not reach Australia or the Americas. It could survive in temperate climates but not in Arctic and sub-Arctic ones, usually prefering to live in savanna, steppe and open woodlands: the same hand-ax technology was widespread. However in southeast Asia it adapted to tropical forest life, using flake and chopper tools and bamboo. The isolated *Homo erectus* populations began to evolve in different ways after 500,000 years ago. In Africa and Europe a variety of large-brained forms showed a mixture of archaic and modern human characteristics. In Europe between 230,000 and 150,000 years ago, archaic *Homo sapiens* evolved into *Homo sapiens neanderthalensis*, its physique adapted to life on the cold steppes and tundras of Ice Age Eurasia. These Neanderthals developed the Mousterian toolmaking technique, which was also widely used by hunter–gatherer groups in North Africa and the Middle East (often called the Near East by archeologists). In Africa archaic humans evolved until anatomically modern humans, *Homo sapiens sapiens*, appeared by 135,000 years ago ∎

The earliest known anatomically modern *Homo sapiens sapiens* had appeared in Africa by 135,000 years ago (ya). By 90,000 years ago anatomically modern humans existed in the Middle East; by 75,000 years ago they were in east Asia and by 40,000 in Europe and Australia. By the end of the Ice Age 10,000 years ago, only some oceanic islands, Antarctica and some parts of the high Arctic remained completely uninhabited.

Two rival explanations have been offered for these facts. One argues that the modern human races developed directly from the regional *Homo erectus* populations: modern Africans evolved from *Homo erectus* via African archaic *Homo sapiens*, modern Europeans from *Homo erectus* via European archaic *Homo sapiens* and Neanderthals and so on. Critics point out that parallel evolution of this sort over such a wide area is implausible and that there is no supporting fossil evidence. The second explanation, known as the single-origins or "out of Africa" model, is supported by genetic evidence suggesting that all modern humans derive from African ancestors who lived between about 285,000 and 150,000 years ago, and that all modern non-African humans are descendants of a single group of this ancestral population that migrated out of Africa around 100,000 years ago. According to this model, the descendants of this group spread across Eurasia. The anatomically modern humans had better developed speech abilities than the archaic natives, who could not compete with the newcomers and gradually became extinct.

This model is more compatible with the fossil and archeological evidence than the first. Between 120,000 and 90,000 years ago the African climate was more moist than it is today and bands of hunters and gatherers could have crossed the Sahara. The earliest known fossils of modern humans outside Africa date to about 90,000 years ago and were found in Israel – just the place and date predicted by the single-origins theory. Only in Africa have forms intermediate between archaic and modern humans been found. In Europe, the Neanderthals and early modern humans formed distinct populations that coexisted for over 10,000 years: the Neanderthals did not evolve into modern humans. In east and southeast Asia, the *Homo erectus* populations were replaced by modern humans with no trace of intermediate forms.

When the first modern humans reached the Middle East, the global climate was beginning to enter one of the most severe glacial periods of the Ice Age. Human technology was probably inadequate for survival in the arctic climates of Europe and central Asia, and these areas were left to the hardier Neanderthals. Instead the moderns moved east, reaching China and southeast Asia around 75,000 years ago. Here they developed boat- or raft-building skills and

BERINGIA
modern humans reach Alaska around 15,000
Bluefish Cave 15–12,000
Cordilleran Ice Sheet
ice free corridor opens c.12–14,000
Laurentide Ice Sheet
Marmes 10,500
Folsom
Clovis
Clovis sites occupied around 11,500–11,000
Little Salt Spring
Tepexpan 11–10,000
Pedra Pintada 14–13,000
Guitarrero Cave c.10,000
modern humans reach Patagonia 11,000
Fell's Cave 11,000

**TIMELINE**

115,000 Onset of the last glaciation of the (Pleistocene) Ice Age

90,000 Anatomically modern humans living at Qafzeh, Israel

40,000 Anatomically modern humans begin to colonize Europe: they live alongside the indigenous Neanderthals

32,000–14,000 Period of cave art traditions in Europe

The Americas
Europe
Middle East
Africa
East and South Asia

100,000 years ago
80,000 ya
60,000 ya
40,000 ya
30,000 ya.

c.120,000 Middle Stone Age flake-tool technology is well established in tropical Africa

120,000–90,000 Periods of higher rainfall make the Sahara habitable by humans

c.75,000 Glaciation causes Africa to become arid: the Sahara becomes impassable by humans

75,000 Anatomically modern humans inhabit China and southeast Asia

45,000 Date of the oldest known musical instrument, a flute, found in north Africa

35,000 Anatomically modern humans hunt large game in Eurasia

35,000 Australian aboriginal hunter–gatherer traditions emerge

28,000 The Solomon Islands are settled

**vegetation zones 18,000 ya**

- tundra
- forest
- grassland
- semidesert
- desert

- ice cap 18,000 ya
- ice cap 12,000 ya
- ice cap 10,000 ya

- selected fossil sites of anatomically modern humans, with date
- other early modern human sites, with date
- Paleoindian fluted point tradition sites, 12,000–10,000 ya
- migration of anatomically modern humans, 100,000–11,000 ya
- possible marine migration route
- range of Neanderthals, c.100,000 ya
- limit of habitation, c.10,000 ya
- ancient coastline at peak of the last glaciation, 18,000 ya
- *SUNDA* ancient land bridge

Greenland Ice Sheet

Taymyr Ice Sheet

Scandinavian Ice Sheet

BERINGIA

Bisovaya 14,000

Dyukhtai Cave 18,000

Berelekh 14,000

Malaya Siya 34,000

Mal'ta 21,000

Cresswell Crags 12,000
early modern humans in Europe 40,000

Mladec 33,000

Cro Magnon 25,000

early modern humans in Middle East 90,000

early modern humans in central Asia 35,000

Zhoukoudian 18,000

Zasaragi 50,000

Dar es-Soltane 40–30,000

Haua Fteah 47,000

Skhul 90,000

Qafzeh 90,000

Okinawa 32,000

Linjiang 67,000 ?

early modern humans in Southeast Asia 75,000

Omo 130,000

Tabon 24–22,000

Niah Cave 40,000

origin of ancestral modern humans 200,000–135,000

SUNDA

early modern humans reach Solomon Islands 28,000

Madagascar

Bobangara 38,000

SAHUL

Wadjak 50–25,000

early modern humans reach Australia and New Guinea 40,000

Border Cave 115,000

Devil's Lair 34,000

Lake Mungo 33,000

Bluff rockshelter 30,500

Kow Swamp 14,000

Klasies River Mouth 120,000

TASMANIA 31,000

**11,000–9000** Folsom culture replaces Clovis culture among Paleoindians

**11,500** Beginning of Clovis culture in North America

**15,000** Possible date of the first settlement of North America, at Bluefish Cave (Alaska)

**28,000** The last Neanderthals become extinct, in southern Spain

20,000 ya

10,000 ya (8000BC)

**20,000–14,000** Dyukhtai tradition: earliest settlement of northeast Asia

**18,000** Height of the last glaciation: sea levels are 100–130m lower than today

**10,000** The beginnings of agriculture in the Middle East

**10,000–3000 ya** Higher rainfall makes the Sahara habitable again

by 40,000 years ago had reached New Guinea and Australia (then linked into one vast island continent), probably by a series of island-hopping voyages. Though the distances to be covered were relatively short as the sea levels were lower than today (a large amount of water was locked up in ice caps), these early sea voyages were a great achievement, even if possibly accidental.

About 40,000 years ago, modern humans moved into Europe. By this time they had evolved modern mental characteristics and sufficient technology to flourish on the frigid Eurasian steppes and tundras. Within 12,000 years the Neanderthals were extinct. The Eurasian steppes and tundras were favorable for late Ice Age hunters because of the herds of reindeer, horse, bison and mammoth that ranged across them. By 35,000 years ago hunting bands had reached deep into central Asia and by 20,000 years ago others, perhaps moving north from China, had entered northeastern Siberia. The area now covered by the Bering Straits was a cold plain which some bands crossed to reach the Americas by 15,000 years ago. Further progress into the Americas was blocked by massive ice sheets. Between 14,000 and 12,000 years ago these began a retreat and hunting–gathering bands – the Paleoindians – could reach the heart of North America. The earliest Paleoindian sites are characterized by beautifully worked fluted projectile points used for big-game hunting. The Paleoindians spread rapidly through the Americas and had reached Patagonia in South America by 11,000 years ago ▪

Anatomically modern humans from Africa reached what is now the Middle East some 90,000 years ago, but it was not until the beginning of the Upper Paleolithic period, about 40,000 years ago, that they were able to move into Europe. Unlike the indigenous Neanderthals, who were physically adapted to the harsh Ice Age climate, the early anatomically modern humans were poorly equipped to survive in Europe until, some 50,000–40,000 years ago, they also acquired a fully modern human mental capacity. This enabled them to adapt to the cold climate through technological and social innovation, and compete on more than equal terms with the Neanderthals. The Neanderthals became extinct about 28,000 years ago. Whether it was as a result of a war of extermination or because superior modern human hunting techniques drove them into marginal environments is a subject of debate: current archeological opinion favors the latter.

Two parallel toolmaking traditions, the Châtelperronian and the Aurignacian, are found in Europe during the 10–12,000 years that modern humans and Neanderthals shared the continent. The Châtelperronian is apparently a development of the Mousterian tool culture and is thought to have been used by the Neanderthals. The Aurignacian has similarities with contemporary tool cultures in the Middle East and is therefore thought to have been introduced to Europe by anatomically modern humans. The Aurignacian and the succeeding Gravettian tool cultures both are fairly uniform over wide areas but later Upper Paleolithic tool cultures show greater variety between different regions. These variations are often in style rather than function and probably served as a way of expressing emerging ethnic identities. Typical Upper Paleolithic stone tools include scrapers, sharpened blades, burins – engraving tools used for antler harpoons – and bone points and needles were also used. The Solutrean culture introduced a sophisticated technique of pressure flaking which produced beautiful leaf shaped spear heads.

The most impressive characteristics of the Upper Paleolithic cultures are their art traditions, both decorated artifacts and cave-wall painting. The earliest Upper Paleolithic art dates from around 31,000 years ago but the traditions reached their peak in the Magdalenian (17,000–11,000 years ago), in the cave paintings of sites such as Lascaux and Altamira. The

**Upper Paleolithic, 40,000–10,000 years ago**

- ▨ Levantine Aurignacian culture
- ▢ Aurignacian culture
- ◆ cave site
- ✋ cave site with painting
- ● open site
- ▲ open site with structure
- ⚱ "Venus" figurine find

**Mesolithic, 10,000–6000 ya (8000–4000 BC)**

- ⚱ major site
- 🐚 site with shell midden

- ▢ maximum extent of ice sheet during last glaciation, c.18,000 ya
- ▨ extent of ice sheet, 7000 BC
- ⋯⋯ northern limit of deciduous woodland, c.18,000 ya
- ⋯⋯ northern limit of deciduous woodland, 7000 BC
- ➤ migration of anatomically modern humans from Middle East, c.40,000 ya
- --- ancient course of Thames/Rhine, 7000 BC
- —— modern coastline and drainage where altered

```
0                    800 km
0                        600 mi
```

greatest concentration of Upper Paleolithic cave art is to be found in southwest France and northern Spain, an area with a particularly dense population at the time. The function of cave art is unknown but it is thought to have played a religious role. The most distinctive decorated artifacts are female "Venus" figurines made around 25,000 years ago. These have been found across Europe – evidence, perhaps, of a widespread religious cult.

Despite the cold, the tundras and steppes of Ice Age Europe were a very favorable environment for hunters, being filled with easily tracked herds of large grazing mammals. Upper Paleolithic hunters used a combination of semi-permanent base-camps – often sited at bottlenecks on animal migration routes, such as river crossings – and seasonal camps where particular game species were intensively exploited. Caves and south-facing rock shelters were favored camp sites, but in more exposed areas tents and huts were built.

The end of the last glaciation, around 10,000 years ago (8000 BC) marks the end of the Upper Paleolithic and the beginning of the Mesolithic

"VENUS" figurines with exaggerated sexual characteristics were a feature of the Gravettian culture and probably symbolized fertility. This example is from Willendorf in Austria.

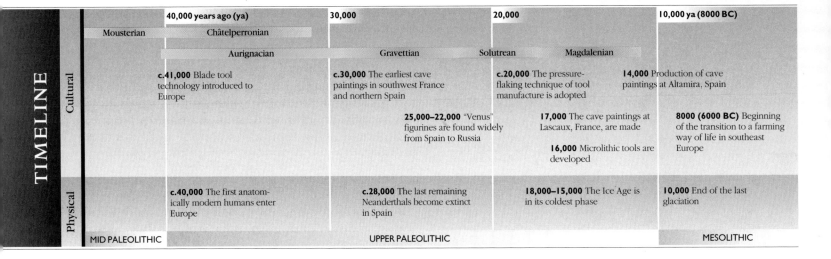

| | | 40,000 years ago (ya) | | 30,000 | | 20,000 | | 10,000 ya (8000 BC) |
|---|---|---|---|---|---|---|---|---|
| | | Mousterian   Châtelperronian | | | | | | |
| | | Aurignacian | | Gravettian | | Solutrean   Magdalenian | | |
| **TIMELINE** | **Cultural** | **c.41,000** Blade tool technology introduced to Europe | | **c.30,000** The earliest cave paintings in southwest France and northern Spain | | **c.20,000** The pressure-flaking technique of tool manufacture is adopted | **14,000** Production of cave paintings at Altamira, Spain | |
| | | | | **25,000–22,000** "Venus" figurines are found widely from Spain to Russia | | **17,000** The cave paintings at Lascaux, France, are made | **8000 (6000 BC)** Beginning of the transition to a farming way of life in southeast Europe | |
| | | | | | | **16,000** Microlithic tools are developed | | |
| | **Physical** | **c.40,000** The first anatomically modern humans enter Europe | | **c.28,000** The last remaining Neanderthals become extinct in Spain | | **18,000–15,000** The Ice Age is in its coldest phase | **10,000** End of the last glaciation | |
| | | MID PALEOLITHIC | | UPPER PALEOLITHIC | | | | MESOLITHIC |

period. As the climate became warmer, sea levels rose and dense forests advanced over most of Europe, bringing the big-game hunting way of life to an end. Large mammals were now fewer and more elusive, but a far greater diversity of plant foods, shellfish, fish, birds and small mammals was available. Mesolithic hunter–gatherers introduced many new devices to exploit these new food sources. The most important technological change was a reliance on microliths – small stone blades or flakes – used in combination to make composite tools such as knives, harpoons, fish spears and lightweight arrow heads. Nets, fish traps, shellfish scoops and dug-out canoes also came into widespread use for the first time in the Mesolithic.

Many areas of northern Europe which had previously been uninhabitable because of extreme cold or ice sheets received their first modern human inhabitants during the Mesolithic, while some which had been relatively densely populated, such as southwest France and the southwest steppes, became comparatively depopulated. The densest population moved to areas such as the Atlantic coast and southern Scandinavia. Hunter–gatherers here were able to adopt an increasingly sedentary way of life, making fewer and shorter migrations between camps. In southern Scandinavia and eastern Europe there were even permanent settlements occupied all year round. Task groups set out from these settlements to spend short periods at temporary seasonal camps to exploit locally abundant food resources.

The Mesolithic period came to an end with the adoption of the Neolithic farming way of life, a process which began about 6000 BC in southeast Europe and about two thousand years later in the British Isles and Scandinavia. In extreme northerly areas, an essentially Mesolithic way of life continued until the domestication of the reindeer early in the Christian era.

**1** In the Upper Paleolithic, southwest France had light woodland for fuel, sheltered valleys with many caves, and lay across major animal migration routes; it was therefore Europe's most densely populated area.

**2** Upper Paleolithic hunters used temporary camps to exploit particular game species. Solutré was a base for horse hunters, Predmosti for mammoth.

**3** Cave paintings of woolly rhinoceros, horses and buffalo found at Vallon Pont d'Arc in 1994 are, at 30,000 years old, the oldest yet found.

**4** On the treeless steppes, mammoth bones were used to build huts; a well-known example, c.18,000 years old, was found at Mezhirich.

**5** The well-preserved Mesolithic settlement of Lepenski Vir includes many fish-head sculptures, perhaps indicating worship of a fish-deity.

**6** Denmark, with marine, freshwater and terrestrial food sources in close proximity, was densely populated in the Mesolithic.

**7** The first cemeteries, such as those at Cabeço da Arruda and Oleneostravski (about 170 burials each) date from the late Mesolithic (c.4250 BC).

**8** Late Mesolithic hunter-gatherers (c.4000–3400 BC) visited Oronsay island several times a year for fish and shellfish.

See also 2 (peopling the earth);
7 (Neolithic Europe)

arming communities arose independently in many parts of the world between 10,000 and 5000 BC as a response to the environmental changes that followed the end of the Ice Age. The warmer climate was a mixed blessing: sea levels rose as the ice sheets melted, flooding huge areas of lowland hunting grounds. The savannas, steppes and tundras, all abundant in big game, shrank as the forests advanced.

In many areas, hunter–gatherers began to exploit small game birds, fish and plants to a greater extent than before. It was among these communities that agriculture first arose. Probably the first stage was planting the seeds of favored wild plant foods to guarantee their continuing availability. Next was the domestication of food plants by breeding strains with desirable characteristics. Because their seeds had a high carbohydrate content and were easy to store, the most important domesticated plant foods were strains of the cereals – wheat, barley, oats, rice, millet and maize – that still form the staple food crops today. Relatively few animal species have been domesticated; most of those have been herd animals, whose tendency to "follow the leader" makes them easier to manage. Animal domestication began with the management and selective culling of wild herds. Penning the animals followed, then selective breeding for desirable qualities. Most early centers of agriculture were rich in wild plants and animals suitable for domestication. Elsewhere agriculture relied on the introduction of crops and livestock from established farming areas.

Some communities of hunter–gatherers moved from casual cultivation of wild plants (incipient agriculture) to a full farming economy far more quickly than others. Farmers have to work harder than hunter–gatherers, and few made the transition willingly. Rising populations probably forced many to adopt cultivation to supplement wild food supplies. In the Fertile Crescent of the Middle East, where farming first developed, the transition from incipient agriculture to dependence on domesticated cereals took only three centuries, 8000–7700 BC, and domesticated animals replaced hunted wild animals a millennium later. In Mesoamerica a full farming way of life developed within a few centuries of the domestication of maize (▷ 17). In eastern North America hunting and gathering remained the main source of food for some three millennia after the first cultivation of domesticated food around 2500 BC. Even farmers who grew most of their food still exploited wild food sources.

Agriculture led to far-reaching technological developments. Most hunter–gatherers had to carry everything from camp to camp: farmers were sedentary, so weight became less critical. New tools, such as polished stone

**EASTERN N AMERICA**
goosefoot
gourds
marsh elder
sumpweed
sunflowers
c.1000

Hawaiian Islands

Bahamas

Cuba   Hispaniola
   Puerto Rico
Jamaica

c.2300

c.1000

**MESOAMERICA**
avocados
beans
cotton
gourds
maize
peppers
pumpkins
squashes
tomatoes
turkeys

c.3500

c.4000

**LOWLAND S AMERICA**
manioc
peanuts
pineapples

c.3000

c.2000

**ANDES**
alpacas
beans
chili peppers
gourds
guinea pigs
llamas
potatoes

c.1000

c.500

---

**5400–4500** Bandkeramik culture: first farmers of central Europe

**6000** Farming spreads across southern Europe

**c.6000** The first cattle are domesticated in the Middle East

**9000** Wild sheep flocks are managed in the Zagros mountains, Iraq

**6200** Copper smelting and textile manufacture in Chatal Huyuk (Turkey)

**9000–8000** Incipient agriculture (cultivation of wild cereals) in the Fertile Crescent

**10,000 BC** Natufian hunter–gatherers harvest wild cereals in Syria

**8000-7700** Wheat and barley are domesticated in the Fertile Crescent

**5000** Irrigation agriculture begins on the Mesopotamian plains

The Americas
Europe
Middle East
Africa
East and South Asia

10,000 BC    8000    6000    4000

**c.12,000 BC** Jomon hunter–gatherers make the first pottery in Japan

**8000** End of the last glaciation, worldwide

**6500** Rice cultivation in the Yangtze valley

**4500** Farming is adopted in the Ganges plain

**6000** Wheat, barley and sheep farming begins in Egypt

**3800** The earliest bronze working is carried out in the Middle East

**6000** Earliest evidence for farming in the Indian subcontinent

transition to agriculture beginning,

before 8000 BC
before 6000 BC
before 3000 BC
before 500 BC

hunters and gatherers
uninhabited

textile find, with date

cotton
linen
silk
wool

earliest pottery, with date

earliest evidence for the adoption of plow, with date

rice   early domestication of plant or animal

earliest use of the potter's wheel, before 3000 BC

earliest centers of copper/bronze metallurgy, 6000-2000 BC

early spread of wheeled vehicles, 4th millennium BC

Greenland
Iceland

SW STEPPES
horses

S EUROPE
cattle
geese
grapes
oats
olives
rye

CENTRAL ASIA
Bactrian camels
yaks

CHINA
millet
rice
silk worms
soybeans

W AFRICA
African rice
oil palms
water melons
yams

SAHARA
bulrush millet
cattle

MIDDLE EAST
asses
barley
date palms
dogs
dromedary camels
flax
goats
lentils
onions
peas
pigs
sheep
wheat

INDIA
cotton
zebus

E AFRICA
sorghum

Ceylon

SE ASIA
chickens
pigs
rice
taros
water buffalo
waterchestnuts

Philippine
Islands

SE ASIAN
ARCHIPELAGO
bananas
breadfruit
coconuts

NEW GUINEA
sugar cane
sweet potatoes

Borneo   Celebes
Sumatra
Java
Timor
New Guinea

Madagascar

**750** Nomadism becomes the dominant way of life on the Eurasian steppes

**1000–800** Maize is introduced to South America

**1200** Maize is introduced to southwest North America

**1500** Pastoral farmers spread across the Eurasian steppes

**2700** Maize is domesticated in Mesoamerica

**2000** Farming becomes the main source of food in Peru

**3650** Wheeled vehicles in use on the Russian steppes

2000

**3000** Copper and silk manufacture are known in China

**2000** Farming and pastoralism begin in sub-Saharan Africa

**2500** Desertification of the Sahara drives nomadic herding groups to the edges of the desert

**1500** Rice cultivation is adopted in Korea

axes for clearing forest, hoes, sickles and grindstones, appeared in early farming cultures. Pottery became common in early farming settlements where it was needed for storage and cooking. Pottery led to other technological breakthroughs: the kilns that were developed in some areas for baking pots also provided the means for smelting and casting metals – copper and gold first, then bronze and finally iron. The wheel too was first used as an aid to making pottery; only later was it applied to transport. The spinning and weaving of plant and animal fibers to make textiles also became important in early farming communities.

The social implications of the adoption of agriculture were just as far-reaching. Farming peoples accumulated material possessions on a scale far beyond anything possible among most hunter–gatherers. As a result, differences in social status became more marked and the equality of hunter–gatherer society gave way to complex and hierarchical social structures. Most significantly, farming made possible an enormous increase in the human population. A single hunter–gatherer may need 25 square kilometers to make a living even in favorable terrain. In contrast, even the most primitive forms of agriculture can support up to 20 people on one square kilometer. Where food production could be intensified by plowing or by irrigation, still greater populations were possible. If the typical unit of hunter–gatherer society was the nomadic band of 30–50, simple farming methods could support villages of hundreds of people, and intensive methods, towns of thousands of people ■

The world's first cities and states emerged in the region of Sumeria in southern Mesopotamia in the Uruk period (4300–3100), named for the oldest and largest Sumerian city. States, with their social classes, centralized government and well-organized trade, became important mechanisms for coordinating flood control (important in this region) and other public works. Early Sumerian cities were dominated by temple complexes, and the priesthood probably took the lead in this organization. The Tigris and Euphrates rivers are subject to violent floods and unpredictable changes of course, events which must have seemed like the acts of capricious gods (the biblical story of the flood is of Sumerian origin). The priests claimed to be able to propitiate the gods, and this may have given them the authority to be accepted as rulers of their cities.

Most Sumerian cities of the Uruk period had a population between two and eight thousand people, although Uruk itself, the largest, had over 10,000; by 2700 BC this had risen to about 50,000. Most of these were farmers who traveled out each day to the surrounding fields. However, the food surpluses they produced were great and Sumerian society became the first to have the resources to support large numbers of people in specialist occupations: sculptors, potters, bronze-casters, stonemasons, bakers, brewers and weavers.

The temples became centers of redistribution where the surplus food of the countryside and craft products were gathered to be given out as rations, or traded abroad for raw materials that could not be found locally. These trade links ranged from India and Afghanistan to Egypt, and played an important part in spreading the influence of Sumerian civilization throughout the Middle East. It was a complex task to manage the redistribution of produce. Keeping track of all the transactions was beyond the ability of unaided memory and by around 3400 a system of pictographic writing, probably derived

**Map legend:**

- ▨ area of strongest Sumerian cultural influence
- ⬭ kingdom of Lugalzagesi, c.2350
- 🏘 city named in the Sumerian King List (compiled c.2100)
- 🏘 other city
- **Mari** site of major temple
- <u>Kish</u> site of palace

origins of writing

- ► hollow clay spheres and impressed tablets (token system)
- ► inscribed clay tablets (Sumerian pictographic script), 3400–2900
- ► inscribed clay tablets (proto-Elamite script), 3100–2900

- —— trade route
- *copper* imports to Mesopotamia
- grain exports from Mesopotamia
- ▢ area of alluvial soils
- —— modern coastline and drainage where altered

```
0                              300 km
0                      200 mi
```

*Mediterranean Sea*

*copper from Anatolia*

*silver*

*Ceyhan*

TAURUS MTS

*timber*

Habuba Kabira

*Orontes*

Ebla   4

*copper*

Cyprus

*shells* Ugarit

Hama

*Syrian*

Byblos

*timber*

KINGDOM OF EGYPT (c. 3000 BC)

*alabaster diorite gold*

Memphis

*copper*

---

from an earlier token system, had been developed.

Sumerian civilization entered a new and troubled phase in the Early Dynastic period (2900–2334 BC). Massive defensive walls were built around the cities, bronze weapons were produced in increasing quantities and war begins to feature prominently as a subject of official art with rulers often being shown trampling on their enemies. This period also saw writing applied to purposes other than administration, as rulers began to record their glorious deeds to ensure their posthumous reputations. The gap between rich and poor widened and slavery appears in the records for the first time. Secular leaders now appear alongside the priest-kings. Some had the title *sangu* (accountant), suggesting that bureaucrats had achieved equal status with the priests. Others were called *lugal* (literally "big man"): these may have been war leaders, elected in times of emergency in the past, who had succeeded in making their power permanent. To show that their rule had divine approval these secular rulers built palaces next to the temple precincts, where they lived in opulence. In death they were given rich burials, such as those excavated at the Royal Cemetery at Ur, accompanied by the luxuries of their everyday lives and even their sacrificed retainers. Lacking the spiritual authority of the priesthood, the new secular rulers established their authority through law codes,

---

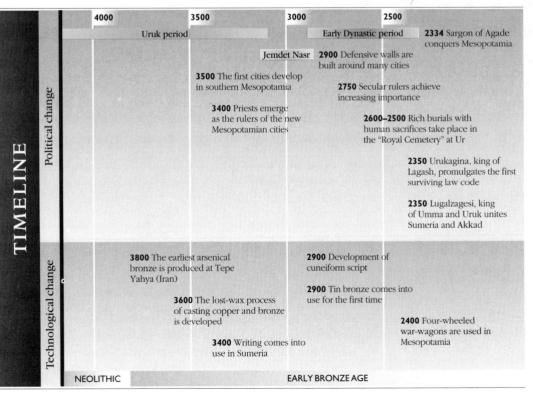

## TIMELINE

| | 4000 | 3500 | 3000 | 2500 |
|---|---|---|---|---|
| | | Uruk period | | Early Dynastic period   **2334** Sargon of Agade conquers Mesopotamia |

**Political change**

- Jemdet Nasr   **2900** Defensive walls are built around many cities
- **3500** The first cities develop in southern Mesopotamia
- **2750** Secular rulers achieve increasing importance
- **3400** Priests emerge as the rulers of the new Mesopotamian cities
- **2600–2500** Rich burials with human sacrifices take place in the "Royal Cemetery" at Ur
- **2350** Urukagina, king of Lagash, promulgates the first surviving law code
- **2350** Lugalzagesi, king of Umma and Uruk unites Sumeria and Akkad

**Technological change**

- **3800** The earliest arsenical bronze is produced at Tepe Yahya (Iran)
- **2900** Development of cuneiform script
- **3600** The lost-wax process of casting copper and bronze is developed
- **2900** Tin bronze comes into use for the first time
- **2400** Four-wheeled war-wagons are used in Mesopotamia
- **3400** Writing comes into use in Sumeria

NEOLITHIC       EARLY BRONZE AGE

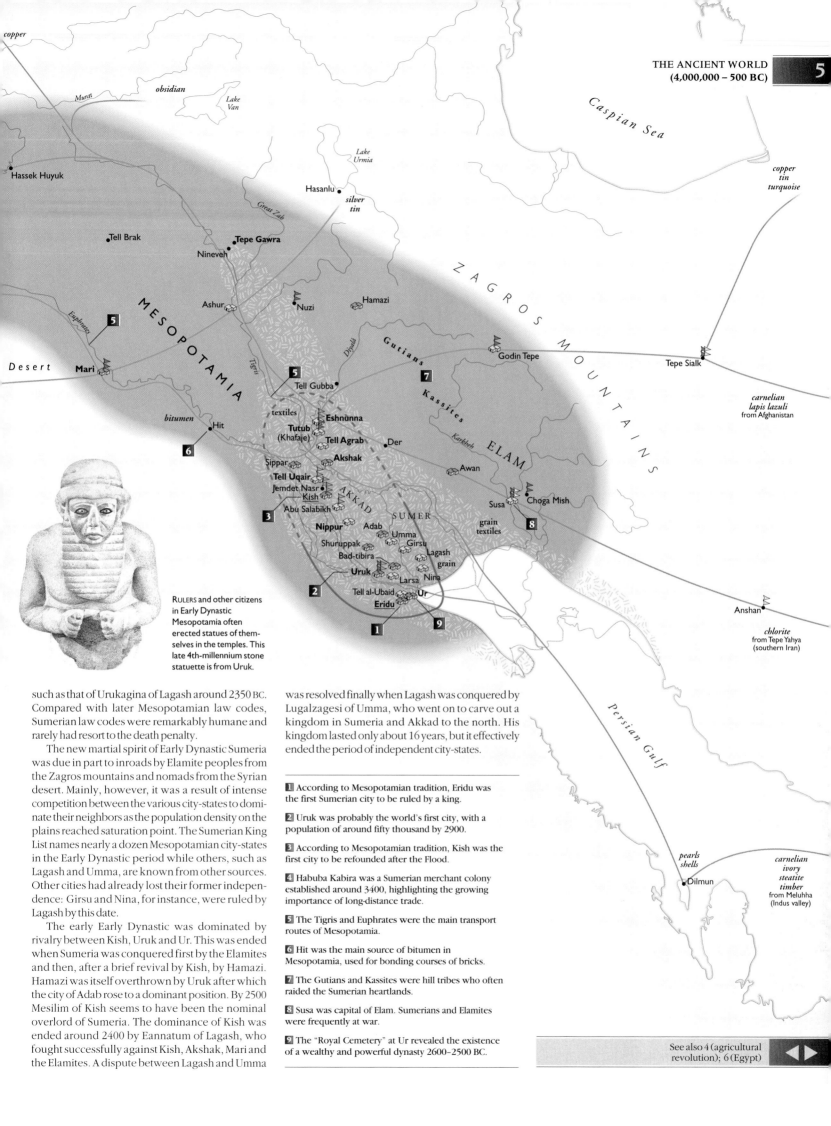

*copper*

*Murat*

*obsidian*

*Lake Van*

Hassek Huyuk

*Caspian Sea*

*copper tin turquoise*

Hasanlu

*silver tin*

*Great Zab*

Tell Brak

**Tepe Gawra**

Nineveh

M E S O P O T A M I A

Ashur

5

*Euphrates*

Nuzi

Hamazi

Z A G R O S   M O U N T A I N S

Godin Tepe

Tepe Sialk

*Desert*

**Mari**

*Tigris*

*Diyala*

*Gutians*

7

*Kassites*

E L A M

*carnelian lapis lazuli from Afghanistan*

5

Tell Gubba

*bitumen*

Hit

*textiles*

**Tutub**
(Khafaje)

**Eshnunna**

**Tell Agrab**

Der

*Karkheh*

6

**Akshak**

Sippar

**Tell Uqair**

Jemdet Nasr

**Kish**

A K K A D

Awan

Susa

Choga Mish

*grain textiles*

8

Abu Salabikh

3

**Nippur**

Adab

S U M E R

**Nippur**

Shuruppak

Umma

**Girsu**

Bad-tibira

Lagash

*grain*

**Uruk**

Larsa

Nina

2

Tell al-Ubaid

Ur

**Eridu**

1

9

Anshan

*chlorite from Tepe Yahya (southern Iran)*

*Persian Gulf*

RULERS and other citizens in Early Dynastic Mesopotamia often erected statues of themselves in the temples. This late 4th-millennium stone statuette is from Uruk.

*pearls shells*

Dilmun

*carnelian ivory steatite timber from Meluhha (Indus valley)*

such as that of Urukagina of Lagash around 2350 BC. Compared with later Mesopotamian law codes, Sumerian law codes were remarkably humane and rarely had resort to the death penalty.

The new martial spirit of Early Dynastic Sumeria was due in part to inroads by Elamite peoples from the Zagros mountains and nomads from the Syrian desert. Mainly, however, it was a result of intense competition between the various city-states to dominate their neighbors as the population density on the plains reached saturation point. The Sumerian King List names nearly a dozen Mesopotamian city-states in the Early Dynastic period while others, such as Lagash and Umma, are known from other sources. Other cities had already lost their former independence: Girsu and Nina, for instance, were ruled by Lagash by this date.

The early Early Dynastic was dominated by rivalry between Kish, Uruk and Ur. This was ended when Sumeria was conquered first by the Elamites and then, after a brief revival by Kish, by Hamazi. Hamazi was itself overthrown by Uruk after which the city of Adab rose to a dominant position. By 2500 Mesilim of Kish seems to have been the nominal overlord of Sumeria. The dominance of Kish was ended around 2400 by Eannatum of Lagash, who fought successfully against Kish, Akshak, Mari and the Elamites. A dispute between Lagash and Umma

was resolved finally when Lagash was conquered by Lugalzagesi of Umma, who went on to carve out a kingdom in Sumeria and Akkad to the north. His kingdom lasted only about 16 years, but it effectively ended the period of independent city-states.

**1** According to Mesopotamian tradition, Eridu was the first Sumerian city to be ruled by a king.

**2** Uruk was probably the world's first city, with a population of around fifty thousand by 2900.

**3** According to Mesopotamian tradition, Kish was the first city to be refounded after the Flood.

**4** Habuba Kabira was a Sumerian merchant colony established around 3400, highlighting the growing importance of long-distance trade.

**5** The Tigris and Euphrates were the main transport routes of Mesopotamia.

**6** Hit was the main source of bitumen in Mesopotamia, used for bonding courses of bricks.

**7** The Gutians and Kassites were hill tribes who often raided the Sumerian heartlands.

**8** Susa was capital of Elam. Sumerians and Elamites were frequently at war.

**9** The "Royal Cemetery" at Ur revealed the existence of a wealthy and powerful dynasty 2600–2500 BC.

See also 4 (agricultural revolution); 6 (Egypt)

Ancient Egypt was totally dependent on the Nile. Below the First Cataract, the Nile flows through a narrow valley and, except where it broadens out into the Delta, its flood plain is nowhere more than a few kilometers wide, often less. The flood plain was probably the most favorable area for agriculture anywhere in the ancient world. The Nile flooded annually in the late summer, falling in the autumn and leaving the fields moist and fertilized with fresh silt ready for sowing. The crops grew through the warm Egyptian winter and were harvested in the spring before the next cycle of flooding. Egypt had little need of the complex irrigation systems and flood defenses of Mesopotamia, where the rivers flooded in spring, after the start of the growing season. Canals, however, were used to spread the floodwaters and increase the cultivable area. High yields were possible year after year: the farmers' surpluses were taken to state storehouses for distribution to administrators, craftsmen and priests, for trade or to build up reserves against the famine that would follow if the Nile flood failed. The Nile was also Egypt's main highway. The prevailing winds in Egypt blow north to south, enabling boats to travel upstream under sail and return downstream with the flow. Few settlements were far from the river, making it relatively easy to transport heavy loads of grain or stone over long distances. On either side of the narrow 800-kilometer (500-mile) fertile strip was the desert which isolated Egypt from the influence of other civilizations and protected it from invaders: Egyptian civilization was over 1,300 years old before it suffered its first major invasion.

Farming began in the Nile valley before 6000 BC and by 4000 BC it was populated by subsistence farmers. Chiefdoms and towns appeared by 3300. In the narrow confines of the valley competition was probably intense. Eventually, the southern chiefdoms amalgamated into an Upper Egyptian kingdom, which gained control over Lower Egypt. The first king known to have ruled all Egypt was Narmer, king of Upper Egypt who may have conquered Lower Egypt about 3000. This unification was consolidated by the foundation of Memphis as a new capital.

By the same date the hieroglyphic system of writing had appeared. The system worked on similar

THIS pottery lion, with a stylized mane resembling a headcloth, was found in the temple at Hierakonpolis. It dates from about the 3rd Dynasty.

*Mediterranean Sea*

to Libya

principles to the Sumerian pictographic script; hieroglyphs were developed for use in record keeping and as labels in the late Predynastic period. Early hieroglyphs appear on a slate palette which Narmer had carved to commemorate his victories. This palette shows that the principle of theocratic kingship that would be the basis of the ancient Egyptian state was already well established. During the ensuing Early Dynastic period (2920– 2575) the kings developed an efficient administration which made possible a dramatic increase in royal power at the beginning of the Old Kingdom (2575–2134), named for the kingdom ruled from Memphis by a succession of four dynasties.

The annual Nile flood was seen as a gift from the gods. The king claimed to be able to control the flood, but if the flood failed, his authority could be called into question. He was believed to be of divine descent and was held to be immortal. At his death immense effort was put into preserving his body and to providing it with a suitably regal tomb furnished with the luxuries of everyday life. Early royal tombs were built on platforms known as *mastabas*, but these were superseded by pyramids in the reign of King Djoser (r.2630–2611). Pyramid building climaxed in about 2550 with the 146-meter-high Great Pyramid, built for Khufu, and the slightly smaller pyramid of his son Khephren. These enormous

buildings are impressive evidence of the power the kings exercised over their subjects. However the large pyramids strained the resources of the kingdom: later ones were more modest and no more royal pyramids were built after the 17th century BC, by which time ideas of the afterlife had changed.

Egypt was governed by an efficient central and local bureaucracy. The kingdom was treated as the personal property of the king and the central bureaucracy was an extension of the royal household. The highest official was the vizier, who supervised the administration of justice and taxation. Below the vizier were chancellors, controllers of stores and other officials, supported by a staff of scribes trained in mathematics and writing. For the purposes of local government, Egypt was divided into provinces, or *nomes*, under governors selected from the royal or noble families.

During the 5th Dynasty (2465–2323) the monarchy was weakened by granting out lands as rewards and favors to the nobility. The provincial governorships became hereditary and drifted out of the control of the king. A period of low Nile floods then began around 2150, bringing famine and starvation, and the remaining royal authority crumbled. The Old Kingdom state collapsed and Egypt was divided between rival dynasties in Upper and Lower Egypt in what is known as the First Intermediate period.

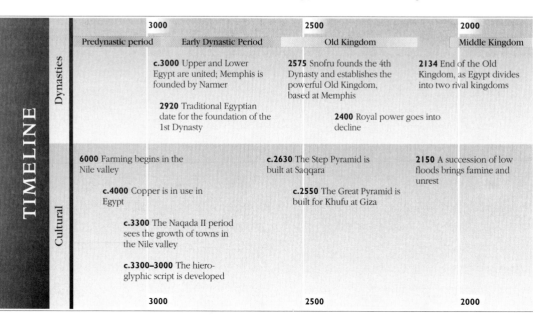

## TIMELINE

| | | 3000 | 2500 | 2000 |
|---|---|---|---|---|
| | | Predynastic period | Early Dynastic Period | Old Kingdom | Middle Kingdom |
| **Dynasties** | | **c.3000** Upper and Lower Egypt are united; Memphis is founded by Narmer | **2575** Snofru founds the 4th Dynasty and establishes the powerful Old Kingdom, based at Memphis | **2134** End of the Old Kingdom, as Egypt divides into two rival kingdoms |
| | | **2920** Traditional Egyptian date for the foundation of the 1st Dynasty | **2400** Royal power goes into decline | |
| **Cultural** | | **6000** Farming begins in the Nile valley | **c.2630** The Step Pyramid is built at Saqqara | **2150** A succession of low floods brings famine and unrest |
| | | **c.4000** Copper is in use in Egypt | **c.2550** The Great Pyramid is built for Khufu at Giza | |
| | | **c.3300** The Naqada II period sees the growth of towns in the Nile valley | | |
| | | **c.3300–3000** The hieroglyphic script is developed | | |
| | | 3000 | 2500 | 2000 |

**1** The First Cataract was the traditional southern frontier of Egypt through most of its history.

**2** Hierakonpolis and Naqada were the first towns to develop in Egypt, c.3300.

**3** Saqqara is the site of the oldest pyramid, the Step Pyramid, c.2630.

**4** Giza is the site of the largest pyramids, including the Great Pyramid of Khufu.

**5** The mountains of the Eastern Desert were the chief source of minerals.

**6** Graffiti show that the Egyptians were exploiting Sinai's mineral wealth as early as the 3rd Dynasty (2649-2575).

**7** The Egyptians maintained a trading post at Buhen in Nubia during the Old Kingdom.

**8** Memphis was capital of Egypt for most of the Early Dynastic period and Old Kingdom.

to the Levant

timber
from Lebanon

Tell el-Rub'a

Buto

Nile River Delta

LOWER
EGYPT

natron

SINAI

Great Bitter
Lake

natron

Wadi
Natrun

Heliopolis

**4**

Abu Rawash

Giza

quartzite
limestone

Zawyet el-Aryan    Abusir
                    Memphis

Saqqara

**8**

**3**

Dahshur

Maidum

Seila

basalt
dolerite
gypsum

Faiyum

Birket Qarun
(ancient shoreline)

Abu Rawash

Dishasha

Herakleopolis

flint

Sawaris

Gebel el-Teir

Tihna

Zawyet el-Amwat

MIDDLE EGYPT

Bahariya
Oasis

Bahr Yusuf

Beni Hasan

limestone

Deir el-Malik

Sheik Sa'id

alabaster

Sheik Atiya

Quseir el-Amarna

Deir el-Gabrawi

Meir

Dara

Asyut

Hammamiya

Qaw el-Kebir

Akhmim

Western
Desert

Farafra
Oasis

Nag el-Deir

Hagarsa

Eastern
Desert

copper
turquoise

**6**

copper

Gulf of Suez

copper

Red Sea

porphyry
granite
jasper

copper

lead

**5**

copper

granite

Dendara    Nag el-Gaziriyah

Koptos

Naqada    Tukh

**2**

Thebes

Abydos

**2**

limestone

UPPER EGYPT

Gebelan    El-Mo'alla

limestone

El-Kab

El-Kula    Hierakonpolis

**2**    Edfu

gold
feldspar
emeralds

to the Red Sea

alum

El-Kharga
Oasis

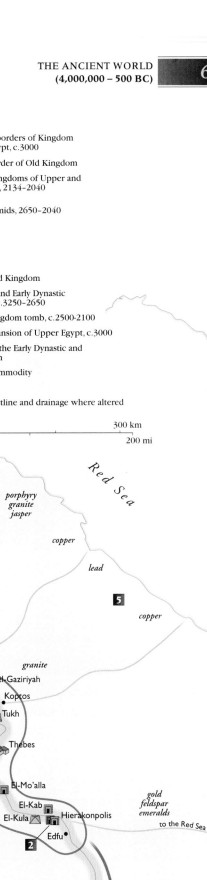

Kurkur
Oasis

Qubbet el-
Hawa

lead
granite
diorite
steatite
quartzite

amethyst

Elephantine
1st Cataract

**1**

**7**

to Buhen

El-Dakhla
Oasis    Balat

ebony
gold
ivory
from Nubia

### Legend

| | fertile area |
| | conjectural borders of Kingdom of Upper Egypt, c.3000 |
| | southern border of Old Kingdom |
| | border of Kingdoms of Upper and Lower Egypt, 2134–2040 |

Old Kingdom pyramids, 2650–2040

| | single |
| | multiple |
| | non-royal |

| | capital of Old Kingdom |
| | Predynastic and Early Dynastic royal tomb, c.3250–2650 |
| | later Old Kingdom tomb, c.2500–2100 |
| | military expansion of Upper Egypt, c.3000 |
| | campaign in the Early Dynastic and Old Kingdom |
| lead | source of commodity |
| | desert route |
| | modern coastline and drainage where altered |

0 ——— 300 km
0 ——— 200 mi

See also 5 (Mesopotamia);
10 (Middle and New Kingdoms); 15 (Bible lands)

The spread of agriculture through Europe was a complex process of small-scale migrations by farming peoples and the adoption of farming techniques by Mesolithic hunter–gatherers. It took time to develop crop strains suited to the colder and wetter climates of central, western and northern Europe. Hunter–gatherers readily adopted some aspects of the material culture of neighboring farmers, such as pottery and polished stone axes, but only adopted food production when natural food sources were in short supply. In many areas, Mesolithic hunter–gatherers were already semi-sedentary, so the transition to a settled farming way of life was probably easily made when it became necessary.

Farming, based on cereals, legumes, sheep, goats and cattle, first began in Europe in Greece and the Balkans around 6500 BC. This pattern of farming spread from the Balkans around the Mediterranean coasts to southern France and Spain by 5000. Whether the adoption of farming in Europe was an indigenous development or was influenced by the farming societies of the Middle East is doubtful. Southeastern Europe was within the range of wild einkorn wheat, cattle, pigs and sheep and farming may have developed as a result of experimentation with cultivation and animal husbandry by indigenous hunter–gatherers. Cattle may have been domesticated independently in southeast Europe but some crops, such as emmer wheat and barley, were certainly introduced from the Middle East.

The earliest farming culture of central Europe is the Bandkeramik or Linear Pottery culture. This originated in the northern Balkans around 5400 BC and over a few centuries spread north and west across the band of fertile and easily worked loess soils that extends across Europe from Romania to the Rhineland. When the population of a village became too large, a daughter settlement was simply founded a few kilometers away. The indigenous Mesolithic hunter–gatherer bands were not displaced by the Bandkeramik people, who settled on vacant lands between them, usually along rivers. However, the steady encroachment by the farmers placed pressure on the hunter–gatherers' resources and they were gradually forced to adopt farming too: gradually the two populations became assimilated. After a delay of several centuries, the farming way of life spread from central Europe into western Europe, then Britain and Scandinavia and the southwest steppes.

Farming in central and northern Europe was very different from that in the south. The cold winters led to spring sowing of crops (autumn sowing prevailed in southern Europe, the Middle East and north Africa) and there was greater emphasis on cattle and pigs, which were better suited to grazing in woodland than sheep and goats.

Neolithic settlements were generally small, with populations of only forty to sixty. The most common type of building was the wooden longhouse that accommodated both people and livestock. Except in treeless areas such as the Orkney Islands, where stone houses were built, settlements have left few traces; burials and ritual structures provide most evidence of the nature of Neolithic societies. In most of Europe the dead were buried in individual graves in cemeteries with offerings of stone tools, pottery and ornaments. There is little variation in the quantity and quality of grave goods, indicating that these communities were not divded between rich and poor. In many areas the dead were buried communally in megalithic tombs which remained in use for many generations. The tombs were usually covered with mounds of earth, and may have served as territorial markers as well as burial places, the presence of the community's ancestors legitimizing the ownership of the present generation. The Atlantic coast of western Europe, where the earliest megalithic tombs were built, was already relatively densely populated in Mesolithic times. Population pressure may have been felt after the introduction of agriculture, leading to a new concern with territoriality.

In the later Neolithic and the early Bronze Age, northwest Europe saw the construction of megalithic stone circles and circular earth structures known as henges. Some circles have astronomical alignments or form part of a complex ritual landscape but their exact functions are unknown. Some monuments are so large that they must have been built by chiefdoms able to command the resources

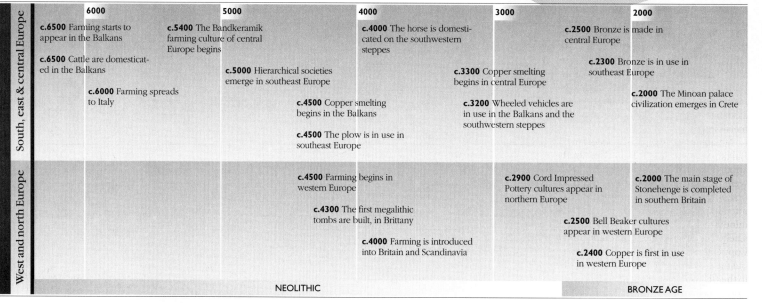

## TIMELINE

### South, east & central Europe

| 6000 | 5000 | 4000 | 3000 | 2000 |
|---|---|---|---|---|
| **c.6500** Farming starts to appear in the Balkans | **c.5400** The Bandkeramik farming culture of central Europe begins | **c.4000** The horse is domesticated on the southwestern steppes | | **c.2500** Bronze is made in central Europe |
| **c.6500** Cattle are domesticated in the Balkans | **c.5000** Hierarchical societies emerge in southeast Europe | | **c.3300** Copper smelting begins in central Europe | **c.2300** Bronze is in use in southeast Europe |
| **c.6000** Farming spreads to Italy | **c.4500** Copper smelting begins in the Balkans | **c.3200** Wheeled vehicles are in use in the Balkans and the southwestern steppes | | **c.2000** The Minoan palace civilization emerges in Crete |
| | | **c.4500** The plow is in use in southeast Europe | | |

### West and north Europe

| 6000 | 5000 | 4000 | 3000 | 2000 |
|---|---|---|---|---|
| | | **c.4500** Farming begins in western Europe | **c.2900** Cord Impressed Pottery cultures appear in northern Europe | **c.2000** The main stage of Stonehenge is completed in southern Britain |
| | | **c.4300** The first megalithic tombs are built, in Brittany | | **c.2500** Bell Beaker cultures appear in western Europe |
| | | **c.4000** Farming is introduced into Britain and Scandinavia | | **c.2400** Copper is first in use in western Europe |

**earliest farming cultures**

- early Aegean and Anatolian Painted Ware cultures, 7000–6000
- Balkan Painted and Impressed Pottery cultures, 6500–4000
- Impressed Pottery cultures, 6000–4000
- Bandkeramik or Linear Pottery culture, 5400–4500
- Bowl cultures, 4500–3300
- Tripolye–Cucuteni cultures, 4200–3800
- Funnel-necked Beaker cultures, 4200–2800

- megalithic monument building, 4300–2000
- stone circle or alignment
- megalithic tomb
- excavation of early farming village
- other site
- spread of copper working by 4500
- spread of copper working by 3000
- general direction of the spread of farming, 6000–3000

0        600 km
0        400 mi

BELL-BEAKER drinking cups with incised decoration have been found in graves all over western Europe. Pollen grains found in the bottom of some indicate that they had contained a mead-like drink.

and populations of wide areas. The emergence of more hierarchical societies in the later Neolithic is also reflected in burial practices. In cultures such as the Cord Impressed Ware culture of eastern Europe and the Bell Beaker cultures in western Europe, variations in the quality and quantity of grave goods in burials indicate differences of wealth and status in farming societies. In many areas these changes are associated with the introduction of copper and gold metallurgy.

Metallurgy developed separately in the northern Balkans around 4800 BC and in southern Spain about fifteen centuries later. Both copper and gold were used to make small tools and ornaments. At first only native metals were used, cold-hammered into shape, but by 4500 copper ores were being mined in the Balkans for smelting. Copper was smelted in Spain, Italy and probably Britain by 2400. Copper tools had few advantages over stone ones, but the elites valued metal for display objects. Only in the Bronze Age did metal tools begin to replace stone tools in everyday use.

**1** Starcevo was one of the earliest farming settlements in the Balkans, 6000–4000 BC. Hunting and gathering, cereals and cattle were all important.

**2** Horses were domesticated in the Tripolye-Cucuteni cultures in the 4th millennium BC.

**3** Incised clay tablets from Tartaria show that a simple system of notation had developed in the Balkans by 5000.

**4** Copper ores were being mined at Rudna Glava in 4500 BC, the earliest known in the world.

**5** A major stone temple complex was built at Tarxien c.3500–2400 BC.

**6** Some three thousand standing stones aligned in multiple rows make Carnac one of the largest megalithic sites. Its purpose is unknown.

**7** The stone circle at Stonehenge was built in several phases spanning the Neolithic and Bronze Age (c.3000–1500 BC).

**8** An "ice man", whose body was found in 1991, froze to death in the Otztaler Alps c.3350–3120 BC.

See also 3 (Mesolithic Europe); 4 (spread of agriculture); 12 Bronze Age Europe

The first civilization of east Asia developed in the Yellow river valley in the 18th century BC from indigenous Neolithic cultures. Farming began as early as 5800 BC on the broad band of loess soils that stretches across the Yellow river basin. By 5000 millet farming villages of the Yangshao culture were spread across much of the region. At the same time rice farming communities were spreading among the wetlands of the Yangtze valley. Rice farming spread to the Yellow river valley in the late 4th millennium and the Longshan cultures emerged. In favorable areas, the Longshan cultures practiced intensive rice cultivation using irrigation. The population rose, copper came into use, regional trading networks developed and a warrior class emerged. There is evidence of warfare, such as rammed earth fortifications and massacres of prisoners. A system of divination based on the use of "oracle bones" was developed.

According to Chinese traditions, civilization was founded by the emperor Huang Di around 2698 BC while the first dynasty, the Xia, was founded by Yu the Great in about 2205. However, there is no evidence for states in China in the 3rd millennium BC.

The first historically and archeologically attested Chinese dynasty is the Shang. This was founded about 1766 BC by King Tang, around the time of the appearance of the Erlitou culture. Cities with monumental buildings began to develop craft specialization and advanced bronze-casting techniques were adopted. The appearance of rich burials points to the emergence of a powerful ruling elite. A pictographic script came into use: the modern Chinese script is its direct descendant. Shang cultural influence extended across most of northern China and as far south as the Yangtze river. Like many early states, the Shang kingdom combined directly run provinces and vassal states.

Around 1122 the Shang king Di-xin was defeated and overthrown by his vassal king Wu of Zhou. The dynasty established by Wu became the longest lived of Chinese history and the early centuries of its rule were looked back on as a golden age. To legitimize their rule after their usurpation of the Shang, the Zhou rulers introduced the theory of the "Mandate

rice farming, 6500-3000

Yangshao Neolithic culture, 5000-3200

Longshan Neolithic cultures, 3200-1800

Erlitou culture, c.1800-1650

Shang bronze working

Shang city

PI    administrative subdivision of Shang kingdom

Anyang    rich burial of the Shang period

spread of rice farming

source of copper

source of tin

area of loess soils

modern coastline and drainage where altered

0 ————————— 800 km
0 ————————— 600 mi

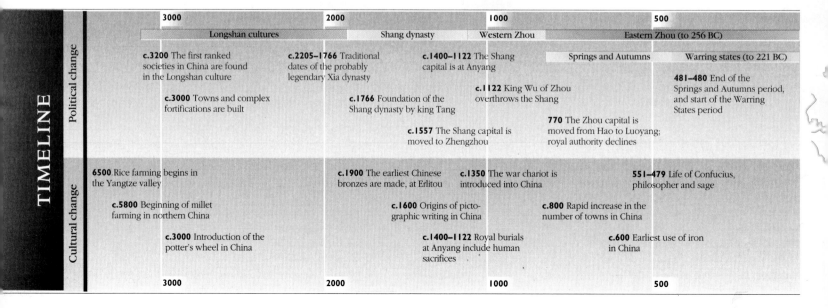

| | 3000 | 2000 | 1000 | 500 |
|---|---|---|---|---|
| | | Longshan cultures | Shang dynasty | Western Zhou | Eastern Zhou (to 256 BC) |
| **Political change** | **c.3200** The first ranked societies in China are found in the Longshan culture | **c.2205–1766** Traditional dates of the probably legendary Xia dynasty | **c.1400–1122** The Shang capital is at Anyang | Springs and Autumns    Warring states (to 221 BC) |
| | **c.3000** Towns and complex fortifications are built | **c.1766** Foundation of the Shang dynasty by king Tang | **c.1122** King Wu of Zhou overthrows the Shang | **481–480** End of the Springs and Autumns period, and start of the Warring States period |
| | | | **770** The Zhou capital is moved from Hao to Luoyang; royal authority declines | |
| | | **c.1557** The Shang capital is moved to Zhengzhou | | |
| **Cultural change** | **6500** Rice farming begins in the Yangtze valley | **c.1900** The earliest Chinese bronzes are made, at Erlitou | **c.1350** The war chariot is introduced into China | **551–479** Life of Confucius, philosopher and sage |
| | **c.5800** Beginning of millet farming in northern China | **c.1600** Origins of pictographic writing in China | **c.800** Rapid increase in the number of towns in China | |
| | **c.3000** Introduction of the potter's wheel in China | **c.1400–1122** Royal burials at Anyang include human sacrifices | **c.600** Earliest use of iron in China | |
| | 3000 | 2000 | 1000 | 500 |

TIMELINE

**Legend:**

- borders, 770–481
- Zhou state, 770–481
- Zhou royal domain, 770–481
- other state
- extent of Chinese cultural influence
- state capital
- city
- WU  state with non-Chinese population
- (1–5)  order of hegemons, late 8th to mid 6th century BC
- Mixu  barbarian tribes
- barbarian attacks, late 9th to early 8th century BC
- barbarian attacks, 7th to early 6th century BC
- modern coastline and drainage where altered

Xianyun, Sanggan, Yuxian, Wuzhong, YAN, Ji, Yellow, LÜLIANG MTS, Wuzhong, Yellow river before 602 BC, Bo Hai, Hutuo, TAIHANG MTS, JIN (3, 5), Xing, Yellow river after 602 BC, present Yellow river, QI (2), Linzi, Di, Fen, Jing, Chaoge, Zhang, Qufu, LU, Mixu, Jiang, WEI, Cao, Teng, Tan, Qin, QIN, [4], ZHOU, Luoyang, Xinzheng, ZHENG (1), CAO, TENG, Wei, Hao, [5], Xu, SONG, Shangqiu, Lirong, QIN MTS, XU, Ying, CHEN, DABA MTS, Han, CAI, Chen, Huai, Lake Hongze, Yangtze, CHU (4), Xincai, WU [6], Lake Tai, Wu, Yangtze, BA, Ba, Baipu, Ying, YUE, Guiji, Lake Dongting, Lake Pengli, Dongyi, Yellow Sea

Scale: 0 — 400 km / 0 — 300 mi

SKILLED bronze casting was common to both the Shang and the Zhou dynasties. This ritual wine bucket is of early Zhou manufacture, c.1000.

of Heaven". The ruler was the "Son of Heaven" and "All under Heaven" was his lawful domain so long as he was just and moral. Should a ruler become unjust, Heaven would send him a warning and if he failed to reform, the Mandate would be given to another. Di-xin had been a sadist so Heaven had transferred the right to rule to the Zhou. This theory, which could be used both to condemn disobedience to the ruler and to justify successful usurpation, remained central to Chinese imperial ideology.

The Zhou kingdom was a decentralized feudal state, divided into fiefs governed by dukes chosen from among the king's relatives and trusted supporters. Only the royal domain was directly ruled by the king. In 770 barbarian attacks on Hao forced the Zhou to move their capital to Luoyang. This event was a turning-point in the history of the dynasty and marks the beginning of the period of disorder and fragmentation known as the Springs and Autumns period (after the title of tne annals of the state of Lu).

Luoyang was more centrally situated than Hao but it removed the dynasty from its traditional heartland in the west; its authority began to decline. By this time the king controlled less land than most of his dukes who now became, in effect, the rulers of independent states, making almost constant war on one another. However, the dukes continued to recognize the sovereignty of the king and also recognized the duke of the leading state of the time as hegemon (with general primacy over all other states). The Springs and Autumns period turned into the Warring States period (480–221), which saw the decline of feudal relationships and the rise of a professional bureaucracy.

The Springs and Autumns period was a brutal age but it saw great creativity in literature and religious and philosophical thought. The end of the period saw Confucius found the ethical system, which remains fundamental to Chinese thought. Iron working was adopted around 600, probably in Wu, though iron tools and weapons did not replace bronze in everyday use until the 2nd century BC.

1 More than a hundred wet-rice farming villages (using flooded fields) were established in this region 6500–4000 BC.

2 Erlitou was the site of the first Chinese bronzes c.1900 BC; it was probably also the first Shang capital.

3 The city and ritual offering pits at Sanxingdui, discovered in the 1990s, are evidence of a bronze-using civilization contemporary with the Shang.

4 Hao, in the original Zhou heartland, was abandoned as the capital in 770 after barbarian attacks. The move initiated a decline in Zhou authority.

5 The Zhou royal domain was limited to a small area around Luoyang by the 7th century.

6 Wu, the dominant state in southern China in the late 6th century, was destroyed by Yue in 473 BC.

See also 4 (agriculture),
26 (Warring states and after)

**B**y 2000 BC the revolutionary impact of agriculture had become clear. Farming was practiced on every continent and would overtake hunting and gathering as the way of life of most people well before the Christian era.

Not all early farming societies developed the same level of complexity. Poor soil, climate, endemic diseases of humans or livestock or a lack of suitable crops limited development in many areas. The greater the resources possessed by a society, the more complex it could become; in a few favorable environments (such as the northwest of North America), hunter-gatherer societies too achieved greater levels of social complexity.

Most early farming societies were kinship-based tribes of hundreds or a few thousand people living in villages or dispersed homesteads. Although they recognized ties of kinship, religion or language with others, each tribe was essentially independent. Differences of rank and status existed but leaders could rarely exercise coercive power over other tribes' people. Archeologically, such societies (known to anthropologists as "segmentary societies") can be recognized by communal burial practices, the remains of permanent homesteads and villages and communal works such as the megalithic tombs of prehistoric western Europe. In 2000 BC segmentary farming societies were dominant in south and southeast Asia, New Guinea, north Africa, northern Europe and parts of Mesoamerica and South America.

Where intensive agricultural techniques could be used, largescale hierarchical communities of up to 20,000 people, known as "chiefdoms", could develop. Rank and status were linked to lineage: the senior person of the senior lineage was the chief, who was thereby the ruler of the whole community. Chieftains could exercise coercive power, often through a warrior class, and support specialist craftsmen. Archeologically, chiefdoms show major construction projects requiring large resources of labor and wealth, such as Stonehenge in southern Britain (▷ 7 ). In chiefdoms the quantity and quality of grave goods placed with burials indicate the rank and status of the individual and a few burials are lavishly furnished. Chiefdoms commonly had a dominant central site such as a stronghold or ceremonial center, and smaller satellite settlements. In 2000 BC chiefdoms were established in the Middle East and southwest central Europe, in China and the Andes. In western Europe segmentary farming societies were giving way to chiefdoms at this time.

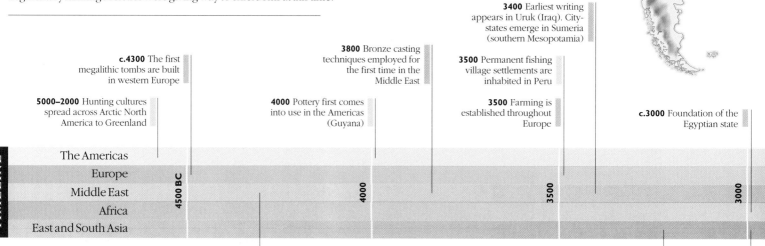

**3400** Earliest writing appears in Uruk (Iraq). City-states emerge in Sumeria (southern Mesopotamia)

**3800** Bronze casting techniques employed for the first time in the Middle East

**3500** Permanent fishing village settlements are inhabited in Peru

**c.4300** The first megalithic tombs are built in western Europe

**5000–2000** Hunting cultures spread across Arctic North America to Greenland

**4000** Pottery first comes into use in the Americas (Guyana)

**3500** Farming is established throughout Europe

**c.3000** Foundation of the Egyptian state

| TIMELINE | | | | |
|---|---|---|---|---|
| The Americas | | | | |
| Europe | 4500 BC | 4000 | 3500 | 3000 |
| Middle East | | | | |
| Africa | | | | |
| East and South Asia | | | | |

**4300–3100** Uruk period in Mesopotamia. The first cities are built.

**3200–1800** Chinese Longshan advanced farming cultures; first towns are built in China

**3000** Ancestral Austronesians migrate from Taiwan to the Philippines

**3000–1700** Pastoral farming is established on the central Asian steppes (Afanasevo culture)

hunter-gatherers
nomadic pastoralists
simple farming societies
complex farming societies/chiefdoms
state societies
uninhabited
extent of bronze working, c.2000 BC

Greenland

Iceland

*Arctic marine mammal hunters*

*Finno–Ugrian taiga hunter-gatherers*

*Paleo–Siberian taiga hunter-gatherers*

*early Bronze Age Unetice culture*

*late Neolithic corded ware cultures*

*Afanasevo culture (pastoral farmers)*

*Bell Beaker cultures (late Neolithic farmers)*

*Catacomb grave culture (pastoral farmers)*

*Bronze Age cultures*

*Steppe Pastoralist cultures*

*Paleo–Asiatic hunter-gatherers*

Koreans

*Greeks*

Hittites

Hurrians

*Central Asian farmers*

*late Jomon hunter-gatherers*

Berbers

city states

Chinese

*Longshan late Neolithic cultures*

Minoan palace civilization

UR

Kassites

*Tibeto–Burmese*

Amorites

ELAM

EGYPT

*pastoral nomads*

Indus valley civilization

Thais

*Austro-Asiatic rice farmers*

Taiwan

Nubians

south Semites

Dravidians

Austronesians

*Pastoral nomads*

*tropical forest hunter-gatherers*

Ceylon

Sumatra

Borneo

Celebes

Java

New Guinea

Timor

*Khoisan hunter-gatherers*

Madagascar

*Australo–Melanesian Neolithic farmers and hunter-gatherers*

*Australian Aboriginal hunter-gatherers*

*Tasmanian hunter-gatherers*

**2300** Beginning of the Bronze Age in Europe

**2334–2279** Sargon of Akkad conquers Mesopotamia, and sets up the world's first empire

**2000** Completion of the main stage of Stonehenge megalithic monument (southern Britain)

**2600** The earliest monumental buildings are built at Aspero, Peru

**2000** Early Greeks settle the Peloponnese

2500

2000

**c.2630** The first pyramid is built at Saqqara (Egypt)

**2600–1800** The Indus valley civilization flourishes

**2575–2134** The Old Kingdom in Egypt

**2040–1640** The Middle Kingdom in Egypt

**2500** The earliest bronze tools are found in southeast Asia

**2000** Austronesians settle in Melanesia

In river floodplains where agriculture could support communities of tens of thousands, cities could develop. In these large-scale societies the first states and civilizations developed. Ties of kinship and lineage were insufficient to bind them, and rulers devised ideologies to define the rights and obligations of their subjects. Writing and mathematics were developed for administration. Although most people still worked on the land, specialist occupations – craftsmen, shopkeepers, merchants, soldiers, priests and bureaucrats – and social classes emerged. Public building projects, such as city walls, roads, canals, temples and palaces, could be undertaken for economic, defense, religious reasons, or for prestige.

In 2000 BC states existed in only a few areas. Independent city-states had developed in Sumeria (southern Iraq) around 3400 and were widespread in the Middle East by 2500, but declined in importance in Mesopotamia as militaristic rulers began to create territorial kingdoms and empires. In Egypt, the territorial kingdom formed the basis of the state from the start. A centralized kingdom was created in about 3000, and by 2800 it held sway throughout the Nile valley north of Nubia (▷ 20). By 2300 a state civilization had also developed in the Indus valley.

Pastoral nomadism, an important form of intensive animal husbandry in which farmers constantly move their herds from one poor pasture to another, developed out of sedentary (single-center) pastoral farming, probably in the Sahara where desertification spread after 3000 BC ■

The reunification of Egypt in 2040 BC by Mentuhotpe II (r.2061–2010), of the Theban dynasty of Upper Egypt, marks the start of the Middle Kingdom. A few decades later royal authority and political stability had been restored and the power of the provincial governors reduced. To rebuild a loyal administration, the Middle Kingdom rulers promoted propagandist literature, while statuary presented the king as the care-worn "good shepherd" of his people. Pyramid building was revived, though more modestly than in the Old Kingdom.

Egypt's neighbors were now becoming organized into chiefdoms and petty kingdoms, and the Middle Kingdom rulers had to pursue a more aggressive foreign policy than their predecessors. Under Amenemhet I (r.1991–1962), Lower Nubia was conquered; the frontier at the Second Cataract was garrisoned and heavily fortified by his successors. Egyptian influence was extended over the Levant during the reign of Senwosret III (r.1878–1841) and local rulers were forced to become vassals of Egypt. During the 18th century the bureaucracy began to grow out of control and for much of the time the effective rulers of Egypt were the viziers. In the 17th century there was considerable immigration from the Levant into the Delta. Most immigrants were absorbed into the lower classes of Egyptian society but one, Khendjer, became king around 1745 BC.

From around 1640 much of Egypt was ruled by the Hyksos, a Semitic people from the Levant, who gradually took over Lower Egypt, which they ruled from their capital at Avaris. Upper Egypt remained independent under a Theban dynasty but control over Lower Nubia was lost to the nascent kingdom of Kush. Hyksos rule, in what is known as the Second Intermediate period, made Egypt more open to foreign influences. Bronze came into widespread use, war chariots were introduced, as were weapons such as the composite bow and scale armor. New fashions in dress, musical instruments, domestic animals and crops were adopted through Hyksos influence. Otherwise, the Hyksos accepted Egyptian traditions and historical continuity was unbroken.

Under the Theban king Seqenenre II (died c.1555) the Egyptians began a long struggle to expel the Hyksos which was finally completed by Ahmose in 1532. This victory marks the beginning of the New Kingdom, under which the power and influence of ancient Egypt reached its peak. The Hyksos invasion had shown the Egyptians that their borders were no longer secure, and the New Kingdom was overtly militaristic and expansionist, reaching its greatest extent around 1500 under the warrior king Tuthmosis I. Tuthmosis conquered the entire Levant and established a frontier on the Euphrates. Lower Nubia was reconquered and Kush was overrun to beyond the Fourth Cataract. The primary motive of expansion into the Levant was to establish a buffer zone between Egypt and the aggressive powers of the Middle East; in Nubia, which had rich gold deposits, the motive was economic. In the Levant, local rulers were kept under the supervision of Egyptian officials and key cities were garrisoned. Nubia was subjected to full colonial government under a viceroy directly responsible to the king. Nubia was a great source of wealth to the New Kingdom, but the Egyptians faced a constant struggle to control the Levant, against local rebellions and expansionist powers such as the Hittite empire.

The power of Egypt declined after the reign of Amenophis IV (r.1353–1335). Amenophis, who changed his name to Akhenaten, was a radical religious reformer who attempted to replace Egypt's traditional polytheism with the monotheistic cult of the Aten, or sun disk. Akhenaten founded a new capital and promoted radically new art styles to symbolize the break with the past, but there was little popular enthusiasm for the new religion, which was abandoned after his death. In the ensuing period of political instability, Egypt lost control of the Levant to the Hittites. Campaigns by the kings (or pharaohs as they were now known) Sethos I (r.1306–1290) and Ramesses II "the Great" (r.1290–1224) to restore the Egyptian position were only partially successful and Ramesses eventually made peace with the Hittites.

Around 1200 the entire region was disrupted by

**Middle Kingdom (12th Dynasty, 1991-1783)**

- zone of direct control
- zone of dominance

**Second Intermediate period**

- Hyksos Kingdom (15th Dynasty, 1640-1532)
- Theban (17th Dynasty, 1646-1550)
- Kingdom of Kush
- maximum extent of New Kingdom under Tuthmosis I, 1504-1492
- royal capital, with dynasty
- city

royal tomb
- Middle Kingdom
- New Kingdom

fort or garrison
- Middle Kingdom
- New Kingdom
- sacked c.1200, probably by Sea Peoples

Giza   temple

- desert route used for communication between the Hyksos and Kushite allies
- gold deposit
- major migration
- modern coastline and drainage where altered

Libyans

0         300 km
0         200 mi

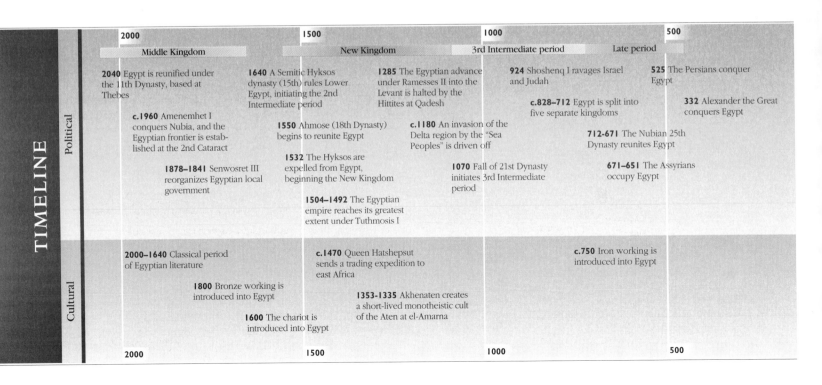

TIMELINE

| | 2000 | 1500 | 1000 | 500 |
|---|---|---|---|---|
| | Middle Kingdom | New Kingdom | 3rd Intermediate period   Late period | |

Political

**2040** Egypt is reunified under the 11th Dynasty, based at Thebes

**c.1960** Amenemhet I conquers Nubia, and the Egyptian frontier is established at the 2nd Cataract

**1878–1841** Senwosret III reorganizes Egyptian local government

**1640** A Semitic Hyksos dynasty (15th) rules Lower Egypt, initiating the 2nd Intermediate period

**1550** Ahmose (18th Dynasty) begins to reunite Egypt

**1532** The Hyksos are expelled from Egypt, beginning the New Kingdom

**1504–1492** The Egyptian empire reaches its greatest extent under Tuthmosis I

**1285** The Egyptian advance under Ramesses II into the Levant is halted by the Hittites at Qadesh

**c.1180** An invasion of the Delta region by the "Sea Peoples" is driven off

**1070** Fall of 21st Dynasty initiates 3rd Intermediate period

**924** Shoshenq I ravages Israel and Judah

**c.828–712** Egypt is split into five separate kingdoms

**712-671** The Nubian 25th Dynasty reunites Egypt

**671–651** The Assyrians occupy Egypt

**525** The Persians conquer Egypt

**332** Alexander the Great conquers Egypt

Cultural

**2000–1640** Classical period of Egyptian literature

**1800** Bronze working is introduced into Egypt

**1600** The chariot is introduced into Egypt

**c.1470** Queen Hatshepsut sends a trading expedition to east Africa

**1353-1335** Akhenaten creates a short-lived monotheistic cult of the Aten at el-Amarna

**c.750** Iron working is introduced into Egypt

| 2000 | 1500 | 1000 | | 500 |

Sea peoples
c.1180

HITTITE EMPIRE

MITTANI

Carchemish

Aleppo
Alalakh

Ugarit
Hamath

Cyprus

*Syrian
Desert*

Euphrates

Arvad
Qadesh
1285

*M e d i t e r r a n e a n   S e a*

Byblos

*L E V A N T*

Sidon
Damascus

Tyre
Hazor

Acco
5

Megiddo
c.1456
Beth-shean

Jerusalem
Joppa
Amman

6
1180
Gaza

Buto
Sakha
14

Raqote

Sais
Tanis
Sile

Kom el-Hisn
Bubastis
Avaris
15, 19, 20

Athribis
Heliopolis

*L O W E R
E G Y P T*

Giza
Memphis
12, 13, 18, 19

Dahshur
El-Lisht
12, 13

Hawara

Kom Medinet Ghurab
El-Lahun

Herakleopolis

*Hyksos*
17th century

*Hebrews*
late 13th century

*S I N A I*

Serabit

*Bahariya
Oasis*

El-Ashmunein

El-Amarna
18

7

*Farafra
Oasis*

Asyut

*Western
Desert*

Akhmim

*Eastern
Desert*

Mersa Gawasis

Abydos

8
Karnak

Valley of the Kings

Thebes
11, 17, 18

*Red Sea*

Armant
2

*El-Dakhla
Oasis*
Balat

*El-Kharga
Oasis*

Luxor

Hierakonpolis
El-Kab

Edfu

*U P P E R   E G Y P T*

Elephantine

1st Cataract

*Kurkur
Oasis*

Beit el-Wali

*Dunqul
Oasis*

Gerf Hussein

Ikkur
Quban

3

Aniba

*L O W E R
N U B I A*

Abu Simbel

Buhen
Faras

Kot
Meinarti

*Salima
Oasis*

Mirgissa
Dorginarti
2nd Cataract

Uronati
Semna
1

Kumma

Sai

Amara West

*U P P E R
N U B I A*

Amara East

Soleb

Sesebi

Tombos
3rd Cataract
Kerma

Kawa
4

*K U S H*

4th Cataract

Napata

5th Cataract

WAR chariots and the powerful bow were introduced to Egypt by the Hyksos. This painting of the boy-king Tutankhamun portrays him using both.

waves of migrations. In the 1180s the northern Delta was invaded by the Sea Peoples, a coalition of Aegean, Anatolian and Levantine peoples. They were driven off after a naval battle by Ramesses III but he could not prevent them settling around Gaza.

During the New Kingdom large tracts of land were granted to the temples, and by the 11th century they controlled a third of Egyptian land: the temple of Amun at Karnak effectively controlled all Upper Egypt. By now the priesthood had become heredi- tary and was largely out of the king's direct control.

The Third Intermediate period (1070–712) was a time of weak monarchies and decentralized power. The New Kingdom empire was completely lost by 1000. Although the kingdoms of the Levant posed no threat to Egypt, the Nubian kingdom of Kush developed into a powerful Egyptianate state which eventually conquered Egypt in 712. This conquest marked the beginning of the Late period (712–332) which saw foreign influence in, and over, Egypt increase. Spells of Nubian, Assyrian and Persian rule were followed by revivals under native dynasties, but after the conquest by Alexander the Great in 332, Egypt was permanently under foreign rule until modern times..

**1** The 2nd Cataract, long treacherous rapids, was heavily fortified by the 12th Dynasty 1991–1783.

**2** Thebes became capital of Egypt at the start of the Middle Kingdom; by the New Kingdom it was Egypt's most important religious center.

**3** The fort at Aniba was the administrative capital of the Nubian province during the New Kingdom.

**4** Kerma was the capital of the kingdom of Kush in the 2nd Intermediate period.

**5** The rebellious king of Qadesh was defeated by Tuthmosis III at Megiddo in c.1456, and the city fell after a seven-month siege.

**6** Ramesses III defeated the Sea Peoples in a naval battle in 1180, after which they settled near Gaza.

**7** El-Amarna was founded as a new capital by the "heretic" pharaoh Akhenaten c.1350 and was abandoned after his death.

**8** The Valley of the Kings contains 62 tombs, mostly of members of the royal family of the 18th–20th Dynasties, including Tutankhamun's (r.1333–1323).

See also 6 (Old Kingdom Egypt);
15 (Bible lands); 18 (Persia)

E urope's first cities and states developed on the Aegean island of Crete around 2000 BC, where the Minoans developed a system of intensive agriculture based on wheat, olives and vines. Olives and vines grew well on rough hillsides and produced valuable commodities for long-distance trade, allowing good plowland to be kept for wheat production. Sheep were kept on Crete's mountain pastures and their wool supplied a textile industry that exported cloth to Egypt. Minoan pottery and metalwork was in demand throughout the eastern Mediterranean.

By 2000 BC Minoan society was controlled from palaces at Knossos, Phaistos, Mallia and Khania, probably the capitals of small kingdoms. A number of smaller palaces were probably subordinate centers. The palaces, which incorporated vast storehouses for grain, oil and other products, were centers for redistributing produce collected as taxes or tribute for rations to support administrators, craftsmen or traders. The Minoans had a hieroglyphic script by 2000, but this was superseded by a syllabic script three centuries later. Neither script has been deciphered so the ethnic identity of the Minoans is unknown, but they did not speak an Indo-European language and were therefore not Greeks.

Around 1700 most of the Minoan palaces were destroyed by fire, probably as a result of warfare between the palace states; they were subsequently rebuilt, but only Knossos regained its former splendor, taking control of the whole island and reducing the other palaces to tributary status. In 1626 the palaces were damaged by ash falls and earthquakes resulting from a volcanic eruption on the nearby island of Thera. The palaces were rebuilt and the Minoan civilization endured until it collapsed in about 1450 after conquest by the Mycenaeans.

The Mycenaeans, or Achaeans as they probably called themselves, were a Greek-speaking people who had moved to the Greek peninsula from the Balkans around 2000 BC. By around 1600 small kingdoms based on fortified towns were beginning to develop and a system of writing, based on the Cretan syllabic script, had been adopted. The earliest

## TIMELINE

### Crete

| 2000 | | 1500 | | 1000 |
|---|---|---|---|---|
| | | Minoan civilization | | |
| c.6000 The first settlement of Crete | | | | |
| 3000 Stone tombs are built on Crete, and trade develops with the Levant | 2000 The first palaces are built on Crete | 1700 Minoan Linear A script develops | c.1450 The Mycenaeans conquer Crete, and the palaces are destroyed | |
| | 2000 The Minoan hieroglyphic script develops | 1700 Knossos is rebuilt as the main palace on Crete | | |
| | 2000 A Minoan colony is established at Kastri on Kythera | 1626 Eruption of the volcano at Thera disrupts Cretan life | | |

### Greece and the Aegean

| | | | | |
|---|---|---|---|---|
| c.2300 Bronze enters use in the Aegean region | | Mycenaean civilization | | Greek dark ages |
| | 2000 The Achaeans (Mycenaeans) move south into Greece | 1650 Emergence of Mycenaean urban life | c.1200 Invasions of the Sea Peoples | |
| | | c.1600 Rich shaft grave burials at Mycenae | c.1200 Fall of Mycenaean civilization and decline of urban life in Greece | |
| | | c.1450 The earliest Mycenaean palaces are built | c.1100 The Dorian peoples occupy Greece | |
| | | c.1450 The Mycenaean Linear B script is developed | 1000 Iron is in widespread use in Greece | |
| | | 1400 Walls are built around the Mycenaean cities | | |

| 2000 | | 1500 | | 1000 |

## MINOAN CRETE

Crete

Khania

Knossos

Mallia

Monastiraki

Arkhanes

Palaikastro

Hagia Triadha    Phaistos    Gournia

Myrtos    Kato Zakro

**1**

0        60 km

0        40 mi

*S e a*

### Legend

- Minoan civilization, c.1600
- Minoan influence, c.1600
- Mycenaean civilization, c.1300
- Mycenaean colonization, late 13th century BC
- Minoan city, with palace
- other Minoan settlement
- Mycenaean city, with palace
- other Mycenaean settlement
- **Knossos** capital city
- Troy fortified settlement
- site damaged or destroyed by Mycenaeans, c.1450

- site damaged or destroyed by invaders from the north, or "Sea Peoples", c.1200
- mountain-top shrine on Crete
- sacred cave on Crete
- shipwreck
- probable trading route of the Ulu Burun ship
- *ivory* source of objects in the cargo of the Ulu Burun wreck, 14th century BC
- major migration, c.2000
- major migration, c.1200
- area affected by ash falls from the eruption of Thera, 1626

HITTITE EMPIRE

Sea Peoples

Carchemish

Sea Peoples

Mersin    Tarsus

Alalakh    Aleppo

**6**

Kas

Cape Gelidonya

Sea Peoples

*tin ingots*

*Orontes*

Ugarit

Hamath

Sea Peoples

Mycenaeans

Lapethos    Chytroi

Soloi    Enkomi

**8**    Idalion

Tamassos    Kition

Paphos    Amathous

Kourion    *Cyprus*
*copper ingots,*
*pottery*

*amphoras, bronze, dye, glass, ivory, olives, resin, weapons*

EVIDENCE of a wealthy and powerful kingdom is offered by this gold death mask from Mycenae, c.1500 BC.

*cylinder seals*
*from Mesopotamia*

Sea Peoples

PALESTINE

1180

*bronze weapons, ebony, scarab brooches*

Gaza

Avaris

**3**

EGYPT

Memphis

0        300 km

0        200 mi

*Nile*

---

evidence of Mycenaean civilization is a series of richly furnished shaft graves at Mycenae, dating to between 1650 and 1550. The grave goods reveal a wealthy warrior society and include hoards of bronze weapons, gold, silver and electrum tableware, jewelry and gold deathmasks. Mycenaean warriors rode to battle in horse-drawn chariots, but fought on foot with spear, sword and dagger. The towns were well defended, especially after the 14th century, by strong walls, built with massive blocks of stone and bastioned gateways. From the 15th century, Mycenaean rulers were buried in vaulted *tholos* (beehive shaped) tombs in which rituals related to a cult of kingship could be performed.

Each Mycenaean stronghold was ruled over by a king with a warrior aristocracy. The kings controlled many craftsmen – the king of Pylos employed about four hundred bronzesmiths – and hundreds of mainly female slaves. The royal palaces were smaller than those on Crete. According to a survey preserved in Homer's *Iliad*, known as the Catalog of Ships, there were some twenty kingdoms theoretically acknowledging the leadership of Mycenae.

Around 1450 the Mycenaeans expanded in the Aegean, conquering Crete and founding Miletos on the Anatolian coast: they may also have raided Egypt and the Hittite empire and, perhaps, they sacked Troy. They traded throughout the eastern Mediterranean and as far west as Malta, Sicily and Italy.

The Mycenaean civilization came to a violent end around 1200. Most of the major centers were sacked, town life came to an end and writing fell out of use. The whole Aegean entered a dark age which lasted about four centuries. The attackers were probably the Sea Peoples who also brought chaos to Egypt and the Levant. Some Mycenaeans sought refuge on Cyprus and on the coast of Anatolia; others may have joined with the Sea Peoples – Mycenaean influence is evident in Palestine where some of them settled. A power vacuum developed in Greece into which another Greek-speaking people, the Dorians, migrated around 1100, overrunning the Peloponnese, Crete and Rhodes: of the old Mycenaean centers only Athens retained its independence.

---

**1** Knossos, the greatest of the Cretan palaces, was first built around 2000 and was rebuilt several times after earthquake damage or war.

**2** The Minoan city of Akrotiri was preserved by ashfalls after the volcanic eruption on Thera in 1626.

**3** Avaris was an Egyptian city which contained a Minoan colony founded in about 1550.

**4** Mycenae had rich tombs and massive defenses built between 1600 and 1200. According to Homer, its king Agamemnon led the Greeks in the Trojan War.

**5** A defensive wall was built across the Isthmus of Corinth in the late 13th century to protect the Peloponnese from invasion from the north.

**6** A 14th-century shipwreck found at Ulu Burun near Kas had a cargo from around the east Mediterranean.

**7** Troy was sacked twice in the 13th century, and again in 1100.

**8** Mycenaeans reached Cyprus in the 15th century but the main settlement was 300 years later.

See also 10 (Egypt); 12 (Bronze Age Europe);
16 (Greek city-states)

The Bronze Age saw chiefdoms and warrior elites established across most of Europe. Beyond the Aegean, states were not formed until the Iron Age was well advanced and in northern and eastern Europe not until the early Middle Ages. The chiefdoms were competitive communities: fortifications were built in great numbers and new weapons such as swords and halberds were invented. Superb crafted display objects – ornaments, weapons, "parade-ground" armor, tableware, cult objects – made of bronze and precious metals, express the competitiveness of the period. Long-distance trade, particularly in tin and amber, arose to satisfy the demand for metals and other precious objects in areas where such resources were lacking. The increase in trade aided the spread of ideas and fashions and led to a high degree of cultural uniformity.

The earliest known use of bronze in Europe, in the Unetice culture in central Europe about 2500 BC, was probably an independent development and not the result of influence from the Middle East. Bronze came into use in southeast Europe, the Aegean and Italy two hundred years later, followed by Spain and, finally, the British Isles in about 1800. Scandinavia, with no workable deposits of copper or tin, continued in the Stone Age until the middle of the 2nd millennium BC. By this time bronze had entered Scandinavia, brought by traders in exchange for amber and, probably, furs.

Bronze technology led to a rapid increase in the use of metals. Bronze weapons and tools kept an edge better than stone or copper, could easily be resharpened and when broken could be melted down and recast. It was expensive, however, and its use was largely confined to the social elites in the early Bronze Age. Stone tools, sometimes copying the style of prestigious bronze tools, continued in everyday use. Large quantities of bronze artifacts, often of the highest quality, were buried or sunk in bogs as offerings to the gods.

The social distinctions of Bronze Age society are apparent in burial practices: a minority of burials being richly furnished with grave goods and the majority with few offerings. In the earlier Bronze

**early Bronze Age cultures, c.2300–1800**

- late megalithic cultures
- Bell Beaker cultures
- Nordic late Neolithic cultures
- Cord Impressed Pottery cultures
- Catacomb Grave cultures
- Unetice culture
- Danubian–Carpathian Bronze Age cultures
- Balkan Bronze Age cultures
- early Aegean Bronze Age cultures
- North Italian Bronze Age cultures
- South Italian Bronze Age cultures

**spread of Urnfield cultures in late Bronze Age**

- by 14th century
- by 12th century
- by 9th century

- early Bronze Age barrow burial
- fortified site
- late Bronze Age urnfield
- metal hoard
- shipwreck
- ○ settlement
- • other site
- source of tin
- source of copper
- source of gold
- source of amber
- Mycenaean trade route
- — main amber trade route

0                600 km
0                400 mi

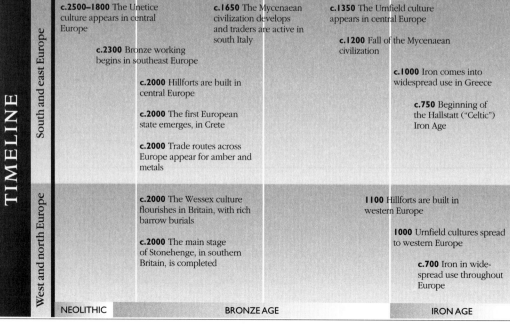

| | 2000 | 1500 | 1000 |
|---|---|---|---|
| **South and east Europe** | c.2500–1800 The Unetice culture appears in central Europe | c.1650 The Mycenaean civilization develops and traders are active in south Italy | c.1350 The Urnfield culture appears in central Europe |
| | c.2300 Bronze working begins in southeast Europe | | c.1200 Fall of the Mycenaean civilization |
| | c.2000 Hillforts are built in central Europe | | c.1000 Iron comes into widespread use in Greece |
| | c.2000 The first European state emerges, in Crete | | c.750 Beginning of the Hallstatt ("Celtic") Iron Age |
| | c.2000 Trade routes across Europe appear for amber and metals | | |
| **West and north Europe** | c.2000 The Wessex culture flourishes in Britain, with rich barrow burials | | 1100 Hillforts are built in western Europe |
| | c.2000 The main stage of Stonehenge, in southern Britain, is completed | | 1000 Urnfield cultures spread to western Europe |
| | | | c.700 Iron in widespread use throughout Europe |

TIMELINE

NEOLITHIC            BRONZE AGE            IRON AGE

Age three distinct burial practices are found. In southeast Europe the normal practice was burial of rich and poor alike in flat grave cemeteries. In most of eastern, northern and western Europe, the poor were buried in flat graves but the rich were buried under earth mounds known as barrows. Barrows required a communal effort to build and are evidence of the power of the elites. In some parts of western Europe Neolithic-style communal burials in megalithic tombs continued until about 1200 BC.

In southern and central Europe, large villages, often fortified, developed but in northern and western Europe the settlement pattern was one of dispersed homesteads. Population rose across Europe and agricultural settlers moved into many marginal upland areas. These were abandoned late in the Bronze Age, perhaps because of climatic deterioration or because the poor soils had been exhausted. As agricultural land rose in value, clear boundaries were laid out between communities in sub-Neolithic forest hunters and gatherers

Rickeby
Hallunda
Tromøy
Vänern
Vättern
Kvarnby
Bulbjerg
Lake Peipus
Rezne
Trundholm
Egtved
Brudevaelte
Voldtofte
Kivik
Western Dvina
Pustinka
**4**
Drenthe
Barger-Oosterveld
Perleberg
Ivanja
Moska
Dnieper
Donec group
Biskupin
Jankowo
Kamieniec
**3**
Nieder-Neundorf
Schweinert
Miejsce
Rostov
Toterfout
Court St Etienne
Leubingen
Grossenheim
Iwanowice
Bad Nauheim
Helmsdorf
Gedinne
Flörsheim
Postoloprty
Spissky Stvrtok
Havré
Heidesheim
Unetice
Velatice
Barca
Usatove
Mannheim
**5**
Blucina
Veterov
Hagenam
Kelheim
Unter-Radl
Malé Kosihy
Wasserburg
Ettins
Nitriansky Hrádok
Mohi
Tudoromo
Rixheim
Baldegg
Caka
Füzesabony
Kamenka
**1**
Volders
Vál
Suciu du Sus
Cortaillod
Hölting
Monteoru
Crestaulta
Ledro
Wittnauer Horn
Kisapostag
Tószeg
Bled
Angarano
Czorvas
Periam
Polada
Dobova
Gomalova
Vattina
Fontanella
Sava
Gîrla Mare
Ezerovo
Bismantora
Cîrna
Tarnava
Danube
Luni
Ezero
Corsica
Danja Slatina
Filitosa
Allumiere
Narce
Black Sea
Nuraghe
Albucci
Phlegraean Fields
Scoglio del Tonno
ANATOLIA
Barumini
Sardinia
**6**
Hittites
Lipara
Millazzo
Sicily
Troy
Borg in-Nadur
Malta
Mycenae
Cyprus
Mediterranean Sea
Crete
Knossos
Minoan civilization

ALPS
Rhine
Danube
Elbe
Oder
Vistula
Po
CARPATHIAN MTS

VOTIVE offerings, thrown into the bogs, include this bronze and gold "chariot of the sun" from Trundholm (Denmark).

many areas, especially northwest Europe, and farmland was enclosed into small fields that could be managed more intensively. Farmers benefited from the introduction of heavier plows, wheeled vehicles and horses. European wild oats were domesticated at this time, probably as horse fodder.

Around 1350 the Urnfield culture, named for its distinctive burial practices, appeared in Hungary. Bodies were cremated and the ashes buried in funerary urns in flat grave cemeteries of hundreds, even thousands, of graves. As with earlier Bronze Age burial customs, a minority of graves included rich offerings, weapons and armor. Some of these graves were covered with barrows, demonstrating a degree of continuity with the past, but this was by no means universal: the powers enjoyed by chieftains in the early Bronze Age may have been undermined to an extent by the emergence of a warrior class. By the 9th century Urnfield customs had spread over most of continental Europe. Except in the west where it

was probably taken by migrating Celtic peoples, the Urnfield culture spread mainly as a result of the wide-ranging contacts on trade links. The later Bronze Age saw increased militarization, with extensive fortress building in western Europe and the introduction of the bronze slashing sword. Bronze armor was introduced, but probably for display only: it offers less protection than leather.

Small numbers of iron artifacts appeared in many areas about 1200. However, iron tools first became common only around 1000 in Greece and two hundred and fifty years later in northern Europe.

**1** Bronze Age settlements along the northern fringes of the Alps were often built on islands in lakes for defense.

**2** One of the last megalithic tombs to be used was at Island, in Ireland; it was still in use about 1200 BC about a millennium later than most megalithic tombs.

**3** At Leubingen, an early Bronze Age barrow contains the remains of an elderly man accompanied by a girl, pottery, stone and bronze tools and weapons, and gold jewelry.

**4** A late Bronze Age dismantled wooden "temple" was deliberately sunk into a peat bog at Barger-Oosterveld.

**5** The Urnfield cemetery at Kelheim of 900–800 BC had more than 10,000 burials.

**6** Defensive towers called *nuraghe* were built about 1800 BC in Sardinia; similar structures are found in Corsica and the Balearic islands.

**7** A shipwreck from 800 BC off the southwest coast of Spain included more than 200 bronze weapons made in the Loire region.

See also 7 (Neolithic Europe); 11 (Minoans and Mycenaeans); 25 (Celts)

The fragility of the first civilizations was evident during the second millennium BC. Sumeria had vanished as a political entity shortly before 2000 BC, though its achievements were built upon by the Babylonian and Assyrian states which arose in the early second millennium. The rivalry between these two states was to endure until the middle of the first millennium. The other major power of the Middle East was the Hittite kingdom of Anatolia. One of the secrets of Hittite success is thought to have been their early mastery of iron working, in about 1500 BC. Meanwhile, Egypt expanded far south into Nubia and north into the Levant (▷ 6). In the eastern Mediterranean, the Minoans of Crete were replaced by the Mycenaean civilization that emerged on the Greek mainland around 1600. Around 1400 the Mycenaeans conquered Crete and introduced the Greek language; they also settled on Cyprus and in Anatolia (▷ 11).

This civilized world was thrown into chaos about 1200 by a wave of invasions. Mycenae was destroyed by invaders from the north, plunging Greece into a 400-year-long "dark age". Thracians, Phrygians and Anatolian Luvians overthrew the Hittite empire and nomadic Aramaeans occupied much of Mesopotamia. Egypt was invaded by mysterious Sea Peoples. Their fleets were driven from the Nile, but they settled in the Levant where they were known as the Philistines.

By 1000 stability was returning. The Hittites survived though as a shadow of their former selves. The Aramaeans had settled and were assimilating with the urbanized peoples of the conquered territories: their language became the common tongue of the Middle East for the next millennium. Assyria and Babylon were beginning to recover. The Levant was a mosaic of tiny states: of these, the Phoenician city-states and Israel acquired a historical importance out of all proportion to their size (▷ 15). Egyptian power was in decline and the Nubians, after a millennium of Egyptian domination, set up the kingdom of Kush. In sub-Saharan Africa, the transition to a farming way of life was beginning.

In Asia, the Indus valley civilization had collapsed around 1700; about 200 years later the Aryans, an Indo-European pastoralist people, migrated into India. In northern China the Neolithic Longshan cultures developed into the urbanized Shang state around 1766, marking the start of Chinese civilization. Around 1122 the Shang dynasty was ousted by the ruler of the Zhou sub-kingdom (▷ 8).

The Austronesian farming peoples continued to colonize the southeast Asian archipelagoes; by 2000 they had bypassed New Guinea and settled the western Pacific Bismarck archipelago around 1500 BC. The Lapita culture,

**2000–1500** Wessex culture introduces bronze working to the British Isles

**2300–1500** Emergence of the first permanent farming villages in Mesoamerica

**1800** U-shaped ceremonial centers are built on the Peruvian coast

**c.1900** Ashur, capital of Assyria, is founded

**1600** Emergence of the Mycenaean civilization on the southern mainland of Greece

**c1600** The proto-Canaanite phonetic alphabet is developed in the Levant

**1400** Olmec culture emerges in Mesoamerica

**1500–700** Poverty Point culture, Louisiana

The Americas

Europe

Middle East

Africa

East and South Asia

TIMELINE

2000

1800

1600

1400

**2040–1640** The Middle Kingdom in Egypt

**2000–1600** The Minoan palace civilization flourishes on Crete

**2000** Cattle raising begins in highland east Africa

**1766** The Shang dynasty begins its dominance in China's northern plain

**1700** Fall of the Indus valley civilization

**1600** Foundation of the Nubian kingdom of Kush

**1532–1070** The New Kingdom in Egypt

**1500–1000** Lapita culture spreads to Vanuatu, Tonga and Samoa

**1400** The Mycenaeans conquer Crete

hunter-gatherers
nomadic pastoralists
simple farming societies
complex farming societies/chiefdoms
state societies
uninhabited
extent of bronze working, c.1000 BC
extent of iron working, c.1000 BC

Greenland

Iceland

Lapps

Finno-Ugrian taiga hunter-gatherers

Paleo-Siberian taiga hunter-gatherers

Arctic marine mammal hunters

Bronze Age cultures

Urnfield cultures

Cimmerians (pastoralists)

Karasuk culture (transhumant pastoralists)

Paleo-Asiatic pastoralists (ancestral Turko-Mongol)

Koreans

late Jomon hunter-gatherers

Celtiberians

Illyrians

Thracians

Phrygians

URARTU

Hittites

ASSYRIA

BABYLONIA

Iranians (pastoralists)

Tibetans (transhumant pastoralists)

ZHOU

Wu

Berbers

Greeks

Aramaean kingdoms

Minor kingdoms

ELAM

EGYPT

KUSH

SABA

Pastoral nomads

Vedic Aryans

Burmese

Thais

Austro-Asiatic rice farmers

Taiwan

Dravidians

Ceylon

Pastoral nomads

cereal farmers

Ethiopian highland farmers

pastoralists

Philippine Islands

Austronesians

Borneo

Celebes

Sumatra

Java

Timor

New Guinea

Papuan-Melanesian Neolithic farmers

Lapita culture (ancestral Polynesian)

Madagascar

Khoisan hunter-gatherers

Australian Aboriginal hunter-gatherers

Tasmanian hunter-gatherers

**1200** Earliest Olmec ceremonial centers in Mesoamerica

**1200** Collapse of Mycenae and the beginnings of the Greek "dark ages"

**1200–1100** Hebrew tribes settle west of the river Jordan (Canaan)

**1000** Spread of Phoenician trading colonies in the Mediterranean

**c.1000** Iron working in southern Europe

**c.1100** Hillfort construction begins in western Europe

**1100** Development of the influential Phoenician alphabet

1200

1000

**1350–1250** The Hittite empire reaches its peak

**1200–800** Karasuk culture introduces advanced bronze working to the Asian steppes

**1180** The Egyptians defeat invasions of the Sea Peoples

**1122** Beginning of the Zhou dynasty in China

**1100** Iron working on the Ganges plain

ancestral to the Polynesian culture, developed here by 1500 and spread by voyages of trade and exploration as far east as Samoa and Tonga by 1000. This expansion was made possible by the invention of the ocean-going outrigger canoe.

On the east Asian steppes the ancestors of the Turko-Mongol peoples took up pastoral farming during the second millennium, under the influence of the Iranian pastoralists of the western steppes. By 1000 far-reaching changes were underway on the western steppes: the people of the Karasuk culture (probably Iranians) adopted transhumance, or seasonal migrations between summer and winter pastures – only a step away from true pastoral nomadism.

In northern Europe the bronze-using Urnfield cultures (named for their burial practices) spread across much of central, southern and western Europe. By 1000 bronze working was almost universally practiced among European farming cultures, most of which were now aristocratic chiefdoms (▷ 12).

In the Americas the Archaic period came to a close soon after 2000 BC, with the emergence of fully developed regional hunter–gatherer cultures. Some of these, such as the Poverty Point culture on the Mississippi, were developing a degree of social complexity by 1000. In Mesoamerica, permanent farming villages appeared after 2000. By 1250 chiefdoms had emerged among the Olmecs, farmers of the fertile floodplains by the Gulf of Mexico. In South America complex societies continued to develop on the Pacific coast and in the Andes, and farming spread into the Amazon basin (▷ 17) ■

By the 10th century the Aramaeans had begun to abandon their nomadic lifestyle and to settle in city-states across a wide area of the Levant and northern Mesopotamia. Simultaneously the Chaldeans were undergoing the same process in southern Mesopotamia. By settling down, the Aramaeans and Chaldeans lost most of the advantages that their loose nomadic organization had given them over the old military powers, and these now began to revive.

Like the Amorites a millennium earlier, the Aramaeans and Chaldeans adopted Mesopotamian culture but the Aramaeans, at least, kept their identity; their language and alphabet was the common tongue of the region by 500 BC. Mesopotamia experienced no further immigrations in this period but Anatolia and Iran saw the arrival of several waves of Iranian peoples, including the Medes and the Persians, who had both formed powerful kingdoms by the 6th century.

Of the Hittites, Assyria and Babylon, the three powers who had dominated the region before 1200, the Hittites made the least impressive recovery. With their heartland lost to the Phrygians, the Neo-Hittites (as they are now called) formed a number of small states in southern Anatolia, of which the most successful were Carchemish, Kummukhu (Commagene) and Khilakku (Cilicia). The Neo-Hittites were conquered by Assyria in the 8th century after which their identity became lost.

The Assyrian heartland around Ashur and Nineveh had survived the Aramaean invasions relatively unscathed and formed a strong base for recovery. The old pattern, established during the Middle Assyrian period, of expansion under able warrior kings followed by contraction under weak kings was continued in the new Assyrian empire.

Expansion began again in the reign of Adad-nirari II (r.911–891) and by the reign of Ashurnasirpal II (r.883–859) the empire dominated northern Mesopotamia and received tribute from the Levant as far south as Tyre. During Ashurnasirpal's reign Ashur, Assyria's ancient capital, declined in importance and was superseded by a new purpose-built capital at Kalhu.

In 854 a coalition of Levantine states tried to halt the expansion of Assyrian power in the region. The coalition met Shalmaneser III (r.858–824) in battle at Qarqar on the Orontes and, though Shalmaneser claimed complete victory, Assyrian power in the Levant did suffer a setback. Relations between Assyria and Babylon had been good since about 911 when the two states became allies. Shalmaneser gave military support to the Babylonians against the Chaldeans and also gave them assistance against internal enemies.

After Shalmaneser's reign Assyria was crippled by internal problems and went into decline for sixty years. Recovery and expansion began again in the reign of Tiglath-pileser III (r.744–727), who assumed overlordship over Babylon, reconquered the Levant and exacted tribute from Israel and Judah. Tiglath-pileser was responsible for a complete overhaul of the administration of the empire to assert central power. Hereditary provincial governors in the Assyrian heartlands were replaced by a hierarchy of officials under direct royal control. Traveling inspectors were sent out to examine the performance of local officials. A post system was introduced and officials were required to send regular reports to the capital. Representatives were appointed to the courts of vassal states to safeguard the interests of Assyria. Large numbers of subject peoples were resettled to prevent local opposition. Finally, in

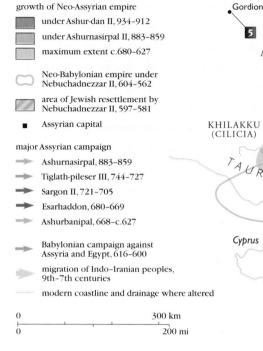

growth of Neo-Assyrian empire

■ under Ashur-dan II, 934–912

■ under Ashurnasirpal II, 883–859

■ maximum extent c.680–627

Neo-Babylonian empire under Nebuchadnezzar II, 604–562

area of Jewish resettlement by Nebuchadnezzar II, 597–581

■ Assyrian capital

major Assyrian campaign

→ Ashurnasirpal, 883–859

→ Tiglath-pileser III, 744–727

→ Sargon II, 721–705

→ Esarhaddon, 680–669

→ Ashurbanipal, 668–c.627

→ Babylonian campaign against Assyria and Egypt, 616–600

→ migration of Indo-Iranian peoples, 9th–7th centuries

---- modern coastline and drainage where altered

0                    300 km
0                    200 mi

perhaps the greatest break with the imperial traditions of the past, rebellious vassal states lost their nominal independence and were reorganized as provinces of Assyria, directly ruled by officials appointed by the king.

Under Sargon II (r.721–705) Assyrian power reached its zenith. Sargon broke the power of the Armenian kingdom of Urartu and expanded Assyrian dominions with campaigns against the Chaldeans (who had seized Babylon), Elamites and Hebrews. Sargon's last campaign ended in defeat, however, and he was killed in battle in Anatolia in 705. Sargon's successor Sennacherib (r.704–681) was preoccupied with rebellions in Judah, with Babylon

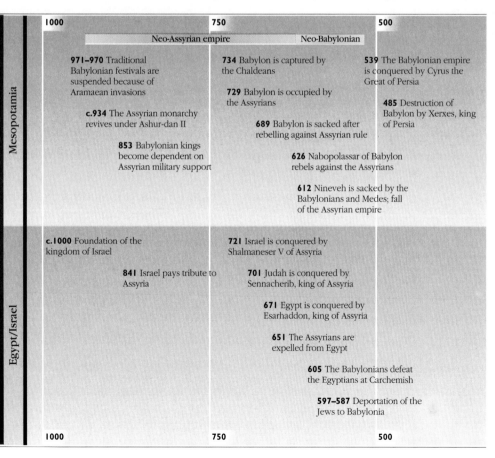

## TIMELINE

| | 1000 | 750 | 500 |
|---|---|---|---|
| | | Neo-Assyrian empire | Neo-Babylonian |
| **Mesopotamia** | **971–970** Traditional Babylonian festivals are suspended because of Aramaean invasions | **734** Babylon is captured by the Chaldeans | **539** The Babylonian empire is conquered by Cyrus the Great of Persia |
| | **c.934** The Assyrian monarchy revives under Ashur-dan II | **729** Babylon is occupied by the Assyrians | **485** Destruction of Babylon by Xerxes, king of Persia |
| | **853** Babylonian kings become dependent on Assyrian military support | **689** Babylon is sacked after rebelling against Assyrian rule | |
| | | **626** Nabopolassar of Babylon rebels against the Assyrians | |
| | | **612** Nineveh is sacked by the Babylonians and Medes; fall of the Assyrian empire | |
| **Egypt/Israel** | **c.1000** Foundation of the kingdom of Israel | **721** Israel is conquered by Shalmaneser V of Assyria | |
| | **841** Israel pays tribute to Assyria | **701** Judah is conquered by Sennacherib, king of Assyria | |
| | | **671** Egypt is conquered by Esarhaddon, king of Assyria | |
| | | **651** The Assyrians are expelled from Egypt | |
| | | **605** The Babylonians defeat the Egyptians at Carchemish | |
| | | **597–587** Deportation of the Jews to Babylonia | |
| | 1000 | 750 | 500 |

Phrygians

**ANATOLIA**

Cimmerians, c.705–c.695

*Kizil Irmak*

Scythians, late 7th century

*Caspian Sea*

KUMMUKHU
(COMMAGENE)

*Murat*

*Lake Van*

Tushpa

× 714 *Lake Urmia*

**URARTU**

**4**

MANNEA

*Tigris*

714

*Ceyhan*

Neo-Hittites

**CARCHEMISH**

Nisibis

*Great Zab*

Dur-Sharrukin

**1**

Medes, 9th century

Harran

608

Medes, 614–612

MTS

Carchemish × 605

Nineveh

Arbil

**8**

Hamadan
(Ecbatana)

**7**

Aleppo

*Orontes*

Aramaeans

Kalhu

Z A G R O S

Qarqar
× 854

601

605

*Euphrates*

**ASSYRIA**

Ashur

Arrapha

710–707

Ugarit

Aramaeans

*Syrian Desert*

**SYRIA**

Tadmor
(Palmyra)

Mari

M E S O P O T A M I A

*Diyala*

M O U N T A I N S

Arvad

605

729

615–612

*Karkheh*

Byblos

**LEVANT**

Riblah

**ARAM**

653, 648–647

Susa

Phoenicians

Sidon

600

Damascus

605

Der

**ELAM**

Tyre

Sippar

Dur-Kurigalzu

**3**

Babylon

Nippur

Karkheh

**PHILISTIA** 601

**ISRAEL**

Borsippa

**2**

**BABYLONIA**

Jerusalem

MOAB

Lachish

Uruk

Gaza

Ur

**JUDAH**

**Chaldeans**

EDOM

Persians 8th century

**A r a b s**

Taima

*Red Sea*

*Persian Gulf*

LION hunting was symbolic to the
Assyrians of royal power and only kings
(Ashurbanipal in this bas-relief) were
shown killing the animals.

and with Chaldean and Elamite attacks in the south. Assyrian expansion was renewed under Esarhaddon (r.680–669), who began the conquest of Egypt, and Ashurbanipal (r.668–c.627), who completed it and took great stores of booty back to Nineveh. This last conquest, however, succeeded only in over-extending the empire while Ashurbanipal's increasingly tyrannical rule spread discontent everywhere. Egypt regained its independence by 651 and, despite his subsequent conquest of Elam in 648, Ashurbanipal's reign ended in chaos. The Babylonian king Nabopolassar (626–605) rebelled against Assyrian rule and after ten years of fighting drove the Assyrians from Babylon.

In 615 Nabopolassar took the offensive and,

supported by the Medes, took Nineveh in 612. A rump kingdom held out at Harran until 609, but after that Assyrian resistance ended. The pharaoh Necho II (r.610–595) seized the opportunity offered by the collapse of Assyrian power to reoccupy the Levant but was defeated by the Babylonian crown prince Nebuchadnezzar at Carchemish in 605. The Babylonians followed up their victory by occupying virtually all of the territory previously held by Assyria. Nebuchadnezzar came to the throne in the following year and spent his reign (r.604–562) consolidating his empire, rebuilding the city of Babylon in imperial splendor and ruling very much within the Assyrian tradition.

Nebuchadnezzar's dynasty lasted only until 556 when it was overthrown in a palace coup. An official, Nabonidus (r.555–539), was chosen as king but his religious unorthodoxy soon made him unpopular in the Babylonian heartland. When the Persian king Cyrus the Great invaded in 539, Babylon surrendered without a fight, bringing to a quiet end an imperial tradition that was almost two thousand years old. Mesopotamian civilization survived for some centuries but gradually declined under the influence of Persian, and subsequently Hellenistic, culture, and had died out by the beginning of the Christian era.

**1** The Assyrian capital moved: Ashur (c.1363–c.878); Kalhu (c.878–707); Dur-Sharrukin (707–705); Nineveh (705–612, when it was sacked by the Babylonians and Medes).

**2** Though overshadowed militarily by Assyria before 626, Babylon was the dominant religious and cultural center of Mesopotamia.

**3** Tyre was the leading Phoenician city; in the 9th century the Phoenicians established trade routes to the western Mediterranean.

**4** Urartu developed as a rival to Assyria in the 8th century; its power was broken by Sargon II in 714.

**5** Gordion was the capital of the Phrygians; its last king Mitas (Midas) killed himself after being conquered by the Cimmerians around 695.

**6** Thebes, the most southerly point reached by the Assyrians, was sacked by Ashurbanipal in 663.

**7** Pharaoh Necho II's attempt to seize the Levant was ended by the Babylonians at Carchemish.

**8** Hamadan became the capital of a powerful Median empire after the fall of Assyria.

See also 15 (Bible lands); 10 (Egypt);
18 (Persians)

The Hebrew kingdoms of the Bible lands were dwarfed in scale and longevity by the great empires of the Middle East, yet their significance in world history is at least as great. The period of the independent monarchy, from the time of David to the Babylonian conquest in 587, was a formative time for Judaism and gave Jews a sense of historical destiny, driving them to preserve their religion and identity through centuries of foreign rule, exile and worldwide dispersal. Christianity and Islam both owe so much to Judaism that neither religion would have its present form had Judaism not survived.

The Hebrews migrated into Canaan in the early 12th century BC, a time when the great powers of the region were neutralized by troubles of various kinds. In their initial attacks under Joshua, the Hebrews occupied most of Canaan, which they settled in tribal units under chieftains (the "judges" of the biblical Book of Judges). However, many Canaanite enclaves remained and Hebrew expansion to the southwest was blocked by the Philistines who had settled in the area after being repulsed from Egypt in 1180. Most of the Canaanite enclaves were mopped up in the 11th century, but the Hebrews began to lose ground in the southwest to the Philistines.

The need for effective defense against the Philistines led the Hebrew tribes to unite under a monarchy. According to the Bible, the first king of the Hebrews was Saul (r.c.1020–c.1006), but it was his successor David who was responsible for consolidating the monarchy and creating the first Hebrew state. David conquered the Philistines, Ammonites, Moabites and Edomites and forced several of the Aramaean tribes of the Levant to accept his overlordship. These were great achievements, but he was aided by the temporary impotence of the powers who might otherwise have intervened. It was also to his advantage that the Aramaeans of the Levant (who had moved into the area after the fall of the Hittite empire) had settled in urban communities by 1000, and so were more vulnerable to attack than the still-nomadic Mesopotamian Aramaeans. Perhaps the most important event of David's reign was his capture of Jerusalem from the Canaanite Jebusites. By making Jerusalem his capital David ensured its lasting importance as a religious center.

David was succeeded by his son Solomon. Solomon's reign was largely peaceful, but maintaining his splendid court life and ambitious building projects, including the temple at Jerusalem, proved burdensome to his people. Some Hebrews were used as forced labor and territory was ceded to Tyre in return for supplying craftsmen and materials. He was criticized for tolerating the pagan religious practices of the many non-Hebrew wives he had acquired from diplomatic marriages. When his successor Rehoboam (r.928–911) dealt tactlessly with the economic complaints of the northern tribes, the kingdom split in two halves, Israel and Judah, and most of the non-Hebrew provinces fell away.

probable border of the kingdom of Saul, c.1006

kingdom of David and Solomon
— border, 1006–928
under direct rule
vassal states and tributaries
campaigns of David, c.1006–965
Canaanite enclaves conquered by David
area ceded to Tyre by Solomon
fortress built by Solomon
other major building project by Solomon

0                    200 km
0                    150mi

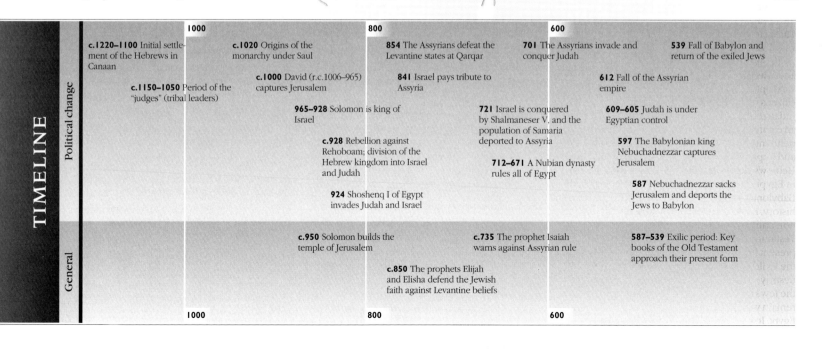

**Political change**

| | | | |
|---|---|---|---|
| 1000 | 800 | 600 | |
| c.1220–1100 Initial settlement of the Hebrews in Canaan | 854 The Assyrians defeat the Levantine states at Qarqar | 701 The Assyrians invade and conquer Judah | 539 Fall of Babylon and return of the exiled Jews |
| c.1020 Origins of the monarchy under Saul | 841 Israel pays tribute to Assyria | 612 Fall of the Assyrian empire | |
| c.1150–1050 Period of the "judges" (tribal leaders) | c.1000 David (r.c.1006–965) captures Jerusalem | 721 Israel is conquered by Shalmaneser V. and the population of Samaria deported to Assyria | 609–605 Judah is under Egyptian control |
| 965–928 Solomon is king of Israel | | | 597 The Babylonian king Nebuchadnezzar captures Jerusalem |
| c.928 Rebellion against Rehoboam; division of the Hebrew kingdom into Israel and Judah | 712–671 A Nubian dynasty rules all of Egypt | | 587 Nebuchadnezzar sacks Jerusalem and deports the Jews to Babylon |
| 924 Shoshenq I of Egypt invades Judah and Israel | | | |

**General**

| | | |
|---|---|---|
| c.950 Solomon builds the temple of Jerusalem | c.735 The prophet Isaiah warns against Assyrian rule | 587–539 Exilic period: Key books of the Old Testament approach their present form |
| c.850 The prophets Elijah and Elisha defend the Jewish faith against Levantine beliefs | | |

1000                    800                    600

**Legend:**
- border of former kingdom of Solomon
- greatest extent of kingdom of Israel
- greatest extent of kingdom of Judah
- border of state gaining independence from kingdoms of Israel or Judah
- kingdom of Egypt, 924
- Assyrian empire, 722
- Babylonian empire, 597

campaigns in Israel and Judah
- pharaoh Shoshenq I, 924
- Sennacherib, 701

0 _____ 150 km
0 _____ 100 mi

Aleppo

Orontes

Euphrates

6

Ugarit ×Qarqar 854

Hamath      Syrian     Desert

ARAM

Arvad

Tadmor

Riblah

Byblos

Sidon      Damascus

Cyprus

Mediterranean Sea

Tyre    •Dan

Acco    Hazor    7

Sea of Chinnereth (Sea of Galilee)

Megiddo

Beth-shean

8

Samaria    Shechem

Joppa    5    AMMON
KINGDOM OF ISRAEL    Rabbah

Eltekeh 701    Gezer    9

Ashkelon    •Jerusalem
    Bethlehem

Gaza    Lachish×    MOAB
    independent of
    Israel, 843 BC

Arad

Salt Sea (Dead Sea)

PHILISTIA

KINGDOM OF JUDAH

EGYPT

EDOM
independent of
Judah, 843 BC

Ezion-geber

Disunity was a luxury the Hebrews could ill afford, as the power of both Egypt and Assyria was reviving. In 924 the pharaoh Shoshenq I (r.945–924) led a campaign through Philistia, Judah and Israel, sacking many cities and imposing tribute, although both kingdoms survived. In the 9th century relations between Israel and Judah was usually hostile and Israel often suffered attacks from Aram–Damascus, which was frequently allied to Judah. Under Omri and Ahab Israel became the most powerful kingdom in the region and played a leading role in attempts by the Levantine states to check the growing power of Assyria under Shalmaneser III. However, under Ahab's successor Jehu, Israel was forced to pay tribute to Assyria. In the early 8th century the kingdoms enjoyed relative peace and prosperity with Assyria in a period of decline, until Tiglath-pileser III (r.744–727) overran the Levant and forced vassal status on Israel and Judah. When Hoshea, king of Israel, rebelled against Assyria in 724 his capital Samaria was taken after a three-year siege and its population deported to Assyria. Despite receiving Egyptian support, a rebellion by Hezekiah, the king of Judah, was also put down by the Assyrians. As Assyrian power entered terminal decline in the 630s, Judah briefly regained independence under Josiah (r.640–609) who extended his authority over the old kingdom of Israel until he was killed in battle with the Egyptians at Megiddo. The Egyptians occupied the Levant but were defeated by the Babylonians at Carchemish in 605, after which Judah became a vassal state of Babylon.

In 597 Judah rebelled against Babylonian rule and was crushed by Nebuchadnezzar. Jerusalem was captured, the temple plundered and many of its citizens were deported to Babylonia. Ten years later Judah rebelled again but Jerusalem was taken after an eighteen-month siege. This was the end for independent Judah. Its last king Zedekiah was blinded and imprisoned with most of his nobles and more Hebrews were deported. Many others fled into exile in Egypt. Though a disaster in political terms, the Babylonian captivity was a creative period in Jewish history. Exile caused a great deal of religious reflection and it was the period when much of the Old Testament was written up in something close to its present form. Nor perhaps were the conditions of the exile extremely harsh. When Cyrus of Persia destroyed the Babylonian empire in 539 and gave the Jews leave to return home, thousands chose to remain where they were. Many others remained in Egypt. It was the beginning of the Diaspora.

HEBREW captives march into exile after the fall of Lachish in 701. Sennacherib commissioned this relief to record his triumph.

**1** Saul was killed in battle against the Philistines at Gilboa c.1006.

**2** Hebron was David's capital before his capture of Jerusalem from the Jebusite Canaanites c.1000.

**3** The Aramaeans of Hamath submitted after David defeated the Aramaeans of Zobah and Damascus.

**4** Solomon built a fleet at Ezion-geber to trade on the Red Sea with east Africa and Arabia.

**5** Northern tribes rebelled against Rehoboam and formed the breakaway kingdom of Israel.

**6** A coalition of Levantine states including Israel briefly checked Assyrian expansion at Qarqar, 854 BC.

**7** Aram–Damascus emerged as a major rival to Israel in the 850s, but was conquered by Assyria in 732.

**8** Samaria, the capital of Israel, was taken by the Assyrians in 721 after a three-year siege.

**9** Jerusalem, capital of Judah, was sacked after the rebellion of 587, and its population deported to Babylon; they stayed until 539 when the victorious Achemenid Persians allowed them to return.

See also 10 (Egyptian empire);
14 (Assyrians and Babylonians)

During the dark ages (1200–800 BC), the Greeks lived in tribal communities under chiefs or kings who combined the roles of warleader and chief priest but who had to consult a council of elders and the warrior aristocracy. Their subjects sometimes paid tribute to the kings, but there was no regular system of taxation. There were no palaces, and kings lived in houses distinguished from those of their subjects only by their greater size. Town life almost ceased and such long-distance trade as survived was controlled by the Phoenicians. War, hunting and lavish displays of hospitality were the hallmarks of dark-age Greek culture. One of the most important developments of the period was that iron replaced bronze.

By the 9th century power began to pass to the hereditary aristocracy, and by the end of the 7th century only Sparta, Argos and Thera still had monarchies. Little is known about the institutions of aristocratic government but it was under their rule that trade and city life revived in Greece and that Greek colonization overseas began. The *polis* (city-state) became the dominant form of political organization. The cities dominated the countryside and became the main centers of political power, commerce and cultural life. The revival of trade made it necessary to re-invent writing in the 8th century, as the Mycenaean script had been entirely forgotten. The Greeks adopted the Phoenician consonantal alphabet and by adding separate signs for vowels turned it into a far more flexible and simple writing system. As a result writing became a common accomplishment in Greece. This was to be a major factor in the brilliant flowering of Greek civilization in the 6th and 5th century.

In the 7th century aristocratic government became unpopular. New military tactics, involving large numbers of heavily armed infantry, deprived them of their status as a warrior elite. There was discontent also among the newly rich who, not having aristocratic birth, were excluded from political power. In many Greek city-states these discontents led, between 660 and 485, to revolutions under popular leaders known as "tyrants" (a term describing rulers who had gained power through their own efforts, rather than by virtue of birth). Most tyrannies endured only a few decades before they were overthrown and replaced with "oligarchies", in which the aristocracy was influential but had no monopoly on power. Other Greek city-states reformed their constitutions without revolutions and by the 6th century most were ruled by oligarchies: the remaining strongholds of aristocratic power were in the north of Greece, where there were few cities, and in Sicily.

The most far-reaching political upheavals took place in Athens. Faced with mounting internal problems, the Athenians sought to avoid revolution by

| | area of Greek settlement, 6th century BC |
| | Greek territory under royal or aristocratic rulers, c.600 |
| | Spartan territory, 505 |
| | allies of Sparta, 505 |
| | major city-state, 6th century BC |
| Athens | tyranny at some time between 660–485 |
| — | Persian conquests by 513 |
| ▲ | site of pan-Hellenic festival |
| ▪ | Amphictonic shrine, with associated god named |
| ▫ | other major temple or shrine, with associated god named |

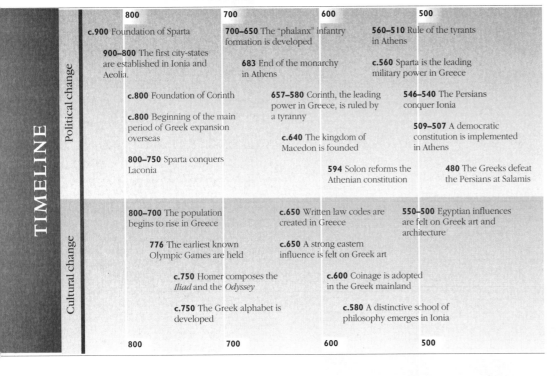

**TIMELINE**

**Political change**

| 800 | 700 | 600 | 500 |
|---|---|---|---|
| c.900 Foundation of Sparta | 700–650 The "phalanx" infantry formation is developed | 560–510 Rule of the tyrants in Athens | |
| 900–800 The first city-states are established in Ionia and Aeolia. | 683 End of the monarchy in Athens | c.560 Sparta is the leading military power in Greece | |
| c.800 Foundation of Corinth | 657–580 Corinth, the leading power in Greece, is ruled by a tyranny | 546–540 The Persians conquer Ionia | |
| c.800 Beginning of the main period of Greek expansion overseas | c.640 The kingdom of Macedon is founded | 509–507 A democratic constitution is implemented in Athens | |
| 800–750 Sparta conquers Laconia | 594 Solon reforms the Athenian constitution | 480 The Greeks defeat the Persians at Salamis | |

**Cultural change**

| 800 | 700 | 600 | 500 |
|---|---|---|---|
| 800–700 The population begins to rise in Greece | c.650 Written law codes are created in Greece | 550–500 Egyptian influences are felt on Greek art and architecture | |
| 776 The earliest known Olympic Games are held | c.650 A strong eastern influence is felt on Greek art | | |
| c.750 Homer composes the *Iliad* and the *Odyssey* | c.600 Coinage is adopted in the Greek mainland | | |
| c.750 The Greek alphabet is developed | c.580 A distinctive school of philosophy emerges in Ionia | | |

**1** A century of far-reaching political reforms transformed Athens from a backwater in 600 into a leading state in 500.

**2** Regarded by the Greeks as a barbarian kingdom, Macedon had a mixed population of Illyrians, Thracians and Dorian Greeks.

**3** Olympia was the wealthiest religious center in Greece; pan-Hellenic games were held in honor of Zeus every four years from 776 BC to AD 393.

**4** The oracle of Apollo at Delphi was widely consulted by the Greek states on important political matters; it was famous for its ambiguous answers.

**5** Corinth benefited from its strategic position on the isthmus between the Gulf of Corinth and the Aegean Sea to become a major trading power.

**6** The Ionians were the most culturally sophisticated Greeks in the 7th and 6th centuries, taking advantage of close links with the Middle Eastern civilizations.

**7** Argos was a bitter rival of Sparta for control of the Peloponnese from the 7th to the 5th century.

**8** Coinage was introduced by Lydian kings in about 700; its use had spread to Greece by about 600.

BURIED under the ruins of the Acropolis when the Persians attacked Athens in 480, this marble *kore* (maiden) would once have been brightly painted.

*Black Sea*

*Danube*

Thracians

*Marista*

Herakleia

Byzantium

Chalcedon

*Strymon*

Abdera

Thasos

Thasos

Lampsakos

Cyzicus

Sestos

Samothrace

*Imroz*

Abydos

*Lemnos*

Lake Prespa

MACEDON

2

Poteidaia

Mt Olympos
(Zeus)

Lesbos

AEOLIA

Mytilene

*Vjose*

Corcyra

Dodona
(Zeus)

*Pinios*

EPIRUS

*Corfu*

THESSALY

*Northern Sporades*

*Aegean Sea*

Chios

Phokaia

LYDIA
conquered by Persians
547–546

8

Ambracia

Chios

Klasomenai

ACARNANIA

AETOLIA

PHOCIS

Anthela
(Apollo)

4

Alacomenae
(Apollo)

*Euboea*

Delphi
(Apollo)

*Kephisos*

Chalcis

Kolophon

*Menderes*

BOEOTIA

Eretria

Ephesos
(Artemis)

*Kephallenia*

ACHAEA

Thebes

5

Megara

ATTICA

Eleusis (Demeter)

Athens

*Andros*

Samos

IONIA

Miletus

Sikyon

Nemea
(Zeus)

Corinth
(Poseidon)

Didyma
(Apollo)

*Ikaria*

6

ELIS

*Zakynthos*

Olympia
(Zeus)

ARCADIA

Argos
(Hera)

Aegina

1

Epidauros (Asclepios)

Delos
(Apollo)

Naxos

Halikarnassos

Mantineia

Calauria
(Poseidon)

*Paros*

*Naxos*

Kos

Kos

Tegea

7

*Melos*

Knidos
(Aphrodite)

LYCIA

3

Ialysos

MESSENIA

KYNOURIA

*Thera*

Kameiros

*Rhodes*

Sparta

LACONIA

Lindos

KYTHERA
(Aphrodite)

*Carpathos*

*Mediterranean Sea*

Crete

Kydonia

Knossos

Itanos

Gortyn

*Olt*

appointing Solon to reform the constitution in 594. The result was a compromise that satisfied nobody and in 546 the tyrant Peisistratus seized power. Peisistratus was an effective and popular ruler who broke the aristocratic hold on power and did much to address the problems of the peasantry. Peisistratos was succeeded by his less able son Hippias who was overthrown by an aristocratic faction in 510. After three years of internal strife the aristocratic party was defeated. The reformer Kleisthenes "took the people into partnership" and introduced a democratic constitution which gave all 45,000 male citizens the right to attend the assembly and vote on all major decisions and appointments.

By actively involving its citizens in government, Athens had become a self-confident and assertive

state by 500, but for most of the 6th century the most powerful state was Sparta, which had taken the lead in developing new infantry tactics in which armored spearmen fought in a close-packed phalanx, presenting an impenetrable hedge of spears to the enemy. Sparta formed a league of similar cities based on a hoplite franchise, through which it dominated the Peloponnese.

The first Greeks to fall under Persian power were the Ionians on the Anatolian coast. Since about 600 the Ionians had paid tribute to the kings of Lydia but relations were good: the Greeks adopted coinage as a result of Lydian influences and the Lydians themselves became increasingly Hellenized. Persian rule was not particularly oppressive but it was more unpopular than the loose control of the Lydians.

Despite their rivalries, Greeks had a strong sense of common identity by the 8th century, expressed through the name they gave themselves – Hellenes – and by religion. All Greeks worshiped the same gods and celebrated pan-Hellenic festivals, such as the Olympic Games, during which hostilities had to cease. The neutrality of shrines of pan-Hellenic importance was protected and supported by leagues (*amphictonies*) of neighboring states, such as the Amphictony of Delphi. A cultural heritage had also emerged, epitomized by the epic poems of Homer, which were composed in the 8th century.

See also 11 (Minoans and Mycenaeans);
12 (Bronze Age Europe); 18 (Persia)

The domestication of maize around 2700 made possible the development of permanent farming villages in Mesoamerica by 2300. Most early farmers practiced slash-and-burn agriculture, which cannot support dense populations. However, on fertile river flood-plains in the tropical forests of southeastern Mexico, reliable rainfall and year-round warmth made it possible to raise four crops of maize a year, which provided the economic base for the Olmec civilization.

By 1250 BC the Olmec lived in chiefdoms or small states ruled by a powerful hereditary elite. The most important sites were ceremonial centers with earth pyramid mounds and monumental stone sculptures of gods and chiefs. Associated with the ceremonial centers were settlements of two to three thousand people. The ritual centers were periodically destroyed and sculptures defaced or buried. Though possibly due to warfare between chiefdoms or states, it is more likely that this served a ritual purpose, marking the end of calendrical cycles, the death of a ruler or the accession of a new dynasty. Trade and gift exchange played an important part in the Olmec way of life. The Olmec lands have few natural resources and the raw materials for everyday tools, stone sculpture and status enhancing display objects had to be imported over long distances. Gift exchange played an important part in the diffusion of Olmec culture as the emerging elites of neighboring communities took up Olmec beliefs and artifacts to enhance their prestige. Late in their history, the Olmec developed a rudimentary hieroglyphic script which was used mainly for astronomical inscriptions. They used – and may have originated – both the Mesoamerican 260-day sacred year and the 52-year "long-count" calendar.

The Maya originated about 1200 BC in the Guatemalan highlands, developing from earlier Archaic cultures, and began to spread out into the lowlands of the Yucatán peninsula around 1000. By draining and canalizing swamps the Maya were able to

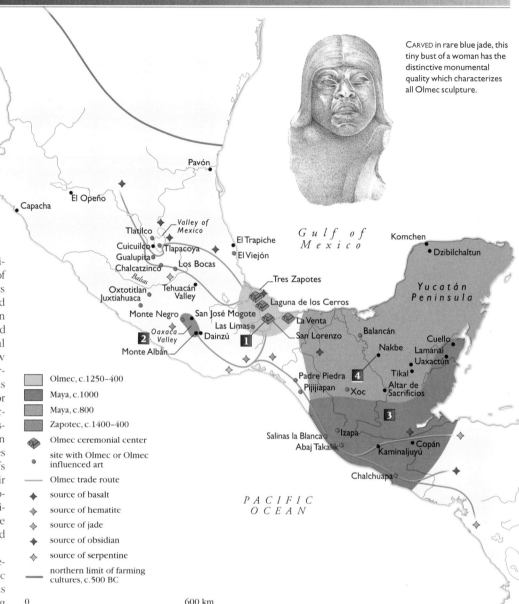

CARVED in rare blue jade, this tiny bust of a woman has the distinctive monumental quality which characterizes all Olmec sculpture.

Map labels:
Pavón
Capacha
El Opeño
Tlatilco
Valley of Mexico
Cuicuilco
Gualupita
Tlapacoya
Chalcatzinco
Balsas
Los Bocas
Oxtotitlan
Juxtiahuaca
Tehuacán Valley
Monte Negro
San José Mogote
Oaxaca Valley
Dainzú
Monte Albán
Las Limas
El Trapiche
El Viejón
Tres Zapotes
Laguna de los Cerros
San Lorenzo
La Venta
Gulf of Mexico
Komchen
Dzibilchaltun
Yucatán Peninsula
Balancán
Nakbe
Cuello
Lamanai
Uaxactún
Tikal
Padre Piedra
Pijijiapan
Xoc
Altar de Sacrificios
Salinas la Blanca
Izapa
Abaj Takalik
Kaminaljuyú
Copán
Chalchuapa
PACIFIC OCEAN

Legend:
Olmec, c.1250–400
Maya, c.1000
Maya, c.800
Zapotec, c.1400–400
Olmec ceremonial center
site with Olmec or Olmec influenced art
Olmec trade route
source of basalt
source of hematite
source of jade
source of obsidian
source of serpentine
northern limit of farming cultures, c.500 BC

0 — 600 km
0 — 400 mi

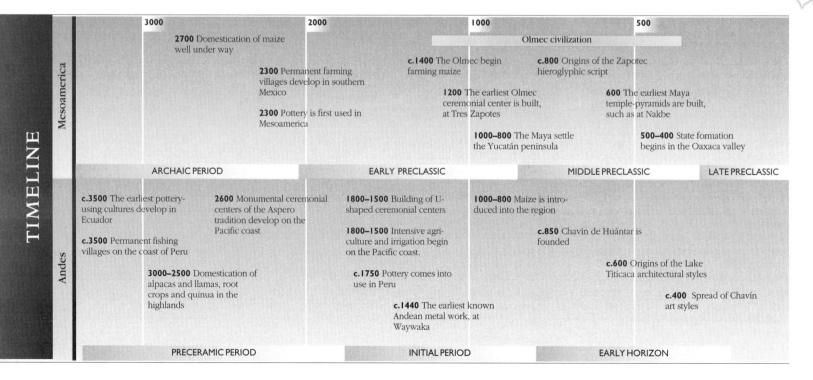

TIMELINE

| | 3000 | 2000 | 1000 | 500 |
|---|---|---|---|---|

**Mesoamerica**

2700 Domestication of maize well under way

Olmec civilization

c.1400 The Olmec begin farming maize

c.800 Origins of the Zapotec hieroglyphic script

2300 Permanent farming villages develop in southern Mexico

1200 The earliest Olmec ceremonial center is built, at Tres Zapotes

600 The earliest Maya temple-pyramids are built, such as at Nakbe

2300 Pottery is first used in Mesoamerica

1000–800 The Maya settle the Yucatán peninsula

500–400 State formation begins in the Oaxaca valley

ARCHAIC PERIOD — EARLY PRECLASSIC — MIDDLE PRECLASSIC — LATE PRECLASSIC

**Andes**

c.3500 The earliest pottery-using cultures develop in Ecuador

c.3500 Permanent fishing villages on the coast of Peru

2600 Monumental ceremonial centers of the Aspero tradition develop on the Pacific coast

1800–1500 Building of U-shaped ceremonial centers

1800–1500 Intensive agriculture and irrigation begin on the Pacific coast.

1000–800 Maize is introduced into the region

c.850 Chavín de Huántar is founded

3000–2500 Domestication of alpacas and llamas, root crops and quinua in the highlands

c.1750 Pottery comes into use in Peru

c.600 Origins of the Lake Titicaca architectural styles

c.1440 The earliest known Andean metal work, at Waywaka

c.400 Spread of Chavín art styles

PRECERAMIC PERIOD — INITIAL PERIOD — EARLY HORIZON

produce sufficient food to support a complex society and by 600 towns, such as Nakbe and Komchen, with monumental temple pyramids, were developing. Complex societies also developed among the Zapotec people of the Oaxaca valley by the 1st millennium BC. Here food production was increased by simple irrigation techniques and terracing. By 400 BC there were at least seven small states in the valley, the most important of which was centered on Monte Albán, and a system of hieroglyphic writing had been developed. In the Valley of Mexico highly productive agriculture using *chinampas* – raised fields built on reclaimed swamps – led to the development of trading networks, a market economy, craft specialization and large villages by around 200 BC.

The earliest complex societies in South America developed on the desert coast of Peru in settled fishing communities during the Preceramic period (3750–1800 BC). The marine resources of this area are unusually rich and these communities were able to free labor for the construction of temples and ceremonial centers under the direction of village leaders. One of the earliest such centers was built at Aspero around 2600: it consisted of six mounds nine meters high, topped with masonry ceremonial structures. Cotton, squash and gourds (used as floats for fishing nets) were cultivated but farming did not make a significant contribution to the diet. In the highlands, herding alpacas or llamas and cultivation of root crops such as potatoes, ullucu and oca or quinua, a cereal, gradually replaced hunting and gathering during the Preceramic; permanent villages with small ceremonial buildings also developed.

During the Initial Period (1800–800 BC) the area of cultivable land in the coastal lowlands was greatly extended through irrigation works, diverting water from the rivers which flowed from the Andes through the desert to the coast. Pottery was adopted. Huge U-shaped ceremonial centers, requiring the control of considerable resources of labor, food supplies and raw materials, were constructed: one at Garagay is estimated to have required 3.2 million work-days to complete. These sites were probably focal points for local chiefdoms but burial practices show few distinctions of wealth or rank. Interaction between the fishing communities on the coast and the farming communities in the desert river valleys and the mountains was considerable, with salt, seaweed and dried fish from the coast being exchanged for carbohydrate foods such as root crops and grain from the highlands and river valleys.

The Early Horizon (about 800–200 BC) saw the development of sophisticated architecture and complex sculptural styles at the highland ceremonial center of Chavín de Huántar. The Chavín style was the culmination of styles which had originated as early as 1200 in other Andean and coastal sites and by 400 its influence had spread over a wide area of coastal and highland Peru. Chavín had a population of two to three thousand at its peak in the 4th century but thereafter it declined, without developing into a full urban civilization. Complex societies, united by common beliefs, also developed in the Lake Titicaca basin during the Early Horizon. Particularly important is the ceremonial center at Chiripa, built 600–400 BC, in which can be seen the origins of the architectural styles of the 5th-century AD Tiahuanaco state. Maize became an important crop in the Andes during this period.

Valdivia tradition, 3800–1700

Preceramic

Aspero tradition, 3000–1800

Kotosh tradition, 2300–1200

El Paraiso tradition, 2000–1800

Chinchoros tradition, 3000–500 (ceramic after 1200)

site with monumental building

other important site

Initial Period and Early Horizon

El Paraiso, 1800–850

Chorrera culture, 1200–300

Chavín culture, 900–200

Paracas culture, 650–150

Yaya-Mama religious traditions, 600–400

site with monumental building

other important site

possible trans-Andean route

coastal desert

tropical rainforest

0                    600 km
0                    400 mi

FANGED gods with human-animal attributes rendered in complex geometry, are found in the widespread Chavín style, seen here on a textile design.

1 San Lorenzo was the first Olmec ceremonial center with earth pyramid mounds and monumental sculpture, flourishing c.1200–900.

2 The Zapotec script, the earliest in the Americas, was developed in the Oaxaca valley c.800–700.

3 The Maya originated in the Guatemalan highlands and settled the Yucatán peninsula by 800.

4 By the 7th century the Maya were constructing temple pyramids and other monumental buildings at sites such as Nakbe.

5 Valdivia has given its name to a culture, with early use of pottery (c.3000 BC), fishing, shellfish-gathering and maize-farming.

6 The earliest evidence of metal-working in the Andes is from Waywaka, where tools and beaten gold from c.1440 BC have been found.

7 Chavín de Huántar was a large ceremonial center occupied 850–200; its distinctive art style was adopted over a wide area of Peru c.400 BC.

8 More than four hundred mummies have been found at the necropolis of Paracas.

9 Chiripa was a mound-top ceremonial center of c.600 BC, with many features common to later civilizations in the region.

See also 4 (agriculture);
39 (later South America)

The Persians who took Babylon in 539 were comparative newcomers to the region. An Indo-Iranian people, the Persians had followed their close relations the Medes from central Asia to Iran in the 8th century. The founder of the Persian monarchy was Achemenes, who gave his name to the dynasty, but it is uncertain when he ruled. In 648, when Ashurbanipal destroyed the Elamite kingdom and occupied western Elam, the Persians seized the opportunity to take its eastern territories. Despite this Persia was overshadowed by, and often subject to, the powerful Median kingdom. It was in the reign of Cyrus the Great that Persia rose to empire.

Cyrus' career as a great conqueror started when his nominal overlord, the Median king Astyages, invaded Persia around 550 following a rebellion. Astyages was deserted by his army and captured when he met Cyrus in battle at Pasargadae. Cyrus followed up this easy victory by taking the Median capital at Hamadan (Ecbatana). Cyrus was now the most powerful ruler in the region. In 547 he repulsed an invasion of Media by King Croesus of Lydia, who withdrew to his capital Sardis and disbanded his army for the winter. Cyrus, however, had nothing against winter campaigns and, when he arrived unexpectedly, Sardis fell after a siege of only fourteen days. Leaving his generals to complete the conquest of Lydia and the Ionian Greeks, Cyrus marched east to push deep into central Asia. In 539 he crowned his career by conquering Babylonia. Discontent over the religious unorthodoxy of its king Nabonidus was rife and, by posing as a servant of the god Marduk and restorer of orthodoxy, he was even welcomed in Babylon.

In little more than a decade Cyrus had built the largest empire the world had yet seen, with remarkably little hard campaigning. Clearly the close relationship between the Medes and Persians aided in what was more of a dynastic takeover than a conquest, and in Mesopotamia the experience of incorporation in the Assyrian and Babylonian empires had long-since mixed cultures, weakened local identities and accustomed people to imperial rule. As a result there was little spirit of resistance to what amounted, in practice, to no more than the advent of

a new imperial dynasty. Cyrus was diplomat as well as soldier and the consolidation of his empire owed much to his moderation. Demands for tribute were modest, he did not interfere with local customs, upheld the rights of the local priesthood and left local institutions of government intact.

Cyrus was killed in 530 on campaign against the Sakas in central Asia and was succeeded by his son Cambyses. Cambyses added Egypt and Libya to the empire before dying in mysterious circumstances,

Persia at the accession of Cyrus, 559
conquered by Cyrus, 559-550
conquered by Cyrus, 550-530
conquered by Cambyses, 530-522
conquered by Darius, 521-486
tributary region or vassal state
border of pre-Achemenid state
uncertain border of pre-Achemenid state
border of Persian empire, 496
royal road
■ capital of Persian empire
**Susa** major royal palace
**LYDIA** conquered state
Caria region paying tribute to Persia in 500
modern coastline and drainage where altered

major Persian campaign
Cyrus
Cyrus, conjectural
Cambyses
Darius
Darius, conjectural
Xerxes

**TIMELINE**

**Persian empire**

**c.850** The Medes migrate into Iran from central Asia.

**c.750** The Persians migrate into southern Iran from central Asia

**c.640** Persia becomes a vassal state of Media

**c.630–553** Life of Zoroaster, the prophet of Iran and founder of the Parsee religion

**559** Accession of Cyrus, who seizes the Median throne in 550

**547–546** Cyrus captures Lydia

**539** Cyrus takes Babylon

**525–523** Cambyses (r.530–522) conquers Egypt

**520** Darius (r.521–486) campaigns against the pointed-hat Scythians

**518** Conquest of the Indus valley by the Persians

**513** Darius invades southeast Europe

**499** The Ionian Greeks rebel against Persian rule

**490** The Greeks defeat the Persians at Marathon

**480** The Greeks halt Xerxes (r.486–465) at Salamis

**General**

**612** Fall of Nineveh and collapse of Assyria's empire

**562** Decline of Babylon after the death of Nebuchadnezzar

**520** Darius links the Nile and Red Sea by a canal

**507** Kleisthenes lays the basis for democracy in Athens

0        600 km
0        400 mi

GOLD bracelets like this were shown as part of the Lydians' tribute, depicted on reliefs at Persepolis

*Aral Sea*

**Sakas**

Sogdiana
horses, jewelry, weapons

**3** • Kyreskhata

• Marakanda
(Samarkand)

Pointed-hat
Scythians
250 talents of silver,
clothing, jewelry,
horses

**Pointed-hat
Scythians**

*Caspian Sea*

**Bactria**
360 talents of silver,
camels, vessels

• Bactra

*HINDU KUSH*

*Indus*

C A U C A S U S   M T S

Colchis
25 boys, 25 girls

*Araks*

Chorasmia
300 talents of silver with
Parthia and Aria, horses,
jewelry, weapons

*Amu Dar'ya*

Aria
camels, lionskin cloaks,
vessels

Capisa

Peshawar
(Caspatyrus?)

*Turan Lowland*

546–539

Kabul •

• Taxila

Armenia
400 talents of silver,
clothing, horses, vessels

*Murat*

Lake
Van

• Van

Lake
Urmia

M E D I A N

Media
450 talents of silver, animal
hides, clothing, jewelry,
vessels, weapons

Parthia
camels, vessels

• Herat

520

Gandhara
170 talents of silver,
bulls, weapons

*Chenab*

*Jhelum*

547

*Tigris*

• Nineveh
• Arbil

*Diyala*

E M P I R E

Hamadan

*Dasht-e Lut*

*Helmand*

Assyria
animal hides, cloth,
eunuchs, metals,
rams, vessels

BABYLONIAN
EMPIRE

539

Elam
300 talents of
silver, lioness &
cubs, weapons

550

Drangiana
camels, lionskin cloaks,
vessels

• Kandahar

*Sutlej*

c.518

*Desert*

*Euphrates*

539 Opis

Sippar •

• Nippur

Susa

Babylon

Sagartia
600 talents of silver,
cloth, horses

Arachosia
animal hides, camels,
vessels

Sind
360 talents of gold dust,
axes, weapons

HINDU
KINGDOMS

Babylonia
1000 talents of silver with
Assyria, bulls, cloth,
eunuchs, vessels

550 **1** Pasargadae

• Persepolis

PERSIA

*Indus*

*Persian Gulf*

Maka

*Gulf of Oman*

*Arabian
Sea*

possibly murdered by his brother Smerdis. Smerdis was quickly overthrown and killed by Darius (r.521–486), a member of a junior Achemenid house. Darius faced rebellions from one end of the empire to the other but suppressed them all within a year. By 520 he was secure enough to campaign against the Caspian Scythians. In 518 he extended Persian control as far as, and possibly a little beyond, the Indus and in 513 he crossed into Europe; though he conquered Thrace, the expedition failed in its main objective of subduing the Black Sea Scythians. This failure encouraged a rebellion by the Ionian Greeks in 499. This was put down in 494 and Darius dispatched an expedition to punish the mainland Greeks for supporting the rebels. When this force was defeated by the Athenians at Marathon in 490, Darius began to plan for the conquest of Greece. The expedition was finally launched by his son Xerxes, but the decisive defeat of his fleet at Salamis in 480 and of his army at Plataea the following year brought the expansion of the empire to a halt.

Darius reorganized the empire into about twenty provinces under governors, or satraps, often relatives or close friends of the king. The system of taxation was regularized and fixed tributes, based on the wealth of each province, were introduced. Only Persia, which was not a conquered province, was exempt. The Assyrian imperial post system was expanded and the roads improved. Local garrison commanders remained directly responsible to the king. The official capital of the empire under Cyrus had been Pasargadae, but Hamadan was effectively the administrative capital. Darius moved the administrative capital to Susa and founded a new official capital at Persepolis. Under Darius the imperial administration used various local languages transcribed into cuneiform and written on clay tablets for documents, but his successors abandoned this system in favor of writing on parchment using the widespread Aramaic language and alphabet.

The Persian empire was a thoroughly cosmopolitan state which united elements of all the major civilizations of its time except the Chinese. By throwing together peoples from so many backgrounds, the empire promoted the diffusion and mixing of cultures and ended the isolation of the old civilizations.

**1** Astyages, king of Media, was defeated by Cyrus at Pasargadae; Cyrus then took Hamadan and seized the Median throne.

**2** Cyrus repulsed a Lydian invasion at Pteria, then captured the Lydian capital Sardis and King Croesus.

**3** Kyreskhata was the strongest of a chain of forts built by Cyrus to protect the northern frontier.

**4** After a hard-fought battle at Pelusium Cambyses captured Memphis (525) and took pharaoh Psammeticus III to Susa in chains.

**5** A Persian force sent by Cambyses to capture Siwa vanished in the desert.

**6** Darius built a bridge of boats over the Bosporus (513) to invade Europe; Xerxes did the same over the Hellespont in 480.

**7** Persian expansion to the west was decisively halted by the Greeks at the naval battle of Salamis.

See also 15 (Babylon); 16 (Greece);
20 (invasion of Greece); 21 (Alexander)

The number and size of organized states in the Middle East, India and the Mediterranean rose sharply between 1000 and 500 BC. A succession of empires dominated the Middle East. The first was the Assyrian empire which stretched from the Zagros mountains to Egypt by the 7th century. Assyrian rule was harsh and in 625 the Babylonians rebelled and seized most of the empire for themselves (▷ 14). Then the Iranian Medes pushed west, conquering the Caucasus and eastern Anatolia. In 550 Cyrus II "the Great", an Iranian king, seized the Median kingdom and founded the Persian empire. He then took western Anatolia and the Babylonian empire. By 500 the Persian empire extended from Egypt to the Indus (▷ 18).

State-organized societies had also spread throughout the Mediterranean world. By 700 Greece was a patchwork of independent city-states: by 500 these cities, and Athens in particular, entered a period of intellectual creativity unparalleled in world history (▷ 16). The Greeks and Phoenicians also founded trading colonies throughout the Mediterranean. Although the Phoenicians lost their independence by 500, Carthage, their colony in north Africa, was the leading power of the western Mediterranean. The Greek cities of Sicily and southern Italy had a powerful influence, notably on the Etruscans who dominated northern Italy by 500. North of the Alps the Urnfield cultures of central Europe were replaced by the aristocratic iron-using Celtic Hallstatt culture c.600.

States reappeared in the Indian subcontinent in the 9th century. The focus this time was the Ganges plain where Vedic Aryan chiefdoms began to coalesce into kingdoms and republics. By 500 the largest was the kingdom of Magadha. At the same time the Aryans extended southward, conquering the Dravidians and imposing Hindu religion on them. The Chinese Zhou kingdom expanded to the southeast after 1000, but what it gained in area it lost in internal cohesion. The Zhou kingdom was a decentralized feudal state and by the 8th century the powerful warlords had so undermined the power of the monarchy that it was powerless to prevent the kingdom from breaking up (▷ 8). Meanwhile the first chiefdoms emerged around 500 in Korea and in Van Lang in southeast Asia.

One far-reaching development of the early first millennium was the change in lifestyle of the Iranian peoples (Scythians, Sarmatians, Sakas and Yue Qi) of the Eurasian steppes from transhumant (seasonal) pastoralism to nomadic pastoralism. The steppe peoples had been pioneers in the use of horses: they had domesticated them for their meat around 4000 BC, they had harnessed them to wagons (4th millennium) and war chariots (2nd millennium) and by 1000 BC they had mastered

## Map labels

Arctic marine mammal hunters
Aleuts
sub-Arctic forest hunter-gatherers
west coast foraging, hunting and fishing peoples
Plateau fishers and hunter-gatherers
desert hunter-gatherers
plains bison hunters
east woodlands hunter-gatherers
Adena complex
Bahamas
Cuba
Jamaica
Hispaniola
Puerto Rico
Caribbean hunter-gatherers
maize farmers
Hawaiian Islands
Zapotec culture
Olmec culture
Maya
maize farmers
manioc farmers
Chorrera culture
Chavin culture
Paracas culture
Chinchoros tradition
Yaya–Mama religious tradition
savanna hunter-gatherers
shellfish gatherers
Andean hunter-gatherers
pampas hunter-gatherers
shellfish gatherers and marine mammal hunters

## Timeline

700–100 Adena culture burial mound builders in the eastern woodlands of North America

800 Zapotecs develop hieroglyphic script in Mesoamerica

700 City-states flourish in Greece and the Aegean

800–500 Greek colonization of the Mediterranean and Black Sea

c.750 Emergence of the Celtic Hallstatt Iron Age culture north of the Alps

800 Emergence of the Etruscan civilization in Italy

750–705 Assyrian power reaches its peak

900–700 Nomadism becomes the dominant way of life on the Eurasian steppes

1000 Emergence of the kingdom of Israel

612 The collapse of the Assyrian empire

| TIMELINE | | 1000 | | 900 | | 800 | | 700 | | 600 |
|---|---|---|---|---|---|---|---|---|---|---|
| The Americas | | | | | | | | | | |
| Europe | | | | | | | | | | |
| Middle East | | | | | | | | | | |
| Africa | | | | | | | | | | |
| East and South Asia | | | | | | | | | | |

1000–500 Formative period of Hinduism

900 The first states emerge on the Ganges plain

814 Foundation of the Phoenician colony of Carthage

712–671 Egypt is ruled by a Kushite dynasty from Nubia

600 Iron and bronze working develop in west Africa

800 The Aryans expand into southern India

600 Introduction of iron working into China

770–481 The "Springs and Autumns" period in China: the Zhou kingdom breaks up into minor states

c.590 The Nubian capital established at Meroë

hunter-gatherers
nomadic pastoralists
simple farming societies
complex farming societies/chiefdoms
state societies
uninhabited
empire
extent of bronze working, c.500 BC
extent of iron working, c.500 BC

Greenland

Iceland

Lapps

Finno–Ugrian taiga hunter-gatherers

Arctic marine mammal hunters

Paleo-Siberian taiga hunter-gatherers

Proto-Germans
Balts
Finns
Slavs
Hallstatt culture (Celts)
Etruscans
Illyrians
Scythians
Sarmatians
Sakas
Turko-Mongol transhumant pastoralists
Greeks
Italics
Greeks
Thracians
Yue Qi (Kushans)
Koreans
Celtiberians
CARTHAGINIAN EMPIRE
Berbers
Silk Route
Zhou states
Late Jomon hunter-gatherers
PERSIAN EMPIRE
Tibetan transhumant pastoralists
MAGADHA
Burmese
Pastoral nomads
Arabs
Hindu kingdoms and republics
Thais
Taiwan
MEROE
SABA
Van Lang
Philippine Islands
cereal farmers
Bantu-speaking people
Ethiopian highland farmers
Ceylon
Austro-Asiatic rice farmers
Austronesians
Pastoralists
Celebes
New Guinea
Sumatra
Borneo
Papuan-Melanesian Neolithic farmers
Madagascar
Java
Timor
Lapita culture (ancestral Polynesian)
Khoisan hunter-gatherers
Australian Aboriginal hunter-gatherers
Tasmanian hunter-gatherers

pastoral nomads

507 A democratic system of government is established in Athens

509 Foundation of the Roman republic after the last king is expelled

525–404 Egypt is conquered by the Persians

539 Babylon is conquered by the Persians

550 Cyrus the Great founds the Achemenid Persian empire

550

500

c.563 Birth of Siddhartha Gautama, the Buddha, in northern India

551 Birth of Confucius in China

c.540 Magadha becomes the dominant kingdom in the Indian subcontinent

500 The Bantu-speaking peoples begin to expand from their west African homeland

riding on horseback. This development made the nomadic life possible by giving sufficient speed and mobility to manage large herds over vast ranges. By 500 BC the Iranian nomads had created a relatively homogeneous culture area from the Balkans almost to the borders of China. Nomadism had both beneficial and destructive consequences for the settled peoples of Eurasia. The nomads helped to forge trade links across Asia and by 500 BC Chinese silks found their way to the west along what would become known as the Silk Route. The mobility of the nomads also made them formidable raiders: Europe, the Middle East and China were troubled by their attacks for two thousand years.

Around 600 sub-Saharan Africa moved directly from the Stone Age to the Iron Age and the expansion of the Bantu-speaking peoples from their west African homeland continued. Over the next 1,500 years they became, through migration and cultural assimilation, the main linguistic group in Africa.

In Mesoamerica the Maya and Zapotec cultures emerged (▷ 17). Both Mesoamerican and Andean chiefdoms built impressive ceremonial centers. Farming was established in the Amazon basin by 500 BC and in several areas of North America cultivated plants were important supplements to wild foods. In the eastern woodlands hunters, gatherers and cultivators lived in semiperma-nent villages and developed complex cultures: the Adena people built com-munal burial mounds and ritual earthworks, made pottery and worked copper. Full farming economies, though, did not appear for many centuries ■

## Part 2

# THE CLASSICAL

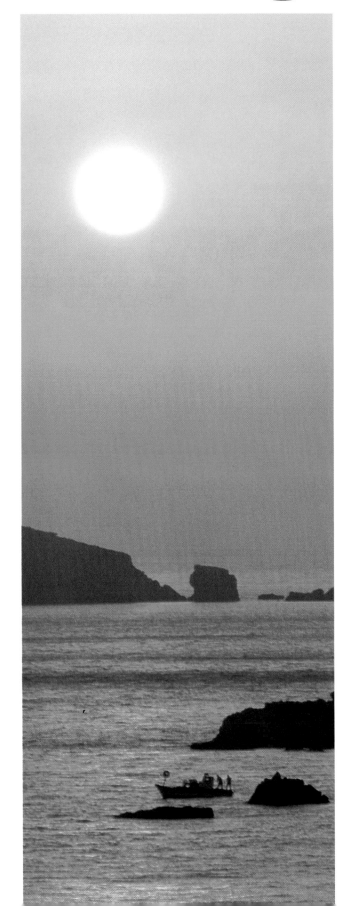

I n the thirty generations between 500 BC and AD 600, populations increased across the globe; states with complex systems of social and economic control emerged; food production intensified, allowing artists, architects, poets and thinkers to develop their skills. All the major religions, with the exception of Islam, took root.

Amidst the vivid mass of detail, certain themes recur. In certain areas, favored by their access to natural resources and their position astride trade routes, centers of social or economic innovation sprang up. Powerful chiefs often commanded discrete territories. They copied and competed with one another, often acquiring prestige goods for display, in life and on death, for others to wonder at. Conspicuous consumption and ritual destruction of luxuries by burying them with chieftains meant that ever more prestige goods were needed. This gave momentum to trade and, sometimes, to warfare.

In some areas chiefdoms were transformed into states through a complex phase of warfare and social reordering. Thus the Mycenaean chiefdoms of the late second millennium BC became the young city-states of Greece two centuries later. On the other side of the world in about 500 BC, in the Oaxaca valley of Mesoamerica, three competing chiefdoms came together to found a new political capital on the mountain-top of Monte Albán; it remained preeminent for more than a thousand years. The unification of rival polities under a single authority was seen throughout the world. In 408 BC, a century after the foundation of Monte Albán, three rival Greek cities on the island of Rhodes agreed to found the city of Rhodes.

A dynamic relationship arose between these innovating centers and the peripheries around them. A complex state needed raw materials and human power to maintain it. A

THE AEGEAN SEA, scene of the ancient Greek experiments in civilization.

# WORLD

regular supply of rare metals, exotic stones and woods, furs and fabrics was essential to support the structure of the social hierarchy, while human power, in the form of slaves or a supply of food for a free workforce, was needed to support the state's bureaucrats, soldiers, priests or scholars. The demands of centralizing powers thus encouraged trade with the surrounding peripheries. African and Indian communities were drawn into the economic sphere of the Roman empire, despite knowing little of the state that gave them pottery, coins and trinkets in return for raw materials and slaves. Communities closer to the centers were in a better position to learn from their neighbors and imitate them.

There was a continual drift of creative energy from the center to the periphery, as the seeds of innovation took root in the fertile periphery while the core decayed. The early core of Europe developed in the Greek cities around the Aegean; later, the focus for innovation was on the Greek mainland. Power then shifted to the central Mediterranean where Rome emerged preeminent. Six centuries later power moved to the peripheral Black Sea region, with the rise of Constantinople and the Byzantine empire. In Mesoamerica the same pattern can be seen, in the move of power from the Oaxaca valley to the Valley of Mexico and then the Maya area of the Yucatán.

The cycle of growth and decay and the inexorable shift of centers of power were accelerated by warfare and invasion. The Celtic tribes who attacked the Greco-Roman world in the fourth and third centuries BC confronted energetic states well able to defend themselves; but the Germanic peoples who attacked around AD 400 found the Roman empire in a state of decay. They rapidly overran Rome and set up a number of new kingdoms within the carcass of the old empire.

The collapse of empires – a common theme in this period – is a subject of great fascination. Each case is different and the reasons are always complex: natural catastrophy, population decline, economic over-extension, invasion, disease. In the prehistoric context of Mesoamerica, archeologists speculate about "ecological overshoot" and the destructive role of parasitic elites; whereas in China, detailed written records reveal the processes leading to the collapse of the Han empire – foreign wars, internal power struggles and peasant rebellions as the empire disintegrated into rival factions of local warlords.

Yet it is possible to turn the notions of center and periphery inside out and to see the states and empires of Europe, India and China not as centers but as developments on the periphery of the huge, central landmass of Asia – an unending steppe land, home of horse-riding nomads who for century after century moved out to strike terror into the hearts of their sedentary, civilized neighbors. In Europe the first recorded invaders were the Cimmerians, around 700 BC. Then followed the Scythians, the Sarmatians, the Alans and the Huns, the last contributing to the chaos at the end of the Roman era. Other groups moved into India, while the northern boundaries of China were constantly at risk – a threat which the Great Wall was eventually designed to avert. The history of Old World civilization was intimately bound up with the population pressures of the deepest Eurasian steppes.

During the millennium 500 BC–AD 600, many foundations of the modern world were created. Bronze and iron became widely available and steel was developed in Han China. The powers of wind and water were harnessed; horse-riding was transformed by the development of the stirrup; and science, astronomy and mathematics made enormous strides in the Hellenistic world, India, China and Mesoamerica. By AD 600 a plateau had been reached. There was to be little further advance until the fifteenth century when the arts of navigation and seamanship opened up the world ■

After Cyrus, founder of the Persian empire, conquered Lydia in 546 BC, his generals mopped up the relatively insignificant Greek cities of Ionia, but in 499 they rebelled again under the leadership of Aristagoras of Miletos and introduced democratic rule. The rebels received aid from Athens and this provoked the Persian king Darius (r.521–486) to plan a punitive invasion of Greece after the revolt had been crushed in 494.

Darius' first invasion, in 492, was defeated by the weather when the fleet supporting his army was destroyed in a storm rounding Mount Athos. After a second expedition was humiliatingly defeated by the Athenians at Marathon in 490, Darius decided that the conquest of the whole of Greece was needed to secure the Persian position in Ionia. He died before his preparations were complete and it was left to his son Xerxes to carry out his plans. Meanwhile the Greeks prepared for an invasion, with Themistocles persuading Athens – by far the largest and wealthiest *polis* or city-state – to invest in an urgent naval building program.

The history of this invasion was memorably recorded by the Ionian-born Herodotos, the first major Greek prose writer and historian, later in the 5th century. Xerxes' army, said to have been 200,000 strong, was one of the largest forces ever assembled in antiquity and was supported by a fleet of perhaps a thousand ships. Faced with this vast force, most of the northern Greek states opted for neutrality or (in a few cases) alliance with Persia. The southern Greek states, however, united under the leadership of Athens and Sparta and prepared to resist the Persians. The resulting struggle was less uneven than expected. The very size of the Persian army proved a serious handicap; it was difficult to supply and impossible to control effectively on a battlefield; the quality of its troops varied enormously and only around 10,000 were elite troops. In contrast the Greeks, though greatly outnumbered, were heavily armed, experienced, disciplined and highly motivated: they were citizens defending their states, homes and families.

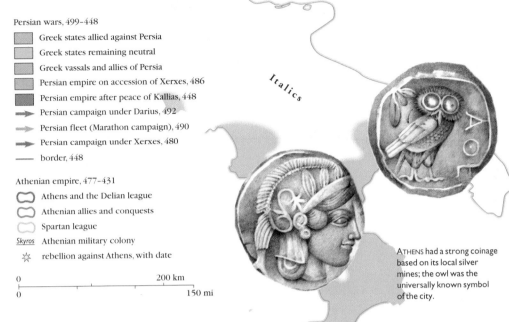

**Persian wars, 499-448**
- ▢ Greek states allied against Persia
- ▢ Greek states remaining neutral
- ▢ Greek vassals and allies of Persia
- ▢ Persian empire on accession of Xerxes, 486
- ▢ Persian empire after peace of Kallias, 448
- → Persian campaign under Darius, 492
- → Persian fleet (Marathon campaign), 490
- → Persian campaign under Xerxes, 480
- — border, 448

**Athenian empire, 477-431**
- ▢ Athens and the Delian league
- ▢ Athenian allies and conquests
- ▢ Spartan league
- *Skyros* Athenian military colony
- ✩ rebellion against Athens, with date

```
0                    200 km
0              150 mi
```

ATHENS had a strong coinage based on its local silver mines; the owl was the universally known symbol of the city.

The Greeks, led by Sparta, attempted to halt the Persian invasion at Thermopylae but were defeated after heroic resistance. The Persians went on to occupy Athens, although its population had been evacuated to Salamis. The Persian fleet, which was needed to outflank Spartan defenses on the Isthmus of Corinth, was now ambushed and destroyed by the Athenian navy at Salamis. Since it was clear that Greece could not now be conquered in a single campaign, Xerxes returned to Asia with half of the army: the remainder wintered in Greece only to be defeated decisively by a Spartan-led army at Plataea in the following year. The threat to Greece ended, the old rivalries of the Greek world resurfaced and Sparta and most of the other states withdrew from the war against Persia. Athens and its allies continued hostilities, destroying the last Persian garrisons in Europe, re-opening the Bosporus to Greek shipping by 475, and freeing the Ionian Greeks from Persian rule in 468. The Athenians also intervened unsuccessfully against the Persians in Egypt in 454 and captured Cyprus in 450. Hostilities came to a formal end in 448 when the Persians recognized Ionian independence.

To pursue its war aims, Athens created the anti-Persian Delian league of Aegean cities, with a common treasury on the island of Delos to which all members contributed. As its richest member and greatest naval power, Athens dominated the league and came increasingly to regard it as its empire. Some states, such as Aegina, were forcibly enrolled, and if a dissatisfied member tried to withhold contributions, the Athenian fleet was sent to enforce obedience. When the Athenians moved the treasury to Athens in 454 its domination became even more apparent. Despite this, many members remained loyal, being grateful to Athens for its role in the Persian wars and for introducing democracy. After the end of the war with Persia the league became as much a commercial as a military organization, although still serving Athenian interests. Athenian coinage, weights and measures were introduced throughout the league.

Under the leadership of the highly nationalistic Pericles, Athens also extended its power on the mainland and by 460 had achieved a dominant position in central Greece. Sparta – unusual in still having a monarchical constitution – had the strongest army in Greece and was unwilling to surrender its primacy to the increasingly arrogant Athenians. Throughout the 460s the Spartans were preoccupied with a *helot* (serf) revolt, but moves to increase the influence of Athens within the Peloponnese led to the outbreak of war between the two rivals in 457.

Athens was unable to sustain a war against Persia and Sparta at the same time, but the peace treaty with Persia in 448 in some ways weakened the Athenian position. Without the fear of a return to Persian rule, many members of the Delian league felt less closely bound to Athens. Sparta, which had no navy, concentrated its attack on the Athenian position on the mainland of central Greece while attempting to foment rebellion in the league. The Athenians successfully put down rebellions in

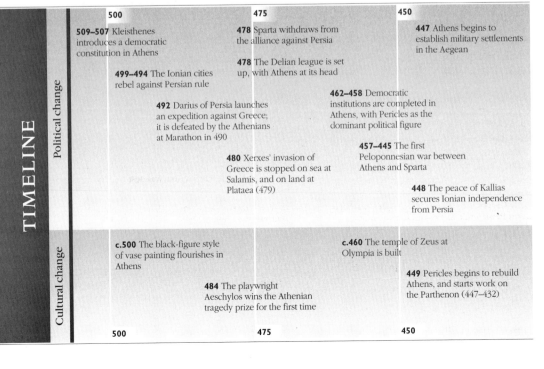

**TIMELINE**

**Political change**

| 500 | 475 | 450 |
|---|---|---|
| **509–507** Kleisthenes introduces a democratic constitution in Athens | **478** Sparta withdraws from the alliance against Persia | **447** Athens begins to establish military settlements in the Aegean |
| **499–494** The Ionian cities rebel against Persian rule | **478** The Delian league is set up, with Athens at its head | |
| **492** Darius of Persia launches an expedition against Greece; it is defeated by the Athenians at Marathon in 490 | **462–458** Democratic institutions are completed in Athens, with Pericles as the dominant political figure | |
| | **457–445** The first Peloponnesian war between Athens and Sparta | |
| **480** Xerxes' invasion of Greece is stopped on sea at Salamis, and on land at Plataea (479) | **448** The peace of Kallias secures Ionian independence from Persia | |

**Cultural change**

| 500 | 475 | 450 |
|---|---|---|
| **c.500** The black-figure style of vase painting flourishes in Athens | | **c.460** The temple of Zeus at Olympia is built |
| | | **449** Pericles begins to rebuild Athens, and starts work on the Parthenon (447–432) |
| **484** The playwright Aeschylos wins the Athenian tragedy prize for the first time | | |

**Map labels:**

Illyrians · Thracians · Apollonia · Black Sea · Bosporus · Byzantium 440 · Epidamnos · Lake Ohrid · Lake Prespa · Marista · Pella · MACEDON Persian vassal, 492 · Amphipolis · Eion · Abdera · 465 Thasos · 9 · Cyzicus · Chersonesos · 3 · Hellespont · Abydos · Apollonia · Vjose · Aliakmon · Axios · 7 · Akanthos · Methone · Poteidaia 432 · 2 · Imbros · Troy · Aegean Sea · Lemnos · EPIRUS · PINDOS MOUNTAINS · Pinios · Larissa · Kosthanaia · Mt Athos · LYDIA · Corcyra · THESSALY · Northern Sporades · Mytilene · Ambracia · Acheloos · Artemisium 480 · Lesbos · Phokaia · Sardis · Anaktorion · ACARNANIA · Thermopylae 480 · 4 · Oreos · Euboea · Skyros · IONIA · Gediz · Delphi · PHOCIS · Chios · Erythraia · Buyuk Menderes · Kephallenia · LOKRIS · Chalcis · EUBOEA 447 · Ephesos · 6 · Plataea 479 · BOEOTIA · Eretria · Marathon 490 · Samos · Elis · ACHAEA · Thebes · ATTICA · Samos 440 · Zakynthos · ELIS · Corinth · Megara · 5 · Athens · Mycale 479 · Miletos · ARCADIA · Salamis 480 · Laurion · Andros · Ikaria · 8 · Halikarnassos · Argos · Aegina · Troizen · Delos · Kos · Tegea · PELOPONNESE · Sparta · 469 Naxos · Rhodes · SPARTA · Carpathos · Mediterranean Sea · Crete

---

Euboea and Thasos, but by 445 they had lost control in central Greece and agreed to peace terms which recognized Spartan dominance in the Peloponnese.

Despite being almost constantly at war, Athens flourished economically in the 5th century as a result of its dominance of eastern Mediterranean and Black Sea trade and its own rich silver mines – worked by more than 20,000 slaves – at Laurion in Attica. Athenian democratic institutions continued to be developed and by 458 all citizens (excluding slaves, women and foreigners) were eligible to vote for and (except for the poorest) to serve in the highest offices of the government and the judiciary. The triumph in the war with Persia led to an exceptional outburst of cultural confidence in Greece as a whole, and especially in Athens, where vase-painting, sculpture and drama all reached new heights. The

city, and notably its Acropolis, were rebuilt and the "classical" style of art and architecture matured. No other Greek city-state saw such a program of public building at this time.

**1** The Greek cities of Ionia, led by Miletos, rebelled against Persian rule in 499 and sacked Sardis.

**2** A Persian fleet was destroyed rounding Mt Athos in 492. To avoid the same thing happening in 480, the Persians dug a canal across the peninsula neck.

**3** A bridge of boats was built across the Hellespont for Xerxes' expedition in 480.

**4** At Thermopylae, the Greeks under Leonidas of Sparta were outflanked; most withdrew, but the Spartans' heroic stand inspired later Greek defense.

**5** At the comprehensive Greek victory of Plataea, the Persian general Mardonios was killed and the leading Theban allies of the Persians were executed.

**6** The last of the Persian fleet was destroyed at Mycale in 479.

**7** Eion, the last important Persian stronghold in Europe, was captured by the Athenians in 475.

**8** The common treasury of the Delian league was kept on Delos, but was removed to Athens in 454.

**9** Delian league member Thasos rebelled in 465, but the Athenians invaded and tore down the city walls.

See also 16 (archaic Greece);
18 (Achemenid Persia)

In only eight years of tireless campaigning, Alexander of Macedon (r. 336–323) conquered the Persian empire and the Indus valley. Although his empire broke up on his death, Alexander's conquests determined that Hellenism would be the dominant cultural influence in the Middle East well into the Christian era.

Alexander was eighteen years old when his father, Philip II, was assassinated. He was bold, imaginative, well educated – Aristotle had been his tutor – and a promising soldier. In the first two years of his reign Alexander proved his abilities by securing Macedon's northern borders and subduing the rebellious Greeks. In 334, his home base now stable, Alexander launched his father's planned invasion of Persia, routing the army sent to stop him at the river Granicus. He then marched down the Anatolian coast, liberating and restoring the Greek cities of Ionia. Only Miletos and Halikarnassos, where the garrisons had been supplied by the Persian fleet, offered serious resistance. To prevent further naval interference, Alexander proceeded to conquer Phoenicia and Egypt, after first crushing a large Persian army, commanded personally by Darius III, at the river Issus in 333. With Persian naval power eliminated, Alexander marched into the heart of the Persian empire in 331, and at Gaugamela inflicted another humiliating defeat on Darius. Persian resistance crumbled, and Babylon and the Persian treasury at Susa were captured.

The following year, at the Persian Gates pass, Alexander destroyed the last sizeable Persian army and swept on to loot and burn the Persian capital, Persepolis. It took Alexander three more years of tough campaigning in Bactria and Sogdiana to complete his conquest of the Persian empire, before invading the Indus valley in 327. There, in 326, Alexander won his last major battle, over King Porus at the river Hydaspes. Alexander wanted to press on and invade the Ganges plain, but his soldiers, after marching 25,000 kilometers (15,000 miles), had had enough and they refused. Instead Alexander marched down the Indus to the sea and turned west, reaching Babylon in 324, where, the following year, aged only 32, he died, an overweight alcoholic.

Shortly before his death his adoption of the styles of oriental kingship had lost him the loyalty of some of his original Macedonian followers.

The most important factor in Alexander's success was his military genius, but he was also aided by the centuries-long tradition of imperial rule in the Middle East, which had weakened local identities and loyalties. The provincial populations of the Persian empire were used to foreign rule and, as Alexander respected local customs and did not make unreasonable demands for tribute, a change from Persian to Macedonian rule was a matter of indifference to them. Alexander's empire broke

**TIMELINE**

**Political change**

**330**
**334** Alexander invades Anatolia, repulsing a Persian army at the Granicus river
**333** Darius III is defeated at the Battle of Issus
**332** Alexander conquers Egypt and founds the city of Alexandria
**331** At Gaugamela, Alexander defeats Darius again, and goes on to sack Persepolis
**329** Alexander conquers Bactria and Sogdiana

**315**
**326** Alexander, in the Indus valley, abandons his planned conquest of India
**323** Alexander dies in Babylon
**321–316** Alexander's empire breaks up as his generals seize territory
**312** Seleucos captures Babylon and founds the Seleucid kingdom

**300**
**307** Democracy is restored in Athens
**c.304** Seleucos cedes the Indus valley to Chandragupta
**301** The kingdom of Antigonos falls after the battle of Ipsus

**Cultural change**
**335** Aristotle founds his school of philosophy in Athens
**c.325–300** Pytheas of Massilia circumnavigates Britain
**312** Zeno, the first Stoic philosopher, arrives in Athens
**306** The philosopher Epicuros establishes his school in Athens
**300** Ptolemy I founds the Museum of Alexandria

Sarmatians

Sakas

*Aral Sea*

ALEXANDER, one of the world's greatest generals, is portrayed in this Roman mosaic (believed to be a true likeness) at the Battle of Issus.

*Caspian Sea*

CAUCASUS MTS

Satrapy of Armenia

Satrapy of Atropatene

Parni

Lake Van

Murat

*Araks*

Lake Urmia

Nisibis

Nineveh

Gaugamela
331

Arbela

*Diyala*

*Tigris*

Dura Europos

*Euphrates*

ZAGROS MOUNTAINS

Ecbatana

330

Rhagae

330

Damghan

Zadrakarta

Susia

Parthia

**5**

PERSIAN EMPIRE
c.336

Alexandria
(Merv)

Bactra

Termez

*Amu Darya*

Sogdia

Sogdiana

Marakanda

329

Kyreskhata

Alexandria
Eschata
(Kokand)

328

Sogdian
Rock

328

Drapsaca

Aornus
327

Nicaea

Bactria

HINDU KUSH

*Indus*

Katgala
Pass

Khyber
Pass

328

Alexandria
(Ghazni)

330

Alexandria
Areion
(Herat)

Drangiana

*Dasht-e Lut*

Arachosia

*Helmand*

Alexandria
Prophthasia
(Farah)

Alexandria
(Kandahar)

Taxila

Bucephela

Hydaspes
326

KINGDOM
OF PORUS

Alexandria
Nicaea

*Chenab*

**6**

326

*Sutlej*

Alexandria

MAURYAN
EMPIRE
after 324

Seleucia

**8**

Babylon

Susa

330

Uruk

Alexandria
Susiana
(Charax)

324

**4**

Pasargadae

Persian Gates
330

Persepolis

324

Persia

Alexandria
(Gulashkird)

Pura

Gedrosian Desert

*Persian Gulf*

325

325

*Gulf of Oman*

Alexandria
(Rambagh)

Pattala

**7**

*Indus*

*Arabian Sea*

up within a few years of his death, but this was for dynastic reasons; there were no popular rebellions against his successors. Alexander founded cities of Greek colonists (usually named after himself) throughout his empire, and his successors founded dozens more. These cities were scattered from the Mediterranean to central Asia, and became the agents for the vast expansion of Greek cultural influence over west Asia that was perhaps the most important consequence of Alexander's conquests.

Alexander left as his heirs a posthumous son and a mentally ill brother, neither of whom was capable of ruling in his own right. The regent Perdiccas maintained the central administration until his murder in 321, but under his successor, Antipater (d.319), the governor of Macedon, power in the provinces was seized by the generals and the empire fragmented in a series of conflicts known as the Wars of the Diadochi ("successors"). By 304 five successor kingdoms had arisen. Cassander, Antipater's son, ruled in Macedon; Lysimachos in Thrace; Antigonos had seized power in Anatolia; Seleucos in Mesopotamia and the east; and Ptolemy in Egypt. Of the five, only Antigonos aspired to recreate Alexander's empire, but this simply united the other Diadochi against him. When Antigonos was killed in battle against the combined armies of Seleucos, Lysimachos and Cassander at Ipsus in 301, his kingdom was divided up among the victors: Lysimachos taking Anatolia, Seleucus Syria and Cilicia, and Ptolemy, who had been campaigning separately, Palestine and Cyprus. Although the battle

of Ipsus did not bring an end to the struggles of the Diadochi, it did set the seal on the break-up of Alexander's empire.

During the chaos that followed his death, Alexander's empire had also begun to fray at the edges. His conquests had been rapid and the rulers of the northern satrapies of Bithynia, Paphlagonia, Cappadocia, Armenia and Atropatene had been allowed to retain their provinces after making only token submission. Alexander's early death prevented these provinces being brought into full submission, and during the Diadochan wars they became fully independent kingdoms. The Indus valley was also lost by the Greeks after Alexander's death. Preoccupied with the war against Antigonos, Seleucos ceded the Indian provinces to the Mauryan empire in 304 in return for a herd of war elephants (which he used to good effect at Ipsus). In Greece, now only a small part of the Hellenistic world, the cities of the Corinthian league rebelled unsuccessfully against Macedonian control in 323 and then defected to Antigonos in 307. However, after the defeat of Antigonos at Ipsus, Macedonian control was restored.

**1** Alexander won control of Anatolia after defeating an army sent to intercept him at the river Granicus.

**2** Founded in 332, Alexandria was to become the largest and richest Greek city in the 3rd century.

**3** The oracle of Amun at Siwa claimed Alexander to be son of the god and heir to the Egyptian throne.

**4** The burning of the palace of Xerxes at Persepolis in 330 marked the end of the Panhellenic war of revenge but not of Alexander's personal desire for conquest.

**5** Darius III was murdered at Damghan by his courtiers as he fled, seeking refuge in Bactria.

**6** Only when Alexander's exhausted and homesick army refused to follow him into the Ganges valley did he at last relent and turn back.

**7** Nearchos built a fleet of more than 100 ships at Pattala to explore and control the Gulf coast.

**8** Alexander died in Babylon in 323, having caught a fever after several days of heavy drinking.

See also 18 (Achemenid Persia);
20 (Persian wars and Greece)

In 500 BC the world's most impressive state was the Achemenid empire of Persia, extending from Libya to the Indus. The empire's first setback occurred when Xerxes I invaded Greece (▷20). The quarrelsome Greek city-states united in the face of the common enemy and defeated the Persians at sea at Salamis and on land at Plataea. The Greeks went back to their quarrels and did little to follow up their victory: Persia lost its foothold in Europe but continued to dominate the Middle East for eighty years. Then, in 404, Egypt rebelled and Persian control was not restored until 343. In 380 Persia's Indian provinces were lost.

Late 5th-century Greece was dominated by rivalry between Sparta and Athens, culminating in the Peloponnesian war which engulfed most of the Greek world but settled nothing. Further indecisive wars between shifting alliances ensued. Meanwhile, the Balkan kingdom of Macedon rose unopposed under Philip II and in 338 all the Greek city-states were forcibly enrolled in the Macedonian-dominated Hellenic league. Philip planned to invade Persia but his assassination in 336 left it to his son Alexander to carry out his plans. In only six years he conquered almost all the Persian empire, opening the whole Middle East to Greek influence (▷21).

By the 4th century the old south Arabian kingdom of Saba had been joined by the new states of Qataban and Hadramaut, driven by a demand from the Mediterranean for the precious gums, frankincense and myrrh, which were produced in the region. By the same period Sabean influence was seen in Damot on the African Red Sea coast.

Through most of the 5th and 4th centuries the main power in the western Mediterranean was Carthage. Carthage was more interested in commerce than conquest and its empire grew little between 500 and 323. Most of central and western Europe was now dominated by Celtic peoples. Around 400, Celts crossed the Alps and invaded Italy, breaking the power of the Etruscans and settling the Po valley. Though still insignificant on the map, by 323 Rome was a major power in Italy, having conquered its Latin and Etruscan neighbors earlier in the century (▷23).

The strongest state in India in 500 was Magadha in the lower Ganges plain. From 364 it brought most of northern India under its control. Southern India was a mosaic of minor states and chiefdoms with little urban development. The Zhou kingdom of China, which had broken up into a dozen competing states in the 8th century, was still disunited, although many of the smaller states had been absorbed by the bigger players (▷26). The continual warfare stimulated

*Hawaiian Islands*

*Arctic marine mammal hunters*

*Aleuts*

*sub-Arctic forest hunter-gatherers*

*west coast foraging, hunting and fishing peoples*

*Plateau fishers and hunter gatherers*

*desert hunter-gatherers*

*plains bison hunters*

*eastern woodlands hunter-gatherers*

*Adena complex*

*maize farmers*

Valley of Mexico

*Bahamas*

*Cuba*    *Hispaniola*    *Puerto Rico*

Zapotec states
Olmec culture
Maya chiefdoms and states

*Caribbean hunter-gatherers*

*maize farmers*

*manioc farmers*

*Chorrera culture*

*Chavín culture*

*Paracas culture*

*Pukara culture*

*savanna hunter-gatherers*

*Fiber-tempered pottery culture*

*South Andean hunter-gatherers*

*shellfish gatherers*

*pampas hunter-gatherers*

*shellfish gatherers and marine mammal hunters*

## TIMELINE

**500–400** Mesoamerican state formation occurs in the Oaxaca valley (Monte Albán and Zapotec civilization)

**509–507** Foundation of democracy in Athens

**c.450** Beginning of the La Tène phase of Celtic Iron Age culture

**450–400** Domestication of the reindeer in the Sayan Mountains of central Asia

**480–479** The Greeks defeat the Persian invasion

**431–404** The Peloponnesian war takes place, between Athens and Sparta

**c.400** Olmec civilization in steep decline

**c.400** The Celts settle northern Italy; decline of Etruscan civilization

| The Americas |
| Europe |
| Middle East |
| Africa |
| East and South Asia |

500 · 450 · 400

**525** Egypt comes under Achemenid Persian control

**c.515** The Achemenid Persian empire is at its height

**483** Death of Siddhartha Gautama, the Buddha, in India

**480–221** China breaks into competing kingdoms in the "Warring States" period

**479** Death of Confucius, Chinese philosopher

**400–300** Iron working is practiced in east Africa

**399** Death of Socrates, Greek philosopher, in Athens

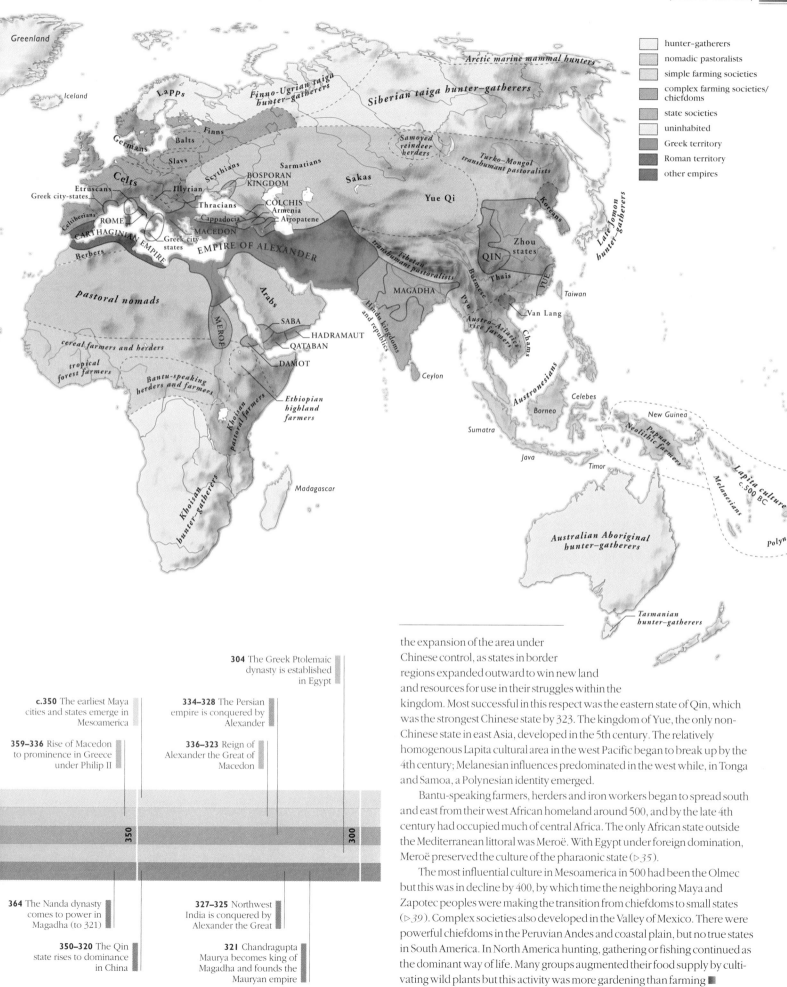

Greenland

Iceland

Lapps

Finno-Ugrian taiga
hunter-gatherers

Arctic marine mammal hunters

Siberian taiga hunter-gatherers

Germans

Balts

Finns

Slavs

Celts

Scythians

Sarmatians

Samoyed
reindeer
herders

Turko-Mongol
transhumant pastoralists

Etruscans

Illyrian

BOSPORAN
KINGDOM

Sakas

Yue Qi

Koreans

Late Jomon
hunter-gatherers

Greek city-states

Thracians

COLCHIS
Armenia

Cappadocia

Atropatene

Zhou
states

QIN

Celtiberians

ROME

MACEDON

Greek city-
states

EMPIRE OF ALEXANDER

Tibetan
transhumant pastoralists

Burmese

Thais

YUE

Taiwan

CARTHAGINIAN EMPIRE

Berbers

MAGADHA

Pyu
Austro-Asiatic
rice farmers

Chams

Van Lang

pastoral nomads

Arabs

MEROË

SABA

HADRAMAUT

QATABAN

Hindu kingdoms
and republics

Ceylon

Austro-Asiatic
rice farmers

Austronesians

cereal farmers and herders

DAMOT

tropical
forest farmers

Bantu-speaking
herders and farmers

Ethiopian
highland
farmers

Khoisan
pastoral farmers

Sumatra

Borneo

Celebes

New Guinea

Papuan
Neolithic
farmers

Lapita culture
c. 500 BC

Melanesians

Madagascar

Java

Timor

Khoisan
hunter-gatherers

Australian Aboriginal
hunter-gatherers

Polynesians

Tasmanian
hunter-gatherers

hunter-gatherers
nomadic pastoralists
simple farming societies
complex farming societies/
chiefdoms
state societies
uninhabited
Greek territory
Roman territory
other empires

---

c.350 The earliest Maya cities and states emerge in Mesoamerica

359–336 Rise of Macedon to prominence in Greece under Philip II

304 The Greek Ptolemaic dynasty is established in Egypt

334–328 The Persian empire is conquered by Alexander

336–323 Reign of Alexander the Great of Macedon

350

300

364 The Nanda dynasty comes to power in Magadha (to 321)

350–320 The Qin state rises to dominance in China

327–325 Northwest India is conquered by Alexander the Great

321 Chandragupta Maurya becomes king of Magadha and founds the Mauryan empire

---

the expansion of the area under Chinese control, as states in border regions expanded outward to win new land and resources for use in their struggles within the kingdom. Most successful in this respect was the eastern state of Qin, which was the strongest Chinese state by 323. The kingdom of Yue, the only non-Chinese state in east Asia, developed in the 5th century. The relatively homogenous Lapita cultural area in the west Pacific began to break up by the 4th century; Melanesian influences predominated in the west while, in Tonga and Samoa, a Polynesian identity emerged.

Bantu-speaking farmers, herders and iron workers began to spread south and east from their west African homeland around 500, and by the late 4th century had occupied much of central Africa. The only African state outside the Mediterranean littoral was Meroë. With Egypt under foreign domination, Meroë preserved the culture of the pharaonic state (▷35).

The most influential culture in Mesoamerica in 500 had been the Olmec but this was in decline by 400, by which time the neighboring Maya and Zapotec peoples were making the transition from chiefdoms to small states (▷39). Complex societies also developed in the Valley of Mexico. There were powerful chiefdoms in the Peruvian Andes and coastal plain, but no true states in South America. In North America hunting, gathering or fishing continued as the dominant way of life. Many groups augmented their food supply by cultivating wild plants but this activity was more gardening than farming ∎

Founded probably around 800 BC, Rome had by about 600 BC fallen under the control of an Etruscan dynasty. Rome benefited from its strategic position on the lowest crossing point of the Tiber but remained a minor city. In 509 the monarchy was overthrown by an aristocratic coup and a republic was founded. The first century of its history was dominated by a struggle between the lower classes (the plebeians) and the leading families (the patricians). By the end of the 5th century the senate had codified the law and granted the plebeians their own representatives: the tribunes. In the 4th century the plebeians also won the right to run for the major offices of state – though voting in the popular assembly was structured to favor the richer classes. The extension of rights to the plebeians helped build a community of interest between the classes that sustained the republic through many crises.

Roman expansion began as a series of minor wars against its immediate neighbors. There was no imperial masterplan at this stage: these wars were intended primarily to make Rome more secure from attack. Around 400 BC, Gauls crossed the Alps and made extensive settlements in the Po valley, which became known as Cisalpine Gaul (Gaul "this side of the Alps") to distinguish it from the Gaulish homeland to the north. The Gauls raided widely, even sacking Rome in 390, but mainly they weakened the Etruscans. In 354 the Romans allied against the Gauls with the Samnites, a powerful tribal confederation, but the alliance did not last. The Romans and Samnites had competing interests in central Italy, which led to the inconclusive First Samnite War (343–341). Rome conquered the Latins (340–338), before renewing its conflict with the Samnites in the Second (327–304) and Third (298–290) Samnite wars. A Roman victory at Sentinum in 295 was followed by the collapse of Samnite power and by 290 Rome dominated central Italy. The Romans planted colonies of Roman citizens in subdued territories

Roman territory, c. 500 BC
gains by 290
gains by 272
gains by 218
gains by 201
Carthaginian territory, c. 264
Carthaginian territory, c. 218
Carthaginian territory, c. 201
area of Gaulish settlement in Italy, c. 400
campaign by Pyrrhus of Epirus, 280-275
campaign of Hannibal, 218-203
campaign of Scipio Africanus, 210-206
campaign of Scipio Africanus, 204-202
Roman victory
Roman defeat
Roman roads in 201
Greek city
Rome    independent city-state

0        400 km
0        300 mi

and awarded their allies half-citizenship rights which could, if loyalty was proved, eventually be increased to full Roman citizenship.

The Romans began to bring the Greek cities of southern Italy under their sway. The Greeks appealed for protection to King Pyrrhus of Epirus. In 280 Pyrrhus invaded Italy after a hard-fought battle at Heraclea. The king's losses were so great that he remarked after the battle that a few more victories like this and he would lose the war. This is what in fact happened: the Romans resisted doggedly and in 275 Pyrrhus withdrew. Three years later the Romans took Tarentum, completing their conquest of peninsular Italy. Rome was now a Mediterranean power.

In 264 Rome went to war with Carthage, the major naval power of the western Mediterranean, over a dispute about spheres of influence in Sicily. The Romans called the Carthaginians "Poeni" (Phoenicians) – and the wars with Carthage came to be known as the Punic wars. Rome had no tradition of naval warfare but learned quickly, and in 260 its newly built fleet won its first victory over the Carthaginians at Mylae. In 255 the Romans tried to bring the war to a quick conclusion by invading north Africa but were repulsed. The war dragged on until 241, when the Carthaginians were vanquished at sea off Lilybaeum. Sicily became a Roman province; and in 238 the Romans also occupied Corsica

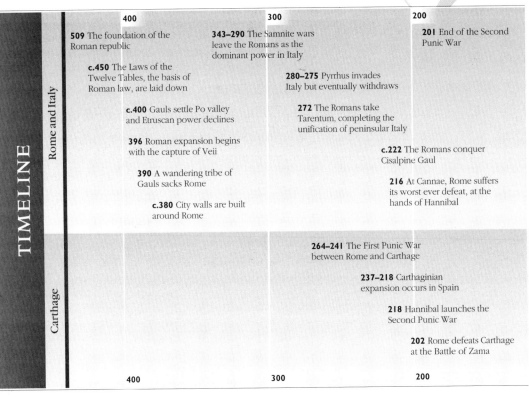

TIMELINE

| | 400 | 300 | 200 |
|---|---|---|---|
| **Rome and Italy** | **509** The foundation of the Roman republic | **343–290** The Samnite wars leave the Romans as the dominant power in Italy | **201** End of the Second Punic War |
| | **c.450** The Laws of the Twelve Tables, the basis of Roman law, are laid down | **280–275** Pyrrhus invades Italy but eventually withdraws | |
| | **c.400** Gauls settle Po valley and Etruscan power declines | **272** The Romans take Tarentum, completing the unification of peninsular Italy | |
| | **396** Roman expansion begins with the capture of Veii | **c.222** The Romans conquer Cisalpine Gaul | |
| | **390** A wandering tribe of Gauls sacks Rome | **216** At Cannae, Rome suffers its worst ever defeat, at the hands of Hannibal | |
| | **c.380** City walls are built around Rome | | |
| **Carthage** | | **264–241** The First Punic War between Rome and Carthage | |
| | | **237–218** Carthaginian expansion occurs in Spain | |
| | | **218** Hannibal launches the Second Punic War | |
| | | **202** Rome defeats Carthage at the Battle of Zama | |
| | 400 | 300 | 200 |

Gauls (Celts)

ALPS

GAUL

Rhône

Massilia

Narbo

Emporiae (Ampurias)

Arausio

Ticinus River 218 ⊗

Mediolanum

CISALPINE GAUL

Ligurians

Genua

Po

Trebia River 218 ⊗

Aquileia

Venetians

Sava

Illyrians

Danube

**6**

**5**

Pisa

Ariminum

Ancona

Metaurus River 207 ⊗

Sentinum 295 ⊗

Etruscans

Lake Trasimenus 217 ⊗

Umbrians

Castrum Novum

Saturnia

Cosa

Sabines

**1**

Aleria
Corsica

Veii
Rome

Samnites

Corfinium

Cannae 216

Adriatic Sea

Epidamnus

MACEDON

Ostia

Latins

**2**

Capua

Benevento

Caudine Forks 321 ⊗

Apollonia

Neapolis

Paestum

Lucanians

Tarentum

Heraclea 280

Messapians

Brundisium

**7**

EPIRUS

Ambracia

Sardinia

Balearic
Islands

Carales

Bruttians

Croton

MAGNA GRAECIA

Panormus

Mylae 260 ⊗

Rhegium

Drepanum 249 ⊗

Messana

*Mediterranean Sea*

Lilybaeum 241 ⊗

**3**  *Sicily*

Agrigentum 262 ⊗

Catana

Syracusae

Ecnomus 256 ⊗

Malta

Hippo Regius

Utica

Carthage

Bagradas 255

Cirta 203 ⊗

Zama 202 ⊗

Hadrumetum

*Malta*

NUMIDIA

**8**

Kingdom of
Syphax

Kingdom of
Massinissa

Leptis Magna

ELEPHANTS carried soldiers to battle, but were used to scare the enemy rather than as cavalry. This Roman plate shows one carrying a fort.

and Sardinia. In the 230s Carthage began to recoup its losses by expansion in Spain; and in the 220s Rome conquered Cisalpine Gaul. In 226 Rome and Carthage agreed on respective spheres of influence, but when Hannibal, Carthage's foremost general, attacked Saguntum, a city within Carthage's sphere but friendly to Rome, the Second Punic War broke out. Roman naval power compelled Hannibal to invade Italy by marching overland and crossing the Alps. In Italy Hannibal found ready allies in the newly conquered Gauls in the north and the Greek cities in the south – and also in the kingdom of Macedon, which viewed with concern the expansion of Roman power into Greece in the 220s. Hannibal was a brilliant general but lacked the strength to take Rome itself and so win the war. The Romans, after a catastrophic defeat at Cannae, did their best to avoid facing Hannibal in open battle, trying simply to contain him in southern Italy. The main Roman counterattack was aimed at Carthage's Spanish possessions. The decisive campaign began in 210 under Scipio Africanus, and by 206 the Carthaginians had been driven out of Spain. Then in 204 Scipio launched an invasion of north Africa and persuaded the Numidian king Massinissa to side with Rome. Hannibal was recalled from Italy to face Scipio, and in 202 the two generals met in battle at Zama. The result was a crushing defeat for Hannibal and

Carthage surrendered on harsh terms. Rome annexed Spain and the Balearic Islands, and the Numidians were given most of Carthage's north African territory. Carthage itself was reduced to a heartland in modern Tunisia: it had to disband its fleet and agree not to go to war without Rome's permission. Although in Spain the Romans faced rebellions – which for seventy years frustrated their attempts to gain control of their new possessions – Rome now dominated the western Mediterranean.

**1** The capture of nearby Veii, an Etruscan city, in 396, was the first step in the Roman conquest of Italy.

**2** Rome disputed control of Italy with the Samnites, a confederation of the Caraceni, Caudini, Hirpini and Pentri tribes, in a series of wars, from 343 to 290.

**3** In the growing rivalry between Rome and Carthage, Sicily was the flashpoint that led in 264 to the outbreak of the First Punic War.

**4** In 226 the Ebro was the agreed border between Roman and Carthaginian spheres of influence.

**5** A Roman campaign against Illyria was mounted in 229-228 to suppress pirates infesting the Adriatic Sea.

**6** Hannibal's crossing of the Alps took 15 days: only a handful of his original 38 elephants survived.

**7** Hannibal's base for operations in southern Italy was at Tarentum until the Romans retook the city in 209.

**8** Numidia's Berber kingdoms, longtime suppliers of cavalry to Carthage, sided with Rome at Zama in 202.

See also 12 (Bronze Age Europe);
29 (growth of the Roman empire)

Alexander's empire did not survive his death in 323 – the immediate cause of its breakup being his failure to provide an heir – and within a few years his generals had become the rulers of independent kingdoms). Seleucos built a state which incorporated most of Anatolia, Mesopotamia, and Iran and extended into central Asia; despite successful rebellions by the Bactrian Greeks in 239 and the Parthians in 238, the Seleucid kingdom was still the largest of the successor states in 200. Ptolemy seized Egypt and founded a dynasty which was to last until 31 BC, ending only with Cleopatra's suicide after the battle of Actium. Macedon itself fell to Antipater, who reasserted Macedonian supremacy in Greece in the face of an Athenian-led rebellion. Macedon was still the leading power in Greece in 200.

The leading power in the western Mediterranean by 200 was Rome. The Romans had completed the conquest of peninsular Italy in 272, and in 264 were drawn into a war with Carthage over Sicily. This, the First Punic War, dragged on for over twenty years until the Romans had wrested control of Sicily, Sardinia and Corsica. Carthaginian expansion in Spain, arousing Roman hostility once again, led in 218 to the outbreak of the Second Punic War. The Carthaginian general Hannibal surprised the Romans by attacking Italy from the north, but counterattacks in Spain and north Africa brought Rome crushing victory, and Carthage was shorn of its empire (▷23).

Several centuries of stability on the Eurasian steppes came to an end in the 3rd century as the Sarmatians began to push westward against the Scythians. On the far eastern steppes the Turko-Mongol pastoralists made the transition to a horse-mounted fully nomadic way of life around 300, and by 200 they were united in the powerful Xiong-nu confederation. Their use of the composite bow gave the Xiongnu a decided military advantage over their nomadic Iranian neighbors to the west and made them a formidable adversary for the newly united Chinese.

In 321 Chandragupta Maurya (321–c. 293) seized the throne of the kingdom of Magadha, overthrowing the Nanda dynasty. Chandragupta spent most of his reign building a strong central administration, but he defeated a Seleucid invasion, adding all of northwest India to his domains. His son Bindusara also conquered much of southern India. Under Ashoka the Mauryan empire reached its greatest extent. Appalled by his bloody conquest of the east coast kingdom of Kalinga in 261, Ashoka abjured further warfare and, becoming a Buddhist, tried to impose Buddhist standards of behavior on his people. Little is known about

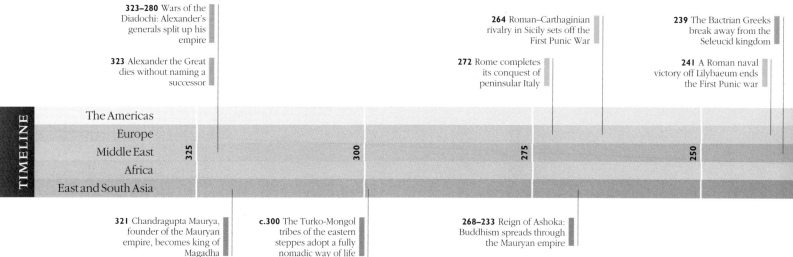

323–280 Wars of the Diadochi: Alexander's generals split up his empire

323 Alexander the Great dies without naming a successor

264 Roman–Carthaginian rivalry in Sicily sets off the First Punic War

272 Rome completes its conquest of peninsular Italy

239 The Bactrian Greeks break away from the Seleucid kingdom

241 A Roman naval victory off Lilybaeum ends the First Punic war

TIMELINE

The Americas
Europe
Middle East
Africa
East and South Asia

325
300
275
250

321 Chandragupta Maurya, founder of the Mauryan empire, becomes king of Magadha

c.300 The Turko-Mongol tribes of the eastern steppes adopt a fully nomadic way of life

268–233 Reign of Ashoka: Buddhism spreads through the Mauryan empire

c.300 Beginning of rice farming in Japan

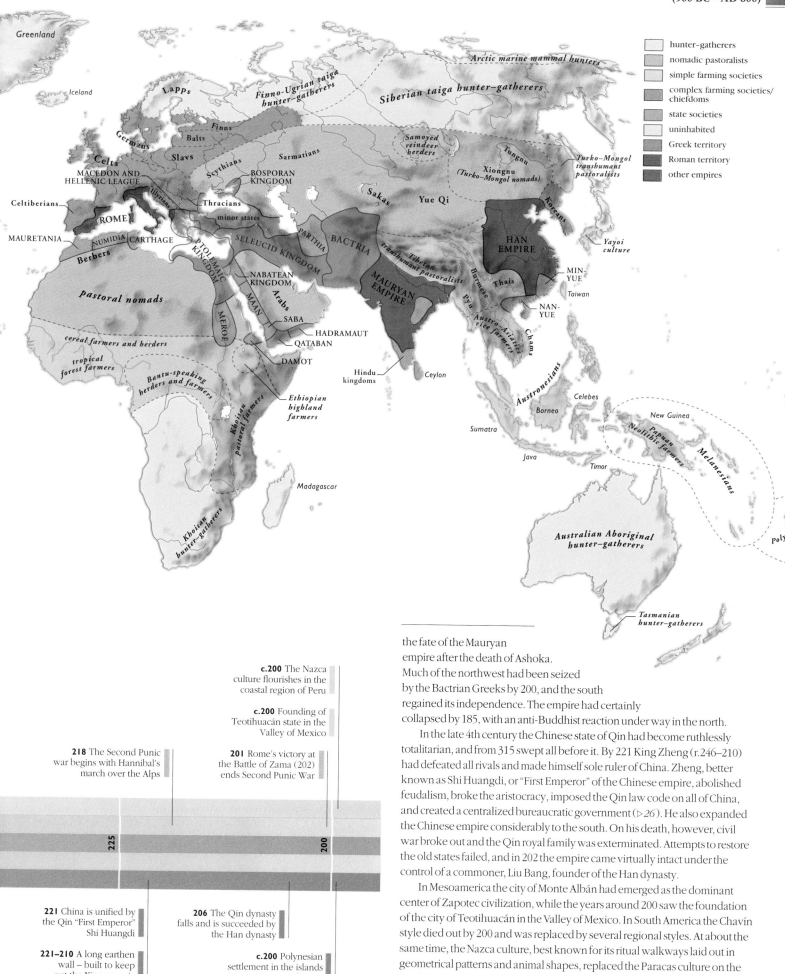

hunter-gatherers
nomadic pastoralists
simple farming societies
complex farming societies/
chiefdoms
state societies
uninhabited
Greek territory
Roman territory
other empires

Greenland
Iceland
Lapps
Finno-Ugrian taiga hunter-gatherers
Siberian taiga hunter-gatherers
Arctic marine mammal hunters
Germans
Balts
Finns
Slavs
Samoyed reindeer herders
Tungnu
Turko-Mongol transhumant pastoralists
Celts
Scythians
Sarmatians
Xiongnu (Turko-Mongol nomads)
MACEDON AND HELLENIC LEAGUE
BOSPORAN KINGDOM
Sakas
Yue Qi
Koreans
Celtiberians
Illyrians
Thracians
minor states
HAN EMPIRE
ROME
MAUCETANIA
NUMIDIA CARTHAGE
PARTHIA
BACTRIA
Yayoi culture
Berbers
PTOLEMAIC KINGDOM
SELEUCID KINGDOM
Tibetan transhumant pastoralists
MIN-YUE
Pastoral nomads
NABATEAN KINGDOM
MAAN
MAURYAN EMPIRE
Burmese
Thais
Taiwan
Arabs
SABA
Pyu
NAN-YUE
cereal farmers and herders
MEROË
HADRAMAUT
QATABAN
Austro-Asiatic rice farmers
Chams
tropical forest farmers
DAMOT
Hindu kingdoms
Ceylon
Bantu-speaking herders and farmers
Austronesians
Ethiopian highland farmers
Celebes
New Guinea
Khoisan pastoral farmers
Borneo
Papuan Neolithic farmers
Melanesians
Sumatra
Madagascar
Java
Timor
Polynesians
Khoisan hunter-gatherers
Australian Aboriginal hunter-gatherers
Tasmanian hunter-gatherers

c.200 The Nazca
culture flourishes in the
coastal region of Peru

c.200 Founding of
Teotihuacán state in the
Valley of Mexico

218 The Second Punic
war begins with Hannibal's
march over the Alps

201 Rome's victory at
the Battle of Zama (202)
ends Second Punic War

225

200

221 China is unified by
the Qin "First Emperor"
Shi Huangdi

206 The Qin dynasty
falls and is succeeded by
the Han dynasty

221–210 A long earthen
wall – built to keep
out the Xiongnu – is
completed in China

c.200 Polynesian
settlement in the islands
of Tahiti

the fate of the Mauryan
empire after the death of Ashoka.
Much of the northwest had been seized
by the Bactrian Greeks by 200, and the south
regained its independence. The empire had certainly
collapsed by 185, with an anti-Buddhist reaction under way in the north.

In the late 4th century the Chinese state of Qin had become ruthlessly
totalitarian, and from 315 swept all before it. By 221 King Zheng (r.246–210)
had defeated all rivals and made himself sole ruler of China. Zheng, better
known as Shi Huangdi, or "First Emperor" of the Chinese empire, abolished
feudalism, broke the aristocracy, imposed the Qin law code on all of China,
and created a centralized bureaucratic government (▷ 26). He also expanded
the Chinese empire considerably to the south. On his death, however, civil
war broke out and the Qin royal family was exterminated. Attempts to restore
the old states failed, and in 202 the empire came virtually intact under the
control of a commoner, Liu Bang, founder of the Han dynasty.

In Mesoamerica the city of Monte Albán had emerged as the dominant
center of Zapotec civilization, while the years around 200 saw the foundation
of the city of Teotihuacán in the Valley of Mexico. In South America the Chavín
style died out by 200 and was replaced by several regional styles. At about the
same time, the Nazca culture, best known for its ritual walkways laid out in
geometrical patterns and animal shapes, replaced the Paracas culture on the
south coast of Peru ∎

The name Celts was used by Greek writers from the 5th century BC onward to describe a group of peoples of central and western Europe. Roman writers called the same peoples Gauls. The origins of the Celts are uncertain but are probably to be found in the northern Alps in the Bronze Age Urnfield (from mid-2nd millennium BC) and the late Bronze–early Iron Age Hallstatt cultures (1200–450 BC). There were at least two waves of Celtic migration out of central Europe. The first, from around 1000, took the Urnfield culture across western Europe into northern Spain by the 7th century; and a second, beginning in the 8th century, had by 500 BC spread the Hallstatt culture across France, Spain, Portugal, Germany, the Low Countries, and southern Britain.

A new phase of Celtic history began around 450 BC with the development in Germany and France of the La Tène culture. This was distinguished by a vigorous art style based on geometrical patterns and stylized animal images. It developed from Hallstatt art but also showed the influence of Etruscan and Scythian styles. The La Tène culture spread quickly across central and western Europe and reached the British Isles by about 400 BC, passed on partly by trade contacts and partly by smallscale migrations of continental Celts, such as the Parisii, who settled in Yorkshire. The La Tène culture did not spread to Spain, where the earlier Celtic settlers and the native population had become assimilated, forming a distinctive Celtiberian culture.

Around 400 BC there were major migrations of Celtic peoples into Italy and the lower Danube region. In Italy the Celts raided widely, sacked Rome, permanently weakened the Etruscans, and settled densely in the Po valley. The Celts on the lower Danube began to migrate into the Balkans in the 3rd century BC. A major raid on Delphi was repulsed, but the Hellenistic kingdom of Thrace was destroyed by their attacks. Three tribes crossed the Dardanelles and settled in central Anatolia, from where they raided the surrounding kingdoms.

The early 3rd century marked the high tide of Celtic expansion. The Romans began the conquest of the Celts of the Po valley at the battle of Telamon in 225 and captured the last center of resistance in Italy at Bononia (modern Bologna) in 192. The Thracians restored their kingdom around 220; and the Anatolian Celts were pacified by Pergamon in 230. In the 230s the Carthaginians began the conquest of the Celtiberians, and this was continued by the Romans after they had expelled the Carthaginians from Spain in 206. The Roman victory at Numantia in 133 brought them control of most of Spain, but Celtiberian resistance continued in the northwest until 19 BC. By the first century AD the continental Celts were caught firmly in a vise between the northward expansion of the Roman empire and the southward and westward expansion of the Germanic tribes and the Dacians. Between 58

formative area of Hallstatt culture, 1200–750 BC

extent of Hallstatt culture, early 5th century BC

Celts, c.500 BC

Celtiberians, c.500 BC

maximum extent of Celtic related peoples, 100 BC

formative area of La Tène culture, 450 BC

La Tène culture, 2nd century BC

area of Celtic state formation, 100 BC

surviving Celtic languages, c.AD 600

migration of Celtic peoples, with date

*Boii*   Celtic peoples

*Slavs*   non-Celtic peoples

Celtic *oppidum*

other important Celtic site

La Tène vehicle burial

northern limit of Roman empire, 60 BC

northern limit of Roman empire, AD 79

expansion of non-Celtic peoples, with date

0 —————— 600 km
0 —————— 400 mi

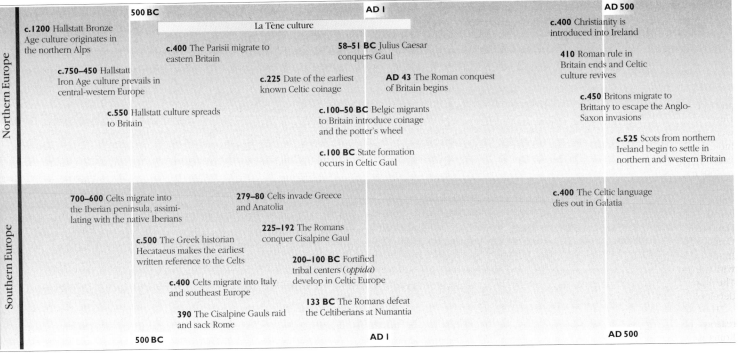

TIMELINE

**Northern Europe**

**500 BC**

La Tène culture

**AD I**

**AD 500**

**c.1200** Hallstatt Bronze Age culture originates in the northern Alps

**c.400** The Parisii migrate to eastern Britain

**58–51 BC** Julius Caesar conquers Gaul

**c.400** Christianity is introduced into Ireland

**c.750–450** Hallstatt Iron Age culture prevails in central-western Europe

**c.225** Date of the earliest known Celtic coinage

**AD 43** The Roman conquest of Britain begins

**410** Roman rule in Britain ends and Celtic culture revives

**c.550** Hallstatt culture spreads to Britain

**c.100–50 BC** Belgic migrants to Britain introduce coinage and the potter's wheel

**c.450** Britons migrate to Brittany to escape the Anglo-Saxon invasions

**c.100 BC** State formation occurs in Celtic Gaul

**c.525** Scots from northern Ireland begin to settle in northern and western Britain

**Southern Europe**

**700–600** Celts migrate into the Iberian peninsula, assimilating with the native Iberians

**279–80** Celts invade Greece and Anatolia

**c.400** The Celtic language dies out in Galatia

**225–192** The Romans conquer Cisalpine Gaul

**c.500** The Greek historian Hecataeus makes the earliest written reference to the Celts

**200–100 BC** Fortified tribal centers (*oppida*) develop in Celtic Europe

**c.400** Celts migrate into Italy and southeast Europe

**133 BC** The Romans defeat the Celtiberians at Numantia

**390** The Cisalpine Gauls raid and sack Rome

**500 BC**       **AD I**       **AD 500**

HORSES, chariots and armor were important elements in the Celtic love of display. This bronze head comes from Yorkshire, Britain.

**1** The Celts (Gauls) sacked Rome in 390 BC, after defeating a Roman army at the river Allia.

**2** An invasive Celtic migration as far south as Delphi was turned back by Greek resistance in 279 BC.

**3** Celtic raids in Anatolia ceased after the victory of Attalus I of Pergamon around 230 BC.

**4** Survivors of the Celtic attack on Delphi in 279 founded a kingdom in Thrace that lasted until 213 BC.

**5** The main Celtiberian resistance to Roman rule was broken when, after a 20-year siege, Numantia fell in 133 BC.

**6** Trade contacts with the Roman empire led to the formation of tribal states in southern Gaul in the 1st century BC.

**7** Julius Caesar's victory over Vercingetorix at Alesia in 52 BC, the climax of an eight-year campaign (58–51 BC), secured Roman control of Gaul.

**8** The Iceni, led by their queen, Boudicca, rebelled unsuccessfully against Roman rule in AD 60.

**9** Celtic culture and art revived in Britain after the end of Roman rule in AD 410.

and 51 BC Julius Caesar conquered the Celts of Gaul. Under Augustus the tribes of the Alps and Pannonia were brought under Roman rule. By AD 1 the only independent Celts on mainland Europe were enclaves in German territory north of the Danube.

Celtic society was hierarchical and competitive and by the 2nd century BC was in the early stages of state formation. Fortified centers, or *oppida*, spread across Europe: some, such as Manching on the Danube, were large towns by the 1st century BC. Coinage and, in some areas, writing came into use. In southern Gaul small tribal states in direct contact with the Roman empire had developed by 60 BC. The Roman conquest prevented the Celts from developing a full urban civilization of their own.

The Celtic resistance to Rome failed for two main reasons. The Celts were politically disunited and the Romans easily exploited rivalries between states or tribes to their own advantage. Also, Celtic warriors saw war as an opportunity to seek personal glory and this put them at a disadvantage to the drilled and disciplined legions. After the Roman conquest the La Tène culture died out on the continent and Celtic language was gradually replaced by Latin; but Celtic religion continued to be practiced. *Oppida* were superseded by planned Romanized towns.

Apart from two punitive raids by Caesar in 55–54 BC, it was AD 43 before the Romans began to subjugate the Celts in Britain. By this time contacts with the Romans across the Channel had already led to considerable Romanization of the southern British tribes and to the development of *oppida* and small tribal states. The Romans could never conquer all of Britain: the closest they came was in AD 83 when they defeated the Caledonians at "Mons Graupius". Harsh weather, mountainous terrain and long lines of communication meant that the highland tribes of Scotland stayed independent, as did the Celts in Ireland, where pagan Celtic culture survived into the early Middle Ages. La Tène art died out in southern Britain in the 2nd century AD, but Celtic art traditions continued in the far north and Ireland, while Celtic languages survived throughout the British Isles. After the end of Roman rule in Britain in 410, Celtic art revived but was strongly influenced by late Roman and Anglo-Saxon art. The introduction of Christianity to Ireland in the 5th century inspired the development of a Celtic monastic civilization which, through missionary activity, had begun to exert a strong influence in Britain and the continent by 600.

See also 29 (growth of the Roman empire);
38 (Dark Ages)

Zhou China (1122–256 BC) was a decentralized feudal state: the king exercised direct authority only over his own domain, while the provinces were held as fiefs by dukes who ruled in his name. Gradually the dukes became, in effect, the rulers of independent states; the Zhou king reigned from his capital at Luoyang but did not rule. The Warring States period (480–221 BC) saw the stronger states eliminate the weaker and absorb their territory: by 300 eleven states were left, and by 256, when the last Zhou king was deposed, there were seven. By 221 one state – Qin – was supreme.

Qin's rise to dominance began under Xiao (r.361–338). Shang Yang, Xiao's prime minister, ended the power of the feudal aristocracy and enacted a series of reforms that turned Qin into a centralized state based on a settled and productive peasantry and a strong army. Qin's frontier position gave it opportunities for expansion at the expense of the tribal peoples to the west, while its mountainous borders protected it from the aggression of other states. By 315 it was the strongest of the surviving states. The Qin dukes had already abandoned the pretence of subservience to the Zhou by adopting the title of king. In the 3rd century Qin waged almost constant warfare against the other Chinese states, which failed to combine against it and were picked off one at a time. The unification of China was completed in a series of lightning campaigns by Zheng (r.246–210) between 230 and 221, after which he adopted the title Shi Huangdi, the "First Emperor".

Shi Huangdi is regarded as the founder of the Chinese empire and the pattern of centralized totalitarian government he established has endured to the present day. Qin laws and institutions were extended to the whole of China. The aristocracies of the defeated states were deported, the remnants of feudalism were abolished and a non-hereditary central and local bureaucracy was created. The empire was divided into 36 districts or commanderies, governed by civilian and military officials responsible directly to the autocratic emperor. Coinage, weights and measures, scripts and even the axle sizes of wagons were standardized. In an attempt to ensure that Chinese history began with him, Shi Huangdi

A TERRACOTTA army, six thousand men and horses strong, was buried with Shi Huangdi at Xianyang.

ordered the destruction of all works of history, along with all "subversive" works of literature: scholars who protested were executed. Military campaigns extended the empire in the south while armies of conscripted laborers linked the frontier walls, which had been built by the Warring States against nomad invasions, into a continuous defensive system.

The cost of Shi Huangdi's reforms ruined the economy and his despotic rule caused such discontent that, after his death in 210, a civil war broke out. In 206 rebels massacred the entire Qin royal family. However, there was no restoration of the old states and the empire passed intact under the rule of Liu Bang, a commoner who had become a Qin official, and who became the first ruler of the Han dynasty. Gaozu (to use his more common posthumous title) ameliorated the severe Qin laws, reduced taxes and introduced reforms to restore prosperity. He rewarded some generals and bureaucrats with small fiefs but these were strictly controlled and the centralized state of Shi Huangdi was preserved.

The Former Han period (206 BC–AD 9) saw major territorial gains in central Asia and the south but northern China suffered severely from raids by the Xiongnu nomads until they were pacified in a long series of Han campaigns between 128 and 36 BC.

Jin, c.500 BC
Warring States border, c.300 BC
Qin state, c.350 BC
Qin gains by 300 BC
Qin gains, 300–250 BC
Qin gains, 230–221 BC
Qin gains by 206 BC
empire of the former Han dynasty, c.AD 6
Han protectorates, c.59 BC–AD 23, AD 73–127
territorial gains of Later Han dynasty
independent kingdom of Nan-yue, 206–113 BC
Warring States capital
capital of Zhou empire
capital of Qin dynasty
capital of former Han dynasty and Later Han dynasty
Qin fort
frontier wall
Chinese campaign
Xiongnu campaign
modern coastline and drainage where altered

Turfan
Cherchen
Dunhuang
Changye
Wu-su
Gansu Corridor
QILIAN MTS
Lake Qinghai
Yue Qi
Tibetans
105 BC
108 BC
6
8

## TIMELINE

|  | 400 BC | 200 BC | AD I | AD 200 |
|---|---|---|---|---|
|  | Warring States period | Former Han | Later Han | Three kingdoms period |
| **Political change** | c.500 Jin becomes the leading Chinese state | 230–221 King Zheng of Qin unifies China | 117–115 BC Han conquer Gansu corridor | 126 Peasant revolts against landowners |
|  | c.400 Breakup of the Jin state | 221–210 Zheng unites China under the Qin dynasty and takes the title Shi Huangdi | 57 BC Traditional date for foundation of the first Korean state, Silla | 189 Provincial warlords seize the Han capital, Luoyang |
|  | 361–338 Shang Yang turns Qin into a militaristic state | 209–202 Civil war: the Qin dynasty is overthrown and Han dynasty established | AD 9 Courtier Wang Mang overthrows Han dynasty | 190 General Tung Cho installs a puppet emperor on Han throne |
|  | c.350–315 Qin becomes the leading state in China |  | AD 23 Restoration of Han dynasty | 220 Deposition of last Han emperor: China splits into three kingdoms |
|  | 256 Qin deposes the last Zhou king | 128–36 BC The Han launch a series of campaigns to pacify the Xiongnu |  |  |
| **Cultural change** | c.500 Sun Tzu writes The Art of War | 175–150 Iron weapons and tools come into widespread use in China | | c.100 Introduction of Buddhism to China |
|  | 371–289 Mencius (Mengzi), Confucian philosopher | c.100 Sima Qian writes the history of China from the beginning to his own times | | |
|  | c.350 Crossbow invented | | | |
|  | 400 BC | 200 BC | AD I | AD 200 |

Mo Bei
119 BC

*Inner Mongolian
Plateau*

Hsien-pi

Xiongnu

119 BC

127 BC

*Gobi Desert*

201 BC

Koguryo
(kingdom c.37 BC)

Long Wall of Yan, built c.290 BC

175–170 BC

315 BC

4

Long Wall of Zhao, built c.300 BC

Xiangping

Ordos
Desert

Wuyuan

conquered
213 BC

Liangzhou

ZHONGSHAN
conquered by Zhao,
296 BC

Datong
201 BC

Diangxiang

YAN
conquered by Qin,
222 BC

Shanggu

Ji

Youbeiping

7

Luolang
conquered by Han,
109–106 BC

*Sanggan*

Yellow river
602 BC–AD 11

present course of Yellow river

Silla
(kingdom c.57 BC)

Long Wall of Wei, built c.353 BC

*Yellow*

ZHAO
conquered by Qin,
228 BC

Jinyang

QI
conquered by Qin,
221 BC

Zichuan

*Fen*

2

Handan

AD 200

Linzi

279 BC

*Y e l l o w
S e a*

Paekche
(kingdom 18 BC)

Jincheng

WEI
conquered by Qin,
225 BC

Gaoping
260 BC

Puyang

*Ji*

wall built by Qi,
c.450 BC

ZHOU
conquered
by Qin, 256 BC

Anyi

Luoyang

341 BC

354 BC

LU
conquered by
Chu, 286 BC

Qufu

Xie

1

Qin

QIN

Xianyang

Chang'an

3

Xinzheng

Daliang

Shangqiu

Pei

*Lake
Hongze*

5

*QIN MTS*

207 BC

SONG
conquered by
Chu, 286 BC

Gaixia
202 BC

Shouchun

Guangling

Nanjing

The costs of territorial expansion and campaigns
against the nomads put the economy under strain
and were responsible for the dynasty's temporary
overthrow by Wang Mang in AD 9. The Later Han
period (AD 23–220) saw a recovery but the empire's
economic problems resurfaced in the 2nd century
and peasant rebellions became more common after
126. The emperors were isolated from events by
elaborate court ritual and power passed to the
generals and court factions. In 189 two provincial warlords seized the capital and the empire
collapsed into anarchy. The last, powerless Han
emperor was deposed in 220 and the empire
broke up into three kingdoms.

The most important cultural development of
the Warring States period was the establishment of
Confucianism as the basis of Chinese pilosophical
and ethical thought. The culture of the Han period
was conservative but it saw the development of the
first systematic history writing in China, exemplified
by the *Historical Records* of Sima Qian.

SHU
conquered by Qin,
316 BC

*DABA MTS*

HAN
conquered by Qin,
230 BC

*Lake
Tai*

Wu

Shu

Danyang

CHU
conquered by Qin, 223
BC

Guiji

*Han*

Ying

AD 219

Nanjun

Pengli

*Yangtze*

*Yangtze*

*Lake
Dongting*

Red Cliffs
AD 208

*Lake
Pengli*

Ba

independent
mountain tribes
conquered by Han, 136–82 BC

1 Qin was the first capital of the Qin state, but the
imperial capital was moved to Xianyang to the east.

2 At the battle of Gaoping in 260 BC, the Qin
reputedly buried alive 400,000 Zhao soldiers.

3 Luoyang, the Zhou capital, was also the capital of
the Later Han.

Lingling

Guiyang

conquered by Han, 110 BC

Viets

4 Early walls to protect northern China from the
nomads were earth ramparts; the stone Great Wall
was not built until the 16th century AD.

Yizhou

conquered by Qin, 213–209 BC

MIN-YUE

5 At Gaixia in 202, Liu Bang defeated his rival Xiang
Yu and consolidated Han authority over China.

6 Chinese campaigns to central Asia had a major aim
of capturing horses for breeding.

*Thai-
speaking tribes*

Nanhai

7 Peasant colonies, such as Luolang (now
Pyongyang), were founded to consolidate the Han
hold on newly conquered territory.

Viets

NAN-YUE

8 In 117–110 BC, a new wall was built to protect the
Gansu corridor, China's main route to the west.

Jiaozhi

Zhuyai

*Hainan*

Juizhen

0        600 km

0        400 mi

See also 8 (Zhou China);
27 (religions of the ancient world)

The years 1000 BC–AD 600 saw the emergence of every major world religion except Islam (a world religion is one that has endured and influenced diverse civilizations). Hinduism and Judaism had earlier roots but assumed their present form at this time; Christianity, Buddhism, Zoroastrianism, Daoism and Confucianism all arose 600 BC–AD 600.

Early Hinduism was based on the Vedas, hymns of the Aryans who invaded India around 1500 BC, but was also influenced by indigenous Dravidian traditions. Vedic Hinduism looked forward to a future existence in heaven; it was not until the 6th century BC that the belief in *karma* and rebirth, central to modern Hinduism, developed. The complex rituals of early Hinduism gave rise to a distinctive feature of Indian civilization, the caste system – the priestly Brahmins forming the highest caste. By 500 BC Hinduism dominated the Indian subcontinent, but discontent with Brahminical traditions grew on the Gangetic plain, where urbanization created a more materialistic society. New sects developed there, the most successful of them being Buddhism.

The founder of Buddhism was Siddhartha Gautama, known as the Buddha, or "Enlightened One." Many legends have become associated with the Buddha and little is known for certain of his life: even his original teachings are a matter of debate as the canon of Buddhist scripture was not written down until four centuries after his death. Buddhism remained a minor sect until the Mauryan emperor Ashoka converted in 260 BC. Under his patronage Buddhist missionaries spread the religion throughout India and to Ceylon and the Iranian nomads in central Asia. In northern India Buddhism supplanted Hinduism as the majority religion. It then spread from central Asia along the Silk Route, reaching China in the 1st century AD; Indian seafarers took it to southeast Asia in the 4th century. By the 3rd century AD Buddhism had divided into two schools: Theravada (Doctrine of the Elders), which adhered strictly to the established Buddhist canon, and Mahayana (Great Vehicle), a more liberal, eclectic

THE MENORAH symbolizes the survival of the Jewish people through the vicissitudes of history, including the Diaspora of the 1st century AD.

tradition. Hinduism responded to the rise of Buddhism by becoming more flexible and tolerant, and by AD 400 it was beginning to recover in India. In the 5th century Hinduism spread to southeast Asia.

The central influence on Chinese thought was the ethical teaching of Confucius. Its emphasis on respect for legitimate authority and moral education made this the official orthodoxy under the Han dynasty (206 BC–AD 220). In the disorder following the fall of the Han, Confucianism declined and Buddhism became a stronger influence in China. Buddhism was itself influenced by Chinese philosophies, particularly Daoism, a system inspired by the teachings of Lao Zi, a philosopher of the 6th century BC. The traditional Chinese practice of ancestor worship remained strong throughout these changes.

Although it was the religion of a minor and relatively unimportant people, the Hebrews, Judaism was the most influential religion of the Middle East. It was the first major monotheistic religion and its

## TIMELINE

### Middle East and Europe

| 600 BC | AD 1 | AD 600 |
|---|---|---|
| **c.630–553** The life of Zoroaster, founder of Zoroastrianism | **c.6 BC–AD 30** The life of Jesus of Nazareth | **313** The Roman empire under Constantine officially tolerates Christianity |
| **587** The Jews are deported to Babylonia by Nebuchadnezzar. This marks the beginning of the Diaspora | **AD 1–100** Mithraism spreads to the Roman empire | **c. 405** St Jerome completes the Vulgate Latin translation of the Bible |
| | **AD 42–62** St Paul undertakes his missionary journeys throughout Asia Minor, Greece and to Rome | **c. 570** The birth of the prophet Muhammad |
| | **AD 70–100** The Christian Gospels are written | **596** The English conversion to Christianity begins |
| | **220–40** Zoroastrianism is the Persian state religion | |

### South and east Asia

| 600 BC | AD 1 | AD 600 |
|---|---|---|
| **800–400** The *Upanishads* of Hinduism are composed | **260** The Mauryan emperor Ashoka becomes a Buddhist and sends Buddhist missions to Ceylon and central Asia | **253–333** The life of Ko Hung, founder of religious Daoism |
| **6th century** The life of Lao Zi, the inspirer of Daoism | | **259** Chinese Buddhists begin pilgrimages to India |
| **c.563–483** Life of Siddhartha Gautama, the Buddha | **c.240 BC** The *Dao De Jing*, the basic text of Daoism, is composed | **300–500** The Hindu epics the *Ramayana* and the *Mahabharata* are written down in their final form |
| **551–479** The life of the Chinese sage Confucius | **AD 1–100** Mahayana Buddhism develops | |
| **600 BC** | **AD 1** | **AD 600** |

*Map labels:*

5th century AD Clonard AD 520 / Iona AD 563 / 6th century AD / Whithorn AD 360–432 / ATLANTIC OCEAN / 4th century AD / 3 / Canterbury AD 596 / Marmoutier AD 372 / 5 / Massilia AD 415 / Vercelli AD 360 / Danube / CARPATHIAN MTS / Goths c.AD 350 / Dnieper / Nursia AD 480 / Rome / Mediterranean Sea / Monte Cassino AD 529 / Nola AD 394 / Black Sea / CAUCASUS MTS / Aral Sea / Volga / Thagaste AD 388 / Carthage / ROMAN EMPIRE Christianity tolerated AD 313, Official religion AD 391 / Athens / Constantinople / Chalcedon AD 400 / Caspian Sea / Ephesus / Caesarea AD 360 / Armenia c.300 AD / 6 / Antiochia / Nisibis AD 325 / Gushnasp / Salamis AD 335 / Sidon / Hamadan / Alexandria / 4 / Jerusalem / Ctesiphon / Susa / Wadi Natrun AD 320 / Bethlehem AD 386–420 / Tigris / PERSIA / Scetis AD 330 / Euphrates / Bishapur / Firuzabad / Nile / NOBATIA c.AD 550 / MAKKURA c.AD 550 / Red Sea / ARABIA / ALWA c.AD 580 / AXUM c.AD 350 / 8

**1** Although Hinduism is an ancient religion, few physical traces survive before the medieval period.

**2** Ellora is the site of rock-cut temples of Buddhist, Hindu and Jain origin, dating from the 6th-8th centuries AD.

**3** Southern Britain became Christian by the 4th century but reverted to paganism following the settlements of the Anglo-Saxons in the 5th century.

**4** Christian monasticism originated on the edges of the Sahara desert, which developed from communities of hermits in the early 4th century.

**5** Mithraism was popular in the Roman army: several Mithraic sites have been discovered on the strongly garrisoned Rhine frontier.

**6** Armenia became the first state to adopt Christianity as its official religion, in about 300.

**7** A major early Buddhist center developed around *stupas* (mounds) built by Ashoka to house relics of the Buddha and his followers.

**8** Sacred Fire, believed to be a manifestation of Ahura Mazda, was the focus of ritual in Zoroastrian temples.

**9** The influence of Daoism led Chinese Buddhists to found monasteries on mountains such as at Lingjiu (Vulture Peak).

Jewish settlement, 500 BC

important area of Jewish settlement by AD 600

largely Christian by AD 300

largely Christian by AD 600

spread of Christianity

early monastic site, with date

Patriarchal see, AD 600

largely Hindu, 500 BC–AD 600

strong Hindu influence by AD 600

sacred Hindu site, AD 600

largely Zoroastrian, 500 BC–AD 600

Zoroastrianism introduced by Sasanians after AD 226

Mithraic site, 1st–3rd centuries AD

Zoroastrian fire temple

largely Buddhist by 3rd century BC

largely Buddhist by AD 600

formative area of Mahayana Buddhism, 1st–3rd centuries AD

spread of Buddhism

Buddhist site, 300 BC–AD 600

Confucianism and Daoism from 3rd century BC

mountain associated with Daoism

teachings provided the basis of Christianity and Islam. Judaism was a national religion and did not actively seek converts among non-Jews; yet the Hebrews' turbulent history meant that it became very widespread in the Mediterranean and Middle East by AD 600. The Diaspora, or dispersal of the Jews, began in the 6th century BC when communities of exiles from Palestine were established in Egypt and Mesopotamia. The greatest dispersal of Jews occurred in the 1st and 2nd centuries AD, following rebellions in Palestine against Roman rule.

Christianity originated in the teachings of a Jew, Jesus of Nazareth, who rejected the current practice of Judaism. Christianity developed initially as a Jewish sect, but the influence of St Paul and others made

the religion more attractive to non-Jews, and by AD 70 its separation from Judaism was complete. Because of their refusal to pay formal homage to the state gods, Christians often faced persecution by the Roman emperors. Despite this Christianity was well established, especially in the eastern empire, by 312 when the emperor Constantine converted, introducing formal toleration the following year. Christianity made rapid progress after this, and in 391 it became the Roman empire's official religion. Christians came to believe that God had created the Roman empire specifically for the purpose of spreading Christianity.

An early rival to Christianity in the Roman empire was Mithraism, a derivative of the Persian Zoroastrian religion. Zoroaster, the religion's founder,

reformed the ancient Iranian religion, dividing the pantheon into good and evil deities. It developed into a dualist religion which taught that the chief god Ahura Mazda, aided by Mithra, was locked in combat to protect the world from his evil rival Ahriman. Zoroastrianism became the religion of the Achemenid rulers of Persia and flourished under the Parthians and Sasanians. Although in its pure form it won few converts outside Persia, its teaching on the nature of good and evil had an important influence on Hellenistic, Jewish, Christian and Islamic thought.

See also 30 (the Christian empire); 31 (early India); 44 (medieval world religions)

A decisive Roman victory at the battle of Cynoscephalae in 197 BC had broken the power of Macedon, who had supported Carthage in the Second Punic War. This victory opened the way for Roman domination of Greece. In 146 Rome brought the whole of Greece under direct control; and in the same year ruthlessly destroyed Carthage, though it had long ceased to be a threat (▷23). The Hellenistic kingdoms of the east were also powerless to prevent Roman expansion. By 64 BC most of Anatolia and the Levant were under Roman rule and Egypt had been made a protectorate. Direct rule was imposed on Egypt in 30 BC (▷29).

Rome's successes put its republican system of government – designed for a city-state, not a world empire – under increasing strain: and a succession of civil wars between 50 and 31 BC brought about the collapse of the Roman republic. The eventual victor, Octavian, created a new form of government – in effect, an absolute monarchy. King in all but name, he took the titles *princeps* (first citizen) and Augustus. His successors used the title *imperator* (commander or emperor).

In northern Europe, the Celts found themselves caught between the Romans, who were expanding northward, and the Germans, who were pushing south: by 1 BC the only remaining independent Celts were in the British Isles (▷25).

In Africa, the Sabean colonies had developed into the kingdom of Axum around 100 BC. At about the same time the dromedary camel was introduced to the northern Sahara, transforming the lives of the desert nomads much as horse riding had earlier changed the steppe pastoralist way of life, enabling them to range widely and raid settled peoples almost at will. By 1 BC pastoralism had spread among the Khoisan-speaking peoples as far south as the Transvaal region and Bantu-speaking peoples had begun to settle on the east African plateau (▷35).

Following his victory in the civil war in China (202), Liu Bang restored prosperity by introducing a series of agricultural and administrative reforms but, despite heroic efforts, failed to stop damaging raids by the nomadic Xiongnu who continued to be a serious threat to China until 38 BC. The Han period saw Chinese expansion in the south (▷26), where the non-Chinese kingdoms of Min-yue and Nan-yue were conquered, and in Korea. Small kingdoms had begun to develop in parts of Korea not under Chinese occupation by 50 BC.

The rise of the Xiongnu had a destabilizing effect on the Iranian nomads to the west. In 170 the Xiongnu inflicted a crushing defeat on the Yue Qi, who fled westward, unsettling the Sakas, before overrunning the Bactrian kingdom around 135. The Sakas headed south, first invading the Parthian empire and,

**Timeline**

c.135 The westward-driven Yue Qi overrun the Bactrian kingdom

170–141 The Parthians conquer the Seleucid kingdom

146 Roman control is extended throughout Greece

c.100 Foundation of the Moche state in the region of Peru

| TIMELINE | | 200 | 150 | 100 |
|---|---|---|---|---|
| The Americas | | | | |
| Europe | | | | |
| Middle East | | | | |
| Africa | | | | |
| East and South Asia | | | | |

c.185 Fall of the Mauryan dynasty after Bactrians invade the Punjab

149–146 The Third Punic War: Rome levels the city of Carthage to the ground

101 China under the Han dynasty conquers Van Lang

170 The Hsiung-nu defeat the Yue Qi and dominate the eastern steppes

c.141 The Sakas invade the Parthian empire and northern India

c.100 The beginning of camel nomadism in the Sahara desert

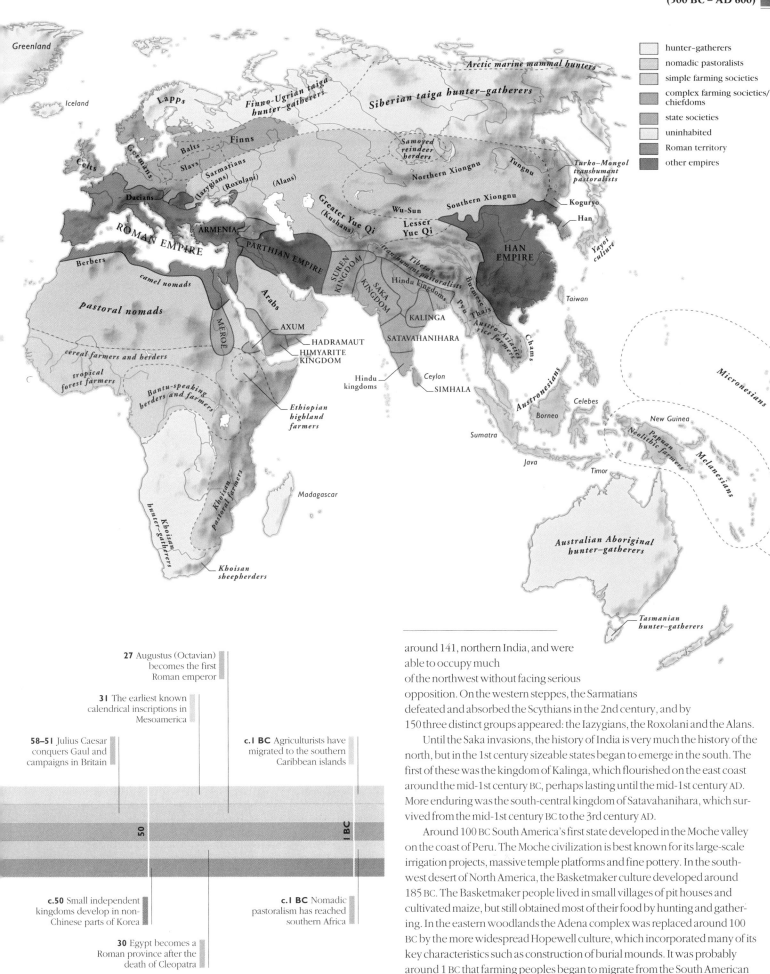

hunter-gatherers
nomadic pastoralists
simple farming societies
complex farming societies/chiefdoms
state societies
uninhabited
Roman territory
other empires

Greenland

Iceland

Lapps

Finno-Ugrian taiga hunter-gatherers

Siberian taiga hunter-gatherers

Arctic marine mammal hunters

Balts

Finns

Celts

Germans

Slavs

Sarmatians
(Iazygians)
(Roxolani)

(Alans)

Samoyed reindeer herders

Northern Xiongnu

Tungnu

Turko-Mongol transhumant pastoralists

Dacians

Greater Yue Qi
(Kushans)

Wu-Sun

Southern Xiongnu

Koguryo

Han

ROMAN EMPIRE

ARMENIA

PARTHIAN EMPIRE

SUREN KINGDOM

Tibetan transhumant pastoralists

HAN EMPIRE

Yayoi culture

Berbers

camel nomads

Arabs

SAKA KINGDOM

Hindu kingdoms

Burmese

Pyu

Thais

Taiwan

Pastoral nomads

MEROË

AXUM

HADRAMAUT
HIMYARITE KINGDOM

KALINGA

SATAVAHANIHARA

Austro-Asiatic rice farmers

Chams

cereal farmers and herders

tropical forest farmers

Bantu-speaking herders and farmers

Ethiopian highland farmers

Hindu kingdoms

Ceylon
SIMHALA

Austronesians

Micronesians

Sumatra

Borneo

Celebes

New Guinea

Papuan Neolithic farmers

Melanesians

Java

Timor

Madagascar

Khoisan pastoral farmers

Khoisan hunter-gatherers

Khoisan sheepherders

Australian Aboriginal hunter-gatherers

Polynesians

Tasmanian hunter-gatherers

around 141, northern India, and were able to occupy much of the northwest without facing serious opposition. On the western steppes, the Sarmatians defeated and absorbed the Scythians in the 2nd century, and by 150 three distinct groups appeared: the Iazygians, the Roxolani and the Alans.

Until the Saka invasions, the history of India is very much the history of the north, but in the 1st century sizeable states began to emerge in the south. The first of these was the kingdom of Kalinga, which flourished on the east coast around the mid-1st century BC, perhaps lasting until the mid-1st century AD. More enduring was the south-central kingdom of Satavahanihara, which survived from the mid-1st century BC to the 3rd century AD.

Around 100 BC South America's first state developed in the Moche valley on the coast of Peru. The Moche civilization is best known for its large-scale irrigation projects, massive temple platforms and fine pottery. In the southwest desert of North America, the Basketmaker culture developed around 185 BC. The Basketmaker people lived in small villages of pit houses and cultivated maize, but still obtained most of their food by hunting and gathering. In the eastern woodlands the Adena complex was replaced around 100 BC by the more widespread Hopewell culture, which incorporated many of its key characteristics such as construction of burial mounds. It was probably around 1 BC that farming peoples began to migrate from the South American mainland to the Caribbean islands ■

27 Augustus (Octavian) becomes the first Roman emperor

31 The earliest known calendrical inscriptions in Mesoamerica

58–51 Julius Caesar conquers Gaul and campaigns in Britain

c.1 BC Agriculturists have migrated to the southern Caribbean islands

50

1 BC

c.50 Small independent kingdoms develop in non-Chinese parts of Korea

c.1 BC Nomadic pastoralism has reached southern Africa

30 Egypt becomes a Roman province after the death of Cleopatra

S oon after the Second Punic War, Rome was drawn into further wars to protect its position in Italy, Spain and Greece. Cisalpine Gaul was reconquered by 191. The need to protect the new Spanish provinces from native attack drew Rome into a piecemeal conquest of the whole peninsula. Rome also launched a punitive campaign in 200 against Macedon, which had allied itself with Carthage in the Second Punic War. In 197, after the battle of Cynoscephalae, Macedon was forced to liberate the Greek city-states. At this time Rome took no territory for itself. However, the weight of constant disputes among the Greek cities and the Hellenistic kingdoms had become so onerous by 146 that the Romans imposed direct rule on Greece: opposition was ruthlessly suppressed. Also in 146 a Roman army, which had been besieging Carthage for three years, finally razed the city to the ground, its territory becoming the Roman province of Africa. Expansion into the Middle East began in 133, when the last king of Pergamon bequeathed his kingdom to Rome, and Pergamon became the province of Asia. Southern Gaul was conquered and became the province of Gallia Narbonensis in 121.

As the empire grew, the booty of successful campaigns – treasure and slaves – flooded back to Rome. The largest class of the early republic had been peasant freeholders, but they could not compete with the new slave-run estates of the rich and were forced off the land to swell the ranks of the urban poor. Demands for constitutional reform led to bitter class conflict in Rome, as defenders of aristocratic privilege resorted to acts of violence, such as the murder of the reformist tribune Tiberius Gracchus in 133. Gaius Marius then reformed the Roman army, opening recruitment for the first time to landless citizens. These soldiers looked to their commanders to reward their service with grants of land to settle on when discharged. This had a dramatic effect on Roman politics as successful generals could usually count on their armies to support their political ambitions. Success in war was now the surest route to political power: it was the main motive for Pompey's

campaigns in Anatolia and Syria (67–64 BC), Julius Caesar's conquest of Gaul (58–51 BC) and Crassus's ill-fated attack on Parthia, which ended in his death at Carrhae, in 53 BC. The generals' need to reward their veterans led to the foundation of colonies throughout the empire in the late republic: these became important agents of Romanization.

The competition for power between generals led to civil war in 49 BC and ultimately to the fall of the republic. The victor was Caesar, who defeated his opponent Pompey at Ilerda in Spain (49 BC) and Pharsalus in Greece (48 BC). By 44 BC Caesar had crushed all military opposition, but a month after he declared himself dictator for life he was murdered by republican conspirators. Instability and civil war continued until Caesar's nephew Octavian, later known as Augustus, defeated Mark Antony and Cleopatra at Actium in 31 BC. In 27 BC Augustus introduced a new constitutional settlement, which he claimed "restored the republic" but in reality

**Legend:**
- Roman empire, c.201 BC
- gains by 100 BC
- gains by 44 BC
- gains by AD 14
- gains by AD 117
- temporary gain, with dates held
- kingdom of Pontus under Mithradates VI, 112–66 BC
- pre-Augustan Roman colony
- Augustan Roman colony
- post-Augustan Roman colony
- Roman provincial boundary, early 2nd century AD
- Roman provincial capital
- Roman legion stationed, early 2nd century AD
- rebellion against Roman rule, with dates
- AC   Alpes Cottiae (Roman province)
- AM   Alpes Maritimae (Roman province)
- AP   Alpes Poeninae (Roman province)

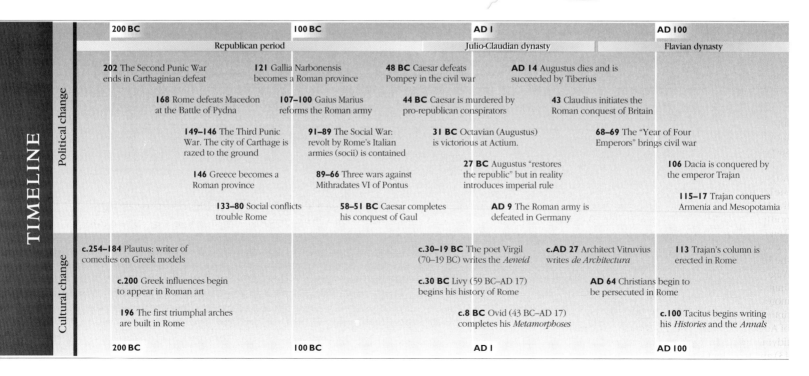

| | 200 BC | | 100 BC | | AD I | | AD 100 |
|---|---|---|---|---|---|---|---|
| | | Republican period | | | Julio-Claudian dynasty | | Flavian dynasty |
| **Political change** | **202** The Second Punic War ends in Carthaginian defeat | **121** Gallia Narbonensis becomes a Roman province | | **48 BC** Caesar defeats Pompey in the civil war | | **AD 14** Augustus dies and is succeeded by Tiberius | |
| | | **168** Rome defeats Macedon at the Battle of Pydna | **107–100** Gaius Marius reforms the Roman army | | **44 BC** Caesar is murdered by pro-republican conspirators | **43** Claudius initiates the Roman conquest of Britain | |
| | | **149–146** The Third Punic War. The city of Carthage is razed to the ground | **91–89** The Social War: revolt by Rome's Italian armies (socii) is contained | | **31 BC** Octavian (Augustus) is victorious at Actium. | **68–69** The "Year of Four Emperors" brings civil war | |
| | | **146** Greece becomes a Roman province | **89–66** Three wars against Mithradates VI of Pontus | | **27 BC** Augustus "restores the republic" but in reality introduces imperial rule | | **106** Dacia is conquered by the emperor Trajan |
| | | **133–80** Social conflicts trouble Rome | **58–51 BC** Caesar completes his conquest of Gaul | | **AD 9** The Roman army is defeated in Germany | | **115–17** Trajan conquers Armenia and Mesopotamia |
| **Cultural change** | **c.254–184** Plautus: writer of comedies on Greek models | | | **c.30–19 BC** The poet Virgil (70–19 BC) writes the *Aeneid* | **c.AD 27** Architect Vitruvius writes *de Architectura* | | **113** Trajan's column is erected in Rome |
| | | **c.200** Greek influences begin to appear in Roman art | | **c.30 BC** Livy (59 BC–AD 17) begins his history of Rome | | **AD 64** Christians begin to be persecuted in Rome | |
| | | **196** The first triumphal arches are built in Rome | | | **c.8 BC** Ovid (43 BC–AD 17) completes his *Metamorphoses* | | **c.100** Tacitus begins writing his *Histories* and the *Annals* |
| | **200 BC** | | **100 BC** | | **AD I** | | **AD 100** |

TIMELINE

*Vänern*

*Vättern*

*Lake Peipus*

*Baltic Sea*

*Western Dvina*

*Volga*

*Dnieper*

*Volga*

GAULS were respected opponents of the Romans in the west and in Anatolia; this statue of a dying Gaul was made in Pergamon, 2nd century BC.

Germania
12 BC–AD 9

Noviomagus  Teutoburgerwald ✕ AD 9

Colonia Agrippina

Moguntiacum

Augusta Treverorum

AD 21  Agentorate

*Elbe*

*Oder*

*Rhine*

Agri Decumates

Germania Superior

Raetia

Castra Regina

*Danube*

Augusta Vindelicorum  Vindobona

Virunum

Noricum

Carnuntum

Aquincum
AD 6–8 ✕

Pannonia Superior

Pannonia Inferior

AD 6–8 ✕

*Sava*

C A R P A T H I A N

Dacia

Sarmizegethusa

Singidunum

Viminacium

*Danube*

Novae

Moesia Superior

Moesia Inferior
(capital not known)

Troesmis

Durostorum

M T S

*Black Sea*

KINGDOM OF BOSPORUS
(Roman vassal state)

Panticapaeum

Sinope

Trapezus **3**

Satala

Armenia
AD 115–117

AP

Axima

C

AM

Cemenelum

A L P S

Mediolanum

Aquileia

Segusio

*Po*

Florentia

Italia

Rome

90 BC ✕

91–89 BC ✕

73–71 BC ✕

Pompeii

**2**

Brundisium

Corsica

Aleria

Corsica

*Sardinia*

126–122 BC,
115–111 BC ✕

Sardinia

Carales

**5**

Carthage

Africa

Sicilia

136–132 BC,
104–101 BC ✕

Syracusae

*Sicily*

*Malta*

Aquileia

Dalmatia

Salonae

Thracia

Byzantium

Perinthus

Macedonia

Pydna
168 BC

Thessalonica

Cynoscephalae
✕ 197 BC

Pharsalus
✕ 48 BC

Epirus

Actium
31 BC ✕

**4**

Achaea

Athens

Corinth

*Mediterranean Sea*

*Crete*

Creta  Gortyn

Nicomedia

Bithynia and Pontus

Nicopolis
68 BC ✕

Ancyra

Galatia

Pergamon

Magnesia
✕ 190 BC

Asia **1**

Ephesus

Aphrodisias

Myra

Lycia and Pamphylia

Paphus

*Cyprus*

Cyprus

A N A T O L I A

Cappadocia

Melitene

Caesarea

Tarsus

Cilicia

Samosata

Cyrrhus

Antiochia

Syria

Emesa  Palmyra

Tigranocerta

Edessa

Carrhae
✕ 53 BC

Mesopotamia
AD 115–117

Ctesiphon

Judaea

Caesarea

AD 66–74 ✕
Jerusalem

Bostra

Arabia

Leptis Magna

Cyrene

Cyrenaica

Alexandria

✕ AD 172
AD 66

Aegyptus

0            600 km
0        400 mi

---

introduced a monarchical type of government. He took the title *princeps* (first citizen), leaving it to his successors to call themselves *imperator* (emperor).

Expansion continued under the emperors. In Augustus' reign Egypt and Galatia were annexed, the last native resistance was extinguished in Spain, the Alpine tribes were conquered, and the empire's northern frontier was pushed to the Danube. Augustus also tried to conquer Germany but gave up the attempt after a humiliating defeat at the battle of the Teutoburgerwald in AD 9. This defeat convinced Augustus that the empire had reached its natural limits and he advised his successors not to seek any more territories. Despite this advice, the empire continued to expand for another century after the death of Augustus. Much of the expansion was simply a tidying-up operation. The annexation of Lycia (AD 43) and the client kingdom of Mauretania (AD 44)

gave Rome control of the entire Mediterranean coastline. In AD 43, Claudius, a weak emperor who needed a triumph to strengthen his position, began the conquest of Britain but only the southern two-thirds of the island were actually brought under Roman rule. The last emperor to pursue an all-out expansionist policy was Trajan. Between 101 and 106 Trajan conquered the Dacian kingdom, which posed a threat to the security of the Danube frontier. His ambition was to conquer the Parthian empire, and he brought Armenia and Mesopotamia under Roman rule. However, his successor Hadrian (r.117–38), judging these eastern conquests to be undefendable, withdrew from all of them except Edessa. Later in the 2nd century the border was pushed northward in Britain, and northern Mesopotamia was wrested from the Parthians, but from this time on the empire was mainly on the defensive.

**1** Willed to the empire by the king of Pergamon, Asia became Rome's first Anatolian province in 133 BC.

**2** Rebellions – the "Social War" – forced Rome to concede equal political rights to non-Roman Italians.

**3** Mithradates VI of Pontus fought Rome in three wars from 89 until his final defeat in 66 BC.

**4** Augustus' victory at Actium in 31 BC ended the civil war and brought Egypt under Roman rule.

**5** Carthage, refounded as a Roman colony, became the center of Roman administration in Africa in 29 BC.

**6** The Roman conquest of Britain began in AD 43, nearly a century after Caesar's raids in 55 and 54 BC.

See also 27 (religion);
30 (later Roman empire)

After Hadrian withdrew from Trajan's eastern conquests in 117, the borders of the Roman empire remained stable for almost 150 years. The only significant change was in the east, where successful campaigning by Septimius Severus between 195 and 198 wrested northern Mesopotamia from the Parthians. The 2nd century was a time of unrivaled peace and prosperity for the empire but this was not to last. The wealth of the empire was attractive to the Germanic tribes along the Rhine and Danube frontiers, and these began to unite in powerful confederations and raid Roman territory. In 167 Marcomannic raiders crossed into Italy, and though the emperor, Marcus Aurelius, successfully secured the borders, pressure on the northern frontier was thereafter continuous. Another problem was the imperial succession: there was no accepted way of deposing an incompetent or tyrannical emperor, nor of selecting a new emperor if a dynasty died out or was overthrown. When the incompetent, tyrannical Nero was overthrown in AD 68 the frontier armies promoted their own candidates for the succession, who then fought it out in a civil war. The same happened after the murder of the mad Commodus.

Pressure on the northern frontiers became critical in the 3rd century, and a new threat appeared in 226 when the Parthians were overthrown by the aggressive Persian Sasanian dynasty. In these conditions, the emperor had to be above all a good soldier. While rival candidates for power, promoted by different legions, fought each other for control of the empire, the borders were left undefended and open to invasion. For example, when Valerian (r. 253–60) withdrew troops from the Rhine to fight a usurper, the Franks immediately invaded Gaul. The efforts of emperors to buy the loyalty of their troops led them to debase the coinage to raise money, but this added runaway inflation to the empire's woes. Urban life now declined, especially in the west, where many towns shrank to a fortified administrative core. Civil war and invasion were incessant between 235 and 284: of the twenty-six emperors who ruled in this period all but one died by violence.

Not all the usurpers aimed at control of the whole

empire. After Valerian was captured by the Persians at Edessa in 260, defense of the east devolved on Odenathus, ruler of the desert city of Palmyra. He defeated the Persians but then built an independent kingdom for himself. Under his wife and successor Queen Zenobia, it came to include Egypt, Syria and much of Anatolia. In the west the usurper Postumus founded an independent Gallic empire, winning over the people of Gaul, Britain and Spain; he promised to concentrate on defending the frontiers and not to march on Rome.

The Roman empire began to revive in the reign of Aurelian, with the reconquest of Palmyra (272) and the Gallic empire (274), though Dacia was permanently abandoned to the Germans. Political and economic stability were restored by Diocletian (r. 284–305), who reformed the whole structure of the empire. Diocletian greatly expanded the army and reformed the tax system to pay for it. Price regulation was introduced to curb inflation, though it drove goods off the markets. To restore respect to the imperial office, elaborate court ritual was introduced and the idea of the emperor as "first citizen" was abandoned: he was now "lord and god." Civilian and military

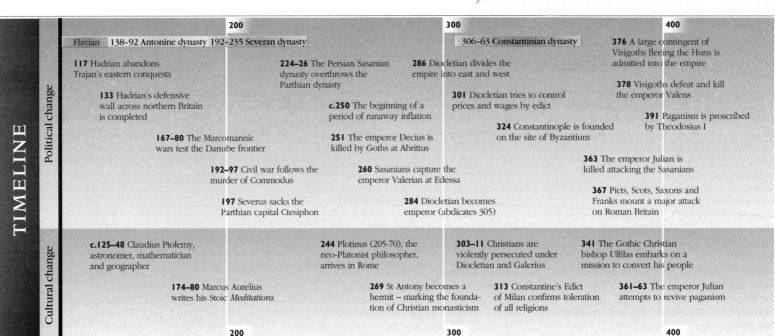

Legend:
- Roman empire, c.235
- Roman territory lost permanently, 163–378
- kingdom of Palmyra, 260–72
- Gallic empire, 260–74
- strong Christian communities by 300
- **Goths** major Germanic peoples, 3rd century
- **Picts** other barbarians, 3rd century
- attacks on Roman empire, with dates
- city sacked
- Roman victory
- Roman defeat
- battle between Roman forces
- frontier wall or rampart
- *Italia* Diocletianic diocese
- borders of Diocletianic dioceses

0 ———— 600 km

**TIMELINE**

| | 200 | 300 | 400 |
|---|---|---|---|

**Political change**

Flavian    138–92 Antonine dynasty    192–235 Severan dynasty    306–63 Constantinian dynasty

**117** Hadrian abandons Trajan's eastern conquests

**133** Hadrian's defensive wall across northern Britain is completed

**167–80** The Marcomannic wars test the Danube frontier

**192–97** Civil war follows the murder of Commodus

**197** Severus sacks the Parthian capital Ctesiphon

**224–26** The Persian Sasanian dynasty overthrows the Parthian dynasty

**c.250** The beginning of a period of runaway inflation

**251** The emperor Decius is killed by Goths at Abrittus

**260** Sasanians capture the emperor Valerian at Edessa

**286** Diocletian divides the empire into east and west

**301** Diocletian tries to control prices and wages by edict

**324** Constantinople is founded on the site of Byzantium

**284** Diocletian becomes emperor (abdicates 305)

**376** A large contingent of Visigoths fleeing the Huns is admitted into the empire

**378** Visigoths defeat and kill the emperor Valens

**391** Paganism is proscribed by Theodosius I

**363** The emperor Julian is killed attacking the Sasanians

**367** Picts, Scots, Saxons and Franks mount a major attack on Roman Britain

**Cultural change**

**c.125–48** Claudius Ptolemy, astronomer, mathematician and geographer

**174–80** Marcus Aurelius writes his Stoic *Meditations*

**244** Plotinus (205–70), the neo-Platonist philosopher, arrives in Rome

**269** St Antony becomes a hermit – marking the foundation of Christian monasticism

**303–11** Christians are violently persecuted under Diocletian and Galerius

**313** Constantine's Edict of Milan confirms toleration of all religions

**341** The Gothic Christian bishop Ulfilas embarks on a mission to convert his people

**361–63** The emperor Julian attempts to revive paganism

**Balts**

**1** In the late 3rd century a chain of forts built on the east and south coasts of Britain was organized into an anti-piracy command, later known as the Saxon Shore.

**2** After the Marcomanni attacked Aquileia in 167, the northern frontier was constantly threatened.

**3** The importance of Rome declined in the 3rd and 4th centuries as it was abandoned by the emperor in favor of bases closer to the troubled frontiers.

**4** Dacia could not be defended, and in 272 Aurelian abandoned it to the Goths and the Gepids.

**5** Frankish invaders seized ships at Tarraco in 260 to launch pirate raids on north Africa.

**6** Constantine the Great chose the small town of Byzantium as the site of a new capital for the empire.

**7** After the emperor Julian was killed at Phrygia in 363 his army bought its freedom by ceding eastern Mesopotamia.

**8** A network of ramparts, ditches, military roads and forts was built in the 3rd century to defend Rome's African frontier.

CHRISTIANITY spread widely before toleration was introduced in 313. This 2nd-century carving shows the *khi-rho* symbol for Christ.

authority were separated: provinces were subdivided and organized in dioceses under "vicars" who were directly responsible to the emperor. Diocletian realized that the problems of defending the empire were too great for one ruler and in 286 he appointed Maximian as co-emperor to rule the west while he concentrated on the east.

In the 4th century the empire underwent a cultural transformation as traditional paganism was supplanted by Christianity. The pagan Roman empire was a tolerant state and was prepared to accept any religion that did not involve human sacrifice, so long as its devotees were prepared to pay lip-service to the state gods. Christians were not prepared to do this and had faced frequent persecutions as a result, one of the worst being ordered by Diocletian. Despite this, Christianity had spread steadily through the urban lower and middle classes, and by 300 it was well established throughout the empire. In 312 the emperor Constantine (r. 306–37) became convinced that the Christian God had helped him win a victory over a rival at the Milvian Bridge, and in 313 he granted Christian toleration. Constantine subsequently presided over church councils, founded churches and was baptized on his deathbed. There is no reason to doubt the sincerity of his conversion, but he may also have seen Christianity as a unifying force for the embattled empire. Constantine's successors continued to promote Christianity, and the new religion began to exert a strong influence on all aspects of Roman life, from personal morality to art and literature. Christianity finally became the empire's official religion in 391, when Theodosius I abolished pagan worship.

See also 27 (world religions); 29 (earlier Roman empire); 33 (fall of the empire)

Around AD 50 the Kushans made northwest India part of an empire stretching from the Ganges to the Aral Sea. They were a clan of the Yue Qi nomads who had overrun the Greek kingdom of Bactria around 135 BC. The Kushan state was set up in Bactria around AD 25 by Kujala Kadphises, who invaded India and conquered Gandhara and the Northern Sakas around AD 50. Kujala's successor, Vima Kadphises (r.c.75–100), conquered the Indus valley and much of the Gangetic plain. The empire reached its peak under Kanishka (r.c.100–130). He was a devout Buddhist and a patron of the arts, supporting both the Indo-Hellenistic school of Gandhara and the Hindu school of Mathura. Under Kanishka's successors, the Kushan empire maintained its borders until the 3rd century, when most of the empire's western provinces were conquered by the Sasanian King Shapur I. Although the Kushans briefly regained their independence in the 4th century, the united Kushan empire was not restored.

The Kushan empire was never highly centralized and the king ruled through a host of dependent sub-kings or *yaghbus*. Kushan rulers used an eclectic range of titles, including *maharaja* (great king), *rajatiraja* (king of kings), the Greek title *basileus* (king) and *kaisara* (from the Latin *caesar*). They also instituted a cult of ruler worship and used the title *devaputra* (son of God). Kushan culture was equally eclectic, mixing Hellenistic, Indian and central Asian styles. Kushan rulers were tolerant in matters of religion. Most of the early rulers were Buddhists and the later ones Hindus, but all showed respect for a wide range of Persian, Greek and even Roman deities. The empire was always wealthy, prospering by its control of all the major trans-Asian overland trade routes. High-quality gold coinage was made by melting down gold Roman coins flooding into the empire to pay for luxury goods such as Chinese silk.

The Kushans did not have a monopoly on east–west trade. By the 1st century AD, Mediterranean seafarers had discovered how to exploit the monsoon winds to sail across the Indian Ocean, bringing increased trade between the Roman empire and southern India. The region's most valuable exports were spices, which the Romans paid for in gold. South Indian rulers did not issue their own coinage and Roman coins circulated freely. The most powerful south Indian state at this period was Satavahanihara; but the influx of wealth led to the formation of several small tribal kingdoms and cities in the region.

The decline of Kushan power made possible the rise of the Gupta kingdom in the 4th century. Minor princes in the Varanasi area in the later 3rd century, the Guptas may have been feudatories of Magadha. The dynasty began with the reign of Chandragupta I (r.320–35), who made an advantageous marriage alliance with the Licchavis. This brought him control of Magadha, the fertile and densely populated heartland of the former Mauryan empire. Chandragupta was succeeded by his son Samudragupta (r.335–80), whose long reign saw the kingdom expand across northern India, reducing the Kushans to tributary status. Samudragupta also fought a major campaign in the southeast, reducing many rulers to tributaries. He formed strong alliances with the Sakas and the Vakatakas (in power in Satavahanihara), but his son and successor, Chandragupta II (r.380–414), turned on the Western Sakas, conquered their kingdom and imposed direct rule. The empire ruled by Chandragupta II was almost as large as the Mauryan empire, but was very loose-knit. Gupta inscriptions approximately cover the area in which the dynasty exercised direct rule – the rest of the empire was ruled by tributary kings and barely-subdued tribes.

The Guptas were patrons of the arts and sciences and the period was one of great creativity. They were devout Hindus and some of the main features of Hinduism, such as image-worship, appeared under their rule. The Hindu epics of the *Ramayana* and the *Mahabharata* reached their final form at this time. Sanskrit poetry and drama flourished, causing the Gupta period to be regarded as the classical age of Indian literature. Advances were made in astronomy and mathematics, including the invention of the decimal system of numerals, later adopted by the Arabs and, through them, by the Europeans.

After the death of Chandragupta II, the empire ceased expanding but remained powerful, and under Skandagupta (r.c.455–67) defeated a major Hunnish invasion. However, a war of succession followed Skandagupta's death and the empire went into decline as tributary kings and nominally conquered tribes reasserted their independence. The final blow came from an invasion of the Hunas (Ephthalite Huns) in 505–11, who founded a kingdom in northwest India, destroying the last remnants of the Kushans. In 528 a coalition of Indian princes defeated the Hunas, but the Guptas played only a minor role in this campaign. Gupta rulers continued in Magadha until around 720, but only as mere princes. Except for a brief period under Harsha (r.606–47) of Kanauj, who united the states on the Gangetic plain, no supraregional state reappeared in India until the 13th century.

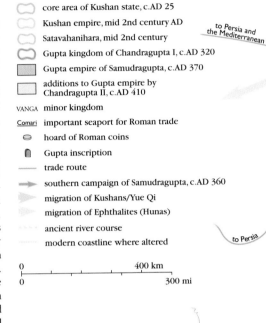

core area of Kushan state, c.AD 25

Kushan empire, mid 2nd century AD

Satavahanihara, mid 2nd century

Gupta kingdom of Chandragupta I, c.AD 320

Gupta empire of Samudragupta, c.AD 370

additions to Gupta empire by Chandragupta II, c.AD 410

VANGA minor kingdom

Comari important seaport for Roman trade

hoard of Roman coins

Gupta inscription

trade route

southern campaign of Samudragupta, c.AD 360

migration of Kushans/Yue Qi

migration of Ephthalites (Hunas)

ancient river course

modern coastline where altered

to Persia and the Mediterranean

to Persia

0      400 km

0      300 mi

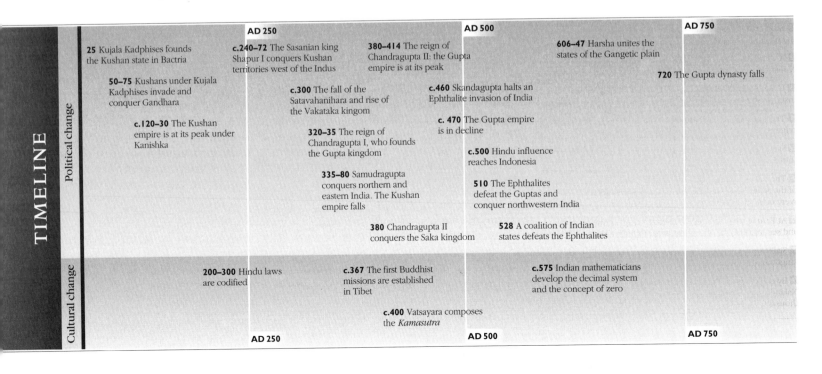

TIMELINE

**Political change**

AD 250

AD 500

AD 750

25 Kujala Kadphises founds the Kushan state in Bactria

50–75 Kushans under Kujala Kadphises invade and conquer Gandhara

c.120–30 The Kushan empire is at its peak under Kanishka

c.240–72 The Sasanian king Shapur I conquers Kushan territories west of the Indus

c.300 The fall of the Satavahanihara and rise of the Vakataka kingom

320–35 The reign of Chandragupta I, who founds the Gupta kingdom

335–80 Samudragupta conquers northern and eastern India. The Kushan empire falls

380 Chandragupta II conquers the Saka kingdom

380–414 The reign of Chandragupta II: the Gupta empire is at its peak

c.460 Skandagupta halts an Ephthalite invasion of India

c. 470 The Gupta empire is in decline

c.500 Hindu influence reaches Indonesia

510 The Ephthalites defeat the Guptas and conquer northwestern India

528 A coalition of Indian states defeats the Ephthalites

606–47 Harsha unites the states of the Gangetic plain

720 The Gupta dynasty falls

**Cultural change**

200–300 Hindu laws are codified

c.367 The first Buddhist missions are established in Tibet

c.400 Vatsayara composes the *Kamasutra*

c.575 Indian mathematicians develop the decimal system and the concept of zero

AD 250

AD 500

AD 750

Tashkent

Marakanda

c.135 BC

Kashgar

to China

to China

Merv

AD 484

Surkh Kotal

BACTRIA

Bactra

HINDU

KUSH

AD 25

AD 505

Kabul

c.AD 50

c.AD 460

Peshawar

GANDHARA

Khalatse

Srinagar

Taxila

AD 510

c.AD 25

Kandahar

Sialkot

8

Northern Sakas

AD 510

c.AD 75-100

HIMALAYAS

KUNLUN MTS

AD 90

Khotan

Indus

Tibetans

CARVED wooden figures of
musicians exemplify the
congenial atmosphere for
Hindu learning and the arts
provided by the Gupta court.

KIRTHAR RANGE

SULAIMAN RANGE

Chenab

Sutlej

PANCHALA

Ahichhattra

Ganges

Sravasti

Kusinagara

NEPALA

PUNDRA

Thar Desert

Bairat

Mathura

KOSALA

Kanauj

Ayodhya

Licchavis

Guptas

Pataliputra

9

Campa

Prayaga

4

Varanasi

Nalanda

Rajgir

MAGADHA

Bodh Gaya

VANGA

Kausambi

Yamuna

Pattala

7

AD 511

Pusyamitras

Tamralipti

Barbaricum

AD 510

Vidisha

Eran

UTKALA

Western Sakas

Narmada

Ujjain

Mahanadi

Tosali

Bay of
Bengal

Valabhi

Junagadh

3

Girnar

Barygaza

Tapti

DECCAN

KALINGA

Palura

Arabian Sea

Bhogavardhana

Pratisthana

Godavari

Vakatakas

6

Simhapura

Suppara

Kalliana

Pistapura

EASTERN GHATS

Byzantium?

Tagara

Krishna

Amaravati

Machilipatnam

WESTERN GHATS

Banavasi

5

Pallavas

Kaveri

1

southern border uncertain

Arikamedu

Ceras

Cholas

Kaveripatnam

Muziris

Madurai

Ceylon

Pandyas

Korkai

Anuradhapura

SIMHALA

Sigiriya

Comari

**1** Arikamedu was a trading port in the 1st century
AD: many Roman artifacts have been excavated there.

**2** A Chinese army defeated the Kushans in AD 90 at
Khotan, halting Kushan expansion in central Asia.

**3** Junagadh is the site of the earliest known Sanskrit
inscription, erected c.150 by the Saka king Rudraman.

**4** The main source of information on Samudragupta's
reign (c.335-75) is a pillar inscription at Prayaga.

**5** Samudragupta's southern campaign (c.360) saw
thirteen kings and princes brought under Gupta rule.

**6** The Vakatakas dominated central India after the fall
of the Satavahanihara kingdom in the 3rd century and
were close allies of the Guptas.

**7** At Eran in 510 the Hunas defeated a Gupta army
and secured control of northwestern India.

**8** Sialkot was the capital of the short-lived Huna
kingdom (c.505-30).

**9** By c.600 a great Buddhist monastic university at
Nalanda, patronized by Gupta kings, housed thirty
thousand students.

See also 21 (Alexander's conquests);
27 (religions)

The area of the – now Christian – Roman empire in AD 400, though slightly greater than in 1 BC, disguises Rome's true position. Although the emperor Diocletian (r.284–305) had given the empire a new lease of life by dividing it into eastern and western halves and completely reforming the administration and army, Rome was a state under siege. Pressure on the empire's borders was constant and the cost of maintaining defenses ruinous, especially in the poorer west. When the Huns, a Turkic-dominated nomad confederation from somewhere in central Asia, arrived in eastern Europe around 372, destabilizing the Germanic tribes, the empire was plunged back into crisis (▷30). To the east, the Sasanians, who had overthrown the Parthian empire in 226, were also posing a threat.

From around AD 50 the Kushan clan, which had become dominant among the Yue Qi, established an empire extending from the Aral Sea to the Indian Ocean and into northwest India. The empire had fallen by the late 4th century. Northern India continued to be divided into small states, until around 350, when Samudragupta (d.c.380) founded the Gupta empire (▷31), which by 410 had reached its greatest extent under Chandragupta II (r.380–414).

Farther east, the authority of the Han dynasty, which had reached the summit of its power in the 1st century, began to decline. In 189 the empire collapsed in chaos as army and court factions struggled to control an isolated and powerless emperor. The dynasty was overthrown in 220, when the empire split into three kingdoms. In 280 unity was briefly restored, but civil war again broke out, giving the Xiongnu the opportunity to conquer the north of the country. A second wave of nomads – the Turkic Toba tribes – arrived in 386 and won control of the north. The Toba Wei state itself was threatened by the Juan-juan, a Mongol-dominated nomad confederation which arose in the late 4th century and controlled the eastern steppes by 400.

Small states sprang up in southern Japan in the 2nd or 3rd centuries, though most of these had been incorporated into the Yamato kingdom of Honshu by 400. The first southeast Asian states – the trading kingdom of Funan and the Cham kingdom of Champa – had developed by the 2nd century. Madagascar had been discovered and settled by Austronesian peoples from Indonesia in the 1st century AD, a voyaging feat to be matched by the Polynesians, who by 400 had colonized Hawaii and Easter Island.

In Africa the kingdom of Meroë collapsed around 350 as a result of nomad

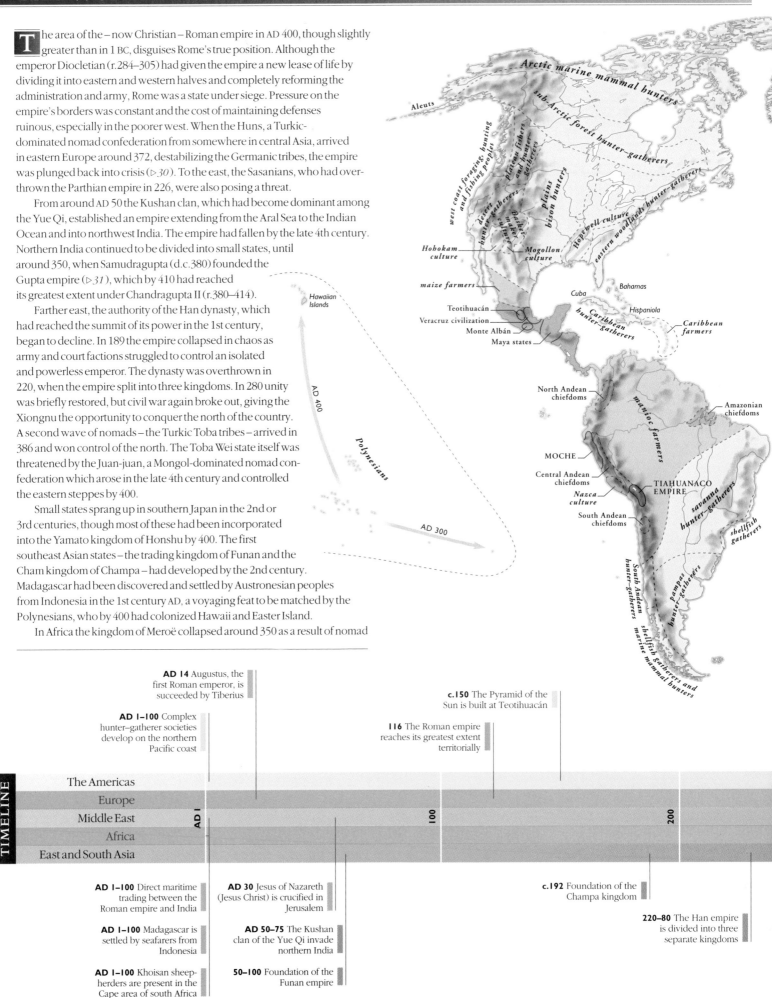

## TIMELINE

**AD 14** Augustus, the first Roman emperor, is succeeded by Tiberius

**AD 1–100** Complex hunter–gatherer societies develop on the northern Pacific coast

**c.150** The Pyramid of the Sun is built at Teotihuacán

**116** The Roman empire reaches its greatest extent territorially

The Americas

Europe

Middle East

Africa

East and South Asia

**AD 1–100** Direct maritime trading between the Roman empire and India

**AD 30** Jesus of Nazareth (Jesus Christ) is crucified in Jerusalem

**c.192** Foundation of the Champa kingdom

**AD 1–100** Madagascar is settled by seafarers from Indonesia

**AD 50–75** The Kushan clan of the Yue Qi invade northern India

**220–80** The Han empire is divided into three separate kingdoms

**AD 1–100** Khoisan sheep-herders are present in the Cape area of south Africa

**50–100** Foundation of the Funan empire

Greenland

Iceland

Lapps

Finno-Ugrian taiga hunter-gatherers

Arctic marine mammal hunters

Siberian taiga hunter-gatherers

Samoyed reindeer herders

Finns

Cells

Germans

Balts

Slavs

Huns

WESTERN ROMAN EMPIRE

EASTERN ROMAN EMPIRE

Berbers

Kushan Principalities

Ephthalites

Juan-juan confederation (Mongols)

Tú-yü-hun

TOBA WEI

Turko–Mongol transhumant pastoralists

Ainu

KOGURYO

SILLA

PAEKCHE

Yayoi culture

YAMATO

SASANIAN EMPIRE

Tibetan transhumant pastoralists

JIN EMPIRE

camel nomads

Arabs

GUPTA EMPIRE

Burmese

Pyu

Mons

Thais

Taiwan

Nubian kingdoms

AXUM

HIMYARITE KINGDOM

VAKATAKA

Hindu kingdoms

Ceylon

SIMHALA

FUNAN

CHAMPA

cereal farmers and herders

tropical forest farmers

western Bantu-speaking herders and farmers

Ethiopian highland farmers

Austronesians

Micronesians

Celebes

Borneo

New Guinea

Papuan Neolithic farmers

Melanesians

eastern Bantu-speaking herders and farmers

Sumatra

Java

Timor

minor states and chiefdoms under Indian influence

Australian Aboriginal hunter-gatherers

Madagascar

Austronesians, 1st century AD

Khoisan herders and gatherers

Khoisan hunter-gatherers

Polynesians

Tasmanian hunter-gatherers

- hunter-gatherers
- nomadic pastoralists
- simple farming societies
- complex farming societies/ chiefdoms
- state societies
- uninhabited
- Roman territory
- other empires
- Greco-Roman trade routes
- India-China trade routes
- migration

**410** Visigothic invaders under Alaric besiege and sack Rome

**313** Constantine becomes the first Roman emperor to accept Christianity

**c.375** Foundation of the Tiahuanaco empire in the Peru region

**c.300** The beginning of the Classic period of Maya civilization

**372** The Huns invade and conquer the western steppes

**300–400** Buddhism is introduced into south-east Asia

**c.350** Axum overthrows the weakened kingdom of Meroë

**c.300** The first states have appeared in Japan

**386–397** The nomadic Toba tribe conquer the Wei state in north China

**320** Foundation of the Gupta kingdom in northern India

300

400

invasions. The city of Meroë itself fell to Axum, which was extending its power west and south over the Ethiopian highlands. Bantu herders and iron workers had appeared in southern Africa by 400, having displaced or assimilated the Khoisan-speaking peoples of east Africa. Herding also began to replace hunting and gathering among the Khoisan people of southwest Africa (▷35).

In North America the Hohokam culture developed in the southwest deserts around 300. Like the Basketmaker peoples to their north, the Hohokam combined maize cultivation with hunting and gathering. The Hopewell culture of the eastern woodlands was now in decline in its homeland in the Ohio and Missouri valleys, but elsewhere derivative cultures were flourishing. During the 1st century, fishing peoples on the Pacific coast began to develop complex hierarchical societies with sophisticated material cultures.

The Mesoamerican civilizations entered their classic age in the early centuries AD. Teotihuacán entered its greatest period around 100. By 300 it was probably the world's fifth largest city, with a population of about 200,000. City-states with warlike ruling dynasties had developed across most of the Maya territories as the Classic period of Maya civilization began around 300. About 200 the Zapotec capital Monte Albán had a population of around 30,000. In South America, the coastal Moche state was at its peak from 200 to 400, and the Tiahuanaco state, in the Lake Titicaca highlands, was beginning a period of imperial expansion (▷39) ∎

The fragile stability of the 4th-century empire was maintained at great cost to its citizens. Taxation was kept at a high level to pay for the large armies needed to defend the frontiers against increasingly well organized Germanic barbarians; yet the economy, particularly in the west, was in decline. The rich used their political influence to avoid paying taxes, so the tax burden fell heavily upon the poorer classes. Even in Egypt's fertile Nile valley, peasant farmers could not afford to pay their taxes and abandoned their fields. The empire's population contracted and manpower shortages began to affect the armies. The western army relied increasingly on barbarian mercenaries to fill its ranks.

In the 370s pressures on the empire's northern frontier increased dramatically. The Huns, a Turkic nomad people, migrated to the eastern European steppes from central Asia and, around 372, crushed the Ostrogoths. The defeat of this the most powerful Germanic tribe caused panic among the rest. In 376 the Visigoths, seeking sanctuary from the Huns, requested permission to settle in the Roman empire. The eastern emperor, Valens, who saw the Visigoths as a valuable source of recruits for the army, settled them on vacant lands in Thrace. There, however, they were treated badly by the corrupt officials in charge of their settlement; and in 378 they rebelled, defeating and killing Valens in battle at Adrianople. Under a new agreement in 382 the emperor Theodosius gave the Visigoths the status of federates (allies); but they rebelled again in 395 under their ambitious new leader, Alaric. He had previously commanded Gothic troops in the Roman army, but now ravaged Greece and Dalmatia before invading Italy in 401. Stilicho, a Roman general of Germanic origin, drove the Visigoths back into Dalmatia; but the situation deteriorated in 406 when a coalition of Vandals, Suevi and Alans invaded Gaul before crossing the Pyrenees into Spain in 409. They were followed into Gaul by Franks, Burgundians and Alemanni. In 410 Alaric rebelled yet again, and when his demands were refused the Visigoths sacked Rome. Though no longer the administrative capital of the empire, Rome remained a potent symbol of its history and power, and the attack was deeply shocking. Alaric died soon afterward, and his successors were more inclined to cooperate with the Romans. In 418 the Visigoths, as allies of the Romans, attacked the Suevi, Alans and Vandals in Spain, before being settled on rich lands in Aquitaine as federates under nominal Roman suzerainty.

Although the Huns were indirectly responsible for the empire's woes, they initially maintained good

--- border of Roman empire, 378
- - division between eastern and western Roman empires, 395
--- northern limit of Germanic peoples, c.376
[ ] eastern Roman empire, 480
[ ] kingdom of Odoacer, 480
[ ] kingdom of Syagrius, 480
[ ] Burgundian kingdom (Germanic), 480
[ ] Franks (Germanic), 480
[ ] Ostrogoths (Germanic), 480
[ ] Vandal kingdom (Germanic), 480
[ ] Visigothic kingdom (Germanic), 480
[ ] other Germanic peoples, 480
[///] temporary settlement of Vandals, with date
[///] federate settlement of Visigoths, with date
▷ Hun migration
▷ Alan, Suevi and Vandal migration
▷ Visigoth migration
▷ other migration
**Goths** major Germanic people, 4th century
**Huns** other barbarian peoples
■ capital city

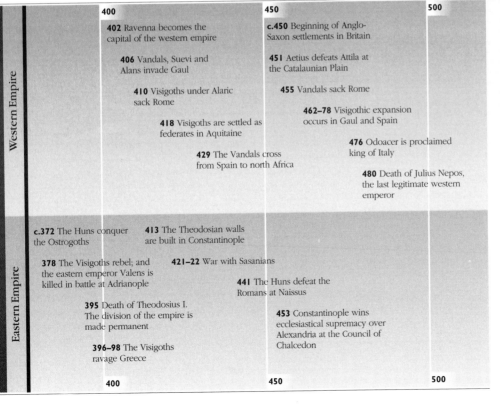

TIMELINE

**Western Empire**

400

**402** Ravenna becomes the capital of the western empire

**406** Vandals, Suevi and Alans invade Gaul

**410** Visigoths under Alaric sack Rome

**418** Visigoths are settled as federates in Aquitaine

**429** The Vandals cross from Spain to north Africa

450

**c.450** Beginning of Anglo-Saxon settlements in Britain

**451** Aetius defeats Attila at the Catalaunian Plain

**455** Vandals sack Rome

**462–78** Visigothic expansion occurs in Gaul and Spain

**476** Odoacer is proclaimed king of Italy

**480** Death of Julius Nepos, the last legitimate western emperor

500

**Eastern Empire**

**c.372** The Huns conquer the Ostrogoths

**378** The Visigoths rebel; and the eastern emperor Valens is killed in battle at Adrianople

**395** Death of Theodosius I. The division of the empire is made permanent

**396–98** The Visigoths ravage Greece

**413** The Theodosian walls are built in Constantinople

**421–22** War with Sasanians

**441** The Huns defeat the Romans at Naissus

**453** Constantinople wins ecclesiastical supremacy over Alexandria at the Council of Chalcedon

**1** The arrival of the Huns in eastern Europe around 370 completely destabilized the Germanic tribes, causing many to seek refuge in the Roman empire.

**2** In 402 the capital of the western empire was moved from Rome to Ravenna, allowing more rapid communication with the northern frontier and Constantinople.

**3** Most of Britain's garrison was withdrawn in 407 by the usurper Constantine to fight in a civil war. In 410 Honorius told the Britons to see to their own defenses.

**4** Rome was sacked twice in the 5th century: in 410 by the Visigoths; and in 455 by the Vandals.

**5** Saxons, Angles and Jutes from north Germany and Denmark began to settle in eastern Britain c.450.

**6** The position and strong fortifications of Constantinople saved Anatolia from barbarian invaders in the 5th century.

**7** In the 460s Visigoths, settled by the Romans in Aquitaine in 418, expanded into Gaul and Spain.

**8** In 476 Italy came under the rule of Odoacer, a barbarian general, who deposed the "last" western emperor: the puppet usurper Romulus Augustulus, who was still a boy.

Götar

Jutes

Danes

Baltic Sea

Balts

Western Dvina

Slavs

5

Angles

Frisians

Saxons

Slavs, c.450–75

Slavs, c.450–75

Huns, c.370–76

Vistula

Franks

Colonia Agrippina

Lombards

Suevi

Oder

Slavs, c.450–75

Ostrogoths

Huns, c.370–76

Alans

Augusta Treverorum

Burgundians

Huns, 451–52

Elbe

c.400

Dnieper

STILICHO, part-Roman, part-Vandal, commanded the western empire's armies, but was beheaded by the emperor Honorius in 408.

Vangiones 436

Alemanni

Siling Vandals

Vandals, c.400

Rhine

Alans & Vandals, 401

Danube

Quadi

Rugians

Alans, c.400

Huns, c.370–76

BURGUNDIAN KINGDOM

ALPS

Huns, 451–52

Nedao 454

Asding Vandals

1

Huns c.376–454

Gepids

CARPATHIAN MTS

Alans

Mediolanum

Aquileia

408–10

Sava

Ostrogoths

Sirmium

Visigoths

Black Sea

Po

Visigoths, 412

settled 401–08

DALMATIA

Danube

Ravenna

2

Naissus 441

settled 376–96

6

Nicomedia

KINGDOM OF ODOACER

Corsica

Rome

8

Dyrrhachium

Huns, c.440

Adrianople 378

Constantinople

4

Vandals, 455

Visigoths, 398–401

Thessalonica

ANATOLIA

Sardinia

Visigoths, 410

Visigoths, 396–98

Edessa

settled 398–401

EASTERN ROMAN EMPIRE

WESTERN ROMAN EMPIRE

Athens

Corinth

Ephesus

Antiochia

Sicily

Sparta

SASANIAN EMPIRE

Vandals, 455

Rhodes

Hippo Regius

468

Carthage

Cyprus

VANDAL KINGDOM

Malta

Crete

Mediterranean Sea

Jerusalem

Alexandria

Nile

Arabs

0        600 km

0     400 mi

relations with Rome. The Roman general Aetius used Hun mercenaries widely in the 430s to impose federate status on the Burgundians and other barbarian settlers in Gaul, but in 441 Attila turned on the empire, ravaging the Balkans and pushing his western border to the Rhine. In 451 Attila invaded Gaul but was defeated by a coalition of Romans, Visigoths, Burgundians and Franks under Aetius at the Catalaunian Plain. After Attila's death in 453 the Huns' German subjects rebelled, breaking their power at the battle of Nedao in 454. The collapse of the Huns in fact worked against Rome: fear of them had kept Rome's Germanic allies reasonably loyal, now they had less cause to be cooperative.

In 429 the Vandals had crossed from Spain to Africa and in 439 captured Carthage and set up a completely independent kingdom. This was the most serious blow the barbarians had so far struck against the empire, as north Africa was Italy's main source of grain. The Vandals turned to piracy, and in 455 went on to sack Rome itself. The assassination in

this year of Aetius, the west's most able general, and of Valentinian III, last of the Theodosian dynasty, were further blows. The western empire now began to crumble and by the 470s was reduced to little more than Italy. The last legitimate western emperor, Julius Nepos, was driven out of Italy in 475 by a palace coup which placed a boy usurper, Romulus Augustulus, on the throne. The following year Odoacer, a barbarian general, deposed Augustulus and was proclaimed king by his soldiers. Odoacer recognized the suzerainty of the eastern emperor Zeno and offered to rule Italy as imperial viceroy. The deposing of Augustulus in 476 is widely accepted as marking the end of the western Roman empire, but Julius Nepos continued to rule a rump empire in Dalmatia from 475 until his death in 480. Dalmatia then became part of Odoacer's kingdom.

The main cause of the fall of the western Roman empire was its exposure to barbarian attack – far greater than in the east, which had only a short northern frontier. This problem was exacerbated by

the division of the empire in the 4th century, which deprived the poorer, less populated and more vulnerable west of the resources of the richer east. Eastern emperors did assist their western colleagues, but their main priority was ensuring that the east did not go the same way as the west. The west was also politically less stable than the east. From the time of Honorius onward western emperors were dominated by overbearing generals. After the death of Valentinian III in 455, the western emperors became the puppets of barbarian generals: when they outlived their usefulness or tried to act independently, they were murdered. The high cost of defending the empire undermined positive loyalty to it. There was little popular resistance to the barbarians and, as they were inefficient tax collectors, most people probably felt themselves better off without the empire.

See also 30 (the later Roman Empire); 34 (rise of Byzantium)

For twelve years after Odoacer's takeover of Italy, Zeno, the eastern emperor, did nothing. Then in 488 he commissioned Theodoric, king of the Ostrogoths, to overthrow Odoacer and rule Italy until he, the emperor, was able to claim sovereignty in person. By 493 Odoacer was dead and Theodoric was master of Italy. Under Theodoric, who wished to preserve Roman civilization, Italy enjoyed peace and prosperity, but there was no assimilation between Roman and Goth. The main barrier was religion. The Goths had converted to Christianity in the 4th century but were followers of the teachings of Arius, who denied the divinity of Christ – which their Roman subjects regarded as heretical. The Burgundians, Visigoths and Vandals were also Arians and assimilation was equally limited in those kingdoms. Arianism also prevented good relations between the barbarian kingdoms and the eastern emperor, who regarded himself as the guardian of orthodox Christianity. The only barbarians to escape the taint of heresy were the Franks, who converted directly from paganism to orthodox Christianity around 500. This earned them the friendship and support of the eastern emperors and the loyalty and cooperation of their Gallo-Roman subjects. Because of this the Frankish kingdom became the strongest power in western Europe by 600.

Although it was frequently at war with Sasanian Persia, the eastern empire prospered after the fall of the west. The emperor Anastasius (r. 491–518) even managed to cut taxes and still leave his successor, Justin (r. 518–27), with a full treasury. Justin was succeeded by his nephew Justinian (r. 527–65), the last great Roman emperor. Justinian had a very clear idea of the responsibilities of a Roman emperor, chief of which was maintaining the territorial integrity of the empire. To Justinian it was a disgrace that the western provinces of the empire were occupied by barbarians and he launched a concerted effort to recover them. In 533 he sent a force under Belisarius which, against expectations, destroyed the Vandal kingdom in north Africa. The Vandal campaign had been made possible by the cooperation of the pro-Roman Ostrogothic queen Amalasuntha,

who allowed the invasion fleet to use Sicily as a base. Amalasuntha's murder in 534 was used as a pretext for the invasion of Italy in 535. By 540 the Ostrogoth capital at Ravenna had fallen, but resistance was revived by Totila (r. 541–52). War with Persia diverted Roman forces to the east and the resulting stalemate in Italy was only broken in 552 when a new Roman army under Narses arrived from Constantinople. By 554 all of Italy south of the Po was in Roman hands, but north of the river Ostrogothic resistance continued until 562. The last of Justinian's conquests was southern Spain, seized opportunistically during a Visigothic civil war in 554.

Justinian's reconquests restored Roman control of the Mediterranean but put the empire under serious economic strain. The concentration of forces in the west left the Balkans exposed to Slavic raiding and settlement, and the Persians made serious

incursions in the east. Italy was devastated by years of war and much of the province was soon lost again following an invasion by the Lombards in 572. However, north Africa and Sicily proved to be valuable additions to the empire's resources.

In about 560 a new wave of nomads, the Avars, arrived in eastern Europe. The Romans paid them to wipe out the remnants of the Huns, but in 580 a dispute over possession of Singidunum (modern

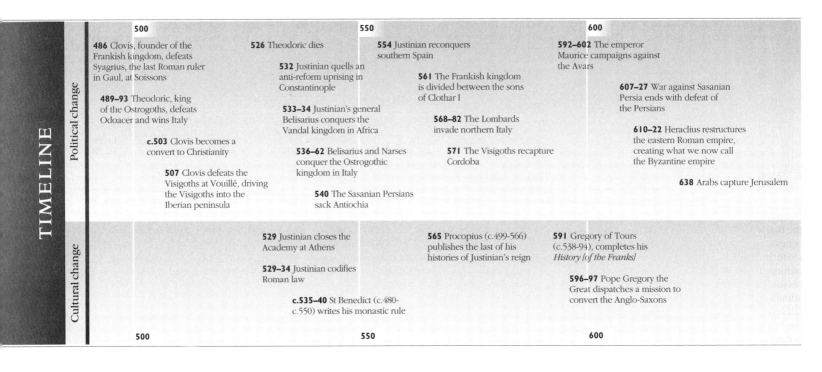

Danes

*Baltic Sea*

Balts

Slavs

*Vistula*

Thuringians

Saxons

*Oder*

*Elbe*

Avars, 533–62

**4**

*Don*

Huns

C A R P A T H I A N   M T S

Lombards

**6**

*Danube*

*Rhine*

*Rhône*

BURGUNDIAN
KINGDOM

A L P S

540s–80s

626

Bulgars

Alans

Gepids

568–72

OSTROGOTHIC
KINGDOM

*Po*

**3**

• Mediolanum

572–82

• Ravenna

Busta
Gallorum
✕ 552

*Sava*

Singidunum

*Danube*

Cherson

*Dnieper*

Naissus

**7**

*Black Sea*

• Salonae

Narses

Adrianople

**8**

Trapezus

*Narses*

**1**

Rome ✚

Corsica

• Salonae

Neapolis

Mons
✕ Lactacius
552

Sardinia

Mediolanum

Thessalonica

Constantinople ✚

Nicomedia
• Nicaea

A N A T O L I A

EASTERN
ROMAN
EMPIRE

*Tigris*

*Euphrates*

Nineveh
✕ 627

626

Antiochia
✚

540

Persians

Palmyra

Ctesiphon

Sicily

**2**

Catana
• Syracusae

Athens

Ephesus •

Rhodes

Cyprus

• Damascus

SASANIAN
EMPIRE

Tricameron
533 ✕

Carthage
✕ ad Decimum
533

*Malta*

Liberius

Crete

M e d i t e r r a n e a n
S e a

VANDAL
KINGDOM

• Cyrene

Jerusalem ✚

Leptis Magna

Alexandria ✚

*Nile*

Arabs

JUSTINIAN was portrayed in this
mosaic at Ravenna, supported by
religious and military forces.

prompted the governor of Africa to equip his son
Heraclius with an army in 610 and send him to
Constantinople to overthrow Phocas.

The reign of Heraclius was a turning point. The
structure of the empire of Diocletian, Constantine
and Justinian could not be revived. Heraclius spent
the first years of his reign rebuilding the administrative and military structure of the empire. Greek,
which had always been the majority language in the
eastern empire, replaced Latin in official documents.
Heraclius worked closely with the patriarch of
Constantinople, who willingly used the wealth and
authority of the church to support the state. While
Heraclius was reforming the empire, the war with
Persia continued to go badly and by 616 Syria,
Palestine and Egypt had been lost. In 622 Heraclius
launched a bold campaign directly into the heart of
the Sasanian empire and five years later destroyed
the Persian army at Nineveh, bringing the war to an
end. Heraclius had saved the empire, but his reforms
are considered to mark the end of the eastern
Roman empire and the beginning of the medieval
Greek Byzantine empire (named for the old Greek
name for Constantinople).

Belgrade) led to war. For ten years the Avars raided
the Balkans until the emperor, Maurice, launched a
series of effective counterattacks in 592. Maurice was
close to breaking Avar power, when his army
mutinied in 602: he was deposed and murdered by
his successor, Phocas, an incompetent despot. The
administrative structure of the empire now began to
fall apart. Slavs and Avars overran the Balkans and
the Persians took the fortresses of Roman Mesopotamia one by one. The chaotic state of the empire

**1** Rome regained importance in the 6th century as
the chief center of Christianity in western Europe.

**2** The Ostrogothic queen Amalasuntha allowed
Justinian's general Belisarius to use Sicily as a base for
his attack on the Vandals in 533.

**3** Ravenna, the Ostrogothic capital, was taken by
Belisarius in 540; resistance continued for many years.

**4** The Avars, a Mongol people, migrated to Europe
after being defeated by the Turks in central Asia (552).

**5** Civil war in the Visigothic kingdom gave Justinian
the opportunity to reconquer southern Spain in 554.

**6** Originally Roman allies against the Ostrogoths, the
Lombards invaded and settled Italy 568–82.

**7** Justinian's concentration on the west left the
Balkans exposed to frequent Slav raids and settlement.

**8** A joint Persian–Avar attack on Constantinople in
626 failed when the Byzantine fleet prevented the two
attacking armies from uniting.

See also 33 (fall of the western empire);
37 (Arab conquests)

The earliest African state formed in Egypt's Nile valley, where a centralized kingdom had emerged by 3000 BC. By this time desertification had turned the Sahara into a major barrier to travel and the only easy land route between Egypt and tropical Africa lay along the narrow valley of the middle Nile through Nubia. By 2500 several chiefdoms had emerged in Nubia. These were consolidated by 1700 into a large state, known to the Egyptians as Kush, whose capital was at Kerma. Nubia was rich in natural resources, especially gold, and was subjected to Egyptian plundering expeditions. It may, therefore, have been the impetus to organize an effective defense against the Egyptians that provided the impetus for state formation in this area. Kush was conquered by the Egyptians about 1500 at the start of Egypt's imperialistic New Kingdom period. When Egyptian power declined at the end of the New Kingdom (1070 BC), Kush regained its independence. In 770 the kings of Kush conquered southern Egypt and in 712 Shabaka (r.712–698) brought the whole kingdom under Nubian rule. Assyrian attacks on Egypt drove the Nubians from northern Egypt, and by 657 they had lost control of the whole country. The Egyptians expelled the Assyrians in 653 and launched campaigns into Nubia, forcing the Nubians to move their capital south to Meroë around 590. The kingdom of Meroë, as Kush is subsequently known, remained a major power that was taken seriously by the Persians, Greco-Macedonians and Romans who in turn ruled Egypt after 525 BC. In the 4th century Meroë suffered attacks from desert nomads; it collapsed about 350, after the capital was taken by the Axumites. Three small states, Nobatia, Makkura and Alwa, arose as successors to Meroë but Makkura conquered Nobatia in the 8th century.

Nubia was strongly influenced by Egyptian religion, kingship and culture. Until about 200 BC, when an indigenous Meroitic script was developed, Egyptian scripts and language were used for inscriptions, and the use of pyramids for royal burials continued into the Christian era, long after the practice had ceased in Egypt. Christianity was introduced to Nubia in the 6th century and remained strong until the region was put under pressure by the Arabs in the 13th century.

The second state to develop in tropical Africa, Axum emerged in northern Ethiopia in the 1st century AD. Urban development had begun at sites such as Yeha in the 5th century BC and the cultural development of the area was strongly influenced by the Sabeans of Arabia, whose alphabet, architecture and religion were adopted. In the 1st century AD the port of Adulis was exporting ivory, rhinoceros horn, tortoise-shell, obsidian and aromatic resins to the Roman empire via Red Sea trade routes. The city of Axum itself included complexes of monumental buildings and palaces. Among the most remarkable monuments at Axum are monoliths carved to resemble multistory buildings: the tallest still standing is 69 feet (21 meters) high. The kingdom of Axum reached a peak in the reign of King Ezana around 350. About this time also, Ezana converted to Christianity, the first African ruler to do so. In 522 the Axumites invaded and conquered the Yemen and held it until driven out by the Sasanians in 574. In the 8th century, attacks by the Arabs accelerated the decline of Axum, and by the 10th century power had shifted to the Ethiopian highlands.

Another area of Africa in which state formation occurred was the Maghrib, where the Berber kingdoms of Numantia and Mauretania emerged around 200 BC in the power vacuum left by the defeat of Carthage in the Second Punic War (226–201 BC). However, these states were soon swallowed up by the expanding empire of Rome. The most significant development in north Africa was the introduction of the camel to the Sahara around 100 BC. Camels were ideal for desert warfare, and settled communities on the fringes of the desert soon suffered badly from nomad raids. Camels also had the endurance for long desert crossings – horses, mules and bullocks had previously been the main beasts of burden in the Sahara. Now cross-desert trade began to expand, and by AD 500 camel caravans forged strong trade links between the Mediterranean and west Africa

Nok early Iron Age culture, 6th century BC–5th century AD

maximum extent of Nubian power, 712–671 BC

kingdom of Meroë, 590 BC–AD 350

kingdom of Axum under Ezana, c.AD 350

Axumite occupation, AD 522–74

kingdom of Numidia, 2nd century BC

kingdom of Mauretania, 2nd century BC

origin of Bantu-speaking peoples, 2000 BC

northwestern Bantu by AD 500

eastern Bantu by AD 500

western Bantu by AD 500

spread of Bantu, with date

Niger–Kordofanian languages, 2nd millennium BC

border of Roman empire, AD 1

sub-Sahara African early Iron Age site

with evidence of iron production

other site

trading post, 1st–3rd century AD

early Christian church, 4th–6th century AD

probable trans-Saharan route

sea route

desert

tropical rainforest

Cape Bojador

Akjouj

*Senegal*

*Gambia*

0                  1000 km

0                     800 mi

(maritime links were never established, because of adverse winds south of Cape Bojador).

The earliest Iron Age culture of west Africa, the Nok culture of Nigeria (c. 500 BC– AD 400), is noted for its sophisticated terracotta sculptures, which are often seen as being ancestral to the art styles of the medieval Ibo and Yoruba peoples. By AD 600 many areas of west Africa had dense farming populations, and one city, Jenne-jeno, had developed as a regional trading center. Many large burial mounds in this region point to the emergence of powerful elites and the beginnings of state formation.

The major development in Africa south of the Equator was the expansion of the Bantu-speaking peoples, mixed farming and, later, iron working. The Bantu languages belong to the Niger-Kordofanian group, confined to tropical west Africa in the second millennium BC. The original homeland of the Bantu was in southern Nigeria and Cameroon, but around 2000 BC Bantu-speakers began to spread into central and east Africa, and by AD 500 they had reached southern Africa. Bantu languages were spread partly by migrations of iron-using farmers, but also by the assimilation to Bantu culture of the Khoisan-speaking Stone Age herders and hunter–gatherers of eastern and southern Africa.

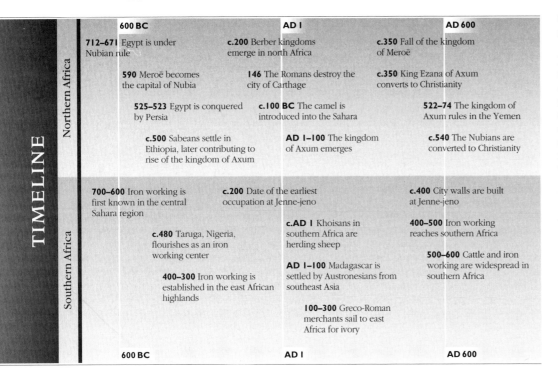

**TIMELINE**

| | 600 BC | AD 1 | AD 600 |
|---|---|---|---|
| **Northern Africa** | **712–671** Egypt is under Nubian rule | **c.200** Berber kingdoms emerge in north Africa | **c.350** Fall of the kingdom of Meroë |
| | **590** Meroë becomes the capital of Nubia | **146** The Romans destroy the city of Carthage | **c.350** King Ezana of Axum converts to Christianity |
| | **525–523** Egypt is conquered by Persia | **c.100 BC** The camel is introduced into the Sahara | **522–74** The kingdom of Axum rules in the Yemen |
| | **c.500** Sabeans settle in Ethiopia, later contributing to rise of the kingdom of Axum | **AD 1–100** The kingdom of Axum emerges | **c.540** The Nubians are converted to Christianity |
| **Southern Africa** | **700–600** Iron working is first known in the central Sahara region | **c.200** Date of the earliest occupation at Jenne-jeno | **c.400** City walls are built at Jenne-jeno |
| | **c.480** Taruga, Nigeria, flourishes as an iron working center | **c.AD 1** Khoisans in southern Africa are herding sheep | **400–500** Iron working reaches southern Africa |
| | **400–300** Iron working is established in the east African highlands | **AD 1–100** Madagascar is settled by Austronesians from southeast Asia | **500–600** Cattle and iron working are widespread in southern Africa |
| | | **100–300** Greco-Roman merchants sail to east Africa for ivory | |
| | **600 BC** | **AD 1** | **AD 600** |

## Map labels

Tingis
Caesarea
Hippo Regius
MAGHRIB
Carthage
MAURETANIA
NUMIDIA
Timgad
ATLAS MTS
Berbers
Leptis Magna
Cyrene
*Mediterranean Sea*

Alexandria
EGYPT
Memphis
Petra

Myos Hormos
Thebes
Berenice
Medina

Elephantine
Gebel Adda
Qustul
Ballana
Nobatia
Kerma
NUBIA
Napata
Makkura
Jebel Barkal
Old Dongola
MEROË
Meroë 600 BC
Wad Ban Naqa
Naqa
AXUM
Wad Ban Naqa
Alwa
Soba
Kohaito
Adulis
Axum
Yeha
Yeha

Mecca
Red Sea
Sabeans
6th century BC
SABA
HADRAMAUT
Miswar
Zafar
Qana
Muza

Mosyllon
Avalites
Malao
Opone
ETHIOPIAN HIGHLANDS

TASSILI MASSIF
Libyans
SAHARA DESERT
TIBESTI MASSIF

Do Dimmi
c.700–600 BC

TERRACOTTA heads from the Nok
culture of northern Nigeria are
among the earliest surviving
sub–Saharan artworks.

_ar Tichit
Tondidara
Koumbi Saleh
Jenne-jeno
Niani
Lake Chad
Niger
Yelwa
Nok
Benue
Samu Dukiya
Taruga
WEST AFRICAN RAINFOREST

Uele
Congo
2000 BC onwards
2000 BC onwards
CENTRAL AFRICAN RAINFOREST
Mouila 200 BC
Lualaba

Lake Turkana
Uruwe
Lake Victoria
Ndora
4th century AD
Katuruka
5th century BC
Kwale
Rhapta

Sarapion
Nikon
Shabelle
Juba

ATLANTIC OCEAN

AD 1–500
AD 1–500
Sanga
Lake Tanganyika
Kalambo Falls
Lake Malawi

Isamu Pati
Victoria Falls
Gokomere
Great Zimbabwe
AD 1–500

Khoisan–speaking
herders and
hunter–gatherers
Kalahari Desert

Broederstroom
5th century AD
Castle Cavern
c.AD 400

Austronesians
1st century AD

## Numbered notes

1 Sailing conditions made it difficult for Mediterranean ships of the period to trade beyond Cape Bojador.

2 Little trans-Saharan trade occurred before camel caravans became common in the first century AD.

3 Jenne-jeno, the earliest-known town in sub-Saharan Africa, had become a walled city by about AD 400.

4 A temple complex and royal pyramid burials at Jebel Barkal mark the site of Nubia's religious center from the 7th century BC to the 3rd century AD.

5 Axum became an early center of Christianity in Africa when King Ezana converted, around AD 350.

6 Taruga was the earliest and most important center of iron production in tropical west Africa c.480 BC.

7 Rhapta, somewhere on the Zanzibar channel, was a major ivory market used by Greco-Roman merchants.

8 The iron-production center at Castle Cavern (c.AD 400) was one of the earliest in southern Africa.

9 Khoisan-speaking peoples continued using late Stone Age technology despite the arrival of iron-mining peoples in southern Africa.

See also 27 (religion);
37 (rise of Islam)

The western half of the Roman empire, altogether poorer and less populated than the east, was also more exposed to Germanic barbarian attack. In 406 German tribes – Goths, Franks, Vandals and others – overran the Rhine frontier and by 476 the western Roman empire was almost entirely under their control. The wealthy eastern half of the Roman empire survived more or less unscathed and its emperor Justinian counter-attacked against the barbarians in the 530s, restoring Roman rule in Italy, north Africa and southern Spain (▷34). However, the empire was put back on the defensive after Justinian's death; much of Italy fell to the Lombards and most of southern Spain to the Visigoths by 600. The most successful of the Germanic invaders were the Franks, who had settled northern Gaul in the early 5th century. From 486 they were united by Clovis, who extended his kingdom into southern Gaul and east into Germany. By 600 the Frankish kingdom stretched from the Pyrenees almost to the Elbe. The end of Roman rule in Britain saw a revival of Celtic culture but in about 450 Angles and Saxons from north Germany began to settle the fertile east of Britain, driving the Celts to the hillier west.

Fear of the Huns drove the Germanic peoples to invade the Roman empire. The Huns extended their control as far west as the Rhine – further west than any steppe nomads in history – and raided both halves of the Roman empire under Attila (r. 433–453). However, after his death the Hun confederation broke up and returned to the steppes. Between 460 and 515 the Ephthalite (or "White") Huns destroyed the last Kushan principalities of central Asia, raided the Sasanian empire and conquered northwest India, only to be driven out in 528. On the eastern steppes, the Mongol-dominated Juan-juan confederacy was broken by a rebellion of the Turks in 552. By 600 the Turks had destroyed the Ephthalites and dominated the steppes as far west as the Aral Sea. The Khazars, another Turkic people, were established on the Caspian steppes. A part of the Juan-juan, the Avars, fled from the Turks and arrived on the European steppes in about 562 where they mopped up the remnants of the Huns and raided the Balkans. North of the Caucasus the Alans – the sole remnant of the Iranian peoples who had once dominated the steppes – re-emerged from Hunnic dominance in the 450s.

In Africa, Christianity had spread to Nubia and Axum by the 6th century, strengthening cultural and political links with the eastern Roman empire (▷35). With Roman encouragement, the Axumites conquered southwest Arabia in 528 but were expelled by the Sasanians in 574, ending Christian influence in Arabia just four years after the birth of Muhammad at Mecca. In west Africa intensive dry-rice farming led to a rising population on the upper Niger and the foundation of large villages in the 3rd and 4th centuries. One of these, Jenne-jeno, became the center of a wideranging network of west

**c.500** Foundation of the Huari empire in the highlands of Peru

**481–511** Reign of Clovis, undisputed Frankish king of Gaul from 486

**476** Fall of the western Roman empire when the the emperor Romulus is deposed

**c.450** The Angles and Saxons begin to settle eastern Britain

**410** The Visigoths, led by Alaric, sack Rome

**533–54** Roman emperor Justinian reconquers most of north Africa and Italy

TIMELINE

The Americas
Europe
Middle East
Africa
East and South Asia

400    450    500    550

**c.400** Iron working reaches southern Africa

**c.400** Jenne-jeno flourishes as the first town in west Africa

**429** A wealthy Vandal kingdom is set up in north Africa

**460–528** The Ephthalite Huns ("Hunas") invade northwest India

**c.470** Decline of the Gupta empire in northern India

**531–79** Sasanian Persia achieves its maximum extent under Chosroes I

**c.540** Christianity is introduced into Nubia

**c.550** The Turkish khanates are dominant throughout central Asia

Aleuts

Arctic marine mammal hunters

sub-Arctic forest hunter-gatherers

west coast foraging, hunting and fishing peoples

plateau fishers and hunter gatherers

desert hunter-gatherers

Basket makers

Plains bison hunters

Hopewell culture

eastern woodlands hunter-gatherers

Hohokam culture

Mogollon culture

maize farmers

Teotihuacán

Veracruz civilization

Monte Albán

Maya states

Cuba

Bahamas

Hispaniola

Puerto Rico

Caribbean hunter-gatherers

Caribbean farmers

Hawaiian Islands

North Andean chiefdoms

Amazonian chiefdoms

manioc farmers

MOCHE

HUARI EMPIRE

Polynesians

TIAHUANACO EMPIRE

savanna hunter-gatherers

farming (replacing hunter-gatherers)

South Andean hunter-gatherers

pampas hunter-gatherers

shellfish gatherers and marine mammal hunters

**hunter-gatherers**
**nomadic pastoralists**
**simple farming societies**
**complex farming societies/chiefdoms**
**state societies**
**uninhabited**
**Roman territory**
**other empires**
India-China trade route

Greenland
Iceland
Anglo-Saxons
Celts
Lapps
Scandinavians
Finns
Balts
Slavs
Saxons
Avars
Huns
Lombard principalities
FRANKISH KINGDOM
VISIGOTHIC KINGDOM
Berbers
EASTERN ROMAN EMPIRE
Alans
Khazars
Samoyed reindeer herders
Siberian taiga hunter-gatherers
Arctic marine mammal hunters
Kirghiz
Eastern Turk Khanate
Western Turk Khanate
Khitans (Mongols)
Turko-Mongol transhumant pastoralists
Ainu
Yayoi culture
KOGURYO
SILLA
PAEKCHE
YAMATO
Tú-yü-hun
SASANIAN EMPIRE
Arab nomads
camel nomads
HEJAZ
MAZUN
NOBATIA
MAKKURA
Jenne-jeno
cereal farmers and herders
ALWA
AXUM
Sasanian dependencies
TIBETAN KINGDOM
KANAUJ
Hindu kingdoms
SHASKANKA
CHALUKYAS
PALLAVAS
DVARAVATI
Hindu kingdoms
SIMHALA
Ceylon
SUI EMPIRE
Burmese pyu
Thai kingdoms
Mons
Taiwan
CHEN-LA (Khmer kingdom)
CHAMPA (Austronesians)
minor states and chiefdoms under Indian influence
Sumatra
Java
Borneo
Malays
Austronesians
Celebes
Timor
New Guinea
Papuan farmers
Micronesians
Melanesians
Polynesians
tropical forest farmers
western Bantu-speaking herders and farmers
eastern Bantu-speaking herders and farmers
Khoisan herders and gatherers
Khoisan hunter-gatherers
Madagascar
Austronesians
Australian Aboriginal hunter-gatherers
Tasmanian hunter-gatherers

**574** The Sasanian Persians conquer the Yemen

**c.570** Birth in Mecca of Muhammad, founder of Islam (dies 632)

**562** The Avar people invade the Balkans from the steppes

**622** The *hijra*, or flight of Muhammad from Mecca to Medina, marks the start of the Islamic era

**610** Accession of Heraclius in Constantinople: the Roman empire is now known as the Byzantine empire

**c.600** Mayan civilization is freed from Teotihuacán influence and reaches its greatest achievements

600

**570–620** Foundation of the Tibetan state

**589** The Sui dynasty reunites China, with a capital at Chang'an

**618** The Tang dynasty replaces the Sui in China

African trade routes; by 600 it was a walled city of ten thousand people.

The Gupta empire of India suffered a damaging war of succession in 467 and its authority never recovered (▷31). The empire stayed intact until the end of the century but by 530 northern India had fragmented. Successful barbarian conquerors of China tended to be assimilated by the far more numerous native population. Within a century of conquering the north the Toba Wei were thoroughly assimilated and acting much like any other Chinese dynasty, determined to fend off the steppe nomads. In 534 the Toba Wei kingdom split into two and by the 550s the Toba rulers had been replaced by native dynasties. However, China remained divided until reunified by Yang Jian, the founder of the Sui dynasty, in 589. In the mid-6th century a combination of rebellion and a shift of trade routes to the Malacca Straits caused the fall of the kingdom of Funan. In its place arose the Mon kingdom of Dvaravati and the Khmer kingdom of Chen-la. Both the Thai and Tibetan peoples formed their first kingdoms during the 6th century and several small states arose in Indonesia.

In Mesoamerica Teotihuacán reached its peak in the early 5th century but its power went into decline in the late 6th century and by 600 its influence on the Maya had ceased (▷39). By this time four main centers of Maya power had emerged. In Peru, climatic instability in the 6th century caused the decline of the coastal Moche state and power shifted to the highlands where the cities of Tiahuanaco and Huari had built considerable empires by 600 ∎

## Part 3

# THE MEDIEVAL

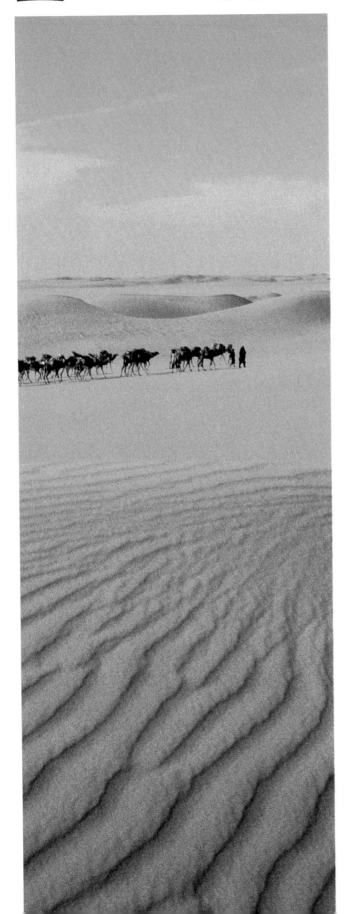

**S**hortly after AD 600, the Islamic community was founded in Medina under the leadership of prophet Muhammad. For many centuries Islam and other civilizations farther east were the world's most dynamic cultures. The year 1492, however, saw Columbus reach the Antilles, the prelude to the conquest and settlement of the New World by Europeans; six years later Vasco da Gama sailed around Africa to India. The foundation of western hegemony was thus laid by the end of the fifteenth century.

Just as the "barbarian" invasions of the fifth century AD led to the eclipse of the classical civilization of Europe, so the Muslim Arab expansion ended the domination of old Persian empires in the Middle East and the surviving Roman empire in the eastern Mediterranean. The intensity of the success of Islam is still unexplained, but there is no doubt about its significance. The unification of large parts of the Mediterranean, the Middle East, and the Indian Ocean by the Umayyad and Abbasid caliphates was a cultural, technological, and economic as well as a political achievement. The use of the Arabic language played an important role: the Bedouins of the Arabian peninsula, the Berber converts of north Africa, Arab conquerors in Andalusia, the Copts of Egypt, the Nabateans of Mesopotamia, and the converted Iranians all shared the Koranic prayers recited in Arabic and a common body of family and civil law.

Islam revitalized old cities and founded new ones. Both Medina and Mecca attracted a huge number of pilgrims each year, while Damascus became the first Islamic capital under the Umayyads, greatly enlarged by successive caliphs. Under the Abbasids, the capital shifted to Baghdad, the first planned capital city to be built by Muslims. This in turn was followed

THE CAMEL CARAVAN drew east and west together in trade and culture.

# WORLD

by Samarra. The Islamic world's great cities included Basra, Alexandria, Fustat, Cairo, Tunis, and Córdoba.

The urban gravitation of Islamic expansion required an economic surplus and food resources. This was achieved by bringing new land under cultivation and reviving existing regions of agricultural production. Arab engineers and farmers proved skilful in constructing irrigation projects. New plants such as hard wheat, sugar cane, citrus fruits, vegetables, and legumes were imported from India and southeast Asia and disseminated throughout the oasis agriculture of north Africa and into the arid areas of southern Spain.

Similar developments took place in China and southeast Asia. The Chinese perfected ways of containing the rivers of northern China to develop the rice-growing areas of Szechuan and the Yangtze valley. Population expansion, combined with the instability of climate, created a problem of feeding the world's most advanced empire. The Song emperors knew this problem to be a product of previous agricultural success, which had created crowded cities and rural areas. Relief in times of scarcity was provided by the state, which encouraged the cultivation of a strain of rice that ripened in two months, as against the three to six taken by traditional varieties.

Chinese civilization and administration was a matter of wonder to the rest of the world. China developed a class of professional bureaucratic administrators who were given formal instructions in writing and who had to report to the imperial court through written memoranda. Science, mathematics, and engineering flourished, and papermaking, the moving-type printing press and gunpowder were invented.

China's capacity for industrial production was evident in the quality of its porcelain and silk textiles. The Indian subcontinent had a similar lead in the production of cotton textiles. These products sustained a trade from the South China Sea to the eastern Mediterranean. Luxury goods were not the only articles of international trade. A network of trading cities grew up in response to the needs of this trade. Chinese ports such as Hangzhou were linked to Malacca in the tip of Malay peninsula, in turn connected to the seaports of India, the Gulf and the Red Sea. The city-states in east Africa completed the commercial rectangle.

The Mongol conquests dealt a severe blow to the ancient civilizations of the Indian Ocean and prepared the way for a resurgent Europe, where Arab intellectual knowledge had slowly penetrated through the intermediary of Jewish scholars and scientists living and working in Spain.

Europe's main contribution to world history to this point was its fighting technique. The adoption of the stirrup made it possible gradually to increase the armament of the mounted warrior using a heavy lance. A new breed of powerful horses appeared and the mounted knights were successful against the Turks during the Crusades. European success in the New World and the Indian Ocean later owed a great deal also to the invention of square-rigged ships armed with artillery capable of bombarding towns and cities. The reinforced hull made it possible to pierce gunports and add a gun-deck without encroaching on the vessel's cargo capacity. The result was a floating fortress that was also a floating warehouse.

European expansion was embedded in a larger process of scientific and intellectual advance. The new navigational methods – the use of compass, marine charts, mapmaking and astronomical navigation – were linked to the development of fighting ships. As a result, when, in the 15th century, Europeans sought routes to the east that would avoid the hostile Ottoman lands, the technology was at hand to enable them to dominate these new waters. The consequences were soon to be dramatically evident ■

The great empires of the Mediterranean and the Middle East had for centuries been accustomed to raids by Arab border tribes. Though troublesome, these raids were prevented from becoming a serious threat by the political disunity of the Arabs. However, this situation changed dramatically in the early 7th century as a result of the rise of Islam.

The faith of Islam (meaning "submission to the will of God") was founded by Muhammad (c.570–632), a member of the Meccan Quraysh tribe. From about 610, Muhammad began to experience the revelations that formed the basis of the *Koran*. Muhammad's espousal of monotheism met with opposition from the Quraysh, so to escape persecution the prophet and his followers fled in 622 to Medina, a commercial rival of Mecca. This event, the *hijra* (flight), marks the beginning of the Muslim era and is the first year of the Islamic calendar. Muhammad used Medina as a base to fight the Quraysh and in 630 he returned to Mecca in triumph. However, Muhammad continued to live at Medina, which became the capital of a theocratic Islamic state. In the last two years of his life, Muhammad used diplomacy and force to spread Islam to other Arab tribes.

Muhammad was succeeded by his father-in-law Abu Bakr, the first *caliph* (successor). After putting down an anti-Islamic rebellion, Abu Bakr completed the political and religious unification of the Arabs. Under the next two caliphs, Umar and Uthman, the Arabs began an explosive expansion which saw the Byzantine empire lose the rich and populous provinces of Syria, Palestine, Egypt and Libya, and the complete destruction of the Persian Sasanian empire. On Uthman's death civil war broke out between supporters of the caliph Ali, Muhammad's son-in-law, and Muawiya, a member of Uthman's Umayyad family. After Ali's murder in 661, Muawiya became caliph, founding the Umayyad dynasty. Ali's son Husain tried to win the caliphate on Muawiya's

death but was killed in battle with the Umayyads at Karbala in 680. Consequently, Islam split into its two main branches: the Sunnites (from *sunna*, "tradition of Muhammad"), who formed a majority, and the Shiites (from *shi'atu Ali*, "party of Ali").

Arab expansion continued under the early Umayyads and by 715 the Islamic caliphate, extending from the Indus and central Asia to the Pyrenees, was the largest state the world had yet seen. Yet their attempts to complete the conquest of the Byzantine

empire and the west failed, with two unsuccessful sieges of Constantinople in 677 and 717 and defeat by the Franks at Poitiers in 732.

The caliphs were both religious and political leaders. Whereas the early caliphs had been elected, the Umayyads introduced hereditary succession, claiming divine appointment and demanding total obedience. By adapting Byzantine bureaucracy, they created an administrative system capable of ruling a world empire. As this empire could not be ruled effectively from the remote Arabian city of Medina, Muawiya moved the capital to Damascus in 661. The Umayyad period saw the beginning of the successful Arabization of the conquered populations through conversion to Islam, the adoption of Arabic as a common language, and by intermarriage. The Arabs in turn were influenced by the Persian and Byzantine civilizations that they had conquered. One of the most important cultural developments of

**1** Mecca was an important trading city and the main cult center for the pre-Islamic Arabs' pagan religion.

**2** Arab military settlements, such as Al-Fustat (Cairo), were sited close to the edge of the desert, where the Arabs could take refuge in the event of rebellions.

**3** The Taurus mountains proved an effective barrier against further Arab conquests in Anatolia.

**4** The last Sasanian king, Yezdegird III, was murdered near Merv in 652, so ending Persian resistance.

**5** Karbala became a major pilgrimage site for Shiite Muslims after Husain, Muhammad's grandson, was killed there by the Umayyads.

**6** With the transfer of the Arab capital to Damascus in 661, Arabia gradually declined in significance.

**7** The two attempts by the Arabs to take the heavily fortified city of Constantinople were costly failures.

**8** Berber resistance to the Arabs was fierce; they were only subdued and converted to Islam in 702.

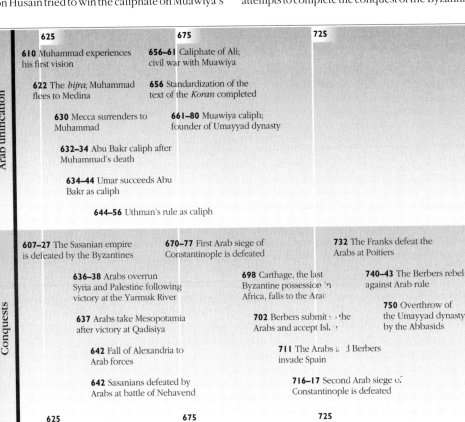

## TIMELINE

### Arab unification

| 625 | 675 | 725 |
|---|---|---|
| **610** Muhammad experiences his first vision | **656–61** Caliphate of Ali; civil war with Muawiya | |
| **622** The *hijra*; Muhammad flees to Medina | **656** Standardization of the text of the *Koran* completed | |
| **630** Mecca surrenders to Muhammad | **661–80** Muawiya caliph; founder of Umayyad dynasty | |
| **632–34** Abu Bakr caliph after Muhammad's death | | |
| **634–44** Umar succeeds Abu Bakr as caliph | | |
| **644–56** Uthman's rule as caliph | | |

### Conquests

| 625 | 675 | 725 |
|---|---|---|
| **607–27** The Sasanian empire is defeated by the Byzantines | **670–77** First Arab siege of Constantinople is defeated | **732** The Franks defeat the Arabs at Poitiers |
| **636–38** Arabs overrun Syria and Palestine following victory at the Yarmuk River | **698** Carthage, the last Byzantine possession in Africa, falls to the Arabs | **740–43** The Berbers rebel against Arab rule |
| **637** Arabs take Mesopotamia after victory at Qadisiya | **702** Berbers submit to the Arabs and accept Islam | **750** Overthrow of the Umayyad dynasty by the Abbasids |
| **642** Fall of Alexandria to Arab forces | **711** The Arabs and Berbers invade Spain | |
| **642** Sasanians defeated by Arabs at battle of Nehavend | **716–17** Second Arab siege of Constantinople is defeated | |

Slavs

Bulgars

Alans

Khazars

*Black Sea*

Aral Sea

WESTERN TURK KHANATE

FERGHANA

early 8th century

CAUCASUS MTS

*Caspian Sea*

713

710

Bukhara 710

Samarkand 710

SOGHD

Balkh 652

Merv 650

652

HINDU KUSH

*Indus*

KASHMIR

7

Constantinople 670–677, 716–717

716

ANATOLIA

3

TAURUS MTS

ARMENIA

Ardebil 643

TABARISTAN

Qazvin 643

731

Rayy 643

637–43

KHORASAN

Herat 650

650

SEISTAN

Kabul 664

Battle of the Masts 655

670

*Cyprus*

Edessa 639
Dabiq
Harran

Aleppo 638

Antioch 638

Hamah 635

Tripoli 638

MESOPOTAMIA

ZAGROS MTS

Jafula 638

*Tigris*

*Euphrates*

Nehavend 642

SASANIAN EMPIRE

PERSIA

Multan 713

*Yamuna*

EMPIRE OF HARSHA

6

Karbala 680

Ctesiphon 637

Wasit

637

Persepolis 648

650

*Helmand*

Gurjaras

Yarmuk 636

Damascus 635

Minya
Ramallah
Jerusalem 638

Alexandria 642

42–43

Al-Fustat 642

2

Kufa 638

633–38

Al Qadisiya 637

Quseir Amra

Qasr el Mshatta

Ajnadain 634

Mu'tah 629

Heliopolis 640

EGYPT

652

*Nile*

*Red Sea*

640

*Ghassan*

*Kalb*

*Lakhm*

*Bakr*

Battle of the Camel 657

*Persian Gulf*

Basra 638

Siraf

643

SIND

*Indus*

MAKRAN

Valabhi

5

633–38

637–43

HEIJAZ

*Ghatafan*

632–33

*Juheina*

*Kinda*

BAHRAYN

*Hanifah*

Al-Yamama 632

OMAN

Mt Uhud 625

Medina

Bedr 624

Mecca

*Sulaym*

*Quraysh*

ARABIA

*Hawazin*

*Azd*

633–38

632–33

*Mahrah*

NOBATIA

Dongola

MAKKURA

ALWA

AXUM

HADRAMAUT

YEMEN

*Himyar*

BEDOUIN nomad tribesmen in Arabia (shown in this illuminated manuscript) were united by Islam.

0        900 km
0        600 mi

—— border at the death of Muhammad, 632

▨ Arabs practicing Islam, 632

growth of the Arab caliphate

▨ at the death of Abu Bakr, 634

▨ at the death of Uthman, 656

☐ at the fall of the Umayyad dynasty, 750

▨ Monophysite Christians within the Byzantine empire

➔ Arab campaign or raid, with date

⌂ Amsar (Arab military settlement), 638–670

⌂ Umayyad mosque

⌂ Umayyad palace

Kufa Umayyad cultural center

⊗ Arab victory

⊗ Arab defeat

⊗ battle between Arabs

*Azd* Arab tribe

➔ expansion of Chinese Tang empire

the Umayyad period was the construction of the first mosques as centers for Islamic worship.

Many factors explain the swift rise of the Arabs in the 7th century. Before Islam, inter-tribal feuding had played a major role as a means of winning status and booty. Muhammad's unification of the Arabs channeled the warrior tradition into raids on the neighboring Byzantine and Sasanian empires. The united Arab armies, now larger and more effective, rapidly overran new territories. Both empires were completely unprepared for the Arab invasions. The Sasanian empire was torn by civil war after its defeat by Byzantium, and organized resistance quickly collapsed after the Arab victory at Nehavend in 642. The Byzantine empire also had internal problems. The Monophysite Christian populations of Syria, Palestine and Egypt, who had suffered years

of persecution by Constantinople, welcomed the Arabs as liberators. Similarly, the Visigothic kingdom of Spain also collapsed through internal divisions. Moreover, Arab soldiers were motivated by Muhammad's pledge that Islamic warriors who died in battle would win immediate entry to paradise.

While the barbarian invasions of the 5th century began the collapse of the Classical world, it was the Arab conquests that marked the final break with the past. As a result of these, a new religion, language and culture were imposed on the Middle East, north Africa and Spain. Few of the areas claimed by the Arabs for Islam have since been lost to it.

See also 38 (Carolingians);
44 (world religions); 47 (Turkish empires)

O f the Germanic kingdoms set up within the territory of the western Roman empire in the 5th century, only the Frankish and the Visigothic still survived in 600. The Visigothic kings preserved the late Roman administrative structure but, in contrast to the Franks, who were able to win the cooperation and loyalty of their subjects, they remained distant from their Hispano-Roman subjects. This was a fatal weakness. Faced with an invasion of Muslim Arabs and Berbers from North Africa in 711, the Visigoths received no support and the kingdom abruptly collapsed. The invaders took only two years to overrun most of the Iberian peninsula, bringing it within the Umayyad caliphate. Only in the mountains of the far north was there substantial resistance. Here the small Christian kingdom of Asturias developed, based at Oviedo. By 800 it had won back a sizable part of the northwest peninsula from the Arabs.

Since the mid 5th century the Merovingian dynasty had ruled the Frankish kingdom. They followed the Germanic custom of dividing the kingdom between all male heirs, leading to a complex sequence of subdivisions as generation succeeded generation. The succession was rarely a simple matter, and civil wars and assassinations were frequent. In the mid 7th century real authority passed into the hands of court officials known as the mayors of the palace. Frankish power declined and some peripheral areas of the kingdom were lost. Most were recovered early in the 8th century but Aquitaine, which broke away in 670, was not taken back until 768. The most successful of the mayors was Pepin II of Herstal (mayor 679–714), who was effective ruler of the entire kingdom by 687. Founder of the Carolingian dynasty, he began an expansion of Frankish power which continued under his son Charles Martel (mayor 714–41). In 732 he turned back an Arab invasion at Poitiers, ending Muslim expansion in the west.

Charles' successor Pepin III (r.741–68) formed an alliance with the papacy in 751. The year before, the

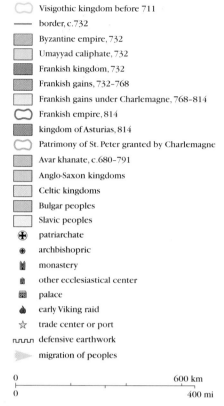

Visigothic kingdom before 711
border, c.732
Byzantine empire, 732
Umayyad caliphate, 732
Frankish kingdom, 732
Frankish gains, 732–768
Frankish gains under Charlemagne, 768–814
Frankish empire, 814
kingdom of Asturias, 814
Patrimony of St. Peter granted by Charlemagne
Avar khanate, c.680–791
Anglo-Saxon kingdoms
Celtic kingdoms
Bulgar peoples
Slavic peoples
⊕ patriarchate
✳ archbishopric
🏰 monastery
🏛 other ecclesiastical center
🏯 palace
🌢 early Viking raid
☆ trade center or port
⌇⌇ defensive earthwork
➤ migration of peoples

0                         600 km
0                         400 mi

Lombards (rulers of most of Italy since 568) had conquered the Byzantine exarchate of Ravenna and were threatening Rome itself. In return for military aid, the pope authorized Pepin to depose the last Merovingian king and assume the kingship of the Franks himself. Pepin died in 768, and the kingdom was divided between his two sons, Charlemagne and Carloman. On the latter's death in 771 Charlemagne was sole ruler; he doubled the size of the Frankish realm in thirty years of campaigning. He

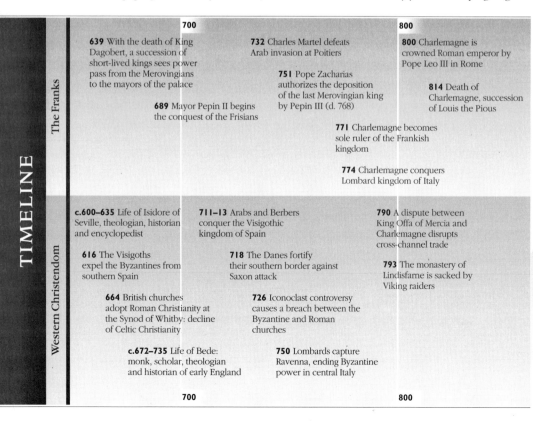

**TIMELINE**

**The Franks**

**700**

**639** With the death of King Dagobert, a succession of short-lived kings sees power pass from the Merovingians to the mayors of the palace

**689** Mayor Pepin II begins the conquest of the Frisians

**732** Charles Martel defeats Arab invasion at Poitiers

**751** Pope Zacharias authorizes the deposition of the last Merovingian king by Pepin III (d. 768)

**771** Charlemagne becomes sole ruler of the Frankish kingdom

**774** Charlemagne conquers Lombard kingdom of Italy

**800**

**800** Charlemagne is crowned Roman emperor by Pope Leo III in Rome

**814** Death of Charlemagne, succession of Louis the Pious

**Western Christendom**

**c.600–635** Life of Isidore of Seville, theologian, historian and encyclopedist

**616** The Visigoths expel the Byzantines from southern Spain

**664** British churches adopt Roman Christianity at the Synod of Whitby: decline of Celtic Christianity

**c.672–735** Life of Bede: monk, scholar, theologian and historian of early England

**711–13** Arabs and Berbers conquer the Visigothic kingdom of Spain

**718** The Danes fortify their southern border against Saxon attack

**726** Iconoclast controversy causes a breach between the Byzantine and Roman churches

**750** Lombards capture Ravenna, ending Byzantine power in central Italy

**790** A dispute between King Offa of Mercia and Charlemagne disrupts cross-channel trade

**793** The monastery of Lindisfarne is sacked by Viking raiders

**700**                    **800**

was also an energetic legislator and administrator and was devoutly religious, even intervening in matters of doctrine. He promoted missionary activity among the pagan Saxons in the northeast and, anxious to improve the quality of the clergy, encouraged the revival of classical learning known as the Carolingian renaissance. Charlemagne made considerable donations of land to the papacy and, influenced by Byzantine ideas of rulership, had himself crowned emperor by the pope on Christmas Day 800, an act he probably saw as restoring the Roman empire in the west. In line with Frankish custom, Charlemagne made provisions for his empire to be divided between his three sons after his death but was survived by only one, Louis the Pious.

In the British Isles, the Anglo-Saxons had overrun most of the fertile lowland zone by 600 and were

**Norse**

**Svear**

**Götar**

**Danes**

**Finns**

**Slovianians**

**Mazovians**

**Pomeranians**

**Wiltzites**

**Poles**

**Derevlians**

**Volhynians**

**Balts**

**Abodrites**

**Sorbs**

**Bohemians**

CHARLEMAGNE, king of the Franks, controlled most of Christian western Europe by 800. This bronze statue is from Metz.

Kaupang
Vänern
Birka
Vättern
North Sea
Baltic Sea
Grobin
Ribe
Reric
Hedeby
Frisians
Bardowick
Scheessel
734
782
Utrecht
Dorestad
Domburg
Saxons
Paderborn
Magdeburg
Aachen
Cologne
Herstal
Erfurt
Fulda
Prüm
Thuringia
Frankfurt
Mainz
Lorsch
Regensburg
St Emmeram
Metz
Thionville
Alemannia
Salzburg
Bavaria
St Gall
Lorch
Carinthia

Nechtansmere 685
disfarne
ORTHUMBRIA
row
Whitby
ork
MERCIA
EAST ANGLIA
amworth
Ipswich
ondon
Canterbury
KENT
amwih
8
Quentovic
Austrasia
Rouen
eustria
Reims
Paris
Sens
Langres
ours
ourges
Poitiers 732
QUITAINE
Lyon
Vienne
Burgundy
Besançon
Moissac
Arles
ulouse
Marseille
epti-nania
Narbonne
Gerona
Barcelona
Balearic Islands
813

**Slovianians**

I. Ladoga
Staraja Ladoga
9
Lake Peipus
Western Dvina

**Avar Khanate**

Danube
Pannonia
Sava
Croats
Serbs
Vlachs

**Bulgar Khanate**

Pliska
Danube

**Goths**

Magyars, c.800
CARPATHIAN MTS

Milan
Pavia
Po
Venice
Bobbio
Comacchio
Ravenna
Aquileia
KINGDOM OF THE LOMBARDS
Luna
Exarchate of Ravenna
Spoleto
Farfa
DUCHY OF SPOLETO
806, 807
Corsica
Rome
1
Monte Cassino
Benevento
Bari
Naples
Salerno
DUCHY OF BENEVENTO
Sardinia
Cagliari
Palermo
Reggio
Sicily
Syracuse
Tunis
Malta

Split
Ragusa
Dyrrhachium
Thessalonica
Athens
Corinth

**Black Sea**

Constantinople
Abydos
ANATOLIA
BYZANTINE EMPIRE
(Eastern Roman empire before 610)
Ephesus
Rhodes
Cyprus
Crete

*North Sea*

*Baltic Sea*

*Vistula*
*Oder*
*Elbe*
*Rhine*
*Danube*
*Loire*
*Rhone*

*Mediterranean Sea*

## UMAYYAD CALIPHATE

beginning to form regional kingdoms, the most powerful being Northumbria. The Anglo-Saxon migrations into southern Britain had cut off British Christianity from contact with the Roman church. The Celtic church developed a distinctive identity and in Ireland fostered the creation of a monastic civilization that was to have significant influence on cultural and religious life in Europe. Irish and Roman missionaries both won converts among the Anglo-Saxons in the 7th century, and it was only with difficulty that the Celtic church was persuaded to rejoin the Roman church in 664. Northumbrian power declined after defeat by the Picts in 685, and in the 8th century the Mercian kingdom rose to dominance under Aethelbald (r.716–57) and Offa (r.757–96).

Frankish overrule brought a modest revival of trade and towns to western Europe, most marked around the southern North Sea and the Baltic, where ports and seasonal trading places developed by 800. Though threatened by the Viking raids that broke out in the 790s, it was the start of the process that shifted the focus of economic life from the Mediterranean to the North Sea and Atlantic coasts.

**1** Rome found a new role as the seat of the papacy and the spiritual capital of western Christendom.

**2** The Asturian victory at Covadonga is regarded as the beginning of the Christian reconquest of Spain.

**3** King Offa of Mercia built a 240km (185 mile) earth and timber rampart on his frontier with the Welsh.

**4** The Bretons fiercely resisted Frankish expansion: subdued by Charlemagne in 799, they revolted in 812.

**5** Charlemagne built an impressive palace, administrative and ecclesiastical complex at Aachen in the 790s.

**6** Charlemagne set up a chain of customs posts to regulate trade with the Slavs in 806.

**7** Córdoba, the capital of Muslim Spain, was the largest city in western Europe by the 9th century.

**8** Trading centers such as Hamwih and Quentovic were evidence of the growing commercial importance of northern Europe.

**9** Scandinavian merchants were established at the Finnic settlement of Staraja Ladoga by 750.

See also 33 (fall of Roman empire); 37 (Arab conquests); 41 (Viking age)

The most sophisticated of the pre-Columbian civilizations of the Americas was the Maya of Guatemala, Petén and Yucatán. By draining and canalizing the swamplands, agricultural production rose in the Middle Preclassic period (700–300 BC), making it possible to support large populations. Chiefdoms and small states appeared and the first towns and monumental structures were built. During the Late Preclassic (300 BC–AD 300) powerful city-states emerged, writing came into use, advanced mathematical and astronomical studies were pursued, and a calendrical system was adopted. The new states were competitive and warlike and many cities were fortified. Underlying these developments may have been such factors as population pressure, agricultural intensification, long-distance trade and increased warfare. The main influences on the development of Mayan civilization were the Olmecs and the Zapotecs, from whom the Maya received, among other things, the 52-year "long count" calendar, writing and the sacred ball game.

The most important Maya center of the Late Preclassic period was the city of El Mirador, occupied 150 BC–AD 150. It had large temple pyramids, a fortified palace area, marketplaces and a population approaching 80,000. Causeways known as *sacbes* linked El Mirador with its subordinate villages. Although there is some evidence of writing at El Mirador, the best evidence for its use by the Preclassic Maya comes from the southern highland area, where many *stelae* (stone monuments) were erected at sites like Kaminaljuyú, in the 1st and 2nd centuries AD, to commemorate royal ancestors. The earliest known inscription, found at El Baul, carries a "long-count" date equivalent to AD 36. The Maya did not invent writing themselves, but their hieroglyphic script was the only pre-Columbian script that could fully express the spoken language. The Mayan script included both ideographic and phonetic elements. About 800 glyphs are known. The southern Maya declined in the 3rd century AD and the tradition of erecting commemorative *stelae* died out. The cause was probably a volcanic eruption that blew apart

Mount Ilopango, covering thousands of square kilometers with ash and ruining agriculture for years.

Commemorative *stelae* with hieroglyphic inscriptions began to be erected by the Maya in the central lowland rainforest area around AD 300, a development that marks the beginning of the Classic period (AD 300–800). The earliest show clear stylistic links with the highland Maya. Until about AD 400 *stelae* were only erected at Tikal, Uaxactún and a few nearby centers, but thereafter the practice spread throughout the central area. Palenque, Yaxchilán, Copán and Calakmul all developed into major regional powers, but the dominant city-state for much of the Classic period was Tikal, with a population of 75,000–100,000. At its peak under King Stormy Sky (r.411–57), Tikal dominated most of the central area and maintained cultural and trade links with Teotihuacán, the greatest power in Mesoamerica. Tikal went into decline after its defeat by Caracol in 562; and although it recovered under Ah Cacau (r.682–723) it did not regain its preeminence.

Warfare was common among the Classic Maya city-states, although the aim was more often to exact tribute and take prisoners than to annex territory permanently. The normal fate of prisoners was ritual torture and mutilation, after which they were sacrificed to the gods. Human sacrifices were needed to dedicate new temples, to accompany the dead and to mark important events such as the completion of calendrical cycles. Mayan rulers were expected to take part in painful bloodletting rites as a means of communicating with ancestral spirits. Marriage alliances were the usual means of forging friendly relations between states.

| | |
|---|---|
| ◈ | late Preclassic site with monumental sculpture, 300 BC–AD 300 |
| ○ | other late Preclassic site, 300 BC–AD 300 |
| ▨ | area of Classic Maya civilization, AD 300–800 |
| ▨ | Puuc style |
| ▨ | Chenes style |
| ▨ | Rio Bec style |
| ▨ | Cotzumalhuapan style |
| ◈ | major Classic site |
| ● | minor Classic site |
| ◈ | pre-eminent regional center |
| ▨ | influence of Tikal, 5th century AD |
| Tikal | dynastic histories deciphered |
| —— | city-state border, AD 790 |
| ---- | trade route |
| *cacao* | source of traded commodity |

area with intensive agriculture

| | |
|---|---|
| ▢ | raised fields |
| ▢ | stone-faced terraces |

0                    200 km
0                              150 mi

MOSAIC jade mask found at Palenque, possibly a representation of Pacal, ruler of Palenque in the 7th century.

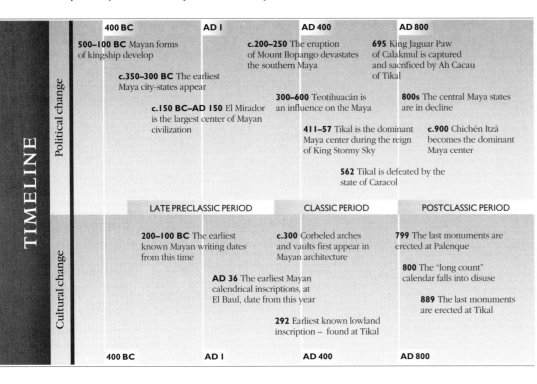

## TIMELINE

|  | 400 BC | AD I | AD 400 | AD 800 |
|---|---|---|---|---|
| **Political change** | **500–100 BC** Mayan forms of kingship develop | | **c.200–250** The eruption of Mount Ilopango devastates the southern Maya | **695** King Jaguar Paw of Calakmul is captured and sacrificed by Ah Cacau of Tikal |
| | **c.350–300 BC** The earliest Maya city-states appear | | | |
| | | **c.150 BC–AD 150** El Mirador is the largest center of Mayan civilization | **300–600** Teotihuacán is an influence on the Maya | **800s** The central Maya states are in decline |
| | | | **411–57** Tikal is the dominant Maya center during the reign of King Stormy Sky | **c.900** Chichén Itzá becomes the dominant Maya center |
| | | | **562** Tikal is defeated by the state of Caracol | |
| | | LATE PRECLASSIC PERIOD | CLASSIC PERIOD | POSTCLASSIC PERIOD |
| **Cultural change** | **200–100 BC** The earliest known Mayan writing dates from this time | | **c.300** Corbeled arches and vaults first appear in Mayan architecture | **799** The last monuments are erected at Palenque |
| | | **AD 36** The earliest Mayan calendrical inscriptions, at El Baul, date from this year | | **800** The "long count" calendar falls into disuse |
| | | | | **889** The last monuments are erected at Tikal |
| | | | **292** Earliest known lowland inscription – found at Tikal | |
| | 400 BC | AD I | AD 400 | AD 800 |

**1** El Mirador was the largest Maya center in the Late Preclassic period, before being abandoned c.AD 150.

**2** Lake Ilopango now fills the crater left by the catastrophic eruption of Mount Ilopango c.AD 200–250, which caused the decline of the southern Maya .

**3** Tikal was the largest Maya city. It reached its peak under King Stormy Sky (r.AD 411–57) and dominated the central Maya until conquered by Caracol in 562.

**4** Classic Maya ceremonial centers were often aligned on astronomical events. The earliest such center, at Uaxactún, was aligned on the midwinter, equinoctial and midsummer sunrises.

**5** Copán, a major Maya center during the Classic period, was supplanted by Quirigua in 738.

**6** The raised causeway, or *sacbe*, linking Cobá with Yaxuná runs for some 100 kilometers (62 miles).

**7** Murals at Bonampak celebrating a victory of King Chan Muan c.790 provide vivid evidence of the warlike character of Maya civilization.

**8** Power and population moved to the north in the Early Postclassic period (AD 900–1200), when Chichén Itzá became the dominant Maya center.

Komchen
Dzibilchaltún
Izamal
Acanceh
*feathers slaves*
Chichén Itzá
Cobá
*feathers slaves*
Oxkintok
Yaxuná
Uxmal
Mul-Chic
Chacchob
Isla de Cozumel
Kabah
Loltun
Jaina
Xcalumkin
Sayil
Chacmultún
Keuic
Labná
Xcichmook
Xcocha
Tancah
Yucatán Peninsula
Xtampak
Dzibilnocac
Huntichmul
Edzná
NORTHERN AREA
Hochob

*Gulf of Mexico*

Pechal
*cacao*
Becan
Xpuhil
Hormiguero
Pasión del Cristo
Rio Bec
Uaacbal
Cohunlich
Cerros
Candelaria
Oxpemul
La Muñeca
Nohmul
Cuello
Calakmul
El Palmar
Colhá
Naachlún
Altamira
Bellote
Balakbal
Altun Ha
Comalcalco
Ucal
Rio Azul
Jonuta
Balancán
El Mirador
La Honradez
Lamanaí
Morales
*cacao*
Tortuguero
Pomoná
CENTRAL AREA
Nakum
Xullún
San José
Palenque
Chinikhá
PETÉN
Uaxactún
Baking Pot
El Porvenir
El Perú
Tikal
Naranjo
Piedras Negras
Uolaritún
Yaxhá
Xunantunich
La Mar
El Cayo
Mótul de San José
Mountain Cow
Toniniá
Yaxchilán
*Lago Peten Itzá*
Caracol
Chiapa de Corzo
Lacanhá
Bonampak
Pomona
San Augustin
Agua Escondida
Itzán
El Caribe
*cacao*
Sacul
Santa Elena
La Armelia
Seibal
Ixtutz
Poco Uinic
Altar de Sacrificios
Nimli Punit
Santa Cruz
Dos Pilas
Machaquitá
Lubaantin
*Grijalba*
Aguateca
Cancuén
Pusihá
*marine products and shells*
Chinkultic
Salinas de los Nueve Cerros
*feathers obsidian salt*
*cacao*
Quen Santo
Chamá
*cacao*
Lagartero
Santa Rica
*Lago de Izabal*
Nebaj
Quirigua
Los Higos
*cacao feathers*
La Lagunita
San Agustin Acasaguastián
El Paraiso
*Motagua*
*cacao jade*
Copán
*Guatemalan Highlands*
*jade*
Izapa
*Lago de Atitlán*
*obsidian*
Takalik
Kaminaljuyú
*jade*
Yarumela
El Jobo
Chucumuk
El Baul
Asuncion Mita
Salinac la Bianca
Tiquisate
Pantaleon
Amatitián
*obsidian*
Chalchuapa
*Lempa*
Monti Alto
Obero
Tazumal
Finca Arizona
*Lake Ilopango*

*PACIFIC OCEAN*

Usulutan

The civilization of the Classic Maya was not uniform: several regional decorative styles are known, and there was considerable variation in architectural styles. The Maya were highly skilled craftsmen, producing monumental stone sculpture, jade carving, pottery, paintings and obsidian tools of the highest quality. A few gold and copper objects have been found at Mayan sites, but metals were little used before Postclassic times.

The Classic period came to an end around the beginning of the 9th century, when the city-states of the central lowlands began to collapse. The population declined dramatically, new building ceased, and the tradition of erecting commemorative *stelae* was abandoned. The last monuments were erected at Palenque in 799, at Yaxchilan in 808, at Quirigua 810, at Copán in 822 and Tikal in 889. By 950 all the major central Mayan cities lay in ruins. The "long count" calendar fell out of use.

The collapse is thought to be an indirect consequence of the fall of Teotihuacán around 750. Mayan rulers competed, through warfare and by commissioning more and more ambitious building projects, to fill the power vacuum created by the fall of Teotihuacán. Pressures on the peasantry to supply food and labor increased to such a point that the agricultural economy collapsed; malnutrition, population decline and political collapse followed. Classic Mayan civilization did not die out, but continued to flourish in the semiarid north of the Yucatán peninsula until around 1000, when the area was invaded by the Toltecs, from central Mexico.

See also 17 (first civilizations of Mesoamerica);
55 (Toltecs and late Maya)

The years between AD 600 and 800 saw the final breakup of the world of classical antiquity and the dramatic rise of an Arab Islamic civilization. Islam has its origins in the teachings of Muhammad (c.570–632). Islam united the Arabs and created a theocratic state. Despite civil war after the prophet's death, the caliph or "successor" Umar turned Arab energies outward in campaigns of conquest and conversion (▷ 37).

Circumstances were favorable to Arab expansion. From 602 to 627 the Persian Sasanian empire and the surviving eastern half of the Roman empire were locked in total war. The Romans emerged triumphant but the reforms introduced by the emperor Heraclius created an essentially new Greek state, known as the Byzantine empire. Neither Persia nor Byzantium was thus in a fit state to withstand the sudden invasions of Arab armies, which began with the capture of Damascus in 635. By 642 the Arabs had captured Syria, Palestine and Egypt from the Byzantines and completely destroyed the Sasanian empire. A second wave of conquests began after the Umayyad dynasty came to power in 661. In 698 Byzantine Carthage fell and in 711 the Arabs crossed the Straits of Gibraltar and conquered the Visigothic kingdom of Spain. In the east Arab armies reached the Indus and Samarkand. Failure to take Constantinople in 717 and defeat by the Franks at Poitiers in 732 marked the end of the Arab victories. The unity of the Arab world ended in 749–50 when the Umayyads were overthrown and slaughtered by the Abbasids, except for one who escaped to Spain and founded an independent state. By 800 the Abbasids had also lost control of Morocco and Tunisia.

In 600 the Frankish kingdom was the leading state in western Europe, but dynastic instability led to a decline in the late 7th century (▷ 38). Frankish power recovered under the Carolingian dynasty, named for Charlemagne, who controlled most of Christian western Europe and expanded into the pagan lands of eastern Europe. He was crowned Roman emperor by the pope in Rome on Christmas Day, 800. In the British Isles, the Anglo-Saxons confined the Celts to the hilly west. The Scandinavians were beginning state formation, a by-product of which was the onset of Viking raids on western Europe.

China, divided for almost four centuries, was reunited by the Sui dynasty in 589 (▷ 43). The Sui's ambitions overstretched the empire's resources and they were overthrown by the Tang dynasty in 618. China flourished under the early Tang emperors and campaigns in central Asia extended

**Map labels:**
Arctic marine mammal hunters
sub-Arctic forest hunter-gatherers
Aleuts
plateau fishers and hunter-gatherers
west coast foraging, hunting and fishing peoples
desert hunter-gatherers
plains bison hunters
eastern woodlands hunter-gatherers and cultivators
Anasazi culture
Mississippian temple-mound builders
Hohokam culture
Mogollon culture
desert hunter-gatherers
TOLTEC EMPIRE
Bahamas
maize farmers
Cuba
Carib farmers
Mesoamerican city-states
Maya city-states
Hispaniola
MONTE ALBÁN (Zapotecs)
Hawaiian Islands
north Andean chiefdoms
Amazonian chiefdoms
manioc farmers
Polynesians
HUARI EMPIRE
farming replacing hunter-gathering
TIAHUANACO EMPIRE
savanna hunter-gatherers
pampas hunter-gatherers
shellfish gatherers and marine mammal hunters

**Timeline:**

**622** Muhammad flees from Mecca to Medina (hijra); beginning of the Islamic calendar

**634** Umar, the second caliph, becomes "ruler of the faithful"

**610** Accession of Heraclius; Eastern Roman empire is now known as the Byzantine empire

**661** Caliph Muawiya founds the Umayyad dynasty

**711** The Arabs invade and conquer Spain

| The Americas |
| Europe |
| Middle East |
| Africa |
| East and South Asia |

600 · 650 · 700

**589** The Sui dynasty reunifies China after 400 years of division

**606** Harsha, king of Kanauj, conquers northern India

**618** The Tang dynasty replaces the Sui in China

**636–42** The Arabs conquer Palestine, Egypt and the Sasanian empire

**659** Chinese power reaches its maximum extent in central Asia

**676** The Korean peninsula is united by the kingdom of Silla

**c.700** Teotihuacán, largest city in Mesoamerica, is sacked and abandoned

**c.700** The Huari empire of Peru conquers the Moche state

**c. 700** Emergence of the kingdom of Ghana in west Africa

hunter-gatherers
nomadic pastoralists
simple farming societies
complex farming societies/
chiefdoms
state societies
uninhabited
empires

Greenland

Iceland

Lapps

*Arctic marine
mammal hunters*

*Siberian
hunter-gatherers*

Celtic
kingdoms

Scandinavians

Finns

Balts

Samoyed reindeer
herders

*Tungusic and Yakut
reindeer herders*

*Ainu
hunter-gatherers*

Anglo–Saxon
kingdoms

Slavs

Magyars

Volga
Bulgars

Kirghiz

Khitans
(Mongols)

CAROLINGIAN
EMPIRE

ASTURIAS

Danube
Bulgars

Turkic nomads

Uighurs

PARHAE

SILLA

Khazars

UMAYYAD
CALIPHATE

Lombard
duchies

BYZANTINE EMPIRE

TIBETAN
EMPIRE

TANG
EMPIRE

JAPAN

IDRISID CALIPHATE

AGHLABID
EMIRATE

ABBASID CALIPHATE

Hindu
states

Burmese

NAN
CHAO

*camel nomads*

MAKKURA

GURJARA-
PRATIHARA

Hindu
states

Pyu
state

Thais

CHAMPA

*Austronesians*

GHANA

ALWA

AXUM

Rashtrakuta
state

Mon
state

CHEN-LA

*Micronesians*

*west African chiefdoms*

Pandya
state

DVARAVATI

Pallava
state

Taiwan

*pastoral
nomads*

Sinhalese
kingdoms

Ceylon

Celebes

*western Bantu-speaking
forest farmers*

*eastern Bantu-speaking
herders and farmers*

minor Hindu &
Buddhist states

SRIVIJAYA
EMPIRE

Borneo

New Guinea

*Papuan
farmers*

Sumatra

*Melanesians*

Malagasay

*Madagascar*

MATARAM

Java

Timor

*San hunter-
gatherers*

*Khoisan herders*

*Australian Aboriginal
hunter-gatherers*

*Polynesians*

*Tasmanian
hunter-gatherers*

**750–800** The Toltecs
begin to move into
the Valley of Mexico

**750** The Abbasids usurp
the Umayyad dynasty and
rule most of the Arab
world from Baghdad

**c. 800** Decline of Maya
city-states in the southern
lowlands of Mesoamerica

**732** The Franks defeat
the Arabs at Poitiers,
halting their expansion
in the west

**800** Charlemagne, king
of the Franks, is crowned
Roman emperor

750

800

**751** At the battle
of Talas river near
Samarkand, Chinese
expansion is halted by
the Arab advance

**793** Beginning of Viking
(Norseman) raids on
western Europe

**794** The classical
Heian period in Japan
is established by emperor
Kammu, who moves his
capital to Kyoto

their control as far as Samarkand
by the early 8th century. A defeat by
the Arabs in 751 caused this central Asian
empire to fall, mainly to the Turks and the Tibetans.
By 800 Tibetan control extended south of the Himalayas to the Bay of Bengal.

Although Harsha (r.606–47), ruler of the northern Indian kingdom of
Kanauj, united much of northern India, his achievement did not outlast his
death and in 800 no kingdom was preeminent. The most important kingdoms
of mainland southeast Asia were the Khmer kingdom of Chen-la, the
Austronesian kingdom of Champa and the Thai kingdom of Nan Chao. The
maritime empire of Srivijaya dominated Malaysia and Indonesia.

Complex societies had developed across most of west Africa by 800 and
one state, the kingdom of Ghana, had arisen in the Sahel. Trans-Saharan trade
played a role in state formation in this region but most of the impetus was
local. In South America the Huari and Tiahuanaco empires were at their peaks
in 800, but the Classic Mesoamerican civilizations were in decline.
Teotihuacán was sacked around 700 and a century later the Maya cities of the
central lowlands began to be abandoned. The Toltecs migrated from northern
Mexico into the power vacuum created by the fall of Teotihuacán (▷ 55). The
first North American societies to depend on farming developed in the southwestern deserts in the 7th–8th centuries. In the eastern woodlands maize was
a widespread crop by 800. The Hopewell cultures were replaced by the more
complex Mississippian temple-mound building cultures (▷ 42) ∎

The Vikings – pagan raiders from Denmark and Norway – burst upon western Europe at the end of the 8th century as a bolt from the blue. The targets for their attacks were defenseless coastal monasteries which offered rich plunder. Their first known raid was against the monastery at Lindisfarne, the center of Northumbrian Christianity, in 793. Six years later they raided the Frankish coast, prompting Charlemagne to set up coastal defenses. But the full weight of Viking raids came in the 830s, when they arrived each year in ever greater numbers and began to sail up navigable rivers like the Rhine to sack inland ports such as Dorestad. Viking activity entered a new phase in 865 when the Danish "Great Army" invaded England with permanent settlement rather than plunder in mind. Much of eastern and northern England was overrun and settled (the area known as the Danelaw, with its capital at York) but the Wessex king Alfred (r.871–99) resisted the Danish advance. By 954 Alfred's successors had conquered the Scandinavian settlements and in the process created a united English kingdom. Traders and farmers as well as pirates, the Vikings also established colonies in Normandy, the Shetland and Orkney Islands, Ireland, the Faroe Islands and Iceland. A migration across the Atlantic in about 1000 led to the colonization of Greenland and the first European exploration in the Americas. In eastern Europe, Swedish venturers known as Rus pioneered trade routes along the rivers of Russia to the Black and Caspian Seas, giving their name to the Russian state, which developed at Novgorod around 862.

The Viking raids and settlements were prompted by developments within Scandinavia itself. By the late 8th century power was becoming centralized, creating an intensely competitive society. For many, pirate raids overseas became a means to acquire wealth, a reputation and an armed following to support their ambitions at home. Others, denied the chance to rule at home, sought to conquer lands for themselves and their followers abroad. Trade and land hunger, caused by a rising population, were other important factors in the Viking phenomenon.

During the 10th century Denmark and Norway emerged as stable territorial states, a process completed in Sweden by the 12th century. The same period saw the start of the Scandinavians' conversion to Christianity. Denmark's hegemony briefly included England and Norway under Cnut (r.1016–35). In the east the Slavs assimilated the Rus ruling class and by 1000 Kievan Rus was a powerful Slavic state, strongly influenced by the Byzantines who introduced Orthodox Christianity. In Normandy the

| | |
|---|---|
| ▭▭▭ | borders, c.888 |
| ▭ | Danish Viking settlement, 800-1000 |
| ▭ | Norwegian Viking settlement, 800-100 |
| ▭ | Swedish Viking settlement, 800-1000 |
| ▭ | Byzantine empire, 888 |
| ▭ | Carolingian kingdoms, 888 |
| ▭ | Muslim states, 888 |
| ▭ | Bulgar peoples |
| ▭ | Slavic peoples |
| ▭ | Magyar settlement, c.900 |
| ▱ | temporary gain by Germany, 929-82 |
| ▭ | kingdom of Hungary, 1000 |
| ▭ | empire of Cnut, 1019-35 |
| ▭ | Kievan Rus, c.1050 |
| ▭ | Holy Roman empire, 1050 |
| ▭ | Duchy of Normandy, 1051 |
| → | Viking raids, trade and colonization routes, 793-1000 |
| → | Magyar raids, 899-955 |
| → | Muslim raids, 800-1000 |
| ☆ | Viking controlled trade center |
| ⚓ | Viking ship find |
| | migration of peoples |

0                        600 km
0                        400 mi

BRONZEWORKING was highly developed among the Vikings, as in this decorated brooch from Denmark.

Vikings adopted French culture and language by 1000, but remained effectively independent of the French monarchy, which had passed from the Carolingian line when Hugh Capet became king in 987.

The Viking invasions occurred at a time when the Carolingian empire was weakened by internal squabbles. The emperor Louis the Pious (r.814–40) was not willing, as Charlemagne had been, to contemplate the equal division of the empire between his sons. Louis' younger sons and many of the Franks regarded the settlement as unjust and in 827 civil war broke out. The succession was not resolved until the Treaty of Verdun (843) which saw the empire divided into three parts. By this time royal authority was weakened and defenses against the Vikings had collapsed. Charles the Fat briefly reunited the Carolingian empire from 885–87, but it broke

## TIMELINE

### The Viking world

| | 900 | 1000 |
|---|---|---|
| **830s** Viking raids on English and Frankish coast increase | **911** Charles the Simple allows Viking settlement in Normandy | **c.1000** Norse Greenlanders found shortlived settlement in Newfoundland |
| **845** The Franks buy off raiders by paying Danegeld | | |
| | **954** Fall of Viking kingdom of York | **1014** Danes under Svein Forkbeard conquer England |
| **859–62** Viking raiders in the Mediterranean | | |
| | **965** Harald Bluetooth of Denmark is baptised first Christian king in Scandinavia | **1016–35** Cnut reigns in England, Denmark and Norway |
| **878** Alfred, king of Wessex, defeats the Danes at Edington | | |
| | | **986** Erik the Red founds Norse settlements in Greenland |
| **882** Oleg makes Kiev capital of the Rus state | | |

### Western Christendom

| | 900 | 1000 |
|---|---|---|
| **840** Death of Louis the Pious | **910** Cluny abbey is founded in Burgundy, initiating period of monastic reform | **1002** Umayyad caliphate collapses into petty states |
| **843** Treaty of Verdun divides Carolingian empire into three | | |
| | **911** End of Carolingian rule in Germany and accession of Henry the Fowler, founder of Saxon dynasty | **1027** Arrival of Norman mercenaries in southern Italy |
| **846** Muslim pirates sack the Vatican | | |
| | | **1043** Edward the Confessor is crowned king of England |
| **889** Final breakup of the Carolingian empire | **962** Otto I crowned Roman emperor in Rome: Holy Roman empire founded | |
| **898–99** Magyars invade Italy and sack Pavia | | |

900             1000

**Map labels:**

Trondheim · Finns · Lake Onega · Finns

NORWAY · Svear (Swedes) · Beloozero · Volga

Oseberg · Tune · Sigtuna · Staraja Ladoga · Yaroslavl

Hafrsfjord 885 · Kaupang · Gökstad · Birka · Lake Ladoga · Novgorod · KIEVAN RUS · Bulgar

Vänern · Vättern · Askerkärr · Paviken · Gotland · Izborsk · Pskov · Volga Bulgars

North Sea · Götar · DENMARK · Lake Peipus · 6

Århus · Skuldelev · Lund · Baltic Sea · Balts · Grobin · Western Dvina · Viatchians

EARLDOM OF NORTHUMBRIA · Ribe · Ladby · Roskilde · Gnezdovo

Hedeby · Wolin · Kolobrzeg · Elbing · Prus · KHAZAR KHANATE

Abodrites · Pomeranians · Gniezno · Vistula · Chernigov · Severyans · Don

Hamburg · Bremen · Magdeburg · 924 · Poles · Kiev · Volga

Utrecht · Saxony · Elbe · Oder · Derevlians · Dnieper · Sarkel · Itil

Dorestad · EAST FRANCIA (GERMANY) · Riade 933 · 915 · Prague · Bohemians · Magyars · Pechenegs

Dyle 891 · Cologne · Frankfurt · Franconia · Slovaks · Goths · Tmutorokan

Lorraine · Mainz · Rhine · Regensburg · Danube · Vienna · Gran · Carpathian Mts · 896–907

Reims 955 · Metz · 926 · 1 · Swabia · Lechfeld 955 · Salzburg · Pest · Pannonia · Moravians · BULGAR KHANATE · Black Sea

Luxeuil · Bavaria · St Gall · Croatia · Save · Belgrade · Danube · Pliska

BURGUNDY · Cluny · Aquileia · Venice · Serbs

Lyon · ALPS · Milan · Pavia · Po · KINGDOM OF ITALY · 899 · Patrimony of St. Peter · 921 · Constantinople 860

PROVENCE · 5 · 897 · ANATOLIA

Arles · Marseille · Pisa · Fraxinetum 890–972 Muslim pirate base · Rome · 927 · 921 · Bari 840–71 Muslim pirate base · Euphrates · Tigris

Corsica · 846 · DUCHY OF BENEVENTO · Otranto · BYZANTINE EMPIRE

Sardinia · 827 · Sicily · Cyprus · ABBASID CALIPHATE

AGHLABID EMIRATE · Tunis · Malta · Mediterranean Sea · Crete

up finally in 889 into five kingdoms: West Francia (France), East Francia (Germany), Italy, Burgundy and Provence.

The Vikings were not the only threat facing western Christendom. Muslim pirates from Spain and Tunisia raided the Mediterranean coast and preyed on travelers over the Alpine passes. In the east a nomadic people, the Magyars, crossed the Carpathians around 900 to settle in the Danube plain in the old Roman province of Pannonia, from where they raided Italy, Germany and France. By 1000, however, the Muslim and Magyar threats had ended and Viking activity was limited mainly to the British Isles. Leading the recovery was Germany. With the ending of Carolingian rule there in 911, power passed into the hands of the Saxon kings. Under Otto I (r.936–73) the Magyars were defeated at the battle of Lechfeld (955) and were converted to Christianity. Expansion against the Slavs continued, and Otto annexed the kingdom of Italy in 951–61. Crowned Roman emperor in 962, he founded what became known as the Holy Roman empire. By the 11th century the German emperors had emerged as the clear leaders of western Christendom.

**1** The monastery of Luxeuil was sacked successively by Viking raiders, Muslim pirates and Magyars between 886 and 924.

**2** The Viking raids damaged Ireland's monastic culture, but also founded its first towns at Dublin, Wexford, Waterford and Limerick in the 9th century.

**3** Paris first rose to prominence as a result of its determined resistance to a Viking siege in 885–86.

**4** Conversion of the Poles to Christianity began in 966: the first Polish archbishopric, at Gniezno, was founded in 1000.

**5** German protectorates from 935, Burgundy and Provence were united in a single kingdom in 948 and absorbed into the Holy Roman empire in 1033.

**6** Rus traders traveled down the river Volga to Bulgar to trade slaves and furs with Arab merchants.

**7** Strategically placed, Gotland was an important center of Baltic trade: over 40,000 Arab, 38,000 Frankish and 28,000 Anglo-Saxon silver coins have been found there.

See also 38 (Carolingians); 42 (North America); 44 (world religions)

The initial settlement of North America began around 12,000 years ago as bands of Paleoindians, the ancestors of modern Native Americans, spread south from Alaska. At first, Paleoindian culture was relatively homogeneous, but adaptation to particular environments led to the emergence of well defined regional cultures by the end of the first millennium BC. From early times hunter–gatherers in many areas of North America had cultivated favored food plants on a small scale. Some native plant species, such as sunflowers, had been domesticated by the end of the first millennium BC and maize and beans had been introduced from Mexico. As wild food sources remained abundant, true farming communities were slow to develop.

The first mainly agricultural North American societies developed in the southwest deserts in about AD 300. Maize, beans, squash and cotton were first cultivated close to permanent water sources, but by about 900 elaborate irrigation systems were in use. By the 9th century three main cultural traditions had developed – the Hohokam, Mogollon and Anasazi – together with two subsidiary cultures, the Patayan and the Fremont. In some areas (such as Chaco Canyon) these cultures developed considerable social complexity. Their most distinctive remains are the multi-roomed dwellings known as pueblos, and their fine pottery. Droughts caused their decline from around 1300.

True farming began to emerge in the eastern woodlands once hardier strains of maize and beans appeared after 700. The resulting growth in food production stimulated the rise of North America's first towns, in the Mississippi basin, by the 12th century. These centered around large earthwork temple mounds. The Mississippian cultures shared a common religion known as the Southern Cult, and were hierarchical. Their rulers were buried in mound-top mortuaries with rich grave goods and even human sacrifices. Large Mississippian towns, such as Cahokia, were the centers of powerful chiefdoms. By the 15th century, Mississippian culture was declining and its heartland was depopulated (the so-called "vacant quarter"). By about 1000 permanent farming villages were established throughout the eastern woodlands. Warfare spread and by the time of European contact, defensive tribal confederacies, such as the Iroquois league, were forming.

Elsewhere in North America hunting, fishing and gathering remained the dominant way of life. On the

Pacific coast, ocean resources were so abundant that relatively dense populations and permanent village settlements emerged, with a level of social and cultural complexity far beyond that normally achieved by hunter–gatherer peoples. The Great Plains and the sub-Arctic forests were sparsely populated, though the advent of the bow and arrow in the first millennium AD made big-game hunting more efficient. At the time of European contact buffalo hunting was gradually giving way to farming, but the introduction of the horse (native American horses died out around 10,000 years ago), led many settled Plains peoples to abandon farming for nomadism.

The Paleoindians did not for the most part settle in Arctic North America. The region was uninhabited until about 2500–1900 BC, when the ancestors of

the modern Inuit peoples arrived in Alaska from Siberia. Early Inuit cultures became increasingly well adapted to the Arctic environment, culminating in the Thule tradition which survived to the modern age. This originated during the Old Bering Sea Stage (200 BC–AD 800) among specialized marine mammal hunters on St Lawrence and other Bering Sea islands, from where it spread along Alaska's west coast and north to Point Barrow. From there Thule Inuit migrated east, displacing or assimilating the earlier Dorset Inuit until they reached Greenland in the 13th century. Here they made contact with Norse settlers, with whom they traded and fought. The Norse were not well adapted to life in the Arctic, and by about 1500 their settlements had died out and been occupied by the Thule.

**cultural areas**

- Arctic marine mammal hunters
- sub-Arctic forest hunter-gatherers
- northwest coast salmon fisher-hunter-gatherers
- plateau fisher-hunter-gatherers
- Great Basin hunter-gatherers
- southwest desert farmers
- California fisher-hunter-gatherers
- Great Plains buffalo hunters
- eastern woodland farmer-hunter-gatherers
- Caribbean farmers
- Mesoamerican farming cultures
- uninhabited
- desert
- origin of Thule Inuit culture, 200 BC–AD 800
- Aleut site, AD 600–1500
- Inuit site, AD 600–1800
- Norse settlement, c.AD 1000
- spread of Thule Inuit AD 1000-1500
- Mississippian temple-mound cultures, AD 800-1500
- temple-mound
- the "vacant quarter", c.AD 1450
- Northern Iroquoian territory, c.AD 1000
- site of major bison kill
- Plains farming village, AD 900-1800
- spread of farming

**southwest farming cultures**

- Anasazi, AD 700-1500
- Fremont, AD 400-1300
- Hohokam, AD 400-1450
- Mogollon, AD 300-1450
- Patayan, AD 875-1450
- Pueblo
- ballcourt
- other important site, AD 600-1500

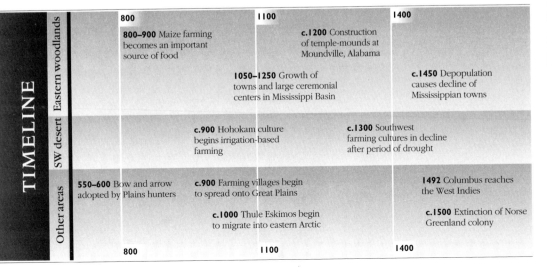

| | 800 | 1100 | 1400 |
|---|---|---|---|
| **Eastern woodlands** | **800–900** Maize farming becomes an important source of food | **c.1200** Construction of temple-mounds at Moundville, Alabama | |
| | | **1050–1250** Growth of towns and large ceremonial centers in Mississippi Basin | **c.1450** Depopulation causes decline of Mississippian towns |
| **SW desert** | | **c.900** Hohokam culture begins irrigation-based farming | **c.1300** Southwest farming cultures in decline after period of drought |
| **Other areas** | **550–600** Bow and arrow adopted by Plains hunters | **c.900** Farming villages begin to spread onto Great Plains | **1492** Columbus reaches the West Indies |
| | | **c.1000** Thule Eskimos begin to migrate into eastern Arctic | **c.1500** Extinction of Norse Greenland colony |
| | 800 | 1100 | 1400 |

**1** Here a cliff was used as a "jump" over which buffalo were stampeded to their deaths, from c.5400 BC to European contact.

**2** A small Norse settlement occupied for about twenty years c.AD 1000 is the only sure evidence that Europeans reached the Americas before Columbus.

**3** Ritual ball courts at Snaketown and Casa Grande indicate that the Hohokam culture was influenced by Mesoamerican civilizations.

**4** From 900-1300, Chaco Canyon was the hub of a network of 125 planned villages linked by 400 kilometers (250 miles) of roads.

**5** Iron ship rivets, textiles and chain mail found at sites at Flagler Bay show contact between the Thule Inuit and the Norse Greenlanders.

**6** Sub-Arctic hunters typically sited their camps at river crossings used by herds of caribou (reindeer).

Greenland

Ellesmere
Island

**5** Inuarfissuaq
Flagler Bay  Thule

Illummersuit

AD 1200–1500

Craig Harbour

Bathurst
Island  Devon Island

Melville  de Blicquy  Maxwell Bay
Island  Resolute  Nunguvik

*Beaufort
Sea*  Banks
Island  AD 1000–1200

Prince of
Wales
Island  Strathcona
Sound

Sermermiut

Mittimatalik

Western
Settlement  Illutalik
Kangeq  Eastern
Settlement
Middle
Settlement

Utqiagvik
Birnick
Point Barrow

Kavik  AD 1000–1200

Kuujja
Memorana  Victoria
Island  Pingitkalik

*Baffin Island*

Yukon

Klo-kut  Jackson  Bell  Pembroke
Clark  Maleruakik

**6**

Lady Franklin
Point  Naujan

Crystal II

*L a b r a d o r
S e a*

Chimi  Southampton
Island

L'Anse aux
Meadows

Silumiut
Iglicligardjuk

GEOMETRICAL design on
pottery was typical of the
Mimbres Valley in the southwest's Mogollon culture.  **2**

Great Bear
Lake

*H u d s o n
B a y*

Newfoundland
Indian
Point

Glacier Bay

Mackenzie

Frank Channel

Great Slave
Lake

Mingan

*COAST MOUNTAINS*

Yukon

Charlot River

Lake Athabasca

Reindeer
Lake

Metabetchouan

Dodge Island

Queen
Charlotte
Islands

Peace  Athabasca

Godard Point

ROCKY MOUNTAINS

Saskatchewan

Tailrace Bay  *Lake
Winnipeg*

*St. Lawrence*  *APPALACHIAN MTS*

Old Women's
Buffalo jump

Nesikep

*Lake
Superior*

Lake
Ontario  Maxon-Derby
Nodwell  Sackett

Vancouver
Island

**1** Head-Smashed-In

Avonlea

*Missouri*

Big Hidatsa

Molander

*Lake
Huron*

*Lake
Erie*

*ATLANTIC
OCEAN*

Ozette  Hoko River

Columbia

*Great Plains*

Vore

Arzberger

*Mississippi*

Proctorville

Netarts Sand
Spit  Wakemap
Mound

Snake

Big Goose
Creek

Glenrock

Platte

*Oneota*

Lake Michigan

*Fort Ancient*
Clay Mound

Old Fort
Cahokia  Angel  Town Creek

Gunther
Island

Hogup Cave  Wardell

Medicine
Creek

Arkansas

*Middle
Mississippian*  Kings Mound  Hiwassee Island
Shiloh  Etowah

San Francisco
Bay

*SIERRA NEVADA*

Colorado

Alkali Ridge
Mesa Verde
Pueblo Bonito
Salmon Ruin  Pecos Pueblo
Canyon de Chelly  Chaco
Canyon

Knapp Mounds

Moundville  *South Appalachian
Mississippian*  Lamar

Santa Barbara

Topoc Maze  Montezuma
Castle  **4**

Mogollon

*Caddoan*

Winterville
*Plaquemine
Mississippian*  Lake Jackson

Pueblo Grande  Snaketown
**3** Casa
Grande  Mimbres
Valley  Garnsey

Emerald Mound  Coles Creek

Safety Harbor

*Rio Grande*

*PACIFIC
OCEAN*

Casas Grandes

*Gulf of
Mexico*

La Candelaria

*Cuba*

0 _____ 1200 km
0 _____ 800 mi

See also 62 (Spanish empire);
70 (European exploration of North America)

The centralized Chinese empire created by Shi Huangdi survived until AD 220, when it split into three rival states. Unity was restored in 589 by Yang Jian, who as emperor Wen (r.589–604) became the founder of the Sui dynasty. Wen, a tyrannical but able ruler, re-established a strong centralized bureaucracy and increased the prosperity of the peasantry through a land redistribution scheme. Granaries were built and the canal system expanded. As a result of Wen's reforms, the economy grew and the state amassed large reserves of cash and commodities. These were squandered on building projects and opulent court life by Wen's successor, Yang (r.604–17). Moreover, a disastrous war against the Korean kingdom of Koguryo caused the peasants of the northeast to rebel. The empire was saved only by the coup of Li Yuan, military governor of Taiyuan, who captured the Sui capital at Luoyang in 617 and became, after Yang's murder in 618, the first emperor of the Tang dynasty (as Gaozu, r.618–26). Gaozong was then deposed by his son Taizong (r.626–49), one of Chinese history's ablest rulers.

Taizong based his government loosely on the Han model but without the feudal elements. At its head was the emperor, whose authority (in theory if not always in practice) was absolute. The central administration consisted of three bodies, the Imperial Chancellery, the Imperial Secretariat and the Department for State Affairs. This latter department supervised the six ministries – officials, finances, religious rites, the army, justice and public works – while a Board of Censors oversaw the actions of officials. The empire was divided into 15 administrative regions or "circuits", under an inspecting commissioner. The examination system became more important for selecting bureaucratic staff, yet the cost of education precluded all but the rich landowning classes from pursuing a career in administration. The

peasantry benefited from further land redistribution and reduced tax and labor dues, and agricultural production rose rapidly. Internal trade flourished, stimulating craft production: silks and ceramics were widely exported.

The Sui had regained the strategic Gansu Corridor. When Turkish nomad power declined after their Uighur subjects rebelled in 627–28, Taizong began to extend Chinese control into central Asia, creating a military protectorate in the Tarim basin. This expansion brought the first extensive contacts between China and Tibet, which had emerged as a powerful centralized kingdom under Sron-btsan-sgampo (r.605–49). Gaozong

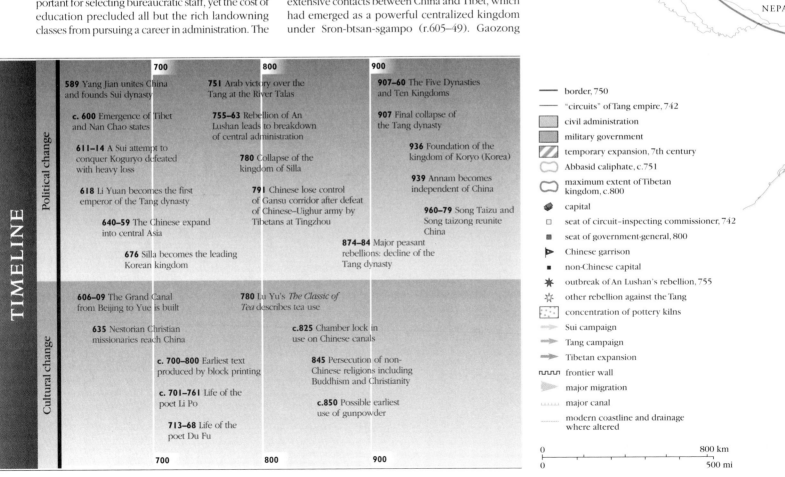

## TIMELINE

### Political change

**589** Yang Jian unites China and founds Sui dynasty

**c. 600** Emergence of Tibet and Nan Chao states

**611–14** A Sui attempt to conquer Koguryo defeated with heavy loss

**618** Li Yuan becomes the first emperor of the Tang dynasty

**640–59** The Chinese expand into central Asia

**676** Silla becomes the leading Korean kingdom

**751** Arab victory over the Tang at the River Talas

**755–63** Rebellion of An Lushan leads to breakdown of central administration

**780** Collapse of the kingdom of Silla

**791** Chinese lose control of Gansu corridor after defeat of Chinese–Uighur army by Tibetans at Tingzhou

**907–60** The Five Dynasties and Ten Kingdoms

**907** Final collapse of the Tang dynasty

**936** Foundation of the kingdom of Koryo (Korea)

**939** Annam becomes independent of China

**960–79** Song Taizu and Song taizong reunite China

**874–84** Major peasant rebellions: decline of the Tang dynasty

### Cultural change

**606–09** The Grand Canal from Beijing to Yue is built

**635** Nestorian Christian missionaries reach China

**c. 700–800** Earliest text produced by block printing

**c. 701–761** Life of the poet Li Po

**713–68** Life of the poet Du Fu

**780** Lu Yu's *The Classic of Tea* describes tea use

**c.825** Chamber lock in use on Chinese canals

**845** Persecution of non-Chinese religions including Buddhism and Christianity

**c.850** Possible earliest use of gunpowder

### Legend

— border, 750

— "circuits" of Tang empire, 742

▨ civil administration

▨ military government

▨ temporary expansion, 7th century

⬭ Abbasid caliphate, c.751

⬭ maximum extent of Tibetan kingdom, c.800

▦ capital

□ seat of circuit–inspecting commissioner, 742

■ seat of government-general, 800

▷ Chinese garrison

▪ non-Chinese capital

✳ outbreak of An Lushan's rebellion, 755

✳ other rebellion against the Tang

▦ concentration of pottery kilns

→ Sui campaign

→ Tang campaign

→ Tibetan expansion

ᜓ frontier wall

▷ major migration

⋯ major canal

⋯ modern coastline and drainage where altered

0          800 km

0          500 mi

Inner Mongolian
Plateau

Karabalghasun

**Uighurs**
**5**

*Gobi Desert*

**Khitans**

KOGURYO
Chinese protectorate
668–76
645–7, 660–8

Yingzhou

Pyongyang

Kyongju

SILLA

*A L T A I   M T S*

Tingzhou
791

Turfan

Anxi

Dunhuang

*Gansu Corridor*

Suzhou

*QILIAN MTS*

Liang

Shan

*Lake
Qinghai*

Wei

Longyou

You

Yun

Jojun
(Beijing)

Sheng

Feng

*Yellow*

Hebei

Hedong

Taiyuan

Heng
Wei

874

Henan

Yan

**6**

Yan

Ling

Guannei

Qing

Yuan

Qin

Jingji

**1**

Chang'an

Liang

Lu

Pu

Shan

Luoyang

Duji

Caizhou

Bianzhou

Yangzhou

Shouzou

Su

Yue
859

**8**

*Yellow
Sea*

*Yellow River (893–1048)*

*Han*

Shanan-Xi

Shanan-Dong

An

Huainan

*Yangtze*

**2**

Song

Li

**Tibetans**

Lhasa

*Brahmaputra*

*H I M A L A Y A S*

*Mekong*

Jiannan

Chengdu

Ya

Li

Sui

Yaozhou

Dali
751

Longyu

Kui

Qian

Qianzhong
868

Gui

Hong
(Nanchang)

Tanzhou

Jiangnan-Xi

*Yangtze*

Fu

*Jiangnan-Dong*

610

*Taiwan*

**NAN CHAO**
**4**

*Red*

Guangzhou

Lingnan

Yong

Rong

Qiongzhou

*Hainan*

Han

*Annam*

*Salween*

**PYU**

*Irrawaddy*

*Mekong*

Indrapura

**CHAMPA**

EARTHENWARE figurines
of dancers (as here),
musicians and foreigners
were placed in Tang-
dynasty tombs, reflecting
the lively culture of the age.

**1** With over one million inhabitants, Chang'an, the Tang capital, was the world's largest city by 750.

**2** Caizhou was one of the last centers of resistance to imperial campaigns to restore central authority after An Lushan's rebellion. It fell in 817.

**3** Tibet emerged as a united kingdom c.600 and reached its greatest extent c.800.

**4** Nan Chao, a Thai kingdom in modern Yunnan province, emerged c.600.

**5** The Uighurs were a Turkic nomad tribe allied with the Chinese against the Turks and Tibetans.

**6** The canal system linked the grain-producing Yangtze valley with the political center of the empire and the northern frontier zone.

**7** The decisive battle at the River Talas, which led to the fall of China's central Asian empire, followed an appeal to the Arabs from the ruler of Tashkent for protection against the Chinese.

**8** The first true porcelain was made in eastern China during the Tang period.

(r.649–83) brought Ferghana and Soghd under Chinese control in 659. However, these conquests over-extended the empire and they were lost by 665. In the east, the Chinese subdued Koguryo in 668 but the Korean kingdom of Silla expelled them in 676.

The Chinese position in central Asia was dealt further blows in 751, with defeats by the Arabs at the River Talas and by the Thai kingdom of Nan Chao at Dali. The Mongol Khitan nomads emerged as a threat in the north in the 8th century. At home, landlord–peasant conflict increased, and the emperors from Gaozong onward proved ineffectual. A rebellion of the general An Lushan in 755 threatened the Tang. It was suppressed in 763 but central authority did not recover and power devolved to around forty semi-independent military governments-general. In 791, the empire lost control of the Gansu Corridor to

the Tibetans following their victory over a Chinese and Uighur army at Tingzhou. In 859, 868 and 874–84 peasant rebellions broke out. The emperor's authority was damaged beyond repair and power was again seized by provincial warlords. The Tang struggled on until 907, finally collapsing in a period of disunity known as the Five Dynasties and Ten Kingdoms (907–960).

The Tang period is regarded as the golden age of Chinese poetry. The dynasty also presided over major achievements in historiography and painting, and restored Confucianism as the state ideology after it had declined during the Period of Disunion.

See also 26 (early imperial China);
44 (the world religions)

The birth of Islam, the most recent of the world religions, dominated the era known to Europeans as the Middle Ages, and it deeply affected all the established world religions.

Islam originated in the teachings of the prophet Muhammad. From 610 Muhammad received a series of revelations which are recorded in the sacred book of Islam, the *Koran*. Islam drew much from Judaism and, to a lesser extent, Christianity. The *Koran* asserts that Muhammad is the last of a line of prophets that included Adam, Abraham, Noah, Moses and Jesus.

By the time of Muhammad's death in 632, Arabs had generally acknowledged him as their religious and political leader and had accepted Islam. Muhammad had no male heir and the decades following his death were marked by prolonged disputes over his successor, which erupted into civil war during the caliphate of Muhammad's son-in-law Ali (r.656–61). When Ali was murdered in 661, his supporters recognized his son Husain as successor (caliph) in preference to Muawiya, founder of the Umayyad dynasty. Husain's death in battle at Karbala in 680 led to his martyrdom, and the development among his supporters of the Shiite tradition of Islam.

Shiism has continued to be distinguished from the majority Sunni tradition by its stress on martyrdom and its radically different theories of religious leadership. In the 9th century doctrinal disputes resulted in the secession from Shiism of the Ismaili sect. Until the 13th century, the Ismailis (who are also known as the Assassins) habitually murdered their enemies. Moreover, the spread of both the Sunni and Shiite Islamic traditions was promoted by the growth, from the 8th century onward, of the mystical movement known as Sufism, which laid a heavy emphasis on piety and zeal.

The rise of Islam halved the area under Christian domination between 600 and 750. Islam tolerated Christians but the social and financial advantages of conversion were great and Christianity soon declined in the areas conquered by the Arabs. However, freedom from Orthodox persecution enabled some minority Christian sects, such as the Nestorians, to spread widely in Asia. Although it regained some ground through missionary work and military conquest – most notably the Crusades that temporarily restored Christian

ATLANTIC OCEAN

Glasgow
Nidaras (Trondheim)
SCANDINAVIA Christianity, c.950–1100
Uppsala
Lincoln  York
Salisbury  London  Roskilde  Novgorod
Rouen  Canterbury
Santiago de Compostela
Paris  Amiens  Saxons Christianity, 785
Chartres  Cologne  Danzig  LITHUANIA Christianity, 1386
León  Bourges  Reims  Ulm  Danzig
Burgos  Strasbourg  Prague  Poles Christianity, c.1000  Moscow
SPAIN Christianity, 750–1492  Freiburg  Regensburg  Russians Christianity, 989
Toledo  Milan  Vienna  Kiev
Seville  Córdoba
Fez  Magyars (Hungarians) Christianity, c.1000
Tlemcen  Rome  KHAZAR KHANATE Jewish ruling dynasty, c.800–1242
Bulgars Christianity, 890
TEKRUR Islam, c.1030  Mt Athos  Constantinople  Black Sea
BYZANTINE EMPIRE Islam, 1071–1453  GEORGIA
Konya  Barda
GHANA Islam, 1076  Nisibis
Niger  Timbuktu  Masyaf  Arbela  Alar
MALI Islam, c.1250  Bethlehem  Damascus  Kirkuk  Ra
Tanta  Jerusalem  Baghdad
Cairo  Karbala  Seleucia  Isfa
AIR Islam, c.1350  Umm Abida  Kaskar
Basra
Rev-Ardashir
Shiraz
Medina
Humaithira
Mecca
MAKKURA Islam, 1317
ALWA  Red Sea
Axum
Lalibela  Socotra
Debre Libanos
ETHIOPIA  Harer
CONGO Christianity, 1490  Somalis Islam, c.1100
Kilwa

**TIMELINE**

| | 700 | 1000 | 1300 |
|---|---|---|---|
| **South and east Asia** | **600–700** Beginning of the Bakhti revival of Hinduism in India | **791** Buddhism becomes the state religion in Tibet | **1191** Zen (Chan) Buddhism is introduced to Japan |
| | **600–800** Spread of Chan and Pure Land Buddhism in China | **843** Manichaeanism in China is destroyed by persecution | **1200–1300** Buddhism dies out in northern India |
| | **c.700** Persian Zoroastrians settle in India: origin of Parsis | **845** Buddhists face persecution in China | |
| | **762** Uighur nomads adopt Manichaeanism as religion | **900–1000** Pilgrimages are established as an important expression of Hindu devotion | |
| **Middle East** | **622** Muhammad's flight (*hijra*) from Mecca to Medina | **c.970** Turks convert to Islam | **1258** Mongols destroy the Abbasid caliphate of Baghdad |
| | **700–800** Growth of the Sufi mystical movement in Islam | **c.1070** Islam spreads to sub-Saharan Africa | |
| **Europe** | **726–843** Iconoclast controversy: destruction of religious images in Byzantine empire | **965** Harald Bluetooth of Denmark is baptized: the first Christian king of Scandinavia | **1209–29** Crusades are launched against Cathar (Manichaean) heretics |
| | | **1054** Roman–Orthodox schism becomes permanent | **1232** The Church sets up the Inquisition to fight heresy |
| | | **1095–99** The First Crusade is called; Jerusalem is taken | **1378–1417** Great Schism damages papal authority |
| | 700 | 1000 | 1300 |

SHIVA, one of the major deities of Hinduism, is seen in his form as Nataraja (Lord of Dance).

Buddhist, c.750
Christian, c.750
Hindu, c.750
Muslim, c.750
area of dense Jewish settlement, c.750
Buddhist, c.1500
Christian, c.1500
Hindu, c.1500
area of dense Jewish settlement, c.1500
Muslim, c.1500
Confucian and Daoist throughout period
860 date of conversion
▲ important Buddhist religious center
🏛 Christian religious center
🏛 Hindu religious center
✳ Manichaean religious center
🏛 Muslim religious center
🏛 Zoroastrian religious center
Rome pilgrimage center
🏯 center of Confucian scholarship, 600–1500
🏛 Lamaist monastery
🏛 Gothic cathedral
🏛 Sufi shrine
🏰 stronghold of the Assassins
✝ Nestorian Christian community
✚ other significant Christian minority
▬ border between eastern Orthodox Church and western Roman Church, 15th century

*Map labels:*

KHANATE OF THE GOLDEN HORDE
Islam, 1313

Naimans and Kereits
Nestorianism, 1000–1300

Mt Fuji
Nara
Heian
Kumano
Liaoyang
Kyongju
Kyongju
Kyoto

Erdeni-dzu

Mongols
Buddhism, 1200–1600

Beijing
Datong
Yellow Sea

Turks
Islam, c.970

Chagatai Mongols
Islam, c.1250

Uighurs
Manichaean, 762–c.1300

Lake Balkhash

Almalik
Hami

Tanguts
Buddhism, 1100–1200

Kaifeng
Yangzhou
Luoyang
Nanjing
Xi'an
Hangzhou
Chang'an

Sudji
Tangut

Aral Sea
Sir Dar'ya
Yasi
Navekath

Khiva
Bukhara
Samarkand
Kashgar
Khotan

CHINA

Amu Dar'ya
Merv
Nishapur
Herat

Tashi-gompa
Darge-gonchen

KASHMIR
Hinduism, 855

TIBET
Buddhism, c.650

Bargo

Guangzhou

PERSIA

Shigatse
Mt Kailas
Gartok
Gangotri
Sakya Gompa
Lhasa
Gyantse

1 Talwandi
Thaneswar
Hardwar
Delhi
Ayodhya
Prayaga
Ajmer
Khajuraho

NEPAL
Hinduism, 1300

6 Varanasi
Nalanda
Bodh Gaya
MAGADHA

Indrapura

South China Sea

INDIA
Islam, 1175–1200

2 Bhubaneswar

Pagan

Somnath
Sanjayanti
Diu
Kalyan
Sthanka

Konarak

Pegu
Dagon
Angkor
Ayutthaya

Islam, 1500

Borneo

Bay of Bengal

Vijayanagara

Mamallapuram

Andaman Sea

Islam, 1414

Java Sea

Bali
Bali

Cranganore
Madurai

INDIAN OCEAN

Polonnaruva
Ceylon

Pasai
Malacca
Islam, 1290
Islam, 1400
Sumatra
Borobudur
Java
Hinduism, 860

0 —————— 1000 km
0 —————— 600 mi

---

control to the Holy Land – Christianity was again in retreat by the 15th century. At this time the Muslim Ottoman Turks overran the Byzantine empire and moved into the Balkans.

The Arab conquests destroyed Zoroastrianism in its Persian homeland, but small communities of emigrants established themselves on India's west coast, where the religion still survives among the Parsis.

The Bakhti (devotional) revival movement in the 7th century caused Hinduism to reassert itself against Buddhism, which had been dominant in the preceding centuries. The 8th-century philosopher Shankara gave impetus to Hinduism's recovery by including popular aspects of Buddhist devotion into Hinduism. An important aspect of the Bakhti revival was the great increase in the popularity of pilgrimages to sacred sites such as Varanasi on the River Ganges. A number of Hindus, especially from the lower castes, converted to Islam following the Muslim conquest around 1200, yet Hinduism remained India's principal religion.

Indian Buddhism, however, was destroyed by the Muslim conquest, continuing to flourish only in Ceylon. Buddhism also declined in southeast Asia following the introduction there of Islam in the 13th century. Chinese Buddhism reached the peak of its influence in the 7th and 8th centuries as a result of patronage by the Tang court. The period saw the spread of the meditative school of Chan (known in Japan as Zen) Buddhism, and the populist Pure Land school, which promised its adherents rebirth in paradise. Some 40,000 Buddhist temples and monasteries, all with tax-exempt estates, sprang up. They proved a severe drain on state income by 800. A brief imperial persecution in 845 closed many of these monasteries and forced 250,000 monks back into secular life. Buddhism recovered but never regained its former prestige.

The most important new converts to Buddhism in this period were the Tibetans. Here elements of Tibetan shamanism were incorporated into Buddhism to form the distinctive tradition of Lamaism.

1 Talwandi was the birthplace in 1469 of Guru Nanak, founder of the Sikh religion.

2 Buddhism declined in its original heartland of Magadha after 600 and had been supplanted by Hinduism and Islam by the 13th century.

3 Jerusalem, site of Jesus' crucifixion, was believed by medieval Christians to be the center of the world.

4 Jews were tolerated in Muslim Spain but faced expulsion or forcible conversion after the Christian reconquest.

5 Constantinople, the greatest Christian city of the East, became a leading center of Islamic culture after its conquest by the Ottoman Turks in 1453.

6 Varanasi is Hinduism's most holy site: pilgrimages to bathe in the Ganges had become popular by 1050.

See also 27 (world religions in 600);
43 (China); 48 (the Crusades)

In the 9th century Christian Europe was under attack from Viking raiders from Scandinavia, Muslim pirates from Spain and north Africa, and steppe nomads, the Magyars and Bulgars (▷ 41). The cultural and economic revival fostered by the Carolingian empire collapsed under the impact of the attacks and the empire itself broke up between 843 and 889. However, by 1000 European civilization was expanding and many of the states of medieval Europe had begun to emerge as stable political units. France was a decentralized, weak feudal kingdom but the German kings built a strong state based on their control of the church. In 962 the German king Otto I adopted the title Roman emperor, founding the Holy Roman empire. He ended the Magyar threat in 955, after which the Magyars founded the Christian kingdom of Hungary. Viking attacks on the British Isles were a catalyst in the formation of the kingdoms of England and Scotland, and by 1000 stable kingdoms had developed in Scandinavia itself. Swedish Vikings founded the first Russian state about 862, but by 1000 this had lost its Scandinavian character and was a Slavic state under Byzantine influence.

The Arab world continued to fragment and by 1000 the Abbasid caliphs were no more than spiritual figureheads. Persia passed under the control of native dynasties; Egypt, Syria and Palestine became independent under the Tulunid emirs in 868; most of Arabia was lost around 900; and the Christian Armenians recovered their independence in 886. Abbasid power revived in the early 10th century and control over Egypt and southern Iran was recovered, but it collapsed for good when the Persian Buwayhids seized Baghdad in 945: they ruled in the name of the caliph who was retained only for his spiritual authority. Between 967 and 973 the Tunisian Fatimid dynasty conquered Egypt, Palestine and Syria and were the most powerful Muslim rulers in 1000. Despite the disunity, the Muslim world continued to expand in the 9th and 10th centuries, the most important gain being the conversion of the Ghuzz Turks.

Despite the collapse of the Tibetan empire around 850, the Tang Chinese empire continued to decline in the 9th century (▷ 43). The government's fiscal problems led to persecutions and expropriation of property belonging to Buddhists, Nestorian Christians and Manichaeans. Landlords began to reverse the earlier Tang land reforms, leading to a peasant uprising in 874–84, which broke the authority of the dynasty. Power devolved to provincial warlords and the empire split into several states. In 916 the far north was conquered by the nomad Khitans (a Mongol people), who founded the

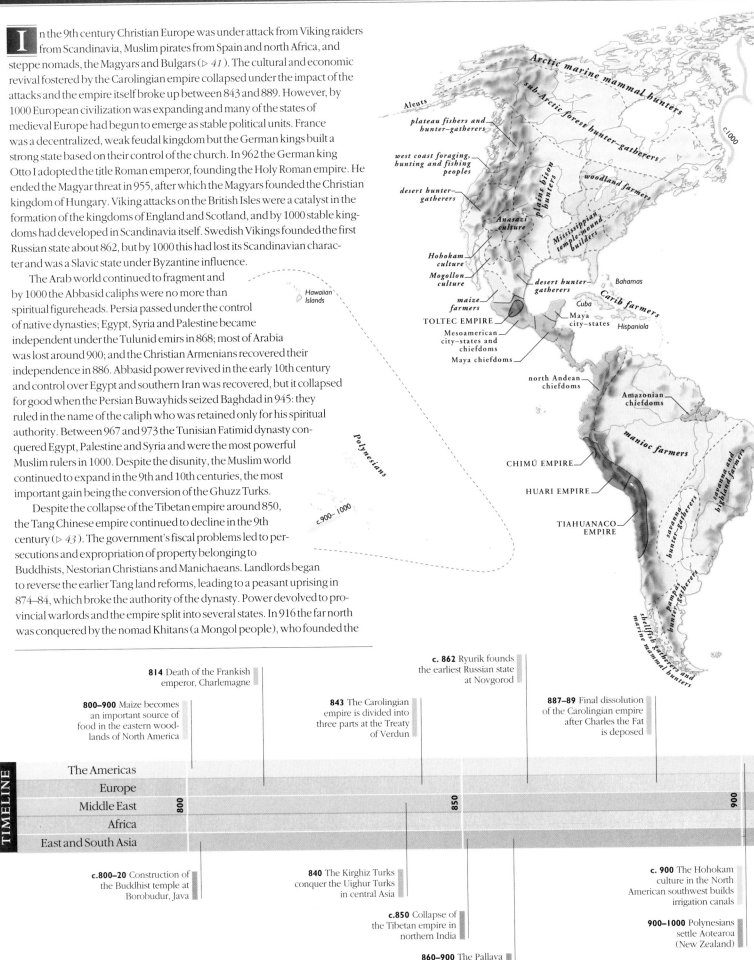

**814** Death of the Frankish emperor, Charlemagne

**800–900** Maize becomes an important source of food in the eastern woodlands of North America

**c. 862** Ryurik founds the earliest Russian state at Novgorod

**843** The Carolingian empire is divided into three parts at the Treaty of Verdun

**887–89** Final dissolution of the Carolingian empire after Charles the Fat is deposed

TIMELINE

| | 800 | 850 | 900 |
|---|---|---|---|
| The Americas | | | |
| Europe | | | |
| Middle East | | | |
| Africa | | | |
| East and South Asia | | | |

**c.800–20** Construction of the Buddhist temple at Borobudur, Java

**840** The Kirghiz Turks conquer the Uighur Turks in central Asia

**c.850** Collapse of the Tibetan empire in northern India

**860–900** The Pallava dynasty in southern India is replaced by the Cholas

**c. 900** The Hohokam culture in the North American southwest builds irrigation canals

**900–1000** Polynesians settle Aotearoa (New Zealand)

**907** The Chinese empire fragments in the period of the Five Dynasties

hunter-gatherers
nomadic pastoralists
simple farming societies
complex farming societies/
chiefdoms
state societies
uninhabited
empires
Norse expansion
Polynesian expansion
AR.  Armenia
BU.  Burgundy
GE.  Georgia
HUN. Hungary
SC.  Scotland

**c.1000** Collapse
of Tiahuanaco and
Huari empires

**967–73** The Fatimids
conquer Egypt and
found Cairo

**c. 1000** The Byzantine
and Holy Roman empires
are at their peak

**962** Otto I, king of
Germany, is crowned Holy
Roman emperor at Rome

**c.1000** Tibetan
Tangut peoples found
the Xixia state

**c. 940** The Mesoamerican
Zapotec capital at Monte
Albán is sacked

**986** Norse settlers reach
southwest Greenland

950

1000

**939** The Annamese
win independence from
China and found the
kingdom of Dai Viet

**999** Mahmud of
Ghazni founds the
Ghaznavid emirate

**960** The Chinese
empire is restored by
the Song dynasty

**c.975** The Christian
kingdom of Axum falls to
pagan invaders

kingdom of Liao, and Annam in the
south became independent. The Chinese
were reunified from 960 by the Song
dynasty, but the Tang frontiers could not be restored.

Angkor became the capital of the kingdom of Chen-la in about 900 and the
Khmer began a period of imperial expansion, becoming the greatest power in
southeast Asia by 1000. The maritime empire of Srivijaya entered a struggle
with the east Javans which left it vulnerable to the rising power of the Cholas of
southern India. In Africa the kingdom of Axum fell to a pagan invasion about
975, but its Christian culture survived in Ethiopia.

In South America climatic instability led to the decline of the Huari and
Tiahuanaco empires, which collapsed around 1000. The Maya city-states also
continued to decline, though Maya civilization survived in north Yucatán.
The last major center of Classic Mesoamerica, the Zapotec capital of Monte
Albán, was sacked and abandoned, and by 1000 the dominant influence was
the Toltec civilization (▷ 55). In North America's eastern woodlands maize
farming grew in importance after 800 and, with Mexican beans as a new crop
about 1000, a full farming economy developed. Large settlements developed
by 1000 in the southwestern deserts and the Mississippi area (▷ 42).

Two large uninhabited landmasses were colonized at this time.
Scandinavians, mainly from Norway, began to settle in Iceland about 870,
and by 1000 had also settled southwest Greenland and reached the American
mainland. At the same time Polynesians reached Aotearoa (New Zealand) ∎

Feudalism was a contractual system by which lord granted a fief (or estate) to a vass usually a knight or nobleman, in return for swo homage and military service. The Carolingian kin used the system to bind the nobility in loyalty to t crown, but under a weak ruler it could undermir royal authority and decentralize power. By the lat 11th century feudalism had been introduced to England and Sicily by the Normans and was highly developed in Spain. It was present, though less dominant, in Scotland, Scandin-avia, northern Italy and eastern Europe. By 1200 the military importance of feudalism was in decline, as kings could raise money to hire professional soldiers, and vassals could make a cash payment in lieu of military service. Fiefs had become heritable and were treated by vassals as family estates.

Decentralization was most extreme in France, where the royal lands (the demesne) were confined in the 11th century to the area around Paris and Orléans, while powerful vassals like the dukes of Normandy and the counts of Anjou and Aquitaine were semi-independent rulers of vast fiefs. When William of Normandy became king of England by conquest in 1066, he became more powerful than his feudal lord, the French king. In the 1150s Henry Plantagenet of Anjou accumulated, through inheri-tance and marriage, fiefs covering half of France, dwarfing the royal demesne. In 1154 he inherited the English throne to become, as Henry II, the most powerful ruler in Europe. Yet he tried to avoid open warfare with the French king, feeling he should not set a bad example to his own vassals. Philip Augus-tus (r.1180–1223) revived the French monarchy and recovered all the Angevin fiefs except Gascony. In 1214 he repulsed a German invasion at Bouvines, making France the strongest power in Europe.

The German kings and emperors avoided the problems of the French monarchy by granting land as fiefs to the church. Literate priests and abbots were well equipped to administer its fiefs, and celi-bate churchmen could not found dynasties, so the lands returned into the gift of the king. As long as the king retained control over ecclesiastical appoint-ments, this system offered a counterweight to the territorial nobility. But when emperor Henry III died in 1056, leaving his son Henry IV (r.1056–1106) in the control of a weak regency, the papacy asserted itself. The ensuing Investiture Contest (1075–1122), a dispute over who had the right to nominate to vacant sees (bishoprics), gave the popes greatly enhanced authority. A sign of their new prestige was the summoning of the First Crusade in 1095, which led to the capture of Jerusalem in 1099.

The Hohenstaufen emperor Frederick Barbarossa (r. 1152–90) found his authority challenged in Germany by powerful terri-torial princes, such as Henry the Lion of the Welf family. He tried to compensate by tightening imperial control in Italy but was defeated by the Lombard league of cities in 1176. His successors did little better. Though the Hohenstaufens won control of the Norman kingdom of Sicily in 1194, they failed to assert their authority over the German princes, and the Holy Roman empire disintegrated into a loose federation of states. The emperor Frederick II (r.1210–50) attempted to consolidate his

HAROLD II, last Anglo-Saxon king of England (r.1066), is shown here being crowned in the Bayeux Tapestry (c.1080).

Faroe Islands

Earldom of Orkney
Orkney Islands

Hebrides

North Sea

SCOTLAND
Perth
Edinburgh

Kingdom of Man

IRISH KINGDOMS & CHIEFDOMS
Dublin

WELSH PRINCIPALITIES

York
Stamford Bridge 1066
ENGLAND
Norwich
Oxford
London
Hastings 1066
Canterbury
Bruges
Bouvines 1214

Rouen   Reim
Bayeux
Normandy   Paris
Brittany   Maine
Loire
Anjou   Tours
FRANCE
Lyon
Clermont
Aquitaine
Bordeaux
Gascony
County of Toulouse
Toulouse
Marseill

ATLANTIC OCEAN

LEÓN
León
NAVARRE
Douro
CASTILE
ARAGON
Barcelona

Coimbra
PORTUGAL
Tagus
Toledo
Valencia
Lisbon
Guadiana
Las Navas de Tolosa 1212

EMIRATE OF MALLORC

**1**
Córdoba
ALMOHAD CALIPHATE until 1230
Granada

## TIMELINE

### Political change

| 1100 | | 1200 | 1300 |
|---|---|---|---|
| **1047–90** Normans conquer southern Italy and Sicily | **1128** Portugal becomes independent of León | **1194** Henry VI conquers Norman kingdom of Sicily | **1253–99** Commercial rivalry leads to war between Genoa and Venice |
| **1066** William the Conquerer, Duke of Normandy, invades and conquers England | **1154** Henry II becomes the first Angevin king of England | **1212** Christian victory at Las Navas de Tolosa breaks Muslim power in Spain | **1254–73** Interregnum in Germany inaugurates period of political chaos |
| **1075–1122** Investiture Contest with popes damages authority of the Holy Roman emperors | **1170** Murder of Thomas Becket, archbishop of Canterbury | **1215** King John of England signs the Magna Carta | |
| **1095** Pope Urban II calls the First Crusade at Clermont | | **1187** Defeat of crusading army by Saladin at the Horns of Hattin leads to fall of Jerusalem to the Muslims | **1230** Union of the kingdoms of Castile and León |
| **1099** Crusaders take Jerusalem | | | **1237–41** Mongols invade Russia and eastern Europe |

### Cultural change

| | | | |
|---|---|---|---|
| **1079–1142** Peter Abelard: theologian and philosopher | **c.1136** Geoffrey of Monmouth's *History of the Kings of Britain* popularizes Arthurian romances | **c.1200–75** Sagas ( fictional-ized family histories of early settlers) written in Iceland | **c.1270–1300** Invention of the mechanical clock |
| **c.1095** "Song of Roland", *chanson de geste*, celebrates chivalric ideals | **c.1140** Abbey church of St Denis near Paris, regarded as first building in Gothic style | **c.1220–92** Roger Bacon: philosopher and early advocate of scientific experiment | **1298** Marco Polo's account of his travels in Asia between 1271 and 1295 becomes an instant success |

| 1100 | | 1200 | 1300 |

Trondheim

*Lake Onega*

NORWAY

Bergen
Christiania

SWEDEN
Uppsala
*Vänern*
*Vättern*
Visby

Finns

River Neva
1240
Åbo

Lake Ladoga
Ladoga

Beloozero

REPUBLIC OF
NOVGOROD

2 Lake
Peipus
1242
*Lake Peipus*
Pskov

Revel
Estonians
Livs

Novgorod

PRINCIPALITY
OF VLADIMIR

*Volga*

Bulgar

Volga
Bulgars

Århus
DENMARK
Roskilde • Lund

*Baltic Sea*

Schleswig
Holstein
Friesland Hamburg
Bremen
Utrecht Saxony
Magdeburg

Wends
Danzig
Stettin
Brandenburg

Königsberg
Prus
*Vistula*

Riga
*Western Dvina*
Lithuanians

Polotsk

PRINCIPALITY
OF POLOTSK
Minsk

Vladimir
Moscow

PRINCIPALITY
OF SMOLENSK
Smolensk

PRINCIPALITY OF CHERNIGOV

Murom
Ryazan

PRINCIPALITY OF MUROM-RYAZAN

*Don*

Cumans
(Turkic)

Cologne
Liège
Lorraine
Mainz
Metz

GERMANY
Frankfurt
Thuringia
Franconia
Nuremberg

*Rhine*
Swabia
*Danube*
Bavaria

Breslau
POLAND

Krakow

PRINCIPALITY OF VOLHYNIA

PRINCIPALITY OF TUROV-PINSK
Pinsk

PRINCIPALITY OF KIEV
Kiev

Chernigov

PRINCIPALITY OF PEREYASLAV
Pereyaslav

PRINCIPALITY OF NOVGOROD-SEVERSK

to Kiev

*Volga*

Cumans
(Turkic)

Prague
BOHEMIA

Vienna
Austria
Salzburg 3 Styria
Carinthia

Gran
Pest

Galich

PRINCIPALITY OF GALICIA

to Kiev

Alans

BURGUNDY
Legnano
1176 Milan
4 Aquileia
Venice
VENICE

KINGDOM OF ITALY
Genoa Bologna
Pisa Florence
PISA

HUNGARY

Belgrade

*Sava*

*Danube*

*Black Sea*

GEORGIA

Ragusa

Zara

BYZANTINE EMPIRE

Duchy of Normandy, 1066

Norman gains in England and southern Italy by 1154

Holy Roman empire, c.1175

5 Rome
Corsica
PAPAL STATES
Sardinia
Naples

Benevento
1266 Bari

KINGDOM OF SICILY 6

Dyrrachium
Thessalonica

Constantinople

Tunis

Palermo
Sicily
Malta

ALMOHAD CALIPHATE
until 1230

*Mediterranean Sea*

Crete

| | Hohenstaufen demesne |
| | Welf demesne |
| | Church land |
| | other |

━━ borders, c.1175

effective Angevin (Anjou) control, c.1175

nominal Angevin control, c.1175

French royal demesne, c.1175

Angevin fiefs in France after 1214

Byzantine empire, 1175

Norwegian territory, 1175

Swedish territory, 1175

Holy Roman empire, 1175

expansion of German settlement, 12th-13th centuries

▪ Lombard league city, 1167

▫ German city founded in 13th century

ARAGON fief of the Papacy during the pontificate of Innocent III, 1198-1216

➡ German and Danish crusades against the pagan Slavs and Balts, 12th-13th centuries

➡ Swedish expansion, 12th-13th centuries

━━ western limit of Mongol conquests, 1240

Spanish states, 1300

| | Aragon |
| | Castile |
| | emirate of Granada |
| | Portugal |
| | controlled by the Teutonic Knights, c.1300 |
| | Russian states |
| | pagan area |

0 ——— 600 km
0 ——— 400 mi

position in Italy but, faced with the hostility of the papacy and the Lombard cities, his reign ended in failure and the dynasty was overthrown in 1266. Despite the political fragmentation of the empire, the 13th century saw German influence expand to the east through the establishment of peasant settlements and new towns, and the activities of traders and the crusading order of the Teutonic Knights in the Baltic.

The Slavic state of Kievan Rus broke up into several principalities in 1132, most of which were overrun by the Mongols in 1237–41. Alexander Nevsky (r.1236–63), ruler of Novgorod, submitted voluntarily to the Mongol invasion, and was therefore able to concentrate his resources on resisting incursions by Swedish forces and the Teutonic Knights. In 1252, he added the principality of Vladimir to his possessions.

1 Lisbon was captured from the Muslims by a fleet from northern Europe *en route* to the Second Crusade in the Holy Land in 1147.

2 Alexander Nevsky's victory at the river Neva in 1240 halted further Swedish expansion eastward.

3 Austria was founded as a duchy by Frederick Barbarossa in 1156 to counter Welf power in Bavaria.

4 The wealthy cities of Lombardy formed defensive leagues in 1167 and 1226 to resist imperial attempts to restrict their freedoms.

5 A major concern of the Papacy was to prevent a political union between the Holy Roman empire and the kingdom of Sicily.

6 Sicily passed to the Normans (1091); to emperor Henry IV (1194); to the Angevin dynasty (1266); to the Aragonese (1282); to independence (1295).

See also 41 (Viking age Europe); 48 (Crusades); 49 (Mongol empire)

Turkish power in the Middle East grew rapidly after the Seljuk invasion of the Ghaznavid emirate in 1037. Three years later, under Toghril Beg (r.1038–63), they had occupied the emirate's western provinces. In 1054–55 the Seljuks, heeding an appeal for help by the Abbasid caliph of Baghdad, drove the Buwayhids from the city. As Sunni Muslims, the Seljuks accorded the caliph greater respect than had the Shiite Buwayhids, but they were no less firm in ruling the city. Under Toghril Beg's successor, Alp Arslan (r.1063–72), the Seljuks overran Syria and routed the Byzantines at Manzikert. Alp Arslan was killed in 1072 repelling a Qarakhanid Turk invasion at Berzem, but in the reign of his successor Malik Shah (r.1072–92), Byzantine Anatolia was occupied and the Fatimids were expelled from Palestine.

Malik Shah's death sparked civil war and the Seljuk sultanate began to fragment. By 1095 the sultanate of Rum and the Danishmend emirate in Anatolia had seceded, and by 1100 there were dozens of independent Seljuk states. The main beneficiaries were the Byzantine empire and the First Crusade, which between them deprived the Seljuks of western Anatolia and northern Syria, and the Fatimids, who retook Palestine in 1098, only to lose it again almost at once to the Crusaders.

Turkish power in the west began to recover under Zangi, the *atabeg* (governor) of Mosul (r.1127–46), who united northern Syria and recaptured Edessa from the Crusaders in 1144. Zangi's son Nur al-Din (r.1146–74) conquered the rest of Muslim Syria and destroyed the Shiite Fatimid caliphate of Egypt. After his death, Saladin, Kurdish governor of Egypt, rebelled against the Zangids and by 1177 controlled the emirate. The Ayyubid dynasty founded by Saladin held power until 1250 when the Mamlukes, a caste of mainly Turkish slave soldiers, seized power. This military elite continued to rule Egypt and Syria until 1517, surviving as a class until 1811. The Seljuks of Rum also recovered their power and

defeated the Byzantines at Myriocephalum in 1176.

In the east Turkish power continued to wane in the 12th century and in 1156 the Abbasid caliphate enjoyed a revival. Although its political authority extended only to Iraq, its spiritual authority enabled it to arbitrate in disputes between the Seljuk states. Then, in the early 13th century, the eastern Seljuk states were absorbed by a new Turkish power, the shahdom of Khwarizm. However, its growth was abruptly halted by the Mongol invasion of 1219. With one stroke, Chingis Khan broke the shahdom's

## TIMELINE

### Political change

| 1100 | 1250 | 1400 |
|---|---|---|
| **1038–40** The Seljuks conquer Khorasan | **1187** Saladin recaptures Jerusalem from the Crusaders | **1354** The Ottomans capture Gallipoli |
| **1055** Seljiks capture Baghdad | **1210** Foundation of the Khwarizm shahdom | **1370–1405** Timur the Lame terrorizes the Middle East |
| **1071** The Seljuks defeat Byzantines at Manzikert | **1243** Seljuk Sultanate of Rum becomes Mongol vassal state | **1389** The Ottoman armies crush the Serbs at Kosovo |
| **1092** Death of Malik Shah; Seljuk sultanate disintegrates | **1258** The Mongols execute the last Abbasid caliph at Baghdad | **1396** The Ottomans defeat the Crusaders at Nicopolis |
| **1099** The First Crusade captures Jerusalem | **c.1280** Foundation of the Ottoman Turkish state | **1402** The Ottomans defeated by Timur at Ankara |
| **1127–46** Zangi, emir of Mosul, unites Turkish emirates of Syria | **1291** The Crusaders are expelled from the Holy Land | **1453** The Ottomans take Constantinople, end of the Byzantine empire |
| **1169–71** Saladin conquers Egypt for the Zangid emirate | | |

### Cultural change

| 1100 | 1250 | 1400 |
|---|---|---|
| **1027–1123** Omar Khayyam: Persian scientist and poet | **1198** Death of Ibn Rushd (Averröes): philosopher | **1352** Ibn Battuta explores the Sahara Desert |
| **1065–67** Nizamayeh academy (Baghdad) is founded | **1273** Death of Djelaleddin Rumi, founder of the order of Dervishes | **1454** Construction of the Topkapi palace is begun at Constantinople |
| **c. 1080** Construction of the Friday Mosque in Isfahan | | |
| | **1347** The Black Death reaches Baghdad | |

### Legend

- Seljuk sultanate at maximum extent, 1092 (upon death of Malik Shah)
- ⎯ border, 1095
- Byzantine empire, 1095
- Seljuk territory lost to Byzantines and Crusaders, 1097–99
- Fatimid caliphate, 1095
- Zangid emirate under Nur al-Din, c.1174 (Ayyubid emirate from 1177)
- Khwarizm shahdom, c.1220
- Ottoman Turks under Osman I, c.1300
- Ottoman empire, c.1360
- Ottoman empire including vassal states, c.1492
- → Seljuk campaigns, with date
- → Mongol invasions, with date
- → route of Ottoman advance into Europe
- ⊗ Turk victory
- ⊗ Turk defeat
- ■ Ottoman capital, with date
- Assassin stronghold

0 — 600 km
0 — 400 mi

Turk nomads

Karakhanids

**5**

Khazars

*Aral Sea*

Jend
1219

1219

Otrar

1219

1221

*Caspian Sea*

1028-38

1220

Tashkent

Urgench

KHWARIZM

Bukhara

1220

Samarkand

1220

SOGHD

Derbent

GEORGIA

1221

1221

**1**

Dandanqan
1040

*Amu Dar'ya*

1258-61

Balkh

1221

*HINDU KUSH*

*Indus*

Ani

Armenia

**2**

Manzikert
1071

*Lake Van*

Tabriz

*Lake Urmia*

**4**

Jurjen

Merv

1220

**1**

Nishapur
1038

Berzem
1072

KHORASAN

1221

1258-61

Herat

Parvan
1221

Kabul

Afghanistan

Ghazni

Peshawar

*Chenab*

Sialkot

Mosul
1042

*Tigris*

1042

JAZIRA

1220

1258-61

Alamut

Rayy
1220

1258-61

1258-61

1258-61

Toghril Beg, 1040-42

*ZAGROS MOUNTAINS*

*Dasht-e Lut*

Punjab

*Sulej*

Kermanshah

lp Arslan, 1064-71

1055

Baghdad

Hamadan

GREAT SELJUK
SULTANATE

Isfahan

PERSIA

SEISTAN

GHAZNAVID EMIRATE

*Helmand*

Multan

Kufa

1229-31

Kerman

Basra

Siraf

SULTAN Mehmet II's capture
of Constantinople in 1453
was decisive in Ottoman
history. His portrait was
painted by the Venetian
Gentile Bellini.

Shiraz

*Persian Gulf*

Arab nomads

*Gulf of Oman*

ARABIA

Muscat

Oman

**1** The Ghaznavids lost their western territories to the Seljuks after defeats at Nishapur and Dandanqan.

**2** Sultan Alp Arslan's victory over the Byzantines at Manzikert began the Seljuk conquest of Anatolia.

**3** Nicaea became the capital of the Seljuk sultanate of Rum ("Rome", from *Romaivi*, as the Byzantine Greeks called themselves) in 1080; when it fell to the Crusaders in 1097, the capital was moved to Iconium.

**4** Alamut was the main stronghold of the Shiite Ismaili Nizari sect (the Assassins).

**5** The Mongol invaders of the 13th century occupied or imposed vassalage on all the Middle East except Palestine, Egypt, Syria and Arabia.

**6** Their defeat by the Ottomans at Kosovo is deeply ingrained on the Serbian national consciousness; for many, it justified the "ethnic cleansing" of Muslims in the Bosnian civil war of 1992-95.

**7** The Ottoman state is named after Osman I (r.1280-1324), a Turkish chieftain who ruled Sögüt.

power. The Seljuks of Rum were reduced to vassals in 1243, the Abbasid caliphate was destroyed, this time for good, in 1258, and in 1260 the Mongols drove the Mamlukes out of Syria. Though the Mamlukes recovered much of this territory after their victory over the Mongols at 'Ain Jalut later that year, the Mongols remained the dominant power in the Middle East until Timur the Lame's death in 1405.

Following the Mongol conquests, the Seljuk sultanate of Rum broke up. The Byzantine empire was now too weak to benefit, while the Serbs, Bulgars and the Latins were busy arguing over the remains of the dying empire. The Ottoman state began its growth under the minor Anatolian chief Osman I, and by the death of Orhan (r.1324–60) the Ottomans occupied most of northwest Anatolia and had begun to expand into Europe, capturing Gallipoli in 1354. In 1361 Murad I (r.1360–89) captured Adrianople and, renaming it Edirne, transferred the capital there. Timur the Lame's invasion in 1402, and his victory at Ankara, led to the temporary collapse of the sultanate but the Ottomans rallied quickly, expanding

again by 1430. Constantinople, and with it the Byzantine empire, fell in 1453. Although further expansion into central Europe was checked by the Hungarians at Belgrade in 1456, the Ottoman sultanate was still a rising power in 1492.

A major factor in Ottoman success was the weakness of the neighboring Christian and Turkish states. The divisions in Europe caused by the Hundred Years' War and the Great Schism precluded a concerted Christian resistance, while the Seljuks were weakened by the Mongols, who subsequently withdrew from Anatolia. Religious zeal was another vital element. Osman I had been a *ghazi*, an Islamic warrior, and commitment to spreading the faith through holy war motivated the Ottoman armies. This was especially true of its elite Janissary corps which was composed of the children of Christians, who were raised as devout Muslims.

See also 48 (the Crusades);
59 (the peak of the Ottoman empire)

The Crusades were holy wars fought to defend the Catholic church and the Christian people against those who were regarded as external and internal enemies of Christendom. Although the main crusading effort was directed against the Muslims in the Holy Land, Crusades were also conducted against the pagan Slavs of the Baltic, Muslim Spain, the Ottoman Turks in the Balkans and heretics, such as the Cathars, within western Christendom itself. Though considered peripheral at the time, it was these campaigns, particularly those in Spain and the Baltic, that were ultimately the most successful. The movement did not die out completely until the 18th century. However, the main period of crusading activity lasted from 1096 to 1291, which saw eight major campaigns and dozens of smaller expeditions.

The Crusaders saw their role as part of the pilgrimage tradition. Pilgrimages to holy places were undertaken as penance and to acquire spiritual merit. The ultimate pilgrimage was to Jerusalem, and when the Turks began to harass pilgrims in the 11th century, an armed pilgrimage to restore Christian control was thought fully justified. This appealed both to the piety and the adventurous spirit of the feudal knightly class, who saw themselves as protectors of Christendom. As an inducement the papacy offered Crusaders spiritual and legal privileges, most important of which was remission of the penances due for sin. This was popularly interpreted as a guarantee of immediate entry to heaven if the Crusader were to die on the expedition.

The First Crusade was called by Pope Urban II at the Council of Clermont in 1095 in response to an appeal from the Byzantine emperor Alexius I Comnenus for military help against the Seljuk Turks. The first army to set out, a motley band of poorly armed pilgrims, was wiped out near Nicomedia. However, the main army, mostly French and Norman knights, fought its way across Anatolia to Antioch and on to Jerusalem, which was taken in 1099. The First Crusade was the most successful, thanks in part to divisions in the Muslim world. Four Crusader states were set up in Syria and Palestine: the Kingdom of Jerusalem, the County of Tripoli, the Principality of Antioch and the County of Edessa.

Muslim unity began to be restored by Zangi, governor of Mosul, who retook Edessa in 1144. This loss prompted the Second Crusade (1147–49), which was badly mauled crossing Anatolia and achieved nothing. The loss of Jerusalem after Saladin's victory at Hattin in 1187 led to the calling of the Third Crusade under Richard I (Lionheart) of England and Philip II Augustus of France. Although this failed to recover Jerusalem, by retaking the coast of Palestine it ensured the survival of the Crusader states.

In the 13th century, Crusaders showed an increasingly sophisticated strategic approach to defense of the Holy Land. It was realized that Christian control of the region could never be secure so long as Egypt remained the center of Muslim power. The Fourth Crusade (1202–04) was the first called with the intention of attacking Egypt but it never reached its destination. Assembled in Venice, the Crusaders were unable to pay for their transit to Egypt, and so agreed to help the Venetians capture the Hungarian city of Zara. Thereafter, the Crusade was diverted to Constantinople in support of a claimant for the Byzantine throne who promised support for the expedition. When this was not forthcoming, the Crusaders sacked Constantinople and made it the center of a Latin Empire. The Fifth Crusade (1217–21) took Damietta at the mouth of the Nile but was defeated by river flooding as it

**Map legend:**

- border, c.1144
- Byzantine empire, c.1144
- Byzantine states, 1204
- Islamic states, 1204
- Venetian territory, 1204
- Crusader territory, 1204
- Crusader territory lost by 1204

**Crusades**
- First, 1096–99
- Third, 1190–91
- Fourth, 1202–04
- Fifth (main army), 1217–21
- Seventh, 1248–54
- Eighth, 1270

- Crusader victory
- Crusader defeat
- castle of the Military Orders
- other Crusader castle or fortified town
- Muslim castle or fortified town
- Assassin castle
- Pisa   city with important trade links to the Holy Land, c.1200

0 ————— 400 km
0 ————— 300 mi

**TIMELINE**

**Eastern Mediterranean**

| | | | |
|---|---|---|---|
| **1095** Pope Urban II calls the First Crusade at Clermont | **1144** Zangi, governor of Mosul takes Edessa | **1217–21** The Fifth Crusade attacks Egypt | **1291** Mamlukes capture Acre: fall of Kingdom of Jerusalem |
| **1098** Crusaders take Edessa and Antioch | **1149** The Second Crusade ends in failure | **1228–29** The Sixth Crusade secures Jerusalem | **1302** Fall of Ruad. Crusaders are expelled from Holy Land |
| **1099** Crusaders capture Jerusalem. Defeat of Egyptian relief army at Ascalon | **1187** Saladin defeats Christians at Hattin and recaptures Jerusalem | **1248–54** Louis IX leads the Seventh Crusade in Egypt | **1310** The Hospitallers are established on Rhodes |
| **1113** Founding of Order of the Hospital of St John in Jerusalem (Hospitallers) | **1190–92** Third Crusade under Richard I: Cyprus captured | **1261** Byzantines recapture Constantinople: fall of the Latin Empire | **1312** The Order of the Knights Templar is dissolved |
| **1118** Founding of the Order of the Knights Templar | **1204** The Fourth Crusade takes Constantinople; founding of the Latin Empire | **1270** Louis IX (St Louis) dies besieging Tunis on the Eighth Crusade | |

**1396** The Ottomans defeat Burgundian–Hungarian Crusade at Nicopolis

**1456** Crusaders defend Belgrade against the Ottomans

**Other Crusades**

| | | | |
|---|---|---|---|
| **1096** Urban II offers privileges to Crusaders fighting the Spanish Muslims | **1208** Pope Innocent III calls a Crusade against the Cathar heretics in southern France | **1309** The Teutonic Knights launch a permanent Crusade against the pagan Lithuanians | **1420** A Crusade is proclaimed against the Hussite heretics in Bohemia |
| **1147** Crusades against the pagan Wends (Slavs) in the Baltic. Crusaders take Lisbon | **1227** The Teutonic Knights begin crusading against the pagan Prussians | | **1492** The fall of Granada completes the Christian reconquest of Spain |

1200        1300        1400

**Map labels:**

CARPATHIAN MTS

Cumans

Alans

HUNGARY

Danube
Drava
Sava
Tisza
Dnieper
Dniester

Belgrade 1456

Spalato

Serbia

Nish

Nicopolis 1396

Danube

Bulgaria

Varna 1444

Black Sea

Cumans

Sinope

Philippopolis

First

Fifth

Bari

Dyrrachium

Pelagonia 1259

Thessalonica

Edirne (Adrianople) to Venice

Rhaidestos

Constantinople 1203, 1204

LATIN EMPIRE

Nicomedia 1096

Nicaea

EMPIRE OF TREBIZOND

Trebizond

Marsivan 1101

Armenians

Mardin

KINGDOM OF THESSALONICA

DESPOTATE OF EPIRUS

Gallipoli to Venice

Fourth

Poimanenon 1225

Dorylaeum 1097, 1147

Ancyra

SELJUK SULTANATE OF RUM

MONGOL ILKHANATE c.1250

Bodonitza

Patras

Thebes

Athens

Corinth

Nauplia

Karitaina

Arcadia

Mistra

Monemvasia

PRINCIPALITY OF ACHAEA

Aegean Sea

EMPIRE OF NICAEA

Smyrna

ANATOLIA

Philomelium

Laodicea

Caesarea

Iconium

Heraclea

LESSER ARMENIA

Sis

Anavarza

Haruniye

COUNTY OF EDESSA

Edessa 1144

Harran

ZANGID SULTANATE OF MOSUL

Bodrum

Third

Rhodes
Rhodes

Castellorize

Seleucia

Tarsus

Antioch 1098

Aleppo

PRINCIPALITY OF ANTIOCH

Euphrates

Crete

Candia

Seventh

Fifth

KINGDOM OF CYPRUS

Kyrenia

Cyprus

Famagusta

Gastria

Kolossi

Limassol

Sahyun

Hamah

Masyaf

Tortosa

Ruad

Tripoli

Homs

Krak des Chevaliers

COUNTY OF TRIPOLI

Mediterranean Sea

Beirut

Sidon

Baalbek

Damascus 1148

Hattin, 1187

'Ain Jalut, 1260

Belvoir

Bastra

Caesarea

Arsuf 1191

Acre

Jaffa

Ascalon 1099

Gaza 1240

Magna Mahumeria

Amman

Jerusalem 1099

Kerak

Arab nomads

Rosetta

Alexandria

Damietta

Mansura 1250

FATIMID CALIPHATE to 1171

Cairo

Nile

Celle

Montreal

KINGDOM OF JERUSALEM

Qal'at al-Jundi

Pharaoh's Island

Aila

MAMLUKE SULTANATE from 1250

MOUNTED Crusaders in heavy armor (seen in a 13th-century manuscript) were poorly equipped for the rigors of the Holy Land.

**1** Magna Mahumeria was a farming settlement of volunteers from France, Spain and Italy, occupied 1120–87 with a population of c.700. Settlers received land on easy terms in return for military service.

**2** The concentric castle was the most important innovation of Crusader military architecture. The earliest, begun in 1168, is at Belvoir.

**3** Food and water shortages and Turkish attacks made Anatolia highly dangerous for Crusaders. After the Second Crusade failed, most went to Palestine by sea.

**4** Occupied by the Hospitallers in 1310, Rhodes became an major Crusader base for campaigns against the Turks until its capture by the Ottomans in 1522.

**5** The fortress island of Ruad was the last Christian stronghold in the Holy Land to fall to the Muslims, being taken by the Mamlukes in 1302.

**6** Malta, the last bastion of the Crusading movement, was home to the Hospitallers from 1530 to 1798, when they were expelled by Napoleon.

advanced on Cairo. The Holy Roman emperor Frederick II gained Jerusalem through diplomacy on the Sixth Crusade (1228–29) but did not win enough territory to ensure its defense once the truce broke down, and the city was lost again in 1244. The Seventh Crusade (1248–54) under Louis IX of France was an exact repeat of the Fifth. The Eighth Crusade (1270), also led by Louis IX and directed against Tunis with the intention of using it as a base for further attacks on Egypt, was also a costly failure. Far more significant than the Crusades in ensuring the survival of the Crusader states in the 13th century were the Mongol attacks on the Muslim world. After decisively defeating the Mongols at 'Ain Jalut in 1260, the Mamlukes turned their full attention to the Crusader states, which finally fell in 1291.

Throughout their existence the Crusader states suffered from a critical shortage of manpower.

Attempts to attract settlers foundered on the extreme inhospitability of the region. Instead, castle building became highly sophisticated; these castles were often garrisoned by military monastic orders, such as the Knights Templars and the Knights Hospitallers, founded to help defend the Holy Land.

The Crusades had considerable effects on the Islamic world, where they briefly revived the concept of the *jihad* (holy war). Nevertheless, Arab historians of the time gave them only scanty attention, and saw the Mongols as a far more potent threat to Islamic civilization.

See also 44 (the world religions); 47 (the medieval Turkish empires)

The dramatic expansion of the Mongols that began under Temujin was the most important event in world history in the 13th century. The son of a minor Mongol chief, Temujin's brilliant leadership in inter-tribal warfare enabled him to unify the Mongol peoples in a ruthless two-year campaign.

To mark his success he was proclaimed Chingis ("universal") Khan in 1206. During his unification campaign, he created what has often been called the finest cavalry army that the world has ever seen. If the army was not to break up, and his khandom with it, he had to find work for it to do and wealth with which to reward it. He therefore adopted a policy of all-round aggression, and by his death in 1227 he had conquered an empire that included most of central Asia and northern China.

His successors, his son Ogedai and grandsons Küyük and Möngke, continued his expansionist policy and by 1259 they had carried the Mongol conquests into Europe and the Middle East. In China, only the southern Song empire stood out against the Mongols, though it too would fall within 20 years. However, Mongol unity was fragile and already the achievement of Chingis Khan had started to unravel.

The Mongol conquests formed the largest land empire in history. The achievement is all the more remarkable in that the Mongols had few governmental institutions and did not even possess basic metalworking skills. They were fortunate in being able to exploit existing disunity among their enemies. China was divided into three hostile kingdoms. The powerful Turkish empires of Kara-Khitai and Khwarizm were mutually hostile and had dynastic problems. Russia, like most of Europe, was a mosaic of quarrelsome states which cooperated only reluctantly and ineffectually against the common enemy.

The key factor in the Mongol success, however, was the magnificent army that Chingis created. Unlike the armies of their opponents, where birth usually determined rank, promotion in the Mongol

army was by merit only. The discipline and mobility of the Mongol army enabled it to execute complex battlefield maneuvers, giving it decisive advantages over any opponent. A frequent tactic was the feigned retreat, used to lure rash pursuers into ambushes on unfavorable ground where they could be destroyed. The Mongols had an excellent long-range weapon in the composite bow, which enabled them to inflict casualties while keeping out of danger themselves. The Mongols also committed horrific atrocities, systematically creating terror to sap their enemies' will to resist. This persuaded many Turks, Uighurs, Kipchaks and Chinese to defect to the Mongols rather than risk defeat.

The Mongol military machine had its limitations. Except in China, the boundaries of the Mongol empire were very close to those of the Eurasian

## TIMELINE

| | 1220 | 1240 | 1260 |
|---|---|---|---|
| **The Mongol world** | **c1167** Birth of Temujin (Chingis Khan) | **1227** Death of Chingis Khan on a campaign in the Jin empire | **1241** Death of Ogedai |
| | **1204–06** Temujin unites the Mongol tribes and is proclaimed Chingis Khan | **1229** Ogedai, second son of Chingis, is elected Great Khan | |
| | | **1235** Ogedai establishes the Mongol capital at Karakorum | |
| **Eastern conquests** | **1209** The Mongols attack Xixia and Uighurs | **1226** The conquest of Xixia is complete | |
| | **1211** The first Mongol attacks on China (Jin empire) | **1234** The Jin capital Kaifeng falls to the Mongols | |
| | **1215** The Mongols capture Dadu (Beijing) | | **1252** The conquest of the Song empire (southern China) begins |
| | **1218** Kara-Khitai empire is conquered by the Mongols | | |
| **The West** | **1219–21** Chingis Khan invades Khwarizm shahdom | **1237–41** The Mongols invade Russia and eastern Europe | **1258** Baghdad falls to the Mongols, and the last Abbasid caliph is executed |
| | **1220–23** Chingis Khan sends a force to Russia | | **1260** The Mongols are defeated by the Mamlukes at 'Ain Jalut |
| | 1220 | 1240 | 1260 |

SHOOTING at the gallop, the Mongolian warrior was unequalled in battle. His horse was his most indispensable possession.

steppes and grasslands, which alone could provide the necessary grazing for the vast herds of horses that accompanied every Mongol army. The defeat suffered by the Mongols at the hands of the Mamlukes at 'Ain Jalut in 1260 was to some extent the result of poor grazing in the Syrian desert. This, rather than the strength of local resistance, was probably also the reason the Mongols never returned to Europe after their invasion of 1241–42. The army also needed plenty of room TO maneuver, so it was less effective in forested, mountainous or intensively farmed areas than it was in open country. This helps to explain, for example, the relative slowness of the conquest of China.

The period of the Mongols' expansion had few beneficial results: they destroyed far more than they built. The most sophisticated civilizations of the time – the Muslim and the Chinese – suffered the worst. The Abbasid caliphate of Baghdad, spiritual, cultural and (for much of the time) political leader of the Muslim world since the 8th century, was overthrown. The ancient cities of central Asia were devastated and never recovered their former prosperity. Depopulation and the neglect of irrigation channels meant that most of Iraq and west Persia was reduced to desert for centuries. Northern China suffered depopulation and the Mongol conquest isolated Russia from the mainstream of European development for almost two centuries. The impact of the Mongols on the rest of Christendom was fleeting, and by disrupting the Muslim world they granted a brief stay of execution to the Crusader states and allowed a shortlived revival of the crumbling Byzantine empire. Eventually, Christendom benefited from the Mongol conquests in Asia, as Muslim control of the silk route ended and the way was opened for westerners such as Marco Polo to travel to east Asia for the first time.

**1** The governor of Otrar provoked Chingis Khan's invasion of the Khwarizm shahdom by executing merchants and envoys from the Mongols in 1218.

**2** Chingis Khan divided his army at Samarkand, despatching a smaller force to pursue the Khwarizm Shah and then cross the Caucasus to gather intelligence in Europe.

**3** Chingis Khan died here in 1227 on campaign against the Jin empire.

**4** Fighting in unfavorable mountainous terrain, it took the Mongols 30 years to force the Koreans to submit. Thereafter the Koreans became close allies.

**5** Karakorum, favorite campsite of Chingis, became the capital of the Mongol empire in 1235.

**6** Using frozen rivers as highways, the Mongols launched the only successful winter invasion in Russian history in 1238–39. The Russians paid tribute to the Mongols for two centuries.

**7** The combined armies of eastern Europe were routed at Legnica and Mohi in 1241. The Mongols withdrew on news of Ogedai Khan's death.

**8** The fall of Baghdad was followed by the massacre of 200,000 captives (20 percent of the population).

**9** The first major defeat of the Mongols was at the hands of the Mamlukes at 'Ain Jalut in 1260.

border, c.1200

Mongol lands, c.1206

conquests of Chingis Khan, 1209–27

Mongol conquests, 1227–59

area of loose Mongol control

⊗ Mongol victory

⊗ Mongol defeat

🔥 city sacked by Mongols

TATARS  Mongol tribe united by Chingis Khan, 1204–06

➤ campaigns under Chingis Khan

➤ Mongol campaigns, 1228–60

silk route

0        800 km

0        500 mi

See also 46 (Europe);
47 (Muslim world)

The early states of Japan and Korea were strongly influenced by Chinese civilization. By 600 Chinese administrative practices and political ideologies were being introduced by Japanese and Korean rulers as they attempted to build centralized states. These endeavors had been largely successful in Korea by the 15th century, but in Japan initial success was followed by progressive decentralization of authority and, in the 15th century, the growth of feudalism. The elite culture of Korea was heavily influenced b that of China in this period. There were similar fo in Japan but also a much greater retention of dist tively Japanese ideas and practices.

In Japan, the attempt to build a centralized state on Chinese lines began late in the Yamato period (AD 300–710). Prince Shotoku (r.593–622) introduced a constitution in 604 asserting the power of the emperor over the nobility. The Taika reforms that followed in 646 brought all land into imperial ownership and instituted a tax system. In 702 the Taiho laws – new civil and penal codes – were introduced. Buddhism was promoted as a way of increasing imperial authority. Finally in 710 a permanent administrative capital, modeled on Chang'an, was established at Nara. Yet the achievement of the Yamato period reformers was superficial and the centralized state was never able to consolidate its authority.

Nara became an important religious center and the Buddhist clergy soon began to exert strong political influence over the emperors. To escape this interference, emperor Kammu moved the court to a new capital at Heian (modern Kyoto) in 794. Here the emperors came under the sway of the aristocratic Fujiwara family, who skillfully strengthened their political influence by marrying into the imperial family. Buddhist monasteries and great families such as the Fujiwara were able to amass extensive landholdings at imperial expense by obtaining *shoen* (private tax-free estates) as rewards for good service.

MELODRAMATIC masks were used in the Korean style of drama, which was imported from China.

# TIMELINE

| | | 800 | | 1200 | | |
|---|---|---|---|---|---|---|
| | Yamato | | Heian | Kamakura | Ashikaga | |
| **Japan** | **604** Prince Shotoku introduces Chinese-influenced constitution | **858** Fujiwara Yorifusa becomes regent | | **1333–36** Go-Daigo tries to restore direct imperial rule | | |
| | **700–800** The Shinto religion is assimilated to Buddhism | | **1010** *The Tale of Genji*, by Lady Murasaki Shikibu | **1333–84** Kan'ami Kiyotsugo, founder of Noh drama | | |
| | **708** The earliest official coinage in Japan is instituted | | **1156–59** Hogen and Heiji insurrections; Taira samurai clan is dominant at court | **1467–77** Onin War: rise of daimyo and feudalism | | |
| | **710** A permanent capital is established at Nara | | **1185** Destruction of the Taira at battle of Dannoura | | | |
| **Korea** | **600–700** Chan (Zen) Buddhism is established in Silla | **c.900** The kingdom of Silla collapses | **1231** Mongol invasions of Korea begin | | | |
| | **660–68** China conquers Koguryo and Paekche | **918** The Koryo dynasty is established at Kaegyong (Kaesong): it unifies Korea in 936 | **1234** Earliest use of cast metal movable type for printing books | | | |
| | **676** Silla expels the Chinese from Korea | **926** Khitan nomads overrun Parhae | **1258** Korea becomes a Mongol vassal state | | | |
| | **694** Establishment of the state of Parhae | | **1446** Korean alphabetical script replaces Chinese script | | | |
| | | **800–900** Populist "New Land" Buddhism established in Silla | | | | |
| | | 800 | | 1200 | | |

Map labels: Khanka, Sanggyong, Khitans 10th century, 12th century, Songhua, Tonggyong, Chunggyong, KOGURYO, Pyongsong, Tumen, Sogyong, Kungnaesong, Liaoyang, 7, 8, Yingzhou, Yalu, Long Wall, 661, 668, 1018, Kusong, Nangyong, Anbuk, The "Six Garrisons", Anbyon, Pyongyang, Imjin, Kaegyong capital 918–1394, Anson, SILLA, Kanghwa, Seoul capital 1394–1910, 9, Sosan, Andong, 660, Annam, Kongju, Naktong, Hakusukinoe (Paek-kang), Yellow Sea, Puyu, Kyongju, 663, PAEKCHE, Masan, 6, Pusan, Tsushima, Ouchi, 5, Yamaguchi, Dannoura 1185, 3, Hakataka Bay 1281, Hirado, Shoni, Hososhima, Oto..., Weifu, Goto Islands, Shimo, Cheju-do, Kagoshima, Shimazu, Satsuma, Kyushu, Osumi Islands

0    300 km
0    200 mi

**Jürchen**
*(pastoral farmers)*

area under control of warrior clans, 1183

Northern Fujiwara

Minamoto Yoritomo

Minamoto Yoshinaka

Taira

—— border of major *daimyo* house, c.1467

—— northern frontier, with date

Toki *daimyo* house

capital

*shoen* of the Fujiwara family, 9th–12th century

Ainu hillfort

early fortress

major late medieval castle, c.1300–1600

coast affected by Japanese piracy and smuggling, 15th century

—— border of the Three Kingdoms, c.350–688

kingdom of Silla, 676–c.900

kingdom of Parhae, 694–926

kingdom of Korea, c.960

gains by Yi dynasty

capital of the Three Kingdoms

"Five capitals" of Parhae

capital of Korea

Koryo regional military command

Koryo border fort

Yi dynasty border fort, c.1450

naval base, c.1450

Seoul cultural center

frontier wall

Chinese invasion, 660–8

Mongol invasion, 1231–54

Mongol invasion, 1274

Mongol invasion, 1281

major migration

**Ainu**
*(hunter-gatherers)*

Hokkaido

Sea of Japan

PACIFIC OCEAN

Ezo

Honshu

Shikoku

1 The Ezo people of Honshu, related to the Ainu, fiercely resisted Japanese expansion but were conquered by the 12th century.

2 The Ainu were an aboriginal hunter-gatherer people, linguistically and physically unrelated to any other east Asian peoples, who were only brought under Japanese rule in the 17th century.

3 The destruction of the Taira at the battle of Dannoura was made the subject of the *Tale of the Heike*, the major literary work of 13th-century Japan.

4 One of the best preserved Japanese medieval castles is White Heron Castle at Himeji (14th century).

5 Fishing villages in the Inland Sea and on Tsushima became bases for smugglers and pirates, breaking tight Korean and Chinese restrictions on trade.

6 The kingdom of Paekche fell after its Japanese allies were defeated by Silla in a naval battle in 663.

7 The Koryo dynasty extended its control to the Yalu River c.960, since when it has remained Korea's northwestern border.

8 The Long Wall was built in 1033–44 to defend Korea against Khitan and Jürchen invasions.

9 During the Mongol invasions, the Korean royal court moved to the greater safety of Kanghwa Island.

The exquisitely refined culture of Heian court life contrasted with growing disorder in the provinces. In the absence of a centralized military system, monasteries and aristocratic houses formed private armies and a class of rural warriors – the *samurai* – developed. Sporadic warfare increased, and with it arose the culture of the warrior.

In the 12th century samurai clans became involved in court politics and Fujiwara influence declined. Following the Gempei war (1180–85) between the Taira and Minamoto clans, Minamoto Yoritomo founded the Kamakura shogunate, beginning a period of military government that would last until 1868. The Kamakura shogunate was overthrown in 1333 and replaced five years later by the Ashikaga shogunate. The shoguns ruled in alliance

with the *shugo* (military constables), who gradually became powerful regional rulers, undermining the authority of the shoguns. When a dispute over the shogunal succession escalated into a fullscale civil war between 1467–77, the shugo lost control of their regional power bases. Control of the provinces fell to new feudal warlords, or *daimyo*. The daimyo feuded almost constantly among themselves, deploying armies of samurai vassals who held small estates in return for military service. The castles of the daimyo became the main centers of government and of warrior culture. Castles attracted craftsmen and merchants and many became a focus for urban development. Though the Ashikaga shogunate survived until 1573, the civil war destroyed its remaining authority and by 1500 Japan had fragmented into

almost 400 effectively independent states. The emperors continued to reign in Heian (Kyoto) but they were powerless and impoverished figureheads.

In Korea three kingdoms – Koguryo, Silla and Paekche – had emerged by 600. In 660 the expansionist Chinese Tang dynasty invaded the peninsula and in alliance with Silla conquered Paekche and Koguryo. On finding that it was not to share in the spoils, Silla drove the Chinese from the peninsula in 676. Silla occupied Paekche and southern Koguryo: northern Koguryo remained in chaos until a successor state, Parhae, emerged in 694. Both Korean states developed as centralized kingdoms on the Tang model. In 780 a struggle between the monarchy and the aristocracy broke out in Silla and in the 9th century the kingdom broke up. A new kingdom was created in 918–36 by Wang Kon (r.918–45), founder of the Koryo dynasty from which Korea gets its name. Parhae was extinguished about the same time by the Khitan nomads. Despite Khitan opposition, Korea had established a heavily fortified frontier on the Yalu River by the early 11th century.

A coup in 1170 deprived the monarchy of real power, leaving Korea leaderless until the military Choe family seized power in 1196. The Choe led resistance to the Mongols but unrest grew more widespread as the wars dragged on. The dynasty was overthrown in 1258 and Korea became a Mongol vassal state. The end of Mongol rule in 1356 brought a return to political instability and the Koryo dynasty was eventually overthrown with Chinese help by the general Yi Songgye (r.1392–98), founder of the Yi dynasty (1392–1910). Under the Yi, Confucianism replaced Buddhism as Korea's main ethical code and was made the basis of the bureaucratic and educational systems. The Yi resumed expansion to the northeast, and by the 15th century the country's, modern borders had been established.

See also 44 (the world religions);
49 (Mongol invasion); 63 (later Japan)

Western Europe's confidence grew in the 11th and 12th centuries, as shown in its Gothic cathedrals and in crusades against the Muslims in the Holy Land and the pagan Slavs in eastern Europe (▷ 48). Spain's Christian kingdoms expanded until by 1279 the Muslims were confined to Granada. The Holy Roman empire looked impressive, but disputes with the papacy undermined its authority. By the mid-13th century the empire was becoming a confederation of semi-independent states. In contrast, England and France had become strong centralized kingdoms (▷ 46).

Although Islam lost ground in Europe it continued to expand elsewhere. The Ghaznavid emirate conquered northwest India and in 1206 a Muslim sultanate was founded at Delhi. By 1279 it was the largest state in India since the fall of the Gupta empire. Islam was spread by merchants to west Africa in the 11th century, and by the 13th century, Timbuktu, the capital of the kingdom of Mali, was a center of Muslim culture. Trade with the Muslim world was a factor in the emergence of the first powerful chiefdom of southern Africa at Great Zimbabwe around 1200.

The dominant Muslim power in the 11th century was the Seljuks (▷ 47). Originally a clan of Ghuzz Turk mercenaries who rebelled against their employer, the Ghaznavid emir, in 1037, the Seljuks overran Persia, the Abbasid caliphate, Syria and the Holy Land, and in 1071 won control of Anatolia. Although the First Crusade, which captured Jerusalem in 1099, allowed the Byzantines to reclaim some lost territory, the empire never fully recovered. By this time Seljuk political unity had broken down, and hostility between them and the Fatimids of Egypt meant that Muslim counterattacks against the Crusaders were ineffective. The Crusaders were put on the defensive after the Seljuk Zangid sultanate of Aleppo overthrew the Fatimids 1169–71 and seized Egypt, but the Zangids were themselves overthrown five years later by Saladin, who retook Jerusalem in 1187. The Crusader states were finally destroyed in 1291 by the Mamlukes who had seized power in Egypt in 1250.

The nomadic Mongol peoples had been gradually expanding westward since the breakup of the Turkish steppe empire in the 8th century. Though superb cavalry fighters, they did not threaten the settled civilizations of Eurasia until they were

## TIMELINE

**1066** Death of Norwegian king Harald Hardrada at Stamford Bridge, England, ends Europe's Viking age

**c.1050** Large ceremonial centers grow up among the Anasazi cultures of southwest North America

**1037** The Seljuk Turks rebel against the Ghaznavid emirate

**1122** End of the investiture dispute with the papacy, which has weakened the authority of the Holy Roman emperors

**1099** Crusaders capture Jerusalem and establish Christian principalities in Palestine

**1187** Saladin, sultan of Syria, recaptures Jerusalem from the Crusaders

The Americas
Europe
Middle East
Africa
East and South Asia

1000    1100    1200

**1044–77** King Anawrahta creates a unified Burmese state based at Pagan

**c.1070** Islam is established in west Africa, carried by trans-Saharan traders

**1071** The Byzantine empire is defeated by the Seljuk Turks at Manzikert

**1127** The Song dynasty loses control of northern China to the Jin

**c.1168** The Toltec state in Mesoamerica falls after its capital Tula is sacked

**c.1200** The Chimú people conquer the coastal valleys of Peru

**c.1200** The Great Enclosure is built at Zimbabwe in southern Africa

**c.1200** The first chiefdoms develop in Polynesia

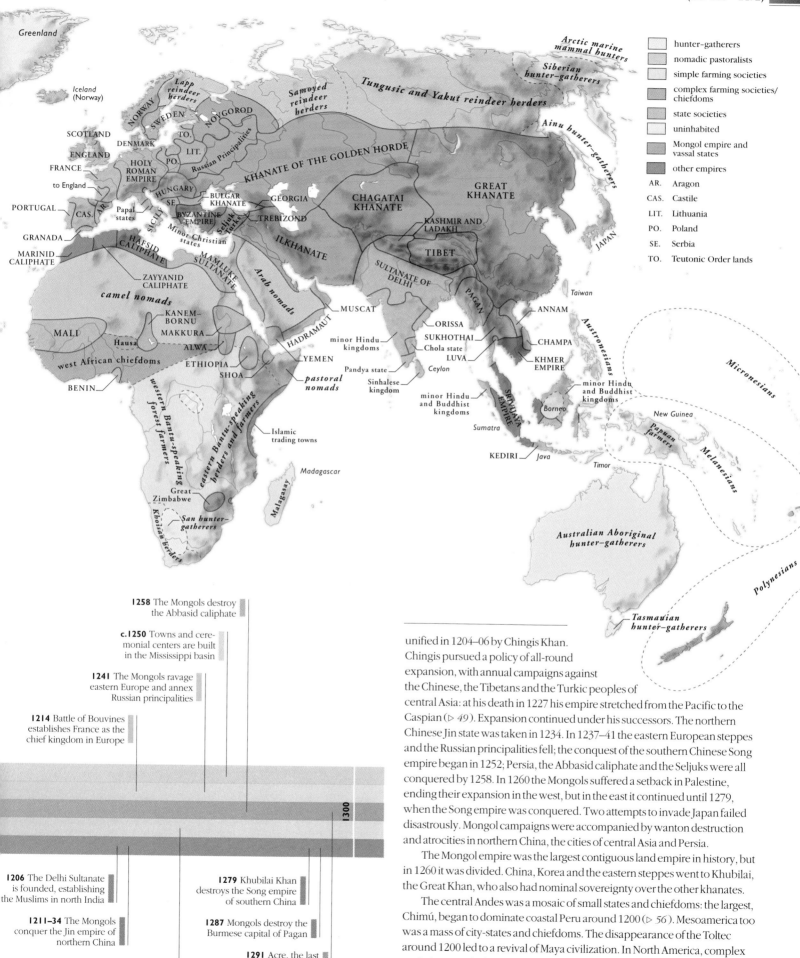

hunter-gatherers
nomadic pastoralists
simple farming societies
complex farming societies/ chiefdoms
state societies
uninhabited
Mongol empire and vassal states
other empires

AR. Aragon
CAS. Castile
LIT. Lithuania
PO. Poland
SE. Serbia
TO. Teutonic Order lands

Greenland

Iceland (Norway)

Lapp reindeer herders
Samoyed reindeer herders
Tungusic and Yakut reindeer herders
Arctic marine mammal hunters
Siberian hunter-gatherers
Ainu hunter-gatherers

NORWAY
SWEDEN
NOVGOROD
TO.
LIT.
PO.
Russian Principalities

SCOTLAND
DENMARK
ENGLAND
FRANCE
to England

HOLY ROMAN EMPIRE
HUNGARY
SE.

KHANATE OF THE GOLDEN HORDE

CHAGATAI KHANATE

GREAT KHANATE

JAPAN

PORTUGAL
CAS.
AR.
Papal states
SICILY
BULGAR KHANATE
BYZANTINE EMPIRE
Seljuk Turks
GEORGIA
TREBIZOND

GRANADA
MARINID CALIPHATE
HAFSID CALIPHATE
Minor Christian states
MAMLUKE SULTANATE
ILKHANATE
KASHMIR AND LADAKH
TIBET

ZAYYANID CALIPHATE
camel nomads
Arab nomads
MUSCAT
SULTANATE OF DELHI
PAGAN
Taiwan

KANEM-BORNU
MAKKURA
Hausa
ALWA
HADRAMAUT
minor Hindu kingdoms
ORISSA
SUKHOTHAI
Chola state
LUVA
ANNAM
CHAMPA

MALI
west African chiefdoms
BENIN
ETHIOPIA
SHOA
YEMEN
pastoral nomads
Pandya state
Sinhalese kingdom
Ceylon
KHMER EMPIRE
minor Hindu and Buddhist kingdoms

western Bantu-speaking forest farmers
eastern Bantu-speaking herders and farmers
Islamic trading towns
minor Hindu and Buddhist kingdoms
Borneo
Sumatra
SRIVIJAYA EMPIRE
New Guinea
Papuan farmers

Madagascar
KEDIRI
Java
Timor
Micronesians
Melanesians

Great Zimbabwe
Malagasy
San hunter-gatherers
Khoisan herders

Australian Aboriginal hunter-gatherers

Austronesians
Polynesians

Tasmanian hunter-gatherers

**1258** The Mongols destroy the Abbasid caliphate

**c.1250** Towns and ceremonial centers are built in the Mississippi basin

**1241** The Mongols ravage eastern Europe and annex Russian principalities

**1214** Battle of Bouvines establishes France as the chief kingdom in Europe

1300

**1206** The Delhi Sultanate is founded, establishing the Muslims in north India

**1211–34** The Mongols conquer the Jin empire of northern China

**c.1235** Rise of kingdom of Mali under Sun Diata Keita

**1279** Khubilai Khan destroys the Song empire of southern China

**1287** Mongols destroy the Burmese capital of Pagan

**1291** Acre, the last Crusader stronghold, falls to the Mamlukes

unified in 1204–06 by Chingis Khan. Chingis pursued a policy of all-round expansion, with annual campaigns against the Chinese, the Tibetans and the Turkic peoples of central Asia: at his death in 1227 his empire stretched from the Pacific to the Caspian (▷ 49). Expansion continued under his successors. The northern Chinese Jin state was taken in 1234. In 1237–41 the eastern European steppes and the Russian principalities fell; the conquest of the southern Chinese Song empire began in 1252; Persia, the Abbasid caliphate and the Seljuks were all conquered by 1258. In 1260 the Mongols suffered a setback in Palestine, ending their expansion in the west, but in the east it continued until 1279, when the Song empire was conquered. Two attempts to invade Japan failed disastrously. Mongol campaigns were accompanied by wanton destruction and atrocities in northern China, the cities of central Asia and Persia.

The Mongol empire was the largest contiguous land empire in history, but in 1260 it was divided. China, Korea and the eastern steppes went to Khubilai, the Great Khan, who also had nominal sovereignty over the other khanates.

The central Andes was a mosaic of small states and chiefdoms: the largest, Chimú, began to dominate coastal Peru around 1200 (▷ 56). Mesoamerica too was a mass of city-states and chiefdoms. The disappearance of the Toltec around 1200 led to a revival of Maya civilization. In North America, complex societies arose in the Anasazi culture of the southwest in the 11th century. Towns developed around ceremonial sites in the Mississippi area (▷ 42) ■

The authority of the papacy – already in decline in the face of royal attempts to build centralized nation-states – faced a further setback in 1303 when it fell under the domination of the French monarchy. In 1309 the papacy took up residence at Avignon. It returned to Rome in 1377, but a disputed papal election led to the Great Schism in 1378, with rival popes at Rome and Avignon. The schism stayed unresolved until 1417 as neither pope would submit to the judgment of a church council. It divided Europe and exacerbated existing political differences. France supported the Avignon papacy, for example, so England – then involved in the Hundred Years War (1337–1453) with France – gave its allegiance to the Roman papacy, while Scotland, antagonistic to England, joined the French party.

The Hundred Years War had been sparked off by French attempts to recover English lands in France. After English victories at Crécy (1346) and Poitiers (1356), the French ceded Aquitaine and Gascony at the treaty of Bretigny (1360). But fighting broke out again and when a 28-year truce was made in 1396 the English held less land in France than they had in 1337. In 1363, the French monarchy stored up future trouble by granting the duchy of Burgundy from the royal desmesne to Philip the Bold, the younger son of John II. Through marriage to the heiress of the Count of Flanders (1369), Philip later added the imperial county of Burgundy (the Franche-Comté) and the wool towns of Flanders to his possessions.

War was endemic throughout the Holy Roman empire. The powerful city-states of northern Italy, where imperial control was now purely nominal, engaged armies of mercenaries to fight one another. The German princes were occupied in dynastic struggles to gain primacy and thus win control of imperial elections. The Wittelsbachs gained the upper hand from the Habsburgs in 1325, only to lose it to the Luxembourgs (1346–1438). From 1377–89 the princes formed a united front to reduce the independence of the cities of south Germany and the Rhineland. In 1388, after a century of rebellion, the Swiss confederation of eight cantons secured their independence from the dukes of Habsburg. In eastern Europe in 1354, the Ottoman Turks took

**Key**

- borders, c.1360–61
- Muslim states
- Orthodox states
- English possessions
- Genoese possessions
- Venetian possessions

Holy Roman empire
- Habsburg lands
- Luxembourg lands
- Wittelsbach lands
- other

Great Schism, 1378
- supporting Avignon papacy
- supporting Roman papacy
- supporting Roman papacy, but with shifting allegiances on a local level

- antisemitic rioting and massacres
- urban revolt
- rural revolt

- lands acquired for Burgundy by Philip the Bold, c.1396
- spread of Black Death, with date
- area relatively lightly affected by the Plague
- Lollard heretic movement, c.1400

**TIMELINE**

**Political change**

| 1325 | 1350 | 1375 |
|---|---|---|
| **1302** Territorial expansion of Muscovy begins | **1326** Cannon first used in Europe by Florentine army | **1378–1417** The Great Schism leads to rival popes at Rome and Avignon |
| **1309–77** The papacy is resident at Avignon | **1331–35** Serbian empire of Stephen Dushan dominates the Balkans | **1380** Muscovites inflict major defeat on Golden Horde at Kulikovo |
| **1310** John of Luxembourg becomes king of Bohemia | **1346–7** Louis IV of Wittelsbach loses imperial title to Charles of Luxembourg | **1389** Serbian defeat at Kosovo makes them vassals of Ottomans |
| **1314–25** War between Wittelsbachs and Habsburgs ends in victory for Louis IV of Wittelsbach | **1347–51** The Black Death devastates Europe | **1397** Union of Calmar unites Scandinavia under the Danish crown |
| **1323** Wars between Scotland and England ends; confirmed by treaty of Edinburgh (1328) | **1356** Charles IV issues the Golden Bull ending papal role in imperial elections | |

**Cultural change**

| 1325 | 1350 | 1375 |
|---|---|---|
| **1305** Frescoes of the Arena Chapel, Padua painted by Giotto | **1348–53** Boccaccio writes the *Decameron* | **1386–1400** Geoffrey Chaucer writes the *Canterbury Tales* |
| **c.1314–21** Dante writes the *Divine Comedy* | **1351** Petrarch, Italian poet, moves from Rome to Provence and begins his *Rime* | |

| 1325 | 1350 | 1375 |

**1** A Genoese attempt to destroy the power of its trading rival Venice was defeated at Chioggia in 1380.

**2** Bohemia, acquired in 1310, served as the Luxembourgs' power base in Germany. Under their rule Prague became a major European cultural center.

**3** The success of English archers over French armored cavalry at Crécy in 1346 showed the increasing importance of infantry in late medieval warfare.

**4** Moscow owed its independence to Prince Daniel (r.1263-1304) who began its territorial expansion.

**5** The Lithuanians, Europe's last pagans, resisted the attempt of the Teutonic Knights to convert them by force, but voluntarily adopted Christianity in 1386.

**6** Defeat at Bannockburn in 1314 forced the English to recognize Scottish independence in 1328, but both kingdoms continued to raid each other's territory.

**7** A Castilian invasion of Portugal was defeated in 1385, securing its future as an independent state.

NORWAY
1380 in union with
Denmark
Bergen

Christiania

SWEDEN
1397 in union with
Denmark

Åbo

Lake
Ladoga

REPUBLIC OF
NOVGOROD

ROSTOV

VLADIMIR-SUZDAL

KHANATE OF THE
GOLDEN HORDE

Stockholm

1350

Novgorod

Lake
Peipus

TVER

MUROM

1351

Visby
1361

Gotland
to Denmark

PSKOV

Riga

Moscow

MUSCOVY

Ålborg

Revel

late 1349

Århus

Calmar

Teutonic Knights

Kulikovo
1380

RYAZAN

mid 1348

Copenhagen

DENMARK

Baltic Sea

western Lithuania

Königsberg

4

1347

Danzig

Vilna

1346

Lübeck

Hamburg

Bremen

Vistula

Warsaw

LITHUANIA

Saxony

Brandenburg

Sarai

Saxony

Brunswick

Magdeburg

5

Volga

HOLY ROMAN
EMPIRE

Elbe

POLAND

Kiev

Cologne

Silesia

Oder

Krakow

RUTHENIA

1350

Frankfurt

Prague

2

Lemberg

Dnieper

Mainz

Nuremberg

Bohemia

Regensburg

Ulm

Bavaria

Vienna

mid 1349

Pest

MOLDAVIA

mid 1348

Swabia

Salzburg

Austria

Buda

late 1349

Basle

Constance

Styria

HUNGARY

late 1348

1347

Kaffa

BLACK DEATH victims – shown in
this French wall-painting – were
buried immediately, often in
unconsecrated ground.

Tyrol

Carinthia

Sava

Milan

mid 1348

Swiss
Confederation

1347

Belgrade

WALLACHIA

Danube

1346

Mantua

Venice

Chioggia
1380

Parma

VENICE

Zara

BOSNIA

Nish

Nicopolis
1396

BULGARIAN STATES
1393 Ottoman vassals

Black Sea
1347

GEORGIA

Genoa

1

Florence

Kosovo
1389

Trebizond

GENOA

Pisa

RAGUSA

SERB STATES
1397 Ottoman vassals

Tuscany

PAPAL
STATES

Constantinople

Corsica

Rome

NAPLES

Durazzo

Thessalonica

Ankara

OTTOMAN
SULTANATE

Gallipoli

Byzantine Empire

Naples

BENEVENTO

Sardinia
to Aragon

TURKISH EMIRATES

Smyrna

Tigris

1347

Palermo

Messina

to Sicily

LESSER
ARMENIA

Euphrates

1347

SICILY

Sicily

DUCHY OF
ACHAEA

to Byzantine
empire

KNIGHTS OF
ST JOHN

Rhodes

CYPRUS

Cyprus

Famagusta

Tunis

Malta
to Sicily

Crete

1347

Mediterranean Sea

JALAYRID
SULTANATE

1347

MAMLUKE SULTANATE

1347

Alexandria

Cairo

Gallipoli on the European shore of the Dardanelles; by the end of the century they had overrun most of the Balkans. Political conflicts and the paralysis of the papacy ensured that there was no purposeful response to the Ottoman threat apart from the unsuccessful Crusade of Nicopolis, led by John the Fearless of Burgundy to support Hungary in 1396.

But the event that dominated the 14th century was the Black Death, a combined epidemic of bubonic and pneumonic plague that broke out on the east Asian steppes in the 1330s and spread along the Silk Road to reach the Genoese port of Kaffa in the Crimea in late 1346. From here it was carried (by the parasitic fleas that infested ships' rats) to Venice, Genoa and Marseille, all ports with strong links to the east, and then spread amazingly quickly along the main trade routes of Europe. One factor explaining the Black Death's rapid inroads may lie in the

series of crop failures earlier in the century, which caused extensive famines in areas where overpopulation was rife. The effects of malnutrition probably weakened resistence to the disease. The impact of the Black Death was catastrophic: even in the most lightly affected areas, ten to fifteen percent of the population died, and in the areas worst affected (Tuscany, East Anglia and Norway) mortality may have been fifty percent or more. Overall, around a third of Europe's population died between 1346 and 1351. The plague remained endemic in Europe for 250 years and many cities had still not regained their pre-plague population levels by the 16th century.

Outbreaks of the plague were often accompanied by religious hysteria, and blame fell on Jews and foreigners who were subjected to attacks. Depopulation caused prices and rents to fall and

wages to rise, loosening the traditional bonds of service. Social disruption increased and urban and rural uprisings such as the Jacquerie wars in northern France (1358), and the English peasants' revolt of 1381, were frequent. Mob violence was mainly directed at landlords, tax officials and rich urban oligarchies, and there was often an element of anticlericalism, found also in the rise of heretical movements such as the Lollards in England. In eastern Europe, in contrast, a largely free peasantry had serfdom imposed upon them by lords who were anxious not to lose tenants.

See also 46 (Feudal Europe); 47 (the Turkish empires); 53 (the medieval economy)

Over 90 percent of the population of medieval Europe were peasant farmers. The manorial system – by which a lord divided up an estate (the manor) between individual peasants who farmed it – was widespread, though there were regional variations. The lord was expected to protect his peasants in times of war, provide relief in times of famine and administer justice in return for payments of produce, labor and money. Many peasants were unfree serfs or villeins, tied for life to the land on which they worked and passing their servile status onto their descendants, but they were not slaves and had certain established rights. By the end of the Middle Ages serfs had been replaced by tenant farmers and wage laborers in the British Isles, Italy and Iberia, but serfdom survived into the 18th century in some parts of western Europe and in Russia until 1861.

A number of agricultural improvements took place in the early Middle Ages. Most important was the widespread adoption around the year 700 of a three-field system of crop rotation, in which one field was used for cereals, one for vegetables such as beans and the third left fallow, to preserve soil fertility. The introduction of the wheeled plow, and later of the padded shoulder collar that enabled horses – 50 percent more efficient than oxen – to be used for plowing, allowed the heavy soils of northern Europe to be worked more efficiently. In these ways productivity was boosted far beyond the levels achieved in Roman times and peasant prosperity increased steadily. Most surplus agricultural produce was sold at local markets but wool, hides, wine, dairy products, salt, fish and grain were traded in large quantities over long distances. Moving goods by land was slow and expensive, so most bulk trade went by sea or river boat. Various industrial activities such as mining, ore smelting, logging, charcoal burning, quarrying and salt extraction were also important in the countryside. Both agriculture and rural industry benefited from technological improvements that

## Trade and commerce

| 1100 | 1200 | 1300 | 1400 |
|---|---|---|---|
| **1081** Venetians negotiate trade privileges in Constantinople | **1155** Earliest recorded fire insurance (in Iceland) | **1230** Lübeck and Hamburg form alliance – the beginning of the Hanseatic league | **c.1300** Italian merchants develop double-entry bookkeeping: basis of modern accountancy |
| **c.1100** Guilds of artisans and craftsmen begin to develop in towns | **1242** Earliest recorded use of convoy system to protect merchant ships from piracy | **c.1350** Marine premium insurance begins in Genoa | **1414** The Medici of Florence become papal bankers |
| **1133** St Bartholomew's Fair, London founded (until 1853) | **1253** Florence and Genoa introduce gold coinage | **1380** Hans Fugger founds a banking concern at Augsburg; Europe's largest financial house by 1500 | **1441** Portuguese slave trade with west Africa begins |
| | | | **1455** First European printing shop is set up at Mainz |

## Society

| 1100 | 1200 | 1300 | 1400 |
|---|---|---|---|
| **c.1000** European population is about 42 million | **c.1180** Windmills in common use in Europe | **1300** European population is approximately 73 million | **c.1435** Three-masted square-rigged ships, capable of oceanic voyaging, come into use |
| **1086** Domesday Book provides a detailed survey of English agriculture and land ownership | **c.1240** Water-powered sawmills come into use in Europe | **1346–51** Around 24 million die in the Black Death | **c.1450** European population is about 50 million |

LÜBECK was a center of the Hanseatic trade in the Baltic, using sturdy ships called cogs, as shown on this seal of 1258.

made possible greater use of water and wind power to mill grain and work pumps, bellows and sawmills.

Except in Italy, urban life declined dramatically in western Europe during the late Roman empire and did not fully recover until the 11th century. Italy remained the most urbanized region of Europe throughout the Middle Ages. Compared with contemporary towns in the Arab world and China, medieval European towns were small and, outside northern Italy and Flanders, rarely had populations above 10,000. They were unhygienic places and, as deaths exceeded births, they relied on immigration from the countryside to maintain their populations. Townspeople were free of servile obligations but citizenship, and with it a right to participate in local government, was normally restricted to property owners. The trade and craft activities of towns were regulated by associations of merchants or craftsmen known as guilds. These dictated standards of quality and training and provided members with welfare benefits, but their principal function was to protect their members by excluding outside competition. Manufactured goods produced in towns were generally intended for the local market but production of high-quality goods for export was important in some areas, such as Flanders, where there was a flourishing woolen textile industry. Seasonal trade fairs were important commercial events, attracting merchants from a far wider area than the weekly town markets; some, for example the Champagne fairs, developed into major centers of international business.

One of the most powerful trade associations of the Middle Ages was the Hanseatic league, membership of which extended to 37 north German and Baltic towns at its peak in the 14th century. The league negotiated trading privileges for its members, prepared navigational charts, suppressed piracy and even waged war. It maintained offices called *kontors* in London, Bergen, Bruges and Novgorod, where its merchants lived and traded permanently, as well as subsidiary depots in many other cities. The league's power declined at the end of the Middle Ages, when it was faced with greater competition from England and the Netherlands. In the Mediterranean, maritime trade was dominated by Venice and Genoa. Both took advantage of the Crusades to build up trade links with Asia, the source of luxury products such as silks, spices and gems, and maintained a bitter rivalry between them.

By the 13th century merchants were assuming the role of capitalists to finance craft production, so that productivity increased but craftsmen lost their independence. International banking houses such as the Medici and the Fuggers emerged, and the principles of modern insurance and accountancy were established.

**1** Flanders was a leading center of Europe's growing textile industry; its prosperity was enshrined in grand town halls, as at Ghent.

**2** England's prosperity resulted from it being Europe's main source of wool for cloth-making.

**3** The Arabs introduced papermaking to Europe at Valencia in the 12th century.

**4** The church's prohibition on eating meat on fast days maintained demand for salted fish from the Baltic and North Seas.

**5** The fairs of Champagne flourished as centers of north–south trade in the 12th and 13th centuries.

**6** The importance of the Black Sea as a trading area increased after the 13th-century Mongol invasions improved access to the east for European traders.

See also 52 (war, revolt and plague);
66 (European economy 1500–1800)

population density per sq km, early 14th century

- over 30
- 21–30
- 11–20
- 10 or under

■ city with population over 10,000, c.1300
○ branch of Fugger bank
● branch of Medici bank
Kiev city with important trade fair
■ major Hanseatic league member
● other Hanseatic league member
★ Hanseatic *kontor* (foreign depot)
★ Genoese trading center
★ Venetian trading center
grain exporting area
wine exporting area
woollen cloth producing area
*furs* main trade commodity

borders, c.1325
Hanseatic trade route
Genoese trade route
Venetian trade route
Gascon wine route
other trade route

0       600 km
0       400 mi

The Renaissance, the great cultural movement of 15th-century Europe, had its origins in the revival of interest in classical philosophy, science and literature that first emerged during the 12th century. But its immediate roots lay in 14th-century Italy in the work of artists such as Giotto and humanist scholars such as Petrarch. By the early 15th century, men like Masaccio and Donatello in Florence were evolving new styles of painting and sculpture, while Brunelleschi was leading the revival of classical forms of architecture. In the course of the century Italy's city-states came to be ruled by dynastic princes. Italian Renaissance rulers – whether the powerful Medici family in Florence or the heads of ducal courts such as Mantua or Urbino – dispensed patronage as an arm of government, to secure prestige and influence. In Venice, a large urban aristocracy was keen to publicize its wealth and status. The technology of printing, developed in Germany in the mid-1450s, aided the spread of the new arts and learning outside Italy. By the early 16th century these arts were beginning to find their place in the courts of Europe's "new monarchs", who were emerging from periods of dynastic rivalry and civil war with strong centralized governments.

In the early 15th century France was divided by the rivalry between the Burgundian and Armagnac families, who disputed control of mad king Charles VI (r.1380–1422). Henry V of England (r.1413–22), anxious to secure the legitimacy of the Lancastrian dynasty established by his father Henry IV in 1399, seized the opportunity to reopen the Hundred Years War. His major victory at Agincourt (1415) and conquest of northern France led to his recognition as Charles VI's heir in 1420. After Henry's death and the revival of French morale under the leadership of Joan of Arc, English fortunes declined. By 1453 they had lost all their French possessions except Calais. Defeat provoked dynastic wars in England (the Wars of the Roses) until Henry VII (r.1485–1509), founder of the Tudor dynasty, restored stable government.

The dukes of Burgundy profited from France's troubles to enhance their own position by forming an alliance with the English which lasted until 1435. Under Philip the Good (r.1419–67) they acquired further territory in the Netherlands. His successor Charles the Bold wanted to establish an independent kingdom and tried to build a corridor of lands to link his southern and northern possessions, but died in battle against the Swiss at Nancy in 1477. When his heiress Mary married Maximilian of Habsburg, the Burgundian lands descended to the Habsburgs. They had ruled the Holy Roman empire since 1438, having already united their lands with those of Luxembourg. Louis XI (r.1461– 83) seized and retained the lands of the duchy of Burgundy in France. Franche-Comté was ceded to France on the betrothal of the *dauphin* (later Charles VIII) to Mary's daughter in 1482, but reverted to the Habsburgs when the engagement was revoked.

- ═══ borders, 1429-33
- ▨ Burgundian territory, 1429
- ☐ English territory, 1429
- ☐ nominally English territory, 1429
- ▤ Aragonese territory, 1430
- ▨ Byzantine empire, 1430
- ▨ Genoese territory, 1430
- ▨ Habsburg territory, 1430
- ▨ Hungarian territory, 1430
- ☐ Muscovy, 1430
- ▨ Ottoman empire, 1430
- ☐ Poland-Lithuania, 1430
- ▨ Venetian territory, 1430
- ▨ Polish acquisition, 1466
- ▨ Habsburg acquisition, 1477
- ▨ temporary Hungarian gain under Matthias Corvinus, 1477-90
- ⌒ maximum extent of Burgundian kingdom under Charles the Bold, 1477
- ⌒ kingdom of Aragon & Castile, 1492
- ⌒ kingdom of France, 1492
- ⌒ Muscovy, 1492
- ⌒ Ottoman empire, 1492
- ⌑ Portuguese base
- ⌂ printing center, with date
- Milan   early Renaissance cultural center
- ➡ Tatar campaign
- ⬚ Hussite movement, 1415-36

0              600 km
0              400 mi

## TIMELINE

### Political change

| 1425 | 1450 | 1475 |
|---|---|---|
| **1405–06** Florence captures Pisa, giving it an outlet to the sea | **1453** Ottoman Turks capture Constantinople, bringing the Byzantine empire to an end | **1478** Foundation of the Spanish Inquisition |
| **1429** Joan of Arc relieves the siege of Orléans: turning point of Hundred Years War | | |
| **1417** The Council of Constance ends the Great Schism of the papacy | **1455–85** The Wars of the Roses in England | **1492** Fall of Granada. Columbus' first voyage to the New World |
| **1434** Cosimo de' Medici becomes the ruler of Florence (d.1464) | | |
| **1419** John the Fearless, Duke of Burgundy, murdered during peace conference with Armagnacs | **1463–79** Venice loses Euboea and the Greek islands to the Ottomans | **1494** Beginning of the Italian Wars between France and the Habsburgs |
| **1438** Albert II of Austria, a Habsburg, is elected Holy Roman emperor: the office remains with the Habsburgs until it is abolished in 1806 | **1469** Ferdinand of Aragon marries Isabella of Castile | **1497–98** Vasco da Gama sails to India |

### Cultural change

| 1425 | 1450 | 1475 |
|---|---|---|
| **1411–66** fl. Donatello, Florentine sculptor | **1455** First commercially printed book, the *Gutenberg Bible*, is published at Mainz | **1476** William Caxton sets up the first printing press in London |
| **1435** Rogier van der Weyden's *Descent from the Cross* (wooden altarpiece) painted | | |
| **1420–36** Brunelleschi builds dome on Florence cathedral | **1456–57** Botticelli, Florentine painter, completes *Primavera* | |
| **1422–40** fl. Jan van Eyck, Netherlandish painter | | **1495–97** Leonardo da Vinci paints *The Last Supper* in Milan |

1425                     1450                     1475

Norway

Bergen

**KINGDOM OF DENMARK**
(Union of Calmar)

Christiania **1**

*Vänern*

Sweden

Åbo

Helsinki

Revel

*Lake Ladoga*

PRINCIPALITY OF NOVGOROD
1478 to Muscovy

Novgorod

MUSCOVY

1463–74
to Muscovy **4**

Yaroslavl

Rostov

Kazan

Stockholm
1483

*Lake Peipus*

Pskov

Tver
1483 to Muscovy

Moscow

1408, 1447, 1451, 1465, 1472, 1480

*Vättern*

Denmark

Calmar

Copenhagen
1493

Holstein

Bremen

Lübeck

Hamburg
1491

Stettin

Riga

Smolensk

Ryazan

RYAZAN

KHANATE OF THE
GOLDEN HORDE
Tatars

Haarlem

Amsterdam

Deventer
1477

Utrecht
1472

Ghent

Cologne
1466

Antwerp
1466

Brussels

Brandenburg

Berlin

TEUTONIC KNIGHTS

Danzig **2**

Königsberg

Tannenberg
1410

*Vistula*

Warsaw

*Western Dvina*

Vilna

*Dnieper*

Sarai

Luxembourg

Frankfurt

HOLY ROMAN
EMPIRE

Leipzig
1481

Breslau

*Oder*

Krakow

Lemberg

POLAND–LITHUANIA

GERMAN and Italian armorers
brought plate armor to its
highest development in the
15th century. This finely-
crafted plumed helmet was
made for Ferdinand of Aragon.

Mainz
1455

Bamberg
1460

Nuremberg
1470

Prague
1478

Bohemia

Nancy
1477

Strasbourg
1460

Augsburg
1468

Munich
1482

Salzburg

Vienna
1482

*Danube*

Austria

MOLDAVIA

Basel
1462

Cluny
1483

**3**

Constance

Zürich

Innsbruck

Tyrol

Franche-
Comté

Swiss
Confederation

Geneva
1478

Savoy

Milan
1470

Milan

Mantua
1469

Venice
1469

VENICE

Ferrara

**7**

Rimini

Urbino

Zagreb

*Sava*

Buda

Pest

HUNGARY

Belgrade

WALLACHIA

*Danube*

1444

Varna

Kaffa
1475 to Ottomans

*Black Sea*

GEORGIA

Genoa

Zara

Split

Bosnia

Serbia

Nish

Montenegro

Sofia

Trebizond

TREBIZOND

Avignon

Provence

Pisa

Florence
1471

Siena

PAPAL
STATES

Florence

Rome
1467

Subiaco
1465

Corsica

NAPLES
1442 to Aragon

RAGUSA

ALBANIA

OTTOMAN

Adrianople

Constantinople
1488
1453 to Ottomans

Ankara
1402

TURKISH
EMIRATES

Naples

BENEVENTO

Otranto

EMPIRE

Sardinia

ATHENS

*Euboea*

Palermo

Reggio
1480

Sicily

*Morea*

KNIGHTS OF
ST JOHN

*Rhodes*

CYPRUS
1489 to Venice

Cyprus

MAMLUKE
SULTANATE

Tunis

Malta

*Mediterranean Sea*

Crete

---

In the Iberian peninsula a century or more of rivalry between Castile and Aragon (which added the kingdom of Naples to its extensive Mediterranean empire in 1442), came to an end in 1469 with the marriage of Ferdinand of Aragon to Isabella of Castile. Under their joint leadership, Granada, the last Muslim state in Spain, was conquered in 1485–92. Portugal, prevented from expanding in the peninsula by Castile, turned its attention to North Africa, beginning with the capture of Ceuta in 1415. In the 1430s Portuguese navigators began to explore the African coast and in 1487 entered the Indian Ocean. Even more significant was the voyage of Columbus, commissioned by Isabella of Castile, which led to the discovery of the New World in 1492.

Eastern Europe saw the creation of a strong but short-lived kingdom: Poland–Lithuania, under Casimir IV (r.1447–92) the largest state in Europe.

Hungary, which resisted Ottoman expansion in the Balkans, dominated central Europe under Matthias Corvinus (r.1477–90). By the end of the century Muscovy had absorbed most of the other Russian principalities. With the fall of the Byzantine empire in 1453, it was left as the only significant Orthodox state. Ivan III married a Byzantine princess in 1472, adopting the title of *czar* (caesar).

**1** The Union of Calmar, proclaimed in 1397, was unpopular in Sweden, where it led to several revolts before its final collapse in 1523.

**2** The defeat by Poland–Lithuania of the Teutonic Knights at Tannenberg saw the start of their decline.

**3** The burning for heresy of the Bohemian religious reformer Jan Hus at Constance in 1415 sparked a 20-year revolutionary uprising by his followers.

**4** In 1480 Ivan III of Muscovy ceased paying tribute to buy off the Golden Horde, by now a shadow of its former strength.

**5** In 1492, after their victory over the Muslims, Ferdinand and Isabella expelled from Spain around 150,000 Jews who refused to convert to Christianity.

**6** England's preoccupation with war in France in the 15th century allowed much of Ireland to achieve effective independence.

**7** The patronage of the wealthy Medici family made Florence the leading cultural center of the age, as well as a center for banking and trade, and the dominant political entity of central Italy.

See also 53 (economy of medieval Europe);
58 (Reformation Europe)

The destruction of Teotihuacán in the 8th century left a power vacuum in central Mexico, which allowed new peoples to migrate to the region. The Chichimeca and the Nonoalca settled to the north of the Valley of Mexico, where they merged to form the Toltec nation. By around 900 a Toltec state was established around Tula, from where they expanded over the Valley of Mexico. Little is known of the history of the Toltecs, but their legends feature prominently in the traditions of the Aztecs, who claimed descent from them. The most important legend concerns the Toltec ruler Topiltzin-Quetzalcóatl, a real person born in 935 or 947, who soon came to be identified with the god Quetzalcóatl ("feathered serpent"). His opposition to human sacrifice offended the god Tezcatlipoca, who overthrew him: Topiltzin-Quetzalcóatl fled east overseas, vowing to return one day to reclaim his kingdom. Intriguingly, Mayan records show that in 987 a man called Kukulcán ("feathered serpent" in Mayan) conquered Yucatán. Whether or not this was the Toltec Quetzalcóatl, archeological evidence confirms that in about 1000 the main Mayan city of Chichén Itzá was occupied by Toltecs.

Tula was sacked in about 1168 and the Toltec empire was supplanted by many rival city-states. Around 1200 the Aztecs, a farming people from the west, moved into the Valley of Mexico, eventually founding a permanent settlement at Tenochtitlán in 1325. First serving as mercenaries for Tezozomoc, ruler of Azcapotzalco, the Aztecs allied with Texcoco to destroy Azcapotzalco after Tezozomoc's death in 1426. Two years later Itzcóatl established a strong Aztec monarchy. In 1434 Tenochtitlán, Texcoco and Tlacopan formed the Triple Alliance, imposing tributary status on the other states of the Valley of Mexico. Expansion continued under Itzcóatl's successors; by 1500 the alliance ruled over some 10 million people. The empire peaked under Moctezuma II (r.1502–20) but was abruptly ended by Hernán Cortés' invasion of 1519–21. Though Cortés had great advantages in weaponry and armor, these were not decisive against overwhelming Aztec superiority of numbers.

Moctezuma vacillated, believing Cortés to be the returning Quetzalcóatl, whom the legends described as fair-skinned and bearded. The Mesoamerican custom of taking prisoners for sacrifice also hampered the Aztecs against the conquistadors, who fought to kill. Moreover, Cortés found willing allies in the Tlaxcallans, the Aztecs' main source of sacrificial victims. Finally, diseases such as smallpox, brought by the Spanish, decimated the Aztecs.

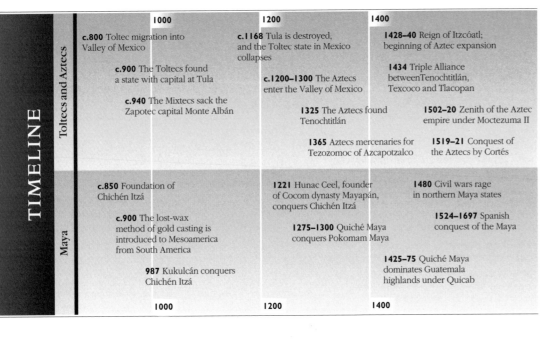

At the time of the conquest, Aztec society was a class-based hierarchy. Relatives of the king formed the aristocracy, while the commoners (the largest class) comprised members of 20 clans. Each clan had its own quarter of the city with its own schools, temples and communal farms. The lowest class were conquered peoples, who served the aristocracy as farmers and laborers. There were also slaves, usually war captives, and a merchant class, the *pochteca*.

After the Classic Maya cities of the Petén lowlands were abandoned in about 800, Mayan civilization continued in northern Yucatán. Around 850–900 the Putún or Itza Maya settled at Chichén Itzá, which quickly became the dominant Maya center. Around 1000 Yucatán was conquered by the Toltecs, whose rule ended in 1221 with the fall of Chichén Itzá to Hunac Ceel, ruler of Mayapán. The Cocom dynasty he founded dominated Yucatán for over 200 years. When the Spanish landed on Yucatán in 1517, the northern Maya were divided into 16 rival states. This made them harder to subdue than the Aztecs, as there were no key institutions. Thus, Tayasal, the last independent Maya state, did not fall until 1697.

## TIMELINE

### Toltecs and Aztecs

| | | |
|---|---|---|
| **c.800** Toltec migration into Valley of Mexico | **c.1168** Tula is destroyed, and the Toltec state in Mexico collapses | **1428–40** Reign of Itzcóatl; beginning of Aztec expansion |
| **c.900** The Toltecs found a state with capital at Tula | **c.1200–1300** The Aztecs enter the Valley of Mexico | **1434** Triple Alliance between Tenochtitlán, Texcoco and Tlacopan |
| **c.940** The Mixtecs sack the Zapotec capital Monte Albán | **1325** The Aztecs found Tenochtitlán | **1502–20** Zenith of the Aztec empire under Moctezuma II |
| | **1365** Aztecs mercenaries for Tezozomoc of Azcapotzalco | **1519–21** Conquest of the Aztecs by Cortés |

### Maya

| | | |
|---|---|---|
| **c.850** Foundation of Chichén Itzá | **1221** Hunac Ceel, founder of Cocom dynasty Mayapán, conquers Chichén Itzá | **1480** Civil wars rage in northern Maya states |
| **c.900** The lost-wax method of gold casting is introduced to Mesoamerica from South America | **1275–1300** Quiché Maya conquers Pokomam Maya | **1524–1697** Spanish conquest of the Maya |
| **987** Kukulcán conquers Chichén Itzá | | **1425–75** Quiché Maya dominates Guatemala highlands under Quicab |

**VALLEY OF MEXICO**

Citlaltepec · Tizayucan · Coyotepec · Xoloc · Teoloyucan · Cuautitlan · Chiconautla · Tepexpan · Teotihuacan · Ecatepe · Tenayuacan · Xaloztoc · Texcoco · Azcapotzalco · Tepeyacac · Tlacopán · Tenochtitlán · Chalpultepec · Culhuacan · Chimalpan · Coyohuacan · Ixtapalucan · Zapotlan · Xico · Chalco · Xochimilco · Atlapulco · Tezompa

*Lake Zumpanco* · *Lake Xaltocan* · *Lake Texcoco* · *Lake Xochimilco* · *Lake Chalco*

0 — 30 km
0 — 20 mi

Isla de Sacrificios

*Gulf of Mexico*

Mixtlan

✕ 1519

TABASCO

Atazta / Xicallanco

PUTÚN MAYA (ITZA)

Toltec-Nonoalca

Chiapa de Corzo

San Juan · Coatzacoalcos

*Sierra Madre*

*Grijalba*

Xoconochco

Huiztlan

Mazatlan

MAM MAYA

Zacaleu

QUICHÉ MAYA

CAKCHIQUEL MAYA

Utalán

Iximché

Mixco Viejo

*Lago de Atitlán*

*Motagua*

POKOMAM MAYA

Cilvituk

*Candelaria*

Itzamkanac

MAYA

PETÉN

*Usumacinta*

TAYASAL · Topoxté

Tayasal

AH KIN CHEL / CEH PECH

CHAKAN

HOCABÁ

Motul · Dzibilchaltún · Izamal · CHIKINCHEL · CUPUL · TASÉS · Isla Mujeres · from Cuba

Tihoo · Chichén Itzá · Balankanché · ECAB

Mayapán · SOTUTA · Cobá · Tancah · San Miguel

*Isla de Cozumel*

AH CANUL · Uxmal · Mani · Tulum · Muyil

TUTUL XIUH · COCHUAH · Chacmool

CANPECH · *Yucatán Peninsula* · HUAYMIL

CHAMPUTÚN

Ichpaatun · Tzibanché · Santa Rita · CHETUMAL · Lamanai

Wild Cane Cay

*Lago de Izabal* · Nito · Naco

Quirigua

HIEROGLYPHS were most fully developed among the Maya; this example is from a Mixtec manuscript.

**Legend**

- Toltec empire, c.1200
- Aztec empire under Itzcóatl, 1427–40
- expansion under Moctezuma I, 1440–68 and Axayacatl, 1469–81
- expansion under Ahuitzotl, 1486–1502 and Moctezuma II, 1502–20
- late Postclassic Maya states
- borders, c.1520
- major Postclassic Maya site
- other Postclassic Maya site
- major Toltec site
- other Toltec site
- major Aztec site
- other Aztec site
- other major Postclassic site
- other site
- Aztec garrison
- Tlacopán  city of the Triple Alliance
- Putún Maya trade route
- migration, c.900
- Toltec migration, c.980–1200
- route of Cortés, April to November 1519

**1** Xoconochco was a rich province of the Aztec empire, conquered for its cocoa.

**2** The Aztecs allowed Tlaxcallan to remain independent so that they could raid it for sacrificial victims.

**3** Chichén Itzá: founded by the Putún Maya c.850, it was the Toltec capital of Yucatán c.987–1221. Many of its buildings were modeled on the old Toltec capital of Tula.

**4** Isla de Cozumel was settled by the Putún Maya, who used the island as a storage depot for their coastal trade routes.

**5** The key to Aztec power was intensive agriculture on fertile reclaimed swampland, or *chinampas*, on the southern shores of Lake Texcoco.

**6** The Maya Cocom dynasty, founded by Hunac Ceel, ruled Yucatán from Mayapán from 1283 until their empire broke up in 1441.

**7** The Toltec state, founded at Tula c.900, became the model for the later Mesoamerican states of the Aztecs and northern Maya.

**8** With a population of 500,000 at the time of the Spanish conquest, Tenochtitlán ("place of the high priest Tenoch") was far larger than most contemporary European cities. Its site is now buried under Mexico City.

See also 39 (early Mesoamerica); 62 (Spanish empire)

The collapse of the highland Tiahuanaco and Huari empires in about 1000 ushered in a long period of political fragmentation in the Andean civilizations. Both in the highlands and on the coast many local states emerged, most of which, like the Sicán state of Lambayeque, controlled no more than a single valley. Around 1200 the Chimú state, centered on Chan Chan in the Moche valley, began a period of gradual imperial expansion, until in the 15th century, it controlled over a thousand kilometers (620 miles) of the Peruvian coast. Around the same time that the Chimú began to expand, a semi-legendary figure, Manco Capac, founded the Inca state at Cuzco in the Killke cultural area of the highlands. For most of its history the Inca state controlled little more than the valley around Cuzco, but in the 15th century it became the greatest of all the empires of the pre-Columbian Americas. It was also destined to be the last.

At its peak in around 1500, the Inca empire encompassed much of modern Peru and Bolivia, together with sizable portions of Chile, Argentina and Equador, and ruled over some 12 million people. The Incas' remarkable territorial expansion took place almost entirely during the reigns of Pachacutec (r.1438–71) and his equally able son Tupac Yupanqui (r.1471–93). The Incas overcame the Chimú, their only serious rivals as an imperial power, with little difficulty, capturing their capital Chan Chan in 1470. By the end of Tupac's reign the Inca empire was reaching the practicable limits of its expansion. The Amazonian rainforest to the east and the southern Andes had sparse, mobile populations that would have proved difficult to control and had environments that were unsuited to the settled intensive agriculture that might make their conquest and colonization worthwhile.

Some new territorial gains were made in the north under Huayna Capac (r. 1493–1525), but on his death a bloody civil war broke out between his sons Atahuallpa and Huáscar. Atahuallpa finally triumphed in 1532, but he had no opportunity to restore the weakened empire. In the same year the Spanish conquistador Francisco Pizarro invaded and captured Atahuallpa in a daring assault on Cajamarca. In 1533 the Spanish executed Atahuallpa and installed a puppet ruler at Cuzco. However, when he rebelled in 1536, they assumed direct rule. Inca resistance continued from inaccessible mountain strongholds but was finally crushed in 1572.

There are many reasons for the Incas' spectacular rise and equally rapid decline. They were fortunate in having able generals as rulers. Inca nobles were brought up in the art of war and a standing army was maintained, so the empire was able to react quickly to any threat. Uniquely among Andean states, the Incas built a network of strategic roads estimated to have been more than 20,000 kilometers (12,500 miles) long – second only in size to the Roman empire's among pre-industrial civilizations – which allowed troops to move quickly to quell trouble on the borders or in the provinces. Conquests were ensured by deporting rebellious populations to the heart of the empire where they could be supervised, while their lands were resettled by loyal Inca subjects.

Probably the main factor in Inca success, however, was their complex administrative system. It was maintained without any type of writing, and with record-keeping done using an elaborate system of knotted strings known as *quipu*, which allowed them to marshal the empire's human resources with great efficiency. Inca society was highly centralized and rigidly hierarchical. At its head was the semidivine emperor. Below the emperor, and directly answerable to him, were the prefects of the

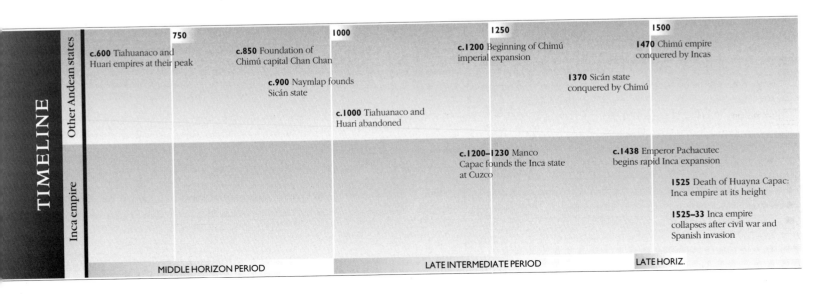

TIMELINE

| | 750 | 1000 | 1250 | 1500 |
|---|---|---|---|---|
| **Other Andean states** | c.600 Tiahuanaco and Huari empires at their peak | c.850 Foundation of Chimú capital Chan Chan | c.1200 Beginning of Chimú imperial expansion | 1470 Chimú empire conquered by Incas |
| | | c.900 Naymlap founds Sicán state | 1370 Sicán state conquered by Chimú | |
| | | c.1000 Tiahuanaco and Huari abandoned | | |
| **Inca empire** | | | c.1200–1230 Manco Capac founds the Inca state at Cuzco | c.1438 Emperor Pachacutec begins rapid Inca expansion |
| | | | | 1525 Death of Huayna Capac: Inca empire at its height |
| | | | | 1525–33 Inca empire collapses after civil war and Spanish invasion |
| | MIDDLE HORIZON PERIOD | | LATE INTERMEDIATE PERIOD | LATE HORIZ. |

Four Quarters, and below them provincial governors, followed by district officers, local chiefs and, at the bottom, foremen each responsible for supervising ten families. Farmland was divided into thirds, for the support of the state, the gods and the people. All Inca men and women contributed taxation in the form of labor on those parts of the land allocated to the state and the gods. Able-bodied men also paid tax through a labor draft known as *mit'a*. This could last for months and range from military service to work on major construction projects, such as roads and fortresses, or agricultural improvements, such as terracing steep hillsides. This system enabled the empire to raise and supply large armies and keep them in the field for long campaigns.

Although Pizarro was fortunate in having his invasion coincide with the end of a long and destructive civil war, the centralized hierarchy of the Inca empire was also partly responsible for its swift demise. No major decision could be taken without the emperor, whch meant that the empire was paralyzed once Atahuallpa had been captured. Diseases also contributed to the Incas' defeat; as in Mesoamerica, the indigenous population had no resistance to epidemics brought by the Spanish. Indeed, the civil war that first weakened the Inca empire was indirectly caused by a disease introduced from Europe: Huayna Capac died of a smallpox epidemic that spread south from the Spanish base at Panama.

**1** Chan Chan was the capital of the Chimú empire from c.850-1470: at the heart of the city were ten walled palace-mausoleum compounds.

**2** The Inca capital Cuzco was regarded as the center of the universe, from which radiated the "Four Quarters" of the world. In the Quechua language of the Incas (still widely spoken in the Andes), *cuzco* means "navel".

**3** *Tambos*, roadside hostels and storehouses, were sited at intervals of one day's journey on all the empire's roads; one of the largest and best preserved is Tambo Colorado.

**4** The oracle of the god Pachacamac, dating to around AD 200, was a major pilgrimage center and rival to the Incas' state solar cult.

**5** The Lambayeque valley was the center of the wealthy Sicán state from c.900 until its conquest by the Chimú in c.1370.

**6** The Inca increased the area of farmland by terracing mountainsides: many, as at Pisac, are still farmed today.

**7** Machu Picchu, the most famous Inca site, was a remote mountain-top religious center and frontier outpost.

**8** The victory of Atahuallpa's forces over his rival Huáscar at Cotabambas ended the Inca civil war.

Late Intermediate period, c.900-1475

- ○ Chimú site
- ◉ Lambayeque site
- ○ other site

- ⌇ Aymara kingdoms
- ⌇ Chimú empire, c.1470
- ⌇ Chiribaya
- ⌇ Huanca
- ⌇ Ica
- ⌇ Killke

- ▨ Inca territory under Manco Capac, c.1230
- ▨ expansion under Yahua Huyacac, c.1400
- ☐ expansion under Pachacutec and Tupac Yupanqui, 1438-71
- ☐ expansion under Tupac Yupanqui, 1471-93
- ☐ expansion under Huayna Capac, 1493-1525
- ─── border of Inca empire, 1525
- ─── border of empire Quarter, 1525
- <u>Cuzco</u> Inca capital
- ▪ known Inca provincial capital
- ● other Inca town or city
- 🏛 *tambo* (hostel)
- ─── Inca road
- ➤ Pizarro's invasion, 1532-33
- ⣿ coastal desert

PERUVIAN gold was one of the great attractions of the region for the conquistadors: this intricate knife showed the moon- or sun-god.

0                    400 km
0                    300 mi

See also 62 (Spanish empire)

A t the end of the 13th century Islam began to spread through Malaya and the islands of southeast Asia, gradually supplanting Hinduism and Buddhism. At the same time, the Mongols tried to expand into southeast Asia, but with little success. Their vast empire broke up in the 14th century. In China they were overthrown by the native Ming dynasty in 1368, following peasant rebellions and internal power struggles. The Ming ruled in the tradition of the Tang dynasty and reasserted Chinese power in southeast Asia. One of their first acts was to forbid Chinese from traveling abroad. This isolated China, ruined Chinese trade and led to a fateful neglect of maritime matters just as the Europeans were about to begin their own oceanic exploration. By the time the interdict was lifted in 1567, the initiative had passed irretrievably to the Europeans.

The Mongols remained a power on the eastern steppes and the khanates of the Chagatai and the Golden Horde survived at the end of the 15th century, but their mainly Turkic subjects had already reasserted their independence. In the Middle East the Mongols converted to Islam and were assimilated by their Persian and Turkic subjects. Fragmentation followed and by 1350 the Ilkhanate had dissolved into a number of Turkish, Persian and nominally Mongol states. One of these, the Ottoman Turk sultanate, had by 1400 conquered most of Anatolia and the Balkans and reduced the Byzantine empire to its capital Constantinople (▷ 47). Attempts to build a united Christian front to counter this new Muslim threat to Europe foundered amid international rivalries. The Ottomans, however, were defeated in 1402 by Timur the Lame (r.1361–1405), ruler of Samarkand, who claimed Chingis Khan as his ancestor. Timur saw himself as restorer of the Mongol empire, though he was culturally more Turk than Mongol. In a devastating reign of terror, Timur rebuilt the Ilkhanate, broke the power of the Delhi sultanate and was only prevented from invading China by his death. His empire broke up shortly after.

Ottoman power revived after Timur's death and the advance into Europe began again. In 1453 Constantinople fell after an epic siege and the Byzantine empire finally died. In 1475 the Ottomans crossed the Danube and pushed west. Although Byzantium had fallen, much of its heritage survived in the

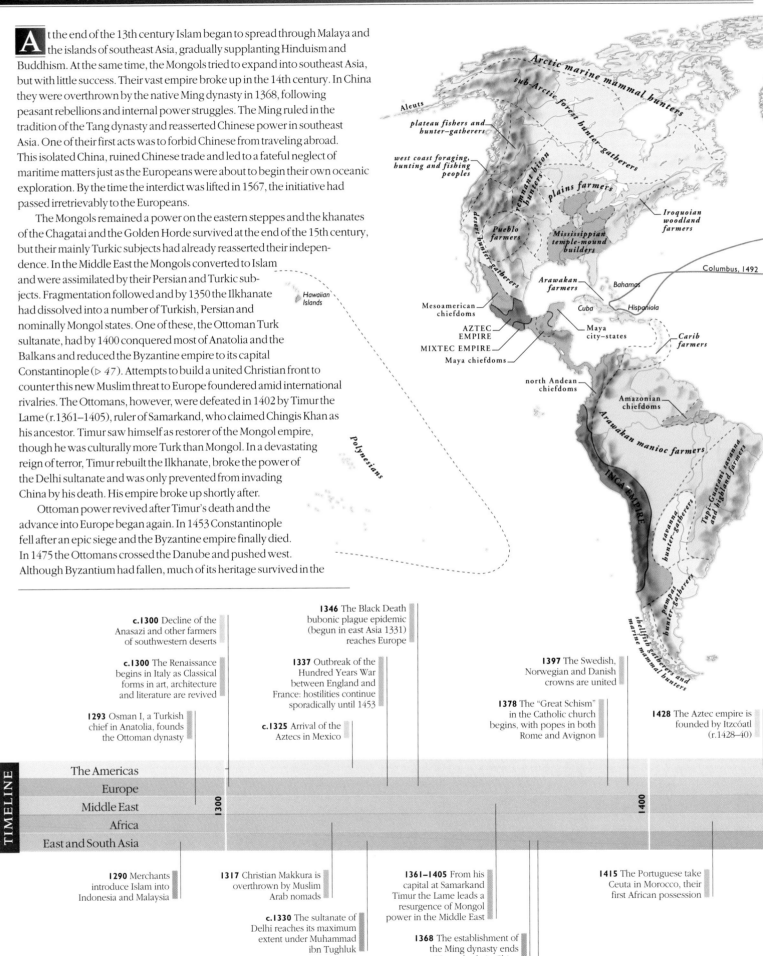

**TIMELINE**

c.1300 Decline of the Anasazi and other farmers of southwestern deserts

c.1300 The Renaissance begins in Italy as Classical forms in art, architecture and literature are revived

1293 Osman I, a Turkish chief in Anatolia, founds the Ottoman dynasty

1346 The Black Death bubonic plague epidemic (begun in east Asia 1331) reaches Europe

1337 Outbreak of the Hundred Years War between England and France: hostilities continue sporadically until 1453

c.1325 Arrival of the Aztecs in Mexico

1397 The Swedish, Norwegian and Danish crowns are united

1378 The "Great Schism" in the Catholic church begins, with popes in both Rome and Avignon

1428 The Aztec empire is founded by Itzcóatl (r.1428–40)

The Americas
Europe
Middle East
Africa
East and South Asia

1300

1400

1290 Merchants introduce Islam into Indonesia and Malaysia

1317 Christian Makkura is overthrown by Muslim Arab nomads

c.1330 The sultanate of Delhi reaches its maximum extent under Muhammad ibn Tughluk

1361–1405 From his capital at Samarkand Timur the Lame leads a resurgence of Mongol power in the Middle East

1368 The establishment of the Ming dynasty ends Mongol rule in China

1370 The kingdom of Vijayanagara dominates southern India

1415 The Portuguese take Ceuta in Morocco, their first African possession

**hunter-gatherers**
**nomadic pastoralists**
**simple farming societies**
**complex farming societies/chiefdoms**
**state societies**
**uninhabited**
**empires**
→ Chinese voyage
→ Portuguese voyage
→ Spanish voyage

HUN.   Hungary
Ps.    Papal states
TO.    Teutonic Order lands
VE.    Venice

**1492** Columbus, sailing on behalf of the Spanish monarchy, reaches the Caribbean

**c.1455** Johannes Gutenberg develops movable type, leading to the first printed books

**1480** Russians stop paying tribute to the Golden Horde, ending Mongol power in eastern Europe

**1438** Pachacutec begins the expansion of the Inca empire

**1470** The Incas conquer the Chimú empire in coastal Peru

**1441–43** Portuguese navigators explore the coast of west Africa

**1490** King Nzinga Nkuwu of Congo becomes Christian as a result of Portuguese influence

**1453** The Ottoman Turks take Constantinople and end the Byzantine empire

**1464** Songhai eclipses Mali as the chief power in west Africa

1500

principality of Moscow. By 1478, when it refused to pay tribute to the Golden Horde, Moscow had absorbed most of the Russian principalities and was expanding east.

Resurgent Muslim power in the eastern Mediterranean drove western Christendom to seek a way of outflanking the Islamic world. Portugal took the lead, beginning in 1415 with the capture of Ceuta in Morocco. Expeditions to explore the African coast followed. In 1487–88 Bartholomew Dias rounded the Cape of Good Hope and found the African coast turning northward, proving that sea voyages between Europe and the east were possible. The Genoese navigator Christopher Columbus believed the east could also be reached by sailing west. Eventually he was given a fleet by Isabella of Castile in 1492. What he found, though he did not realize it, was the American continent.

The greatest power in the Americas was the Inca state. This originated in Peru around 1200 and began its imperial expansion in the 15th century. The Chimú empire was conquered in 1470, and by 1492 the Inca empire was the largest yet seen in the Americas (▷ 56). Mesoamerica was dominated by the Aztecs (▷ 57), who settled the valley of Mexico about 1325 and became an imperial power under Itzcóatl (r.1428–40). The complex cultures of the south-western deserts of North America collapsed at the end of the 13th century after prolonged droughts. The towns of the Mississippian cultures were in decline by 1492 and the region's center had lost its population. Buffalo-hunting on the Great Plains was dying out as farming spread along river valleys (▷ 42) ■

## Part 4

# THE EARLY

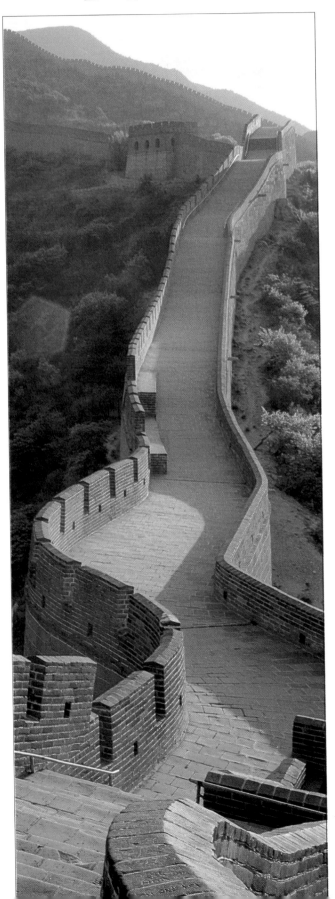

**T**he three centuries between 1492 and 1783 saw the different parts of the world interact as never before, and at the same time witnessed a decisive rise of European power. The period (often called the "early modern period") began with the European "discovery" of the New World by Christopher Columbus, and ended, ironically, with the throwing off by Britain's North American colonies of European rule.

The rise of Europe and the shrinking of the world were linked. First Spain and Portugal, and later England, France and the Dutch all conquered and settled important portions of North and South America. It was through the projection of Portuguese naval power that European military strength began to make its impact in the Indian Ocean; again, the other powers, notably the Dutch and British but also the French and Spanish, soon followed in their wake.

The result was a shift in global power. For much of the preceding millennium, Europe had been fairly insignificant on the world stage. In the fifteenth century Europeans had been unable to prevent the advance of the Ottoman Turks into the Balkans, a process that had led to the fall of Constantinople, last bastion of the old Roman empire, to Mehmet II in 1453. At that time, no European king matched Mehmet's power. And at the same date, Chinese ships dominated Asian waters; and Chinese fleets, far larger than any contemporary European one, sailed the Indian Ocean.

Over the next 150 years, the impact of Europe on the rest of the world grew enormously. Spain made dramatic gains in the New World in the early decades of the sixteenth century, overthrowing the Aztecs of Mexico and the Incas of Peru. The supply of precious metals from these two regions sustained

THE GREAT WALL OF CHINA, built to keep out the nomads of central Asia.

# MODERN WORLD

the European economy throughout the century. When Spain began to take control of the Philippines in the 1570s, King Philip II of Spain – for whom the islands were renamed – became the world's first ruler of an empire on which the sun never set. Meanwhile Portuguese warships destroyed the leading Indian fleets of Calicut and Gujarat, and those of Egypt and Turkey; Portugal also laid claim to the coast of Brazil.

The tide of transoceanic European maritime activity and territorial expansion was maintained through the next two centuries. England and France set up colonies – initially little more than fragile footholds but eventually growing to lay claim to much of the eastern seaboard – in North America, while the Dutch took over some of the spice-producing regions of the East Indies, regions that brought with them a fantastically profitable trade. Russian power too expanded across Siberia to the Pacific, as a result of which even China acquired a land-frontier with a European state.

In the New World in the eighteenth century, the Portuguese pressed into the interior of Brazil, the Spaniards expanded into California and the English and French competed for supremacy in the Great Lakes region. In India, the British took over Bengal and became the leading power on the southeast coast. Europe's only serious defeat occurred in North America, where the Thirteen Colonies fought their way into independence from Britain. Yet, even this defeat was at the hands of people of European descent, armed with European weapons and allied to a European state, France.

Europeans were not victorious everywhere . Their control in Africa was still limited, even though the demands of the slave trade to the New World had political and demographic ramifications deep in the interior of the continent. In east Asia the most expansive state in the eighteenth century was still China. The Persians resisted the Russians spiritedly while the

Turks showed great resilience against Austria.

But the world was increasingly one where the crucial links were controlled or created by Europeans. A "world economy" developed as distant regions traded with one another under European auspices. Thus the British shipped tea from India to North America or the Dutch moved Chinese porcelain to Europe. This trade was to the profit of the European maritime powers that controlled it, and maritime rivalry was the source of several conflicts between Britain, France and the Netherlands. Eventual British dominance in this trade helped make London the world's dominant financial center and ensured that Britain was well placed for the rapid economic growth that would lead to the Industrial Revolution.

The theme of European expansion might appear exaggerated. Much of the world had never seen a European. European maps of central Asia or of inland Africa were either blanks or full of errors. To talk of European power would have seemed curious in Tibet, conquered by China in 1720; in Mombasa, whence the Omani Arabs expelled the Portuguese in 1698; or in west Africa where the kingdom of Dahomey dominated European trading posts from 1720.

Yet, however limited their impact in some respects, Europeans were to be found off the coast of Asia, not Asians off that of Europe. Europeans charted the oceans, explored their dark side of the world – the Pacific – and acquired the knowledge that helped them to profit from their strength. The world was renamed by Europeans. Many of the consequences of European ambition were unattractive, most obviously the slave trade. Today we can consider the rise of Europe without applauding it; but it is difficult to challenge its importance. At this era Europeans remolded the world, and created new political, economic, religious and cultural spaces, forging links that still affect our world today ∎

As the 15th century neared its close, the monarchies of western Europe consolidated their positions and brought civil wars within their territories to an end. Louis XI of France (r.1461–81) overcame his Burgundian rivals, Henry Tudor brought England's long Wars of the Roses to an end in 1485, and Ferdinand of Aragon and Isabella of Castile oversaw the unification of their kingdoms and the final conquest of Moorish Granada in 1492. As feudal relationships continued to break down, the near-independence of the great nobles in times of weak kings was gradually curtailed by the rise of administrators and financiers. Europe's monarchs became distributors of patronage in a world where finance was beginning to count for more than fealty.

The territorial kingdoms of 16th-century Europe were very different from the monolithic states of today. Material conditions, slow communications and the stubborn survival of local customs, economies and even laws limited royal power. The nation-state was still a novelty.

The old notion of a secular empire transcending the state endured. Charles VIII of France invaded Italy in 1494 in pursuit of such an aim, prompting a long struggle in which French, Spanish and German armies rampaged through the peninsula, almost destroying the achievements of the Italian Renaissance. In 1519, Charles of Habsburg, grandson both of Ferdinand of Aragon and Emperor Maximilian I, became Emperor Charles V. The empire itself was weak and fragmented, but Charles now held the Austrian Habsburg lands in Spain, the Netherlands, Franche-Comté and much of Italy, as well as Spain's new overseas possessions, creating a power bloc that dominated Europe until the late 17th century.

Alarmingly, though, the defeat of Louis II of Hungary by the Ottomans at Mohács in 1526 raised the specter that the empire that would unify Europe might not even be a Christian one. In both central Europe and the Mediterranean (where Barbarossa's

**major faith, 1550**

- Anglican
- Catholic
- Calvinist
- Lutheran
- Muslim
- Orthodox
- mixed

- ● state with significant Catholic minority, 1550
- ● state with significant Protestant minority, 1550
- ═ borders, 1560
- territory controlled by Christian military orders, 1500
- Austrian Habsburg land
- Spanish Habsburg land
- Ottoman empire, 1492
- European territory lost to Ottomans by 1560
- ⊗ Christian defeat by Ottomans
- ⛊ major Ottoman siege
- → Ottoman advance against Christian Europe
- popular uprising, with date
- 📖 major printing center, 15th–16th centuries
- Spanish *presidio* fort

**Italian wars**

- ⊗ French victory
- ⊗ Spanish Habsburg victory
- ⊗ Venetian victory
- ➡ invasion route of Charles VIII of France, 1494

| 0 | | 600 km |
| 0 | | 400 mi |

LUTHER was caricatured as the Devil's plaything in this typically grotesque woodcut of 1525.

*ATLANTIC OCEAN*

Ireland
Irish Pale
Dublin
Wale[s]
1549, Western Rebellion
Bristol
Brittany 1491 to France
La Rochelle
Bordea[ux]
La Coruña
Santander
Pamplona
Navarre 1512 to Sp[ain]
Burgos
1521–22, Comunero revolt
Douro
SPAIN
Arago[n] 1479 to Sp[ain]
Madrid
Tagus
PORTUGAL
Lisbon
Castile 1479 to Spain
Valencia
Córdoba
Seville
Granada
Granada 1492 to Spain
Cartage[na]
Tangier
Asilah
Ceuta
Oran 1509 to Spain
Melilla 1497 to Spain

victory at Prevesa in 1538 ensured Ottoman and Barbary corsair domination), Charles V shouldered the responsibility for halting the Ottoman advance.

Against this background of imperial commitments, the greatest event of the 16th century, the Reformation, was played out. What began as a challenge by a monk, Martin Luther, to corrupt practices in the church became an expression of German nationalism, and then of local interests asserted against the emperor. The Peasants' Wars, uprisings partly fueled by religious unrest, were vigorously put down by the German nobility, who then began to adopt the reformed faith themselves, often for political reasons. Charles won a crushing victory at Mühlberg over the Protestant nobles, but otherwise did little to halt the spread of reform.

The papacy faced Luther's challenge hamstrung

## TIMELINE

**Habsburg lands**

| 1500 | 1530 | 1560 |
|---|---|---|
| **1492** The conquest of Granada completes Spain's *reconquista*; Castile and Aragon are united by the marriage of Ferdinand and Isabella | **1521** Protestant Reformation begins as Luther is outlawed | **1547** Charles V defeats the Schmalkaldic league of Protestant princes at Mühlberg |
| | **1524–25** The Peasants' War breaks out across Germany | **1555** The Peace of Augsburg allows each prince in the Holy Roman empire to select the faith of his subjects |
| **1509** Spain takes Oran, beginning a campaign to take key bases in North Africa | **1527** Imperial troops sack Rome | |
| | **1529** Vienna is besieged unsuccessfully by the Turks | **1556** Charles V abdicates; he is succeeded by Philip II in Spain, and by Ferdinand I as emperor |
| **1517** Martin Luther writes his 95 Theses against abuse in the Catholic Church | **1530** German Protestants publish 28 articles of faith to avoid a split with the Church | |
| **1519** Charles of Habsburg, king of Spain since 1516, is elected Holy Roman emperor | **1534** Anabaptists seize control of Münster, prophesying the end of the world | |

**Other lands**

| 1500 | 1530 | 1560 |
|---|---|---|
| **1494–95** Charles VIII of France invades Italy, initiating a series of wars with Spain | **1525** Francis I is captured by the Spaniards at Pavia; he is held for a year | **1558** The Protestant Elizabeth I succeeds her Catholic sister Mary to the English throne |
| **1503** Pope Alexander VI, a Borgia, dies; Julius II becomes pope | **1534** Henry VIII asserts his claim to be the supreme head of the Church in England | **1559** The treaty of Cateau-Cambrésis ends Italian wars |
| **1515** Francis I of France defeats Swiss at Marignano to control northern Italy | **1541** Calvin introduces a puritan Protestant society to Geneva | |

| 1500 | 1530 | 1560 |

Christiania

Revel
ESTONIA

Novgorod

SWEDEN
Stockholm

LIVONIA

Vänern
Vättern
Gotland

Riga
Pskov
1510 to Russia

RUSSIA

Lake
Peipus

Moscow

SCOTLAND
North
Sea

COURLAND
Western Dvina

Polotsk
Smolensk

Edinburgh
Flodden
1513

Baltic Sea

Königsberg
Königsberg

Vilna
Minsk

Copenhagen

DENMARK–NORWAY

Danzig
ROYAL
PRUSSIA

Lithuania

Gomel

York

ENGLAND

1536,
Pilgrimage of
Grace

Hamburg
Emden
Bremen

Stettin

Brandenburg

Elbe

Berlin

Warsaw

POLAND

Norwich

1549,
Ket's Rebellion

Amsterdam
Leiden
Deventer
Münster

HOLY
ROMAN
EMPIRE

Vistula

Kiev

Oxford
London

1549,
Wyatt's
Rebellion

Utrecht

Leipzig
Wittenberg
Mühlberg
1547

Lusatia
Dresden

Silesia

Krakow
Lemberg

Ukraine

Netherlands
Antwerp
Brussels
Cologne
Bonn

Saxony

Prague

Bohemia

Moravia

Calais
1558 to
France

Picardy
1482 to France

Luxembourg

Mainz
Frankfurt
Worms
Nuremberg
Bamberg

1526 to Austrian
Habsburgs

MOLDAVIA
1504 Ottoman Vassal

Jedisan
1526 to Ottoman empire

Rouen

1524–25,
Peasants War

Danube

TRANSYLVANIA
1541 to
Ottoman empire

Jassy

Paris

FRANCE

Strasbourg
1482 to France
Augsburg
Ulm

Bavaria

Austria

Vienna

Gran
Buda

Chambord
Orléans

Loire

Basel

Munich

IMPERIAL HUNGARY

HUNGARY
1541 to Ottoman empire

1527 to
France

Franche-
Comté
Zürich
Swiss
Confederation

Tyrol

Guns
1532

Mohács
1526

WALLACHIA

Bucharest

Bourbon
Charolais
Berne
Geneva

Pieve di Cadore
1509

1529

Belgrade

Danube

La Marche

Lyon

Marignano
1515

Trent
Venice

Nish

Bulgaria

527 to
France

Savoy
Pavia
1525

Milan

VENICE

Ravenna
1512

Sofia

Black Sea

Auvergne

Forez

Parma
Genoa

Modena

URBINO

Ragusa
Montenegro

OTTOMAN

1527 to
France

Saluzzo
1559 to France

PAPAL

Adrianople

Avignon
Provence
1481 to France

Florence
Piombino
Siena
Piombino

STATES

Thessalonica

Constantinople

Roussillon
1493 to Spain

Orbetello

Rome
Subiaco

NAPLES

Rumelia

ANATOLIA

Perpignan
ANDORRA

Corsica
to Genoa

Garigliano
1503

Cerignola
1503

Izmir

Barcelona

Naples

BENEVENTO

EMPIRE

SARDINIA

Sardinia

Cagliari

Corfu
1537

Athens

Prevesa
1538

Morea

Balearic
Islands

Palermo
Messina
Reggio

SICILY

Sicily

Monemvasia

1522
Rhodes

BARBARY COAST

Crete
to Venice

Candia

Algiers
1510 to Spain
1541 to Ottoman
empire

Bougie
1510 to Spain
1555 to Ottoman empire

Tunis
1535 to Spain

MALTA
1551
1530 to Knights
of St John

Mediterranean
Sea

by a decline in the need for a unified church (literacy, once the church's preserve, had become more widely diffused in the previous two centuries) and by the widespread perception that the pope was merely a cynical participant in the complex web of Italian politics. The authority of the church was challenged even by rulers with no particular religious motive. First by Ferdinand of Aragon, who threatened in 1508 to withdraw his kingdoms from obedience to the pope; by Gustavus Vasa's 1527 seizure of church lands in Sweden; and by Henry VIII of England, who repudiated papal authority in 1532.

The Reformation was driven by a shift in religious sensibilities, as the spread of printing gave the new demands for a more personal spirituality an unprecedented mobility and resilience. Even as political compromise between the faiths was agreed in

1555 within the empire (the Peace of Augsburg) and between France and Spain in Italy in 1559 (the treaty of Cateau-Cambrésis), the Catholic response to church reform was taking shape. The Council of Trent formulated a statement of Catholic doctrine and the Jesuit Order was adopted by the papacy as the spearhead of a new pastoral effort.

**1** A defeat at the hands of the English at Flodden ensured Scotland did not interfere in English affairs for most of the Tudor period.

**2** Martin Luther, an Augustinian monk, nailed his *95 Theses* to the Wittenberg cathedral door in 1517, challenging church abuses and initiating the Reformation.

**3** The château of Chambord, built by Francis I from 1519, is a classic of French Renaissance architecture.

**4** The Christian stronghold of Rhodes fell to the Ottomans in 1522, after vigorous defense by the Knights of St John.

**5** The unexpected defeat and capture of Francis I of France by Spanish forces at Pavia in 1525 was the climax of the Italian wars.

**6** The brutal sack of Rome in 1527 by Spanish and German mercenaries in the service of Charles V shocked the whole of Europe.

**7** In three sessions from 1545, the Council of Trent decrees laid the basis of modern Catholicism in doctrines directly opposing Protestantism.

See also 54 (Renaissance Europe);
59 (Ottoman empire)

The rise of the Ottoman Turkish state from a regional power in Asia Minor in the mid-15th century to the greatest empire in Europe and the Middle East by the mid-16th was a dramatic one. In less than a century, the house of Osman had destroyed Byzantium and become unquestioned leaders of the Islamic world, wealthy patrons of a confident culture and rulers of an empire stretching from the Atlas Mountains to the Caspian Sea.

The key moment in this transformation is often considered to be the capture of Constantinople by Mehmet II in 1453, but the second decade of the 16th century perhaps has a better claim. Between 1516 and 1520 the armies of Selim I (r.1512–20) drove the Safavid Persians out of Kurdistan, destroyed empire of the Mamlukes on the battlefields of Marj Dabiq and al-Raydaniyya, and secured from the *sharif* of Mecca recognition of their sultan as caliph, or leader of the Islamic faithful.

The conquest of Syria and Egypt from the Mamlukes made the Ottoman territories an integral part of a vast network of overland caravan routes from Morocco to the gates of Beijing. At one end of this network were the spices, drugs, silks and (later) porcelain of the east. At the other end were the traders in gold dust, slaves, gems and other products of the African interior, and the shipments of textiles, glass, hardware, timber and currency from Europe.

Christian Europe responded ambivalently to the Ottomans. Venice was anxious to retain as great a share as possible of trade with the Levant – even, ultimately, at the expense of Venetian territory – while Francis I of France openly allied himself with

Legend:
- Ottoman empire, 1492
- Ottoman conquests by 1520
- Ottoman conquests, 1520-66
- Ottoman conquests, 1566-1640
- Habsburg territory, 1550
- Venetian territory, 1550
- Safavid territory, 1512
- Safavid territory conquered by Ottomans but regained before 1640
- Crimean Tatar territory lost to Zaporogian Cossacks before 1640
- Ottoman-Safavid border, 1639
- borders, 1600
- Ottoman administrative center
- Ottoman victory
- Ottoman defeat
- Ottoman siege
- center for Ottoman trade with Europe
- Spanish *presidio* fort
- Spanish *presidio* fort captured by Ottomans
- *gems* trade commodity in the Ottoman empire
- Ottoman/Tatar campaign or raid
- trade route

0 — 800 km
0 — 600 mi

## TIMELINE

### Constantinople and the west

**1499** War between the Ottomans and an alliance of Venice and Hungary

**1512** Selim I ("the Grim") becomes sultan

**1516** The Mamlukes, allied with Persia, are defeated at Marj Dabiq

**1520** Suleiman I ("the Magnificent") becomes sultan

**1526** The Ottomans defeat Hungary at Mohács

**1533** Suleiman makes peace with Ferdinand of Habsburg

**1535** Emperor Charles V captures Tunis

**1536** Suleiman forms an alliance with Francis I of France

**1538** The Ottomans defeat a Christian fleet at Prevesa

**1566** Suleiman dies on campaign in imperial Hungary

**1571** The Holy league defeats the Ottomans at Lepanto

**1572** Don John of Austria reoccupies Tunis (to 1574)

**1573** Venice withdraws from the Holy league, abandoning Cyprus (fell 1571)

**1574** Ottomans retake Tunis and complete the occupation of the north African coast

**1595** Mehmet III murders 27 brothers to gain power

**1604** Protestant Hungarians support the Ottoman protégé Stephen Bocskay, forcing the Habsburgs to abandon Transylvania

**1623** Murad IV succeeds to the throne and embarks on a campaign against the Janissaries

**1639** Murad abolishes the tribute of Christian children (*devshirme*) as part of his campaign to reduce Janissary power

### Eastern empire

**1514** Selim wages war against the Safavids, winning a decisive victory at Chaldiran

**1517** The *sharif* of Mecca surrenders to Selim

**1538** An Ottoman naval expedition attacks Portuguese possessions in India

**1559** Suleiman's son Selim has his brother Bajazid murdered in Persia

**1590** Peace is agreed between Ottomans and Safavids

**1602–18** Shah Abbas of Persia captures Mesopotamia

**1639** The treaty of Qasr-i Shirin finally establishes a permanent border between the Ottoman and Safavid empires

**1** Rhodes was captured by the Ottomans in 1522, when help from Europe failed to arrive for the defending Knights of St John (Hospitallers).

**2** At the Battle of Lepanto, Ali Pasha's Ottoman fleet was defeated by a Don John of Austria. Casualties included writer Miguel de Cervantes, who lost an arm.

**3** The Ottomans were initially welcomed by many of the inhabitants of the Balkans; in Bosnia, descendants of the Bogomil heretics voluntarily converted to Islam.

**4** After the Spanish fort of Peñon d'Argel was taken by the Ottoman admiral Khaireddin in 1529, Algiers became a major base for Barbary corsairs.

**5** The deployment of artillery – which their opponents lacked – was decisive in the Ottoman victories of Chaldiran and at al-Raydaniyya.

**6** An expedition to Muscat in 1551 secured Ottoman control of Oman and raided Portuguese bases in India, but the Ottomans failed to expel the Portuguese from the Indian Ocean or to dominate the region's trade.

SULEIMAN I was renowned as a lawgiver, soldier and art patron. The Venetian artist Titian painted his portrait.

Suleiman the Magnificent (r.1520–66) against the Habsburgs. Reformation and Counter-Reformation helped to weaken the crusading spirit that had once united Europe against Islam. Suleiman reduced Hungary to vassal status after his victory at Mohács in 1526, then conquered a swathe of European territory from Croatia to the Black Sea. His siege of Vienna in 1529 was broken more by the winter weather and the length of Ottoman supply lines than by Habsburg action. Ultimately, though, it was the Ottoman commitment to a savage and apparently endless religious war with Safavid Persia that saved Habsburg central Europe.

The Ottoman–Christian frontier on the Danube achieved a kind of equilibrium after the death of Suleiman. In the Mediterranean, Ottoman conquest of the north African coast was facilitated by the naval victory at Prevesa, but Charles V's initially successful offensive at Tunis (1535) and the Christian victory at Lepanto (1571) restored the *status quo*. A rough division of the sea was made along a line through Italy, Sicily and Tunisia. The Ottoman fleet was quickly rebuilt, but there was no new naval confrontation.

The wars between Ottomans and Christians never entirely halted trade between Europe and the Levant. European merchant ships continued to arrive at Iskanderun or Tripoli in Syria, or at Alexandria, and to unload cargoes of European goods and quantities of Spanish–American gold and silver destined for Asia. These cargoes were carried through the Ottoman and Safavid empires in caravans forbidden to Europeans, meticulously organized, secure, regular and often faster than the European sea routes. The same system of caravans brought Asian goods back for export to Europe from Mediterranean ports. Until the mid-17th century, this trade flourished, enriching the Ottoman empire and ensuring that European technology remained available to the sultan.

The most costly of the Ottoman–Safavid wars broke out in 1602; the reorganized and re-equipped armies of the Persians reversed almost all the Ottoman gains of the previous century before a peace came. Constantinople was devastated by plagues and economic crises. The empire was further weakened by instability, which derived both from the lack of a clear custom of succession (fratricide often settled the matter) and from the growing independence and political influence of the Janissaries. These were originally an elite military and administrative caste recruited from the *devshirme* system, by which children of Balkan Christians were surrendered as tribute to Constantinople. This caste increasingly played the role of the empire's kingmakers. From the mid-16th century, too, the caravan routes' profitability began to wane under pressure from alternative routes to the East through Russia and around the Cape of Good Hope. By the death of Murad IV (r.1623–40), the Ottoman empire was starting to fall behind its European rivals in military technology, in wealth and even in political unity.

See also 47 (rise of the Ottomans);
58 (16th-century Europe)

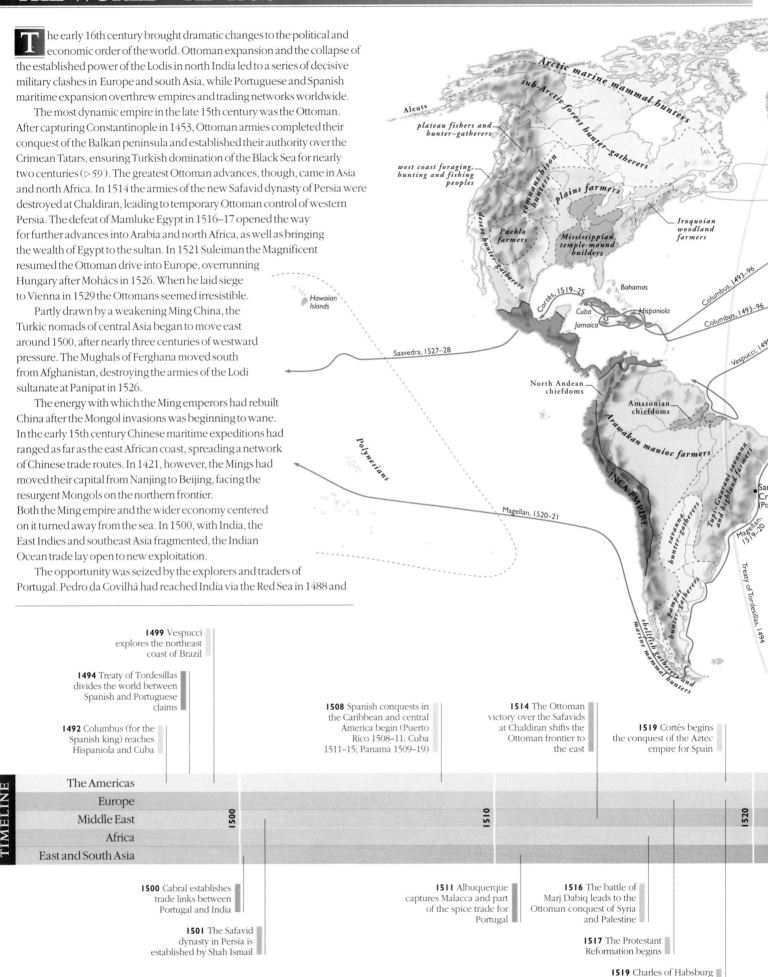

The early 16th century brought dramatic changes to the political and economic order of the world. Ottoman expansion and the collapse of the established power of the Lodis in north India led to a series of decisive military clashes in Europe and south Asia, while Portuguese and Spanish maritime expansion overthrew empires and trading networks worldwide.

The most dynamic empire in the late 15th century was the Ottoman. After capturing Constantinople in 1453, Ottoman armies completed their conquest of the Balkan peninsula and established their authority over the Crimean Tatars, ensuring Turkish domination of the Black Sea for nearly two centuries (▷ 59). The greatest Ottoman advances, though, came in Asia and north Africa. In 1514 the armies of the new Safavid dynasty of Persia were destroyed at Chaldiran, leading to temporary Ottoman control of western Persia. The defeat of Mamluke Egypt in 1516–17 opened the way for further advances into Arabia and north Africa, as well as bringing the wealth of Egypt to the sultan. In 1521 Suleiman the Magnificent resumed the Ottoman drive into Europe, overrunning Hungary after Mohács in 1526. When he laid siege to Vienna in 1529 the Ottomans seemed irresistible.

Partly drawn by a weakening Ming China, the Turkic nomads of central Asia began to move east around 1500, after nearly three centuries of westward pressure. The Mughals of Ferghana moved south from Afghanistan, destroying the armies of the Lodi sultanate at Panipat in 1526.

The energy with which the Ming emperors had rebuilt China after the Mongol invasions was beginning to wane. In the early 15th century Chinese maritime expeditions had ranged as far as the east African coast, spreading a network of Chinese trade routes. In 1421, however, the Mings had moved their capital from Nanjing to Beijing, facing the resurgent Mongols on the northern frontier. Both the Ming empire and the wider economy centered on it turned away from the sea. In 1500, with India, the East Indies and southeast Asia fragmented, the Indian Ocean trade lay open to new exploitation.

The opportunity was seized by the explorers and traders of Portugal. Pedro da Covilhã had reached India via the Red Sea in 1488 and

**TIMELINE**

**1499** Vespucci explores the northeast coast of Brazil

**1494** Treaty of Tordesillas divides the world between Spanish and Portuguese claims

**1492** Columbus (for the Spanish king) reaches Hispaniola and Cuba

**1508** Spanish conquests in the Caribbean and central America begin (Puerto Rico 1508–11; Cuba 1511–15; Panama 1509–19)

**1514** The Ottoman victory over the Safavids at Chaldiran shifts the Ottoman frontier to the east

**1519** Cortés begins the conquest of the Aztec empire for Spain

| The Americas |
| Europe |
| Middle East |
| Africa |
| East and South Asia |

1500     1510     1520

**1500** Cabral establishes trade links between Portugal and India

**1501** The Safavid dynasty in Persia is established by Shah Ismail

**1511** Albuquerque captures Malacca and part of the spice trade for Portugal

**1516** The battle of Marj Dabiq leads to the Ottoman conquest of Syria and Palestine

**1517** The Protestant Reformation begins

**1519** Charles of Habsburg is elected Charles V, Holy Roman emperor

Greenland

Iceland
(Denmark)

*Lapp
reindeer
herders*

*Arctic marine
mammal hunters*

*Siberian
hunter-gatherers*

*Siberian reindeer herders*

*Ainu hunter-gatherers*

DENMARK-NORWAY
SWEDEN
RUSSIA

SCOTLAND
ENGLAND
Cabot, 1497

POLAND-LITHUANIA

*Sibir Tatars*

*Kazan Tatars*

*Nogais*
*Astrakhan Tatars*

*Eurasian steppe and desert nomads*

*Mongols*

HOLY
ROMAN
EMPIRE

FRANCE
HUNGARY

VENICE

*Turkomans*
*Kirghiz*
*Uzbegs*

*Kalmyks*

KOREA

PORTUGAL

Azores
(Portugal)

SPAIN
Papal
states

OTTOMAN
EMPIRE

SAFAVID
EMPIRE

MUGHAL EMPIRE

TIBET

MING
CHINESE
EMPIRE

JAPAN

Canary Is
(Spain)

MOROCCO ALGIERS TUNIS
TRIPOLI

*camel nomads*

*Arab nomads*

RAJ.

*Islamic and Hindu states*

*Shan states*

Taiwan

Cape
Verde Is
(Portugal)

Cacheu SEN.
(Portugal)

MALI
Mossi
states

SONGHAI

AIR

KANEM-
BORNU

DARFUR

WADAI

FUNJ

ETHIOPIA

OMAN

GHARRA

MAHRA
HADRAMAUT
Covilhã, 1488-90

YEMEN

ADAL
Galla

OYO

Hausa
states

BENIN

AKAN

Elmina
(Portugal)

MOROCCO

*western Bantu-
speaking herders
and farmers*

OROMO

*eastern Bantu-
speaking herders
and farmers*

Mombasa
(Portugal)

*Islamic city-
states*

da Gama, 1497-98

Covilhã, 1488-90

BENGAL

ORISSA

VIJAYANAGARA

Goa
(Portugal)

Colombo
(Portugal)
SAYLAN

Ceylon
Lopez de Sequeira,
1509-10

PEGU

LAOS

AYUTHAYA

ANNAM

CAMBODIA

Perestrello,
1514-16

del Cano,
1521

Philippine
Islands

Magellan, 1520-21

Saavedra, 1527-28

Micronesians

Fernando Póo
(Portugal)

CONGO

LUNDA

LUBA

Mozambique
(Portugal)

MWENEMUTAPA

*San hunter-
gatherers*

*Khoisan
herders*

Madagascar

Malagasy

da Gama, 1497-98

del Cano, 1521-22

da Gama, 1497-98

ACEH

MALACCA

Malacca
(Portugal)

Sumatra

Borneo

Java

*Malaysian
Islamic states*

Timor

New Guinea

*Papuan
farmers*

Melanesians

*Australian Aboriginal
hunter-gatherers*

*Tasmanian
hunter-gatherers*

*Maori chiefdoms*

Polynesians

del Cano, 1521-22

**Legend:**

- hunter-gatherers
- nomadic pastoralists
- simple farming societies
- complex farming societies/chiefdoms
- state societies
- uninhabited

empires
- Portuguese
- Spanish
- other

→ English route of exploration
→ Portuguese route of exploration
→ Spanish route of exploration

RAJ. Rajputana
SEN. Senegambian states

**1521** The Portuguese begin to colonize Brazil, in the reign of João III

**1521** The Ottomans capture Belgrade

**1520s** The Inca empire reaches its greatest extent, in the reign of Huayna Capac

**1531** The Spanish conquest of the Inca empire of Peru begins

**1529** The Ottomans unsuccessfully besiege Vienna for the first time

1530

**1522** del Cano completes the voyage around the globe begun by Magellan in 1519

**1526** The Ottomans defeat Hungary at the battle of Mohács

**1526** The Mughal leader Babur defeats the Lodis at Panipat and overruns northern India

Vasco da Gama via the east African coast in 1498; Afonso de Albuquerque secured the spice port of Malacca in 1511, and Portuguese trade routes to southern China were pioneered in the next few years. A network of trading bases was set up, and Arab and Ottoman merchants were kept away by Portuguese warships. By 1510, Venetian economic supremacy, built on control of spice imports via the Levant ports, was ended. The Portuguese used Antwerp as the depot for spice shipments, and it became the new center of European finance.

Portuguese bases on the west coast of Africa began to draw the trade in gold dust away from Songhai, the southern terminus of caravan routes across the Sahara. The Hausa states inflicted a defeat on their weakened neighbor in 1517, and the power of Songhai began to decline (▷ 72). In the Horn of Africa Ahmed Gran of Adal launched a *jihad* against the Christian kingdom of Ethiopia. Portugal supplied firearms to Ethiopia and the Ottomans to Adal, but the struggle left both sides prey to the incursions of the nomadic Galla.

While Portuguese mariners pioneered routes to the east, the Spanish successors of Columbus and Vespucci soon came into contact with the empires of the Americas. The Aztec state collapsed in the face of Hernán Cortés in 1519–24, and in Peru the Incas, divided by a succession struggle, were ill-prepared to resist the expedition being organized by Francisco Pizarro in 1530. Spain was on the verge of a huge territorial expansion, and about to tap a source of silver that would drive the world's economy for over a century (▷ 62) ∎

The eastward migration of Mongols and Tatars in the late 15th and early 16th centuries meant that the Mughals, a people descended from Timur's Mongols, were driven out of the principality they had established in Ferghana. Under their leader Babur (r.1501–30), the Mughals conquered an area around Kabul in 1504, and made the first of several exploratory invasions of India in 1519, culminating in a fullscale attempt in 1526. The Indian subcontinent at the time was a patchwork of warring Muslim and Hindu states. Among these the Rajput lands southwest of Delhi, the ancient Hindu kingdom of Vijayanagara in the south and the Afghan Lodi sultanate of Delhi were the most powerful. Babur's force of 12,000 men, supported by artillery, overcame the army of Ibrahim Shah Lodi at Panipat in 1526. Mughal conquest thereafter was swift; by Babur's death, all the former Lodi lands had been subdued, while his son Humayun (r.1530–40; 1555–56) invaded Gujarat in 1535, taking the fortress of Champanir. In the 1540s, however, a rebellion of the Afghan Sur dynasty of south Bihar against their new masters almost spelled the end of the Mughal dynasty. The Surs captured the Gangetic plain and Delhi, and forced Humayun to take refuge in Persia. Only in 1555 did Humayun succeed in reoccupying Delhi, but his reconquest was cut short by his death.

Babur's grandson Akbar (r.1556–1605) not only managed to regain all the lands lost to the Surs, but created one of the world's most powerful states. In 1572 the conquest of Gujarat brought access to the sea, while control of Bengal in 1576 secured India's richest region for the Mughals. By 1605 their advance into the Deccan had begun with the subjugation of Khandesh and Berar, with the loyalty of the Rajputs assured by military force and dynastic intermarriage. Akbar's reign brought administrative efficiency and social reform. The empire was divided into provinces (subahs) which were administered by professional civil servants who were appointed on merit. Moreover, though himself a devout Muslim, the sophisticated Akbar promoted religious toleration throughout his empire.

Other external powers also arrived in India after 1500. The Portuguese acquired trading bases at Goa, Daman and Diu in the early 16th century. Conflict ensued; the Portuguese defeated a combined Indian and Mamluke Egyptian fleet off Diu in 1509, and repulsed an Ottoman-Gujarati attack on the same base in 1538. In general, though, the Indians found mercantile benefits in cooperating with Europeans. By 1500 Indian banking and credit facilities supported a commercial network that covered most of Asia and east Africa, and extended as far as Moscow. Since Roman times Europeans had exchanged silver or gold for Indian silks, cottons, spices and dyes, and European access to the silver mines of Latin America made possible a huge increase in this trade. Trading links with European companies became more and more important in the Mughal economy.

Mughal agriculture was highly efficient (cereal yields were higher than those of Europe until the 19th century), and cash crops (indigo, cotton, sugar, opium, pepper and later tobacco) were developed within a centrally controlled internal market. Indian industry, based on cheap labor and proven, low-level technology, included both the world's largest textile industry (whose products were exported worldwide) and an iron industry producing high-quality steel and cannon the equal of any in Europe. The Mughals kept a standing army of about one million men who were equipped with weapons that, until the 18th century, rivaled European arms. Yet the vast Mughal empire was already fragmenting by the death of the last great emperor, Aurangzeb (r.1658–1707). Religious intolerance had grown under Akbar's successors Jahangir, Shah Jahan and Aurangzeb himself, leading to increasingly frequent revolts, even as the empire reached its greatest territorial extent with the conquest of Ahmadnagar (1636), Bijapur (1686) and Golconda (1687). As bases of the Dutch and English East India companies spread in the later 17th century, largely displacing the Portuguese, the Hindu Marathas of the Western Ghats were already asserting their independence of the Mughal empire.

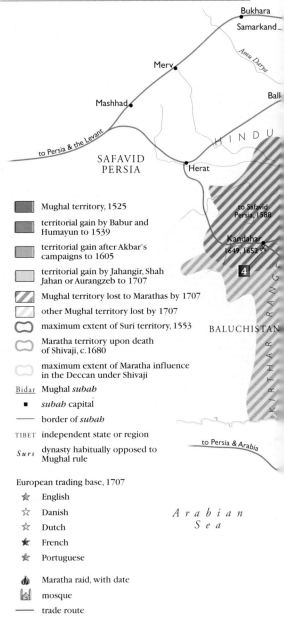

Mughal territory, 1525

territorial gain by Babur and Humayun to 1539

territorial gain after Akbar's campaigns to 1605

territorial gain by Jahangir, Shah Jahan or Aurangzeb to 1707

Mughal territory lost to Marathas by 1707

other Mughal territory lost by 1707

maximum extent of Suri territory, 1553

Maratha territory upon death of Shivaji, c.1680

maximum extent of Maratha influence in the Deccan under Shivaji

Bidar   Mughal subah

■   subah capital

——   border of subah

TIBET   independent state or region

Surs   dynasty habitually opposed to Mughal rule

European trading base, 1707

☆   English

☆   Danish

☆   Dutch

★   French

★   Portuguese

Maratha raid, with date

mosque

——   trade route

## Mughal empire

| 1525 | 1600 | 1675 |
|---|---|---|
| **1504** The Mughals under Babur are expelled from Ferghana by the Uzbegs | | |
| **1556** Mughals under Akbar rout the Suri army at Panipat | **1598** The Mughal capital is moved to Agra | **1659–70** The Hindu Maratha leader Shivaji defeats Bijapur and sacks Surat |
| **1526** Babur defeats Shah Ibrahim Lodi of the sultanate of Delhi at Panipat | | |
| **1568–69** Akbar captures the Rajput fortresses of Chittaurgarh and Rathambhor | **1632** Shah Jahan begins the Mughal conquest of Deccan | **1669–78** Religious persecution prompts rebellions by the Jats and Sikhs |
| **1535** Humayun invades Gujarat | | |
| **1571** Construction of new capital Fatehpur Sikri begins | | **1679–1709** War between the Mughals and Hindu Rajputs |
| **1539** Suri Afghans of Bihar under Sher Shah rebel and reconquer much Mughal territory | **1572** Conquest of Gujarat gives the Mughals a seaport | **1707** Death of Aurangzeb marks the start of the disintegration of the Mughal empire |
| | **1576** The Mughal conquest of Bengal is completed | |

## Europeans in India

| 1525 | 1600 | 1675 |
|---|---|---|
| **1498** A Portuguese expedition under Vasco da Gama reaches the Malabar Coast | **1608** The English East India Company receives its first trading concessions in India | **1661** The English East India Company gains a base at Bombay |
| **1509** The Portuguese under Francisco de Almeida defeat Egyptian–Indian fleet at Diu | **1612** The English East India Company defeats a Portuguese fleet at Surat | **1664** The French East India Company is founded |
| **1538** The Portuguese defeat an attack on Diu by Ottoman and Gujarati forces | | **1685** The English are expelled from Surat by Aurangzeb |

Tashkent
FERGHANA
Kokand
Andijan

to Beijing

KHANATE OF
TURFAN

Kashgar
KHANATE OF KASHGAR
Yarkand

Khotan

KUNLUN MTS

independent from
late 17th century

Badakhshan
KUSH
Baltistan

Kabul
Kabul
Khyber
Pass
Peshawar
Mughals
Pathans
Kashmir
(sub province)
Srinagar
Ladakh

TAPESTRY and carpet design was
inspired by Persia, but often
demonstrated an informality and
realism that was entirely new,
as seen in this detail.

TIBET

Lhasa

to Safavid
Persia,
1618–38
and from
1649

SULAIMAN RANGE

Lahore
Lahore
Chenab

Indus

HIMALAYAS

Brahmaputra

Multan
Multan
Sutlej

Delhi
1526, 1556
Sikhs
Panipat

Delhi
Sambhal

Gurkhas

Kathmandu

Koch

Ahoms
recovered by
Ahoms, 1669

Nagas

Shans

TOUNGOU

Bhakkar

Satnamis

2
Jats

Oudh
Ayodhya

Salween

Thatta
ub province)

Rathors
Rajputs

Thar Desert
Jaisalmer

Ajmer

Fatehpur
Sikri
Agra
4

Jaipur

Surs

Patna

Gaur

Dhaka

Chittagong

Thatta

Ajmer
Jodhpur
Ranthambhor
1569
3
Agra

Yamuna

Ganges

Allahabad
Varanasi
Bihar

Bihar
Cossimbazar

Baharampur

Bengal
Hooghly
Chinsura

Chittaurgarh
1568
Udaipur

Sisodiyas

Malwa
Ujjain
1703

Sironj
1703

Allahabad

Bundelas

Chandannagar
Calcutta

ARAKAN

Irrawaddy

Rann of
Kutch

Gujarat
Ahmadabad

Narmada

Mandla

Gondwana

Baleshwar

to southeast Asia China & Japan

Ahmad
Shahis
Vadodara
1706
Mandu
Asirgarh
1601

Mahanadi

Cuttack

Bharuch
1685
Champanir
1
Surat
1664
Diu
1509
Daman

Gawilgarh
Burhanpur
1670
Imad Shahis
Khandesh
Karanja
1670

DECCAN
Berar

Pipli

Orissa

Bay of
Bengal

Vasai
Bombay
Chaul

Nizam
Shahis
Ahmadnagar
5
Aurangabad
1685

Bimlipatam
Vishakhapatnam

to Arabia, East Africa & Europe
via Cape of Good Hope

WESTERN GHATS

Maratha's

Ahmadnagar
1657

Qutb Shahis

Golconda

Kakinada

6

Bidar
1687
Golconda

EASTERN GHATS

Godavari

Palakollu
Machilipatnam

Bijapur
1686
Bidar
Bijapur
1666

Krishna

to southeast Asia

Adil Shahis
Hubli
1673
Koppal
1677

Aravidus

Vengurla
Goa

Anjidiv
Island
Karwar

Vijayanagara
Chitradurga
1695
Sira

Pulicat

Coondapoor

Madras

Mangalore

Mysore
Cannanore
Tellicherry

MYSORE

MALABAR COAST

Bangalore

Vellore
1677
Arani
1677

to Udaiyars,
1672
Gingee

Sadras

Pondicherry
Fort St David
Porto Novo
Tranquebar

Udaiyars

Kaveri

Calicut
Cranganur
Cochin
Porakad
Kayankulam
Quilon
Anjengo

MADURAI

Pallipuram
Madurai

Tanjore
1677

Nagappattinam

Jaffna

Mannar

Trincomalee

Tuticorin
Kayalpatnam

Manapadu
Negombo
Colombo

Savulus

Puttalam

Batticaloa

Ceylon

Galle
Matara

to southeast Asia

to Arabia, East Africa, & Europe
via Cape of Good Hope

0        400 km
0        300 mi

**1** Surat was the major trading port of Mughal India,
and also the departure point for pilgrimages to Mecca.

**2** Akbar's monumental capital at Fatehpur Sikri, built
between 1571 and 1584, was only occupied for 14
years, as it lacked a reliable water supply.

**3** Agra was the Mughal capital for most of the period
between Akbar's accession and the foundation by
Shah Jahan of a new city at Delhi, Shahjahanabad.

**4** Kandahar was a major base for the Mughal
reconquest of India under Humayun and Akbar.

**5** Despite the loss of their capital Aurangabad in
1600, the Nizam Shahis resisted Mughal conquest
until 1633.

**6** Maratha hostilities against the Mughals began in
1657; in 1689 the Mughals conquered most of their
territories, but were unable to halt widespread
Maratha raids.

**7** Bases in Ceylon were seized by the Dutch in
1655-60, after the Savulus requested their help in
expelling the Portuguese.

See also 69 (Manchu China);
83 (19th century India)

Spanish conquest in the New World profoundly affected both the region itself and Europe. Spain's empire was the largest in world history to date other than that of the Mongols. It destroyed ancient cultures and decimated native populations, who proved disastrously vulnerable to diseases introduced from the Old World. Meanwhile, the mining of huge silver deposits financed Spanish Habsburg ambitions and underpinned the whole of European trade. Nor was the traffic in disease all one-way: syphilis, caught by Spanish sailors in the Caribbean, became a feared killer in Europe from the early 16th century.

Spain's incursion in the Americas began with royal sponsorship of the voyages of the Italian navigator-merchants Christopher Columbus and Amerigo Vespucci at the end of the 15th century. In particular, Columbus' discovery of the West Indies for Spain soon led to permanent settlements. Colonization of the Caribbean islands began on Santo Domingo (Hispaniola) and provided a foretaste of Spanish rule on the mainland. Administrative, legal, and religious structures were rapidly put in place, while the aboriginal Arawak and Carib peoples fell victim to maltreatment and disease.

The Spanish empire was territorial from the outset, concerned with the government, economic exploitation and religious conversion of its native subjects. It was perhaps less careless of the welfare of its subject peoples than were some other colonial empires. Paradoxically, its rapid growth depended on existing political structures and communications networks. Hernán Cortés and Francisco Pizarro encountered, in the Aztec and Inca empires respectively, centralized, populous and formidable states, yet internal divisions helped them swiftly to destroy any resistance. Beyond their boundaries, the population was sparse and the environment hostile and virtually impenetrable to Europeans. These hinterlands were still only partially conquered by 1800.

The prosperity of the empire was built above all on Mexican and Peruvian gold and silver. These precious metals had been extracted on a modest scale by the Aztecs and Incas for use in ceremonial artifacts, but were now mined and shipped in huge

quantities by the Spanish. This enterprise required regular commercial fleets with permanent naval escorts, linking Seville and Veracruz on the east coast of Mexico, and Peru and the west coast of the Central American isthmus. The maintenance and protection of these fleets was one of the great maritime and commercial achievements of the age.

Challenges by Spain's European rivals to the Spanish–American empire itself were frequent but largely unsuccessful; indeed, Spanish America proved more resilient than Spain's European territories to challenges from the other powers. From the

1570s, major ports were subjected to numerous assaults. The English capture of Jamaica in 1655 was an important strategic loss, but the empire remained largely secure until the Seven Years War (1756–63). In 1762, the British occupied Havana; Spain only regained control by ceding Florida. However, the demise of France as a colonial power in America allowed Spain to acquire Louisiana while, in the American War of Independence, it regained Florida and checked British expansion on the Mississippi.

Spain was not the only significant colonial power in South America. In 1494, Spain and Portugal

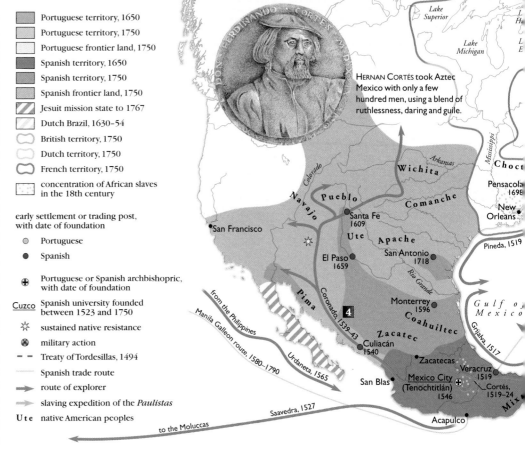

**Key**

- Portuguese territory, 1650
- Portuguese territory, 1750
- Portuguese frontier land, 1750
- Spanish territory, 1650
- Spanish territory, 1750
- Spanish frontier land, 1750
- Jesuit mission state to 1767
- Dutch Brazil, 1630–54
- British territory, 1750
- Dutch territory, 1750
- French territory, 1750
- concentration of African slaves in the 18th century

early settlement or trading post, with date of foundation
- ○ Portuguese
- ● Spanish
- ⊕ Portuguese or Spanish archbishopric, with date of foundation
- Cuzco Spanish university founded between 1523 and 1750
- ☆ sustained native resistance
- ⊗ military action
- - - Treaty of Tordesillas, 1494
- —— Spanish trade route
- → route of explorer
- → slaving expedition of the *Paulistas*
- **Ute** native American peoples

HERNAN CORTÉS took Aztec Mexico with only a few hundred men, using a blend of ruthlessness, daring and guile.

---

**TIMELINE**

**Spanish America**

**1508–15** Puerto Rico (San Juan), Jamaica (Santiago) and Cuba are colonized by Spain

**1519–24** Hernán Cortés conquers the Aztec empire

**1531–35** Francisco Pizarro completes the conquest of the powerful Inca empire

**1538** Spanish control is established in Colombia

**1565** Forts are built in Florida to defend Spanish fleets

**1569** Francisco de Toledo establishes a stable Spanish government in Peru

**1577–80** Francis Drake raids Spanish settlements on the Pacific coast

**1655** An English expedition captures Jamaica during Oliver Cromwell's war against Spain

**1670** The English freebooter Henry Morgan sacks Panama

**1716** Spain occupies part of modern Texas in response to French expansion from Louisiana

**1739** A British expedition sacks Porto Bello, but in 1741 fails to take Cartagena

**1762** A British expeditionary force captures Havana

**1780–81** Spanish forces recapture west Florida and the Bahamas from Britain

**Portuguese America**

**1530–32** The first major Portuguese colony is established in the Americas at São Vicente

**1534** The first African slaves are landed in Brazil

**1565–67** Rio de Janeiro is founded by Portuguese

**1615** A French attempt to colonize Maranhão is thwarted by the Portuguese

**1624** A Dutch fleet takes Bahia (recaptured 1625)

**1630** The Dutch briefly overrun most of north-eastern Brazil

**1680** Portugal bans the enslavement of Brazilian native peoples

**1708–09** Portugal suppresses the *Paulistas*

**1711** The French sack Rio de Janeiro during the War of the Spanish Succession

**1750** Treaties of Madrid and San Ildefonso (1777) update the Treaty of Tordesillas

1550          1650          1750

**NORTH ATLANTIC OCEAN**

*Lake Ontario*

Cherokee

Bermuda Islands to Britain

Columbus, 1492

Portuguese Spanish

Cape Verde Islands

**1** Cuba was settled from 1511 by Spanish colonists, including Hernán Cortés, who set out eight years later to conquer Mexico. By 1550, from an original indigenous population of 50,000, only 5,000 survived.

**2** Cumaná was the site of an unsuccessful colony founded in 1521 by the Dominican friar Bartolomé de Las Casas, an advocate of the humane treatment of native Americans.

**3** Havana was, by the mid-18th century, the most important Spanish naval and shipbuilding center (not excluding those of mainland Spain).

**4** Spanish exploration of the area between modern Kansas and the Gulf of California was pioneered by Francisco Vázquez de Coronado in 1540–42.

**5** In 1540–61 the Araucanians of Chile conducted fierce resistance to Spanish colonial expansion.

**6** Potosí, discovered in 1545, remained the world's most important silver mine until the late 17th century. Between 1580 and 1626, some 11 million kilograms of precious metals were shipped to Spain.

**7** The Dutch admiral Piet Hein uniquely succeeded in capturing a Spanish bullion fleet off Matanzas in 1628. It had on board some 4 million gold and silver ducats.

**8** In 1713 Britain was granted a 30-year monopoly of the slave trade, coinciding with the greatest period of slaving in Africa.

St Augustine 1565
Florida
Ponce de Leon, 1512–13
Havana–Cádiz direct route
Bahamas
San Juan 1511
Puerto Rico
Lesser Antilles
Columbus, 1493
Island Carib
Columbus, 1498
**7** 1628
Matanzas 1693
1672
Island Arawak
Cuba
Santo Domingo 1496
Hispaniola
**1**
Havana 1515
**3**
Jamaica
Armada Española route, to 1748
Flota a Nueva España route, 1580–1790
Columbus, 1502–4
Cumaná 1521
**2**
Ojeda & Vespucci, 1499
Paramaribo
Cayenne
Cabral, 1500
Magellan, 1519
rdoba 16
Maya
Miskito
Guatemala 1743
Antigua 1542
Porto Bello 1597
Nombre de Dios 1510
Cartagena 1533
1584, 1740
Bastidas & La Cosa 1501–2
Caracas 1567
Arawak
Carib
Guiana Highlands
Bele do Para 1616
São Luis 1615
Macantão
MARANHÃO
Timbira
Ceará
Natal 1597
Olinda 1537
Recife 1563
1640
1568, 1572, 1595, 1739
Panama 1519
1571
Guahipo
Chibcha
Santa Fe de Bogota 1538
1564
Macu
Manaus 1674
Amazon
Munducurú
Caraja
1667
Bahia 1549
**8**
Tierra Firme y Peru route, to 1746
Pizarro, 1526–27
Witoto
Putumayo
Amazon Basin
Cawahie
Madeira
Brazilian Highlands
Santa Cruz
to India

**PACIFIC OCEAN**

Quito 1534
Guayaquil 1535
Ucayali
Piro
Mato Grosso Plateau
Villa Rica 1698
São Francisco
Portuguese Spanish
0    1400 km
0    1000 mi
ANDES
Pizarro, 1533
Inca
Nambicuara
Rio de Janeiro 1565
São Paulo 1532
São Vicente 1530
Mochica
Cuzco
La Paz
Peru
Aymara
Nazca
Chuquisaca (Charcas/La Plata) 1538
1609
Guarani
Tupinamba
Buenos Aires–Cádiz route from 1778
Callao 1537
1546
Ciudad de los Reyes (Lima) 1535
Arica 1537
Potosí 1545
**6**
Asunción 1538
Paraná
Magellan, 1519–20
Banda Oriental
concluded the Treaty of Tordesillas, under which all land beyond a line immediately west of the Cape Verde islands was assigned to Spain, and all land east to Portugal. Later redrawing of the boundary further west allowed Portugal to claim the coast of Brazil, discovered by Pedro Alvares Cabral in 1500. From about 1530, the Portuguese began to settle Brazil in large numbers. Philip II's acquisiton of the Portuguese crown in 1580 drew the Portuguese colonies into the Dutch–Spanish war, and from the 1620s, Dutch efforts to capture Portugal's possessions provoked a limited but savage war. An alliance between the Portuguese and native Brazilians ultimately prevailed. Later, Portuguese slavers known as *Paulistas* (from São Paulo, their starting point) began to penetrate into the Brazilian jungle to attack Spanish Jesuit missions on the fringes of Spanish possessions. In 1680 the Portuguese authorities banned the enslavement of native Americans and suppressed the *Paulistas* but their expeditions had taken Portuguese control far into the interior of the continent. By 1800, Spanish and Portuguese conflict was imminent in the Banda Oriental and Rio de la Plata areas.

to the Philippines
Araucanians
Córdoba 1573
Buenos Aires 1536
**5**

**SOUTH ATLANTIC OCEAN**

Valparaiso 1541
Santiago 1541
ANDES
Valdivia 1552
Patagonia
Magellan, 1520–21
Spanish Portuguese

See also 55, 56 (Aztecs and Incas); 65 and 66 (Spain); 81 (19th-century Latin America)

The last century of the Ashikaga shogunate (1338–1573) in Japan was dominated by the political fragmentation arising from the Onin war of 1467–77. Following this protracted civil conflict, real power devolved to small, feudal units subject to the changing allegiances of local lords (*daimyo*), while the authority of the emperor and his military commander, the *shogun*, was only nominal. Instability was heightened by ever more frequent popular uprisings, often fomented by the powerful Buddhist monasteries. Both this tradition of religious militancy and the independent merchant guilds provided an alternative focus for popular loyalty.

The lack of political stability did not, however, prevent the steady growth of Japanese trade and industry throughout the later 15th and early 16th centuries, although the proliferation of local customs boundaries did preclude a truly national economy. Japan also remained culturally vibrant, with many great *daimyo* patronizing such diverse art forms as *noh* drama, poetry, the tea ceremony and painting. At the same time, traveling balladeers, preachers and dancers helped create a popular culture that transcended Japan's political fragmentation.

In 1568, the first of a series of leaders powerful enough to attempt the political unification of Japan emerged. Nobunaga, lord of the Oda clan, captured the imperial capital Kyoto in that year, and embarked on the destruction of the Buddhist temples and slaughter of the monks. Warfare in Japan had been transformed by the introduction of firearms by the Portuguese in 1542: muskets were copied in large numbers, and sophisticated new tactics developed to utilize this firepower. Even more significant was the construction by Nobunaga of an entirely new type of castle at Azuchi. In contrast to earlier mountain strongholds, Azuchi was built to dominate the rice fields and communications of the plain, and was an administrative center as well as a fortress. Its importance was such that the age of national

## TIMELINE

### Unification of Japan

**1550**

**1568** Oda Nobunaga takes Kyoto to control central Japan

**1571–82** Hideyoshi conquers lands in western and eastern Japan for Nobunaga

**1582** Death of Nobunaga; he is succeeded by Hideyoshi

**1590** Hideyoshi gains control of eastern and northern Japan

**1592** Hideyoshi's first invasion of Korea fails

**1597–98** A second Japanese invasion of Korea is defeated

**1600** Tokugawa Ieyasu succeeds Hideyoshi

**1650**

**1750**

**1684** Widespread economic hardship follows Buddhist-inspired reforms of the *shogun* Tsunayoshi

**1703** Edo (Tokyo) is almost destroyed in an earthquake and major fire

**1745** Tokugawa rule begins to decline into corruption under Ieshige

**1760** Widespread peasant uprisings break out

### Foreign influences

**1542** First Portuguese traders arrive on Tanegashima

**1548–51** Mission to Kyoto and western Japan converts first Japanese to Christianity

**1570** Nagasaki is opened to foreign trade by local *daimyo*

**1609** A Dutch trading base is established on Hirado Island

**1612–32** Systematic persecution of Christians under Ieyasu and Hidetada

**1637–41** Portuguese traders are expelled from Japan

**1715** Dutch trade with Japan is severely restricted

**1720** Yoshimune allows the import of European books, so promoting advances in science and medicine

**1550**

**1650**

**1750**

*Sea of Japan*

*Sado*

JAPAN

*Honshu*

EUROPEAN traders (seen in
this Japanese painting) and
missionaries were initially
welcomed, but repression
increased in the 1630s.

*PACIFIC OCEAN*

*Shikoku*

**Oda land, 1560**

**area conquered by Nobunaga and
Hideyoshi by 1582**

**main *daimyo* house opposed to Hideyoshi, 1582**

Mori   *daimyo* house, 16th-17th centuries

⟶ campaigns of Hideyoshi, 1584–90

⟶ Hideyoshi's first invasion of Korea, 1592

⟶ Hideyoshi's second invasion of Korea, 1597–98

⟶ Korean and Ming Chinese counteroffensives

⧄ main areas of Korean resistance to Hideyoshi

▮ Japanese base in Korea retained after 1593

⊗ Hideyoshi victory

🏯 castle town

☆ Japanese peasant revolt against
Hideyoshi's land survey

⊗ victory of Tokugawa Ieyasu or his successors

✝ area with significant number of Christian converts

<u>Hirado</u> trading port used by Europeans

—— "Five Highways" of Tokugawa Japan

—— coastal shipping route

0        200 km
0            150 mi

■ Nagasaki was an unimportant fishing village until it
was developed as Japan's main port for foreign trade
by the local lord Omura in 1570.

■ The Dutch East India Company base on Hirado
Island was moved to Deshima Island, near Nagasaki, in
1641. The Dutch officials had to undergo various
symbolic indignities to retain their trading privileges.

■ Hideyoshi's invasion of Korea was commanded by
Kato Kiyomasa and Konishi Yukinaga. Konishi took
Pusan in 1592, but the Ming navy almost destroyed
the Japanese fleet, leaving the army cut off.

■ Azuchi castle, on the shores of Lake Biwa, was
begun by Oda Nobunaga in 1576. This pioneering
castle was widely imitated by other *daimyo* over the
next few decades.

■ Edo (Tokyo) became the administrative and military
base of Tokugawa Ieyasu in 1590. In the 1600s it
became a rival to the ancient capital, Kyoto.

■ Osaka castle, stronghold of Hideyoshi's son
Hideyori, became a center for opposition to the rule
of Ieyasu, until Ieyasu's forces sacked it in 1614-15.

■ The Five Highways (*gokaido*) formed an efficient
transport network converging on the *shogun*'s court;
*daimyo* traveling to the court had their travel papers
checked at control points on the highways.

the Koreans with the help of Ming China. He continued the policies of his predecessor, as did subsequent *shoguns* of the Tokugawa dynasty which he
founded in 1603. Christianity, persecuted under
Hidetada (r.1605–23), was eradicated by the massacre of 37,000 Japanese Christians at Hara castle
(1638). Social and economic stability were maintained by strict segregation of farming and trade, a
ban on private investment and official discourage-
ment of any contact between different parts of the
country that did not use the closely controlled Five
Highways. Portuguese ships were banned from
Japan in 1639, export restricted to Dutch and Chinese bases at Nagasaki, and Japanese citizens were
forbidden to travel abroad (while those long resident
in ports throughout Asia were forbidden to return).
The construction of large ships was banned in 1638
to prevent the Japanese from traveling abroad.

Despite these repressive measures, the early Edo
period (1603–1867) was remarkable for its economic
prosperity and agricultural productivity (led by
growing demand from the booming cities), and for
its technological advancement. The population
grew rapidly in the 17th and early 18th centuries to
nearly 30 million, and a vigorous merchant class had
its heyday in the late 17th century. However, economic and social ills did begin to accumulate. By the
mid-18th century many peasants had left the land,
many samurai had fallen into debt, and unrest was
again becoming common. Lifting both of social stric-
tures and of the ban on European books under the
enlightened shogun Yoshimune (r.1716–45) brought
some relief, but famine, natural disasters and government corruption provoked frequent peasant
uprisings after 1760. The late 18th century saw the
growth of an opposition movement around the
emperor to the rule of the Tokugawa shoguns, and a
new Japanese awareness of the threat from expanding European influence in Asia.

unification is known in Japan as the Azuchi–
Momoyama period, after Nobunaga's castle and its
counterpart built by his lieutenant Hideyoshi.

Hideyoshi, who acquired the surname Toyotomi
("the Wealthy"), was a military genius of humble
origins. Under his leadership, Oda forces overran
the lands of their rivals in central Japan, the Akechi,
Shibata and Mori, and then expanded eastward into
Takeda and Uesugi territory. After Nobunaga's death
in 1582, Hideyoshi became ruler of most of central
Japan in alliance with Tokugawa Ieyasu, his most
dangerous rival. Campaigns against rival daimyo on
the islands of Shikoku and Kyushu followed, and in
1590 Hideyoshi's capture of the Hojo clan's castle at
Odawara also gave him control of eastern Japan.

Hideyoshi's conquests were accompanied by
political changes designed to prevent further unrest.
He disarmed the peasantry and insisted that the
*samurai* (warrior-class) live in castle towns, which
ensured that potentially rebellious farming communities could no longer rely on local samurai support.
Taxation was reformed in an unpopular land survey,
which initially caused widespread unrest. Trade was
brought under government control, and steps were
taken to suppress Christianity, which had spread
from the Portuguese base at Nagasaki (founded
1572) but which now seemed alien and subversive.

Ieyasu succeeded Hideyoshi after two Japanese
invasions of Korea in the 1590s were beaten back by

See also 50 (medieval Japan);
93 (19th-century Japan)

B y 1600, Europe and Asia had enjoyed a century of population growth. European prosperity was matched by a rise in living conditions in Asia, India and the Middle East. African populations and material conditions stayed stable, but in the Americas the Europeans brought demographic catastrophe.

Spanish and Portuguese penetration of the Americas was slow after the collapse of the Inca empire. Beyond the highly-organized Inca and Aztec states, populations were sparse, distances huge and political structures lacking, and the conquistadors had little incentive to explore. Instead they exploited their conquests (▷62). In 1545 production began at the rich mines of Potosí; silver was shipped to Seville and spread through Europe, as the Genoese backers of Spain's voyages multiplied its value by sophisticated credit mechanisms. Spanish silver was also used by Europe's merchants to buy into other trading networks around the world. Antwerp's reign as financial capital of Europe had ended by 1576 when it was sacked by Spanish muti-neers: from 1557 Genoa called the tune in Europe's economy (▷66).

Spanish political and military power reached its peak in the 1580s when Philip II seized the crown of Portugal. For sixty years the two crowns were united, although Portuguese overseas possessions were still administered from Lisbon. As the Netherlands began a campaign of conquest against the Portuguese trading bases worldwide, Portuguese power in Asia declined.

European politics spilled over into the Spanish empire. Dutch and English pirates raided the Spanish–American cities and attempted to seize bullion fleets. French Huguenot (Protestant) colonists reached Florida and the mouth of the Amazon. They were driven from the former by Spanish forces, but the Portuguese could not dislodge them from the latter for over a century. French explorers such as Jacques Cartier penetrated North America via the St Lawrence river, while the Spaniard Francisco Coronado pioneered routes north from Mexico (▷70).

In Africa, the Ottomans steadily reduced the Spanish footholds in North Africa, while Morocco's stunning defeat of a major Portuguese expedition at Alcazarquivir in 1578 led directly to the union of Portugal with Spain. The Moroccans then mounted an even more spectacular expedition across the Sahara in 1590–91 to overthrow the weakened Songhai empire at Tondibi. In sub-Saharan Africa, the Muslim empire of Kanem-Bornu emerged as the most

**1552–56** Russia conquers Kazan and Astrakhan from the Tatars and begins expansion into Siberia

**1566** The Dutch begin a rebellion against Spanish rule (to 1648)

**1565** St Augustine is founded by Spain to prevent French Huguenots from colonizing Florida

**1535** Pizarro completes the conquest of Peru for Spain (begun 1531)

**1545** The Potosí silver mines in Peru begin production

**1580** Philip II of Spain claims the throne of Portugal

| TIMELINE | |
|---|---|
| The Americas | |
| Europe | |
| Middle East | 1540 ... 1560 ... 1580 |
| Africa | |
| East and South Asia | |

**1538** The Ottoman Turks overrun the entire Red Sea coast of Arabia

**1557** A Portuguese trading base is established at Macao, China

**1568** Japanese unification under the control of Nobunaga begins

**1577–80** Drake's circumnavigation of the world includes raids on Pacific Spanish America

**1539–56** The Mughals are driven from northern India by the Afghan Sur dynasty

**1570** Kanem-Bornu begins to reach the peak of its power under Idris III Aloma

**1578** The Moroccans defeat and kill Sebastian I of Portugal at al-Qasr al-Kabir (Alcazarquivir)

**1542** Portuguese traders land at Tanegashima, Japan

**1571** A combined Christian fleet defeats the Ottoman navy at Lepanto

**Map legend:**

- hunter-gatherers
- nomadic pastoralists
- simple farming societies
- complex farming societies/ chiefdoms
- state societies
- uninhabited

empires
- Spanish
- other

→ English route of exploration
→ French route of exploration
→ Spanish route of exploration

GE.  Genoa
SEN.  Senegambian states
SO.  Songhai

**Map labels:**

Greenland

Iceland (Denmark)

SCOTLAND

Cartier, 1534–41

ENGLAND

DENMARK NORWAY

SWEDEN

RUSSIAN EMPIRE

Siberian reindeer herders

Arctic marine mammal hunters

Siberian hunter-gatherers

Ainu hunter-gatherers

FRANCE

HOLY ROMAN EMPIRE

POLAND

Sibir Tatars

Eurasian steppe and desert nomads

Mongols

Kazan Tatars

Nogais

Astrakhan Tatars

Turkomans

Kirghiz

Kalmyks

Uzbegs

KOREA

JAPAN

VENICE

GE.

Portugal

SPAIN

Papal states

OTTOMAN EMPIRE

SAFAVID EMPIRE

TIBET

MING CHINESE EMPIRE

MOROCCO

camel nomads

Arab nomads

MUGHAL EMPIRE

Shan states

Taiwan

AIR

KANEM-BORNU

Oman (Ottoman)

Diu (Portugal)

GHARRA

TOUNGOO

LAOS

Macao (Portugal)

DARFUR

MAHRA

HADRAMAUT

Golconda

Islamic and Hindu states

Philippine Is

acheu SEN.

MALI

SO.

WADAI

ETHIOPIA

Yemen (Ottoman)

Goa (Portugal)

GOLCONDA

ANNAM

AYUTHAYA

(tugal)

OYO

Hausa states

AWSA

BIJAPUR

SAYLAN

CAMBODIA

Drake, 1577–80

AKAN

BENIN

Hindu kingdoms

Ceylon

Micronesians

Elmina (Portugal)

OROMO

western Bantu-speaking herders and farmers

eastern Bantu-speaking herders and farmers

ACEH

Malaysian Islamic states

Celebes

Borneo

New Guinea

Papuan farmers

Mombasa (Portugal)

Sumatra

Melanesians

CONGO

Luanda (Portugal)

LUNDA

LUBA

Mozambique (Portugal)

Java

Timor

MWENEMUTAPA

MATARAM

Madagascar

Mauritius (Netherlands)

Malagasay

Drake, 1577–80

San hunter-gatherers

Khoisan herders

Delagoa Bay (Portugal)

Drake, 1577–80

Australian Aboriginal hunter-gatherers

Tasmanian hunter-gatherers

Maori chiefdoms

Polynesians

**Timeline:**

**1590** The Ottomans and Safavids make peace, leaving the Ottoman frontier at the Caspian Sea

**1588** Philip II of Spain launches an Armada to invade England

**1588** Accession of Shah Abbas I, Safavid Persia's greatest ruler

**1598** Dutch trade with Lisbon is banned by the Spaniards, prompting a Dutch campaign against the Portuguese empire

**1598** The Dutch establish a trading base on the island of Mauritius

1600

**1591** The Moroccans overthrow the Songhai empire at Tondibi

**1592, 1597–98** The Japanese under Hideyoshi invade the Ming vassal state of Korea

**1596** The first Dutch trading expedition reaches the East Indies

powerful state under Idris III Aloma (▷ 72). The first threat to Portuguese control of the coasts came in 1596 with the appearance of Dutch traders in Guinea.

Ottoman expansion along the Red Sea coast had ended the Portuguese presence at Massawa and Aden, but Portuguese warships from Diu and Goa continued to restrict Ottoman trade. In the Mediterranean a series of Ottoman victories was ended by an Austrian, Spanish and Venetian fleet at Lepanto, but the coalition of Christian powers soon fell apart (▷ 59).

The conquest by Russia of the Tatar khanates of Kazan and Astrakhan in the 1550s had brought the Russian frontier to the north shore of the Caspian Sea, and expansion across Siberia now began in earnest.

Mughal domination of north India seemed doomed by the revived Afghan Sur dynasty of Bengal, and the Mughals were briefly expelled from Hindustan until the 1550s, when Humayun and Akbar re-established their control. A prosperous, tolerant Muslim empire was built on foundations that had been laid by the Lodi sultanate.

After 1550 the Chinese Ming empire was assailed both by the Mongols under Altan Khan, and by Japanese pirates. Japan's Hideyoshi Toyotomi devastated the Ming vassal state of Korea. Portuguese trading bases at Macao and in Japan brought the European and Asian economies into direct contact, but, with traditional suspicion of outsiders, both China and Japan acted to keep the European traders under close control (▷67) ■

The "crisis of the 17th century" brought social upheaval, religious violence and economic hardship from Portugal to Russia. Monarchs tried to increase their power at the expense of the nobility, local corporations and the peripheral regions.

Religious tensions abounded, heightened by the uncompromising stances of both Calvinism and Counter-Reformation Catholicism. Religion was, however, seldom the overriding factor in conflict. In England and France it gave an edge to political and social struggles, while in the shifting alliances of the Thirty Years War, religious affiliation was often little more than a kind of badge for armies recruited indiscriminately from all faiths, or for princes prepared to change religion to further a political advantage.

After the assassination of Henry IV in 1610, France underwent a period of weak government until Cardinal Richelieu became chief minister in 1624. Plots against him by the brother of Louis XIII led to a renewal of hostilities between the administration and the nobility. The Huguenots demanded concessions and rose in revolt again. Richelieu laid siege to their chief stronghold, La Rochelle; the defenders were starved into submission. Thereafter Richelieu concentrated on dismembering the Habsburg empire. Offensives against the strategic route to Flanders were narrowly defeated by Spanish and imperialist forces. In the 1640s Richelieu and his successor Mazarin brought the scheme to fruition, with military success in Flanders, the Rhineland, Italy and the Pyrenees, and French-sponsored revolts in Portugal, Catalonia, Sicily and Naples. Spain's empire appeared doomed, but unrest in France showed the cost of these efforts.

Contemporaries recognized the war that broke out in 1618 as one which subsumed all Europe's other conflicts. The Thirty Years War consisted of several stages. First, the Bohemian–Palatinate war (1618–23) in which a Bohemian Protestant and Transylvanian threat to Habsburg Vienna was defeated and the Calvinist Lower Palatinate was conquered by imperial and Spanish troops. Second, the Danish war (1625–29) in which an intervention on behalf of the German Protestants by Denmark was shattered at Lutter, and the Edict of Restitution strengthened the position of the Catholics in Germany. Third, the Swedish war (1630–35) in which Sweden briefly carried the war to the the heart of Catholic southern Germany. Fourth, the French–Swedish war (1635-48), in which the French defeated successive Spanish invasions and undertook counter-offensives against all the Spanish possessions, Sweden defeated the imperialists and various armies spread unprecedented devastation over much of Germany before peace was made.

Spain's role as Catholic champion of Europe was the greatest casualty of the war. The years of relative peace in the early 17th century were wasted and the reform program initiated after 1621 by the chief minister Olivares could not be sustained, as the cost of financing a war effort across the continent escalated while silver revenues dwindled. With the revolts of Catalonia and Portugal in 1640, Spain was forced to divert resources to deal with domestic difficulties.

James VI and I of Scotland and England planted Ulster with Protestant settlers, but avoided commitment to the Protestant cause on Europe's mainland. Constitutional and religious opposition to his son Charles I led to war in Scotland (1639–40), to a massacre of the Ulster Protestants, and then to civil war in England. The victory of his Parliamentary enemies did not end unrest. The king was executed in 1649 (though few sought such a radical solution) and a Commonwealth established under Oliver Cromwell.

The Dutch alone gained from Europe's long, grim war. By weathering years of Spanish assaults they preserved their trading empire and won their independence. They now set about commercial expansion. By 1650 Amsterdam's financiers dominated the entire European economy.

| | Austrian Habsburg territory, 1618 |
| | Spanish Habsburg territory, 1618 |
| | Habsburg allies, 1618 |
| | France, 1618 |
| | German Protestant states |
| | United Provinces, 1609 |
| | Sweden, 1618 |
| | other state hostile to Habsburgs |
| | borders, 1648 |
| | French offensive |
| | Protestant offensive |
| | Spanish offensive |
| | Swedish offensive |
| ⊗ | Habsburg and imperialist victory |
| ⊗ | Habsburg and imperialist defeat |
| ⌂ | major siege |
| | town sacked |
| ✳ | major revolt or unrest |
| | major Dutch fortifications built 1605-06 |
| | Spanish blockade of Dutch trade, 1624-27 |
| | major Habsburg strategic route |
| | major Dutch trade route |
| | Spanish naval patrol |
| | British settlement in Ireland, 1613 |
| | "Plantations" of James I, 1613-25 |
| | Eastern Association of pro-Parliamentary counties, 1643 |
| ⊗ | royalist victory |
| ⊗ | royalist defeat |

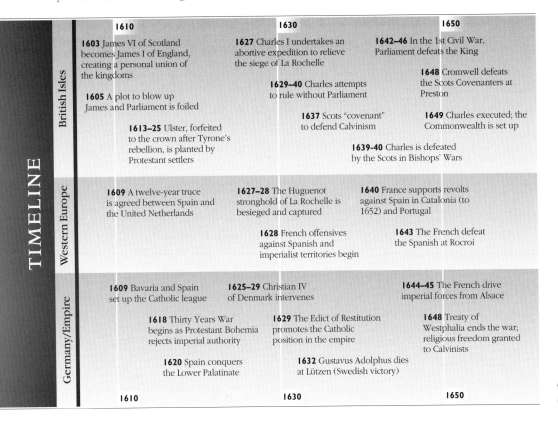

## TIMELINE

|  | 1610 | 1630 | 1650 |
|---|---|---|---|
| **British Isles** | **1603** James VI of Scotland becomes James I of England, creating a personal union of the kingdoms<br><br>**1605** A plot to blow up James and Parliament is foiled<br><br>**1613–25** Ulster, forfeited to the crown after Tyrone's rebellion, is planted by Protestant settlers | **1627** Charles I undertakes an abortive expedition to relieve the siege of La Rochelle<br><br>**1629–40** Charles attempts to rule without Parliament<br><br>**1637** Scots "covenant" to defend Calvinism<br><br>**1639-40** Charles is defeated by the Scots in Bishops' Wars | **1642–46** In the 1st Civil War, Parliament defeats the King<br><br>**1648** Cromwell defeats the Scots Covenanters at Preston<br><br>**1649** Charles executed; the Commonwealth is set up |
| **Western Europe** | **1609** A twelve-year truce is agreed between Spain and the United Netherlands | **1627–28** The Huguenot stronghold of La Rochelle is besieged and captured<br><br>**1628** French offensives against Spanish and imperialist territories begin | **1640** France supports revolts against Spain in Catalonia (to 1652) and Portugal<br><br>**1643** The French defeat the Spanish at Rocroi |
| **Germany/Empire** | **1609** Bavaria and Spain set up the Catholic league<br><br>**1618** Thirty Years War begins as Protestant Bohemia rejects imperial authority<br><br>**1620** Spain conquers the Lower Palatinate | **1625–29** Christian IV of Denmark intervenes<br><br>**1629** The Edict of Restitution promotes the Catholic position in the empire<br><br>**1632** Gustavus Adolphus dies at Lützen (Swedish victory) | **1644–45** The French drive imperial forces from Alsace<br><br>**1648** Treaty of Westphalia ends the war; religious freedom granted to Calvinists |
|  | 1610 | 1630 | 1650 |

1 The offensive of Albrecht von Wallenstein in 1627-28 against the Baltic ports was intended to destroy Dutch trade; instead it prompted Sweden's entry into the war in Germany.

2 Dunkirk was a key Spanish naval base and a threat to both Dutch and English trade until captured by French troops in 1646. Spain retook it in 1652.

3 France actively supported the Neapolitan insurrection of 1647 to break Spain's hold on Italy.

4 The Habsburgs were threatened in 1629-32 by the Swedish advance and French attacks on Mantua and the Valtelline; they revived by 1634.

5 The sack of Magdeburg by the imperialist Count Tilly in 1631 encouraged savage reprisals between Swedes and imperialists for the rest of the war.

6 The Catalan revolt of 1640 was supported by France, and the subsequent French invasion led to a long, inconclusive war.

See also 66 (European economic development); 68 (age of Louis XIV)

Europe's economy in 1783 still rested on a base of semi-subsistence agriculture, poor transport, local economies based partly on barter, lack of development capital and the slow adoption of technological advances. Important developments in agriculture, industry and commerce had taken place since the 16th century, most importantly in Britain and France, but their social impact was still slight.

The population growth of the 16th century had brought pressure on resources, resulting in rising prices and falling wages. Population stagnation in the 17th allowed a slight rise in living standards; but renewed population growth in the later 18th century was not matched by an equivalent increase in production and so brought hardship again. This contributed to the revolutionary explosion at the end of the century. Overall, however, Europe's population doubled between 1500 and 1800. The cities grew most: London and Paris exceeded 250,000 inhabitants by 1700.

It was in the cities that a higher level of economic activity took place. Sophisticated banking and credit systems emerged, providing finance not only for long-distance trade but also for monarchs and governments. Although neither standards of living nor technology were markedly superior in Europe to those in Asia or the Middle East, this new merchant capitalism made possible Europe's transformation into the economic powerhouse of the world.

The economic area dependent on European capitalism underwent an extraordinary expansion after 1492, reaching across the Atlantic to incorporate the Americas and spreading a galaxy of trading bases across south and east Asia. Its center of gravity, having see-sawed between Flanders and northern Italy, finally settled in the north, at Amsterdam in the 17th century and London in the late 18th. A succession of financially dominant cities took European capitalism progressively closer to world domination, in a contest between the nimble city-states of the past and the nation-states of the future; Britain's precocious national economy centered on London finally proved too powerful for its predecessors.

In the late 15th century, the dominant financial powers were still Venice and the Hanseatic league, each controlling a network of trade routes. Flemish and English incursions into Hanseatic areas, and the arrival of Portuguese ships with East Indies spices at Antwerp (bypassing the Venetian spice route through the Levant), resulted in the collapse of their partnership. From 1501 to 1568 European capitalism was dominated by the bankers of Antwerp. The distribution of the American silver flooding into Seville was handled from Flanders, while Dutch and Flemish ships dominated the Baltic grain trade to southern Europe – and reduced the Mediterranean to a peripheral area. In 1557 the pendulum swung back to the south. The first Spanish state bankruptcy damaged the Antwerp banking system, and the Genoese seized their chance. For the next seventy years Europe's finances were managed from Genoa, while the Netherlands subsided into religious war.

Whereas Antwerp and Genoa competed for dominance during the economic upswing of the 16th century, as the downturn gathered pace in the 1620s and silver remittances from Spanish America reduced, Amsterdam emerged as Europe's capitalist powerhouse. Maritime expertise combined with a stable, subtle and flexible credit system led to Dutch control of much European and Asian trade.

The foremost nation-states, Britain and France, made strenuous efforts to compete. The advantages of a stable banking system and an established system of national debt – and the benefit of huge investments after 1688 from the Dutch themselves – finally told in Britain's favor.

population density per sq km, c.1620

- over 40
- 20–40
- under 20

■ city with static population of over 40,000

■ city with significant population growth, 1500–1800

⚓ port for European external trade, 18th century

Genoa̲ city dominating the European financial system at date shown

⚗ pioneering development in steam power

⚙ important development in iron manufacture and use

▦ important development in the mechanization of the textile industry

▪ commercial center for linen industry

〰 area of coastal or marsh reclamation

▨ textile area in the 18th century

▢ grain exporting area in the 16th century

▨ grain importing area in the 16th century

▱ coalfield exploited by the late 18th century

▱ advanced agricultural techniques practiced by the late 18th century

▱ area of iron working in the 18th century

▱ major metallurgical area in the 18th century

◇ copper

◆ lead and zinc

◇ silver

◆ tin

➤ migration

━ major canal built by 1770

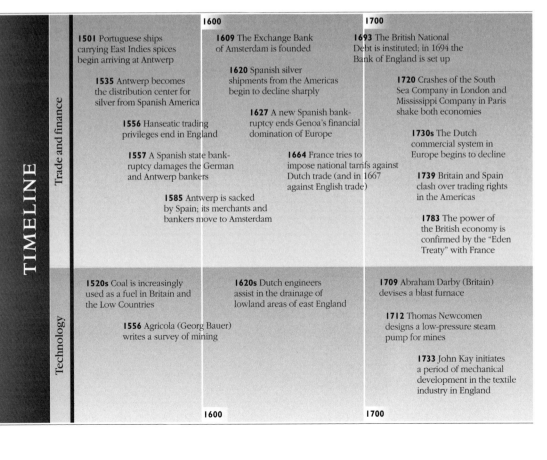

*ATLANTIC OCEAN*

**Trade and finance**

**1501** Portuguese ships carrying East Indies spices begin arriving at Antwerp

**1535** Antwerp becomes the distribution center for silver from Spanish America

**1556** Hanseatic trading privileges end in England

**1557** A Spanish state bankruptcy damages the German and Antwerp bankers

**1585** Antwerp is sacked by Spain; its merchants and bankers move to Amsterdam

**1609** The Exchange Bank of Amsterdam is founded

**1620** Spanish silver shipments from the Americas begin to decline sharply

**1627** A new Spanish bankruptcy ends Genoa's financial domination of Europe

**1664** France tries to impose national tarrifs against Dutch trade (and in 1667 against English trade)

**1693** The British National Debt is instituted; in 1694 the Bank of England is set up

**1720** Crashes of the South Sea Company in London and Mississippi Company in Paris shake both economies

**1730s** The Dutch commercial system in Europe begins to decline

**1739** Britain and Spain clash over trading rights in the Americas

**1783** The power of the British economy is confirmed by the "Eden Treaty" with France

**Technology**

**1520s** Coal is increasingly used as a fuel in Britain and the Low Countries

**1556** Agricola (Georg Bauer) writes a survey of mining

**1620s** Dutch engineers assist in the drainage of lowland areas of east England

**1709** Abraham Darby (Britain) devises a blast furnace

**1712** Thomas Newcomen designs a low-pressure steam pump for mines

**1733** John Kay initiates a period of mechanical development in the textile industry in England

1600  1700

The counterpart to this struggle for the heights of European capitalism was the beginning of a transformation of the European economy itself. New agricultural techniques (notably the enclosure by private landlords of common land, improved crop rotation and animal husbandry techniques, and the drainage of marginal lands) in the 18th century spread across Britain and the Netherlands. At the same time, transportation was revolutionized by the construction of canal networks, and energy use by the exploitation of coalfields once bulk transport on the canals became possible. Thomas Newcomen's steam

Falkirk
Carron Iron Works, 1762
Glasgow
Edinburgh
Watt, 1765
Belfast
Newry–Lough
Neagh canal, 1742
Newcastle
Bolton
Crompton, 1779
Bury
Kay, 1738
Hull
Dublin
Liverpool
Manchester
Bridgewater and
Grand Trunk canal,
Cromford
Arkwright, 1771
Ironbridge
Darby, 1779
King's Lynn
Dudley
Newcomen, 1712
Birmingham
Norwich
Bristol
Southampton
London
from 1763
Plymouth
Savery, 1698
Copenhagen
Königsberg
Vilna
Danzig
Warsaw
Poles
Poles
Vistula
Lübeck
Hamburg
Bremen
Stettin
Elbe–Oder canal,
1745
Berlin
Oder
Breslau
Krakow
Lemberg
Amsterdam
1627–1783
Deventer
Minden
Bielefeld
Elberfeld
Leipzig
Rotterdam
Middelburg
Bruges
Antwerp
1501–68
Cologne
Ghent
Brussels
Jemappe
1729
Liège
Frankfurt
Prague
Serbs
Lille
Cambrai
Valenciennes
Nuremberg
Amiens
Rouen
Péronne
St Quentin
Huguenots
Passy
May/Meeres, 1726
Paris
Strasbourg
Augsburg
Danube
Vienna
Buda
La Havre
St Malo
Troyes
Canal d'Orléans, 1692
Orléans
Ravensburg
Salzburg
Loire
Nantes
St Gallen
Poitiers
Geneva
Swiss
Lyon
Vaucanson, 1742
Swiss
Brescia
Verona
Trieste
Serbs
Bordeaux
Huguenots
Milan
Cremona
Turin
Venice
1378–1510
Po
Rhône
Genoa
1557–1627
Bologna
Toulouse
Montpellier
Nice
Pisa
Florence
Ancona
Marseille
Livorno
Aigues-
Mortes
Piombino
Sofia
Zaragoza
Barcelona
Rome
Albanians
Albanians
Serbs
Thessalonica
Naples
Corsica
Valencia
Palma
Balearic
Islands
Sardinia
Cagliari
Crotone
Athens
Palermo
Messina
Sicily

North
Sea
Vänern
Vättern
Stockholm
Swedes
Baltic
Sea

*Mediterranean Sea*

SELECTIVE breeding contributed
to the agricultural revolution of
the 18th century. This British
illustration shows a prize pig.

| 0 | | 400 km |
|---|---|---|
| 0 | | 300 mi |

engine, which was developed in 1712 in England as
a means of pumping water from mines (and soon
imitated in Europe), was turned into a source of
mechanical power by the Scottish inventor James
Watt and his partner Matthew Boulton in 1776.
Metallurgy was revolutionized by Abraham Darby
and others. Above all, the mechanization of the textile industry initiated by John Kay, Samuel Crompton
and Richard Arkwright led directly to the first
modern-style factories – and the beginnings of the
transformation of work itself in what became known
as the Industrial Revolution.

**1** Portugal broke Venetian control of the spice trade
in the early 1500s, but Venice was a center of trade,
finance and manufacturing until the late 18th century.

**2** English and Dutch merchant ships entered the
Mediterranean in the 1570s to break the dominance of
Venice and Genoa.

**3** After the golden years of the empire, Spain's
economy stagnated, with low investment, little technological innovation and entrenched local interests.

**4** The North Sea and Atlantic fishing and whaling
fleets contributed greatly to Dutch prosperity.

**5** Steam pumps in a mine at Jemappe and the Paris
water works at Passy were among the first to be used.

**6** Agricultural advances transformed Ireland from a
subsistence economy into an efficient supplier of
butter and meat for Britain in the 18th century.

**7** Urbanization, transport and metallurgical advances
gave 18th-century Germany a dynamic economy.

See also 53 (medieval economy); 74 (world
trading networks); 90 (Industrial Revolution)

The first half of the 17th century saw a downturn in material conditions in Eurasia so widespread that many historians consider a global climatic change to be the only sufficient explanation. The population growth of the 16th century was sharply reversed amid widespread famine, plague and warfare. Even Europe's exploration of the wider world came to a halt, with the exception of Tasman's voyage to Australia and New Zealand.

All the great empires were shaken, but the greatest casualty of the "crisis of the 17th century" was Ming China, in 1600 still the most powerful in the world. Mongol and Japanese attacks at the end of the 16th century added to taxation and economic pressures, and from the 1620s peasant revolts and military rebellions threatened the dynasty. In 1644 it was swept away by a nomad people from the north, the Manchus, and by 1650 northern and central China were under Manchu control (▷ 69).

Although Shah Jahan extended Mughal territory in mid-century, religious intolerance and political instability grew rapidly in his reign. Safavid Persia had enjoyed a period of prosperity under Shah Abbas I, but after 1629 the Ottomans retook Mesopotamia and the Safavid empire began to decline rapidly. The Ottoman empire itself was shaken by a series of revolts during the reign of Murad IV, and made little progress in wars with Austria and Venice.

Russia fell into renewed chaos during the early 17th century, with civil strife and military intervention by Poland and Sweden. Russian merchants spread through Siberia, creating an empire tyrannized by its own vast size, but the Russian sphere of influence remained open to exploitation by traders from both Europe and Asia.

In Europe, the tensions of the Protestant Reformation had already brought widespread bloodshed to France, Germany and the Netherlands, and several other regions. The outbreak of the Thirty Years War in 1618, however, devastated much of Europe. Contemporaries were horrified at the scale of destruction. The predominance of Spain was ended, and the Holy Roman empire was torn apart (▷ 65). There were few winners on the Protestant side either: the German Protestant states were ruined, and their backers Denmark and Sweden were exhausted by their military efforts.

The only states to emerge strengthened from the war were France (by its victories over its rivals, the Habsburgs) and the United Provinces

**Map labels:**

Arctic marine mammal hunters
sub-Arctic forest hunter-gatherers
plateau fishers and hunter-gatherers
west coast foraging, hunting and fishing peoples
desert hunter-gatherers
plains hunters
plains farmers
Iroquoian woodland farmers
Acadia
New France
Massachusetts Bay
New Amsterdam
Virginia
Pueblo farmers
Florida
Bahamas
Hawaiian Islands
Cuba
Belize
Jamaica
Hispaniola
Puerto Rico
VICE-ROYALTY OF NEW SPAIN
Essequibo
Surinam
Cayenne
Amazonian chiefdoms
Arawakan manioc farmers
Dutch B.
1642/54 to Po...
Tupi-Guarani savanna and highland farmers
Portuguese Brazil
VICE-ROYALTY OF PERU
Polynesians
savanna hunter-gatherers
pampas hunter-gatherers
shellfish gatherers and marine mammal hunters

**Timeline**

The Americas — Europe — Middle East — Africa — East and South Asia

1600 | 1610 | 1620 | 1630

**1622** English merchants and Persian troops take Hormuz from the Portuguese

**1611** The accession of Gustavus II Adolphus begins Sweden's great power period

**1604–13** The "Time of Troubles" brings political chaos to Russia

**1620** English colonists (the "Pilgrims") arrive at Cape Cod, Massachusetts

**1609** The Netherlands agree a 12-year truce in their rebellion against Spain

**1618** Outbreak of the Thirty Years War, which engulfs much of Europe and severely weakens Spanish power

**1626** The Dutch found the colony of New Amsterdam (New York)

**1600** The English East India Company is established; the Dutch East India Company is set up two years later

**1608** French settlers found the colony at Quebec

**1625** The first French settlements in the Caribbean are founded

**1602–18** Ottomans lose Azerbaijan, Georgia and, temporarily, Baghdad and Mosul in a war with Persia

**1615** The Manchus unite under Nurhachi and begin the conquest of the ailing Ming empire

**1623** The Dutch destroy the English base at Amboina and end English trade in the East Indies, Ayutthaya and Japan

**1603** Foundation of the Tokugawa shogunate in Japan, with its capital at Edo (Tokyo)

**1619** The Dutch build a trading post and headquarters of the Dutch East India Company at Batavia

**1629** The accession of Shah Safi marks the beginning of Safavid decline

*Greenland*

*Iceland (Denmark)*

SWEDEN

DENMARK-NORWAY

SCOTLAND

ENGLAND

U.P.

HOLY ROMAN EMPIRE

POLAND

PRUSSIA

RUSSIAN EMPIRE

*Siberian reindeer herders*

*Arctic marine mammal hunters*

*Siberian hunter-gatherers*

*Ainu hunter-gatherers*

FRANCE

VENICE

GE.

Papal states

PORTUGAL

SPAIN

Algiers

OTTOMAN EMPIRE

*Nogais*

*Turkomans*

*Uzbegs*

*Kirghiz*

*Tatar-Kalmuks*

*Eurasian steppe and desert nomads*

*Kalmyks*

MANCHU EMPIRE

KOREA

JAPAN

MOROCCO

*camel nomads*

SAFAVID EMPIRE

TIBET

MUGHAL EMPIRE

*Post-Ming Warlords*

*Taiwan*

t Louis (France)

TEKRUR

SO.

AIR

Hausa states

BORNU

DARFUR

WADAI

ETHIOPIA

*Arab nomads*

Oman (Ottoman)

GHARRA

MAHRA

HADRAMAUT

YEMEN

AWSA

Goa (Portugal)

*Islamic and Hindu states*

ARAKAN

AVA

*Shan states*

ANNAM

LAOS

rtuguese Guinea

MALI

AKAN

Mossi states

OYO

BENIN

OROMO

GOLCONDA

BIJAPUR

*Hindu kingdoms*

*Ceylon*

CAMBODIA

AYUTTHAYA

Elmina (Netherlands)

*western Bantu-speaking herders and farmers*

*eastern Bantu-speaking herders and farmers*

ACEH

BRUNEI

*Celebes*

*Borneo*

*Philippine Islands*

*Micronesians*

CONGO

Luanda (Portugal)

LUNDA

LUBA

Mombasa (Portugal)

Mozambique (Portugal)

*Sumatra*

MATARAM

*Java*

BANTAM

*Timor*

TIDORE

*New Guinea*

*Papuan farmers*

Tasman, 1642–43

*Melanesians*

*San hunter-gatherers*

*Khoisan herders*

ROZWI

*Madagascar*

*Malagasay*

*Mauritius (Netherlands)*

Tasman, 1642–43

*Australian Aboriginal hunter-gatherers*

Delagoa Bay (Portugal)

Tasman, 1642–43

*Tasmanian hunter-gatherers*

*Maori chiefdoms*

*Polynesians*

hunter-gatherers
nomadic pastoralists
simple farming societies
complex farming societies/ chiefdoms
state societies
uninhabited

empires
Dutch
English
French
Portuguese
Spanish
other

→ Dutch route of exploration
GE. Genoa
U.P. United Provinces
SO. Songhai

---

**Timeline:**

**1643** Accession of Louis XIV as king of France

**1640** The Portuguese successfully reclaim their independence from Spain

**637** Russian traders reach the Pacific coast of Siberia

**1649** Parliament in England executes Charles I and creates a republic

**1648** The Peace of Westphalia ends the Thirty Years War

1640

1650

**1638** The Ottomans under Murad IV retake Baghdad from Persia

**c.1638** Portuguese traders are expelled from Japan

**1642–43** Abel Tasman sails round Australia and discovers New Zealand

**1644** The Ming dynasty in China collapses under pressure from rebels and the Qing (Manchus)

---

(by confirmation of their independence from Spain). Portugal threw off Spanish rule.

The military gains of the Netherlands were insignificant, though, compared with the triumph of the merchants of Amsterdam. When the Spanish state finances collapsed in 1627, Genoese domination of European banking drew to a close and with it the last period of Mediterranean financial power (▷ 66). The Dutch merchant fleet took over much of the European coastal trade, while the Amsterdam bankers established their grip on European finance.

The Dutch campaign against the Portuguese trading empire since the 1590s gained pace. The Dutch East India Company was founded in 1602. By capturing Timor, Malacca, and bases in Ceylon and Taiwan, and by destroying Portuguese and English bases at Amboina, the new company won almost complete control of the spice trade. Dutch occupation of Masulipatam in India and the West African bases further reduced Portugal's trading network (▷ 72).

Only in the Americas did the Dutch advance falter. The colony of New Amsterdam was surrounded by English colonies north and south, while French penetration of the St Lawrence basin prevented expansion inland (▷ 70). The West Indies were largely divided between Spain, France and England, while a Dutch effort to overrun Brazil foundered in the face of guerrilla warfare by the Portuguese (▷ 62) ■

The Thirty Years War concluded the conflicts that had threatened Europe since the Reformation and brought a revulsion against religious and social extremism. Only in Britain, where Cromwell's regime faced mounting discontent until it collapsed in 1660, did the radical opponents of the existing social order achieve power. Instead there was a general extension of royal control over the affairs of the state, and the doctrine of the absolute power of the monarch emerged. The long struggle between kings and territorial magnates was at last resolved, nowhere more so than in France, Europe's most populous and most influential state. Local administration was put in the hands of officials while aristocrats were required to dance attendance on the king at his court, and representative institutions were stripped of the power to criticize the government.

The seven decades after 1648 saw Louis XIV systematically pursue his ambition of supplanting Habsburg Spain as Europe's dominant power. The Netherlands, formerly banker and mainstay of the anti-Habsburg cause, allied itself with Spain against the growing threat of France and England. Under Cromwell and the later Stuart kings, England took a pro-France, anti-Spain stance, leading it into a series of damaging naval wars with the Netherlands. The dramatic accession of the Dutchman William of Orange to the English throne in 1688–89 reversed this pattern and Anglo-French enmity again became a feature of European history. Austria, once the junior partner in Habsburg Europe, emerged as a power while Spanish might waned. Sweden, France's partner against the Habsburgs in the 1630s and 40s, suffered a defeat at Fehrbellin while supporting Louis XIV against the Netherlands, and thereafter shrank from direct involvement in western Europe. In Italy, Savoy eclipsed Habsburg Milan, while the Spanish possessions in the south survived the French-supported revolts of the 1640s and

passed to Austrian control after 1713 as Spain's European territories were shared out between the new Bourbon king of Spain, Philip V, and the Austrian Habsburgs.

Louis' military aggressiveness raised a coalition of hostile powers against him. He achieved much in modernizing the French state, but failed to control and centralize the economy, ultimately ensuring social upheaval and economic collapse for his successors. Furthermore his revocation of the Edict of Nantes led to the flight of 200,000 Huguenots and ended any hope of again enlisting the Protestant German states against the Habsburgs.

Louis relied for most of his reign on a small group of competent ministers: Colbert (responsible for

economic and financial policy, and building up the armed forces), Louvois (minister of war), Vauban (an engineer whose fortresses secured the northern and eastern frontiers for the first time since the Roman era), and a group of exceptional generals (Turenne, Condé, Luxembourg and Villars). France fought four major wars in his reign, making substantial territorial gains and dominating Europe's seas for thirty years. The widespread imitation of Louis' palace at Versailles throughout Europe in the 18th century is a testament to the influence of France during his reign.

In Britain, the accession of William of Orange had other effects than the realignment of foreign policy. In 1714 the equally Protestant George I, Elector of Hanover, came to the British throne, keeping the Catholics from power and involving

## TIMELINE

### France and Spain

| 1650 | 1675 | 1700 |
|---|---|---|
| **1643** Louis accedes to the French throne aged five; Mazarin runs the government | **1672** Louis attacks the Netherlands (except Holland), and occupies most by 1678 | **1701** Outbreak of the War of the Spanish Succession after death of Charles II of Spain |
| **1648** The Fronde, a noble and parliamentary revolt, causes widespread disorder | **1681** France annexes Strasbourg | **1710** Madrid is briefly occupied by the anti-Bourbon alliance |
| **1661** Louis XIV's personal rule begins | **1685** Revocation of the Edict of Nantes ends Huguenot toleration in France | **1713** The Treaty of Utrecht divides Spanish territories between Philip V of Bourbon and the Austrian Habsburgs |
| **1667–68** French War of Devolution against the Spanish Netherlands | **1688–97** War of the League of Augsburg: Sweden, Spain, the Palatinate, Bavaria and Saxony oppose France | |

### Rest of Europe

| 1650 | 1675 | 1700 |
|---|---|---|
| **1649** Execution of Charles I of England and establishment of the Commonwealth | **1675** The Swedes, allies of Louis, are defeated by Brandenburg at Fehrbellin | **1699** Treaty of Karlowitz cedes most of Hungary to Austria |
| **1651** England's Navigation Act leads to the 1st Anglo-Dutch war (1652–54); 2nd war 1665–67; 3rd war 1672–74) | **1683** The Ottoman siege of Vienna is defeated | **1707** Act of Union unites Scotland and England as Great Britain |
| **1660** Restoration of the English monarchy under Charles II | **1688** In England's Glorious Revolution, Stuart King James II is replaced by William III of Orange and Queen Mary | **1714** The Elector of Hanover becomes King George I of Britain |
| **1665** Great Plague in London, followed by the Great Fire in 1666 | **1688** Death of Frederick William, "Great Elector" of Brandenburg since 1640 | |

| 1650 | 1675 | 1700 |

Britain deeply in European politics for the remainder of the century. The deposed Stuart royal family became a focus of political discontent for several decades, with the threat of a counter-coup first manifested in the Earl of Mar's revolt in 1715.

After a series of reforms under Kara Mustafa, the Ottomans advanced a huge army against Vienna in 1683, but the city was relieved by a German and Polish army. Austrian Habsburg forces swiftly reconquered Hungary before Turkish resistance stiffened.

The War of the Spanish Succession (1701–14), fought on the death of the last Habsburg king of Spain, exemplified the changes that had taken place since 1648. Once Europe's predominant power, Spain was now little more than a battleground for French, Austrian, British and Portuguese armies, while Britain, Holland and the Austrian Habsburgs lined up against the house of Bourbon, who claimed the throne with Louis' backing. The Bourbons ultimately succeeded despite several major French defeats, confirming the power-base Louis had built.

**1** Cromwell's alliance with France against Spain allowed England to capture Dunkirk (1658); Charles II kept the alliance but sold the port to Louis (1662).

**2** The Duchy of Hanover and Great Britain were temporarily united in 1714, when dynastic links allowed George of Hanover to succeed Queen Anne.

**3** In 1656 English admiral Robert Blake captured a Spanish bullion fleet off Cadiz, a feat achieved before only by Dutchman Piet Hein in the Caribbean (1628).

**4** The Netherlands were saved from occupation at the hands of Louis, Turenne and Condé (1672) by William of Orange, who flooded much of the country.

**5** In 1704 an anti-Bourbon army led by Marlborough and Eugene of Savoy succeeded in knocking France's ally Bavaria out of the War of the Spanish Succession.

**6** Louis XIV's naval base at Toulon played a major role in French naval campaigns against the Habsburgs.

**7** The War of the Spanish Succession was most bitter in Spain itself; pro-Bourbon Castile prevailed against pro-Habsburg Catalonia.

See also 65 (Thirty Years War); 66 (European economic development)

The Manchus originated as one of the Jürchen tribes – themselves part of a larger group of Tungusic (Siberian) peoples – from the area to the north of the Korean peninsula adjoining the Han Chinese enclave of Liaodong. They began to emerge as a political force under the leadership of Nurhachi (r.1586–1626). Nurhachi imposed a Mongol-style military administration on his people in 1615, and took the title Jin Khan the following year to indicate continuity with the Jürchen Jin (or Ruzhen) dynasty that had ruled northern China in the 12th century.

In the 1620s and 1630s, the peoples united by Nurhachi profited from Ming weakness to establish their control over the Mongol lands just north of the Wall, the Liaodong basin and the Ming vassal state of Korea. Although Nurhachi died in battle, his son Dorgun (r.1628–50) gained control of Beijing in 1644 and acted as regent to his nephew who was installed as the first Manchu (Qing) emperor of China, under the name Shunzhi, in the same year. Over the next 15 years, Ming resistance was suppressed, with the far southwestern province of Yunnan the last to fall.

The Manchus adopted a more subtle approach to administrative reform than that of China's previous conquerors, the Mongols. Manchu officials were given senior posts in existing Ming institutions, and military garrisons were set up in the major provincial cities, but new structures were not imposed whole-sale. The Manchus were initially quick to require cultural changes (such as their characteristic shaven head and pigtail), but their numerical inferiority to the Han Chinese meant that, by the 18th century, their culture had become fully assimilated. Their most significant contribution was to inject an unprecedented dynamism and efficiency into Chinese political and military life.

Resistance to Manchu rule was rekindled in 1674. An attempt by the Beijing government to assert its authority over the southern province of Guangdong, which had been allowed considerable autonomy since its subjugation, prompted a popular revolt led by Wu Sangui, governor of Yunnan and Guizhou. Wu, supported by Shang Zhixin of Guangdong and Geng Jingzhong of Fujian (the "Three Feudatories"), was only defeated after five years of campaigning. At the same time, the government was confronted with a rebellion by the Ming-loyalist warlord Zheng Jing, whose father Zheng Cheng-gong (Koxinga) had expelled the Dutch from Taiwan in 1662.

After this, only the uprising of non-Han tribal peoples in Yunnan in 1726–29 disrupted more than

**Legend:**

Manchu homeland, early 17th century

Manchu territorial expansion

to 1644, with date of acquisition

1644-97, with date of acquisition

1697-1783, with date of acquisition

vassal state acquired before 1644, with date

vassal state acquired or confirmed after 1697, with date

area affected by Wu Sangui's rebellion, 1674-81

area held by Ming loyalists, 1662-83

☆ rebellion of non-Han people against Manchu rule

◆ Manchu national capital

■ Manchu provincial capital

— trade route of the Manchu empire

area of extensive coastal trade

silk major export from Manchu China

rice major import to Manchu China

migration of Kalmyk Tatars, mid-17th century

migration of Oirat Mongols, late 17th to early 18th centuries

internal migration of Han Chinese, 18th century

borders, c.late 18th century

Great Wall

Willow Palisade

Grand Canal

modern coastline and drainage where altered

**Map labels:** Semipalatinsk; Lake Balkhash; Dzungars 1765; Oirat Mongols 1750-57; Ili Protectorate 1755-57; Ili; Issyk Kul; Dzungars 4; DZUNGARIA; territory added to Gansu 1759; Urumqi; TIEN SHAN; KASHGARIA; Aksu; Muslims 1758-59; Turfan; Kashgar 1759; gems, silk, tea to Middle East; Yarkand; 4 Xinjiang 1724-60; EASTERN TURKESTAN; Khotan; gems, silk, tea to Middle East; KUNLUN MTS; LADAKH 1783; Leh; Xizang 1718-20; TIBET; HIMALAYAS; Lhasa; Tashilumpo; NEPAL 1792; SIKKIM; Darjeeling; BHUTAN 1730; Brahmaputra; Ahom

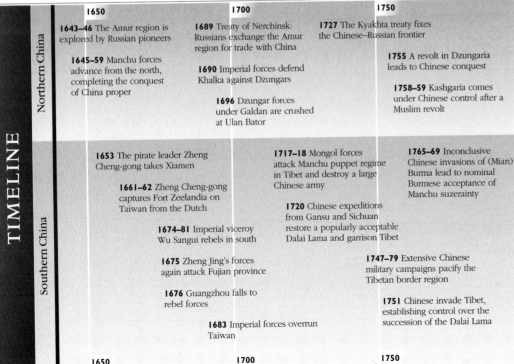

**TIMELINE**

*Northern China*

| 1650 | 1700 | 1750 |
|---|---|---|
| **1643–46** The Amur region is explored by Russian pioneers | **1689** Treaty of Nerchinsk: Russians exchange the Amur region for trade with China | **1727** The Kyakhta treaty fixes the Chinese–Russian frontier |
| **1645–59** Manchu forces advance from the north, completing the conquest of China proper | **1690** Imperial forces defend Khalka against Dzungars | **1755** A revolt in Dzungaria leads to Chinese conquest |
| | **1696** Dzungar forces under Galdan are crushed at Ulan Bator | **1758–59** Kashgaria comes under Chinese control after a Muslim revolt |

*Southern China*

| 1650 | 1700 | 1750 |
|---|---|---|
| **1653** The pirate leader Zheng Cheng-gong takes Xiamen | **1717–18** Mongol forces attack Manchu puppet regime in Tibet and destroy a large Chinese army | **1765–69** Inconclusive Chinese invasions of (Mian) Burma lead to nominal Burmese acceptance of Manchu suzerainty |
| **1661–62** Zheng Cheng-gong captures Fort Zeelandia on Taiwan from the Dutch | **1720** Chinese expeditions from Gansu and Sichuan restore a popularly acceptable Dalai Lama and garrison Tibet | |
| **1674–81** Imperial viceroy Wu Sangui rebels in south | | **1747–79** Extensive Chinese military campaigns pacify the Tibetan border region |
| **1675** Zheng Jing's forces again attack Fujian province | | |
| **1676** Guangzhou falls to rebel forces | | **1751** Chinese invade Tibet, establishing control over the succession of the Dalai Lama |
| **1683** Imperial forces overrun Taiwan | | |

**1** The name "Manchu" is thought to derive from Manjusri, a Buddhist *bodhisattva* recognized in Mongolia from 1579; the term was not used until 1652.

**2** The Willow Palisade around the Liaodong region was retained after the Manchu conquest of China as a barrier to Han Chinese settlement in Manchuria.

**3** The province of Gansu was created in 1715; the large area of former Mongol territory added to the province in 1759 was directly administered by the imperial bureaucracy in Beijing.

**4** The Ili (Dzungaria) and Xinjiang regions remained under military control throughout the Manchu period.

**5** Manchu administrative reforms resulted in the creation of the new provinces of Anhui (1662) and Hunan (1664), as well as Gansu.

**6** The Russian fort built at Albazin in 1651 was ceded to China in return for trade concessions that created a large market for Russian furs in Beijing.

**7** The vast population growth of China in the 18th century stimulated internal migration to outlying areas; Sichuan and Yunnan provinces experienced extensive Han Chinese immigration.

**8** The Manchu conquest of 1683 brought imperial Chinese control to Taiwan for the first time, but the inhospitable eastern side of the island was barely settled by Han Chinese until the late 19th century.

*Amur*
Amur
1689
(to Russia 1650–89)

**Heje
Kiakia**

*Lake
Baykal*

Irkutsk

Chita

Nerchinsk

Aigun

Mergen

*furs, gold, silver*
from Russia

Kyakhta

Solon **6**

Albazin
(Yakesa)

Heilungjiang

Qiqihar

M A N C H U R I A

**Kurka**

*cotton fabrics,
silk, tea
to Russia*

Kobdo

*Songhui*

*ginseng,
soya beans*
from Manchuria

Uliastay

1696 ✕ Ulan Bator

*Inner Mongolian
Plateau*

**Setsen**

Jilin

**Jürchen (Manchus)**

**1**

*Sea of
Japan*

**Khalka**
1697

Shenyang
(Mukden)

**2**

Hunchun

**O U T E R   M O N G O L I A**

Khorchin
1629–30

**Tushiyetu**

*Gobi Desert*

**Chahar**
1635

Dolonnur

Liaodong

Niuzhuang

Jinzhou

Wonsan

**CHAOXIAN
(KOREA)**
1637

Seoul

**RIBEN
(JAPAN)**

Kyoto

**Kalmyk
Tatars**

**I N N E R
M O N G O L I A**

Kalgan

Rehe

*present course of
Yellow river*

Pusan

Anxi

**Alashan
Eleuth**

Ningxia

Beijing

Dengzhou

*cotton fabrics, tea
to Manchuria*

*Yellow
Sea*

Nagasaki

*copper
from Japan*

Suzhou

Ganzhou

*Ordos
Desert*

**Zhili**

*Yellow*

*Sanggan*

Taiyuan 1644

Ji'nan

**Qinghai**
1724

*Lake
Qinghai*

Hui Muslims
1781–84
**3**

Lanzhou

**Gansu**
1649

*Fen*

**Shanxi**
1644–45

**Shandong**
1645

*medicines,
silk, sugar
to Japan*

**Qinghai**

Hui Muslims
1781–84

**3**

Kaifeng

Huai'an

*Huai*

**Shaanxi**
1645–46

Xi'an
(Chang'an)

*Han*

**Henan**
1645

**Jiangsu**
1645

Nanjing

Hefei

**Anhui**
1645

Hangzhou

Mingzhou

*East
China
Sea*

Chamdo

**Sichuan**
1646

Chengdu

Wushan

**Hubei**
1645

Wuchang

*Yangtze*

**5**

**Zhejiang**
1646

Wenzhou

Jin Chuans
1746–49
**7**

Chongqing

*Lake
Dongting*

Tanzhou

Nanchang

*Lake
Pengli*

tribal risings
1726–29

**Guizhou**
1658

**Hunan**
1647–50
**5**

**Jiangxi**
1649–52

Fuzhou

Dali

Guiyang

Ganzhou

**Fujian**
1646

*Taiwan
(Formosa)*
1683
**8**

**Yunnan**
1659
**7**

Guilin
(Guizhou)

Yao
1790

**Guangdong**
1650–55

**Guangxi**
1650–52

Guangzhou
(Canton)

Xiamen
(Amoy)

*aboriginal rising*
1787–88

Fort Zeelandia

**MIAN**
1769

Macao

*Xi*

*cotton fabrics, ironware,
porcelain, silk*
to southeast Asia

**BURMA**

**YUENAN
(ANNAM)**
1666

Qiongzhou

*South
China
Sea*

*porcelain,
silk, tea
to Europe*

**XIENLO
(SIAM)**

**LAOS**

Hainan

*raw cotton,
rice, woods*
from southeast
Asia

*opium, silver*
from India

*Irrawaddy*

*Salween*

*Mekong*

*Yalong*

*Jinsha*

ASTRONOMY was stimulated
by contact with Europeans.
A Jesuit priest equipped the
observatory at Beijing with
the latest devices in the late
17th century.

0 ————————— 1000 km

0 ————————— 800 mi

a century of internal peace and stability for Manchu China. An aggressive campaign of territorial expansion, however, resulted in the creation of the greatest Eurasian land empire since the Mongols. Russian incursions into the Amur region were ended by the Treaty of Nerchinsk in 1689. The Manchus then embarked on a sustained campaign to end the Mongol menace. Military expeditions of great ferocity finally subdued the formidable Dzungars (West Mongols). By 1783 Manchu colonial administration had been extended to Tibet and – nominally at least – its vassal states (Bhutan, Sikkim and Ladakh) and the former Turkic khanates of eastern Turkestan. (This extension of Chinese authority brought its own problems,

in the form of a widespread revolt of the Muslim Hui people in 1781–84.) Burma and Laos were reduced to nominal vassal status, and Manchu troops were poised to invade Nepal and Annam.

Following the conflicts and plagues that had afflicted the region during the 17th century, peace and prosperity caused a demographic explosion within the Manchu empire. The Chinese population swelled from 100 million in 1650 to 300 million in 1800. This expansion created growing tensions. A ban imposed by the Manchus on the settlement of Han Chinese north of the Wall led to largescale internal migrations in the late 17th and 18th centuries from the overpopulated Yangtze basin and south-

east to new agricultural lands in the west and southwest. The authorities maintained Chinese external trade, but were able to restrict foreign merchants to Guangzhou in the south and Kyakhta in the north. The export of Chinese luxury goods for silver continued to ensure a strong monetary economy. At the end of the 18th century, however, Manchu China's decline was about to begin, with growing government corruption, social unrest and the start of the European opium trade to China.

See also 63 (Tokugawa Japan);
94 (19th-century China)

The exploration of North America was unlike other achievements of the age of European expansion. Even though many of the cultures and civilizations encountered in other continents had had little recent contact with Europeans, they were not all wholly alien. Moreover, many had dynamic economies willing to supply in bulk products that Europe lacked. Even in Mexico and Peru, whose cultures were entirely new to Europeans, strong centralized states, a relatively dense population and an available fund of gold and silver were familiar elements. Only the Caribbean islands and the vast, empty interior of South America provided a foretaste of what confronted the first explorers of North America. From the first landing of John Cabot in 1497 until the 18th century, North America remained enigmatic; its true scale was not appreciated for a long time, nor did it offer any immediate returns on the investments of explorers and their backers.

Explorers were driven by a number of pervasive myths, and dogged by a sense of disappointment once their lack of substance was revealed. The earliest chanced upon North America while seeking a route to China; Columbus died convinced that he had found an island off the Asian mainland. After Giovanni da Verrazano had explored the length of the Atlantic seaboard and the first colonial ventures had encountered a densely wooded interior and native peoples hostile to exploration inland, the search began for a route around the continent. A possible northern passage remained an English obsession: Hudson, Davis and Baffin endured hardships in the Canadian north to find a northwest sea passage to China. Even James Cook, mapping the Alaskan coast in 1778–79, felt compelled to explore major inlets in search of the elusive seaway.

French exploration of the St Lawrence river was stimulated by the idea of a sea passage through the heart of the continent. Cartier, Champlain, the Jesuit fathers, the de la Vérendryes and generations of fur trappers progressed down the St Lawrence and

## Map key

extent of European settlement by 1650
- Dutch
- English
- French
- Spanish
- Swedish

⛴ early European landing

European settlement or trading post founded in the 16th or 17th centuries
- ○ Dutch
- ○ English
- ● French
- ● Spanish

route of exploration
(conjectural routes are shown dashed)
- → England
- → France
- → Portugal
- → Russia
- → Spain

→ raid by the Iroquois, 1642–89

Ute native American peoples

0               1200 km
0               800 mi

through the Great Lakes, fueling the myth of a route westward to the Pacific. This myth finally evaporated in the endless expanse of the Great Plains beyond Lake Manitoba. The supreme French achievement, La Salle's descent of the Mississippi in 1682, did reveal a north–south passage, yet his disappointment at finding the Gulf of Mexico, rather than the Pacific, at the mouth of the river was profound.

Initial Spanish exploration of North America from

Mexico and the Caribbean under leaders such as de Soto and Coronado was mounted in a spirit of conquest, gold-lust and missionary zeal. Large military expeditions were equipped to build forts, establish missions and despoil the cities that reputedly lay to the north. After epic journeys, survivors of these expeditions returned exhausted and empty-handed. By the early 17th century, Spanish New Mexico was little more than a string of outposts in the *pueblo* villages around Santa Fé, surrounded by desert. Florida, which the Spaniards initially believed to be an island, was explored (and defended) for strategic reasons to protect the bullion fleet route to Europe. Similarly, the Spaniards began to venture up the Californian coast in the 17th century in response to a British and Russian threat.

By the 1650s the Caribbean and, to a lesser extent, the Atlantic seaboard had attracted settlers in number, but it was in the north that the true wealth of the American continent – rich farmland – began to be exploited. From the outset, the Dutch New Netherland colony encouraged settlement by farmers, while the English colonies quickly developed a European-style agricultural economy. The native peoples welcomed settlers for the trade they brought, but they prevented expansion inland; the Appalachian mountains also remained a formidable barrier. It was 180 years after Cabot's landing before English traders and explorers penetrated the basin of the Ohio, after European diseases and the erosion of native cultures had weakened resistance. In the years following the British conquest of French America, the trickle of pioneers across the Appalachians and into the fertile lands of Kentucky and Tennessee became a flood, marking a new era of truly profitable exploration.

## TIMELINE

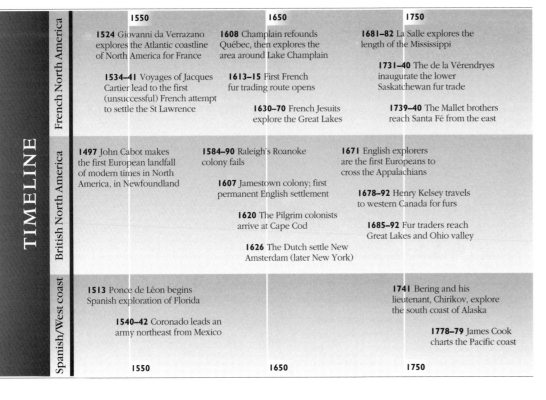

### French North America

| 1550 | 1650 | 1750 |
|---|---|---|
| **1524** Giovanni da Verrazano explores the Atlantic coastline of North America for France | **1608** Champlain refounds Québec, then explores the area around Lake Champlain | **1681–82** La Salle explores the length of the Mississippi |
| **1534–41** Voyages of Jacques Cartier lead to the first (unsuccessful) French attempt to settle the St Lawrence | **1613–15** First French fur trading route opens | **1731–40** The de la Vérendryes inaugurate the lower Saskatchewan fur trade |
| | **1630–70** French Jesuits explore the Great Lakes | **1739–40** The Mallet brothers reach Santa Fé from the east |

### British North America

| 1550 | 1650 | 1750 |
|---|---|---|
| **1497** John Cabot makes the first European landfall of modern times in North America, in Newfoundland | **1584–90** Raleigh's Roanoke colony fails | **1671** English explorers are the first Europeans to cross the Appalachians |
| | **1607** Jamestown colony; first permanent English settlement | **1678–92** Henry Kelsey travels to western Canada for furs |
| | **1620** The Pilgrim colonists arrive at Cape Cod | **1685–92** Fur traders reach Great Lakes and Ohio valley |
| | **1626** The Dutch settle New Amsterdam (later New York) | |

### Spanish/West coast

| 1550 | 1650 | 1750 |
|---|---|---|
| **1513** Ponce de Léon begins Spanish exploration of Florida | | **1741** Bering and his lieutenant, Chirikov, explore the south coast of Alaska |
| **1540–42** Coronado leads an army northeast from Mexico | | **1778–79** James Cook charts the Pacific coast |
| 1550 | 1650 | 1750 |

1 A French colony was established at Fort Caroline in 1564; it was destroyed as a potential threat to the silver fleet route by a Spanish expedition in 1565.

2 English privateer Francis Drake spent five weeks with the Miwok people near modern San Francisco in 1579; he claimed the land and named it New Albion.

3 An English colony was founded on Roanoke Island by Walter Raleigh in 1584. It was resettled in 1587, but by 1590 the colony had vanished without trace.

4 Dutch merchants purchased Manhattan Island from the native Americans in 1626; the New Netherland colony was established by Peter Minuit in 1621.

5 The English Hudson's Bay Company bases were established to trade for furs with the Cree after 1670; a French expedition captured them all in 1686.

6 Spanish settlement of New Mexico was limited in the 17th century and was set back by a major native uprising 1680-1710.

7 Much of modern Texas was explored by Spanish expeditions in 1686-90, determined to end French incursions into the region.

8 Briton James Cook's exploration of "Cook's Inlet" in 1779 was prompted by a contemporary map showing Alaska as an island.

See also 42 (native peoples); 62 Spanish–American empire); 73 (European colonies )

The global demographic crisis became less severe after about 1670. The bubonic plague, which had appeared in India in 1616 and Turkey in 1661 spread as far as London by 1665, then declined – one of the last great plagues in Eurasian history. A great famine of 1709 also proved to be Europe's last. In Asia, the population of China reached 100 million by 1650, and began to expand at a rate that would take it to nearly 300 million by 1800.

Dutch domination of European worldwide trade survived three damaging wars with England. France under Louis XIV, though, was Europe's greatest power, its population in 1700 as large as that of the Spanish and Austrian Habsburg lands combined (▷ 68). But Louis XIV failed to break the hold of the Amsterdam bankers on French trade, revealing the enduring financial power of the last great European city-state.

Dutch might was built on control of trade within Europe, but trade with the rest of the world also grew. As silver production in Spanish America fluctuated and Asia's demand for silver was partially assuaged, the Dutch took over the Asian coastal trade. Bills of exchange from Amsterdam underpinned credit transactions worldwide.

The rise of France pursuing a consistently anti-Habsburg policy upset the balance between Austria and Turkey in the Balkans. After a near-disastrous campaign against Crete (1645–69), Ottoman reforms led to a new, though unsuccessful, siege of Vienna (1683). This, however, was followed by a Russian and Austrian onslaught on Ottoman territory, while in Africa the corsair rulers of Algiers confirmed their independence. After taking Azov from the Turks in 1696, Peter the Great of Russia embarked on war with Sweden. His victory at Poltava marked the end of Sweden's dominance of northern Europe and Russia's rise to the status of great power.

The campaigns of Aurangzeb against the Hindu Marathas extended Mughal frontiers into the Deccan, but his empire began to fall apart on his death in 1707. By 1715 the Marathas were the most powerful of the successor states within the empire's nominal borders. The foundation of British trading bases at Bombay and Calcutta, and French at Pondicherry, however, established both Britain and France as future players in Indian affairs.

Manchu control over southern China was finally confirmed. The Ming warlord Zheng Cheng-gong had driven the Dutch from Taiwan in 1661–62,

**1652–54** The first Anglo–Dutch naval war (second 1665–67; third 1672–74)

**1664** The English take New Amsterdam (New York) from the Dutch

**1664** The French East India Company is set up, competing with the English

**1683** The Ottoman siege of Vienna is defeated, leading to Austrian advances in Hungary

**1652** Cape Town is founded by Dutch settlers

**1656** English forces under Penn and Venables take Jamaica from Spain

**1643** Louis XIV succeeds to the French throne (to 1715)

**1681–82** La Salle explores the Mississippi and claims the whole area for France

| TIMELINE | 1650 | 1670 | 1690 |
|---|---|---|---|
| The Americas | | | |
| Europe | | | |
| Middle East | | | |
| Africa | | | |
| East and South Asia | | | |

**1636** The Mughals begin to expand into the Deccan

**1655** The Dutch expel the Portuguese from their trading posts in Ceylon

**1686** France claims Madagascar after the establishment of Fort Dauphin

**1661** An English East India Company base is set up in Bombay, India

**1689** The Russians withdraw from the Amur basin following the Treaty of Nerchinsk with China

**1661–62** Jeng Cheng-gong takes Taiwan

Arctic marine mammal hunters

sub-Arctic forest hunter-gatherers

plateau fishers and hunter-gatherers

west coast foraging, hunting and fishing peoples

desert hunter-gatherers

Rupert's Land

New France

Newfoundla

Iroquoian woodland farmers

plains hunters

plains farmers

Nova Scotia

British American colonies

Pueblo farmers

Louisiana

South Carolina

Florida

Cuba

Bahamas

Saint-Domingue

Belize

Hispaniola

Jamaica

VICE-ROYALTY OF NEW SPAIN

Mosquito Coast

Guyana

Cayenne

Arawakan-manioc farmers

VICE-ROYALTY OF PERU

Tupi-Guarani savanna and highland farmers

VICE-ROYALTY OF BRAZIL

Hawaiian Islands

Polynesians

savanna hunter-gatherers

pampas hunter-gatherers

shellfish gatherers and marine mammal hunters

hunter-gatherers
nomadic pastoralists
simple farming societies
complex farming societies/
chiefdoms
state societies
uninhabited

empires
British
Dutch
French
Portuguese
Spanish
other

GE.  Genoa
KA.  Kali
MO.  Mossi states
N.   Netherlands
SO.  Songhai
TE.  Tekrur

**1713** Britain takes
over the slave trade
to Spanish America under
the Asiento Treaty

**1710** Britain captures
Acadia from France,
renaming it Nova Scotia

**1709** Russia becomes a
European power, defeating
Sweden at Poltava

**1701–14** The War of
the Spanish Succession,
involving all major
European powers

**1699** The French colony
of Louisiana is founded

1710

**1697** The Manchus
overrun Outer Mongolia
(Khalka)

**1705** Tunis throws
off Ottoman rule

**1709** The Afghans rebel
against Safavid rule and
assert their independence

**1698** The Omanis
drive the Portuguese
from Mombasa and set up
the Zanzibar sultanate

and the Manchu invasion of the
island in 1683 was the last display of
Chinese naval power (▷ 69). Annam came
under Chinese rule, but Manchu ambitions were
focussed on central Asia. In 1689 Russia gave up the Amur valley and Manchu
troops overran Outer Mongolia, driving the Khalka Mongols west.

Dutch reverses in Taiwan were compensated by consolidation in southeast Asia. The destruction of the English settlement at Bantam in 1684 removed
the last European rival in the region, and the final expulsion of the Portuguese
from Ceylon strengthened the Dutch in India.

In Africa, the most important developments were the Dutch foundation of
Cape Town in 1652 and an Islamic revival in the north. Omani Arabs overran
the northern Portuguese settlements on the east coast, setting up the sultanate
of Zanzibar. Along the Niger, however, a revival of the Islamic Fulani peoples
was forestalled by the Bambara kingdoms of Segu and Kaarta (▷ 72).

The decline of Spain had only marginal impact on its colonial empire.
England captured Jamaica and the Mosquito Coast, while France took Saint-
Domingue (Haiti) and established a settlement at New Orleans. In North
America, Frenchman Robert La Salle explored the Mississippi, while English
control of the eastern seaboard was confirmed by the capture of Dutch New
Amsterdam (New York) (▷ 70). The English colonies grew rapidly in popula-
tion; the English built a presence beyond the French-controlled St Lawrence,
and took control of French Acadia, renaming it Nova Scotia in 1710 ∎

The arrival of Europeans in sub-Saharan Africa caused dislocations in old patterns of trade and cultural exchange that were unresolved by 1800. Nonetheless, outside influence was nowhere so extensive or systematic that it overwhelmed indigenous culture: several important African states emerged in this period.

The geographical barriers of the oceans and the Sahara, and Africa's abundance of natural resources, had inhibited the growth of an African seafaring or long-distance trading culture. Even coastal trade was minimal until it was developed by the Portuguese and the Dutch. Nevertheless the empires of the Sahel (the southern fringe of the Sahara), notably Songhai, traded gold, ivory and slaves in exchange for salt, glass and other luxuries. Other states flourished and traded with one another along the great river routes, especially those of west Africa.

Portuguese navigators first appeared off west Africa in the mid-15th century; the coastal bases they established drew trade away from the upper Niger. Following a long struggle with the Hausa people to the east, the Songhai empire was overthrown in 1591 by a Moroccan mercenary army at the battle of Tondibi, and a Moroccan *pashalik* (governorship) was established on the Niger. Neither Morocco nor the new African states on the upper Niger – the short-lived Manding empire and the Bambara kingdoms of Segu and Kaarta – could match the power of Songhai at its height.

The early 16th century saw the emergence of other states to the south of the Sahara, including the Mossi around Ouagadougou and, later, the Oyo states of the Niger delta. Asante and Dahomey emerged in the 17th century, first in the interior and later dominating the coast. By the late 18th century both of these were centralized, bureaucratic kingdoms. South of the Equator was the culturally dynamic Congo kingdom, where rivalry with Ndongo allowed the Portuguese to establish a colony in Angola after 1575, which was to become a major base for the transatlantic slave trade. Nevertheless, Ndongo's Queen Njinga (r.1624–63) prevented any further European expansion here. Further inland, the powerful Lunda empire arose in the mid-18th century, and pressed westward.

**1** The Funj were pagan nomadic cattle-herders who overran the Islamic state of Nubia in the early 16th century, but then converted to Islam themselves.

**2** The Portuguese force sent to support Christian Ethiopia against Ahmad Gran was commanded by Cristoforo da Gama, son of the explorer Vasco.

**3** The Songhai empire rose to prominence under Sonni Ali (r.1464–92); its trading towns, notably Timbuktu, were celebrated centers of Islamic culture.

**4** The Dutch traded on the Guinea coast in 1595 as part of a campaign against Portuguese trading bases; by 1637 the Portuguese had gone.

**5** The Gold Coast–Benin area was the hub of the west African slave trade; in the 18th century 35,000 slaves a year were transported from here.

**6** By 1783 the Dutch colony in the Cape region was the largest concentration of Europeans in Africa.

European influence in the states of the southern edge of the Sahara was minimal, and here Islam made its greatest progress. From 1570, Idris Aloma of Kanem-Bornu created the most purely Islamic state in Africa, and built up its power by importing firearms from the Ottomans. Its conversion of the pagan Wadai and Bagirmi states to the east was one of the few genuine territorial advances of Islam during this period. An Islamic revival, though, took place in Senegambia in the late 18th century.

In east Africa, a direct conflict arose between Islam and Christianity, mainly because of the survival of the ancient Christian kingdom of Ethiopia. The conversion of the Funj to Islam was accompanied by a rebellion of Adal, an alliance of Islamic states, against Ethiopian rule in 1527. Ahmed Gran, an Adali *imam*, ravaged Ethiopia for thirteen years before being killed by a Portuguese–Ethiopian force. On the east African coast, Portugal established a string of bases from Delagoa Bay to Socotra to dominate Indian Ocean trade. These were largely successful until the end of the 17th century, when the sultanate of Oman, semi-independent of the Ottoman empire, capitalized on a fierce conflict between the Portuguese and the Dutch by occupying most of the northern bases. Omani and Indian

trade across the Indian Ocean revived as a result.

The most dramatic impact of the Europeans on Africa was the transatlantic slave trade, which began early in the 16th century. A trade in slaves within Africa had been known long before; but the demand for labor in the plantations in the Americas and the willingness of many African states to deal with Europeans led to a true explosion of the trade in the 17th century. States such as Dahomey used the provision of slaves as part of their own political processes – waging war in their traditional manner to obtain slaves, or enslaving and selling parts of their own populations. The human cost of transporting some ten million people to the Americas is incalculable.

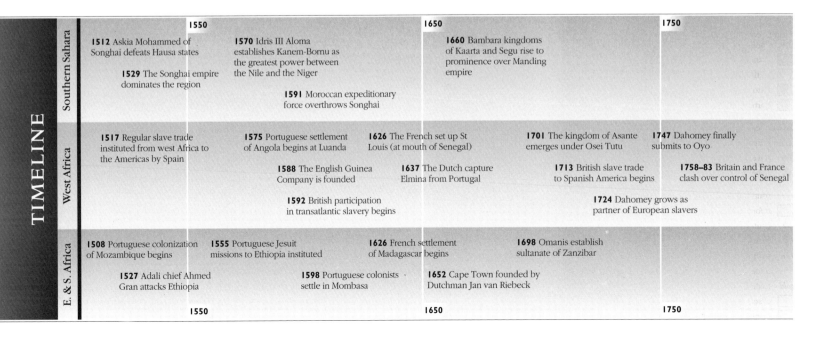

Map labels: arms, cotton, fabrics, guns, hardware from Europe; Banu Hassan Arabs; 1543; Idjil; salt; Cape Blanc; Ouadane; Berber; Arguin; to Portugal, 1617 to Netherlands, 1678 to France; Chinguetti; Cape Verde Islands 1495 to Portugal; salt; 1584; St Louis 1626 to France; Kaédi; Oualat; Gorée 1617 to Netherlands, 1677 to France; WALO; CAYOR; FUTA TORO; KAARTA; gold; West Indies, Central & North America; BAOL; Gambia; Fulani; Bamako; Mali; Fort James 1618 to Britain; Senegal; MANDING; FULA; Niani; Cacheu 1460 to Portugal; Kankan; Portuguese Guinea; FUTA JALON; Bunce Island; Mitomba; Kon; SUSU; iron; gold; Dyo; ivory; kola; ATLANTIC OCEAN; Little Cestos; Cape Palmas; Dutch & Portuguese traders; Brazil; Dutch & Portuguese traders; Brazil, West Indies, Central & North America

**TIMELINE**

| | 1550 | | 1650 | | 1750 |
|---|---|---|---|---|---|
| **Southern Sahara** | **1512** Askia Mohammed of Songhai defeats Hausa states / **1529** The Songhai empire dominates the region | **1570** Idris III Aloma establishes Kanem-Bornu as the greatest power between the Nile and the Niger / **1591** Moroccan expeditionary force overthrows Songhai | | **1660** Bambara kingdoms of Kaarta and Segu rise to prominence over Manding empire | |
| **West Africa** | **1517** Regular slave trade instituted from west Africa to the Americas by Spain | **1575** Portuguese settlement of Angola begins at Luanda / **1588** The English Guinea Company is founded / **1592** British participation in transatlantic slavery begins | **1626** The French set up St Louis (at mouth of Senegal) / **1637** The Dutch capture Elmina from Portugal | **1701** The kingdom of Asante emerges under Osei Tutu / **1713** British slave trade to Spanish America begins / **1724** Dahomey grows as partner of European slavers | **1747** Dahomey finally submits to Oyo / **1758–83** Britain and France clash over control of Senegal |
| **E. & S. Africa** | **1508** Portuguese colonization of Mozambique begins / **1527** Adali chief Ahmed Gran attacks Ethiopia | **1555** Portuguese Jesuit missions to Ethiopia instituted / **1598** Portuguese colonists settle in Mombasa | **1626** French settlement of Madagascar begins / **1652** Cape Town founded by Dutchman Jan van Riebeck | **1698** Omanis establish sultanate of Zanzibar | |
| | 1550 | | 1650 | | 1750 |

MOROCCO

*Mediterranean Sea*

TUNIS
c.1705 semi-independent

TRIPOLI
c.1714 semi-independent

CYRENAICA
c.1714 semi-independent

•Alexandria

Egypt

•Asyut

BAHRAIN
1515–1622 to Portugal

QATAR

Tuareg

×Terhazza

*salt* •Taoudenni

Ghat ⚘

Murzuq ⚘

HOGGAR MASSIF

SAHARA DESERT

TIBESTI MASSIF

⚘Al Kufrah

•El Kharga ⚘

•Aswan

•Medina

Jiddah• •Mecca

ARABIA

*salt*

AIR

Timbuktu
Tondibi
1591
•Gao

1591

Agadez•

*copper*

Sherda•

*salt* Bilma×

Chad Arabs

⚘Ain Galakka

Selima ⚘

Dongola•

•Suakin

FUNJ

*gold, ivory*

•Massawa

•Hodeida
•Zabid

Hodeida
YEMEN

Aden•

*ivory*

EGU

Jenne

SONGHAI

GOBIR

HAUSA STATES

Say

Zinder•

KANEM–BORNU

Lake Chad

WADAI
Wara

DARFUR
El Fasher•

1
Sennar•

Axum
2
Gondar•

×Woina 1543

AWSA
Awsa•

Beilul•

•Berbera

MOSSI STATES

•Ouagadougou

KEBBI

Kano

Kukuwa
Ngarzagamu

ETHIOPIA

ETHIOPIAN HIGHLANDS

*salt*

Harer

Somali

Galla

BORGU

*kola*

Niger

MAHI

*gold*

YORUBA STATES

*gold*

Igala

Benue

BAGIRMI

Biddefi•

OROMO

Nilotes

Lake Turkana

Shebelle

ASANTE
Kumasi•

*gold*

DAHOMEY
Ouidah

OLD OYO

Porto Novo
Lagos
BENIN

*pepper*

IGBO
Bonny
•Old Calabar

Accra•

Axim

São Jorge da Mina (Elmina)
to Portugal, 1637 to Netherlands

Benin
5

Brass

*gold*

BRONZES cast at Benin
reflected African life as
European technology shifted
the balance of power.

Lake Victoria

•Mogadishu

•Baraawe

SULTANATE OF ZANZIBAR

Fernando Póo
to Portugal,
1778 to Spain

Príncipe
to Portugal

São Tomé

Annobón
to Portugal, 1778 to Spain

BOBANGI

Ubangi

CONGO BASIN

Congo

Babwa

Congo

White Nile

RIFT VALLEY STATES

Lomami

Lualaba

Kikuyu

•Pate
•Lamu
•Malindi
•Mombasa

INDIAN OCEAN

LOANGO
KAKONGO

TEKE

MPUMBU

KUBA

RIFT VALLEY

•Zanzibar

Indian traders

Loango
Malembo
Brazil
Cabinda

NGOYO

CONGO

Guango

LUNDA

Kasai

LUBA

Ujiji

Lake Tanganyika

Tabora

•Kilwa Kisiwani

Portuguese traders

Luanda
1574 to Portugal
Brazil

NDONGO
KASANJE

MBUNDU

MBUNDU

Benguela
1587 to Portugal
Brazil

OVIMBUNDU

Zambezi

Kafue

Cuanza

Cuando

Okavango

Ovambo

San

Herero

Kalahari Desert

Khoisan

Zambezi

Luangwa

Lake Malawi

•Ibo

MAKUA

*gold, ivory*

Shona

Zambezi

Tete
1532 to Portugal

Sena
1531 to Portugal

•Mozambique
1508 to Portugal

Vohémar•

*ginger*

Malagasy

Tananarive

*Madagascar*

Hova

Khami
ROZWI

Limpopo

Sofala
1505 to Portugal

Quelimane
1544 to Portugal

Sotho

•Inhambane

Xhosa

Nguni

Vaal

Orange

Delagoa Bay
1544 to Portugal,
1720–30 to Netherlands

Fort Dauphin

Cape Town
1652 to Netherlands
6
Cape of
Good Hope
CAPE COLONY

Brazil

**Legend:**

- Songhai empire at greatest extent, c.1515
- kingdom of Adal at greatest extent, 1543
- kingdom of Mwenemutapa at greatest extent, c.1600
- empire of Kanem-Bornu at greatest extent, c.1600
- *jihad* by Ahmed Gran of Adal against Ethiopia, 1531–43
- Portuguese expedition to Ethiopia, 1541–43
- Moroccan campaign of conquest, 1543–91
- approximate border of state or composite state, 1783 (where known)

territory controlled by non-African power, 1783
- France
- Netherlands
- Ottoman empire
- Portugal

slave trade, 1450–1810
- BAOL state important as a slave source
- slave trade route
- slave depot
- southern limit of Islamic influence, 1783
- reformist Islamic state, late 18th century
- center of Islamic learning
- oasis
- San peoples
- trade route
- *gold* trade commodity
- desert
- tropical rainforest

0        800 km
0        600 mi

See also 74 (slave trade);
89 (19th-century Africa)

From the 1650s most major European wars were also fought in North America. First the smaller colonies were eliminated. After the Netherlands turned against France, the Dutch in 1655 took New Sweden (Delaware) from Louis XIV's European ally. Likewise, the New Netherland colony (in the Hudson River region) was overrun by English forces during the Anglo-Dutch naval wars (1664).

The main rivalry was between the French and the British. Early exploration had created distinct areas of influence on the St Lawrence and the eastern seaboard respectively. As these grew to include claims in the Mississippi basin, Georgia and the Appalachian foothills, some native peoples were drawn into the hostility between the colonists. Sporadic fighting erupted into the conflict known as King William's War (an extension of the War of the League of Augsburg in Europe), when a French expedition sacked English trading forts on Hudson Bay (1686), and French and Huron raids ravaged New England, despite England's alliance with the Iroquois.

Britain seized the opportunity of Queen Anne's War (the War of the Spanish Succession) to overrun the French territory of Acadia in 1710. Renamed Nova Scotia, the peninsula was confirmed as a British possession (together with Newfoundland) by the Treaty of Utrecht in 1713, while the Ile St Jean and Ile Royale remained French. However, the area remained the scene of regular skirmishes for fifty years. In King George's War – the War of the Austrian Succession – the French naval base at Louisbourg on Ile Royale was sacked (1745), a French naval expedition to reconquer Acadia was destroyed by a storm (1746), and an unsuccessful British and Iroquois attack on New France led to widespread French and Huron raids (1746–48). Hostilities continued after the war in the Ohio basin, where the French tried to halt British expansion westward by destroying the advanced post at Pickawillany.

The decisive phase of Anglo-French conflict came with the French and Indian War (1755–63), the American counterpart of the Seven Years War. The European population of New France and Louisiana was only one-tenth that of the British colonies, and despite strategically sited forts and alliances with the indigenous peoples, the French could no longer offset this imbalance. Though France had achieved naval parity after 1748, the Royal Navy was able to blockade both trade and military reinforcements from France. Initially Britain suffered defeat at Fort Duquesne, failed to take Crown Point (1755), and endured successful French counterattacks (1756) and defeat at Ticonderoga (1758). Thereafter, the war swung in Britain's favor. James Wolfe's victory over the Marquis de Montcalm on the Plains of Abraham near Québec in 1759 secured British supremacy. By 1760 the whole of New France was in British hands. At the same time, British naval forces captured all French possessions in the West Indies except Saint-Domingue. When France coerced Spain to enter the war, the British occupied Florida and Havana. In the Treaty of Paris (1763) Britain's control of the whole of North America east of the Mississippi was confirmed. French territories beyond the Mississippi passed to Spain, which also regained Havana in exchange for Florida.

Contact with Europeans initially brought some benefits to indigenous peoples. In the southwest, the Plains peoples reverted to buffalo-hunting after acquiring Spanish horses, while, in the mid-17th century, the Huron people of the Great Lakes were saved by their military alliance with France from destruction by the Iroquois. However, native Americans experienced a steady loss of their traditional lands. King Philip's War of 1675–76 ended native resistance to European encroachment in the northeast. The Tuscarora and Yamassee peoples were driven out of the Carolinas in 1711 and 1715 respectively; and from 1730 to 1755 the Shawnee and Delaware fled west down the Ohio. Only in the west, where French traders encountered the Sioux nation of the Plains, was European impact minimal.

**extent of European settlement in 1713**
- British
- French
- Spanish
- French territory acquired by Britain, 1713

**European territorial claims, 1750**
- British
- French
- Spanish
- British territory after 1763
- Spanish territory after 1763

**settlement or trading post founded in the 18th century**
- British
- French
- Spanish

**French and Indian War, 1755–63**
- British capture of fort or settlement
- French capture of fort or settlement
- British victory
- French victory
- Spanish victory
- raid by French and native allies on British settlements
- British campaign
- Spanish campaign
- Iroquois campaign, 1642–67
- migration of Delaware and Shawnee, 1730–55
- colonial road
- trade route of the native peoples

**Ute** native American peoples

*Lake Athabasca*

*Western Woods Cree*

*Saskatchewan*

*Plai Cre*

*Plains Gros Ventre*

*Crow*

0 ___ 600 km
0 ___ 400 mi

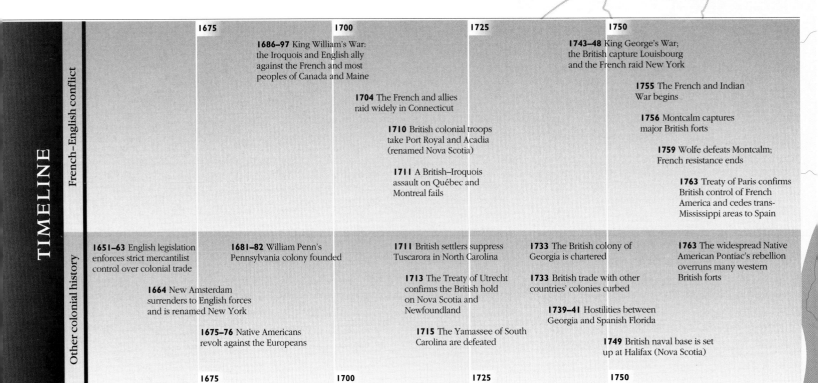

## TIMELINE

### French–English conflict

| 1675 | 1700 | 1725 | 1750 |
|---|---|---|---|

**1686–97** King William's War: the Iroquois and English ally against the French and most peoples of Canada and Maine

**1743–48** King George's War; the British capture Louisbourg and the French raid New York

**1704** The French and allies raid widely in Connecticut

**1755** The French and Indian War begins

**1710** British colonial troops take Port Royal and Acadia (renamed Nova Scotia)

**1756** Montcalm captures major British forts

**1711** A British–Iroquois assault on Québec and Montreal fails

**1759** Wolfe defeats Montcalm; French resistance ends

**1763** Treaty of Paris confirms British control of French America and cedes trans-Mississippi areas to Spain

### Other colonial history

**1651–63** English legislation enforces strict mercantilist control over colonial trade

**1681–82** William Penn's Pennsylvania colony founded

**1711** British settlers suppress Tuscarora in North Carolina

**1733** The British colony of Georgia is chartered

**1763** The widespread Native American Pontiac's rebellion overruns many western British forts

**1664** New Amsterdam surrenders to English forces and is renamed New York

**1713** The Treaty of Utrecht confirms the British hold on Nova Scotia and Newfoundland

**1733** British trade with other countries' colonies curbed

**1675–76** Native Americans revolt against the Europeans

**1715** The Yamassee of South Carolina are defeated

**1739–41** Hostilities between Georgia and Spanish Florida

**1749** British naval base is set up at Halifax (Nova Scotia)

| 1675 | 1700 | 1725 | 1750 |
|---|---|---|---|

*Labrador Sea*

*Newfoundland*

Inuit

Inuit

Inuit

*Southampton Island*

*Coats Island*  *Mansel Island*

*H u d s o n
B a y*

Naskapi

*Newfoundland*  **1**

• St John's

*Belcher Islands*

Fort Churchill •

Chipewyan

Port Nelson •
• Fort York

Fort Severn •

*Eastern Cree*

Rupert's Land
(Hudson's Bay Company)

*Akimiski Island*

**5**

Fort Le Pas •

*Lake Winnipeg*

Fort Bourbon •

Cree

Fort Dauphine •

Fort La Reine •

Assiniboin

Fort St Charles •

Fort Maurepas •

Fort St Pierre •

Fort Kaministiquia •

Sault St Marie •

*Lake Superior*

Fort Albany •

Moose Factory •

Fort Rupert •

Tadoussac •

⊗ 1746

• Louisbourg
1758

*Ile St Jean
(Prince Edward I)*

Ft Beausejour
1755

*Ile Royale
(Cape Breton I)*

Halifax •

Nova Scotia

Port Royal
1710

Plains of Abraham
1759

⊗ 1711

Québec
1759

Trois Riviéres

Montréal
1760

Fort La Tourette •

Fort Népigon •

Ojibwa

Fort Michipicton •

Huron

**2**

Fort William Henry
1756

Fort Frontenac
1758

Crown Point
1759

Ticonderoga
1758

Fort George
1756

1704

New Hampshire

Portsmouth

Boston

Massachusetts

*Lake Michigan*

*Lake Huron*

Fort Rouillé •

Fort Niagara •

Fort Oswego
1756

Fort Ontario
1755

Albany •

*Lake Ontario*

1746–48

New York

Plymouth

Providence

New Haven

Connecticut

Gros Ventre

Mandan

Fort St Croix •

Winnebago

Fort St Joseph •

Ottawa

*Lake Erie*

Fort Presqu'isle

Pennsylvania

**3**

*Hudson*

New York
New Amsterdam until 1664

New Jersey

Arikara

Sioux

Fort Beauharnais •

Fort Pontchartrain •

Fort Duquesne
1758
1755

Fort Necessity

Delaware

Philadelphia •

Delaware •

Cheyenne

*Misouri*

*Mississippi*

Miami  Wyandot

Fort Pickawillany
1752

**7**

Shawnee

*Ohio*

Baltimore •

Annapolis •

Maryland

*ATLANTIC
OCEAN*

Fort St Louis •

Fort Crevecoeur •

Kaintuck

Virginia

Richmond •

Williamsburg •

Jamestown •

*Warrior's Path*

Fort Vincennes •

Tuscarora

North Carolina

New Bern •

Fort Orléans •

Fort Chartres •

*Louisiana*

Cherokee

*Great Trading Path*

Chickasaw

Fort Prudhomme •

*Appalachian Mts*

*Decaneechi Path*

**6**

Wilmington •

South Carolina

Georgetown •

Charleston •

Choctaw

Creek

Fort Augusta •

1742 ⊗  Savannah •

*Georgia*

Fort King George •

Alabama

Yamassee

1740
1743
⊗ St Augustine
1702

Fort Rosalie •

Fort Condé •

Natchez

Pensacola •

New Orleans •

*Florida*

*Gulf of
Mexico*

*Rio Grande*

**4**

**1** European cod-fishing fleets visited Newfoundland from about 1500, but the first permanent settlements were established by the English Newfoundland Company in 1610. France ceded the island to Britain in 1713.

**2** Iroquois campaigns against the Huron in the 1640s and 1650s severely disrupted French exploration and fur trading in modern New York state; French troops halted the Iroquois advance in 1667.

**3** The former Dutch colony of New Netherland, including Manhattan and the Hudson River, was seized by England in 1664; it was reoccupied by the Dutch in 1673, but confirmed to England in 1674.

**4** A French expedition from the Mississippi to the Rio Grande in 1714 provoked Spanish expansion across modern Texas to block French moves westward.

**5** The French established trading forts around lakes Winnipeg and Saskatchewan in 1732–48, diverting much of the rich fur trade of the Cree away from the British bases on Hudson Bay to the French Great Lakes–St Lawrence route.

**6** While cattle and grain-farming dominated the colonial economy north of Delaware, tobacco was the most important crop in Virginia and North Carolina, and rice and indigo in South Carolina and Georgia.

NATIVE Americans were seen as a threat to colonial America; this model was on a Massachusetts weathervane.

See also 70 (exploration); 75 (war of independence); 84 (19th century North America)

Trade between the Mediterranean and the east was of very ancient origin. The "Silk Route" linked the Middle East with China from classical times (▷ 49 ). Ancient Rome, like 16th-century Europe, imported goods from China and paid for them in gold and silver. India developed a money-based economy before the Christian era, despite a lack of local precious metals, by attracting gold through the sale of cheap cotton textiles (▷ 31 ). Credit facilities for merchants, which made long-distance trade possible, developed at an early date in both China and India, and achieved roughly their modern form in Europe by 1200.

The period 1500–1800, however, brought three new developments in world trade, all of them originating in Europe. First was the establishment of regular routes around Africa from Europe to India and China. These routes, and the permanent bases along them, meant that European traders no longer had to rely on the overland caravan routes and Islamic middlemen.

The second development resulted from the Spanish conquests in the Americas. By the second half of the 16th century, as the gold mines of southern Germany and Hungary were nearing exhaustion, vast shipments of silver from Peru and Mexico began to arrive at Seville. Much of the Spanish–American silver found its way into the general European economy, where it made possible a huge increase in the credit available to European merchants, and helped avert financial collapse during the grim 17th century (▷ 66 ).

American silver bought European access to the other world markets. Until 1750, only in shipbuilding did European technology enjoy the superiority over its world rivals that was to characterize the 19th century, and European manufactured goods had little allure for Indian or Chinese merchants. Europeans could only obtain the goods they desired – southeast Asian spices, Indian cottons or Chinese silks and porcelain – by paying in gold or silver. The huge quantities of American silver flowing into Europe after about 1550 therefore flowed out again to the east almost as quickly – some via the Ottoman empire (the old trade routes never completely closed), some (after the opening of Siberia) via Russia, and some by sea. Meanwhile large quantities of American silver were reaching the Asian economies from the Americas, via the Philippines. In the hands of the Dutch, and then their British successors, Spanish–American silver became the means of establishing a permanent

*Hawaiian Islands*

**Map labels:** furs; fish; furs, grain, meat; Québec; timber; Boston; New York; dyes, rice, tobacco; Charleston; cotton; New Orleans; to Manila; silver; Cuba; Havana; Bahamas; Veracruz; sugar; Hispaniola; Acapulco; Jamaica; coffee, cotton, sugar; sugar; Guadeloupe; cacao, dyes; Panama; cacao, dyes; New Amsterdam; Cayenne; sugar; silver; sugar, tobacco; Callao; sugar; Bahia; coffee, sugar; Arica; Potosí; silver; Rio de Janeiro; coffee, diamonds, gold, silver; hides; Buenos Aires; Falkland Islands; £5.0 million; £4.5 mil...; "Middle Passage"

**Timeline entries:**

**c.1550** The first slave-worked sugar plantations are established in Brazil

**1545** The Potosí silver mine in Peru enters production for Spain

**1521** Lisbon and Oporto are licensed as monopoly ports for trade with Brazil

**1503** The Spanish office of American trade is set up at Seville

**1625** British settlement begins in the West Indies: by 1640 plantation-grown sugar is the principal crop

**1602** The Dutch East India Company is founded in Amsterdam

**1600** The English East India Company is set up (its first base is founded at Bantam in 1602)

**1664** The French East India Company (*Compagnie des Indes*) is founded

**TIMELINE**

| The Americas |
| Europe |
| Middle East |
| Africa |
| Asia and Australasia |

1550    1650

**1498** Vasco da Gama reaches Calicut, initiating European maritime trade links with India

**1557** A permanent Portuguese trading base is established at Macao

**1619** The Dutch East India Company headquarters is set up at Batavia on Java

**1575** The slaving town of Luanda is founded in Portuguese Angola to supply slaves for Brazil

**1641** The Dutch capture Malacca to win control of the East Indies trade

**1661–62** The Dutch lose Formosa (Taiwan) to the Chinese

Greenland

Iceland
(Denmark)

*copper,
iron*

*flax, furs,
hemp, timber*

Glasgow

£2.8 million

Liverpool  Hamburg
Bristol
St Malo    Amsterdam
Nantes     Antwerp
           London
Bordeaux   Venice
Oporto  Marseille  Genoa
Lisbon
Seville
Cádiz

*copper,
lead*

Moscow

*furs*

Astrakhan

Constantinople

*gems;
textiles*

Damascus

*salt*

*gold, ivory,
slaves*    *gold, ivory,
           slaves*

St Louis

*gold, ivory,
slaves*

*gold, slaves*

Lagos

Fernando Póo

*coffee, gems,
spices*

Delhi

Surat     *cotton, silk,
Bombay     textiles*
          *cotton,
          textiles*

Goa
Madras
*spices*
Pondicherry

Ceylon

Luanda
*slaves*

Mozambique
*slaves*

Madagascar

Mauritius
(France)

Réunion
(France)

£1.5 million

£2.0 million

£2.2 million

£1.4 million

Cape Town

*furs*

Kyakhta

*porcelain,
silk, tea*

*gems, silk,
tea*

Beijing

Macao

Taiwan
(Formosa)

to Acapulco

Manila

Philippine
Islands

Malacca

Sumatra
Bantam
*spices, sugar*
Batavia
Java

Borneo

Celebes

New Guinea

*spices*

Timor

Australia

**European economic zone,
c.1500**

**economic zones, c.1780**

Chinese
European
Indian
Islamic
Russian

**European trade route, with value of
imports to European trade, 1760-70**

British
Dutch
French
Portuguese
Russian
Spanish

important non-European
trade route

slave trade triangle

*slaves*  source of commodity

☠  area affected by pirates

---

**1714** The office of
American trade is trans-
ferred from Seville to Cadiz

**1690s** Major gold and
diamond strikes are made
in the Minas Gerais region
of Portuguese Brazil

**1764–78** Charles III of
Spain allows trade
between the Americas and
over 20 ports, increasing
trade greatly

1750

**585** The Mughal emperor
urangzeb expels English
traders from Surat; he
grants Calcutta as an East
India Co. base in 1688

**1713** British slavers take
over the slave trade from
West Africa to Spanish
America for 30 years under
the Asiento agreement

**1769** The French East
India Company is
dissolved

---

presence in the Asian economies.
The Dutch East India Company had
gained control of the entire trading economy of the East Indies by the late 18th century by
forcing the native traders out of business, and its British rival similarly had
made great advances in gaining access to India itself.

The third development was the territorial expansion of the European
economic zone itself. Expansion in the Americas allowed a process very
different to the patient game of trading rivalry played by Europeans in Asia.
Large parts of the Americas were converted to single-crop plantations or
heavily exploited sources of raw material for the home market. A labor force
for the sugar plantations was imported forcibly from Africa, replenished constantly because conditions both in the slaving ships and on the plantations
caused high mortality rates among the slaves. Rivalry among the colonial
powers, and the settlement of some areas (notably North America) by
Europeans anxious to reproduce the society and the mixed economy of
Europe, meant that the mercantilist ideal, by which each European nation had
its own colonies dedicated to supplying raw materials to the home market,
was rarely achieved (▷ 62). Attempts to regulate the colonial trade for the
benefit of the mother country in British and Iberian America alike were only
partially successful and provoked covert or open resistance (▷ 73). Even so,
the trade agreements that followed the American Revolution demonstrate how
intimately these colonial economies remained tied to Europe ■

The 18th century witnessed a great increase in the colonial population of North America, particularly with the end of the struggle for supremacy between Britain and France in 1763. In just five years between 1769 and 1774, 152 ships from Irish ports alone brought over 44,000 new colonists. By 1774 Europeans in North America numbered two million – over a quarter of Britain's population. This growth altered the nature of the colonies and the allegiances of their inhabitants. In Pennsylvania, a flood of German and Irish Protestant immigrants in the 1720s outnumbered the original English Quakers. German soldiers sent to the colonies by the Hanoverian dynasty ruling Britain further swelled the non-British populace; Scots and Irish settlers, many with Jacobite (anti-Hanoverian) sympathies, also arrived. After 1775 loyalist support was concentrated in those longer-established colonies whose inhabitants could claim English ancestry. Even so, Virginia and the Carolinas, which attracted few non-British immigrants and were developing a distinctive plantation economy based on mass importation of slaves, showed little enthusiasm for the loyalist cause.

The influx of new immigrants, together with a rising birthrate in the colonies, are evidence of a booming economy. Agriculture was by far the most important activity, but it was commerce (particularly that of New England) that caused Britain most concern. Mercantilist theory maintained that colonial possessions should be developed to supply goods or raw materials unavailable in the home country, that these commodities should be paid for in manufactured goods for the colonists, and that the colonies should be discouraged from engaging in any other form of external trade. From the mid-17th century onward, these theories were imposed on the British colonies through a range of legislation, including the 1651 and 1673 Trade and Navigation Acts and the 1663 Staple Act. Yet the introduction of European-style agriculture into North America compromised the first of these conditions, while application of the second caused a currency shortage that rendered useless any attempts to restrict independent colonial trade. By the 18th century, the economy relied on smuggling: that is, trade other than with Britain. Merchants traded in fish, whale oil, horses, beef and timber to the Spanish, Dutch and French Caribbean in exchange for sugar, molasses, rum and silver coin. By the 1750s, they had begun to export dried fish, grain and flour to Europe in their own vessels, competing with British shippers and often bypassing British ports. In response, customs administration was tightened and a succession of laws passed in Britain from 1763 sought to curb this trade, including the 1764 Sugar Act. Along with the imposition of direct taxation in the Stamp Act of 1763, these caused great resentment in America.

At the same time, the costs that had been incurred in the war to gain control of the French colonies proved a severe drain on Britain's finances. In 1763–65 prime minister George Grenville forced the colonies to bear a greater share of this cost by imposing a series of taxes and other obligations. One that caused particular resentment was the Quartering Act of 1765, providing for the quartering of soldiers in colonial public buildings; it was seen as irrelevant once the French threat had dissipated.

Finally, the British attempted to forestall further hostilities over land with the indigenous peoples by setting limits to colonial expansion. The 1763 Proclamation Line defined a theoretical western boundary to the growth of the colonies. This aroused opposition (and was largely disregarded) in America, where the open frontier had already become an essential element in economic growth and the absorption of new immigrants. The 1774 Quebec Act, which provided for the government of former French colonies and extended Quebec's boundaries to the Ohio and Mississippi, was widely seen as a further attempt to restrict colonial freedom.

These issues combined to produce escalating tension and finally open war between colonists and British troops in 1775. Despite early reverses, the British commanders Sir William Howe and his brother Admiral Lord Howe had regained the initiative by the second year of the war, by capitalizing on the strategic mobility that their naval supremacy afforded. Subsequent campaigns confirmed the difficulty of holding large territories against an increasingly hostile population, but the intervention of France ultimately proved decisive. The victory of a French fleet over the Royal Navy off the Chesapeake Capes forced the surrender of a besieged British army at Yorktown. Although Britain saved the the economically vital West Indies by defeating a French invasion fleet in the eastern Caribbean in 1782, the American colonies were lost irretrievably. The Treaty of Paris of 1783 confirmed the independence of the new United States of America.

Lake Winnipeg

Fort Népigon

Fort William

Winnipeg

Fort St Charles

Mississippi

**1** The seizure of the vessel *Liberty* for smuggling at Boston in 1768 provoked a riot, followed by the refusal of the citizens to billet British troops.

**2** The First Continental Congress met at Philadelphia on 5 September 1774; in 1776, the Second Congress proclaimed the Declaration of Independence.

**3** Bunker Hill, the first engagement of the American revolution, was a British victory. However, as colonial forces inflicted heavy casualties on the British at little cost to themselves, the battle raised American morale.

**4** Colonial forces besieged Québec in 1775-76, but withdrew when their commander was killed.

**5** New York remained a loyalist stronghold after its capture by Sir William Howe in 1776, replacing Boston as the main British base in North America.

**6** George Washington's Continental Army wintered in great hardship at Valley Forge in 1776-77, after its retreat across New Jersey from New York.

**7** After British commander Samuel Hood's failure to prevent the French capture of St Kitts in 1782, George Rodney defeated de Grasse off The Saintes islands.

## TIMELINE

### Military campaigns

**1770**

**1770** The Boston Massacre; Bostonians are killed in fracas with British soldiers

**1773** Boston Tea Party; protest against British tea-dumping in America

**1775** Fighting erupts near Boston between British and colonial forces; Americans take Montréal but fail to capture Québec

**1776** Declaration of Independence; British vacate Boston; Howe captures New York

**1780**

**1777** British advances on the Hudson are halted; Howe occupies Philadelphia

**1778** France gives Americans military support; British forces secure Savannah

**1779** Spain declares war on Britain and retakes Florida

**1780** Charleston falls; Netherlands declares war on Britain

**1781** British surrender after the siege at Yorktown

**1782** British defeat French at The Saintes in West Indies

**1783** The Treaty of Paris confirms US independence

### Legislation

**1763** Direct taxation is imposed on America

**1765** The Stamp Act imposes the first direct taxation on the Brritish colonies

**1766** The Declaratory Act affirms Britain's right to legislate in the colonies

**1774** Massachusetts Government Act removes many rights; Quebec Act ends the growth of several colonies

**1774** The First Continental Congress meets in Philadelphia

**1776** Congress adopts the Declaration of Independence

**1777** Congress adopts the Articles of Confederation, setting up the United States of America

**1770**                    **1780**

BENJAMIN FRANKLIN's cartoon urged the American colonies to "join or die" against the British in the *Pennsylvania Gazette* in 1754.

See also 73 (the Atlantic colonies); 84 (the 19th-century United States)

A fter more than a century of worldwide famine, plague, warfare and hardship, recovery took place in the course of the 18th century. In China, the population rose from 120 million in 1680 to nearly 300 million by 1790. In Europe, perhaps 100 million in 1650 had become 187 million by 1800. Even in the Americas, 13 million inhabitants in 1650 had doubled by 1800. Only in Africa did the overall population of 100 million stay unchanged: here several million were forcibly moved under the slave trade.

It is often said that medical and sanitation advances gave humankind the means to escape the tyranny of plague and high infant mortality. Such advances were indeed made in parts of Europe, but nowhere else. A more general cause may have been climatic, with a gradual rise in the temperature of the planet leading to improved harvests and greater resistance to disease.

Politically, the 18th century brought the struggle between the most dynamic nation-states of western Europe, France and Great Britain, to the world stage. British gains in the Americas were extended during the War of the Austrian Succession (1740–48), but French successes in India and in Europe meant that the Treaty of Aix-la-Chapelle (1748) simply restored the pre-war status quo. In the Seven Years War (1756–63), however, British naval superiority was decisive. James Wolfe's victory at Quebec in 1759 delivered New France to Britain, and all French possessions in the West Indies except Saint-Domingue were taken in 1762. In the same year, British forces captured Havana, heart of the Spanish–American empire, and twelve months later Florida was ceded. In India, the English East India Company, struggling to reverse the French gains of 1748, won a decisive victory at Plassey (1759) over France's ally Siraj ud-Daulah of Bengal. By 1763, France held only Pondicherry in India, and had lost all footholds in North America east of the Mississippi.

Britain's attempts to tighten fiscal control over colonial America and its concern at illicit trade between its American subjects and French, Dutch and Spanish colonies led to war with its largest colonial possession. France, supporting the colonials, sent troops and a fleet to threaten British North America and the economically valuable West Indies. By 1783 Britain had secured the West Indies but lost America (▷ 75).

New powers emerged elsewhere in the world in the 18th century. In Europe, the Prussia of Frederick the Great mounted

## Map labels

Russian America
Arctic marine mammal hunters
sub-Arctic forest hunter-gatherers
plateau fishers and hunter-gatherers
west coast foraging, hunting and fishing peoples
Rupert's Land
Labrador
Newfoundland
Quebec
Nova Scotia
Vice-Royalty of New Spain
UNITED STATES OF AMERICA
Florida
Bahamas
Saint-Domingue
Cuba
Jamaica
Hispaniola
Belize
Mosquito Coast
Guyana
Cayenne
Vice-Royalty of New Granada
Vice-Royalty of Brazil
Vice-Royalty of Peru
Vice-Royalty of Rio de la Plata
Hawaiian Islands
Polynesians
Cook, 1768–69
Cook, 1768
pampas hunter-gatherers
shellfish gatherers and marine mammal hunters
Falkland Islands

## Timeline

**1727** The Turks are driven from Transcaucasia by the Persians

**1747** Oyo defeats Dahomey to become the main power in the Niger delta

**1720** French government finances are crippled by the failure of the Mississippi Company

**1740** Accession of Frederick II "the Great" of Prussia, who raises Prussia to a major European power

**1759** Britain takes Quebec from the French

**1720** Dutch settlers from the Cape reach the Orange river

**1756** Outbreak of the Seven Years War in Europe (to 1763)

| The Americas |
| Europe |
| Middle East |
| Africa |
| East and South Asia |

TIMELINE

1720   1740   1760

**1721** France takes Mauritius from the Dutch

**1736** Nadir Shah becomes ruler of Persia; he campaigns in central Asia, northern India and against the Ottomans

**1757** The British defeat the French in India at Plassey

**1722** The Marathas emerge as the strongest successors to the Mughals in India

**1761** Afghan Ahmad Shah Durrani defeats the Marathas at Panipat

**1739** The Persians under Nadir Shah sack Delhi

hunter-gatherers
nomadic pastoralists
simple farming societies
complex farming societies/
chiefdoms
state societies
uninhabited

empires
British
Dutch
French
Portuguese
Russian
Spanish
other

→ British route of exploration
KO. Kong empire
MO. Mossi states
N. Netherlands
SO. Songhai
RI. Rift Valley states

**1769** The invention of the "spinning jenny" in Britain permits the industrialization of the textile industry

**1768** War breaks out between Russia and the Ottomans

**1768** British sailor James Cook begins exploration of the Pacific

**1783** Under the Treaty of Paris, Britain accepts American independence

**1783** Russia conquers and annexes the Crimea

**1780–84** The fourth Anglo-Dutch war ends Dutch control of European trade

**1776** The American colonies declare their independence from British rule

**765** Bengal comes under the control of the British

**1765–69** The Manchu Chinese invade Burma

**1775** The first Anglo-Maratha war begins in India

**1770s** The slave trade from Africa to the New World is at its height

**1781** British forces take Dutch settlements in west Sumatra

the first effective Protestant offensive against Catholic Europe since 1632, by wresting Silesia from Austria. Prussia survived an Austrian, Russian and French onslaught in the Seven Years War to rival Austria as successor to the Holy Roman empire. Russia, having eclipsed Sweden in the Baltic, had effectively destroyed Poland by the 1770s and pushed back the Ottoman frontier in the southwest, while pioneers crossed the Bering Strait to establish a presence in Alaska.

In India, the Persian troops of Nadir Shah sacked Delhi in 1739 and destroyed the last vestiges of Mughal authority. In 1761 Ahmad Shah Durrani of Afghanistan won the third decisive battle in world history to be fought at Panipat, routing a huge Maratha army. The English East India Company, effective ruler of Bengal after their victory at Plassey, became the greatest power in India, rivaled only by Mysore.

The world's greatest power of the 18th century, however, was China. By 1700, the Manchu had subdued the last Ming warlords, and an extraordinary period of economic and political growth followed. Chinese power reached far into central Asia, the Amur basin was cleared of Russians, Tibet was brought under Chinese control, and imperial authority was, at least nominally, reestablished over much of southeast Asia. Only Burma resisted powerfully (▷ 69).

The 18th century also saw Cook, Bougainville and other European navigators systematically begin to explore the last great area of the planet's surface largely unknown to European mariners, the Pacific ■

## Part 5

# THE NINETEENTH WORLD

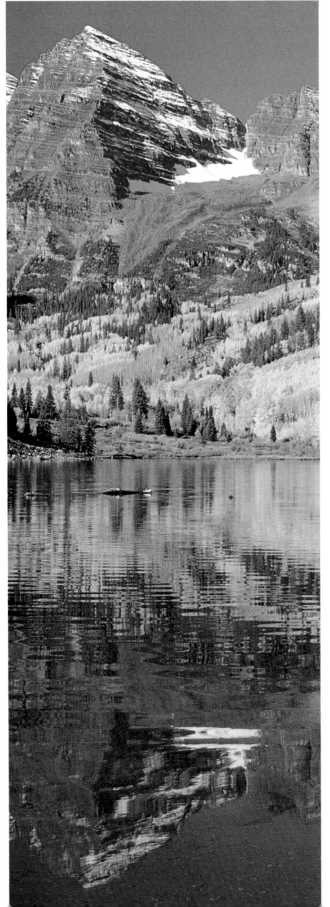

I n 1783 Britain disconsolately accepted the independence of its thirteen colonies in North America. Yet, in the century and a quarter after the emergence of the United States, European powers still dominated the world. Their armies spread their authority, their navies charted the seas and their merchants built a network of trade and investment. A genuinely global economy was the result.

The only part of the world effectively to resist the European powers was North America, but the United States itself was a state ruled by people of European descent, its economy closely linked to and partly financed by Europe, and its culture shaped by European influences. The railroads that effectively made the United States by linking the Atlantic and Pacific coasts owed much to British investment and technology. By 1900, though, the United States had challenged and overtaken much of Europe's economic and technological lead, and was poised to become the most powerful state in the world.

The United States was sustained by migration. Between 1815 and 1901, the United States took over eight million immigrants from the British Isles alone, and many more from Germany, Scandinavia and eastern and southern Europe. European migrants also totally altered the politics, economy and ethnic composition of Australasia and Canada.

Europeans were not the only people to move, but those non-whites who journeyed long distances in pursuit of work – Chinese, Japanese, Indians, Malays as well as Africans – did so only with the consent of the European or North American states. Unlike Europeans who were generally welcomed, despite their poverty, to assist in populating the new lands and building a new society, these non-Europeans were often contract laborers or worse, controlled by strict racial barriers.

THE FRONTIERLANDS of North America drew settlers from Europe.

# CENTURY

The age of migrations reflected the potency of the new technologies of the age. Thanks to the steamship, the oceans shrank; long voyages became faster, safer, cheaper, more comfortable. Barbed wire, invented in the United States in 1873, made possible the fencing in of the prairies and thus the establishment of vast ranches on what had been virgin land. Refrigerated shipholds allowed fresh meat grown on these ranches to be shipped to cities on the other side of the globe. Railroads, too, brought foodstuffs and other raw materials quickly and efficiently to the urban centers.

Trade was not restricted to raw materials. The heavy industry, light engineering, chemicals and textile manufacture that now drove Europe's economy also provided products for the rest of the world. European investment capital acted as the engine of this global economy, financing the creation of the infrastructure for the new trade on every continent. The British empire, which encompassed more than a fifth of the Earth's landmass by 1914 (its political and financial influence pervaded much of the rest) was dominant in this flow of capital, though increasingly challenged by its cultural and political offspring, the United States. As a result English became the international language of business across most of the globe.

The spread of European influence was not always peaceful. There was violent resistance, especially in Africa and China. Yet there was frequently also emulation. This was most apparent in Japan, which embarked on an effective process of westernization from the 1870s. Similar choices were made in Egypt, Persia and Siam, all more or less independent states which saw the benefits of adopting western ways.

The formal European empires ensured that their colonies were educated in European ways of government, law and culture as much as in technology and commerce. This cultural imperialism was often conducted with little thought for the indigenous civilizations, and was barely questioned by the Europeans. The *pax Britannica* was maintained across the globe by a combination of British gunboats and diplomats, but the introduction of British education, religion and the political institutions of Westminster was thought to bring undeniable benefits to the "poor benighted heathen". Although advantages undoubtedly accrued, the forcible imposition of western civilization built up resentments that would grow throughout the first half of the twentieth century and explode after 1945.

In the nineteenth century, humanity sought to use advances in knowledge to mould the environment. Science – conducted mainly in Germany, France, Britain and the United States – made massive advances and its power to change the world became undeniable. Scientific breeding and a thorough knowledge of the needs of plants and animals transformed national economies: Malaya, for example, was changed utterly when the British introduced the rubber tree from South America. Science seemed to hold the key to the future, to the creation and use of goods, new sources of power (electricity, turbines, internal-combustion engines) and new materials (alloys, dyes, fertilizers, explosives). Equally revolutionary were the telegraph, telephone and radio, which shrank distance even more than had railroad and steamships: in 1901 Marconi transmitted radio signals across the Atlantic. Two years later the Wright brothers made the world's first heavier-than-air flight, giving the industrial countries access to a new medium that would have great implications, civil and military.

Every such innovation helped dissolve former certainties, and in 1914, when Europe began the conflict that engulfed the continent, the assumptions of the previous century were destroyed. To survive, the powers drew on the resources of their old colonies in ways that changed the relationships between them for ever ∎

**E**nlightenment thinkers of the mid-18th century often emphasized people's right to self-determination through a system of representative government. In this they expressed a hostility to the repressive forces – clerics, aristocrats and absolute monarchs – that still reigned supreme throughout Europe in the 18th century. Fueled by poverty, inflation and food shortages, and inspired by the successful revolution of American colonists against the British, this discontent was soon to erupt.

Uprisings occurred in 1784, when the Patriot party in the Dutch Netherlands tried to democratize government, and in 1787, when citizens of the neighboring territory of the Austrian Netherlands (Belgium) attempted to establish an independent republic. Neither insurrection achieved its goals.

A more widely based protest began against the *ancien régime* (autocratic royal government) in France when Louis XVI tried to raise taxes to avert state bankruptcy. He summoned the Estates-General – a periodic assembly of deputies from the three "Estates" (clergy, nobility, and commoners) – to approve his plans. However, Louis was faced with a political crisis when the Third Estate (made up of the rising middle class) withdrew to found a National Assembly and institute reform. Parisians feared an attack on the Assembly by Louis' forces and, on 14 July 1789, stormed the Bastille fortress, symbol of Bourbon tyranny. The rebellion spread rapidly .

In August 1789 the Assembly abolished the feudal system and issued its *Declaration of the Rights of Man*. That proclaimed freedom of conscience, property and speech, and established the principle that sovereign power resided in the nation rather than the king. After failing to escape from the country in 1791, Louis was compelled to approve a constitution that divested him of most of his power. By this stage, aristocrats who had managed to flee France had persuaded Prussia and the Habsburg

empire (Austria) to intervene on Louis' behalf. Opposition to revolutionary France soon crystallized into the First Coalition of European powers. The ensuing Revolutionary Wars (1792–1802) saw the French repulse an initial invasion and then go on the attack. The king and queen and many of aristocratic supporters were executed, counter-revolutionary risings were suppressed, internecine struggles broke out among the revolutionaries (the "Terror"), and the French tried to export revolution to their hostile neighbors the Netherlands, Spain and Britain (where they fomented rebellion in Ireland).

The First Coalition was broken by a series of French victories in 1794–95, culminating in a

successful invasion of the Netherlands (ruled by France as the Batavian Republic until 1806). Prussia and Spain sued for peace, leaving Britain and the Habsburg empire isolated. Britain, though, maintained naval supremacy with victories over France, and latter its Dutch and Spanish allies, from 1794–97. In 1798 a Second Coalition was formed.

Napoleon Bonaparte now began to emerge as the greatest of the French commanders through his brilliant campaigns in Italy and Austria. By late 1797, he had forced Austria to cede the Austrian Netherlands to France, in exchange for Venice, in a peace treaty that also created French-ruled states in northern Italy. As a prelude to his planned invasion

**Legend:**
- borders, 1783
- border of Holy Roman empire, 1783
- Austrian Habsburg territory, 1783
- France, 1783
- Brandenburg–Prussia, 1783
- Great Britain & Hanover, 1783
- Ottoman empire, 1783
- Spanish Bourbon territory, 1783
- Russian empire, 1783
- Russian gains by 1795
- Brandenburg–Prussian gains by 1795
- Austrian Habsburg gains by 1797
- French gains by 1800
- Roman Republic — state established by Revolutionary France
- extent of the "Great Fear" within France, 1789
- French counter-revolution, 1793
- French campaign, 1796–98
- Russian campaign, 1798–1800
- town bombarded by Russian Black Sea fleet
- Naval mutiny in Great Britain
- major revolt, riot or disorder

THE SANS-CULOTTE, "man without breeches", symbolized the radical republicans of France in 1790.

**Map labels:** Scotland; Edinburgh; Glasgow; Belfast; Carrick; ×1798; Killala Bay; Newcas[tle]; GREAT BRITAIN & IRELAND; Ireland; Dublin 6; Manchester; Liverpool; Wexford 1798; Birmingham; Wales; Fishguard 1797; Englan[d]; Bristol; Ilfracombe; Spithead 1797; 5; ATLANTIC OCEAN; "First of June" ×1794; 1802; 1796; 1797; 1797; Brest; Quiberon Bay 1795 ×; Loire; Nantes; Vendée 3; Bordeaux; La Coruña; ANDORRA; Ebro; Oporto; Madrid; PORTUGAL; SPAIN; Valencia; Lisbon; Guadiana; Cape St Vincent 1797 ×; Cádiz; Gibraltar to Britain; Tangier; Ceuta to Spain; Melilla to Spain; Oran; MOROCCO

## TIMELINE

| | 1790 | 1795 | 1800 |
|---|---|---|---|
| **Revolts** | **1784–87** Revolts occur in Dutch and Austrian Netherlands<br><br>**1788** Louis XVI of France summons the Estates-General<br><br>**1789** French Revolution begins; the Bastille is stormed | **1793** Execution of Louis XVI; a royalist rebellion begins in the Vendée<br><br>**1794** Tadeusz Kosciuszko leads a national rebellion in Poland | **1797** Mutinies in the British Royal Navy at Spithead and the Nore<br><br>**1798** United Irishmen rebel in a vain effort to win independence from Britain |
| **Revolutionary wars** | | **1792** The Prussians are checked at Valmy; Austrians are defeated at Jemappes<br><br>**1793** France blocks Anglo-Hanoverians at Hondschoote; defeats Austrians at Wattignies<br><br>**1794** Britain beats France at the Battle of the First of June | **1798** The French defeat the Mamlukes at the Battle of the Pyramids but are defeated by British at Battle of the Nile<br><br>**1799** Bonaparte returns to France and seizes power<br><br>**1800** Bonaparte defeats the Austrians at Marengo |
| **Alliances & treaties** | **1783** Britain recognizes the independence of the United States in the Treaty of Paris | **1792** Austria and Prussia ally against France: start of the French revolutionary wars<br><br>**1793** Second Partition of Poland; Spain, Holland, Britain and the empire join First Coalition against France<br><br>**1795** Third Partition of Poland | **1797** Treaty of Campo Formio follows the French defeat of Austria<br><br>**1798** Second Coalition against France |

| 1790 | 1795 | 1800 |

North Sea

SWEDEN

Christiania

Göteborg

Copenhagen

Stockholm

*Vänern*

*Vättern*

DENMARK–NORWAY

Helsinki

Revel

Svenskund 1789, 1790

St Petersburg

*Lake Peipus*

Riga

*Western Dvina*

*Gotland to Sweden*

*Baltic Sea*

Samogitia

Swedish Pomerania

Danzig

Königsberg

New East Prussia from 1795

East Prussia

Ermland

West Prussia

PRUSSIA

Mazovia

Lithuania

Minsk

Black Russia

POLAND

4 ☼ 1794

Warsaw

Podlesia

Volhynia

1795–1806 Batavian Republic

Camperdown 1797

Amsterdam

The Nore 1797

ndon

1787

1784

Brussels

Neerwinden 1793

ondschoote 1793

Jemappes 1792

Liège 1789

Fleurus 1794

Wattignies 1793

Paris

Valmy 1792

2 1789

Versailles 1789

Saarwerden

Salm

Orléans

Montbeliard 1792–93

Rauracian Republic

FRANCE

1

Lyon

Geneva

SWISS CONFEDERATION 1798–1803 Helvetic Republic

SARDINIA-PIEDMONT

Marengo 1800

Turin

Mondovi 1796

Venaissin to Papal States

Avignon 1796

Marseille

Nice 1796

Toulon

Trouillas 1793

Vernet 1793

Corsica 1794–96 to Britain

Ajaccio

Zürich 1799

Tyrol

Milan

Castiglione 1796

Mantua

Rivoli 1797

Arcole 1796

1797

Venice

Campo Formio

1797–1802 Cisalpine Republic

Genoa

GENOA 1797–1805 Ligurian Republic

TUSCANY

1793

Civitavecchia

PAPAL STATES

Fano

Rome

1798–99 Roman Republic

NETHERLANDS

Hamburg

Bremen

Hanover

Brandenburg

Berlin

*Elbe*

Saxony

Dresden

Frankfurt

Nuremberg

Bavaria

Munich

Hohenlinden 1800

Salzburg

Prague

Bohemia

Moravia

Austrian Silesia

Silesia

*Oder*

Netze

Great Poland South Prussia from 1793

Little Poland West Galicia from 1795

*Vistula*

Galicia and Lodomeria

Red Russia

Bukovina

Austria

*Danube*

Vienna

Leoben

Styria

Carinthia

Carniola

VENICE

Venice

HABSBURG EMPIRE

Buda

Hungary

☼ 1790

Croatia

*Sava*

Slavonia

Banat

Transylvania

Jassy

Moldavia

Bessarabia

Sebastopol

*Black Sea*

Wallachia

*Danube*

Varna

Bosnia

Serbia

Bulgaria

Herzegovina

MONTENEGRO

RAGUSA

Rumelia

Üsküb

Edirne

Constantinople

Russian Black Sea fleet, 1798–1800

Russian Black Sea fleet, 1798–1800

Albania

Janina

ANATOLIA

OTTOMAN EMPIRE

Wissembourg 1793

1798

1798

1798

Naples

1798–99 Parthenopean Republic

KINGDOM OF NAPLES AND SICILY

Naples

*Ionian Islands* Venetian, 1797 to France, 1799 to Russia

Morea

Athens

*Cythera* Venetian, 1797 to France, 1799 to Russia

*Rhodes*

*Cyprus*

Palermo

Messina

Sicily, 1799 independent of Naples

Bonaparte, 1798

*Crete*

Barcelona

Minorca 1798 to Britain

SARDINIA-PIEDMONT

*Sardinia*

1793

*Balearic Islands*

Algiers

Tunis

ALGIERS

Tunis

Tripoli

*Malta* Knights of St John, 1798 to France, 1800 to Britain

*Mediterranean Sea*

Acre

Mount Tabor 1798

Jaffa

Bonaparte, 1798

Aboukir Bay (Battle of the Nile) 1798

Alexandria

Battle of the Pyramids 1798

Cairo

*Nile*

Palestine

*Cyrene*

Egypt

1 In July and August 1789, a series of panics known as the "Great Fear" swept the French countryside, caused by rumors of brigands in the pay of aristocrats.

2 The Jacobin Maximilien Robespierre came to power in Paris in July 1793, initiating the revolutionary "Terror" and executing over a thousand people in the following twelve months.

3 The main counter-revolutionary revolt took place in the Vendée region of western France in 1793, and was brutally suppressed.

4 The Polish uprising against Russian rule in 1794 was led by Tadeusz Kosciuszko. Defeated and exiled, he refused to support subsequent attempts by France and Russia to grant Poland nominal independence.

5 Despite victories over France and its allies, harsh conditions in Britain's Royal Navy caused low morale, which led to two serious mutinies in 1797.

6 The French were persuaded by Wolfe Tone to support Irish risings against British rule. The rising of 1798 failed, and Tone committed suicide in prison.

of Britain, Bonaparte threatened Britain's trade route to India by attacking Egypt in 1798. Though victorious against Egypt's Mamluke rulers, his fleet was defeated by the British admiral Nelson at the Battle of the Nile. In response to reverses in Italy and on the Rhine, Bonaparte returned to France, overthrew the committee that had ruled France since 1795 (the "Directory") and installed himself as military dictator.

French military fortunes proceeded to rise; Napoleon's generals blocked an Anglo-Russian expedition to the Batavian Republic and defeated the Russians at Zürich, while he himself masterminded the defeat of the Austrians at Marengo (1800). Yet though his forces were all-powerful on land, his lack

of naval superiority meant that he could not prevent raids from the Russian Black Sea fleet in 1798–1800, or – more importantly – deliver a decisive blow against the Second Coalition.

In eastern Europe, Poland embarked on a course of constitutional reform modeled on Enlightenment ideas in the 1790s. Russia under Catherine II, which had annexed part of the country in 1772, responded by invading in 1792. Further regions were annexed by Russia and Prussia in the Second Partition (1793). A rebellion against the foreign overlords ended with the fall of Warsaw in 1794, and the Third Partition (1795) saw the disappearance of Poland as a sovereign country for over 120 years.

0        600 km

0        400 mi

See also 68 (*ancien regime* Europe); 78 (Napoleonic Europe)

French victories in 1800 virtually secured the defeat of Austria, but British naval power still frustrated Napoleon Bonaparte. His army in Egypt was forced out by the British in 1801, while the Danish fleet he hoped would keep Britain from the Baltic was destroyed at Copenhagen in the same year. A respite from war was confirmed by the Treaty of Amiens in 1802, enabling Britain to implement the Act of Union which incorporated Ireland into the United Kingdom, improving the islands' security.

War broke out again, however, in the spring of 1803. Napoleon revived his plan to invade Britain, which now stood alone against France, but he was unable to put it into action because of the undiminished strength of the Royal Navy. Britain's comprehensive naval victory at Trafalgar (1805), and the formation of the Third Coalition later that year, focussed Napoleon's attention back on the armies of Austria, overwhelming them at Ulm and Austerlitz. In 1806, Napoleon proclaimed the dissolution of the Holy Roman empire, united all the German states (apart from Austria and Prussia) into the Confederation of the Rhine, and then moved north to smash the Prussians at Jena–Auerstädt.

As in his earlier campaigns, Napoleon's generalship was unsurpassed and his army irresistible. The Treaty of Tilsit that followed his defeat of a Russian army at Friedland in 1807 broke the Third Coalition and placed Napoleon at the height of his power. He now turned to blockading all legitimate trade with Britain. The so-called "Continental System," established in Napoleon's Berlin and Milan decrees (1806, 1807), was designed to force the British to buy overpriced smuggled goods, thus depleting their gold reserves. Britain retaliated by prohibiting all French trade between one port and another.

Between 1804 (when he declared himself emperor) and 1814, Napoleon imposed his administrative and political ideas upon a conquered Europe while countering British attempts to probe the weak

points in the continental blockade. In all his vassal states, he introduced the *Code Napoléon*, the French civil code that enshrined the revolutionary principles of equality and liberty, and provided the protection of private property.

A new phase of the Napoleonic wars opened in 1808, when a French army marched across the Iberian peninsula to force Portugal to adopt the Continental System. This sparked a uprising in Spain against the French, while the British under the command of Wellington established a base in Portugal. In a war of shifting fortunes, a number of hard-fought battles drained the reserves of both sides. At the same time, Napoleon was obliged to conduct another campaign against the Austrians, finally overcoming them at Wagram (1809) to reassert his position as master of Europe. Although this victory allowed Napoleon to concentrate his forces on Spain and temporarily reverse his setbacks suffered there, his decision to attack Russia in 1812 – again to enforce the Continental System – radically altered the situation. The campaign was a huge drain on men and supplies; after hunger, winter and Russian resistance forced a withdrawal from Moscow in late 1812, Napoleon's enemies seized the opportunity to create a Fourth Coalition. For the first time since 1795, a united Europe front opposed France.

Even the retreat from Russia did not break Napoleon's power. In 1813, his forces were still able to resist the new coalition at Lützen, Bautzen and Dresden, but suffered heavy casualties in doing so. The loss of troops in Russia, combined with the huge international force ranged against him, finally proved decisive. At Leipzig – in the "Battle of the Nations"– Napoleon suffered his first major defeat and was forced to quit Germany. At the same time, Wellington managed to push north to Toulouse and conclude the Peninsular War. Allied armies pressed home their attack from Germany, and threatened Paris in 1814. Napoleon now abdicated and was sent

into exile on the Mediterranean island of Elba.

While the victorious allies were redrawing the map of Europe at the Congress of Vienna, Napoleon escaped from exile and re-entered France in a final attempt to rebuild his empire. In his so-called "Hundred Days," he reformed his armies and challenged the combined British, Dutch and Prussian forces at Waterloo. The ensuing battle was closely contested, but ended in final defeat for Napoleon. He abdicated for a second time and was exiled to St Helena in the south Atlantic, where he died. Europe was finally at peace after twenty-three years of war.

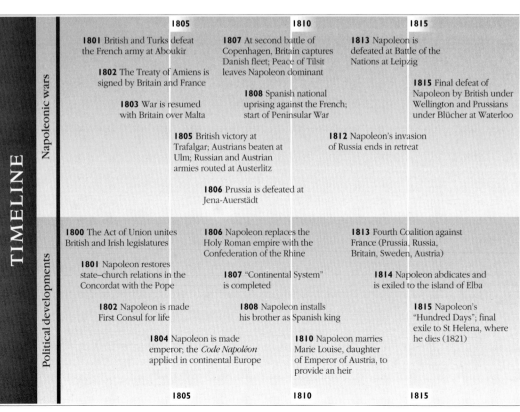

## TIMELINE

### Napoleonic wars

**1805**

**1801** British and Turks defeat the French army at Aboukir

**1802** The Treaty of Amiens is signed by Britain and France

**1803** War is resumed with Britain over Malta

**1805** British victory at Trafalgar; Austrians beaten at Ulm; Russian and Austrian armies routed at Austerlitz

**1806** Prussia is defeated at Jena-Auerstädt

**1810**

**1807** At second battle of Copenhagen, Britain captures Danish fleet; Peace of Tilsit leaves Napoleon dominant

**1808** Spanish national uprising against the French; start of Peninsular War

**1812** Napoleon's invasion of Russia ends in retreat

**1815**

**1813** Napoleon is defeated at Battle of the Nations at Leipzig

**1815** Final defeat of Napoleon by British under Wellington and Prussians under Blücher at Waterloo

### Political developments

**1800** The Act of Union unites British and Irish legislatures

**1801** Napoleon restores state–church relations in the Concordat with the Pope

**1802** Napoleon is made First Consul for life

**1804** Napoleon is made emperor; the *Code Napoléon* applied in continental Europe

**1806** Napoleon replaces the Holy Roman empire with the Confederation of the Rhine

**1807** "Continental System" is completed

**1808** Napoleon installs his brother as Spanish king

**1810** Napoleon marries Marie Louise, daughter of Emperor of Austria, to provide an heir

**1813** Fourth Coalition against France (Prussia, Russia, Britain, Sweden, Austria)

**1814** Napoleon abdicates and is exiled to the island of Elba

**1815** Napoleon's "Hundred Days"; final exile to St Helena, where he dies (1821)

**1805**          **1810**          **1815**

North Sea

Christiania

SWEDEN
1815 union with Norway

Helsinki

St Petersburg

Revel

Lake Peipus

Stockholm

Vänern

Vättern

Göteborg

Gotland

Riga

Baltic Sea

DENMARK–NORWAY
united until 1814
allied to France until 1814

1801–07

Kovno

Vilna

Western Dvina

Vitebsk
1812

Smolensk
1812

Borodino
1812

Moscow
1812

Maloyaroslavets
1812

3

6

RUSSIAN
EMPIRE

Krasnoi
1812

Berezina
1812

Minsk

Kharkov

Kiev

Dnieper

Copenhagen
1801, 1807

5

Heligoland
1807–14 to Britain

MECKLENBURG-
SCHWERIN

Swedish Pomerania
1815 to Prussia

1807–11

Königsberg
Eylau
1807

Friedland
1807

East
Prussia

Tilsit

Hull

Hamburg

Bremen

Pomerania

Danzig

Stettin

PRUSSIA
1807–13 allied
to France

England

Amsterdam

Holland

WESTPHALIA

HESSE

Elbe

Brandenburg

Berlin

1813

Oder

GRAND DUCHY
OF WARSAW
1815 to Russia

Warsaw

London

4

BERG

Frankfurt

Jena
1806

Auerstädt

Lützen
1813

Leipzig
1813

SAXONY

Bautzen
1813

Dresden
1813

Silesia

Vistula

Galicia and Lodomeria

Boulogne

Waterloo
1815

Brussels

Ligny
1815

Amiens

1

Laon
1814

1813

Hanau
1813

WÜRZBURG

1813

Prague

Moravia

Austrian
Silesia

Dniester

Château Thierry
1814

Reims
1814

1814

Mannheim

Bohemia

Austerlitz
1805

Bessarabia
1812 to Russian empire

Paris
1814

Champaubert

La Fère
Champenoise
1814

WÜRTTEMBERG

Ratisbon
1809

Austria

Wagram
1809

1811

Ochakov

Montmirail &
Vauchamps
1814

Ulm
1805

Munich

BAVARIA

Danube

Vienna

Aspern
1809

AUSTRIAN EMPIRE
1809–13 allied to France

Bukovina

Jassy

Moldavia

Sebastopol

Orléans

BADEN

Montereau
1814

Basel

Ebersberg
1809

Salzburg

Buda

Hungary

Transylvania

Zürich

Berne

HELVETIA

Styria

Carinthia

Banat

1806–12 under
Russian occupation

Wallachia

Bucharest

FRANCE

Geneva

Rhine

Illyrian Provinces

Slavonia

Sava

Belgrade

Serbia

Danube

1811

Varna

Black Sea

Lyon

Milan

Venice

Bosnia

Bulgaria

Russian maritime operations, 1800–07

Grenoble

Turin

ITALY

Herzegovina

MONTENEGRO

Genoa

LUCCA

Florence

Tuscany

Rumelia

Edirne

Constantinople

Toulouse
1814

1808

Cannes

PIOMBINO

Papal
States

Rome

Elba

NAPLES

Albania

Janina

ANATOLIA

Andorra

Corsica

Marseille

Ajaccio

Sardinia

Catalonia
1812–13 to France

Barcelona
1808

Naples

BENEVENTO

OTTOMAN
EMPIRE

Balearic
Islands

THE LÉGION D'HONNEUR, an
award for all ranks for notable
service to France, was created
by Napoleon in 1802.

Corfu
to Russia,
1807 to France,
1815 to Britain

Ionian Islands
to Russia,
1807 to France,
1809 to Britain

Morea

Athens

Palermo

Messina

SICILY

Cythera
to Russia,
1807 to France,
1809 to Britain

1800–07

Rhodes

Crete

Algiers

Tunis

Malta
to Britain

Mediterranean Sea

ALGIERS

Tunis

Cyrene

Cyrenaica

Aboukir
1799, 1801

Alexandria

EGYPT

**1** By the Treaty of Amiens (March 1802), Britain and France both agreed to return most conquests made since 1793. Peace, though, lasted barely a year.

**2** The Battle of Trafalgar, in which the French lost over half of their ships, ended Napoleon's plans to invade Britain. British commander Lord Nelson died of injuries sustained in the action.

**3** Borodino was a costly victory for Napoleon, who lost a quarter of his men. Only 30,000 troops of an original French force of 600,000 survived the Russian campaign.

**4** Napoleon planned to invade England from Boulogne in 1804, and assembled a fleet of 2,000 ships; he failed, however, to control the Channel.

**5** Naval bombardment forced Denmark to surrender its fleet to Britain in 1807, further weakening French opposition to British sea power.

**6** Napoleonic armies lived off the land in invaded countries, a strategy that brought disaster in the severe Russian winter of 1812–13. In contrast, British success in the Peninsular War was based on sustaining strong defensive positions with supplies from home.

0        600 km
0        400 mi

See also 77 (revolutionary Europe); 80 (mid-19th-century Europe); 90 (Industrial Revolution)

The early 19th century saw Europe continue to open new markets and exploit new sources of raw materials worldwide. Another aspect of European expansion – colonialism – led many countries to expend considerable resources on the conquest and administration of new territories. Europeanization would influence every other culture in the world in some measure. Some, as in India, were long established and highly sophisticated; others, as in Africa, were at critical stages in their evolution. Many native cultures in North America, Australia and New Zealand would face the threat of displacement or extermination.

Both the United States of America and imperial Russia expanded their continental empires. The United States purchased Louisiana from France in 1803 and expeditions pioneered routes to the Pacific in 1805–12 (▷ 84). Russia and Britain also promoted their North American interests, in Alaska and Vancouver respectively. American commerce grew after the revolution, first with China and then with Europe. Disruption to this trade, by Barbary pirates and the British blockade of Napoleonic Europe, met with a military response. American forces attacked Tripolitania in 1804 and British positions around Lakes Erie and Ontario in 1812.

The Ottomans still claimed authority over Egypt, Tripolitania, Tunis and Algiers, though all were now virtually independent. European penetration of Africa was mainly confined to the voracious demands of the slave trade. Portuguese traders at the mouth of the Congo and the Zambezi made great profits from slavery. British involvement in the trade was also intense until its abolition in 1807, by which time opponents of slavery had founded the state of Sierra Leone as a home for freed slaves.

Africa was in a state of turmoil that was to worsen in the course of the 19th century. In west Africa, the Asante and Fulani empires were dominant; the Omani were rebuilding their trading empire on the east coast; and central African states were jostling for power. Further south, the Lozi and Kazembe empires controlled east–west trade along the Zambezi. Madagascar, gradually being absorbed by Merina, supplied slaves (as did Angola) to Brazil and the United States. Dutch settlers at the Cape were joined by the English (1795), who established a naval base at Simonstown in 1806. Before long they would

**1792** France becomes a republic; French Revolutionary Wars begin

**1792** The first white settlers land at Bay of Islands, New Zealand

**1791** Slave revolt led by Toussaint L'Ouverture on Haiti (St Domingue)

**1789** French revolution; the *ancien régime* is overthrown

**1798** Failed nationalist rebellion in Ireland led by Wolfe Tone

**1798** Napoleon Bonaparte occupies Egypt

**1805** Napoleon defeats Austro-Russian armies at Austerlitz

**1803** Louisiana Purchase; USA buys extensive territories from France

The Americas
Europe
Middle East
Africa
Asia and Australasia

TIMELINE

1790
1800

**1787** First freed slaves settle in Sierra Leone; becomes a colony 1808

**1788** Sydney, Australia, is founded as a British convict settlement

**1793** A British trade delegation to China is rebuffed by the Manchu

**1795** First British settlers land at the Cape of Good Hope; Cape Colony under British control from 1806

**1804** Napoleon proclaims himself emperor of France

**1804** Usman dan Fodio begins *jihad* in Hausaland (northern Nigeria), which results in large Islamic state

*Greenland*

*Iceland (Denmark)*

UNITED KINGDOM

DENMARK-NORWAY
SWEDEN

PRUSSIA
GRAND DUCHY OF WARSAW

FRANCE
R.
AUSTRIA
ITALY
NAPLES

HELVETIA

PORTUGAL
SPAIN

S.

OTTOMAN EMPIRE
SICILY

MOROCCO
ALGIERS
Tunis
Tripoli
Cyrenaica

Egypt

*camel nomads*

Senegal

KAARTA
Mossi states

Hausa states
ASANTE
OYO
FULANI EMPIRE
BENIN
BUNYORO
NKORE
RWANDA
BURUNDI
KAZEMBE
LOZI

uguese Guinea
Sierra Leone

CONGO
Angola

*Khoisan gatherers*
*San hunter-gatherers*
Cape Colony
Dutch settlements
XHOSA
ZULU
Delagoa Bay

Portuguese East Africa
EXPANSIONIST KINGDOM OF MERINA

ETHIOPIA
SOMALIA
BUGANDA
ZANZIBAR

*Arab nomads*
NEJD
YEMEN
OMAN

*Omani trading empire*

RUSSIAN EMPIRE

central Asian khanates

PERSIA
AFGHAN-ISTAN

*Indian Princely states*

India

Goa

KANDY
Ceylon

BURMA
NEPAL
BHUTAN
ARAKAN
SIAM
ANNAM
LAOS
CAMBODIA
COCHIN CHINA

MANCHU EMPIRE

*Ainu hunter-gatherers*

KOREA
JAPAN

Taiwan

*Philippine Islands*

ACEH
Malay states
Sumatra
Borneo
Celebes
Java
Timor

*Dutch East Indies*

New Guinea
*Papuan farmers*

*Melanesians*
Solomon Islands
New Hebrides
New Caledonia
Fiji Islands

*Micronesians*
Marshall Islands
Gilbert Islands
Ellice Islands

*USS Empress of China 1784*

*Australian Aboriginal hunter-gatherers*
New South Wales
Van Diemen's Land

*Polynesians*
Bay of Islands
*Maori chiefdoms*

**Legend:**

hunter-gatherers
nomadic pastoralists
simple farming societies
complex farming societies/chiefdoms
state societies
uninhabited

empires
British
Dutch
French
Portuguese
Russian
Spanish
other

Napoleonic and dependent states
important route
R.  Confederation of the Rhine
S.  Sardinia

---

**1810** Father Miguel Hidalgo leads Mexican Revolution; defeated and executed in 1811

**1808** Peninsular War starts (Spanish, Portuguese, British against French)

**1807** Napoleon's defeat of Russians at Friedland is followed by Peace of Tilsit

**1807** Britain declares the slave trade illegal

1810

**1806** Napoleon's Berlin Decrees deny British right to trade with Europe

**1806** Sayyid Said reasserts Omani power in east Africa

**1812** Anglo–American War; ends in stalemate in 1814

**1812** Napoleon invades Russia; occupies Moscow but fails to defeat the Russians decisively

---

threaten the survival of the San and Xhosa peoples.

China's Manchu empire was still expanding. Chinese colonists settled in Xinjiang; Manchu soldiers clashed in Tibet with invading Gurkhas from Nepal; Burma and Annam accepted Manchu overlordship. Above all, China sought a sustained period of peace in order to restructure its agriculture to feed a population that had grown from 160 million in 1700 to around 300 million by 1812 (▷ 94).

In the Americas, Spanish imperial power began to collapse with insurrection in Mexico (1810), Paraguay (1811) and Venezuela (1810–12). Toussaint L'Overture's slave revolt (1791) won independence for Haiti, but slavery persisted elsewhere in the Caribbean until the late 19th century.

In France, Napoleon Bonaparte assumed power, initially as first consul (1799), and then as emperor (1804). He subjugated Austria and Prussia in succession and expanded into Poland, while his blockade of British trade (the Continental System) guaranteed British hostility from 1803 onward (▷ 78). When Spain and Portugal flouted the system, Napoleon invaded the Iberian peninsula. The Portuguese court fled to Brazil under British naval protection. A British army, advancing through Portugal, pushed back French forces over the next six years. When Czar Alexander I also defied Napoleon, he invaded Russia (1812). Despite initial victory, harsh conditions forced his withdrawal. This encouraged European monarchs to unite and overthrow Napoleon ■

The decades after 1815 saw the emergence of nationalism in the aftermath of Napoleon's imperial rule. Liberals and democrats demanded nation-states that embraced a common racial and linguistic identity and embodied constitutionally guaranteed rights for their citizens. Only a few nation-states were actually created in the early 19th century: Belgium, the Netherlands, Switzerland and Greece. More often, the monarchies restored after the fall of Napoleon (Prussia, Austria and Russia) stifled the nascent democracies. The strongest states to emerge – Italy and the German second empire – did so not through popular nationalist uprisings, but by growing around dynamic existing monarchies (Sardinia–Piedmont and Prussia respectively).

The Congress of Vienna (1814–15), convened at Napoleon's defeat, was intended to create a balance of power. Under the leadership of the conservative Austrian foreign minister Clemens Metternich, the Congress restored hereditary monarchies, created new enlarged kingdoms by unifying Norway with Sweden and Belgium with Holland, and established the "concert of Europe": congresses to deal with threats to political stability. A few concessions were made to nationalism: the Turkish sultan granted a measure of self-government to Serbia (1817) and to Moldavia and Wallachia (1829). However, when revolutions broke out in Naples, Spain and Portugal, the congresses at Troppau, Laibach and Verona authorized intervention. France sent troops to help conservatives suppress a liberal regime in Spain in 1823.

The Greek revolt against Ottoman rule broke out in 1821. The Greeks won control of the Peloponnese (Morea) by early 1822 when they declared Greece a sovereign state, but Turkish forces, bolstered by Egyptian troops, reinvaded in 1825. The conservative nature of the Greek rebellion, combined with strategic machinations against the crumbling Ottoman empire, led the European powers to approve

- borders, 1815
- Austrian empire, 1815
- France, 1815
- Ottoman empire, 1815
- Prussia, 1815
- Russian empire, 1815
- United Kingdom & Hanover, 1815
- German Confederation, 1815
- French territorial gain by 1860
- Prussian territorial gain by 1866
- Belgium, 1830
- Greece, 1830
- Italy, 1861
- German second empire, 1871
- "Concert of Europe" congress
- nationalist revolt or unrest, 1815-49
- revolt or unrest in the United Kingdom, with movement involved
- route of Garibaldi, 1860

an autonomous Greek state. A British, French and Russian naval force destroyed the Turkish–Egyptian fleet at Navarino, and the Ottomans conceded Greek independence in 1832.

Revolutions in Modena, Parma, the Papal States, Poland and some areas of Germany broke out in 1830–31, but were all suppressed. The reactionary regime of Bourbon Charles X in France was ended by the July Revolution of 1830, though this lead not to a new republic but to the accession of the "citizen-king" Louis-Philippe. In the same year, Belgium began its struggle for independence from the Dutch.

The Congress of Vienna had replaced Napoleon's German state with an alliance of 39 states

headed by Austria and Prussia, known as the German Confederation. Prussia gradually gained ascendancy, partly by forming the *Zollverein* free trade zone from 1819–44, isolating protectionist Austria.

The most serious challenge to Metternich came in 1848, the "Year of Revolutions". The catalyst was the fall of Louis-Philippe's regime to republicans in February. Unrest spread to Hungary, Croatia, and the Czech lands, where liberal governments were installed and democratic constitutions were drafted. Metternich was forced to resign and flee abroad. Republics were proclaimed throughout Italy and a

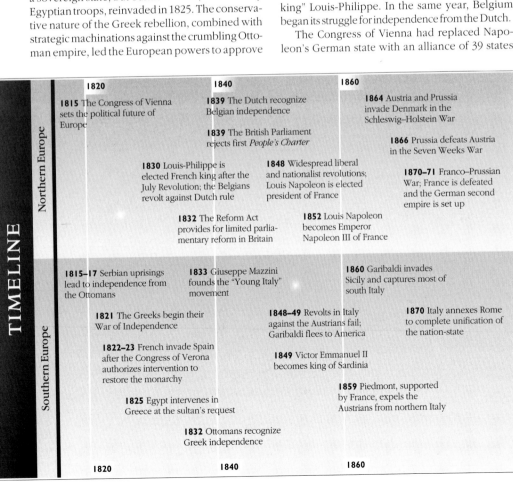

## TIMELINE

### Northern Europe

| 1820 | 1840 | 1860 |
|---|---|---|
| **1815** The Congress of Vienna sets the political future of Europe | **1839** The Dutch recognize Belgian independence | **1864** Austria and Prussia invade Denmark in the Schleswig–Holstein War |
| | **1839** The British Parliament rejects first *People's Charter* | **1866** Prussia defeats Austria in the Seven Weeks War |
| **1830** Louis-Philippe is elected French king after the July Revolution; the Belgians revolt against Dutch rule | **1848** Widespread liberal and nationalist revolutions; Louis Napoleon is elected president of France | **1870–71** Franco–Prussian War; France is defeated and the German second empire is set up |
| **1832** The Reform Act provides for limited parliamentary reform in Britain | **1852** Louis Napoleon becomes Emperor Napoleon III of France | |

### Southern Europe

| 1820 | 1840 | 1860 |
|---|---|---|
| **1815–17** Serbian uprisings lead to independence from the Ottomans | **1833** Giuseppe Mazzini founds the "Young Italy" movement | **1860** Garibaldi invades Sicily and captures most of south Italy |
| **1821** The Greeks begin their War of Independence | **1848–49** Revolts in Italy against the Austrians fail; Garibaldi flees to America | **1870** Italy annexes Rome to complete unification of the nation-state |
| **1822–23** French invade Spain after the Congress of Verona authorizes intervention to restore the monarchy | **1849** Victor Emmanuel II becomes king of Sardinia | |
| **1825** Egypt intervenes in Greece at the sultan's request | **1859** Piedmont, supported by France, expels the Austrians from northern Italy | |
| **1832** Ottomans recognize Greek independence | | |

| 1820 | 1840 | 1860 |

**1** The reunification of the northern and southern Netherlands in 1815 under the Protestant Dutch monarchy caused resentment in Catholic Belgium.

**2** Ferdinand VII, king of Spain (r.1808–33) brutally suppressed liberal opposition after his return from exile in 1814. In 1820, the army he had assembled to reassert his rule in Latin America rose against him.

**3** An early challenge to the rule of Louis-Philippe occurred in Lyon in 1831, when 600 protestors were killed in rioting.

**4** A Roman republic was established by radicals (including Garibaldi) in 1848-49, but was ended when French troops restored Pope Pius IX to power

**5** The head of the Bonaparte dynasty, Louis Napoleon, was elected French president in 1848. He became emperor Napoleon III after a coup (1851), but was exiled after defeat by Prussia in 1871.

LORD BYRON, the British Romantic poet, was inspired by the cause of Greek independence and died at Missolonghi in 1824.

parliamentary assembly met in Frankfurt with the aim of uniting Germany. Yet internal divisions prevailed, and by late 1849 the Habsburgs regained control in Austria, Italy and Hungary (the latter with Russian help). The German assembly collapsed under pressure from Prussia, which consolidated its power by means of swift victories over Denmark, Austria and France.

In Italy, revolutionary movements from 1820 onward, such as the Carbonari, had failed to expel the Austrians or unite the country. In mid-century an unlikely champion of the unification movement (*Risorgimento* or "resurrection") arose: the rich industrial state of Sardinia–Piedmont. The Piedmontese king Victor Emmanuel II and his prime minister Camillo di Cavour instituted liberal domestic reforms and secured the help of Napoleon III's France to drive the Austrians from northern Italy in 1859. The liberal constitutional monarchy sought by Piedmont was threatened when the revolutionary Giuseppe Garibaldi and his "redshirts" took Sicily and overran much of the southern mainland. Yet Garibaldi passed his conquests to Victor Emmanuel II, who effectively became king of a united Italy.

Britain was less affected by nationalist agitation, though the Chartists – supporters of a "People's Charter" – sought universal manhood suffrage after limited parliamentary reform was conceded in 1832. Irish nationalism was given urgency by the famine of 1845–47, and the Irish Republican Brotherhood (Fenians), precursor of the movement that won Irish independence in 1921, was set up in 1858.

See also 78 (Napoleonic Europe);
90 (Industrial Revolution)

apoleon's invasion of the Iberian peninsula in 1808–09 was the catalyst to the independence movements in the American colonies of Spain and Portugal. In the Spanish territories, wars of liberation broke out when Napoleon's brother Joseph Bonaparte took the Spanish throne. Brazil played host to Portugal's prince regent, later JoãoVI, who fled there in 1807 after the French occupied Portugal. When he returned home in 1822, his son Pedro became emperor of an independent Brazil. The new state was recognized by Portugal in 1825.

Mexico's war of independence, led by the priest Miguel Hidalgo, began in 1810. Hidalgo was executed, but his conservative successor Agustín Iturbide united Mexican society and in 1822–23 formed the Mexican empire with himself as emperor. At the same time, the Spanish colonies in Central America proclaimed a Confederation of the United Provinces, which lasted until 1838, when its constituent parts became individual sovereign states.

The principal figure of South American independence, Simón Bolívar (the "Liberator"), began his fight to free his native Venezuela and adjoining territories from Spanish rule in 1811. Bolívar's victory at Boyacá in 1819 heralded the proclamation of the Republic of Gran Colombia, and his defeat of the royalists at Carabobo in 1821 led to the fall of Caracas and to Venezuelan independence. In Argentina, revolutionary forces were led by José de San Martín, a veteran of the Peninsular War. San Martín trained an army and led it across the Andes in 1817 to take Lima in 1821. He proclaimed Peru's independence, then gave up control to Bolívar who established a revolutionary government at Lima. With the final battle of the wars of liberation at Ayacucho in 1824, all Spanish possessions in the Americas were independent, except Cuba and Puerto Rico.

The new states not only inherited the frontiers of the former Spanish and Portuguese administrative regions; their social divisions also remained intact. There was no tradition of pluralistic government, and color was still decisive. Spanish-born whites or *peninsulares* (and *reinóis*, the Portuguese equivalent in Brazil) were dominant. The majority of the people (*mestizos* or Indian–Europeans) had limited

| | Portuguese colony c.1800 |
| --- | --- |
| | Spanish colony c.1800 |
| | Republic of Gran Colombia, 1819–30 |
| | united with Mexico 1821–23, independent as United Provinces of Central America 1823–38 |
| | Confederation of Peru & Bolivia 1836–39 |
| **1838** | date of independence as a nation-state |
| | territory gained by former Spanish colony since independence, with date |
| | territory gained by the United States from Mexico, with date |
| | campaign by Simón Bolívar 1819–24 |
| | campaign by José de San Martín 1817–22 |
| | campaign by United States forces, 1846–48 |
| | battle fought by José de San Martín |
| | battle fought by Bolívar or de Sucre |
| | battle during the Mexican–American War, 1846–48 |
| | battle during the Paraguayan War (War of the Triple Alliance), 1864–70 |
| | battle during the War of the Pacific 1879–83 |
| | border c.1840 |
| | other border |
| | railroad within Latin America by 1914 |
| *oil* | trade commodity |
| | movement of peoples |

SIMON BOLIVAR was a remarkable military leader, and is the only individual to have a state named for him today.

*Galapagos Islands 1832 to Ecuador*

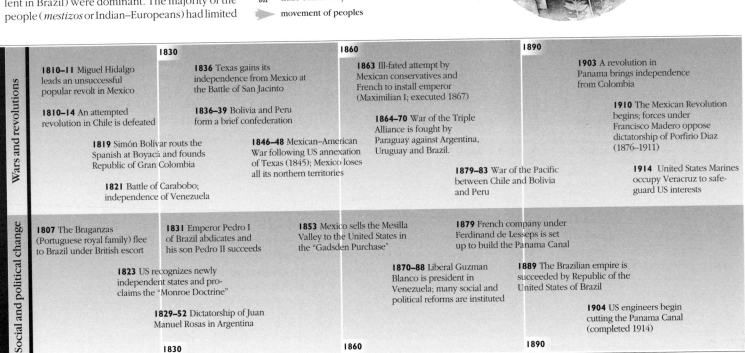

TIMELINE

**Wars and revolutions**

**1810–11** Miguel Hidalgo leads an unsuccessful popular revolt in Mexico

**1810–14** An attempted revolution in Chile is defeated

**1819** Simón Bolívar routs the Spanish at Boyacá and founds Republic of Gran Colombia

**1821** Battle of Carabobo; independence of Venezuela

**1836** Texas gains its independence from Mexico at the Battle of San Jacinto

**1836–39** Bolivia and Peru form a brief confederation

**1846–48** Mexican–American War following US annexation of Texas (1845); Mexico loses all its northern territories

**1863** Ill-fated attempt by Mexican conservatives and French to install emperor (Maximilian I; executed 1867)

**1864–70** War of the Triple Alliance is fought by Paraguay against Argentina, Uruguay and Brazil.

**1879–83** War of the Pacific between Chile and Bolivia and Peru

**1903** A revolution in Panama brings independence from Colombia

**1910** The Mexican Revolution begins; forces under Francisco Madero oppose dictatorship of Porfirio Diaz (1876–1911)

**1914** United States Marines occupy Veracruz to safeguard US interests

**Social and political change**

**1807** The Braganzas (Portuguese royal family) flee to Brazil under British escort

**1823** US recognizes newly independent states and proclaims the "Monroe Doctrine"

**1829–52** Dictatorship of Juan Manuel Rosas in Argentina

**1831** Emperor Pedro I of Brazil abdicates and his son Pedro II succeeds

**1853** Mexico sells the Mesilla Valley to the United States in the "Gadsden Purchase"

**1870–88** Liberal Guzman Blanco is president in Venezuela; many social and political reforms are instituted

**1879** French company under Ferdinand de Lesseps is set up to build the Panama Canal

**1889** The Brazilian empire is succeeded by Republic of the United States of Brazil

**1904** US engineers begin cutting the Panama Canal (completed 1914)

power, while the *mulattoes* (African–Europeans), *zambos* (Indian–Africans), blacks and Indians all suffered discrimination. Sectional interests, such as the military, the church, industrialists, bankers and landlords were often in conflict, and power was frequently seized by *caudillos*, dictators who ruled through patronage and private armies.

The *caudillo* José Francia helped lead Paraguay's struggle for independence and was "el supremo" 1814–40. Bernardo O'Higgins was prominent in Chile's revolution and became "supreme director" 1817–23. The Mexican Antonio de Santa Anna, after a period as an elected president (1833–36), intermittently took dictatorial powers. During his rule

Mexico fought, largely unsuccessfully, against the United States, and ceded large tracts of land by 1850.

Intervention by European powers in Latin American affairs was effectively preempted by the Monroe doctrine of 1823, which signaled US hostility toward any attempt to colonize the region. Most territorial changes that occurred did so as a result of wars between the new sovereign states. Major conflicts of the period were the War of the Pacific, in which Chile defeated Peru and Bolivia, and the War of the Triple Alliance), involving Paraguay, Brazil, Argentina and Uruguay. The 1910–11 Mexican revolution led to chaos, mass slaughter and eventual US intervention, as US president Wilson supported General Huerta, who exterminated the nationalist Zapata rebels while Pancho Villa's bandits ran riot in the north. Wilson sent warships to Tampico and troops to Veracruz in 1914.

Economic change came swiftly to Latin America. Foreign capital funded railroad and harbor construction. The Panama Canal was completed by US engineers in 1914 after an earlier French venture had failed. British firms exploited the natural phosphates and nitrates of Peru and northern Chile, for use in fertilizers and explosives. US investment turned coffee exports into a vital element in Brazil's economy. In Argentina, revenue from wool, leather and beef exports brought a sharp rise in the standard of living. Meat exports grew after refrigerated sea transport was introduced in the 1880s; but a decline in world trade in the 1890s ended the boom years. Immigrants were among the region's greatest assets. Initially they entered Chile and Argentina (which saw a huge influx of Italian immigrants from the 1850s), but Brazil became the preferred destination after slavery was abolished there in 1888. Over one million Europeans arrived in Brazil by 1898. They were favored over the original inhabitants for educational and work opportunities. Chinese and Japanese laborers were also imported in large numbers to work on the railroads and in the mines.

**1** Peruvian *guano* (seabird droppings used as fertilizer) was a major source of foreign revenue after independence, but deposits were exhausted in 20 years.

**2** At the Alamo in 1836, during the Texan War of Independence from Mexico, 180 defenders resisted Mexican forces but were eventually overcome.

**3** The War of the Triple Alliance was the bloodiest conflict in Latin American history. Paraguay lost over 60 percent (300,000) of its population.

**4** Costa Rica was the first Central American republic to export coffee beans. The United Fruit Company developed the country, building its railroad and port facilities. The first elections were held there in 1885.

**5** Manaus, in the Amazon basin, saw great prosperity in the rubber boom of 1890-1920. The town's lavishly appointed opera house was built in 1896.

**6** Mechanization (railroads, steam excavators) and medical provision against malaria were crucial in the success of the US Panama Canal project (1904-14).

See also 62 (the Spanish–American empire); 84 (expansion of the United States)

*Bermuda Islands to Britain*

ATLANTIC OCEAN

HAITI to France, **1804**
*sugar*
Santo Domingo
Puerto Rico 1898 to US
Guadeloupe to France
Martinique to France
Dominica to Britain
Barbados to Britain
Port-au-Prince
DOMINICAN REPUBLIC 1822–44 to Haiti, **1844**
*coffee*
Jamaica to Britain

*Caribbean Sea*

Margarita
Trinidad to Britain
British Guiana (Berbice, Demerara, Essequibo) to the Netherlands, 1814 to Britain
Dutch Guiana to the Netherlands
French Guiana to France

over 3 million immigrants from southern Europe from the mid 1830s

Carabobo 1821
Caracas
Ciudad Bolívar (Angostura)
San Carlos
*coffee*
1904 from Venezuela
Fortaleza (Ceará)
Belém
*cocoa*
*sugar*
Recife (Pernambuco)

Panama Canal Zone 1903 to United States
Panama City
**6**
*coffee*
VENEZUELA 1821 to Colombia, **1830**
*sheep*
1905 from Venezuela
*cattle*
*Guiana Highlands*
*timber*
*cotton*

Boyacá 1819
Bogotá
*cattle*
COLOMBIA **1819**
*cattle*
1904-05 from Colombia
*Negro*
Manaus
*rubber*
**5**
*Amazon*
*rubber*
*Xingu*
*rubber*
*coffee*

Bombona 1822
Pichincha 1822
Quito
*cattle*
1880 from Colombia
*Japurá*
*Putumayo*
*Amazon Basin*
BRAZIL **1822**
*coffee*
*tobacco*
Salvador (Bahia)

*bananas*
ECUADOR 1822 to Colombia, **1830**
Guayaquil
1880 from Peru
*Purus*
*Madeira*
*rubber*
*Tapajós*
*rubber*
*Tocantins*
*Brazilian Highlands*

*sugar*
*copper*
*silver*
*timber*
1903 from Bolivia
1867 from Peru
*rubber*
*Matto Grosso Plateau*
*coffee*

Junín 1824
1880
PERU **1821**
*rubber*
*São Francisco*
*coffee*
Rio de Janeiro

Callao 1880
Lima
Ayacucho 1824
BOLIVIA **1825**
Curupayty 1866
Corumbá
*cattle*
Jundiaí
São Paulo
Santos

Chorrillos 1881
Pisco 1824
La Paz
*copper, silver, tin*
Potosí
1880 to Bolivia
1870 from Paraguay
*coffee*

*nitrates*
Tacna 1880
Arica
Iquique 1879
**1**
PARAGUAY **1811**
Asunción
1874 from Paraguay
*cattle*

1883 from Peru
Paso de Patria 1866
Riachuelo 1865
1874 from Paraguay
*cattle*
Porto Alegre

Antofagasta 1879
1884 from Bolivia
*timber*
Pelotas

*copper, manganese, silver, lead*
ARGENTINA **1816**
*cattle*
**3**
Rio Grande

La Serena
Rosario
URUGUAY **1828**
Montevideo

Chacabuco 1817
San Luis
Campana
*cattle, cereals, sheep*
Buenos Aires

Valparaíso
Santiago
Maipo River 1818
Bahía Blanca
Mar del Plata

CHILE **1818**
Punta Alta
*sheep*

PACIFIC OCEAN

Valdivia
*PATAGONIA*
1902 to Chile
1881 to Argentina

over 4.5 million immigrants from southern Europe from the mid 1850s

Falkland Islands (Malvinas) 1820 to Argentina, 1833 to Britain

*ANDES*

0    1200 km
0    800 mi

The Congress of Vienna (1814–15) dismembered Napoleon's empire and transformed the map of Europe (▷ 78). The German Confederation was formed, an alliance of states dominated by Austria and Prussia. Wholly new nations also arose. Greece wrested sovereignty from the Ottoman empire from 1821–28; Belgium rebelled against Dutch rule (1830) and won international recognition of its independence in 1839. Yet the restoration of autocratic monarchies by the Congress in the name of stability bred resentment, which erupted in a series of revolutions that swept the continent in 1848 (▷ 80). Only Britain and Russia stayed unaffected. Elsewhere, liberals and nationalists exploited economic hardship to foment revolts demanding representative forms of government. Internal divisions caused the revolutions to fail and conservative forces soon regained power.

In contrast, revolutions succeeded in toppling the Spanish and Portuguese empires in Central and South America. Brazil proclaimed an independent empire after King João VI returned to Portugal in 1822. The collapse of Spain during the Napoleonic Wars led to a succession of uprisings against Spanish rule in the Americas. Eleven independent states were formed by 1826 (▷ 81). The disparate nature of the region's cultures and the diversity of the revolutionaries' aspirations prevented the development of the envisaged Hispano–American state. Simón Bolívar's Gran Colombia (comprising modern Venezuela, Colombia, and Ecuador) fragmented in 1830, only eleven years after its formation.

Spain's fall benefited the United States, which gained the territories of East and West Florida in 1819–22. US foreign policy was outlined in the Monroe Doctrine of 1823, which stipulated separate spheres of interest for Europe and the Americas to forestall any renewal of European ambition in the region. The transcontinental expansion of the United States also accelerated during this period, with the annexation of Oregon in 1844, and Texas in 1845 (▷ 84). War with Mexico (1846–48) led to the United States gaining California, where gold deposits were discovered soon after.

In Russia, Czar Alexander I and his successor Nicholas I maintained an implacable opposition to reform at home and abroad. An insurrection in Poland against Russian rule was suppressed (1830–31), while Russian troops were also sent to help Austria quell a Hungarian nationalist uprising in 1848–49. Russian forces

*Hawaiian Islands*

*Marquesas Islands (France)*

*Tuamotu Archipelago (France)*

*Pitcairn Island (Britain)*

Russian America

Arctic marine mammal hunters

sub-Arctic forest hunter–gatherers

west coast foraging, hunting and fishing peoples

plateau fishers and hunter–gatherers

Rupert's Land

Newfoundland

Canada

Nova Scotia
New Brunswick

UNITED STATES

MEXICO

*Bahamas*

British Honduras

Cuba

Jamaica

HAITI

*Puerto Rico*

DOMINICAN REPUBLIC

GUATEMALA
EL SALVADOR
HONDURAS
NICARAGUA

COSTA RICA

VENEZUELA

British Guiana
Dutch Guiana
French Guiana

COLOMBIA

*Galapagos Islands*

ECUADOR

BRAZIL

PERU

BOLIVIA

PARAGUAY

ARGENTINA

CHILE

URUGUAY

pampas hunter–gatherers

Falkland Islands (Britain)

shellfish gatherers and marine mammal hunters

## TIMELINE

**1823** Monroe Doctrine warns against further European expansion in the Americas

**1822** Brazil declares independence from Portugal

**1818** Border between Canada and United States is defined as 49th Parallel

**1830–31** Polish revolt against Russian rule

**1815** Defeat of Napoleon by British and Prussian forces at Waterloo

**1828** Greeks win War of Independence (Ottomans recognize Greece 1832)

**1839–42** Britain fights the First Afghan War to stop the southern spread of Russian influence

The Americas
Europe
Middle East
Africa
Asia and Australasia

1820

1830

**1816–20** Argentina declares its independence from Spain; war of liberation lasts for four years

**1820** British settlers begin to arrive at the Cape in large numbers

**1833** Falkland Islands are occupied by Britain

**1837** Natal Republic is founded by Afrikaners

**1816** Shaka, king of the Zulu, begins to expand the Zulu empire

**1824–26** British fight two unsuccessful wars against the Asante of west Africa

**1833** The Ottoman empire recognizes the independence of Egypt

**1839** Belgian independence is internationally guaranteed

**1816** Britain begins to recruit Gurkha soldiers from Nepal

**1839–42** First Opium War is fought between Britain and China

*Greenland*

Danish
settlement

*Iceland*
(Denmark)

RUSSIAN EMPIRE

Ainu hunter-
gatherers

MANCHU EMPIRE

NORWAY-SWEDEN

UNITED
KINGDOM

D.
N.
B. P.
G.
PRUSSIA

FRANCE

AUSTRIAN
EMPIRE

ITALY

PORTUGAL

SPAIN

Papal
states

OTTOMAN EMPIRE

GREECE

KOREA

JAPAN

Central Asian
khanates

MOROCCO

Algeria

Tunis

Cyrenaica

PERSIA

AFGHAN-
ISTAN

KASHMIR

Tripoli

*Arab
nomads*

BALUCHISTAN

NEPAL

BHUTAN

Taiwan

*camel nomads*

EGYPT

BURMA

*Indian
princely*

KAARTA

MASINA

BORNU

OMAN

LAOS

Senegal

SEGU

Aden

Goa

Tenasserim

ANNAM

SIAM

Philippine
Islands

ambia

Portuguese
Guinea
Sierra
Leone

SOKOTO
CALIPHATE

IBADAN
EMPIRE

ASANTE

ETHIOPIA

CAMBODIA

COCHIN
CHINA

Marshall
Islands

LIBERIA

Ivory
Coast

Gold
Coast

BENIN

Ceylon

ACEH

Malay states

Celebes

Gilbert
Islands

CONGO

BUGANDA

Gabon

*Sumatra*

Singapore
(Britain)

Borneo

New Guinea

Solomon
Islands

ZANZIBAR

Dutch East Indies

*Papuan farmers*

Ellice
Islands

Angola

NDEBELE

LOZI

Portuguese
East Africa

*Madagascar*

*Java*

*Timor*

*Khoisan
herders*

*San hunter-
gatherers*

GAZA
EMPIRE

SWAZILAND
ZULULAND
Natal
(Cape Colony)
BASUTOLAND

Cape
Colony

New
Hebrides

Fiji Islands

New
Caledonia

*Australian Aboriginal
hunter-gatherers*

Western
Australia

South
Australia

New South Wales

Van Diemen's
Land

New
Zealand

hunter-gatherers
nomadic pastoralists
simple farming societies
complex farming societies/
chiefdoms
state societies
uninhabited

empires

British
Dutch
French
Portuguese
Russian
Spanish
other

German Confederation
B. Belgium
D. Denmark
G. German states
N. Netherlands
P. Prussia
S. Switzerland

**1848** Liberal and
nationalist revolutions
sweep Europe

**1846–48** United States is at
war with Mexico; much of
present-day southwestern
USA lost by Mexico

**1846** Slave trade
between west Africa and
Brazil at its height

1840

1850

**1840** Treaty of Waitangi
gives Britain sovereignty of
New Zealand

**1846** Britain annexes
Sind and the Punjab in
western India

**1841** Ibadan empire
expands in West Africa

also began to encroach upon
the central Asian khanates from
1839 onward (▷ 88).

In Africa, France began the conquest of Algeria
in 1830, but European expansion was otherwise still relatively limited. South
of the Sahara, new empires such as the Sokoto caliphate, Ibadan and Masina
dominated west Africa. Southern Africa experienced great instability as a result
of Zulu expansion (the *mfecane*). The Afrikaners of the Cape opposed British
rule and began their "Great Trek" north in 1835. The *voortrekkers* who settled
across the Vaal River came into conflict with the Ndebele, while those who
reached Natal clashed with the Zulu.

British imperial ambitions, frustrated in America, now focussed on Asia.
In 1839–42, the British defended their profitable drug trafficking in China in
the first of the "Opium Wars" (▷ 94). Its conclusion brought the opening of
five "treaty ports" to British trade and the colonization of Hong Kong. British
control of India was consolidated by the acquisition of Sind and the Punjab –
the latter providing access to central Asia via the northwest frontier (▷ 83). The
regions of Arakan and Tenasserim in Burma were also occupied. In Australia,
where most penal colonies had been closed by 1848, fresh waves of migrants
populated new settlements, such as Adelaide and Perth. Conflict with the
Maori in New Zealand resulted in 1840 in a treaty according to which the
Maori recognized Queen Victoria as their sovereign. However, the treaty left
many questions of land ownership and sale unresolved ■

Despite its territorial acquisitions toward the end of the 18th century, the British East India Company still saw its role in the subcontinent as primarily commercial. This was enshrined in the India Act passed by the British Parliament in 1784, which forbade further annexation. Nevertheless, British rule (*raj*) in India continued to grow, as successive governors-general felt obliged to occupy hostile territory or form protectorates to prevent disruption to trade. Thus, when Tipu Sultan of Mysore attacked Travancore in 1789, he saw half his dominions annexed by Lord Cornwallis (governor-general 1786–93) in the ensuing war. Warfare was resumed against the Marathas of central India in 1803.

The fear of an assault on India by Napoleon radically altered British policy. A far more aggressive approach was adopted, in which independent principalities such as Hyderabad were reduced to dependencies by the stationing of British troops there. After the French threat had passed, Company interest turned toward countering Burmese aggression in the east and guarding against Russian incursions from the north. Assam, Arakan, and Tenasserim were acquired from Burma in 1824–26. On the northwest frontier, the First Afghan War (1839–42) was begun against Dost Muhammed. In both this and a later conflict (1878–80), the British occupied Kabul but failed to dominate the country. An attack on Sind secured the Bolan Pass in 1843, while two bloody wars against the Sikhs brought control of the Punjab. Lord Dalhousie (governor-general 1848–56) now evolved the doctrine of "lapse" (when a Hindu prince had no natural heirs his lands passed to the Company) and, on the pretext of ineffective government, annexed Muslim Oudh in 1856.

The East India Company also instituted administrative reforms. These began with revision of land revenue collection (the principal source of public finance) and a reorganization of the judicial system along British lines. Despite a Parliamentary directive urging respect for the people's rights and customs, the Company often disregarded religious and cultural sensitivities – particularly under governor-general Lord Bentinck (1828–35) who tried to ban *suttee* (the immolation of Hindu widows), *thuggee* (ritual robbery and murder) and infanticide. Continuing

Christian conversion efforts, plans to extend roads and railroads and an insistence on English as the language of education and commerce all threatened the traditional ways of life of both Hindus and Muslims.

Opposition to British rule was not, however, anticipated among the Company's *sepoy* (native) armies. Three such armies had been raised in India; those based at Madras and Bombay were largely untroubled by questions of caste and religion. But the Bengal *sepoys* – high-caste Hindus and Shi'ite Muslims – were offended by a rumor that new rifle cartridges (which had to be bitten before use) were greased with pork and beef fat. This violated the dietary proscriptions of their religions. Thus began the most serious challenge to British rule in India.

The Indian mutiny (also known as the First War of Independence) arose in January 1857 among troops stationed at Meerut and rapidly spread through north central India. The army revolt acted as a catalyst to a number of other grievances, and the mutineers were supported by peasant uprisings and some isolated *jihads*. The capture of Delhi and the besieging of the cities of Kanpur and Lucknow were serious blows to British authority. However, the Bombay and Madras armies remained largely loyal, and there was no strategy for a national revolt.

Though brief, the mutiny changed the face of British India; suspicion was now widespread on both sides. The 1858 Government of India Act transferred sovereignty from the East India Company to the British monarch and ended the doctrine of lapse, but other reforms were never instituted. Theoretically, racial impartiality operated in recruitment to the Indian civil service; in practice few Indians were admitted. The insular community of Anglo-Indians shunned contact with the local population and became ever more prosperous, partly through investment in plantations in southeast Asia and Africa. Gurkha and Sikh troops from the northwest of India now formed the backbone of the army.

The British policy in frontier regions continued to be determined by fear of Russian expansion. This led to the Second Afghan War of 1878–80, which ended with the recognition that Afghanistan could not be incorporated within the Indian empire. Similarly, in 1903 the British under Colonel

Younghusband invaded Tibet. After a year's conflict Tibet agreed not to concede territory to a foreign power.

Excluded from the administration of their country, educated Indians turned increasingly toward nationalism. The Indian National Congress was founded in 1885 and Gopal Gokhale, its president in 1905, worked for peaceful constitutional progress towards responsible government. The All-India Muslim League, a similarly constitutional organization, was founded in 1906. The Morley–Minto constitutional reforms (1909) brought in a measure of representative government, but Indians were still

**Map legend:**

- territory under direct Maratha rule, 1785
- British territory, 1805
- British territorial gains by 1838
- British territorial gains by 1857
- British territorial gains by 1914
- British sphere of influence, 1914
- princely state or protectorate, 1914
- border of princely state or protectorate
- border, 1914
- ⊗ battle in the second Maratha War, 1803–05
- disruption to British administration during the Indian mutiny, 1857–59
- *Sepoy* army base remaining loyal to Britain, 1857
- ☼ center of rebellion
- naval station
- *coal* source of commodity
- British campaign
- railroad by 1914

AFGHANISTAN
Kandahar
Quetta
PERSIA
1893 to Britain
Bolan Pass
Baluchistan
1876 British protectorate

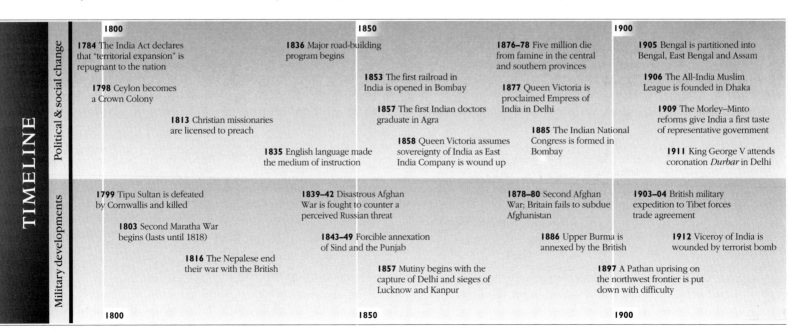

| | 1800 | 1850 | 1900 |
|---|---|---|---|
| **Political & social change** | **1784** The India Act declares that "territorial expansion" is repugnant to the nation | **1836** Major road-building program begins | **1876–78** Five million die from famine in the central and southern provinces | **1905** Bengal is partitioned into Bengal, East Bengal and Assam |
| | **1798** Ceylon becomes a Crown Colony | **1853** The first railroad in India is opened in Bombay | **1877** Queen Victoria is proclaimed Empress of India in Delhi | **1906** The All-India Muslim League is founded in Dhaka |
| | | **1857** The first Indian doctors graduate in Agra | | **1909** The Morley–Minto reforms give India a first taste of representative government |
| | **1813** Christian missionaries are licensed to preach | | **1885** The Indian National Congress is formed in Bombay | |
| | | **1858** Queen Victoria assumes sovereignty of India as East India Company is wound up | | **1911** King George V attends coronation *Durbar* in Delhi |
| | **1835** English language made the medium of instruction | | | |
| **Military developments** | **1799** Tipu Sultan is defeated by Cornwallis and killed | **1839–42** Disastrous Afghan War is fought to counter a perceived Russian threat | **1878–80** Second Afghan War; Britain fails to subdue Afghanistan | **1903–04** British military expedition to Tibet forces trade agreement |
| | **1803** Second Maratha War begins (lasts until 1818) | **1843–49** Forcible annexation of Sind and the Punjab | **1886** Upper Burma is annexed by the British | **1912** Viceroy of India is wounded by terrorist bomb |
| | **1816** The Nepalese end their war with the British | **1857** Mutiny begins with the capture of Delhi and sieges of Lucknow and Kanpur | **1897** A Pathan uprising on the northwest frontier is put down with difficulty | |

**1** Tipu Sultan of Mysore, the East India Company's greatest adversary in south India from the early 1780s, tried to ally himself with the French and was killed at the siege of Seringapatam in 1799.

**2** Gurkha warriors from the hill tribes of Nepal fought fiercely against the British from 1814–16. From 1860 to the present day, Gurkhas have been recruited to form an elite infantry unit of the British Army.

**3** The First Afghan War ended with a humiliating retreat from Kabul to Jalalabad (1842); only 121 men of the entire 20,000-strong British force survived.

**4** Atrocities were committed by both sides during the mutiny; British reprisals included executing mutineers by strapping them to the muzzles of artillery pieces.

**5** Tea has been cultivated as a major commercial crop since the mid-19th century, particularly in the fertile, rainy upper Brahmaputra valley in Assam.

**6** The northwest frontier of India proved the most troublesome to defend for the British. In 1897, 35,000 troops were needed to quell a rising by Pathan tribes.

**7** The British briefly invaded Tibet in 1903–04, to counter Russian influence there by imposing a trading agreement on the Dalai Lama.

**8** Bombay was the site of the Gateway to India, an arch erected in Mughal style in 1911.

RUSSIAN EMPIRE

Kashgar
Yarkand
Khotan
Kabul
Khyber Pass
1842
Jalalabad
Peshawar
Rawalpindi
Jammu
Jullundur
Amritsar
Lahore
Firozpur
Ambala

Kashmir
1846 British protectorate

*silk*
*wheat*

Northwest Frontier Province

**6**

**3**

1878 to Britain

*cotton*

Punjab
1846/49 to Britain

*sugar*
*cotton*
*tobacco*

Bikaner
Saharanpur
Meerut
Delhi
1803
Bareilly
Sitapur
Farrukhabad
1804
Mainpura
Lucknow 1857–58
Kanpur
Agra
Laswari 1803
Kalpi
Azamgarh
Fatehpur
Allahabad
Jhansi
Benares (Varanasi)
Danupur
Patna

Bibi
Khairpur
*wheat*
Thar Desert
Jaipur
Ajmer
Nasirabad
Jodhpur
Gwalior
*barley*
*wheat*
*barley*
Oudh
1856 to Britain
*rice*
*sugar*
*maize*
*silk*
Bundelkhand

Sind
1843 to Britain
Hyderabad
*cotton*
Rajputana
1818 British protectorate
Erinpura
Udaipur
Nimach
*wheat*

Rann of Kutch
*cotton*
Ahmadabad
*tobacco*
Baroda
Bhopal
Jabalpur
Indore
Mhow
Nagpur
Burhanpur
*wheat*
*rice*

Gujarat
Surat
Diu to Portugal
Daman to Portugal
Bombay
**8**
Poone
*cotton*
*rice*
*wheat*
*tobacco*
Aurangabad
Argaon 1803
Amravati
*linseed*
Assaye 1803
DECCAN
*cotton*
Godavari

Bay of Bengal

Orissa
Cuttack

Northern Circars
Bastar

Hyderabad
Hyderabad
Bijapur
*cotton*
Krishna
Yanam to France
*cotton*

Goa
Goa to Portugal
*tobacco*
*coffee*
*cotton*
Mysore
1831 British protectorate
*cotton*
Madras
Madras
*rice*
Vellore
Sepoy mutiny, 1806
Bangalore
Seringapatam 1799
Mysore
**1**
*groundnuts*
Pondicherry to France
Karikal to France
Kaveri
Tellicherry
Mahé to France
*rice*
*tea*
Cochin
*coconuts*
Laccadive Islands
Madurai
Jaffna
Mannar
Trincomalee
*rice*
Anjengo
Trivandrum
Travancore
*tobacco*
*cotton*
Tuticorin
Ceylon
1798 to Britain
1815–1818
Kandy
*coconuts*
Colombo
*rice* *tea*

TIBET
Lhasa
1903–04
**7**
Sikkim
1817 British protectorate
Bhutan
Darjeeling
Kathmandu
Gurkha War 1814–16
**2**
NEPAL
HIMALAYAS
Indus
Chenab
Sutlej
Yamuna
Ganges
Narmada
Mahanadi

Northeast Frontier Agency
1913/14 to Britain
Assam
from 1824 to Britain
*tea*
**5**
Cachar
1868–82 British protectorate
Manipur
1813 to Burma,
1886 British protectorate

*tea*
*tobacco*
*jute*
*rice*
*sugar*
*oil seed*
*sugar*
Baharampur
1857
Chandannagar to France
Dum-Dum
Calcutta
*jute*
Bengal
Dhaka
Chittagong
*rice*
Tripura
Upper Burma
1886 to Britain
Mandalay
Arakan
1826 to Britain
Burma
Chinese tributary until 1886
Lower Burma
created 1862 incorporating Arakan, Pegu and Tenasserim
Pegu
1852 to Britain
Rangoon
Tenasserim
1826 to Britain

Andaman Islands
1857 to Britain

Nicobar Islands
1869 to Britain

MEMBERS of the British Raj (rule) saw themselves as dispensing even-handed justice and the benefits of European civilization to grateful natives.

0    400 km
0    300 mi

See also 61 (Mughal India);
103 (Indian nationalism before 1947)

Two decisions made by the Congress of the embryonic United States of America set up the decisive conflict between white settlers and native Americans. In 1787 the indigenous peoples were promised that their lands and property could only be ceded with their consent. In 1791, however, George Washington authorized expansion westward along the Ohio. Initially the growth of the United States was limited by Spain's (from 1800, France's) possession of lands beyond the Mississippi. Even at this stage, however, trade links existed between the thirteen eastern states of the Union and the Pacific. By 1795, the pattern of territorial gains by the whites and displacement of native Americans to the west was set, a process hastened by Thomas Jefferson's purchase of Louisiana from France in 1803, when the territory of the United States was doubled.

In the ensuing decades further territories were gained by the United States, through purchase or conflict: Florida, Texas, Oregon, the Mexican cession and the Gadsden Purchase. Some 400,000 native people were confronted by the westward thrust of settler culture across the Great Plains.

In Florida, the Seminole people conducted a sustained resistance which was only ultimately suppressed in the 1840s. The forcible removal of the Cherokee to the unsettled "Indian Territory" of Oklahoma in 1838–39, after gold was found in their original homelands, cost four thousand lives (the "Trail of Tears"). The Delaware, Wichita and many others suffered a similar fate. Congress offered free land in return for minimal investment, encouraging claims to be staked to territories on the Great Plains. Railroads further threatened the Plains peoples' main food source, the vast buffalo herds.

The Kiowa, Comanche and Arapaho accepted reservation status at the Medicine Lodge Creek Conference (1867), while Sitting Bull's Dakota Sioux

ceased hostilities in return for permanent occupation of the Black Hills reservation. However, gold prospector incursions in 1874 provoked resistance by the Sioux and Northern Cheyenne in 1876–77. They annihilated General Custer and 200 troopers at the Battle of the Little Bighorn, but their leaders were eventually forced to surrender. Other native peoles in Wyoming, Montana, Oregon and Idaho met similar fates. Cochise and Geronimo of the Chiricahua Apaches in Arizona and New Mexico

conducted guerrilla campaigns until forced to surrender (1872 and 1886 respectively).

Geronimo's surrender marked the end of the Indian Wars. Despair at their situation, however, led many native Americans to follow the cult of the ghost dance which was supposed to make initiates immune to gunfire. The US Seventh Cavalry massacred Sioux ghost dancers and their families at Wounded Knee Creek in December 1890.

Throughout this period the United States thrived. The northeast saw a stream of immigrants from Europe, and new industries arose to feed, house and clothe the growing population. In the south, the high export prices of cotton brought the development of large plantations. The invention of the cotton gin in 1792 to separate cotton fiber from seeds stimulated production. Yet the plantation system relied on slavery, a growing point of contention between North and South. In the 1820s, many had hoped to liberate the slaves, but three decades later the rising value of slaves made this less attractive. California was allowed to join the Union as a "free" state in 1850 in return for harsh laws against fugitive slaves, but the issue exploded into civil war.

Canada's population changed in the late 18th century as a result of Britain's loss of its other colonies. White loyalists from New York and South Carolina, as well as the Mohawks who had fought alongside the British, settled in Nova Scotia, New Brunswick, Cape Breton and Prince Edward Island. Expansion westward began when the Red River Colony, nucleus of what later became Manitoba, was founded in 1812, though further growth was hampered by the rocky terrain of the Canadian Shield.

A United States invasion of Canada in 1812 was followed by a British attack on Washington (1814) and the Battle of New Orleans (1815). Thereafter, border issues were settled peacefully: the 1818 agreement on the 49th Parallel created an undefended US–Canadian frontier from the Lake of the Woods to the Rockies, which the 1846 Oregon Treaty then extended to Vancouver.

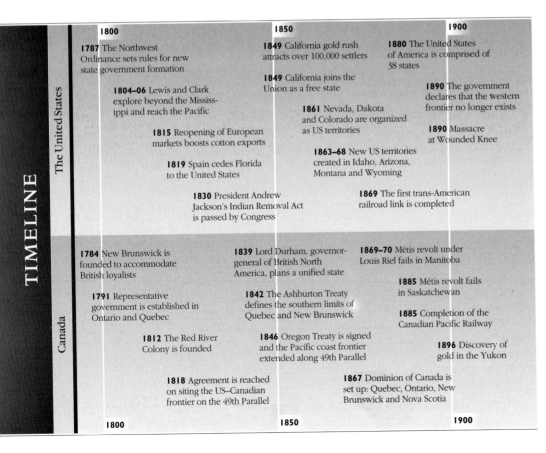

## TIMELINE

### The United States

**1787** The Northwest Ordinance sets rules for new state government formation

**1804–06** Lewis and Clark explore beyond the Mississippi and reach the Pacific

**1815** Reopening of European markets boosts cotton exports

**1819** Spain cedes Florida to the United States

**1830** President Andrew Jackson's Indian Removal Act is passed by Congress

**1849** California gold rush attracts over 100,000 settlers

**1849** California joins the Union as a free state

**1861** Nevada, Dakota and Colorado are organized as US territories

**1863–68** New US territories created in Idaho, Arizona, Montana and Wyoming

**1869** The first trans-American railroad link is completed

**1880** The United States of America is comprised of 38 states

**1890** The government declares that the western frontier no longer exists

**1890** Massacre at Wounded Knee

### Canada

**1784** New Brunswick is founded to accommodate British loyalists

**1791** Representative government is established in Ontario and Quebec

**1812** The Red River Colony is founded

**1818** Agreement is reached on siting the US–Canadian frontier on the 49th Parallel

**1839** Lord Durham, governor-general of British North America, plans a unified state

**1842** The Ashburton Treaty defines the southern limits of Quebec and New Brunswick

**1846** Oregon Treaty is signed and the Pacific coast frontier extended along 49th Parallel

**1867** Dominion of Canada is set up: Quebec, Ontario, New Brunswick and Nova Scotia

**1869–70** Métis revolt under Louis Riel fails in Manitoba

**1885** Métis revolt fails in Saskatchewan

**1885** Completion of the Canadian Pacific Railway

**1896** Discovery of gold in the Yukon

Beaufort
Sea

Queen
Elizabeth
Islands

Baffin
Bay

Devon Island

Parry Islands

Banks
Island

Prince of
Wales
Island

Somerset
Island

Baffin Island

Inuit

Victoria
Island

Kutchin

Inuit

Hare

Inuit

Foxe
Basin

Labrador
Sea

Athabascan

Inuit

Back

Southampton
Island

Inuit

Hudson Strait

Inuit

Dawson

Yukon
Territory
1895–98 district of
Northwest Territories

Great Bear
Lake

Northwest Territories
organized into districts 1882–95

Inuit

Inuit

LABRADOR
1809
to Newfoundland

Inuit

Whitehorse

Yellowknife

Mackenzie

Hudson
Bay

NEWFOUNDLAND
British crown colony

Tlingit

Great Slave
Lake

CANADIAN SHIELD

St John's

Juneau

Liard

60th Parallel

Newfoundland

Sitka

Slavey
Fort Chipewyan

Chipewyan

Churchill

Anticosti
Island

St Pierre &
Miquelon
to France

Kwakiutl

Lake
Athabasca

Reindeer
Lake

Port
Nelson

Cree

Quebec
(Lower Canada)
1867

Cape Breton Island

Beaver

Nelson

Abenaki

British
Columbia
1871

Alberta
1882 district of
Northwest Territories
1905

CANADA

Manitoba
1870

Cree

Prince Edward
Island
1873

Prince
Rupert

Sekani

Saskatchewan
1882 district of
Northwest Territories
1905

Cree

CANADIAN SHIELD

Cree

New
Brunswick
1867

Nova Scotia
1867

ROCKY MTS

1885 Cree

Saskatchewan

Round Lake

Ontario
(Upper Canada)
1867

Québec

1842
to US

Halifax

St John

Edmonton

1885 1885
1885

Lake
Winnipeg

Maine
1820

Haida

Sarcee

Blackfoot

Saskatoon

Ojibwa

Fraser

Calgary

Regina

Lake
Manitoba

Fort William

Ojibwa

Timmins

Montréal

Vermont
1791

New Hampshire, 1788

Queen
Charlotte
Island

Tlingit

Medicine
Hat

Assinboine

Winnipeg 1869–70

Mandan

Huron

Sudbury

Ottawa

Boston

Vancouver
Island

Nootka
Sound

Vancouver

Trail

49th Parallel

Red River Colony
1818 to United States

Lake
Superior

Sault Ste Marie

Lake
Huron

Ottawa

Ottawa

New
York
1788

Massachusetts, 1788

Nootka

Victoria

Blackfoot

1783
to US

Michigan
1837

Toronto
(York)

Lake
Ontario

5

Buffalo

Rhode Island, 1790

Seattle

Kellogg

Missouri

North
Dakota
1889

Minnesota
1858

Duluth

Wisconsin
1848

Ottawa

Fort Erie

New York
US capital 1785–90

Connecticut, 1788

Olympia

Washington
1889

Helena

Bismarck

Lake
Michigan

Detroit

Milwaukee

Fox

Lake Erie

Fallen
Timbers
1794

Cleveland

Pennsylvania
1787

Philadelphia
US capital 1790–1800

Fort Clatsop

Columbia

Montana
1889

Sioux

Minneapolis

Chicago

Ohio
1803

Pittsburgh

West Virginia
1863

Delaware, 1787

Portland

Salem

Idaho
1890

South Dakota
1889

Sioux

Tippecanoe
1811

Fallen

Indianapolis

Illinois

Indiana
1816

Cincinnati

Maryland, 1788

Oregon Country
–46 joint Canadian
and United States
occupation,
46 to United States

Oregon
1859

Flat Head

Little Bighorn
1876

Pierre

1

Iowa
1846

Des
Moines

Mississippi

Illinois
1818

Shawnee

Virginia
1788

Washington
US capital from 1800

Bermuda Islands
to Britain

Boise

Crow

Wounded Knee
1890

Nebraska
1867

Omaha

Missouri

St Louis

Ohio

Kentucky
1792

North
Carolina
1789

Raleigh

Modoc

Modoc War
1872–73

Snake

Wyoming
1890

Plains

Lincoln

Missouri
1821

Jefferson
City

Nashville

ATLANTIC
OCEAN

Promontory
Point

4

Cheyenne

Kansas City

Topeka

Tennessee
1796

Cherokee

South
Carolina
1788

Californian Trail

Reno

Nevada
1864

Cheyenne

Salt Lake
City

Denver

Kansas
1861

Sand Creek
1864

Arkansas

Memphis

Chickasaw

Alabama
1819

Georgia
1788

Atlanta

Charleston

Sacramento

Carson City

Utah
1896

Colorado
1876

Colorado

Arapaho

UNITED
STATES

Oklahoma
City

Little
Rock

Mississippi
1817

Montgomery

Savannah

San Francisco

Stockton

Miwok

Arizona
1912

Navajo

Santa Fe

Kiowa

Oklahoma
1907

Arkansas
1836

Jackson

Creek

Choctaw

Jacksonville

California
1850

Mojave

New Mexico
1912

Wichita

Red

Louisiana
1812

Mobile

Tallahassee

Florida
1845

Los Angeles

Phoenix

Comanche

Dallas

Baton
Rouge

New Orleans

Seminole

Miami

San Diego

Apache

Tucson

El Paso

Texas
1845

Colorado

Brazos

Houston

Nassau

Bahamas
to Britain

PACIFIC
OCEAN

MEXICO
to Spain,
1821 independent

Rio Grande

Austin

San Antonio

**1** Meriwether Lewis and William Clark were commissioned by Thomas Jefferson to explore beyond the Mississippi in 1804.

**2** The "Five Civilized Tribes" of the southeast United States – Choctaw, Cherokee, Chickasaw, Creek, and Seminole – were socalled for their adaptation to white culture. Even so, they were forcibly relocated in 1830.

**3** Alaska was bought from czarist Russia in 1867 for US$7.2 million.

**4** In 1869, the Union Pacific and the Central Pacific railroads met at Promontory Point in Utah.

**5** In 1866–70, the Fenian Brotherhood, an American arm of the Irish Republican Brotherhood, carried out raids in Canada, trying to change British policy on Irish independence. The first attack was at Fort Erie.

The American Civil War proved a decisive factor in Canadian unification. The Federal victory in 1865, attacks by the Fenian Brotherhood on Canadian territory (1866–70) and the westward expansion of the United States together caused Canada to press for a coast-to-coast union to ensure national security. In 1867 Nova Scotia, New Brunswick, Quebec and Ontario were united in the Dominion of Canada. Manitoba joined in 1870, British Columbia in 1871 and Prince Edward Island in 1873. The first government of the new dominion promoted a "national policy" aimed at peopling the Canadian Shield and the Far West, building a transcontinental railroad and introducing tariffs to protect farm prices.

The long-promised Canadian Pacific Railway was completed in 1885. The railroad consolidated the western frontier, created new towns along its route and provided a tangible link between British Columbia and the east.

Canada continued to expand to the north. In 1912 Manitoba advanced to the 60th Parallel (to match Saskatchewan and Alberta). In the same year Quebec and Ontario were extended to the Hudson Bay and the Arctic. Another frontier developed as Canada's northernmost territories, home to the Inuit, were encroached upon first by fur-trappers and then thousands of gold prospectors. Oil reserves, too, were found in Alberta in 1912–14.

See also 85 (American Civil War); 87 (the United States in the later 19th century)

The demand for cotton as an export crop made the economy of the states south of the Mason–Dixon line (the border between Pennsylvania and Maryland) dependent on the systematic exploitation of humanity. On plantations and farms and in cities and towns, four million black slaves were denied their rights to a family, education and citizenship. Slavery became a political issue during the westward expansion of the United States. In deference to southern interests, the Constitutional Convention of 1787 prohibited the importation of slaves, but protected slavery in the states from federal interference. In the Missouri compromise of 1820, which admitted Maine and the Louisiana Purchase lands (except Missouri) as free and proclaimed all states above latitude 36° 30' as free, a convention of balancing abolitionist and slave-owning interests was established.

Attitudes toward slavery were polarized; some demanded complete and immediate abolition, while others saw good economic and racial reasons for its retention. The issue was made even more divisive by a number of legislative decisions in the 1850s. The 1850 compromise admitted California as a free state, but took no action to curb slavery in the other territories ceded by Mexico after the war of 1846–48 (Utah and New Mexico). The Kansas–Nebraska Act (1854) gave settlers the right to decide whether or not to permit slavery in a new territory, a situation that led to open warfare between rival groups in "bleeding Kansas." Finally a Supreme Court ruling of 1857 – the "Dred Scott" decision – declared that neither Congress nor the people of a territory could abolish slavery in the territories. This meant the Missouri compromise was unconstitutional and destroyed the artificial balance between free and slave states. This decision threatened the democratic foundation of the Union. Meanwhile, fugitive slaves escaped to the north via the "Underground Railroad" (a network of abolitionist households). In the 1860 presidential elections all the free states – except New Jersey –

returned the Republican Abraham Lincoln, who refused to extend slavery to new territories.

On 20 December 1860, South Carolina seceded from the Union. Georgia, Alabama, Texas, Florida, Mississippi and Louisiana soon followed, creating a Confederacy and electing Jefferson Davis as their president. On 12 April 1861, Confederate forces began hostilities with a bombardment of Fort Sumter. Lincoln called for 75,000 northern volunteers, prompting Virginia, North Carolina, Tennessee and Arkansas to join the Confederacy. Yet not all the slave states seceded: Kentucky declared itself neutral; Delaware, Maryland and Missouri remained loyal, as did the northwestern counties of Virginia (which became the state of West Virginia in 1863).

The civil war that erupted was a devastating conflict: a quarter of all those who saw combat lost their lives. Confederate strategy was to defend itself and win international recognition as an independent state. The Union government thus had no option but to attack the south and restore the rebel states to the Union. The Union had a larger population, less vulnerable railroads and far greater industrial resources than the Confederacy. Lincoln was confident of achieving his two main objectives: to blockade the Confederate coastline and capture Richmond, the Confederate capital. However, superior Confederate generalship caused Union armies several early setbacks, notably their defeat at the two Battles of Bull Run, and their failure to take the key town of Fredericksburg. In January 1863, Lincoln espoused abolition of slavery in his emancipation proclamation, freeing all slaves in the Confederacy. Meanwhile, Confederate armies pushed north into Pennsylvania to take the war to the enemy. This aim was thwarted at the Battle of Gettysburg in July 1863, which marked a turning point in Union fortunes.

At the same time, Union armies were victorious in the west. Under the command of Ulysses Grant, they advanced down the Mississippi. After gaining

control of the area through the battle of Shiloh and the siege of Vicksburg, the North succeeded in cutting off Arkansas, Louisiana and Texas from the Confederacy. William Sherman's campaign in Georgia saw the destruction of Atlanta and the capture of Savannah. Grant fought a series of battles (Wilderness, Spotsylvania, Cold Harbor and Petersburg) against the Confederate commander Robert E. Lee, which left the south with barely 60,000 troops. Richmond fell on 3 April 1865 and Lee surrendered the Confederate army at Appomattox Court House on 9 April. Five days later, Lincoln was assassinated.

Map legend:

- Northwest Territory (slavery forbidden, 1787)
- Mason–Dixon line
- Missouri Compromise line, 1820
- borders, 1861
- Confederate state, 1861, with date of secession
- slave state loyal to the Union
- Union state, 1861
- United States territory, 1861
- Confederate campaign
- Union campaign
- deployment of Confederate troops by rail
- deployment of Union troops by rail
- ⊗ Confederate victory
- ⊗ Union victory
- Confederate fort
- Union fort
- burned by Union troops
- coast blockaded by Union Navy
- ■ capital
- ▪ state or provincial capital
- Mobile slave port
- population density over 18 per sq km, 1860
- cotton growing area, 1860
- 1865 date of abolition of slavery

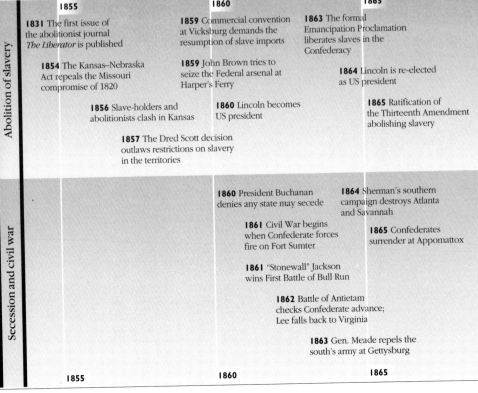

## TIMELINE

### Abolition of slavery

**1831** The first issue of the abolitionist journal *The Liberator* is published

**1854** The Kansas–Nebraska Act repeals the Missouri compromise of 1820

**1856** Slave-holders and abolitionists clash in Kansas

**1857** The Dred Scott decision outlaws restrictions on slavery in the territories

**1859** Commercial convention at Vicksburg demands the resumption of slave imports

**1859** John Brown tries to seize the Federal arsenal at Harper's Ferry

**1860** Lincoln becomes US president

**1863** The formal Emancipation Proclamation liberates slaves in the Confederacy

**1864** Lincoln is re-elected as US president

**1865** Ratification of the Thirteenth Amendment abolishing slavery

### Secession and civil war

**1860** President Buchanan denies any state may secede

**1861** Civil War begins when Confederate forces fire on Fort Sumter

**1861** "Stonewall" Jackson wins First Battle of Bull Run

**1862** Battle of Antietam checks Confederate advance; Lee falls back to Virginia

**1863** Gen. Meade repels the south's army at Gettysburg

**1864** Sherman's southern campaign destroys Atlanta and Savannah

**1865** Confederates surrender at Appomattox

1855    1860    1865

Lake Superior
to Michigan
St Paul
Wisconsin 1848
Iowa 1846
Davenport
Madison • Milwaukee
Peoria
Illinois 1818
Springfield
St Louis
Jefferson City
Missouri 1864
Lake Michigan
Michigan 1836
Lansing
Chicago
Indiana 1816
Indianapolis
Wabash
Ohio
Lake Huron
Detroit
Lake Erie
Cleveland
Ohio 1802
Columbus
Cincinnati
Newport
Louisville
Frankfort
Kentucky
officially neutral though limited support of both sides
Perryville 1862
Bowling Green 1865
Paducah 1862
Cairo
Arkansas seceded May 1861 1865
Tennessee seceded June 1861 1865
Fort Henry Nashville 1864
Fort Donelson
Stone's River 1862–63
Murfreesboro 1863
Little Rock
Memphis 1862
Fort Pillow 1862
Shiloh 1862
Corinth 1862
Chattanooga 1863
Cleveland
Chickamauga 1863
Mississippi seceded Jan 1861 1865
Birmingham
Alabama
Alabama seceded Jan 1861 1865
Montgomery
Meridian
Vicksburg
Jackson
Port Hudson
Baton Rouge
afayette 1863
New Orleans
Mobile Bay 1864
Mobile
Pensacola
Fort Pickens
Fort Morgan
Fort St Philip
Fort Jackson 1862
Gulf of Mexico
Georgia seceded Jan 1861 1865
Chattahoochee
Tallahassee
Florida seceded Jan 1861 1865
Fort Myers
Tampa
Miami
Jacksonville

Canada to Britain
Ottawa
Montréal
Maine 1780
Augusta
New Hampshire 1783
Vermont 1793
Concord
Montpelier
Connecticut
Toronto
Lake Ontario
New York 1799
Albany
Rochester
Buffalo
Massachusetts 1780
Boston
Hartford
Connecticut 1784
Providence
Rhode Island 1784
Hudson
Pennsylvania 1780
Harrisburg
Philadelphia
New York
Long Island
Trenton
Pittsburgh
Gettysburg 1863
New Jersey 1804
Mason–Dixon line
Antietam 1862
Baltimore
Northwestern counties of Virginia became the state of West Virginia in 1863
Harpers Ferry
Washington
Annapolis
Dover
Delaware 1865
Bull Run 1861, 1862
Wilderness 1864
Maryland 1864
Charleston
Chancellorsville 1863
Spotsylvania 1864
Fredericksburg 1862
Virginia seceded Apr 1861 1865
Richmond
Cold Harbor 1862, 1864
Petersburg 1864
Appomattox Confederate surrender, 9 Apr 1865
Hampton Roads 1862
Fort Monroe
Norfolk
Roanoke
Greensboro
Raleigh
Bentonville 1865
North Carolina seceded May 1861 1865
Goldsboro
Fort Hatteras
Fayetteville
South Carolina seceded Dec 1860 1865
Wilmington
Fort Fisher
Fort Macon
Columbia
Charleston
Fort Sumter Confederate attack 12–13 Apr 1861, initiates the Civil War
Savannah
Fort Pulaski
Altamaha
Atlanta 1864
Santee
Savannah
ATLANTIC OCEAN

A UNION soldier storms a Confederate position: the use of accurate rifles meant that casualties were very high.

**1** The Mason–Dixon line – the border between Maryland and Pennsylvania – was drawn in 1763–67 by a British astronomer and his assistant, and came to be regarded as the boundary of the south.

**2** In the Harpers Ferry Raid of 1859, a group led by the anti-slavery activist John Brown attacked the Virginia arsenal; Brown was captured and hanged.

**3** In the first Battle of Bull Run (21 July 1861), the impregnable defensive line of Confederate general Thomas Jackson won him the nickname "Stonewall".

**4** The first battle between ironclad battleships took place at Hampton Roads in March 1862, when the U.S.S. *Monitor* engaged the C.S.S. *Virginia* (formerly the U.S.S. *Merrimac*).

**5** The Gettysburg Address, Lincoln's famous proclamation of democratic rights, was delivered on 19 November 1863 at the dedication of a cemetery for the dead of the Battle of Gettysburg.

**6** General William Sherman's "March to the Sea" in late 1864 destroyed everything in its path in an effort to cripple the economy of the Confederacy.

**7** On 14 April 1865, while attending a theater in Washington, Abraham Lincoln was shot by an actor and Confederate sympathizer, John Wilkes Booth.

Lincoln had preserved the Union and freed the slaves, thousands of whom had served in Union regiments (as had many native Americans). Congress passed several constitutional Amendments: the Thirteenth declared slavery illegal; the Fourteenth (ratified 1868) gave former slaves US citizenship (native Americans had to wait until 1924); the Fifteenth (1869) guaranteed their right to vote. Yet the cultural divide between north and south remained, and Congress could not ensure that African–Americans would be able to exercise their civil rights. Racial discrimination survived for the next hundred years.

See also 84 (early 19th-century United States); 102 (early 20th-century)

Growing urbanization and industrialization, and a dramatic increase in population, were evident throughout the world by 1880. European cities developed rapidly, as ever more people were drawn away from rural life by factory work (▷ 90). Technological advances, especially in communications, impelled industrial development and promoted colonial expansion. By the 1850s, the British had installed the first railroads and telegraph systems in India. Politically, while some ancient entities such as the Tokugawa shogunate in Japan did not survive the advent of the modern age, others – the Chinese Manchu dynasty, the Ottoman empire and czarist Russia – lingered into the 20th century, though torn by internal dissent.

Dynamic new nation-states arose as the 19th century progressed, changing the balance of power in Europe. In Italy, nationalist groupings in the north and south combined to bring about the unification of the country (▷ 80). The struggle for domination in the German Confederation between Austria and Prussia resulted in conflict in 1866, from which Prussia emerged victorious. Another crushing Prussian military victory in 1870–71 against France destroyed the empire of Napoleon III and led to Prussia forming the nucleus of the German "second empire".

Warfare was in the process of being radically altered by mechanization. The American Civil War (1861–65) was the first conflict to utilize the greatly enhanced mobility and firepower afforded respectively by railroads and the mass production of munitions (▷ 85). Fought between the North and the South over the question of slavery and the extent of federal jurisdiction, the war exacted a huge toll in human lives. The North's far superior manpower and industrial capacity eventually allowed it to prevail. Despite the damage caused by the war, however, the United States was fast becoming the dominant power in the Western Hemisphere. Expansion continued with the purchase of the Gadsden Strip from Mexico (1853) and Alaska from Russia (1867). The inauguration of a transcontinental electric telegraph was swiftly followed by the linking of the Union Pacific and the Central Pacific railroads to form a coast-to-coast route in 1869 (▷ 84). In the 1870s and 1880s, the construction of another railroad across the North American continent played a vital role in unifying Canada, joining the new western territory of British Columbia to the eastern provinces that had declared the Dominion of Canada in 1867.

Central and South America were beset by armed conflict. France undertook an imperial adventure in Mexico in 1863–67, which ended disastrously.

**1861–65** American Civil War; northern states fight to preserve Union against secessionist South

**1861** Czar Alexander II undertakes reform by emancipating Russian serfs

**1854–56** Crimean War; Britain and France oppose Russian expansion into Ottoman territories

**1860** Abraham Lincoln elected US president on anti-slavery ticket

**1867** Russia sells Alaska to the United States

**1852** French second empire: Louis Napoleon emperor (Napoleon III)

**1858** Piedmontese premier Camillo Cavour and Napoleon III plan Italian unification

**1866** Austro-Prussian War; Prussia defeats Austria

| TIMELINE | | 1850 | 1860 | 1870 |
|---|---|---|---|---|
| The Americas | | | | |
| Europe | | | | |
| Middle East | | | | |
| Africa | | | | |
| Asia and Australasia | | | | |

**1851–53** Gold rush in Australia

**1857–58** Indian Mutiny; Muslims and Hindus rebel against British rule

**1863** Asante people of west Africa defeat British in Third Asante War

**1868** Japanese Tokugawa shogunate ends; Meiji dynasty restored

**1853** US Commodore Matthew Perry opens up Japan to western trade

**1869** Suez Canal, built by the French, opens

**1870** Unification of Italy as Rome becomes part of the kingdom

Alaska

CANADA

Newfoundland

UNITED STATES

MEXICO

Hawaiian Islands (United States)

Bahamas

British Honduras

Cuba

HAITI

Puerto Rico

Jamaica

DOMINICAN REPUBLIC

GUATEMALA
EL SALVADOR
HONDURAS
NICARAGUA

COSTA RICA

VENEZUELA

British Guiana
Dutch Guiana
French Guiana

COLOMBIA

Galapagos Islands (Ecuador)

ECUADOR

BRAZIL

PERU

Marquesas Islands (France)

BOLIVIA

PARAGUAY

Tuamotu Archipelago (France)

PARAGUAY

URUGUAY

ARGENTINA

CHILE

shellfish gatherers and marine mammal hunters

pampas hunter-gatherers

Falkland Islands (Britain)

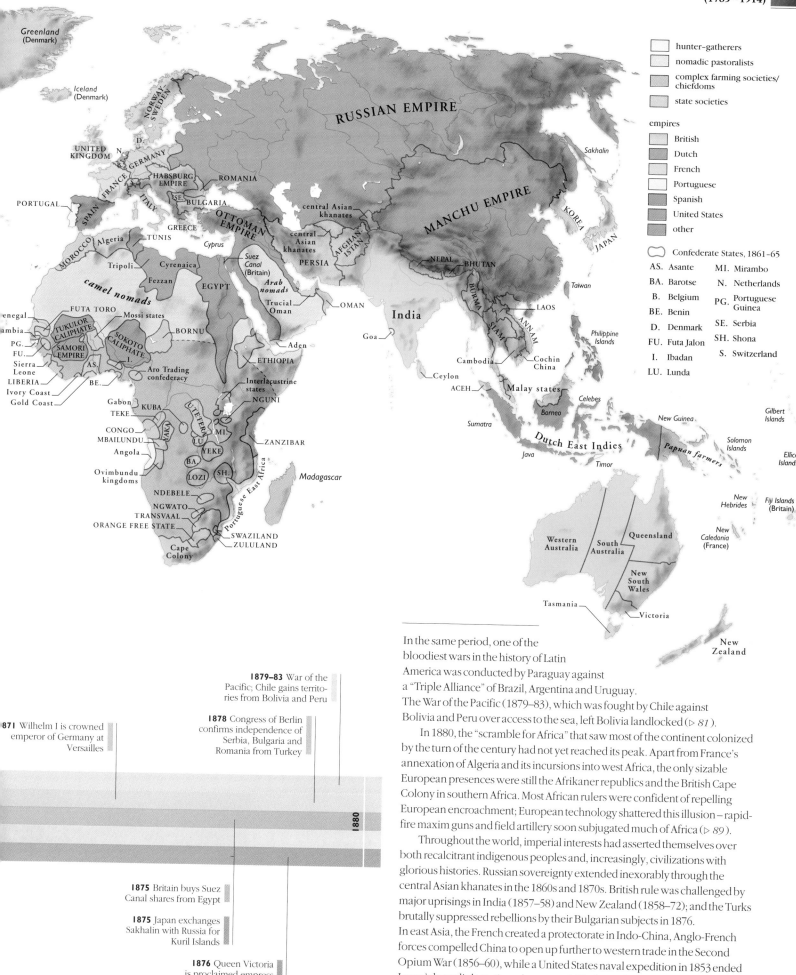

*Greenland*
(Denmark)

*Iceland*
(Denmark)

**RUSSIAN EMPIRE**

*Sakhalin*

UNITED
KINGDOM
N.
D.
B.² GERMANY
FRANCE
HABSBURG
EMPIRE
ROMANIA
PORTUGAL
SPAIN
ITALY
SE.
BULGARIA
GREECE
OTTOMAN
EMPIRE
central Asian
khanates
central
Asian
khanates
**MANCHU EMPIRE**
KOREA
JAPAN

MOROCCO
Algeria
TUNIS
*Cyprus*
Suez
Canal
(Britain)
PERSIA
AFGHAN-
ISTAN
NEPAL
BHUTAN
*Taiwan*

Tripoli
Cyrenaica
Fezzan
EGYPT
*Arab
nomads*
BURMA
LAOS
*camel nomads*
Trucial
Oman
OMAN
India
SIAM
ANNAM
*Philippine
Islands*

enegal
FUTA TORO
Mossi states
BORNU
Aden
Goa
Cochin
China

ambia
TUKULOR
CALIPHATE
SOKOTO
CALIPHATE
Cambodia
PG.
FU.
SAMORI
EMPIRE
I.
AS.
Aro Trading
confederacy
ETHIOPIA
Ceylon
Malay states
*Celebes*
Gilbert
Islands

Sierra
Leone
LIBERIA
Ivory Coast
Gold Coast
BE.
Interlacustrine
states
NGUNI
ACEH
*Borneo*
New Guinea
Solomon
Islands
Ellice
Islands

Gabon
KUBA
UTETERA
*Sumatra*
Dutch East Indies
*Papuan farmers*

TEKE
YAKA
MI.
*Java*
*Timor*

CONGO
LU.
YEKE
ZANZIBAR
New
Hebrides
Fiji Islands
(Britain)

MBAILUNDU
BA.
Angola
LOZI
SH.
*Madagascar*
New
Caledonia
(France)

Ovimbundu
kingdoms
NDEBELE
NGWATO
TRANSVAAL
ORANGE FREE STATE
*Portuguese East Africa*
SWAZILAND
Cape
Colony
ZULULAND
*Western
Australia*
*South
Australia*
*Queensland*
*New
South
Wales*
*Tasmania*
*Victoria*
*New
Zealand*

**Legend:**
- hunter-gatherers
- nomadic pastoralists
- complex farming societies/chiefdoms
- state societies

empires
- British
- Dutch
- French
- Portuguese
- Spanish
- United States
- other

Confederate States, 1861–65

AS. Asante
BA. Barotse
B. Belgium
BE. Benin
D. Denmark
FU. Futa Jalon
I. Ibadan
LU. Lunda
MI. Mirambo
N. Netherlands
PG. Portuguese Guinea
SE. Serbia
SH. Shona
S. Switzerland

**1879–83** War of the Pacific; Chile gains territories from Bolivia and Peru

**1878** Congress of Berlin confirms independence of Serbia, Bulgaria and Romania from Turkey

**871** Wilhelm I is crowned emperor of Germany at Versailles

**1880**

**1875** Britain buys Suez Canal shares from Egypt

**1875** Japan exchanges Sakhalin with Russia for Kuril Islands

**1876** Queen Victoria is proclaimed empress of India

In the same period, one of the bloodiest wars in the history of Latin America was conducted by Paraguay against a "Triple Alliance" of Brazil, Argentina and Uruguay. The War of the Pacific (1879–83), which was fought by Chile against Bolivia and Peru over access to the sea, left Bolivia landlocked (▷ *81*).

In 1880, the "scramble for Africa" that saw most of the continent colonized by the turn of the century had not yet reached its peak. Apart from France's annexation of Algeria and its incursions into west Africa, the only sizable European presences were still the Afrikaner republics and the British Cape Colony in southern Africa. Most African rulers were confident of repelling European encroachment; European technology shattered this illusion – rapid-fire maxim guns and field artillery soon subjugated much of Africa (▷ *89*).

Throughout the world, imperial interests had asserted themselves over both recalcitrant indigenous peoples and, increasingly, civilizations with glorious histories. Russian sovereignty extended inexorably through the central Asian khanates in the 1860s and 1870s. British rule was challenged by major uprisings in India (1857–58) and New Zealand (1858–72); and the Turks brutally suppressed rebellions by their Bulgarian subjects in 1876. In east Asia, the French created a protectorate in Indo-China, Anglo-French forces compelled China to open up further to western trade in the Second Opium War (1856–60), while a United States naval expedition in 1853 ended Japan's long diplomatic and commercial isolation (▷ *93*) ■

At the end of the Civil War, the northern states experienced unprecedented prosperity as American and foreign speculators rushed to invest in a new wave of industrialization. Railroad construction drove the economy. The completion of the first transcontinental link in 1869 encouraged the development of other lines across America; three more were in operation by 1883. Urban centers and rural areas alike benefited. Millions of cattle were transported to slaughterhouses in the new cities of Chicago and Kansas City. By opening up the west to profitable farming, railroads also hastened political change. By 1890 most of the western territories had been admitted as states of the Union. Yet the railroad boom was not without its negative aspects. Corrupt share-dealing provoked a panic and withdrawal of foreign capital in 1873.

The south had been devastated by the civil war. Its principal towns lay in ruins and its economic life destroyed. Opinion in the north was divided on how the rebel states should be treated. President Andrew Johnson (Lincoln's successor) favored reconciliation, while hardliners counseled repression. After a period of radical administration, conservatives reasserted white rule in the south, circumventing the constitutional rights guaranteed by Congress to freed blacks. Reconstruction proceeded slowly, and states were gradually readmitted to the Union.

Towns and cities grew with astonishing rapidity. By 1914, the United States had an urban population of 45 million, most of whom were immigrants – On five occasions the annual total of immigrants – from every corner of Europe – exceeded one million. Desperate for work and willing to take low-paid employment, the newcomers were quickly absorbed into the factories of New York, Chicago, Buffalo, Pittsburgh, Cleveland, Milwaukee, Cincinnati and St Louis. Appalling conditions prevailed in the crowded cities, polluted factories, primitive mining communities and harsh lumber camps. Immigrants often faced discrimination; as early as 1871, the Chinese who had entered through California to work in mining and on the railroads were the

population density per sq km, c.1900

- over 18
- 2–18
- under 2

- ■ city with population over 1 million, c.1900
- ■ city with population of between 250,000 and 1 million, c.1900
- <u>Boston</u> immigrant entry port
- ✳ start of great labor strike, 1877
- ✵ other industrial conflict
- ⛴ oilfield
- coalfield
- iron ore deposits
- center of steel production
- Goodnight-Loving cattle trail
- western cattle trail
- Chisholm cattle trail
- Shawnee or eastern cattle trail
- Sedalia cattle trail, later abandoned
- railroad
- borders, 1914

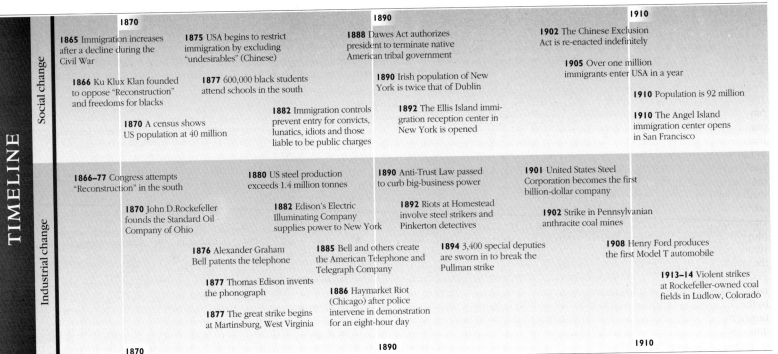

## TIMELINE

### Social change

| 1870 | 1890 | 1910 |
|---|---|---|
| **1865** Immigration increases after a decline during the Civil War | **1888** Dawes Act authorizes president to terminate native American tribal government | **1902** The Chinese Exclusion Act is re-enacted indefinitely |
| **1875** USA begins to restrict immigration by excluding "undesirables" (Chinese) | | **1905** Over one million immigrants enter USA in a year |
| **1866** Ku Klux Klan founded to oppose "Reconstruction" and freedoms for blacks | **1890** Irish population of New York is twice that of Dublin | **1910** Population is 92 million |
| **1877** 600,000 black students attend schools in the south | **1892** The Ellis Island immigration reception center in New York is opened | **1910** The Angel Island immigration center opens in San Francisco |
| **1870** A census shows US population at 40 million | **1882** Immigration controls prevent entry for convicts, lunatics, idiots and those liable to be public charges | |

### Industrial change

| 1870 | 1890 | 1910 |
|---|---|---|
| **1866–77** Congress attempts "Reconstruction" in the south | **1880** US steel production exceeds 1.4 million tonnes | **1901** United States Steel Corporation becomes the first billion-dollar company |
| **1870** John D. Rockefeller founds the Standard Oil Company of Ohio | **1890** Anti-Trust Law passed to curb big-business power | |
| | **1882** Edison's Electric Illuminating Company supplies power to New York | **1902** Strike in Pennsylvanian anthracite coal mines |
| **1876** Alexander Graham Bell patents the telephone | **1892** Riots at Homestead involve steel strikers and Pinkerton detectives | |
| | **1885** Bell and others create the American Telephone and Telegraph Company | **1908** Henry Ford produces the first Model T automobile |
| **1877** Thomas Edison invents the phonograph | **1894** 3,400 special deputies are sworn in to break the Pullman strike | **1913–14** Violent strikes at Rockefeller-owned coal fields in Ludlow, Colorado |
| **1877** The great strike begins at Martinsburg, West Virginia | **1886** Haymarket Riot (Chicago) after police intervene in demonstration for an eight-hour day | |

Map labels:

Saskatchewan · Lake Winnipeg · Lake Winnipegosis · Lake Manitoba · Manitoba · CANADA British dominion · Ontario (Upper Canada) · Quebec (Lower Canada) · New Brunswick · Nova Scotia

Lake Superior · Lake Huron · Lake Michigan · Lake Ontario · Lake Erie · St Lawrence

Maine · Augusta · Montpelier · Concord · New Hampshire · Vermont · New York · Albany · Hartford · Boston · Massachusetts · Providence · Rhode Island · Connecticut · Buffalo · Molly Maguire's 1862–76 · New York · Trenton · Philadelphia · New Jersey · Pennsylvania · Harrisburg · Baltimore · Dover · Delaware · Pittsburgh · Homestead Strike 1892 · Columbus · Washington · Annapolis · Maryland

Montana · North Dakota · Great Northern · Bismarck · Missouri · Northern Pacific · Minnesota · Duluth · Wisconsin · Michigan · Lansing · Detroit · Cleveland · Minneapolis · St Paul · Mississippi · Madison · Milwaukee · Ohio · West Virginia · Richmond · Charleston · Virginia · Cincinnati

South Dakota · Pierre · Iowa · Des Moines · Union Pacific · Haymarket Riot, 1886 · Chicago · Indiana · Indianapolis · Springfield · Louisville · Frankfort · Kentucky · Pullman Strike 1894 · Illinois · St Louis

Wyoming · Nebraska · Omaha · Lincoln · Platte · Kansas City · Sedalia · Jefferson City · Missouri · Ohio · Raleigh · North Carolina

Union Pacific · Cheyenne · Ogallala · Topeka · Abilene · Kansas Pacific · Kansas · Atchison, Topeka & Santa Fe · Nashville · Tennessee · Columbia · South Carolina

Denver · Leadville 1896 · Cripple Creek 1894 · Colorado · Pueblo · Arkansas · Dodge City · Memphis · Arkansas · Atlanta · Georgia · Charleston · Savannah

Ludlow 1913–14 · Santa Fe · Las Vegas · Albuquerque · New Mexico · Atchison, Topeka & Santa Fe · Oklahoma · Oklahoma City · Missouri, Kansas & Texas · Little Rock · Mississippi · Alabama · Birmingham · Montgomery · Jackson · Vicksburg · Mobile · Jacksonville · Tallahassee · Florida

Canadian · Red · Atchison, Topeka & Santa Fe · Pecos · El Paso · Fort Concho · Texas & Pacific · Colorado · Brazos · Dallas · Louisiana · Baton Rouge · New Orleans · Rio Grande · Texas · Austin · Houston · Galveston · Southern Pacific · San Antonio · Laredo

MEXICO · Gulf of Mexico · Cuba · Bahamas to Britain · Miami · ATLANTIC OCEAN

---

victims of race riots. Further Chinese immigration was blocked by the Chinese Exclusion Act of 1882.

The depression that affected Europe in the late 19th century had little effect on the vibrant US economy. This period saw the rise of magnates who made the United States into the world's great industrial power. John D. Rockefeller dominated the oil industry while Philip D. Armour controlled a meat-packing empire. The financier J. Pierpont Morgan underwrote railroads, and Andrew Carnegie was the leading figure in the steel industry. These men took advantage of low interest rates, cheap labor and a largely unregulated market. However, though employers used ruthless business methods and dealt summarily with discontent among their workforces, the age of American capitalism had its benefits. The essential symbol of American enterprise and democracy was the Model T automobile, first made in 1908 by the Detroit mechanic Henry Ford. Also some multimillionaires, such as Carnegie, were philanthropists who gave away part of their fortunes.

Industrial growth brought labor problems. The job losses resulting from the 1873 economic crisis made labor unions hostile to further immigration. Strikes were common, the most damaging in 1877. Railroad employees, enraged by a pay cut, withdrew their labor and were supported in their grievances by a large army of unemployed. Unrest spread to Pittsburgh, Chicago, St Louis, Kansas City, Galveston and San Francisco before militiamen were called out to suppress it. Although this dispute, the first general strike in American history, involved millions and even spread to Canada, its most significant feature was the Federal administration's use of troops. In 1892, workers at the Carnegie steel mill in Homestead were beaten by the state militia. Two years later president Cleveland sent soldiers to put down a strike of railroad workers in Chicago.

The economy, though, stayed buoyant. By 1914, with a population over 97 million, the United States led the world in the manufacture of steel and lumber products, in meat-packing and precious metal extraction, and had more telephones, telegraphs, electric lights and automobiles than anywhere else.

**1** Between 1867 and 1871, about 1.5 million head of cattle were herded on "long drives" along the Chisholm Trail to the railhead at Abilene, Kansas.

**2** Atlanta had been razed by fire during the Georgia campaign of the civil war, but became the center of Federal government activity during reconstruction.

**3** During the great strike of 1877, Pittsburgh was devastated by three days of rioting that destroyed much railroad property and almost leveled the city.

**4** Oklahoma was opened to settlement in 1889; settlers raced across the prairie to stake their claims.

**5** Ellis Island in New York Bay became the country's principal immigration station from 1892 onward.

**6** Utah was admitted to the Union as a state in 1896, after its Mormon inhabitants had promised to relinquish the practice of polygamy.

See also 85 (American Civil War);
102 (the Americas in the early 20th century)

The Russian empire, though ostensibly mighty, had structural weaknesses. Above all, its sheer size made it difficult to govern and prevented ready use of its abundant resources. As a result, corruption was rife and the country remained economically underdeveloped. Territorially, Russia continued to expand throughout the 18th and 19th centuries. Catherine the Great's energetic foreign policy added much of Poland and extended Russia's empire in the south. Czar Alexander I (r.1801–25) suffered Napoleon's invasion of 1812, but secured a share of the spoils after the defeat of France. The Congress of Vienna ceded the remainder of Poland to Russia, thus augmenting its recent acquisitions in Finland and Bessarabia.

Territorial expansion left Russian rulers with a permanent fear of rebellion by conquered peoples. During the 1828–29 war with the Turks, Nicholas I (r.1825–55) was able to field barely 180,000 troops, as half a million frontline soldiers were committed to maintaining security in the Baltic provinces and the Caucasus. In 1830, an uprising in Poland against Russian rule was only suppressed with difficulty. Internal dissent at autocratic rule began to grow. The "Decembrist" revolt of progressive army officers early in Nicholas I's reign was ruthlessly put down.

The principal aim of Nicholas' foreign policy was dominance over the Ottomans to ensure that Russia's grain exports had free passage across the Black Sea and through the Dardanelles to the Mediterranean. Russia endeavored to absorb Turkey's Balkan possessions and to encourage fellow Slavs to rebel against Ottoman rule in Europe. This policy brought Russia into conflict with the western powers. Britain saw its trade with India threatened by Russian expansion into the eastern Mediterranean, while France was concerned in its role as protector of the Catholic church within Turkish territories. Nicholas' decision to occupy the Ottoman

provinces of Moldavia and Wallachia in 1853 provoked Britain and France to invade the Crimea (1854). Once again, mustering sufficient manpower to resist the invaders proved a severe problem.

Russia's defeat in the Crimean War, its withdrawal from Moldavia and Wallachia and the requirement that it "neutralize" the Black Sea compelled Alexander II (r.1855–81) to review his power base. Russian rulers had always depended on the conscription of serfs, but this force was no match for the modern armies of France and Britain. The nobility, whose wealth was grounded in serfdom, was reluctant to innovate or invest in modern industry. To forestall revolution from below, Alexander reformed from above, emancipating the serfs and moving Russia toward a capitalist economy. Even so, millions of former serfs had to pay redemption fees for the lands they tilled. Massive discontent remained, held in check only by conscripts and the secret police. The czar was assassinated in 1881.

Alexander II had begun to tap the vast resources of Siberia, had extended the empire in central Asia and had secured a warm-water port in east Asia. The territory of Alaska was sold to the United States to concentrate development efforts on eastern Siberia and Vladivostok. Alexander's armies gradually sub-

## TIMELINE

### Domestic developments

| 1800 | 1850 | 1900 |
|---|---|---|
| **1796** Death of Catherine II; brief reign of her son Paul I ends in assassination | **1855** Alexander II becomes czar and institutes reform | **1894** Nicholas II, the last czar, ascends the throne |
| **1801** Alexander I ascends the throne; kingdom of Georgia voluntarily unites with Russia | **1861** Russian serfs are emancipated by the "Czar Liberator" Alexander | **1905** Major uprisings sweep the country and lead to limited constitutional reform |
| **1812** Napoleon invades Russia and occupies Moscow, but is forced to withdraw | **1881** Assassination of Alexander II in St Petersburg; Alexander III becomes czar and reasserts autocratic rule | **1911** Pyotr Stolypin, reforming prime minister under the first *dumas*, is assassinated |
| **1825** Accession of Czar Nicholas I; Decembrist revolt of army officers fails | **1891** Trans-Siberian Railroad is begun; completed in 1916 | |

### Foreign policy

| 1800 | 1850 | 1900 |
|---|---|---|
| **1810–50** Russia extends its dominion in central Asia | **1860–70** Russian expansion into Turkestan | **1904–05** Russo-Japanese War; Russian forces are humiliated |
| **1815** Congress Poland is united with Russian empire, but retains its government | **1867** Alaska is sold to the United States for US$7.2 million | **1914** Russia mobilizes its army against Germany; on the outbreak of war it suffers a major defeat at the Battle of Tannenberg |
| **1830–31** Insurrection in Poland is brutally suppressed | **1877–78** Last of a series of Russo-Turkish wars; creation of the vassal state of Bulgaria | |
| | **1849** Russian troops are sent to crush Hungarian liberals | |
| | **1854–56** Crimean War; British and French halt Russian Black Sea expansion | |
| **1800** | **1850** | **1900** |

CANADA

Russian
America
1867 to United States
and renamed Alaska

*Gulf of
Alaska*

**1** Catherine II annexed the Crimea in 1783 and ordered the construction of a huge naval facility at Sevastopol; this base was besieged by Anglo-French forces in 1854-56.

**2** Congress Poland, so-called because it was awarded to Russia by the Congress of Vienna in 1815, lost its constitution after the 1830 revolt, and was entirely absorbed by Russia after another rebellion in 1863.

**3** A strip of mountainous country known as Wakhan was appended to Afghanistan in 1905 to separate conflicting Russian and British interests in the region.

**4** The revolution of 1905 spread to the armed forces; sailors of the battleship *Potemkin* seized control of the ship in Odessa and sought asylum in Romania.

**5** Count Sergei Witte, Minister of Finance 1892-1903, was the driving force behind the Russian rail network and industrial expansion.

**6** The loop of the Trans-Siberian railroad around Lake Baykal was completed in 1915, and the eastern Siberian link in 1916.

**7** Thousands of political dissidents were sent to Siberian labor camps by the czarist regime, including the Bolsheviks Lenin (Shushenskoye), Stalin (Kureika), and Trotsky (Verkholensk).

*Wrangel Island*
1867 to Russian
empire

*Bering
Sea*

*Aleutian Islands*

*PACIFIC
OCEAN*

RUSSIAN EMPIRE

Kureika
Turukhansk
Surgut
Narym
Ob
Yenisey
Tomsk
Novosibirsk
Krasnoyarsk
Shushenskoye
Verkholensk
Lena
Viluisk
Yakutsk
*Sea of
Okhotsk*
Lake
Baykal
Irkutsk
Barguzin
Kara
Chita
Kyakhta
Nikolayevsk
Amur
1858 to Russian empire
1853 to Russian
empire
*Sakhalin*
1875 to Russian
empire, 1905
to Japan
Khabarovsk
*Kuril Islands
Northern islands to Japan 1875*
MONGOLIA
1900–14 under Russian influence
Hami
Gobi Desert
Manchuria
1900–05 Russian
occupation
Harbin
Ussuri
1860 to Russian empire
Yellow
Mukden
(Shenyang)
Vladivostok
Beijing
Port Arthur
(Lushun)
Seoul
KOREA
Tsushima
Strait
1905
*Sea of
Japan*
JAPAN
Edo
(Tokyo)
Lanzhou
MANCHU EMPIRE
Yangtze
*Yellow
Sea*
Chongqing

| | |
|---|---|
| | Russian empire, 1802 |
| | Russian territorial gains, 1809-55 |
| | Russian territorial gains, 1855-1914 |
| | Russian sphere of influence, 1907 |
| | Austro-Hungarian empire, 1853 |
| | Ottoman empire, 1853 |
| | "Big Bulgaria", 1878 |
| | territory under Japanese control by 1910 |
| | Manchu empire, 1912 |
| | British India, 1914 |
| | British sphere of influence, 1907 |
| — | border, 1914 |

Russian urban population, 1914

| | |
|---|---|
| ■ | under 100,000 |
| ▣ | 100,000–500,000 |
| ◆ | over 500,000 |

| | |
|---|---|
| | area of heavy grain export |
| | area of heavy industry, 1914 |
| | coal mining, 1914 |
| | gold mining, 1914 |
| | iron ore mining, 1914 |
| | oilfield, 1914 |
| | port |
| Tula | mutiny or strike, 1905 |
| | czarist prison/labor camp |
| — | railroad by 1917 |
| | trade route |
| ⟶ | Russian campaign, 1853 |
| ⟶ | Anglo-French campaign, 1854 |
| | Jewish Pale of Settlement, subject to pogroms, 1881-1907 |

dued the khanates in Bukhara, Khiva and Tashkent south of Lake Balkhash and the Aral Sea. However, a new war against Turkey and the creation of a client state in Bulgaria so alarmed the other great powers that Alexander let the Berlin Congress of 1878 put a brake on his Balkan ambitions.

Under his successor, Alexander III (r. 1881–94), Russia was poised to exploit trade routes in east Asia. The Trans-Siberian Railroad was begun, giving greater access to the mineral wealth of Siberia and central Asia and helping Russian entrepreneurs to penetrate Manchuria and Korea. This expansion brought Russia into collision with Britain and Japan. When antagonism erupted over the Russian occupation of Port Arthur, Japan humiliated the forces of czar Nicholas II (r. 1894–1917) in 1904–05. Russia lost

south Sakhalin island, the lease of Port Arthur and control of the railroads in southern Manchuria.

Discontent grew in European Russia with news of the defeats in the east. In January 1905, a peaceful demonstration in St Petersburg was fired upon by troops. The authorities eventually gave in to liberal demands and allowed an elected national assembly (*duma*) with limited powers. In its foreign relations, Russia agreed to "spheres of influence" in Persia with Britain in 1907. However, Russian interest revived in seeking access to the Mediterranean through the Balkans. Pan-Slavic Russian involvement with militant Serb groups opposing Austrian domination fueled the Balkan crisis of 1914 that sparked World War I. Within three years, Russia was beaten and the empire of the Russian czars had collapsed.

See also 93 (Russo-Japanese war);
100 (Russian revolution)

In 1884–85 representatives of fifteen European nations met in Berlin to settle rival claims to Africa. The Berlin Conference did not designate specific regions as colonies; rather it established the broad principles of the "scramble for Africa." The hinterland of a coast occupied by a European power was defined as a sphere of influence. To claim it, a power had to show itself capable of protecting "existing rights" and "freedom of trade and transit." This doctrine of "effective occupation" meant the process of colonization was conducted violently. Although the partition of Africa occurred quickly, it was the climax of years of activity by traders, administrators, soldiers and missionaries.

Africans were confronted with sudden piecemeal colonization. Some European governments worked through commercial ventures such as the Portuguese Niassa Company, the German South West and East Africa Companies, the Imperial East Africa Company, the Royal Niger Company and the British South Africa Company. By crudely imposing western practices – abolishing existing currencies, introducing hut taxes and removing middlemen from established trade patterns – these companies sowed the seeds of confrontation and armed resistance. In other cases companies conquered territory without reference to their governments. Sometimes, though, Africans invited the Europeans in, then found them impossible to remove.

The Europeans brought changes in modes of life and work. To pay the new taxes, Africans had to undertake wage labor. Imperial enterprises created a vast demand for unskilled labor: railroads, rubber, sugar and cocoa estates, and mining operations in central and southern Africa were all highly labor-intensive. By forcing Africans into these jobs, Europeans took away their culture and independence.

The response was varied. Some – such as the Bugandans who helped the British take over the states between the Great Lakes and form Uganda in 1903 – collaborated with the invaders. Others put their faith in religion: in the Sudan, Muhammad Ahmed (the *Mahdi*) rebelled against Anglo-Egyptian rule and founded a strict Islamic state. Yet apart from

**1** The British general Charles Gordon, appointed governor of the Sudan by Khedive Ismail Pasha in 1873, was killed when Mahdist forces overran Khartoum in 1885.

**2** In an uprising in 1905-07, Kinkjikitele Ngwale promised his followers that magic water (*maji-maji*) would protect them against machine-guns.

**3** The Uganda railroad was built from 1896–1901, and was the most important factor in opening up the landlocked but fertile area north of Lake Victoria.

**4** German colonization of Africa was characterized by foreign minister Bernard von Bülow in 1897 as the country claiming its right to "a place in the sun".

**5** In 1898, at Fashoda on the White Nile, a confrontation between a French expeditionary force sent from west Africa and British troops almost led to war. The French ultimately withdrew.

the Mahdist revolt and the defiance of the west African Asante, most African resistance was short-lived. Artillery and rapid-fire maxim guns brought many uprisings to a swift end: the Ijebu surrendered in 1892, the Matabele in 1896, the Mandinka (under Samori Toure) in 1898 and the Zulu in 1908.

The Swazi branch of the Zulu nation was never defeated in battle; their state was guaranteed independence by the Transvaal and the British, before becoming a British protectorate in 1905. Only one state successfully defied the Europeans: Ethiopia, led by a modernizing Emperor Menelik II, crushed the Italian army at the Battle of Adowa in 1896. The freed-slave state of Liberia also survived despite losing parts of its territory to Britain and France.

By 1914, virtually the whole continent had come under European control. African raw materials and human resources were exploited for the benefit of European industry and commerce. Portugal shipped thousands of indentured laborers to the cocoa plantations on São Tomé and Príncipe, where they lived and died in appalling conditions. Leopold II of Belgium, who took the Congo Free State as his personal possession in 1885, amassed a fortune in revenues from rubber and ivory. By 1908 when the

QUEEN VICTORIA of Britain, as visualized by a Yoruba craftsman in Nigeria in the late 19th century.

Belgian state annexed the Congo, its population was half what it had been in 1891. Conditions then improved only marginally: thousands of people were moved forcibly to work the copper mines.

With footholds in the west, south and north of Africa, Britain was well placed to acquire half of the new colonies and protectorates during the "scramble". Its Gold Coast colony was the world's top rubber producer by 1895. Threatened by competitors in southeast Asia, the colony switched to cocoa and became world leader in this crop by 1914.

Germany came late to colonization. Among its African possessions was Togoland, where medical reforms, support for missionary schools, new roads and rail links brought some benefits of modern life.

*Map labels: Madeira; Ifni 1912 Spanish protectorate; Agad; Canary Islands 1912 Spanish protectorate; Spanish Sahara; Rio de Oro 1884 Spanish protectorate; Mauritania; Cape Verde Islands; St Louis; Kaédi; Nioro; Dakar; Senegal; Kayes 1881 1891 1883; Fren Sud; Gambia; Fort James; Cacheo; Bamako; Portuguese Guinea; Bai Bureh's war; French Guinea; Conakry; Samori's resistance, 1881–92; Sierra Leone; Freetown; Monrovia; LIBERIA*

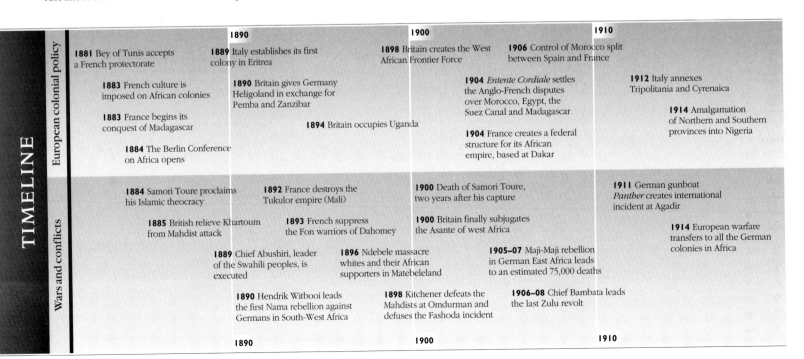

| | | 1890 | | 1900 | | 1910 |
|---|---|---|---|---|---|---|
| **TIMELINE** | **European colonial policy** | **1881** Bey of Tunis accepts a French protectorate | **1889** Italy establishes its first colony in Eritrea | **1898** Britain creates the West African Frontier Force | **1906** Control of Morocco split between Spain and France | |
| | | **1883** French culture is imposed on African colonies | **1890** Britain gives Germany Heligoland in exchange for Pemba and Zanzibar | **1904** *Entente Cordiale* settles the Anglo-French disputes over Morocco, Egypt, the Suez Canal and Madagascar | **1912** Italy annexes Tripolitania and Cyrenaica | |
| | | **1883** France begins its conquest of Madagascar | **1894** Britain occupies Uganda | **1904** France creates a federal structure for its African empire, based at Dakar | **1914** Amalgamation of Northern and Southern provinces into Nigeria | |
| | | **1884** The Berlin Conference on Africa opens | | | | |
| | **Wars and conflicts** | **1884** Samori Toure proclaims his Islamic theocracy | **1892** France destroys the Tukulor empire (Mali) | **1900** Death of Samori Toure, two years after his capture | **1911** German gunboat *Panther* creates international incident at Agadir | |
| | | **1885** British relieve Khartoum from Mahdist attack | **1893** French suppress the Fon warriors of Dahomey | **1900** Britain finally subjugates the Asante of west Africa | **1914** European warfare transfers to all the German colonies in Africa | |
| | | **1889** Chief Abushiri, leader of the Swahili peoples, is executed | **1896** Ndebele massacre whites and their African supporters in Matabeleland | **1905–07** Maji-Maji rebellion in German East Africa leads to an estimated 75,000 deaths | | |
| | | **1890** Hendrik Witbooi leads the first Nama rebellion against Germans in South-West Africa | **1898** Kitchener defeats the Mahdists at Omdurman and defuses the Fashoda incident | **1906–08** Chief Bambata leads the last Zulu revolt | | |
| | | 1890 | | 1900 | | 1910 |

PORTUGAL
SPAIN
Corsica
Sardinia
Balearic Islands
ITALY
SERBIA
BULGARIA
ALBANIA
GREECE
1911
Sicily
Malta
Crete
Cyprus
Mediterranean Sea
OTTOMAN EMPIRE
PERSIA

Tangier
Oran
Algiers
Bone
Tunis
Spanish Morocco
Fez
1912 Spanish protectorate
French Morocco
1912 French protectorate
Laghouat
Tunisia 1881 French protectorate
1881–82
Tripoli
Benghazi
Derna
Tobruk
Alexandria
Cairo
Suez
Syria
Medina
Mecca
Kuwait
1899 British protectorate
Bahrain
Qatar
Riyadh
Trucial Oman
Muscat

1901
Algeria
1902
Tuat
In Salah
1906
Taoudenni
HOGGAR MASSIF
Tamanrasset
1904
Ghat
Murzuq
Fezzan
Tripolitania 1912 to Italy
Cyrenaica 1912 to Italy
1913
SAHARA DESERT
Egypt 1882 British protectorate
Tushki 1889
Wadi Halfa
1896
1897–98
1898
1898
Suakin
Red Sea
ARABIA
Oman 1891 British protectorate
Yemen
Sana
Hadramaut 1888 British protectorate

1904
1904
Timbuktu
1891–94
Gao
Air
Bilma
TIBESTI MASSIF
Rabih resistance, 1892–1900
Dongola
Sudan 1898 Anglo-Egyptian condominium
Omdurman 1898
Khartoum
1899
1898
Eritrea 1889 to Italy
Massawa
West Aden Protectorate 1903 British protectorate
Aden
Socotra 1886 British protectorate

French West Africa
1895 federation of dependencies, reorganised 1904
Segu
Upper Volta
Say
Sokoto
Niger
1899–1900
Zinder
1906
Agadez
Kano
1903
1902
Chad
Lake Chad
French Equatorial Africa 1910 federation of dependencies
1900
1898
Fashoda
1899
1900–01
5
French Somaliland 1884/5 French protectorate
Djibouti
British Somaliland 1884 British protectorate
Addis Ababa
ETHIOPIA
Adowa 1896
1

Samori's resistance, 1892–98
1896
4
Sokoto resistance
Burmi 1903
Nigeria 1914 British colony & protectorate
Ijebu resistance
Fon resistance
Dahomey 1892–94
Lokoja
Benue
1896–98
Ubangi Shari
Ubangi
White Nile
Blue Nile
Shebelle
Italian Somaliland 1889 to Italy
Mogadishu

Gold Coast
1884 protectorate
1901
Asante resistance
1888–90
Kumasi
Togoland 1884–1897
Lomé
Accra
Takoradi
Ivory Coast
1885–86
Lagos
Porto Novo
Itsekiri resistance
Fernando Póo
Spanish Guinea
Príncipe to Portugal
Libreville
São Tomé
Annobón to Spain
Cameroon 1884 to Germany
Douala
1884
4
1884
Gabon
1896–98
to French Equatorial Africa
Middle Congo
Brazzaville
Congo
Belgian Congo (Congo Free State)
1885 to Leopold II, 1908 to Belgium as Belgian Congo
1896–98
Uganda 1894 British protectorate
Entebbe
Lake Victoria
Kisuma
3
Nandi, Embu and Kisii resistance
British East Africa 1895 British protectorate
Nairobi
1890
Lake Turkana

ATLANTIC OCEAN
INDIAN OCEAN

Mahdist state, 1881–98
border, 1914
territory controlled by non-African powers, 1914
Belgium
France
Germany
Italy
Ottoman empire
Portugal
Spain
United Kingdom

Cabinda 1886 to Angola
Kasai
Kwango
Cuango
Leopoldville
Luanda
Benguela
Angola 1886–90 borders determined by treaties
Ujiji
German East Africa 1885 to Germany
4
Lake Tanganyika
Abushiri's resistance
Tanga
Pangani
Dar es Salaam
Kitopi
Kilwa Kisiwani
Maji-Maji rebellion, 1905–07
2
Pemba 1885 to Germany, 1890 to Britain
Zanzibar 1885 to Germany, 1890 to Britain
Mombasa
Comoros 1886 to France

European routes of expansion, 1880–1914
Belgian
British
French
German
Italian
Portuguese
major African resistance
oasis
gold
diamonds
copper
coal
railroads by 1914

Luangwa
Lake Malawi
Northern Rhodesia 1911 to Britain
Lusaka
Zambezi
Tete
Nyasaland 1891 British protectorate
Mozambique
Quelimane
Beira
Cuando
Okavango
Livingstone
Salisbury
Southern Rhodesia 1888 British protectorate
Bulawayo
1896
1896–1903
1891–94 borders determined by treaties, 1907 Portuguese colony
Mozambique
Madagascar 1885 French protectorate, 1896 French colony
Tananarive
1894
Madagascar
Mauritius
Réunion
1894–1906
Fort Dauphin

Herero rebellion, 1904–08
German South-West Africa 1884 to Germany
Boundary war, 1896
Okavango Delta
Bechuanaland 1885 British protectorate
1890
Limpopo
Walvis Bay to Union of South Africa
Windhoek
4
Nama rebellion, 1905–09
Mafeking
Johannesburg
Vaal
Bambata's rebellion, 1906–08
Swaziland 1905 British protectorate
Lourenço Marques
Delagoa Bay

Lüderitz
Bondels–Warts rebellion, 1904
Kimberley
Orange
Union of South Africa 1910 British dominion
Durban
Basutoland 1843 British protectorate, 1868 to Britain
Cape Town
Cape of Good Hope
Port Elizabeth

0        1000 km
0        800 mi

See also 91 (world trade);
104 (early 20th century);

From the last quarter of the 18th century to the outbreak of World War I, Europe was transformed from a series of traditional agrarian communities into a collection of modern industrial nations. Radical changes in the methods by which goods were produced – the widespread adoption of capitalism, mechanization and the factory system – gave rise to a period of unparalleled economic growth, though interrrupted by cyclical depressions. There was also a rapid increase in population and an influx of people from the countryside into the towns and cities that sprang up around the new workplaces.

The Industrial Revolution, as this transformation came to be known, had its origins in Britain. Its effects were first seen in the cotton and woollen industries in the north of the country. Mechanical innovations improved the speed and efficiency of weaving, and required new factories powered first by waterwheels and later by steam engines. These factories brought together the various operations involved in textile manufacture. Britain was ideally placed to pioneer and develop mass production. If possessed abundant natural resources to power the new machinery, favorable terrain on which to construct extensive transport networks (canals in the late 18th and early 19th centuries, and rail from the 1830s onward), and a ready market for manufactured goods. By 1815, Britain's industrialists had already made it the "workshop of the world", with coal mining, textile production and pig-iron smelting exceeding the output of the rest of Europe combined. Industrialization had spread to mainland Europe at the end of the 18th century (for example, in the Belgian armaments industry or cotton weaving in Saxony and northern France). But Britain's embargo on the emigration of skilled artisans and the export of machinery during the Napoleonic period prevented a wider adoption of the new methods of production.

Beginning in the 1820s in Belgium, however, coal mining and the textile and metal industries took root in continental Europe. As in Britain, the new rail network played a prime role in promoting economic expansion. Rail transport allowed rapid distribution of goods, and its con-

## TIMELINE

### Technological change

**1783–84** A new purifying process makes iron smelting more efficient

**1787** Edmund Cartwright (Br) invents the steam-operated weaving loom

**1795** Joseph Bramah (Br) invents the hydraulic press

**1800** Henry Maudslay (Br) invents the precision screw-cutting lathe

**1825** The Stockton and Darlington Railway opens

**1831** Michael Faraday (Br) builds the first electric motor and generator

**1835** Germany's first railroad is opened (Bavaria)

**1837** The first French railroad links Paris with Saint-Germain

**1856** Henry Bessemer (Br) pioneers manfacture of steel from iron ore; first commercial synthetic dye is produced

**1861** Siemens-Martin open-hearth steelmaking process (Ger)

**1876** Nikolaus Otto (Ger) invents the internal-combustion engine

**1878** The first electric street-lighting appears in London

**1883** Orient Express brings rail travel between Paris and Constantinople

**1885** Daimler and Benz develop the automobile (Ger)

**1909** Bakelite, the first commercially viable plastic, is patented (Belgium)

### Social change

**1799–1800** Prohibition of trade unions in Britain

**1833** Britain's Factory Act places restrictions on use of children in industry

**1846** Corn Law repeal in Britain begins free trade era

**1878** Dissolution of the German Social Democratic Party

**1880–89** Bismarck introduces state social welfare system

**1909–10** National strikes by rail and postal workers in France

1800    1850    1900

border, 1914

heavy industrial or mining area

major textile manufacturing area

other large coal deposit

other large iron ore deposit

urban population, 1914
- • under 100,000
- ■ 100,000–500,000
- ■ 500,000–1,000,000
- ◆ over 1,000,000

⚒ oilfield, 1914

⚓ port

⚑ center of socialism

Berlin  research and development center for
the chemical industry

19m  national population (million)
where known, 1914

railroad constructed by 1870

railroad constructed 1870–1914

0         600 km
0         400 mi

CHILD-LABOR was common in the
mines of early 19th-century Britain,
but was banned in 1842.

more hazardous. Employers exploited the large pool of child and female labor to depress wages. Living conditions deteriorated in the vastly expanding new cities, where sanitation failed to keep pace with population growth. Cholera and typhus epidemics were common. A second bout of industrialization after 1870, based on steel and the new power source of electricity, did little to alleviate these problems.

To challenge the effects of capital, both the industrial working classes and the rural peasantry (serfdom did not end in Russia until 1861) organized themselves into trade unions. These efforts met opposition from the state as well as the capitalists. Ideas for alternative ways of structuring society arose during this period. Socialist parties were formed to argue for a more equal distribution of wealth, becoming particularly strong in Germany and France. Karl Marx and Friedrich Engels published their *Communist Manifesto* in 1848, arguing for a class-based revolution in highly industrialized states such as Britain. Anarchists advocated the violent abolition of the state, while syndicalists sought worker-control of industry through general strikes. To forestall social upheaval, some governments enacted legislation to alleviate the worst effects of industrialization. Compulsory free state education was widely instituted; labor in factories and mines was gradually regulated; working hours were cut and wages rose (as did inflation); improved housing also became slowly available. The first decade of the 20th century was marked by widespread unrest, but the old problem of unemployment would be briefly solved by the demands of World War I.

For many people, the solution to poverty was to emigrate. Nearly half a million Poles moved west to find jobs in the industrialized Ruhr, and Italian farmers took harvest work in Germany, France and Austria. Yet far more people left Europe, emigrating in their millions to Australia and New Zealand, but above all to the Americas.

**1** The world's first railroad to use steam locomotive traction was opened for coal traffic in 1825 between Stockton and Darlington in northeast England.

**2** The new country of Belgium, flat and densely populated, was the first continental European state to complete its rail network, in the 1840s.

**3** A major early corporate investment bank was Crédit Mobilier, founded in Paris in 1852; ill-advised speculation led to the bank's collapse in 1867.

**4** In 1856, one of the world's first oil refineries opened in Ploisti. Foreign investment brought rapid expansion of the Romanian oilfields from 1895.

**5** The major iron-ore deposits in Lorraine were a serious loss to France's nascent steelmaking industry after the area was annexed by Germany in 1871.

**6** The German Social Democratic Party was the strongest prewar socialist party, despite laws banning it. The party claimed 1.5 million members in 1890.

**7** Barcelona and Bilbao were the two main industrial centers of 19th-century Spain; Barcelona's powerful anarcho-syndicalist movement was set up in 1910.

**8** A Luddite (machine-wrecker) revolt (1811–12) ended when its leaders were hanged in York 1813.

See also 66 (18th-century European economy);
91 (world trade); 92 (migration)

sumption of materials stimulated further growth. By 1890, nearly all the main rail routes across Europe had been completed.

Private investment lay behind the success of many major industrial ventures, such as some early railroads, but spectacular bankruptcies showed the need for a new method of funding capital projects. Especially in continental Europe, joint-stock limited liability companies, supported by development banks, were founded to provide credit. Free trade (the abolition of import tariffs protecting local producers from competition) was another crucial factor in industrial expansion. Britain lifted its high import duties on corn in 1846. Agreements with France, the Prussian *Zollverein* and Belgium in the 1860s further encouraged the reduction of tariffs. By 1870, most

European countries had expanded foreign trade and industrial production by lowering or abolishing their tariffs – though the position gradually reversed after the Franco-Prussian War (1870–71).

The social effects of the Industrial Revolution were as radical as its technological and financial consequences. The years of growth between 1840–70 also witnessed periodic financial crises and bouts of widespread unemployment. Harvests were critical, causing wild fluctuations in the price of food. Later, the import of cheap foodstuffs from Canada, the United States and Russia undercut agriculture in the industrializing states. New production methods threatened traditional skills, sometimes leading to machine-wrecking by disgruntled workers. As mechanization spread, working conditions became

**B**etween 1830 and 1914 world trade was dominated by the industrialized nations of Europe and the United States. These countries traded manufactured goods and foodstuffs with each other and, increasingly, with the traditional societies of Latin America, Asia and Africa.

The growth in production in the industrialized nations was accompanied by a rise in foreign trade, which had risen from 10 percent of all earnings in 1830 to 33 percent in 1914. This was based in large part on the systematic exploitation of traditional societies and their raw materials. The trade passing through the major ports constructed in China, Latin America and Africa hardly benefited the economies of the host countries. As a result, rural economies were often destroyed – as in Africa, India and the Dutch East Indies – and replaced by westernized agricultural patterns that dictated the nature of the crops grown, and the manner in which they were marketed. Accompanied by colonial warfare, this exploitation was the ultimate expression of imperialism between 1830 and 1914.

The infrastructure of global trade was financed by the industrialized nations. For example, the economic development of Africa required railroads to carry exports to the coast (▷ 89). Rail links were vital, as the continent's great rivers were often ill suited to the mass transportation of freight, especially in sub-Saharan Africa. Similarly, investment by the industrialized nations built harbors, provided ships and established coaling stations worldwide. To handle the new commerce, port facilities were transformed in the industrialized countries themselves as well as in the colonies. Existing harbors, for example those in New York and Barcelona, were enlarged, while entirely new ports were built at Trieste in Italy and Le Havre in France.

Ship design also underwent radical change, with the advent of steam propulsion in 1833, iron hulls in 1837 and steel hulls in 1856. Sailing-ships reached their peak in the fast, elegant "clippers" that competed to transport commodities such as tea from China in record time. Yet by mid-century, purpose-built steamships with efficient engines were beginning to provide stiff competition for sailing vessels. Sail was dealt a further blow when the new canals cut at Suez, Kiel and Panama spared the need for long and often treacherous voyages around land-masses (▷ 81). Between 1850 and 1914 the world's merchant fleet expanded from 9 million net tons to over 35 million tons in 1914.

Increased global trade required changes in the way the world's economy

## TIMELINE

**1834** Official creation of *Zollverein* (customs union; begun 1819) stimulates trade in Germany

**1821** Gold standard is adopted as monetary system for the first time in Britain

**1865** First transatlantic telegraph cable is successfully laid

**1856** Efficient steelmaking process is invented by Henry Bessemer

|  | 1825 | 1850 | 1875 |
|---|---|---|---|
| The Americas | | | |
| Europe | | | |
| Middle East | | | |
| Africa | | | |
| Asia and Australasia | | | |

**1838** *Great Western* launched: first transatlantic passenger steamship

**1853** US naval expedition opens up Japan to world trade

**1869** First transcontinental railroad completed (USA)

**1839–60** China is coerced into foreign trade by two "Opium Wars" with west

**1859** The world's first oilwell is sunk in Pennsylvania (USA)

**1876** Telephone is patented by Alexander Graham Bell; 50,000 in the USA by 1880

**1840** Introduction of postal stamps in Britain initiates efficient mail services

**1859** Port Said (Egypt) founded; becomes world's main ship-coaling station

**1877** Frozen meat is shipped for the first time, from Argentina to France

source of commodity

| | | | | | | |
|---|---|---|---|---|---|---|
| C | cotton | Ft | fertiliser | P | palm products | |
| Co | cocoa | G | gold | R | rubber | |
| Cf | coffee | Gr | grain | Ri | rice | |
| Cu | copper ore | I | iron ore | Sp | spices | |
| D | dairy produce | J | jute | Su | sugar | |
| Di | diamonds | M | manufactured goods | Ti | timber | |
| F | fruit | Mt | meat | To | tobacco | |
| Fi | fish | O | oil | W | wool | |

——— border, 1914
seaway
industrial region
——— railroad, 1914
——— trans-Atlantic cable
gold strike

**1886** The world's first purpose-built oil tanker is launched in Germany

**1885** Internal combustion engine is invented by the German Gottlieb Daimler

**1914** USA is the world's richest economy, with GNP per capita five times the European average

**1914** The international gold standard, adopted in the 1870s, ends with outbreak of World War I

1900

**1890–1914** Natural nitrates are exported from Chile in large quantities, for use in fertilizers and explosives

**1890–1910** Cheap cotton goods produced in China, India and Japan undercut European cotton industry

**1895** Malayan rubber plantations begin production

**1913** Henry Ford introduces conveyor-belt mass production techniques in his automobile plants

was run. The world's most heavily traded currencies were now based on the gold standard. According to this monetary system, bank notes or deposits were convertible into gold on demand. The major gold strikes in California, Australia, South Africa and Canada increased the money supply and so sustained the growth in commercial activity (▷ 84). Adequate gold reserves deposited in the world's financial centers guaranteed that a country could trade without running into debt. Monetary unions, with currencies based on the gold standard, also became popular. The rapidly-industrializing Japanese, convinced that a gold-based currency was invaluable for trade, joined the gold standard in 1897 (▷ 93).

Rapid sea communications, coupled with the effects of migration and the opening up of fertile lands in Canada, the United States, Russia, Australia, the Danube lands and Argentina, meant that cheap food surpluses became readily available to the industrialized countries. One major effect of global trade from the 1870s onward, therefore, was to reduce drastically the price of wheat and most other staple foodstuffs.

Another important result of global trade was the growth in the sales of modern technology to traditional societies. This was frequently in the form of transport technology, such as railroads and engines, or factory machinery, but also increasingly came to include advanced military hardware. The balance of power in regional conflicts was radically altered by this development ▪

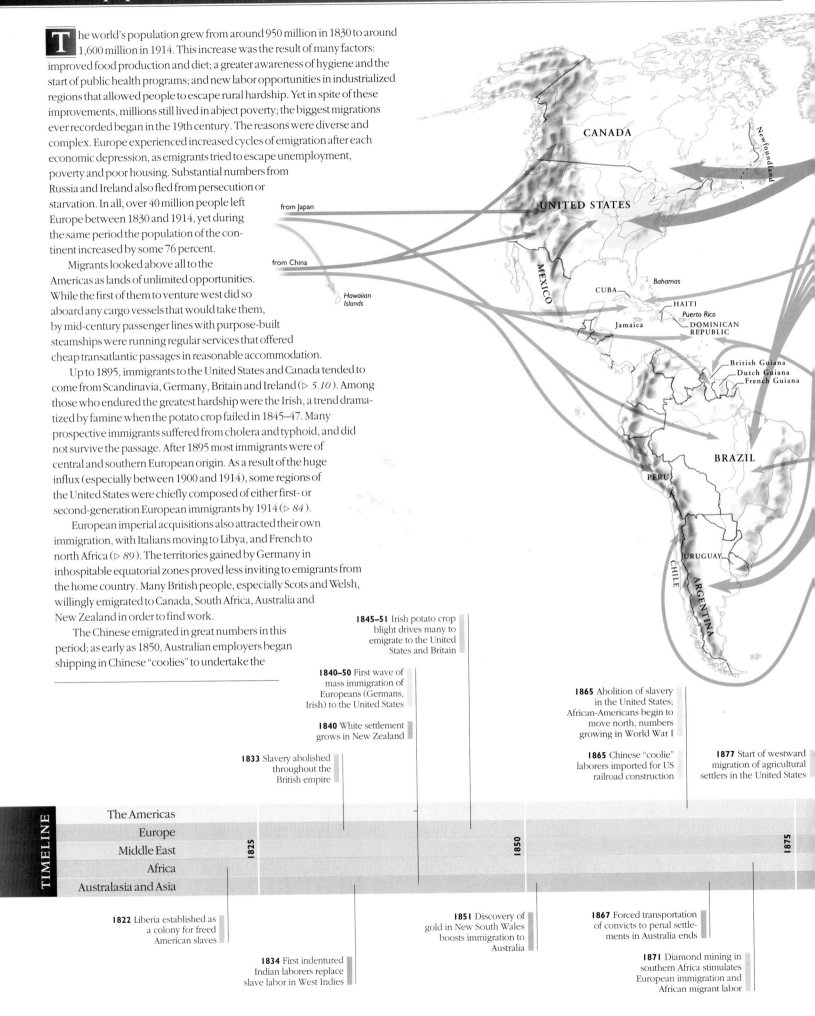

The world's population grew from around 950 million in 1830 to around 1,600 million in 1914. This increase was the result of many factors: improved food production and diet; a greater awareness of hygiene and the start of public health programs; and new labor opportunities in industrialized regions that allowed people to escape rural hardship. Yet in spite of these improvements, millions still lived in abject poverty; the biggest migrations ever recorded began in the 19th century. The reasons were diverse and complex. Europe experienced increased cycles of emigration after each economic depression, as emigrants tried to escape unemployment, poverty and poor housing. Substantial numbers from Russia and Ireland also fled from persecution or starvation. In all, over 40 million people left Europe between 1830 and 1914, yet during the same period the population of the continent increased by some 76 percent.

Migrants looked above all to the Americas as lands of unlimited opportunities. While the first of them to venture west did so aboard any cargo vessels that would take them, by mid-century passenger lines with purpose-built steamships were running regular services that offered cheap transatlantic passages in reasonable accommodation.

Up to 1895, immigrants to the United States and Canada tended to come from Scandinavia, Germany, Britain and Ireland (▷ 5.10). Among those who endured the greatest hardship were the Irish, a trend dramatized by famine when the potato crop failed in 1845–47. Many prospective immigrants suffered from cholera and typhoid, and did not survive the passage. After 1895 most immigrants were of central and southern European origin. As a result of the huge influx (especially between 1900 and 1914), some regions of the United States were chiefly composed of either first- or second-generation European immigrants by 1914 (▷ 84).

European imperial acquisitions also attracted their own immigration, with Italians moving to Libya, and French to north Africa (▷ 89). The territories gained by Germany in inhospitable equatorial zones proved less inviting to emigrants from the home country. Many British people, especially Scots and Welsh, willingly emigrated to Canada, South Africa, Australia and New Zealand in order to find work.

The Chinese emigrated in great numbers in this period; as early as 1850, Australian employers began shipping in Chinese "coolies" to undertake the

**1845–51** Irish potato crop blight drives many to emigrate to the United States and Britain

**1840–50** First wave of mass immigration of Europeans (Germans, Irish) to the United States

**1840** White settlement grows in New Zealand

**1833** Slavery abolished throughout the British empire

**1865** Abolition of slavery in the United States; African-Americans begin to move north, numbers growing in World War I

**1865** Chinese "coolie" laborers imported for US railroad construction

**1877** Start of westward migration of agricultural settlers in the United States

| TIMELINE | | | |
|---|---|---|---|
| The Americas | | | |
| Europe | | | |
| Middle East | 1825 | 1850 | 1875 |
| Africa | | | |
| Australasia and Asia | | | |

**1822** Liberia established as a colony for freed American slaves

**1834** First indentured Indian laborers replace slave labor in West Indies

**1851** Discovery of gold in New South Wales boosts immigration to Australia

**1867** Forced transportation of convicts to penal settlements in Australia ends

**1871** Diamond mining in southern Africa stimulates European immigration and African migrant labor border, c.1900

migration destination
North America
Central and
South America
Australasia
other

persons per sq km, c.1900
over 200
101–200
51–100
11–50
under 10

D. Denmark
P. Portugal
R. Romania

Greenland

NORWAY

SWEDEN

UNITED
KINGDOM

Ireland

D.

GERMANY

FRANCE

SPAIN

P.

AUSTRO-
HUNGARIAN
EMPIRE

ITALY

R.

GREECE

RUSSIAN EMPIRE

Sakhalin

Korea

JAPAN

MANCHU EMPIRE

Morocco

Tunisia

Tripoli

Algeria

Cyrenaica

Rio de
Oro

PALESTINE

ARABIA

India

SIAM

French
Indo-China

Philippine
Islands

Uganda

British East
Africa

Belgian
Congo

German East
Africa

Angola

Madagascar

Celebes

Borneo

New Guinea

Sumatra

Java

Timor

Solomon
Islands

Northern
Rhodesia

German
South-West
Africa

Mozambique

Union of
South Africa

Fiji Islands

AUSTRALIA

NEW
ZEALAND

**1900** Since 1880, over nine
million immigrants have
arrived in the United States

**1882** Attacks on Chinese
miners in the USA lead to
Chinese Exclusion Act

**1881–82** Mass emigration
of Jews from Russia after
first of series of pogroms

**1880–90** Agricultural crisis
in Italy; many migrate to
the USA and Argentina

**1914** Population of Europe
stands at 430 million on
eve of World War I

1900

**1885–1910** Japanese
migration to Hawaii,
Peru and the United States

**1902** Start of the "White
Australia" policy; non-
European immigrants
excluded for over 60 years

hard labor formerly done by convicts.
Laws were soon passed, however, to
prevent further Chinese immigration. In the
United States, the Chinese who had been brought in
to mine the California goldfields and build the transcontinental railroads also
encountered discrimination. Later waves of Chinese migrants joined Indians in
seeking jobs, often as indentured laborers, on the plantations of Cuba, Siam,
British Guiana and French Indo-China. Others worked alongside African
migrants in South African gold mines.

Overpopulation in Japan led to largescale emigration in the 1880s, first to
Hawaii and then to California. However, after the host country threatened total
exclusion, Japanese emigrants went instead to Manchuria, Brazil and Peru.

Russian Jews began to emigrate in large numbers after the pogroms –
organized massacres of their communities – began in the 1880s (▷ 88). Over
two million fled to the United States, while some 60,000 were drawn by the
ideals of the new Zionist movement to establish a Jewish homeland in
Palestine. In Russia, millions of non-Jews sought a new life in undeveloped
regions. Three million emigrated to North America, while many European
workers settled in Russia. Germans and Austrians came to found new
"colonist villages" or to find work in newly established industrial towns.
Europe, the source of so many migrants in the 19th century, was now accustomed to workers, capital and expertise constantly crossing national frontiers,
a situation that would end abruptly with the outbreak of war in 1914 ■

The military bureaucracy (*bakufu*) that had been established at Edo by Tokugawa Ieyasu at the beginning of the 17th century held sway over Japan until the mid-19th century. Under this system, the governor (*shogun*) exercised absolute power and kept close control of the provincial barons (*daimyo*) and the increasingly poverty-stricken *samurai* warrior class. The emperor remained a remote, divine figurehead, residing at Kyoto some 480 kilometers (280 miles) from Edo.

Contact with foreigners was abhorred by this closed society. Russian and American ships that attempted to trade with Japan in 1791–92 were repelled. However, the opening up of California and the 1849 gold rush made the United States conscious that the Pacific offered unexplored commercial opportunities. The arrival at Uraga in 1853 of US Commodore Matthew Perry's "black ships" – a naval expedition to open trade with Japan – brought the question of contact with the outside world to the fore. Perry's return to Edo Bay the following year with a squadron of warships and 4,000 marines forced the *bakufu*'s hand, and the first limited concessions were granted to westerners to trade through the small ports of Shimoda and Hakodate.

The years following Perry's expedition saw resistance to foreign influence, organized by young samurai. Attacks on shipping caused a multinational naval force to bombard the forts at Kagoshima and Shimonoseki in 1863–64. Anti-foreign sentiment grew into concerted opposition to the shogunate. During 1867–68 civil war led to the the shogun being replaced with the emperor, in a development known as the Meiji ("enlightened rule") restoration. The emperor moved to Edo, now renamed Tokyo.

Under the new imperial regime, Japan resolved to compete with the west by industrializing, building a modern army and navy and adopting an aggressive foreign policy. In this way, it was intended that Japan should become the dominant power in east Asia. A pragmatic line was now taken toward foreign influence. Western expertise was harnessed to build Japan's first light industrial enterprise, a silk-reeling factory. The growth of heavy industry also required the import of western plant and materials – steel, steam engines, and railroad rolling stock were all purchased from overseas. Through the offices of a samurai financier, Masayoshi Matsukata, the Japanese government borrowed money from the four giant *zaibatsu*, (financial organizations) that dominated banking, industry and commerce – Mitsui, Mitsubishi, Sumitomo and Yasuda.

Between 1871 and 1914 Japan achieved dominance in east Asia; the country acquired the Ryukyu Islands, the Bonin Islands (Ogasawara), southern Sakhalin and the Kuril Islands. In 1894 the Tonghak revolt in Korea reflected a growing socio-economic crisis at home, but this provoked Chinese and Japanese intervention, with war erupting between the two powers the same year. Japanese ships destroyed the Chinese navy at the Battle of the Yellow Sea, while its army crushed the Chinese in Manchuria. The Japanese took Taiwan and the Pescadores; Korea briefly became independent. Yet intervention by the great powers subsequently deprived Japan of Port Arthur and the Liaodong Peninsula. When Russia was granted a lease of Port Arthur by China and attempted to expand its influence in Korea, Japanese fears grew stronger. Japan negotiated an alliance with Britain in 1902 that effectively neutralized Russia's ally, France, in the event of war, and then resolved to confront and overcome its chief rival in the region.

In 1904 Japanese troops landed in Korea and moved north toward the Yalu. Japanese warships attacked and then blockaded the Russian fleet at Port Arthur. On 1 January 1905 the Russian base surrendered. At Mukden Japan defeated the Russian army. Meanwhile the Russian Baltic Fleet, having sailed halfway around the world, arrived in Tsushima Straits too late to relieve Port Arthur. In one of the most important sea victories in history, Admiral Togo annihilated the obsolescent Russian fleet. In 1905 by the Treaty of Portsmouth (USA), Russia surrendered south Sakhalin and leases on Port Arthur and the South Manchurian railroad (completed in 1904). In 1910 Japan annexed independent Korea. By 1914 Japan had a major sphere of influence in east Asia.

- border, c.1850
- Japanese territory, c.1850
- Japanese territorial gain by 1914
- Japanese sphere of influence by 1914
- Manchu empire, c.1850
- Republic of China, 1914
- Russian empire, c.1850
- Russian territorial gain by 1914
- Russian sphere of influence by 1914
- Russian occupation, 1897–1905
- area allied against *Bakufu*, 1868
- area leased by China to a foreign power
- Commodore Perry's visits to Japan, 1853 and 1854
- Japanese campaign, Sino–Japanese war, 1894–95
- Japanese campaign, Russo–Japanese war, 1904–05
- Russian campaign, 1904–05
- Japanese trading port by 1860
- bombardment by western powers, 1863–64
- battle, 1894–95
- battle, 1904–05
- peasant protest or riot, 1780–1850
- Tonghak revolt, 1894
- Japanese industrial area by 1914
- railroad, c.1914

| 0 | 400 km |
| 0 | 400 mi |

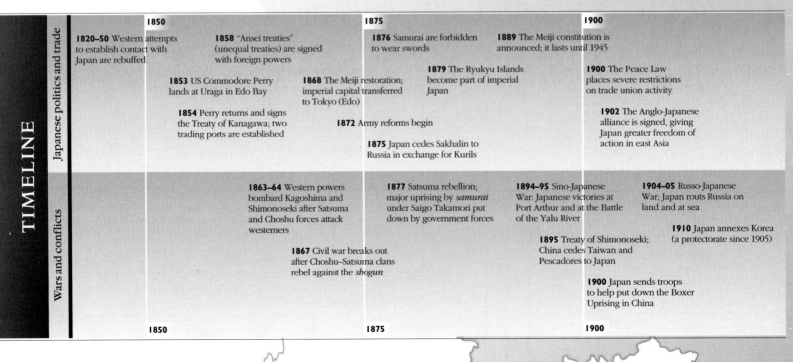

**TIMELINE**

**Japanese politics and trade**

| 1850 | 1875 | 1900 |
|---|---|---|
| **1820–50** Western attempts to establish contact with Japan are rebuffed | **1876** Samurai are forbidden to wear swords | **1889** The Meiji constitution is announced; it lasts until 1945 |
| **1858** "Ansei treaties" (unequal treaties) are signed with foreign powers | **1879** The Ryukyu Islands become part of imperial Japan | **1900** The Peace Law places severe restrictions on trade union activity |
| **1853** US Commodore Perry lands at Uraga in Edo Bay | **1868** The Meiji restoration; imperial capital transferred to Tokyo (Edo) | **1902** The Anglo-Japanese alliance is signed, giving Japan greater freedom of action in east Asia |
| **1854** Perry returns and signs the Treaty of Kanagawa; two trading ports are established | **1872** Army reforms begin | |
| | **1875** Japan cedes Sakhalin to Russia in exchange for Kurils | |

**Wars and conflicts**

| 1850 | 1875 | 1900 |
|---|---|---|
| **1863–64** Western powers bombard Kagoshima and Shimonoseki after Satsuma and Choshu forces attack westerners | **1877** Satsuma rebellion; major uprising by *samurai* under Saigo Takamori put down by government forces | **1894–95** Sino-Japanese War: Japanese victories at Port Arthur and at the Battle of the Yalu River |
| **1867** Civil war breaks out after Choshu–Satsuma clans rebel against the *shogun* | | **1895** Treaty of Shimonoseki; China cedes Taiwan and Pescadores to Japan |
| | | **1904–05** Russo-Japanese War; Japan routs Russia on land and at sea |
| | | **1910** Japan annexes Korea (a protectorate since 1905) |
| | | **1900** Japan sends troops to help put down the Boxer Uprising in China |

THE JAPANESE emperor is shown goading the Russian bear in this European cartoon of the early 20th century.

**1** The goals of Perry's expedition were limited: to secure humane treatment of American whalers ship-wrecked on Japan, and to gain access to trade and supplies at one or two ports.

**2** *Samurai* activists from the feudal domains of Satsuma and Choshu were prominent in the anti-foreigner movement, and later dominated the Meiji regime.

**3** Japan's first railroad was the short line between the port of Yokohama and Tokyo (Edo), built in 1872.

**4** The Osaka steam-powered Cotton Spinning Company began manufacturing in 1883; by 1914 more than eighty Japanese spinning mills were responsible for nearly 25 percent of world output.

**5** The Tonghak ("eastern learning") revolt in Korea mixed Buddhist, Confucian and nationalist ideas, and sought to expel foreign powers from the peninsula.

**6** Port Arthur, leased by Russia from China in 1898, was invaluable to the Russian navy as a warm-water port; Vladivostok was icebound for part of the year.

See also 63 (Tokugawa shogunate);
103 (Japan in the early 20th century)

Under the expansionist Manchu (Qing) dynasty, China enjoyed unrivaled power in east Asia. By 1783, emperor Qianlong (r.1736–96) had settled colonists in Xinjiang and imposed tributary status on Burma and Annam. He restricted foreign merchants to Guangzhou and shunned the industrial innovations offered by western "barbarian" traders. After his abdication, however, imports of opium from British India increased steadily, and eventually led to two "Opium Wars" with China (1839–42; 1856–60). The outcome of the first was the 1842 Treaty of Nanjing, which confirmed Britain's gain of Hong Kong and right to trade through five "treaty ports". The second resulted in two agreements (in 1858 and 1860) for more western commercial footholds.

Russian ambitions focussed on obtaining strategically important Chinese territory. Russian forces annexed the valuable Ili region and advanced into Xinjiang, from which they withdrew in return for cash compensation in 1881. Russia also annexed eastern Siberia (1858–60) to secure ice-free waters in the Sea of Japan. A similar policy of territorial acquisition was adopted by Britain, France and Japan, which began to encroach on the tributary states beyond the Manchu borders. Britain moved into Lower Burma in 1852 and annexed the entire country in 1886. France, entrenched in southern Indo-China, was anxious to open trade with the southern Chinese province of Yunnan. It therefore fought a brief war with China to establish a protectorate over Tongking by 1885. Between 1875 and 1880, Japan annexed the Chinese tributary of the Ryukyu islands and began to weaken Chinese influence in another tributary, Korea. Taiwan and the Pescadores were also lost by China in 1894–95. These concessions and defeats represented unprecedented humiliation for the Qing dynasty.

While foreign powers eroded its frontiers, China faced even greater dangers from within. Official corruption, high taxation and continuing internal migration caused local uprisings. Many were caused by secret societies with political aspirations. The White Lotus sect vowed to overthrow the Qing and restore the Ming dynasty. Their rebellion raged through central China 1796–1804, though some unrest continued to 1813. After 1850 these revolts became so serious as to threaten the survival of the Qing. Hong Xiuquan led the Taiping rebellion, proclaiming the end of Manchu rule and the advent of the "Heavenly Kingdom of the Great Peace." This insurrection and its suppression by Qing forces cost up to 20 million lives. Disaffection with Manchu rule also brought rebellion in Taiwan, Muslim revolts in Xinjiang and Yunnan, Nian peasant risings in Henan and Miao tribal unrest in Guizhou.

The short-lived "self-strengthening movement" instigated by the statesman Li Hongzhang in the 1860s attempted to construct a modern military and industrial state. Yet his plan to purchase foreign armaments and build arsenals and factories met with little support from the dowager empress Cixi (r.1862–1908) and her court at Beijing. Meanwhile, the western clamor for land concessions, mining rights, railroad, building and trade facilities continued. In Cixi's reign, anti-western sentiment took on a republican flavor, and crystallized into the nationalist movement led by Sun Yixian (Sun Yat-sen).

The shame of further territory losses in 1898 led to the Boxer Uprising of 1900–01. This major revolt engulfed several provinces but concentrated chiefly on attacking the foreign legations in Beijing. The outcome of this rebellion, which was supported by the dowager empress, was the International Protocol of 1901, which gave the powers yet more trade concessions and a huge indemnity payment from the Qing. Western soldiers guarded the civilian settlements, while gunboats patrolled the rivers. Merchant and missionary activity increased. Foreign

RUSSIAN EMPIRE

Lake Balkhash

Ili
1854 annexed by Russia
DZUNGARIA

Ili

1871–81
to Russia

TIEN SHAN

Tarim

Xinjiang
**1**

KUNLUN MTS

TRADITIONAL ways of life, including the use of head stocks (known since Han times) for criminals, survived throughout the Manchu era.

**1** With acquisitions of new territories such as Xinjiang by the Manchu, the Chinese population rose to over 400 million by the mid-19th century.

**2** Opium was imported to China not as a narcotic, but as a pharmaceutical. Its addictive properties led to imperial decrees against its import and cultivation from 1800 onward.

**3** Hong Kong was ceded to Britain by China in 1841 (confirmed in 1842); in 1898, the British signed a 99-year lease on the territory.

**4** Shanghai was one of the first treaty ports, opened to western trade in 1842. In these ports, westerners were free from all aspects of Chinese jurisdiction, including taxation.

**5** The Taiping rebellion of 1850–64 took its egalitarianism from Christianity brought by western missionaries. Its leader Hong Xiuquan claimed to be the younger brother of Jesus Christ.

**6** The Boxers – or "League of Righteous Harmonious Fists" – were an anti-foreigner, anti-Christian secret society originating in the Shandong peninsula.

**7** Germany sent a force to occupy the port of Qingdao in 1897. Thereafter the site was heavily industrialized; with the outbreak of war in 1914, Japan (an Allied country) captured the city.

## TIMELINE

### Trade and politics

| 1800 | 1850 | 1900 |
|---|---|---|
| **1793** Emperor Qianlong snubs a British trade mission under Lord Macartney | **1839** Imperial commissioner Lin Zexu sent to Guangzhou to stop opium trade | **1885** Chinese troops defeat a French force at Langson |
| **1796** Qianlong abdicates in order not to rule longer than his grandfather | **1839–42** First Anglo-Chinese War opens up "treaty ports" | **1886** Britain completes its annexation of Burma |
| **1816** Expulsion of British Lord Amherst's trade mission | **1844** France and the United States sign trade agreements with China | **1894–95** Sino-Japanese War: China is defeated and loses Taiwan and the Pescadores |
| **1830** Anglo-American illicit supply of opium increases | **1856–60** Second Anglo-Chinese War | **1896** China, through Li Hongzhang, permits Russia to build a railroad across Manchuria |
| | **1860** An Anglo-French force destroys the imperial palace at Beijing | **1901** An International Protocol is imposed on China |

### Rebellions

| 1800 | 1850 | 1900 |
|---|---|---|
| **1796–1804** The White Lotus rebellion disrupts most of central China | **1850** The Taiping rebellion (*Taiping*: "heavenly kingdom") begins in Jintian; it is crushed by 1864 | **1895** Sun Yixian's attempt at revolution in Guangzhou fails |
| | **1855–57** The Miao rebellion against Manchu in Guizhou | **1900** Boxer Uprising against foreign influence |
| | **1855–57** The Christian, nationalist Hakka rebel against their Manchu overlords | **1908** Death of the dowager empress Cixi |
| | | **1911** Chinese revolution begins |
| | **1863–73** Muslim rebellion in Gansu, Qinghai and Shanxi | **1912** Yuan Shikai president of the new Chinese Republic |

1800    1850    1900

Omsk

Tom

Krasnoyarsk

Trans-Siberian railroad

Tannu Tuva
protectorate
1911 independent,
1914 to Russia

Irkutsk

Lake
Baykal

Chita

completed 1915

Nerchinsk

Ulan Bator

Inner Mongolian
Plateau

MONGOLIA
1912 independent

Gobi Desert

completed 1916

Amur
1858 annexed by Russia

Amur

Manzhouli

Manchuria
1900–05 under Russian influence,
1905–45 under Japanese influence

Aigun

Khabarovsk
founded 1858

Harbin

Suifenhe

Changchun

Hunchun

Nikolayevsk
founded 1850

Sakhalin
1875 to Russia,
1905 southern half
to Japan

Vladivostok
founded 1860

Sapporo

Hakodate

Hokkaido

Sea of
Japan

Honshu

Tokyo
Yokohama

JAPAN

MUSLIM rebellion
1862–73

Gansu

Ganzhou

Pingluo

Ordos
Desert

Yulin

Lake
Qinghai

Shanxi

Hezhou

Kwangtung Territory
1898–1905 to Russia,
1905 to Japan

Beijing
capital city,
focus of Boxer
Uprising

Qinhuangdao

Tianjin

Mukden
(Shenyang)

Niuzhuang

Dandong

Lushun
(Port Arthur)

Dalian

Weihaiwei
1895

Yalu River
1894

KOREA
1905 Japanese protectorate,
1910 Japanese colony

Seoul

Pusan

Shimonoseki

Shikoku

Nagasaki

Kyushu

Kagoshima

Muslim rebellion
1862–73

Hegang

Jinan

Shandong

Dengzhou

Longkou

Chefoo

Qingdao

Weihaiwei
1898 to Britain

Yellow
Sea

Qingdao
1898 to
Germany

IMPERIAL CHINA

Yanguan

Han

Nian rebellion
1853–68

Henan

Zhenjiang

Nanjing

Taiping
rebellion
1850–64

Wuhu

Shanghai

Suzhou

Hangzhou

Anqing

Ningbo
(Mingzhou)

QIN MTS

DABA MTS

Wanxian

Yichang

Lichuan

Hankou

Wuhan

Wuchang

Jiujiang

Taiping
rebellion
1850–64

Mingshan

Chongqing

Luzhou

Shasi

Yeyuang

Nanchang

Lake
Pengli

Wenzhou

Mianning

Lake
Dongting

Tanzhou

Santuao

Fuzhou

Tan-shui

Guizhou

Miao rebellion
1855–57

Taiping
rebellion
1850–64

Assam
1826 annexed by
Britain

Upper Burma
1886 annexed by Britain

Dali

Tengyueh

Muslim
rebellion
1855–73

Yunnan

Mengzi

Manhao

Simao

Linan

Jintian

Hakka rebellion
1855–57

Wuzhou

Sanshui

Nanning

Guangzhou
(Canton)

Xiamen
(Amoy)

Pescadores
1895 to Japan

Shantou
(Swatow)

Aboriginal
rebellion
1862–63

Tainan

Taiwan
1895 to Japan

Longzhou

Tongking
1884–85 French protectorate

Langson

Pakhoi

Kowloon

Macao
to Portugal

Hong Kong

Hong Kong
1841 to Britain

Hanoi

Zhanjiang

Laos
1899 French
protectorate

Lower Burma
created 1862

FRENCH
INDO-CHINA
1887–98 united by
France

Qiongzhou

Hainan

Zhanjiang
1898 to France

Annam
1883–85 French
protectorate

SIAM

South
China
Sea

Philippine Islands
1571–1898 to Spain,
1898 to United States

Manila

**Legend:**

Manchu empire, mid-19th century
former Manchu tributary state
British India, mid-19th century
Japanese empire, mid-19th century
Russian empire, mid-19th century
borders, c.1912
Manchu /Chinese empire, 1912
former Manchu state gaining independence
Manchu territory lost to Britain by 1912
Manchu territory lost to France by 1912
Manchu territory under Japanese control
at some time before 1912
Manchu territory lost to Russian empire by 1912
temporary Russian territorial gain
area leased by China to foreign power

spheres of influence
British
French
German
Japanese

port open to foreign trade under the
Treaty of Nanjing, 1842
treaty port opened from 1858
Taiping marches, 1850–64
anti-Manchu rebellion, with date
center of Boxer Uprising, 1900-01
railroad by 1914
Trans-Siberian railroad sector completed in 1915
Trans-Siberian rail link to Vladivostok,
completed 1916

0                    1000 km
0                    800 mi

See also 69 (the rise of Manchu China);
88 (19th-century Russia)

banks virtually ran China's economy, funding such projects as the rail link across Manchuria between the Trans-Siberian railroad and Vladivostok.

In 1911, an army mutiny in the industrial conurbation of Wuhan was exploited by Sun Yixian's Revolutionary Alliance Party, or Guomindang (KMT), which proceeded to seize power in central and southern China and overthrow the Qing dynasty. Sun Yixian returned from overseas exile to Shanghai, proclaimed the Three Principles of the republican revolution – nationalism, democracy and

people's livelihood – and was duly appointed provisional president of China. On 1 January 1912, the Chinese Republic was founded. However, when the Manchu boy-emperor Pu Yi abdicated on 13 February, General Yuan Shikai was named as president. For the sake of national unity, Sun Yixian voluntarily relinquished the presidency. Yet Yuan Shikai's desire to found a new imperial dynasty led to suppression of the Guomindang. In 1913, Sun Yixian established the first of a series of provisional governments at Guangzhou.

Southeast Asia had suffered extensive foreign intervention by the end of the 18th century. While the Dutch seaborne empire in island southeast Asia remained the major European presence, British entrepreneurs had also set up bases for trade with China. French missionaries and traders, interested in Vietnam since the 17th century, were given more leeway through a 1787 treaty. However, the first major French expedition did not occur until 1858–59, when the empire-building aspirations of Napoleon III resulted in the capture of Saigon. Despite resistance in the Mekong delta area, the French made further gains, establishing a protectorate over the Buddhist state of Cambodia and opening Hanoi and Tourane (Da Nang) as treaty ports. In an undeclared war with China (1883–85), France tried to win control of the whole of Indo-China, a goal achieved in 1887 with the merging of Cochin China, Cambodia, Annam and Tongking as the Indo-Chinese Union (French Indo-China). In 1893 it was extended to include Laos.

At first the French in Indo-China concentrated on modernizing and maximizing profits. Peasants were urged to sell land to boost rice production, so undermining traditional large viable villages. Landless peasants took jobs in salt and opium factories or worked for landlords.

British involvement in mainland southeast Asia began with the purchase of the island of Penang from the sultan of Kedah in 1786. During the Napoleonic Wars (when the Netherlands was under French control), Britain attacked Batavia to win control of Java and safeguard its trade routes to China through the island channels. The administrator Sir Stamford Raffles founded the free port of Singapore in 1819, which rapidly became the commercial center of the region, stimulating demand for British cotton manufactures in southeast Asia and China. In 1824 Britain ceded Benkulen and its claims to Sumatra in exchange for Dutch recognition of British sovereignty over Penang, Port Wellesley, Singapore and Malacca (collectively known as the Straits Settlements). Britain became involved in combating piracy and slavery, and settling disputes among the Malay princely states and sultanates on

Legend:
- sultanate of Aceh, 1873
- Federated Malay States, 1896
- Unfederated Malay States, 1909
- borders, 1914
- British territory, 1914
- British sphere of influence
- Dutch East Indies, 1914
- French Indochina, 1914
- German territory, 1914
- Portuguese territory, 1914
- United States territory, 1914
- area of piracy
- ☆ area of resistance by indigenous peoples
- → British campaign
- → French campaign
- → United States campaign
- *gold* source of commodity
- — trade route through Malacca Straits

Scale: 0 — 600 km / 0 — 400 mi

## TIMELINE

### Indo-China

**1782–1809** Rama I founds Bangkok and increases Siam's influence in Chiangmai, the Lao states and Cambodia

**1786** Britain acquires Penang from Sultan of Kedah

**1795** Britain takes Malacca from the Dutch

**1802** Nguyen Anh unifies Vietnam and rules from Hue as the first Nguyen emperor

**1819** Founding of Singapore by Sir Stamford Raffles

**1820–42** Vietnamese emperor Minh-Manh revives Confucianism and persecutes Christians

**1824** The Anglo-Dutch Treaty confirms British dominance in Malaya (and Singapore)

**1824–25** The British take Rangoon in First Burmese War

**1852–53** Second Burmese War; British gains reduce Burma to an inland state

**1855** King Mongkut (r.1851–68) opens Siam to British trade

**1858–59** French and Spanish naval force bombards Tourane and occupies Saigon

**1873** France begins the occupation of Tongking

**1883** The Treaty of Hue leads to the creation of French protectorates in Annam and Tongking

**1886** Britain annexes Upper Burma in Third Burmese War

**1887** The Indo-Chinese Union is created by France

**1896** Malay states of Perak, Selangor, Negri Sembilan and Pahang are federated

**1909** Anglo-Siamese Treaty; Britain controls Kedah, Perlis, Kelantan and Trengganu

**1914** 100,000 Vietnamese go to France to serve in labor battalions in World War I

### Island southeast Asia

**1811** The Dutch surrender Java to a British invasion force

**1814–16** The Netherlands regains Sumatra and Java

**1841** The sultan of Brunei cedes Sarawak to Brooke

**1859** The Dutch and Portuguese agree to partition island of Timor

**1873** The Dutch attack the Aceh sultanate (to 1907)

**1884** Germany annexes northern New Guinea and the Bismarck Archipelago

**1898–99** US takes Philippines in the Spanish-American War

**1901** Filipino leader Emileo Aguinaldo is captured

**CHINA**

Fuzhou

Taipei

Xiamen

Guangzhou • Swatow

*Taiwan*
*1895 to Japan*

Hong Kong
1841 to Britain

Macao
1887 to Portugal

from San Francisco, 1898

1882–83

1898

*South China Sea*

*gold*
*copper*

*Luzon*

*Philippine Islands*
*1898 to United States*

Manila • **7**

Battle of Manila
Bay, 1898 ✕

*Mindoro* *coconuts*

*Panay* *gold* *Samar*

*coconuts* *Leyte*

*Palawan* *Negros*

1899–1905

1899–1905

*copper*
*Mindanao*

British North
Borneo
1888 British protectorate

Jesselton •

Sandakan •

Beaufort •
*Sulu*

*Sulu Archipelago*

Brunei • *rubber*
*oil*
*oil*

*Celebes Sea*

Brunei
1888 British protectorate

Sarawak
1888 British
protectorate

**2**

*spices*

*spices* *spices*

**Borneo**

*spices*

*rubber*

Banjarmasin ✳ •

*Celebes*
*tobacco*

*nickel*

Macassar •

Bone • ✳

*Dutch East Indies*
*(Netherlands India)*

890–1917

Gresik
Surabaya
*rubber*

Bali

1881–94 Bima

1881–94 ✳ *rubber*

ava

Lombok

*copra*

Sumbawa

*rubber*
Sumba

Manado •

*Minahassa Peninsula*

Tidore •

*rubber*

**Halmahera**

*Sula Islands*

*rice*

*Ceram*

*oil*

Buru
Amboina •

*Kai Islands*

*Banda Sea*

*Aru Islands*

Wetar

*rice*
*Tanimbar Islands*

Flores

*copra*

Alore
*coconuts*

Dili • *rubber*

*East Timor*
*to Portugal*

Timor

Sumatra

Melville Island

*Arafura Sea*

Hollandia •

Dutch New Guinea
1828 to Netherlands

*New Guinea*

German New Guinea
1884 to Germany

*Bismarck Archipelago*

Territory of Papua
1884 to Britain
1888 British colony
1906 to Australia

**4**

Merauke •

Port Moresby •

---

0 ——— 300 km
0 ——— 200 mi

Perlis
1909 to Britain

Port Wellesley
1800 to Britain

Kelantan

Kedah
1909 to Britain

Kelantan
1909 to Britain

Penang

Penang
1786 to
Britain

Kuala
Trengganu

Trengganu
1909 to Britain

Perak

Perak
1875 to
Britain

Pahang
1887 to Britain • Pahang

Selangor
1874 to Britain

Kuala Lumpur •

Negri
Sembilan
1874 to Britain

Malacca • • Johore
1885 to Britain

Malacca
1795 to Britain

Johore
Bahru •

Singapore
1819 to Britain

---

**1** The first of several revolts against Dutch rule on
Java took place in 1825–30 under Dipo Negora, and
was only suppressed with great difficulty.

**2** As a reward for helping the sultan of Brunei put
down a revolt in Sarawak in 1841, the British adven-
turer James Brooke was made *rajah* of the area. The
Brooke "White Rajahs" ruled Sarawak for a century.

**3** In 1858–59, a joint French and Spanish naval force
bombarded Tourane and sailed south to take Saigon.

**4** The Australian state of Queensland's attempt to
annex the east of New Guinea in 1884 to forestall
German expansion was repudiated by the British
government. By the time the British acted, Germany
had already established control of the north.

**5** Rubber began to be commercially grown in Malaya
from 1896 onward, when plants cultivated in England
from South American stock were planted there.

**6** In 1896, France and Britain agreed that Siam should
remain an independent buffer state between their
respective possessions in Indo-China and Burma.

**7** To take the Philippines from the Spanish in 1898,
the United States dispatched 10,000 troops from San
Francisco, while the US Asiatic squadron under
Admiral Dewey left Hong Kong for Manila.

---

the peninsula. In 1896 Federated Malay States was
set up under a British resident-general. Thirteen
years later other states were acquired from Siam;
these formed the Unfederated Malay States. Tin
exports increased after mining was mechanized in
the early 1900s. Rubber also became a major export;
by 1911 nearly half a million hectares of rubber was
being grown, mainly on large, European-owned
estates. The 1824 treaty had also provided a case for
the "white rajah" James Brooke to gain British protection for the state he created in Sarawak in 1841. In
North Borneo commercial competition for concessions from Brunei and Sulu led eventually to an 1881
royal charter for a British North Borneo Company,
which undertook the exploitation of the territory.

To protect India's borders, Britain also annexed
Burma in the course of three brief wars. The first
(1824–26) was in response to a Burmese invasion of
Bengal, and resulted in Burma surrendering large

tracts of territory. Lower Burma was secured by the
British in the second war (1852–53), and Upper
Burma in the third (1885–86). The British adminis-
tered the country as part of India.

Germany and the United States were late beginning their colonial ventures in southeast Asia. Rival
claims to the eastern part of New Guinea eventually
saw Germany occupy the northeast and the adjacent
islands (renamed the Bismarck Archipelago), and a
British protectorate over the southeast of the island.
A crown colony in 1888, British New Guinea became a territory of the Australian Commonwealth in
1906. The United States acquired its first and most
important southeast Asian colony in 1898, when
Admiral Dewey destroyed a Spanish fleet in Manila
Bay to secure the Philippines. Filipino nationalists,
who had been encouraged by the United States to
fight for their independence against Spanish rule,
now felt betrayed by US actions and fierce fighting

ensued on Mindanao during 1902–05. The conflict
wrecked the fragile economy and, in addition to military casualties, 100,000 people died from famine.

After the withdrawal of the British from Sumatra,
the Dutch faced opposition from indigenous people
in the East Indies. Prince Dipo Negoro's rebellion led
to the Java War of 1825–29; Tuanku Imam, Minang-
kabau's militant leader, fought the Dutch 1830–39;
and persistent attacks on merchant shipping by the
state of Aceh led the Dutch to declare war in 1873.
Thirty years of conflict drained the Dutch reserves so
that effective occupation of the islands was still
incomplete by 1914, although the governor-general
J.B. Van Heutsz (1904–09) strove relentlessly to
govern the East Indies as a single state from Batavia.

See also 103 (southeast Asia 1914–41)

Bismarck, who initiated the complex web of alliances that developed after the Franco–Prussian War, now had as his ultimate objective the preservation of peace on the continent. He aimed to prevent France from launching a war of revenge by isolating it from any potential ally.

Bismarck's first step was to form the league of Three Emperors (*Dreikaiserbund*) between Germany, Austria–Hungary and Russia in 1873. In doing so, he had to reconcile a number of conflicting interests. Since the Crimean War, Russia had tried to reassert its position in Europe by championing the cause of Slav freedom from Austrian and Turkish rule. This brought Austria and Russia into conflict, as both empires cherished ambitions to secure the Balkan lands of the moribund Ottoman empire. The loose alliance that Bismarck forged was designed to stabilize southeast Europe, as its members agreed to act in concert against subversive movements in the region. In 1878, however, the Congress of Berlin forced Russia to renounce some of the excessive Balkan gains it had wrested from Turkey in 1877–78.

The chief beneficiary of the Berlin Congress was Austria, which negotiated a secret, defensive Dual Alliance with Germany (who, in World War I, were known as the Central powers). This relationship was to be the main focus of Bismarck's subsequent diplomacy. He publicly renewed the *Dreikaiserbund* in 1881 and distracted France by encouraging its colonial ambitions in north Africa, but secretly created a Triple Alliance between Germany, Austria and Italy.

When the *Dreikaiserbund* expired in 1887, Bismarck replaced it with a bilateral Reinsurance Treaty, which recognized the Balkans as a Russian sphere of influence and confirmed that Russia and Germany would stay neutral unless Germany attacked France, or Russia attacked Austria. This represented the pinnacle of Bismarck's diplomacy, which

sought to secure German predominance in central Europe and avoid dangerous adventurism.

In 1890, a change occurred in the politics of European alliances, when growing antagonism between the headstrong new emperor Wilhelm II and Bismarck brought the latter's resignation. The Reinsurance Treaty was allowed to lapse without renewal and the Russian harvest failed the same year. France offered aid to Russia, so laying the groundwork for a military alliance. This was duly signed in 1894, with the critical provision that if a Triple Alliance country mobilized its armies then Russia and France would do likewise. Mobilization of any armed forces was thus likely to lead to war.

---

border proposed by the Treaty of San Stefano, 1878

borders, 1912

Allied powers, Aug 1914

Central powers, Aug 1914

Schlieffen plan, 1905

⚔ German army position

route of German attack

fortress of the Central powers

fortress of the Allied powers

Belgian fortress

major naval base

major armaments center

○ league of Three Emperors, 1873–87

○ Triple Alliance, 1882–1915

● *Entente Cordiale*, 1904

● Triple Entente, 1907

key railroad line for transferring German troops to Russian front

anticipated Russian attack

Slavic language in central Europe

---

EUROPEAN royalty in the early 20th century had close family ties; Britain's King George V (shown here with Queen Mary) was cousin to Wilhelm II.

Scapa Flow
Cromarty
Glasgow・Rosyt
Edinburgh
Belfast
UNITED KINGDOM
Dublin ・ 3
Birmingham
Bristol・ Lor
Portsmouth
Plymouth ・Portland
Cherbourg
Brest
Lorient
*Loire*
・Nantes
Rochefort
Bordeaux
Santander
Toulouse
Bilbao
ANDOR
Oporto *Douro* *Ebro* Zaragoza
PORTUGAL
SPAIN
Madrid ・ *Tagus*
Lisbon *Guadiana* Valencia
Córdoba ・Alicante
Seville
Cádiz 6
Algeçiras ・Gibraltar
Tangier to Britain
*Spanish* Morocco
1912 *Spanish protectorate*

---

Britain had stood aloof from these alliances but after the death of Queen Victoria in 1901 the new king Edward VII made overtures to France that culminated in the *Entente Cordiale* of 1904. A similar agreement was made with Russia in 1907, forming a Triple Entente (of what became known as the "Allied powers" in 1914) to balance the Triple Alliance.

Several international incidents occurred that tested the commitment of the European powers to peace. Germany's claims to Morocco ran into opposition from both Britain and France, and resulted in the Tangier crisis (1905), settled at the Algeciras conference, and the Agadir crisis of 1911, which resulted in German recognition of France's claim to Morocco. The Balkans, too, continued to provide a highly charged arena. The Balkan peoples tried to organize

---

## TIMELINE

### Alliances and ententes

**1890**

**1873** Bismarck negotiates the League of the Three Emperors (*Dreikaiserbund*)

**1879** Dual Alliance: Germany and Austria-Hungary

**1882** Italy joins the Dual Alliance, thus creating the Triple Alliance

**1887** German Reinsurance Treaty with Russia

**1890** Bismarck resigns over differences with Kaiser Wilhelm II

**1894** Franco-Russian military alliance is announced after France aids Russian famine

**1910**

**1904** *Entente Cordiale* signed between Britian and France

**1907** Agreement between Britain and Russia results in a Triple Entente in Europe

**1902** The Anglo-Japanese Naval Alliance guarantees naval security in east Asia

**1914** Germany pledges total support ("Blank Check") for Austrian actions in Balkans

### Crises and rearmament

**1875–78** Eastern crisis begins when Bosnia and Herzegovina rebel against Turks

**1877–78** Russo-Turkish War ends; Russia gains much from the Treaty of San Stefano

**1878** The Congress of Berlin compels Russia to reduce its recent gains in the Balkans

**1885–86** Tension between Austria and Russia over Bulgaria destroys the *Dreikaiserbund*

**1889** Britain guarantees dominance of the Royal Navy

**1898** Fashoda crisis: a clash between French and British military missions in Sudan causes mutual hostility

**1900** Second German Naval Law (First 1898) confirms growth of the Imperial Navy

**1905–06** German colonial ambitions spark the first Morocco crisis

**1906** HMS *Dreadnought* revolutionizes warship design

**1911** The visit of a German gunboat to Agadir causes the second Morocco crisis

**1914** The Sarajevo crisis leads to Austrian bombardment of Belgrade, Russian mobilization and war

**1908** Austria–Hungary annexes Bosnia–Herzegovina

**1890**　　　　　**1910**

**1** The Treaty of San Stefano concluded between Russia and Turkey in 1878 envisaged the creation of a large new Bulgarian state beholden to Russia.

**2** In France in 1886–89, a vociferous *revanche* ("revenge") movement arose over Alsace-Lorraine, headed by war minister Georges Boulanger.

**3** From 1887–89, British prime minister Lord Salisbury resisted Bismarck's requests for an Anglo-German alliance. Salisbury described Britain's disdain for alliances as "splendid isolation".

**4** One of the greatest European industrial complexes was the Skoda Works in Pilsen, built to produce a new machine-gun for the Austrian army in 1890.

**5** Britain transferred sovereignty of the North Sea island of Heligoland (Helgoland) to Germany in return for Zanzibar in 1890. Germany developed Helgoland into a major naval base.

**6** The *Entente Cordiale* was tested in 1905, when Wilhelm II spoke in Tangier in favor of Moroccan independence. The Algeçiras conference in 1906 upheld French claims to the territory.

into nation-states and the Balkan Wars of 1912 and 1913 radically transformed the map of southeast Europe, arousing the hostility of Austria–Hungary.

Throughout this period, plans were made for war. The most ambitious was devised by the German chief of staff, Alfred von Schlieffen, for a war on two fronts. The Schlieffen plan required a surprise push through neutral Holland, Belgium and Luxembourg to isolate Paris from the coast and encircle the French armies. Troops would then be transferred by rail to reinforce the eastern front against Russia, which was expected to attack near Königsberg.

Rapid developments were also made in armaments. Germany produced medium and heavy artillery of high quality, France excelled in rapid-fire field guns, while all countries were perfecting the

machine-gun. At sea, the British *Dreadnought* class of battleship, begun in 1906, inaugurated a new era of naval design. Heavily armored, equipped entirely with big guns and driven by steam turbines, these ships started a race to build ever more powerful fleets. Wilhelm II was especially keen to develop the navy to challenge the might of Britain's Royal Navy.

Conscription swelled the size of the continent's armies. Most German youth served for three years in the army corps; French conscripts served for two. Both these countries (and Italy) could mobilize a million men within days. Austria and Russia could call on three times this number, though more slowly. The threat of war had loomed for so long over Europe that by 1914 all countries had arsenals and forces of unparalleled size and efficiency.

See also 88 (unification of Germany);
98 (World War I in Europe)

By 1914 the dominion of European peoples had spread throughout the world – the imperial system was at its peak, and expeditions had explored both polar regions. Colonization was most extensive in Africa. The "scramble for Africa" that had begun among European powers after 1870 was formalized at the Berlin Conference of 1884–85, which divided virtually all of the continent between rival claimants (▷ 89). Africans resisted the despoliation of their homelands, but usually to no avail. The Ethiopians successfully repulsed Italian invaders in 1896, but other peoples fought in vain against European troops equipped with superior weapons. Colonial forces also clashed; France and Britain disputed control of the upper Nile, and Germany's vigorous late pursuit of an African empire presaged the conflict to come in Europe. The Second Anglo-Boer War (1899–1902) was the culmination of decades of tension between settlers of Dutch and British origin in southern Africa. The British gained supremacy in a bitter struggle, but their failure to attract mass settlement left the Afrikaners dominant in the new Union of South Africa.

The United States emerged as an imperial power, while the empires of Russia and Britain continued to grow. The British empire reached the height of its power, with important colonial possessions in every continent. The transoceanic remnants of Spain's empire – Cuba, Puerto Rico, Guam and the Philippines – fell to the United States in the Spanish–American War of 1898. In Central America, US technology succeeded in cutting the Panama Canal, which opened for navigation in 1914. The extension of the railroad network throughout the United States by the end of the 19th century was instrumental in opening up new territories. As the 20th century dawned, American engineers pioneered important new forms of transport. The first powered heavier-than-air flight was made in 1903, and mass automobile ownership was a fact by 1914.

Russia's expansion to the east brought it into conflict with Japan (▷ 88). The industrializing and ambitious Japan routed Russian forces in 1904–05 and annexed Korea in 1910. Russia's humiliation sparked the first of a series of revolutions that led to the fall of the imperial regime in 1917.

Britain's prime interest was to protect its trade through the Suez Canal, including the new resource of oil which Britain received from the Persian Gulf. To this end, bases were developed in the Mediterranean. Egypt was also occupied in 1882. Further east, British

Alaska

CANADA

Newfoundland

UNITED STATES

MEXICO

Bahamas

*Hawaiian Islands*
*(United States)*

British Honduras
CUBA
HAITI
*Puerto Rico*
*(United States)*
Jamaica
DOMINICAN REPUBLIC
GUATEMALA
EL SALVADOR
HONDURAS
NICARAGUA
COSTA RICA
PANAMA
COLOMBIA
VENEZUELA
British Guiana
Dutch Guiana
French Guiana

*Galapagos Islands*
*(Ecuador)*
ECUADOR

BRAZIL

PERU

*Marquesas Islands*
*(France)*

BOLIVIA

PARAGUAY

*Tuamotu Archipelago*
*(France)*

*Easter Island*
*(Chile)*

CHILE
ARGENTINA
URUGUAY

*Falkland Islands*
*(Britain)*

## TIMELINE

The Americas
Europe
Middle East
Africa
Asia and Australasia

1885

1895

**1889** Brazil is proclaimed a republic

**1888** Wilhelm II becomes German emperor (*Kaiser*)

**1885** Completion of Canadian Pacific Railway links east and west Canada

**1882** Triple Alliance formed between Germany, Austria-Hungary, and Italy

**1896** Ethiopian defeat of Italians at Adowa secures 40 years of independence

**1896** Klondike gold rush brings flood of prospectors to the Canadian northwest

**1884–85** Berlin Conference divides up Africa between European powers

**1886** Discovery of gold in Transvaal initiates intensive mining activity throughout southern Africa

**1891** Construction of Trans-Siberian railroad begins

**1894** Franco-Russian Alliance formed to counter Triple Alliance threat

**1894–95** Sino-Japanese War; Korea independent and Taiwan is ceded to Japan on Chinese defeat

**1899–1902** Second Anglo-Boer War; British overcome Afrikaners

**1900–01** Boxer Uprising in China against foreigners

nomadic pastoralists
state societies

empires
Belgian
British
Dutch
French
German
Italian
Portuguese
Spanish
United States
other

A. Albania      N. Netherlands
B. Belgium      SE. Serbia
D. Denmark      S. Switzerland
M. Montenegro

Greenland
(Denmark)

Iceland
(Denmark)

NORWAY
SWEDEN
D.
UNITED
KINGDOM
N.
B. GERMANY
FRANCE
AUSTRO-
HUNGARIAN
EMPIRE
ITALY
SPAIN
PORTUGAL
A.
GREECE
M. SE.
ROMANIA
BULGARIA
OTTOMAN
EMPIRE

RUSSIAN EMPIRE

MONGOLIA

CHINESE REPUBLIC

Sakhalin

Korea
(Japan)

JAPAN

Taiwan
(Japan)

TIBET
NEPAL
BHUTAN
Burma

India

Hong Kong
(Britain)

Philippine
Islands

Mariana Islands
(Germany)

Guam
(United States)

Marshall
Islands
(Germany)

Spanish
Morocco
French
Morocco
Algeria
Tunisia
Tripolitania
Cyrenaica
PERSIA
AFGHAN-
ISTAN
Kuwait
Qatar
Arab
nomads
Trucial
Oman
Oman
Aden

Egypt

Rio de
Oro

mbia

French West Africa

Portuguese
Guinea
Togo
Sierra
Leone
LIBERIA
Gold Coast
Nigeria
Cameroon
Rio Muni
French Equatorial
Africa

French
Equatorial
Africa

Eritrea
Sudan
ETHIOPIA

British Somaliland
French Somaliland
Italian Somaliland
British East Africa

Goa
Ceylon
SIAM
French
Indo-China

Malay states
Sumatra
Borneo
Celebes
Java
Timor
Dutch East Indies

Palau
(Germany)

New Guinea
German New
Guinea
Papua

Gilbert
Islands
(Britain)

Solomon
Islands
(Britain)

Ellice
Islands
(Britain)

Uganda
Belgian
Congo
Northern
Rhodesia
German
East
Africa
Angola
Nyasaland
Southern
Rhodesia
Mozambique
Bechuanaland
German
South-West
Africa
Union of
South Africa
Swaziland
Basutoland
Madagascar

AUSTRALIA

New Hebrides
(Britain/France)
New
Caledonia
(France)

Fiji Islands
(Britain)

Tasmania

NEW
ZEALAND

**1906** Launch of
the British battleship
*HMS Dreadnought* revolu-
tionizes naval warfare

**1904** *Entente Cordiale*
is agreed between Britain
and France

**1904–05** Russo-Japanese
War results in a series of
humiliating Russian defeats

**1914** Panama Canal,
joining the Atlantic and
Pacific Oceans, opens

**1914** World War I begins,
sparked by the assassina-
tion of Archduke Franz
Ferdinand in Sarajevo

**1912–13** Balkan Wars;
Ottoman Turks lose most
of their European lands

1905

**1910** Union of South Africa
set up from Afrikaner
republics and Cape Colony

**1910** Japanese annexation
of Korea; lasts until 1945

**1911** Chinese Revolution
overthrows Qing dynasty;
republic established 1912

control of India, the "jewel in
the crown" of the empire, was
consolidated by the construction of railroads. As well as their strategic value, these promot-
ed the export of cotton, jute, tea and coffee from the subcontinent (▷ 83).

The tottering Manchu empire finally fell. Defeated in the Sino-Japanese
War of 1894–95, the Qing dynasty was beset by European demands for land
concessions, mineral rights and trade facilities. A secret anti-foreigner society –
the "Boxers" – rebelled in 1900–01, rampaging through Shanxi and Shandong
provinces. In the European retaliation that swiftly followed, foreign interests
took total control of Chinese affairs (▷ 94). When rebellion came in 1911, most
of China's provinces rose in support of the revolutionaries at Wuhan. The Qing
dynasty fell and a republic replaced the Manchu empire. Mongolia and Tibet
announced their independence.

At the same time, the Ottoman empire lost most of its remaining European
possessions in the First Balkan War (1912–13). In 1913, during the Second
Balkan War, Serbia emerged as the principal state in the region. Hostility
between Serbia and Austria exploded after the murder of the heir to the
Austrian throne at Sarajevo in 1914. When Austria declared war on Serbia,
Russia mobilized its forces. Within a few days all the major European powers,
which had coalesced into two military blocs, were embroiled in World War I
(▷ 98). This devastating global conflict was to bring the collapse of the
Russian, German and Austro-Hungarian empires ∎

## Part 6

# THE MODERN

**M**any of those who went into battle in August 1914 thought the war would be short and glorious. World War I, though, tested human endurance to the limit. The combatant states had the ideological, bureaucratic and technological capabilities, as well as the nationalistic fervor, to mobilize vast human and material resources.

The postwar settlement was built on the principle of national self-determination. But this settlement was partial: totalitarian governments appeared in Germany, Italy and Russia, using the state's resources to foster a virulent nationalism, and committed to revising the precarious status quo.

Germany's invasion of Poland in September 1939 led to a war that soon became truly global and total. Each side sought the unconditional surrender of the other, and the distinction between soldier and civilian collapsed as air power provided the means to strike at the enemy's heartland. This strategy culminated in the atomic destruction of the Japanese cities of Hiroshima and Nagasaki, and the devastation of the social and economic fabric of Germany. Meanwhile six million Jews perished in the Holocaust, a demonstration of the modern totalitarian state's ability to combine ideology, technology and bureaucracy in systematic mass extermination.

The two wars had one positive outcome: the recognition that the propensity of states to destroy one another had to be restrained by means of international institutions to reinforce the rule of law. The League of Nations, created in 1919, failed, but its successor the United Nations raised expectations that a concert of victorious powers could deter and defend against aggressive states.

The Cold War between the United States and the Soviet Union was perhaps a product of misperception: each assumed

SINGAPORE's high rise blocks symbolized the global economy of the 1990s.

# WORLD

the other was bent on aggression. A precarious order ensued, at times threatened by crises in which nuclear disaster was sometimes only narrowly averted. There were, though, other trends in the postwar years whose influence shaped international relations for many years.

First, the United States committed itself to restoring western Europe's battered economies, and equally to the defense of Europe – a reversal of its isolationism after 1919. NATO gave western Europe the confidence to begin economic integration; the European Economic Community was set up in 1957–58. Second, the independence of India, Pakistan and Ceylon from British imperial rule set a precedent for anticolonial struggle elsewhere. By 1968 fifty African states had joined the United Nations. China, too, began a long march to great power status after the Communist victory in 1949. Third, the principle of domestic jurisdiction slowly dissolved, bringing an expansion in the legal competence of bodies such as the UN to intervene when human rights were abused. South Africa's policy of *apartheid* was the catalyst, as new norms entered the vocabulary of inter-state discourse.

The relative stability provided by the threat of "mutually assured destruction" was bought at the expense of the Third World. Nehru in India, Sukarno in Indonesia, Nkrumah in Ghana and Nasser in Egypt hoped to build a third force in international affairs, mediating between east and west, and committed to redressing the inequalities between the rich northern states and the poorer south. Some victories were won: the legal establishment of human rights; the isolation of *apartheid*-ridden South Africa; the recognition that Third World states needed aid and technical assistance to provide a decent life for their peoples.

But the Cold War years also saw wars by proxy fought in Third World states such as Angola, Ethiopia, Somalia and Vietnam, as the superpowers vied to support rival factions in civil wars. And as détente, or relaxation of superpower tension, took hold, the influence of the "nonaligned movement" began to wane, especially as many Third World states failed to deliver social and economic benefits to their people.

Meanwhile, led by Japan, the "tiger" economies – South Korea, Singapore, Taiwan, Malaysia, Hong Kong – underwent an economic miracle via export-led growth and a mix of government intervention and private enterprise. China, too, encouraged market liberalization, though under the strict control of the ruling Communist Party.

In contrast, the Soviet Union was unable to deliver both "guns and butter" to its people. The economy was hamstrung by obsolete state controls, and the arms race of the 1980s placed great burdens on the economy just when conservative western governments – especially in the United States and Britain – were successfully employing free market solutions to boost productivity. Attempts at reform merely led to revolt in several of the Soviet republics and the satellite states of east and south Europe. The fall of the Berlin Wall – symbol of Cold War division – in 1989 heralded a new era, one in which economic activity was global, and free-market capitalism was enshrined as the chief ideology for economic development throughout the world.

As the millennium approached, all governments were constrained by global economic forces. Conventional attack by a neighbor often seemed less threatening than organized crime, drugs and arms trafficking, illegal migration, terrorism and environmental degradation: dangers a nation-state was ill-equipped to cope with. Pressure mounted for the establishment of wider groupings of states, and it seemed possible that such regional associations would be the building blocks for a "new world order" for the twenty-first century ■

Before 1914, Europe had enjoyed unprecedented prosperity, the fruit of industrialization and a century without a general war. Yet two alliances, the Allied powers (the United Kingdom, France and Russia), and the Central powers (Germany, Austria–Hungary and, later, the Ottoman empire), were preparing for war. The main reason was the ambition and the instability of Germany, Europe's newest, and strongest, industrial and military power.

Germany had enjoyed a period of rapid industrialization, replacing Britain as the main motor of Europe's economy. Furthermore, its strength in iron, steel and coal production, and in the new electrical and chemical industries, was matched by a military machine second to none. In peace, Germany's geographical position enabled it to exploit Europe's extensive rail and sea networks. In wartime, however, it faced the prospect of fighting on two fronts.

Germany's rulers believed that its political standing did not match its commercial and imperial ambitions. One of its oldest ambitions (one which brought it into conflict with Russia) was to expand eastward. Germany believed it was encircled by hostile powers and was intent on protecting its interests, and those of Austria–Hungary, in southern Europe, the Ottoman empire and the Middle East.

In a long war, the strain of fighting on two fronts would inevitably tell. Military planners sought to combat this by launching a knockout blow against France and then transporting troops to the east to face the Russian army. But the plan failed when, in August 1914, war broke out following a crisis over Austrian and Russian influence in the Balkans. The exhausted German army was halted 80 kilometers (50 miles) short of Paris. The French army was swiftly mobilized and the transport network used shrewdly – even the Parisian taxi cabs were pressed into service to take soldiers to the front. Stalemate followed on the Western Front; the war was bogged down in trench warfare, as the defensive capabilities of the machine gun dominated the war until

| | | 1915 | 1916 | 1917 | 1918 |
|---|---|---|---|---|---|
| **TIMELINE** | **General** | **1914 (28 June)** Assassination of the Austrian Archduke Franz Ferdinand by a Serb nationalist at Sarajevo | **1915 (Apr)** Allied landings at Gallipoli | **1916 (Apr)** Easter Rising in Dublin against British rule in Ireland | **1917 (Mar)** Czar Nicholas II abdicates in Russia | **1918 (Jan)** US president Wilson publishes a 14-point peace plan |
| | | **1914 (Aug)** Germany declares war on Russia and France; Britain, France and Russia on Germany and Austria–Hungary | **1915 (Apr)** Italy joins the Allied war effort <br> **1915 (May)** US liner *Lusitania* is sunk by a German U-boat | **1916 (May)** The British and German fleets meet at Jutland | **1917 (Apr)** The USA declares war on the Central powers <br> **1917 (Nov)** Bolshevik revolution in Russia | **1918 (Nov)** The Kaiser abdicates and an armistice is signed between Germany and the Allies |
| | **Western Front** | **1914 (Aug)** Germans launch Schlieffen plan <br> **1914 (Sep)** Germans halted at the Battle of the Marne | **1916 (Feb–Dec)** German offensive at Verdun <br> **1916 (July–Nov)** Expensive British offensive on Somme | **1917 (July)** Third Battle of Ypres (Passchendaele) <br> **1917 (Nov–Dec)** Tanks used by British at battle of Cambrai | **1918 (Mar)** Germans threaten Paris in Ludendorff offensive <br> **1918 (Aug)** Allies break through German lines |
| | **Eastern Front** | **1914 (Aug)** The Russian advance into Germany is halted at Tannenberg | **1915 (Oct)** Austria-Hungary invades Serbia | **1916 (Sep)** Central powers defeat Romania <br> **1916 (Oct)** The Russian Brusilov offensive ends | **1917 (July)** Last Russian offensive of the war <br> **1917 (Dec)** Bolsheviks sign an armistice with Germany | **1918 (Mar)** Treaty of Brest-Litovsk ends war in Russia |
| | | 1915 | 1916 | 1917 | 1918 | |

**1** The assassination of the Austrian Archduke Franz Ferdinand on 28 June 1914 by a Serbian began the descent into war. Austria declared war on Serbia; Russia mobilized; Germany declared war on Russia and France, and Britain on Germany, by 4 August.

**2** The German offensive in the west began with the reduction of the Belgian fortresses around Liège.

**3** The French stopped the German advance on Paris on the Marne in September 1914.

**4** The unsuccessful Allied landings at Gallipoli were intended to win control of the Dardanelles and secure a sea route to Russia.

**5** The sinking of the passenger liner *Lusitania* by a German U-boat in 1915 did much to turn American sentiment in favor of the Allies.

**6** The war on the Eastern Front never declined into trench warfare and strategic mobility was preserved; casualties, though, were as heavy as in the west.

**7** Although Britain's fleet suffered heavier losses than Germany's, the Battle of Jutland confirmed Britain's control of the seas.

new offensive tactics, using tanks and artillery more intelligently, were developed in 1917. Despite early victories against the Russians, the Germans now had to cope with war on two fronts.

In the Balkans, victories by the Central powers over Serbia and Romania (and the entry of the Ottomans into the war in 1915) seemed to create the kind of central European political and trading empire that Germany wanted. In 1917 czarist Russia collapsed, its economy and political system exhausted by the demands of the war. Early in 1918, its revolutionary Bolshevik government withdrew entirely from the war, leaving Germany in control of much of the Ukraine and southern Russia. German colonial ambitions in Europe seemed satisfied at last.

Yet the Central Powers could not match the Allies for men, materiel, wealth or opportunities. During 1916 Allied economic power began to assert itself. Britain developed a war economy, supplying munitions and other war materiel manufactured at home or imported from the United States and the British empire. Britain's financial superiority allowed it to bankroll the Allied war effort. The German navy tried to break Allied lines of supply by torpedoing British shipping. When unrestricted submarine warfare began in 1917, the United States was prompted to join the war on the Allied side – though more significantly as a supplier of munitions rather than as a belligerent. The Allies blockaded German ports, intensifying German economic difficulties.

The years 1916–17 saw several desperately costly battles on the Western Front – notably Verdun, the Somme, Ypres – made possible by the huge buildup of arms on the Allied side. The Central powers decided to make a tactical withdrawal on the Western Front and to militarize the economy at home. The result was disastrous. By November 1918, the German army had not retreated to within its own borders (it had in fact made large advances the previous spring), but it was in clear disarray, while food and fuel shortages led to the country collapsing from within. Kaiser Wilhelm II abdicated, as did the emperor of Austria–Hungary. The Allies were clearly in a position to dictate the terms of the peace.

**Legend**

borders, 1914

Allied powers and associates, June 1917

Central powers, June 1917

Central power capitulating before Nov 1918

neutral state

furthest advance of Central powers

furthest advance of Russian forces

Armistice line, 11 Nov 1918

**Western Front**

front line, 5 Sep 1914

front line, 29 Dec 1914

front line, 11 Nov 1918

German offensive, 16 Aug–5 Sep 1914

German offensive, 5 Apr–17 July 1918

furthest extent of German advance, 17 July 1918

Allied counteroffensive, 26 Sep–10 Nov 1918

Russian territory lost at the Treaty of Brest-Litovsk

main area of U-boat activity, 1915-18

naval base

Allied naval blockade

armaments, engineering and metal industry

chemical industry

shipbuilding industry

9.5m maximum mobilized forces (millions)

railroad

shipping route to United States and Canada

0   600 km
0   400 mi

See also 96 (Europe before 1914); 99 (the war outside Europe); 101 (Europe between the wars)

At the beginning of the 20th century the world was dominated by Europe's imperial powers, many of them in the hands of ancient, autocratic monarchies. World War I shattered much of this, and, by its end, revolutions had swept away several monarchies, to be replaced in some states, such as Germany, by fragile democracies and in others (such as Russia) by revolutionary dictatorships (▷ 98 ). Among the factors driving change were the introduction of new technologies, particularly in the field of communications. Continental and oceanic transit networks were completed, and wireless telegraphy and radio were developed. Horse- and steam-power began to give way to gasoline- and diesel-driven transportation systems, and the war brought a rapid advance in air transport, both for civilian as well as military purposes.

Challenges to Europe's empires were already evident before 1914. In the east, Japan was industrializing rapidly, had defeated Russia and advanced into Manchuria as the Manchu dynasty in China collapsed (▷ 103 ). Europe's most formidable challenge, however, came from the United States which, following the defeat of Spain in 1898, became the only power capable of determining the development of the American continent. As a result, the United States built its own informal empire, enforcing its will if necessary by military intervention (▷ 102 ).

During World War I, Britain and France relied on their colonies and on the United States for men and materiel. When they came to make peace in 1919, they could not dictate the settlement alone. The United States was now the world's leading financial, industrial and, potentially, military power, thanks to the boost given to its industry by Allied orders at a time when the European economies were drastically disrupted. While Britain almost bankrupted itself funding the Allied war effort, the United States took over as the world's banker.

The American president Woodrow Wilson used this power to alter the conduct of international relations. On his initiative the League of Nations was set up, an organization of nation-states dedicated to preventing war by substituting mediation for military action. Wilson was also committed to the principle of national self-determination, and promoted the creation of new states such as Czechoslovakia, Yugoslavia and an independent Poland (▷ 101 ). He also tried to discourage imperialism, arguing that Germany's colonies should not be seized as the spoils of war. Instead, he persuaded the victorious powers to mandate these territories to Britain (whose empire thereby achieved its greatest territorial extent), France,

A. Albania
AU. Austria
B. Belgium
C. Czechoslovakia
D. Denmark
E. Estonia
H. Hungary
KS. Kingdom of Serbs, Croats, and Slovenes
L. Luxembourg
LI. Lithuania
N. Netherlands
PG. Portuguese Guinea
S. Switzerland
T. Transjordan
YE. Yemen

Kingsford-Smith and Ulm, 1919

Hawaiian Islands (United States)

French Polynesia (France)

CANADA

Alaska

Newfoundland

UNITED STATES

MEXICO

Bahamas (Britain)

British Honduras

CUBA

Jamaica

HAITI

Puerto Rico (United States)

DOMINICAN REPUBLIC

GUATEMALA
EL SALVADOR
HONDURAS
NICARAGUA
PANAMA
Canal Zone (United States)

COSTA RICA

Galapagos Islands (Ecuador)

VENEZUELA

COLOMBIA

ECUADOR

British Guiana
Dutch Guiana
French Guiana

BRAZIL

PERU

BOLIVIA

CHILE

ARGENTINA

PARAGUAY

URUGUAY

Falkland Islands (Britain)

TIMELINE

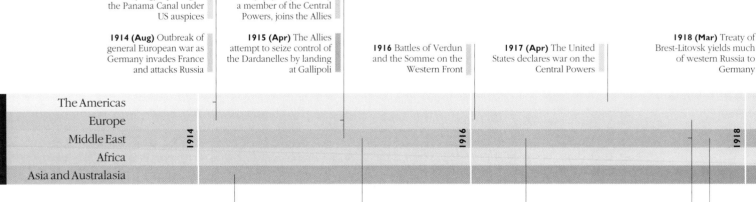

1914 (Aug) Opening of the Panama Canal under US auspices

1915 (Apr) Italy, formerly a member of the Central Powers, joins the Allies

1914 (Aug) Outbreak of general European war as Germany invades France and attacks Russia

1915 (Apr) The Allies attempt to seize control of the Dardanelles by landing at Gallipoli

1916 Battles of Verdun and the Somme on the Western Front

1917 (Apr) The United States declares war on the Central Powers

1918 (Mar) Treaty of Brest-Litovsk yields much of western Russia to Germany

The Americas
Europe
Middle East
Africa
Asia and Australasia

1914

1916

1918

1914 Japan takes over many German colonies in the Pacific

1915 Allied armies advance through Mesopotamia

1916 (Jun) An Arab revolt against the Ottomans begins in the Hejaz

1917 (Nov) Bolshevik revolution in Russia, leading to civil war (to 1921)

1914 Australia takes over the German colony of Kaiser Wilhelmsland

1917 (Nov) The Balfour Declaration commits Britain to the creation of a Jewish state in Palestine

1917 (Dec) British forces occupy Jerusalem

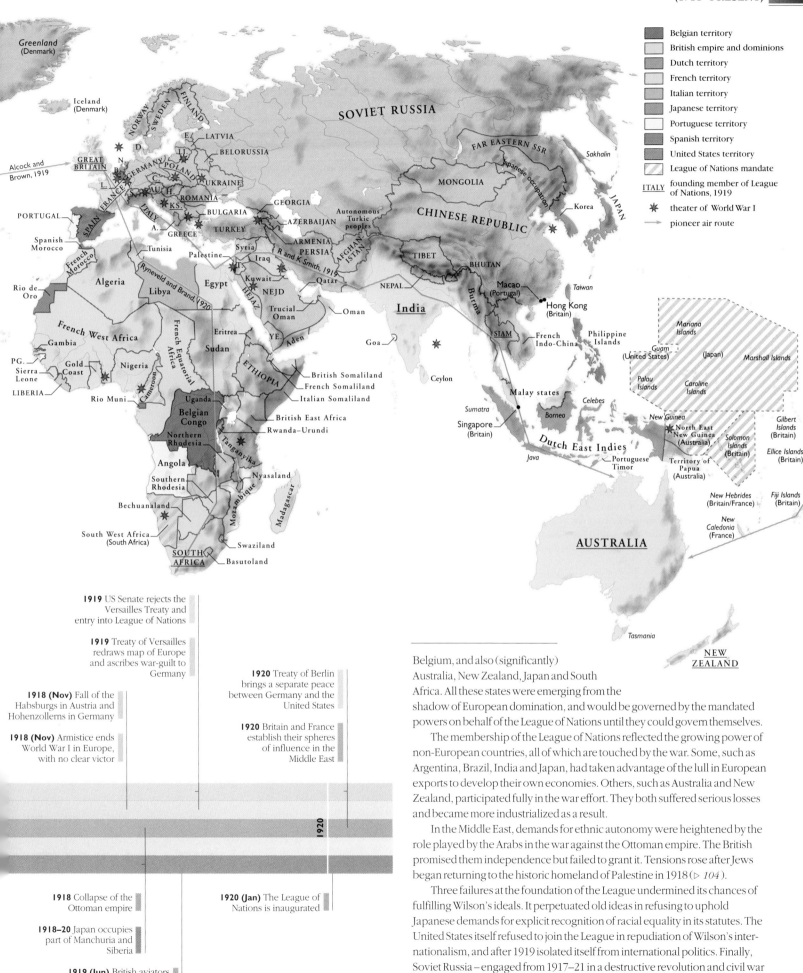

Belgian territory
British empire and dominions
Dutch territory
French territory
Italian territory
Japanese territory
Portuguese territory
Spanish territory
United States territory
League of Nations mandate

ITALY  founding member of League of Nations, 1919

✳  theater of World War I

→  pioneer air route

**1919** US Senate rejects the Versailles Treaty and entry into League of Nations

**1919** Treaty of Versailles redraws map of Europe and ascribes war-guilt to Germany

**1918 (Nov)** Fall of the Habsburgs in Austria and Hohenzollerns in Germany

**1918 (Nov)** Armistice ends World War I in Europe, with no clear victor

**1920** Treaty of Berlin brings a separate peace between Germany and the United States

**1920** Britain and France establish their spheres of influence in the Middle East

1920

**1918** Collapse of the Ottoman empire

**1918–20** Japan occupies part of Manchuria and Siberia

**1919 (Jun)** British aviators Alcock and Brown cross the Atlantic nonstop

**1920 (Jan)** The League of Nations is inaugurated

Belgium, and also (significantly) Australia, New Zealand, Japan and South Africa. All these states were emerging from the shadow of European domination, and would be governed by the mandated powers on behalf of the League of Nations until they could govern themselves.

The membership of the League of Nations reflected the growing power of non-European countries, all of which are touched by the war. Some, such as Argentina, Brazil, India and Japan, had taken advantage of the lull in European exports to develop their own economies. Others, such as Australia and New Zealand, participated fully in the war effort. They both suffered serious losses and became more industrialized as a result.

In the Middle East, demands for ethnic autonomy were heightened by the role played by the Arabs in the war against the Ottoman empire. The British promised them independence but failed to grant it. Tensions rose after Jews began returning to the historic homeland of Palestine in 1918 (▷ 104 ).

Three failures at the foundation of the League undermined its chances of fulfilling Wilson's ideals. It perpetuated old ideas in refusing to uphold Japanese demands for explicit recognition of racial equality in its statutes. The United States itself refused to join the League in repudiation of Wilson's inter-nationalism, and after 1919 isolated itself from international politics. Finally, Soviet Russia – engaged from 1917–21 in a destructive revolution and civil war – was excluded from the peace-making and membership of the League ∎

World War I imposed unbearable social and economic strain on Russia. The czar, who had assumed personal command of the armed forces in 1915, was held responsible for many of the failures of the war, and abdicated following a revolution in Petrograd in March (February in the Russian calendar) 1917. A provisional government took power but its decision to continue the war combined with fear of counterrevolution led to increasing radicalization. Local *soviets* – committees of workers, soldiers and sailors – sprang up in industrial areas. Many were dominated by the radical socialist parties, among whom the anti-war Bolsheviks (led by Vladimir Ilych Lenin since his return in April from exile in Berne) won growing influence. In November (October) 1917, the Bolsheviks overthrew the government.

The Bolsheviks were heavily outnumbered in the Constituent Assembly by the Socialist Revolutionaries representing the peasantry. Lenin therefore dissolved the Assembly and fought a bloody civil war to secure his position. Non-Bolshevik socialists, liberals, aristocrats, national minorities and the peasantry all opposed the regime, and several foreign powers also intervened. Nevertheless, the "Whites" (anti-Bolshevik forces) were too divided geographically and politically to depose the government. Nineteen independent governments were formed but, although at one point the Whites were within 400 kilometers (250 miles) of Moscow, the Bolsheviks ("Reds") recaptured the Ukraine, Caucasus, central Asia and Siberia. They ceded territory to Poland and recognized the independence of the Baltic states, but in 1923 the Union of Soviet Socialist Republics (USSR) was created, comprising the republics of Russia, Ukraine, Belorussia and Transcaucasia.

During the civil war the Bolsheviks adopted a policy of "war communism" and requisitioned food for the army and cities. This brought an arduous struggle with the peasantry which culminated in widespread revolts in 1920–22 and a famine in the Volga region that killed five million people. With the end of the civil war in 1921 Lenin adopted the "new economic policy" (NEP). This reintroduced limited

## TIMELINE

### Political change

**1917** Ukraine, Finland. Latvia, Lithuania claim independence

**1917 (Mar)** First revolution; czar abdicates and provisional government is set up

**1917 (Nov)** The Bolsheviks seize power

**1918 (Mar)** Bolsheviks sign the Treaty of Brest-Litovsk

**1918–21** Civil war between the "Whites" and the "Reds"

**1918** The Caucasus states and Estonia declare independence

**1920** The Red Army invades Poland

**1920–21** Ukraine, the Caucasus states and Turkestan are reconquered; Mongolia expels the Chinese

**1922** Treaty of Rapallo: Soviet–German commercial and military agreement

**1922–23** Formation of the Union of Soviet Socialist Republics (USSR)

**1924** Death of Lenin

**1926** The Soviet Union and Germany sign a neutrality pact

**1934** Start of the "great terror" after the assassination of Leningrad Party secretary Kirov

**1934** The Soviet Union joins the League of Nations

**1936–38** Height of the great purges in the Soviet Union

**1936** Stalin's constitution is promulgated

**1938** Purge of the armed forces by Stalin

**1939** Stalin signs the Nazi–Soviet pact with Hitler

**1939** The Soviet Union occupies eastern Poland and Finland

**1940** The Soviet Union occupies the Baltic states; Finland sues for peace

**1941** Germany invades the Soviet Union

### Economic change

**1918** Depopulation of towns and cities in the civil war

**1920–22** Peasant revolts occur throughout Russia

**1921** The "new economic policy" is introduced

**1928** The first Five Year Plan is announced

**1929** The collectivization of agriculture is announced

**1933** The second Five Year Plan is announced

**1932–33** Famine in the Ukraine and central Asia

**1939** The third Five Year Plan is announced

free trade to encourage the peasants to produce more while the Bolsheviks (soon to be called Communists) tried to modernize the country.

Lenin died in 1924 without leaving an obvious successor, but Joseph Stalin used his post as general-secretary of the Communist Party to secure control of the state. The Communists now had to face the contradiction that they were a workers' government in a peasant country. In 1929 Stalin addressed this issue by ordering the collectivization of agriculture.

Private trade was abolished and peasants forced to give up their private holdings and work on collective farms. Many responded by slaughtering their livestock and planting only enough grain to feed themselves. When this was requisitioned famine ensued, and millions were deported to the *gulag* (prison camps), resulting in around 14.5 million deaths.

Collectivization was intended to cow the peasantry and provide sufficient grain to support a massive program of industrialization as the Soviet Union was built into a modern economic power. Even during the famine, grain was being used to feed the city population and sold abroad to buy western technology. In 1928 Stalin announced the first Five Year Plan, with which he proposed that the Soviet Union should catch up with the west which, he claimed, was "50 to 100 years ahead". Production grew quickly, especially in the heavy and defense industries as old industrial centers were expanded and new ones created in remote regions.

Industrial development was undermined by the purges that Stalin unleashed in 1934. "Subversives" (in the first instance, old Bolsheviks) appeared in show trials, were convicted of fantastic crimes and shot, while millions of others faced deportation to labor camps. Stalin's war with his own population extended across the Soviet Union as he sought scapegoats for the failures of collectivization and industrialization to achieve the targets set out in the Plan. Fear and suspicion led to mass denunciations and the decimation of the upper levels of bureaucracy and Party.

By 1938 a purge of the army and navy began and the country lost most of its officer corps. The following year Stalin agreed to the Nazi–Soviet pact with Hitler and subsequently occupied eastern Poland and the Baltic states. Stalin apparently believed that Hitler would not invade Russia until France and Britain were defeated. He also thought that fascism, which he saw as the highest form of capitalism, must presage the Communist revolution in Europe.

In 1941, though, Hitler did invade. The Soviet Union was in a better position to resist than Russia had been in 1914, despite the depredations of the purges. Communism had been established against all the odds in what had been Europe's most backward country. Stalin's policies, which were mainly an extension of those used by Lenin to win the civil war, were pursued at massive human cost and allowed the Communist Party to prevail.

POSTERS publicized the Bolshevik cause. This image shows Lenin in typical pose.

**1** Petrograd (renamed Leningrad in 1924) was imperial Russia's capital and largest city. It was the conduit for revolutionary ideas and the center of events in 1917.

**2** The Bolsheviks held the central position in the civil war and control of the rail network centered on Moscow (the capital from March 1918), was vital to their cause.

**3** A variety of forces opposed the Bolsheviks: the Czech legion, formed to fight for the Allies during World War I, tried to get home via Vladivostok and in 1918 controlled the trans-Siberian railroad.

**4** Magnitogorsk was the showpiece of Soviet industrializiation, a huge industrial plant built in the shadow of the Urals.

**5** The Soviet "corrective labor camps", known by their acronym (*gulag*), were originally set up by Lenin. They became a key feature of Stalin's economic policy as well as of the eradication of opposition.

**6** Tambov was the focus of violent peasant rebellions in 1920–22.

---

**MAP LABELS:**

New Siberian Islands
Wrangel Island
Ambarchik
Nordvik
Dubinka
Norilsk
Igarka
Tiksi
Kolymskaya
Anadyr
UNION OF SOVIET SOCIALIST REPUBLICS from 1923
Maklakovo
Lena
Krasnoyarsk
Magadan
Sea of Okhotsk
Petropavlovsk
Cheremkhovo
Lake Baykal
Far Eastern Republic 1920–22 independent
Irkutsk
Ulan Ude
Chita
Magdagachi
Nikolaevsk
1925 to Russia
Ulan Bator
MONGOLIA 1924 Communist state under Russian influence
Komsomolsk
Aleksandrovsk
Sakhalin
Sovetskaya Gavan
Khabarovsk
Kuril Islands
Gobi Desert
Manchuria
Harbin
Mukden (Shenyang)
Vladivostok
Yellow
Beijing
Lushun (Port Arthur)
Sea of Japan
Lanzhou
CHINA
Korea Chosen from 1910 to Japan
Tokyo
JAPAN
NORTH PACIFIC OCEAN
Yellow Sea

---

**LEGEND:**

- western frontier of Russian empire, 1914
- principal town where Bolsheviks seized power, Nov–Dec 1917
- area controlled by Bolsheviks, Aug 1918
- advance of anti-Bolshevik armies, 1918–20
- area controlled by Bolsheviks, Oct 1919
- border of temporarily independent area
- Japanese Siberian expedition, 1918–22
- Union of Soviet Socialist Republics, 1939
- border, 1939

- Russian campaign, 1939
- main area of collectivization
- area under *gulag* administration
- new town founded 1925–38
- oilfield
- hydroelectric power station
- railroad

0        800 km
0        500 mi

See also 88 (19th-century Russia);
101 (Europe between the wars)

World War I destroyed the old order in central and eastern Europe: the fall of the Romanovs (Russia), Habsburgs (Austria–Hungary) and Hohenzollerns (Germany) brought political instability that compounded the economic and social dislocation of the war. Extremism flourished across central Europe, with Marxist revolutions in several major cities being countered by a rightwing backlash.

The peace treaties failed to create a lasting settlement, and provided instead the grounds for future discontent. United States president Wilson hoped that ethnically homogeneous nation-states could eradicate the nationalist rivalries and squabbling over territory that appeared to have caused the war; but this proved impossible. Two new states (Czechoslovakia and the Kingdom of the Serbs, Croats and Slovenes – later Yugoslavia) and one reconstituted one (Poland) assembled many ethnic groups within arbitrary borders, and nationalist groups were often disappointed in disputed areas. Everywhere populations were on the move. Italy, its promises from the Allies for territory unfulfilled, set out to take the territory it claimed by force, as did Poland.

The Treaty of Versailles forced Germany to admit guilt for starting the war and to pay huge reparations to the Allies. It was forbidden to ally with Austria and was divided by the Polish Corridor, while three million ethnic Germans remained outside the state.

The League of Nations, set up to resolve the disputes that were bound to arise from the settlement, was hamstrung as the United States, the only power capable of giving weight to its decisions, declined to join. With Russia preoccupied with domestic affairs, Britain and France were left to deal with European issues alone. They were faced with the prospect of a reborn Germany avenging its grievances and filling the power vacuum created by the fall of the imperial monarchies. Both Britain and France were economically weak following the war and they sought to keep Germany weak as well. France occupied the Ruhr in 1923 to enforce payment of reparations, but the hyperinflation that ensued provided fertile ground for extremist groups in Germany. With

**area temporarily independent**

—— border, 1921

**dictatorships by 1 Sep 1939**

- Communist
- fascist
- other

**1924** date of introduction of dictatorship

**democracies, 1939**

- British territories and mandates
- French territories and mandates
- other

- German gain, 1935–1 Sep 1939
- Hungarian gain, 1938–39
- Italian gain, Apr 1939
- Turkish gain, 1923
- Nationalist-held Spain, late 1936
- Nationalist gain by Dec 1938
- demilitarized zone, 1919–35
- area of economic revival
- area of economic decline

SPAIN   country experiencing civil war, with date

☼ strike, riot or other protest action

✳ Communist uprising, 1919–23

✴ international incident

✴ incident of Polish aggression, 1920

♆ city with large Jewish population

—— supply route for Spanish civil war

➤ emigration of more than 200,000 refugees

0                   600 km

0                   400 mi

## TIMELINE

### International affairs

**1919–20** Treaties of Versailles, St Germain, Neuilly, Trianon create the postwar settlement in Europe

**1922** Germany and USSR sign a treaty at Rapallo

**1924** The Dawes plan reduces German reparations

**1925** The European powers guarantee Germany's eastern European borders at Locarno

**1928** The antiwar Kellogg–Briand pact is signed in Paris

**1929** Beginning of the Great Depression

**1932** German postwar reparations are abolished

**1932** France and the USSR sign a nonaggression treaty

**1934** Yugoslavia, Romania, Turkey, Greece sign a Balkan pact against Hitler and Stalin

**1936** The Rome–Berlin Axis is formed

**1938** Munich agreement on Germany's occupation of the Sudetenland

**1939** The Nazi–Soviet pact is signed

### Western Europe

**1920** Abortive Communist revolutions in Germany

**1921** The Irish Free State is set up in southern Ireland

**1923** France occupies the Ruhr; hyperinflation in Germany

**1926** General strike in Britain, led by the miners

**1926** Germany enters the League of Nations

**1929** Lateran treaties between Italy and the Papacy ensure the Vatican's independence

**1931** The Republicans win a landslide victory in Spanish elections; the king flees

**1933** Adolf Hitler is elected chancellor of Germany

**1936–39** The Spanish Civil War follows an attempted rightwing coup by Franco

**1936** German army reoccupies the Rhineland

**1939** Britain and France declare war on Germany

### Eastern Europe

**1920–22** War between Greece and Turkey

**1920–21** Poland and the Soviet Union are at war

**1924–29** Joseph Stalin consolidates his power in USSR

**1926** Josef Pilsudski comes to power in Poland

**1934** Austrian chancellor Dollfuss is murdered by Nazis

**1934** King Alexander of Macedonia is assassinated

**1938** German invasion of Austria (*Anschluss*)

**1939** Germany and Soviet Union invade Poland

1920                          1930                          1940

**alliance system**
- French
- German
- Italian
- Locarno treaty, 1925
- Balkan Entente, 1934
- Baltic Entente, 1922

Britain and France tried to buy them off by conceding small territorial claims (the policy of "appeasement"), but the dictators demanded more. Italy escaped virtually unpunished for invading Ethiopia in 1935 as Britain and France tried (unsuccessfully) to preserve Mussolini as an ally against Germany. Hitler, as well as initiating his anti-Jewish policies, began to challenge the Treaty of Versailles: in 1935 Germany began to rearm and then reoccupied the Rhineland. Further steps to extend German power and territory followed, with the *Anschluss* with Austria (1938) and the partition of Czechoslovakia (agreed with Britain and France at Munich in 1938).

By now Britain and France had lost all credibility. Germany invaded Czechoslovakia in 1939 and the French and British guaranteed the security of several other European states, but to little avail. A French strategy of fencing the Germans in with the "Little Entente" in eastern Europe had already been weakened by a German–Polish non-aggression treaty in 1934. The democracies failed to secure an alliance with the Soviet Union and Stalin, believing Britain and France to be encouraging Hitler to expand to the east, signed a Nazi–Soviet pact in August 1939. Hitler and Stalin partitioned Poland between them, but Hitler failed to anticipate a sea-change in British and French opinion after his annexation of Czechoslovakia. Unexpectedly he had to fight in the west before pursuing his primary objectives in the east.

**1** Budapest saw a Communist takeover in March 1919 under Bela Kun. Hungary then invaded Slovakia and Transylvania; Kun fled abroad in August 1919.

**2** Following a plebiscite in 1920, Schleswig was divided between Germany and Denmark.

**3** Ireland was divided in 1921: the mainly Protestant north elected to stay in the United Kingdom, the south became the Irish Free State. Civil war ensued in the south (1922-23), where many rejected partition.

**4** The Saar became a League of Nations mandate under French rule in 1919, but returned to Germany by plebiscite in 1935.

**5** The town of Guernica was destroyed by German bombers in the first massive aerial attack on civilians.

**6** The Sudetenland of northwest Czechoslovakia, which had a large German minority, was annexed by Hitler following the Munich agreement in 1938.

See also 98 (World War I); 100 (the
Soviet Union to 1941); 105 (World War II)

Germany's prosperity essential for European well-being, reparations were reduced and a limited recovery followed, funded by American loans.

Germany's grievances might have been resolved peacefully. The Locarno pact (1925) guaranteed its western borders and showed that foreign minister Stresemann would work peacefully to revise the Treaty of Versailles, while the Kellogg–Briand pact of 1928 officially, if implausibly, renounced war.

The depression of the early 1930s, caused in part by the withdrawal of American loans, shattered the illusion of stability. Democracy was weakly established in many countries: massive unemployment and protest were now seen, followed by a return to authoritarian government. The dictator Pilsudski had upheld Catholicism in Poland since 1926; now Franco did the same in Spain after a three-year civil war. This bloody conflict showed how polarized politics in Europe was, and became a war by proxy between the Soviet-supplied republic and German- and Italian-supported right. Royal dictatorships also flourished in Bulgaria, Romania and Yugoslavia.

The radical new phenomenon of fascism now threatened the peace. Promising national renewal and fueled by grievances over the peace settlement, Mussolini's movement in Italy had established itself as a totalitarian regime in 1925. Fascist parties formed across Europe and in 1933 Hitler's Nazi party won power in Germany, its appeal magnified by mass unemployment and fear of Communism.

The British and French governments continued to be cautious. In Germany the Nazis eliminated unemployment by means of public work schemes, but in Britain the principles of classical economics still applied. Some economists, led by J.M. Keynes, advocated jump-starting the economy through government spending, but heavy industry did not recover until the armaments boom at the end of the 1930s (newer industries, such as electronics, motor and aircraft production, however, showed rapid growth).

The same caution applied to foreign policy. Unwilling to destabilize the international economy with wars or sanctions, the League proved unable to take a firm line with Germany and Italy in the 1930s.

World War I involved many of the American states, despite an original intention to stay out of the conflict. The Caribbean islands and Canada owed direct allegiance to Britain, but most other countries had divided loyalties and were anxious to preserve their own interests. US president Woodrow Wilson advised neutrality. By 1918 Brazil and several Central American states had joined the Allies; the United States itself stayed out until German U-boat (submarine) attacks drove Wilson to declare war in 1917. The nation was put on a war footing: the government took over the railroads and strikers were faced with the draft. Factories and shipyards converted to warwork, and thousands of African–Americans moved north to the munitions factories.

By the end of the war, there was little enthusiasm for any US involvement in Europe's postwar territorial arrangements. The Treaty of Versailles and the League of Nations, Wilson's brainchild, were both rejected by Congress as Americans sought "normalcy". The "jazz age" of the 1920s brought a quest for consumer goods and material comfort, despite a moral backlash in the form of the Volstead Act, which brought Prohibition in 1920, with intoxicating liquor banned across the country. The result was a rise in political corruption and gangsterism.

In 1929, the Wall St stock market crash threw the country into the Great Depression, which had global repercussions as US loans and investments had propped up the world's trade. The shadow of the depression was felt throughout the Western Hemisphere. In the United States itself, the crisis was exacerbated by drought and storms that devastated parts of Texas and the Mid-West, and created a dustbowl on the Great Plains. Some 12 million Americans lost their jobs, and shanty-towns (Hoovervilles) sprang up around many cities. In 1933, Democrat Franklin D. Roosevelt became president, offering a New Deal to alleviate the depression through unprecedented government spending, giving work to millions on infrastructure projects such as dams and airports. The New Deal could not, however, cure all the economic ills of the country. Agriculture and heavy industry recovered only after 1940, mainly due to US contributions to Britain's war effort, followed by

the outbreak of war with Japan in December 1941.

Canada had suffered in the Great War, and lost 60,000 men by 1918. This experience, followed by the prosperity of the 1920s, encouraged a new spirit of independence. But the country was hit hard by the depression, as it was heavily reliant on the export of wheat and lumber. The great drought of 1934 also wrought havoc on the farmers of the prairies. New political groupings suggested nationalization and the redistribution of income as a cure to national ills, while separatists won a large following in Quebec. The rise in world prices after 1937, and closer economic ties with the United States caused both proposals to be shelved for several decades.

The United States claimed the Caribbean and Central America as its "backyard", intervening to maintain its investments (including the Panama Canal and the oil reserves of Mexico and Venezuela) and building a military base at Guantanamo Bay on Cuba. The region was badly hit by the recession, and strikes and demonstrations were common, especially in the British West Indies. Several countries turned to dictatorships: some, such as Lázaro Cárdenas, ruler of Mexico from 1934–40, tried honestly to improve the condition of their people. Cárdenas restored communal lands to the peasants, and nationalized railroads and oil companies. Venezuela was ruled by Juan Vicente Gómez from 1908–35. He took over the Lake Maracaibo oil reserves, but failed to address the weakness of so many Latin American states: the reliance on a single export commodity.

Colombia became the world's second producer of coffee but, like its main rival Brazil (ruled after 1930 by Getúlio Vargas), tried to reduce the economy's dependence on the fragile coffee trade in the 1930s by industrial diversification and import substitution. Argentina, which had flourished since the 19th century on grain and meat exports, now had to endure austerity measures. Chile too suffered with the fall in copper prices, while its nitrate exports were hit by the discovery of new chemical methods of production. Several South American states engaged in border disputes: Chile and Peru clashed over nitrate resources; the Chaco War between Bolivia and Paraguay in the 1930s was the most

violent conflict to take place in the world between 1918 and 1939; and Ecuador lost the Amazonian region to Peru in 1942.

World War II brought full employment and high wages to North America: by 1943 the USA was outproducing all the enemy nations combined. Millions moved to the cities; African–Americans flooded to California, Detroit and New York. Convoys took troops and supplies to all main theaters of war, and brought aid to Britain and the USSR. To counter enemy submarines operating down the Atlantic seaboard and in the Gulf of Mexico, air patrols were maintained far out to sea. For the Latin American countries the war years were eased by Roosevelt's "good neighbor" policy. The Coffee Accords of 1940 guaranteed US markets; in return Roosevelt gained bases and promises of military support.

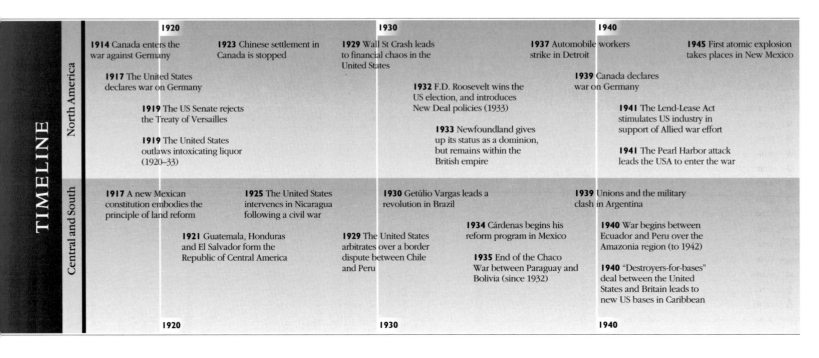

## TIMELINE

### North America

**1914** Canada enters the war against Germany

**1917** The United States declares war on Germany

**1919** The US Senate rejects the Treaty of Versailles

**1919** The United States outlaws intoxicating liquor (1920–33)

**1923** Chinese settlement in Canada is stopped

**1929** Wall St Crash leads to financial chaos in the United States

**1932** F.D. Roosevelt wins the US election, and introduces New Deal policies (1933)

**1933** Newfoundland gives up its status as a dominion, but remains within the British empire

**1937** Automobile workers strike in Detroit

**1939** Canada declares war on Germany

**1941** The Lend-Lease Act stimulates US industry in support of Allied war effort

**1941** The Pearl Harbor attack leads the USA to enter the war

**1945** First atomic explosion takes places in New Mexico

### Central and South

**1917** A new Mexican constitution embodies the principle of land reform

**1921** Guatemala, Honduras and El Salvador form the Republic of Central America

**1925** The United States intervenes in Nicaragua following a civil war

**1929** The United States arbitrates over a border dispute between Chile and Peru

**1930** Getúlio Vargas leads a revolution in Brazil

**1934** Cárdenas begins his reform program in Mexico

**1935** End of the Chaco War between Paraguay and Bolivia (since 1932)

**1939** Unions and the military clash in Argentina

**1940** War begins between Ecuador and Peru over the Amazonia region (to 1942)

**1940** "Destroyers-for-bases" deal between the United States and Britain leads to new US bases in Caribbean

1920    1930    1940

THE NATIONAL RECOVERY ADMINISTRATION (NRA) was set up by Roosevelt to finance New Deal projects in 1933. Its symbol is shown here.

**NRA MEMBER U.S. WE DO OUR PART**

**1** Seattle, in Washington State, flourished after the opening of the Panama Canal expanded Pacific trade; it became a center of aircraft manufacture.

**2** Chicago was a notorious center of gangsterism, built upon the loyalties of existing ethnic communities, in the Prohibition era and into the 1930s.

**3** Manaus had been a center of the rubber industry in the 19th century, but was in decline through the early 20th century.

**4** The apparent discovery of oil in the disputed Gran Chaco region caused Bolivia to attack Paraguayan positions in 1932. By 1935 Paraguayan control was confirmed; but the oil finds proved illusory.

**5** The German East Asian fleet attacked the British coaling station of the Falkland Islands in December 1914, but was defeated by the Royal Navy.

**6** Cuba's reliance on United States imports of sugar in the 1920s left the economy defenseless in the 1930s; World War II boosted exports to the United States.

**7** The Tennessee Valley Authority built dams and hydroelectric plants which, with flood control and land reclamaion schemes, raised living standards in seven states in the 1930s.

**8** Getúlio Vargas used his power base in Minas Gerais to launch a coup in Brazil in 1930.

**countries with territorial changes, 1914–41**

- Bolivia, 1914
- Canada, 1914
- Chile, 1914
- Colombia, 1914
- Ecuador, 1914
- Newfoundland, 1914
- Paraguay, 1914
- Peru, 1914
- border, 1941
- region of Oriente claimed by Peru
- provincial rebellion in Brazil, 1930

**effects of the Depression in North America**

- area of severe economic decline, 1930–40
- area of economic revival, 1930–40
- area affected by drought in the early 1930s
- seat of Pan-American Congress, with date
- West Indian disturbances, 1935–39
- strike or labor unrest
- United States military intervention
- battle of World War I
- battle of World War II
- Lend-Lease aircraft route, 1941–45
- convoy route
- area of Allied shipping losses, 1939–45
- Antigua United States military base, 1940
- center of automobile industry
- center of aviation industry
- oil field
- African-American migration, 1914–18
- migration from the "dustbowl states", 1930s

See also 81 (19th-century Latin America); 87 (19th-century USA); 111 (the postwar Americas)

The Russo-Japanese War of 1904–05 gave Japan protectorate authority over Korea and the lease of Chinese territory in south Manchuria. From these bases the army looked to consolidate its influence in Manchuria and north China. By this time, a new and increasingly militant anti-imperialist nationalism was developing among young Chinese intellectuals, merchants and soldiers. This development was echoed elsewhere in the region, for example in the growth of Indian and Vietnamese national movements. In the case of China, resentment after 1905 was clearly focussed on Japan as the other western powers were preoccupied with European politics and hoped merely to hold onto their Asian interests.

Tokyo's decision to enter World War I was driven as much by interests in China – where the Manchu dynasty had finally fallen three years earlier – as by the desire to help its ally Britain. In August 1914 Japan issued an ultimatum to Germany to hand over territories in Shandong province. Japan then took the German outpost of Qingdao; the whole province was eventually occupied.

As one of the victorious nations, Japan was invited to attend the Versailles peace conference in 1919 and retained the former German territory in Shandong. However, this conference marked a turning point in the position of the European powers in east Asia – Britain, France, the Netherlands, and, to a lesser extent, Portugal. All had been weakened by the war, while the revolution of 1917 ended Russia's imperialism. The League of Nations, created in the aftermath of war, adopted a policy generally critical of colonialism. In the interwar years Britain, while publicly supporting its empire, privately explored ways to enable the Asian colonies to achieve self-governing Dominion status (like New Zealand, since 1907) or Commonwealth status (like Australia). The Dutch, too, were beginning to consider ways of passing power to the native populations.

Nationalist movements in the colonies were given impetus by the severe effects of the worldwide depression of the 1930s and the collapse of European prestige wrought by the carnage of World War I. In India, the Indian National Congress, led by Jawaharlal Nehru and Mohandas "Mahatma" Gandhi, organized a mass self-rule movement in the 1920s and 1930s. In Burma, which was separated from India and given a form of responsible government in 1937, nationalist demands were heightened by the depression. The Dutch East Indies experienced a Communist uprising in 1926–27, and French Indo-China also saw Communist-inspired strikes and rural unrest with the overall objective of national independence. Neither the French nor the Dutch made significant concessions, and – except in India – the nationalist movements appeared divided and unable to make a lasting impression. The United States, though, appeared to support the nationalists, and in 1935 promised independence for its own colony in the Philippines within ten years.

The general unrest in east and southeast Asia led Japan into further military expansion from 1931. After establishing the puppet state of Manzhouguo in Manchuria, however, Japan was criticized by the League of Nations and quit this body in protest. The resulting international isolation made Japan turn for new allies to Germany and Italy and, in China, to pursue an even more aggressive and uncompromising policy toward the Nationalist government which was already engaged in civil war with Chinese Communists. In mid-1937 Japan and China engaged unofficially in a war which Japanese generals confidently promised would be over by the end of the year. Japan's bombing of cities and the massacre of civilians as its forces took the Nationalist cities of Shanghai and Nanjing brought the war to the attention of the world, heightening criticism in the west.

In 1939 Japanese forces landed in French Indo-China to cut off supply routes to the Chinese Nationalists. After the fall of France to Hitler in 1940, the Japanese went on to occupy most of the colony, while maintaining a French administration. Politically, the Japanese exploited the anti-European feeling among the nationalist groups, promising a form of independence such as Burma had been given. Economic prosperity was similarly promised in the Japanese-sponsored Greater East Asian Co-Prosperity Sphere. Some – such as the Indian leader

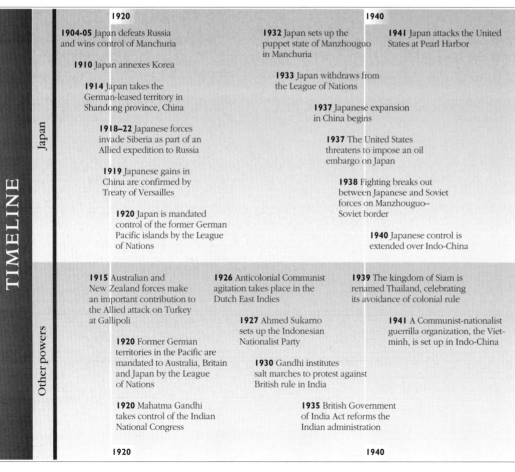

## TIMELINE

### Japan

**1904-05** Japan defeats Russia and wins control of Manchuria

**1910** Japan annexes Korea

**1914** Japan takes the German-leased territory in Shandong province, China

**1918–22** Japanese forces invade Siberia as part of an Allied expedition to Russia

**1919** Japanese gains in China are confirmed by Treaty of Versailles

**1920** Japan is mandated control of the former German Pacific islands by the League of Nations

**1932** Japan sets up the puppet state of Manzhouguo in Manchuria

**1933** Japan withdraws from the League of Nations

**1937** Japanese expansion in China begins

**1937** The United States threatens to impose an oil embargo on Japan

**1938** Fighting breaks out between Japanese and Soviet forces on Manzhouguo–Soviet border

**1940** Japanese control is extended over Indo-China

**1941** Japan attacks the United States at Pearl Harbor

### Other powers

**1915** Australian and New Zealand forces make an important contribution to the Allied attack on Turkey at Gallipoli

**1920** Former German territories in the Pacific are mandated to Australia, Britain and Japan by the League of Nations

**1920** Mahatma Gandhi takes control of the Indian National Congress

**1926** Anticolonial Communist agitation takes place in the Dutch East Indies

**1927** Ahmed Sukarno sets up the Indonesian Nationalist Party

**1930** Gandhi institutes salt marches to protest against British rule in India

**1939** The kingdom of Siam is renamed Thailand, celebrating its avoidance of colonial rule

**1941** A Communist-nationalist guerrilla organization, the Viet-minh, is set up in Indo-China

**1935** British Government of India Act reforms the Indian administration

### Map legend

- borders, 1914
- British territory, 1914
- Dutch territory, 1914
- French territory, 1914
- German territory, 1914
- Japanese territory, 1914
- Portuguese territory, 1914
- United States territory, 1914

territorial gains from Germany by mandate, 1920
- Australian
- Japanese

Japanese territorial expansion in Asia
- temporary occupation, 1915-25
- gains by 1934 (empire of Manzhouguo)
- gains by 1937
- gains by 7 Dec 1941

- under Japanese influence, 1936–40
- Chinese Communist headquarters, 1937
- strong Indian National Congress support
- ○ Allied base
- *oil* strategic resource
- ☆ area of anti-colonial agitation
- Burma road
- → Japanese attack

0 ————— 1200 km
0 ————— 800 mi

Subhas Chandra Bose – were persuaded by this message; others thought that European imperialism was being replaced by a Japanese variety.

The United States proposed an embargo on imports from Japan in 1937, and banned exports to Japan of scrap iron (1940) and oil (1941). The British and Dutch supported the oil embargo, whereupon Japan viewed the oil-rich Dutch East Indies, and the tin- and rubber-producing British colonies of Burma and Malaya as alternative sources of raw materials. Japan realized that any aggression against these would lead to war with the United States itself. But when diplomacy failed, Japan attacked the United States naval base of Pearl Harbor and the Philippines in December 1941, then swept down into Dutch and British colonial southeast Asia.

UNION OF SOVIET SOCIALIST REPUBLICS

Chita

Manzhouli

Khalkin-Gol
1939

Manchuria
1931 Japanese occupation,
1932 republic of Manzhouguo,
1934 empire of Manzhouguo

Khabarovsk

Harbin

coal Sakhalin
Karafuto

Kuril Islands

Iturup
(Etorofu)

to Pearl Harbor
(Hawaii),
Dec 1941

Chahar

coal

Vladivostok

oil

Suiyuan 1938

Jehol
1933 to Manzhouguo

Mukden
(Shenyang)

Chang-ku Feng
1938

Hokkaido

coal

Marco Polo
Bridge
1937

**3**

Beijing

Tianjin

Lushun
(Port Arthur)

Dalian
(Dairen)

Weihaiwei
1930 to China
1938 to Japan

**5**

coal

Pyongyang

Seoul

Sea of
Japan

oil

Yulin

Shanxi

Zhili

Shandong

Korea
Chosen, 1910–45

iron

JAPAN

Honshu

Nagoya

Tokyo

**2**

Yan'an

coal

Qingdao
1914 to Japan

Pusan

Kyoto

Xi'an

Kaifeng

Tai'erzhuang
1938

Yellow
Sea

Shimonoseki

Nagasaki

coal

Shikoku

Kyushu

LHasa

BHUTAN

Bengal
1923–32

Dhaka

Calcutta

Chengdu

Chongqing

Yangtze

Nanjing 1937

Wuhan

Changsha

CHINA
1919–45

1925
Shanghai
1937

**4**

East
China
Sea

Wenzhou

Bonin Islands
to Japan

NORTH
PACIFIC
OCEAN

Ryukyu Islands

Okinawa

Daito Islands
to Japan

Volcano Islands
to Japan

Marcus Island
to Japan

Kunming

Burma

oil

rubber

Mandalay

Lashio

Tongking
1940 under Japanese
occupation

Hanoi

Haiphong

1939

Xiamen
(Amoy)

Fuzhou

Taipei

Taiwan

Shantou
(Swatow)

Tainan

Guangzhou
(Canton)

Hong Kong
to Britain

Macao
to Portugal

Hainan

Luzon

Manila

Philippine
Sea

Mariana
Islands

Rangoon

Laos

tin

SIAM
Thailand from 1939

Bangkok

French
Indo-China
1930

rubber

Phnom Penh

Saigon

rubber

Annam
1941 under Japanese
occupation

South
China
Sea

Philippines

Guam
to United States

Andaman Islands
to Britain

Andaman
Sea

COCHIN CHINA
1941 under Japanese
occupation

Iloilo

Cebu

Palawan

Mindanao

rubber

Davao

Yap Islands

Caroline Islands

Nicobar Islands
to Britain

British North Borneo

Bandar Seri Begawan
(Brunei)

Zamboanga

Sandakan

rubber

Palau Islands

oil
rubber
Medan

Malay
states

Kuala Lumpur

tin

Brunei

oil

Sarawak

oil

rubber

Celebes
Sea

Halmahera

rubber

oil

tin

Singapore

Kuching

Borneo

oil

Jayapura
(Hollandia)

New Ireland

oil

Sumatra
1927

Palembang

Celebes

Ceram

oil

Dutch
New Guinea

Wewak

German
New Guinea

Bougainville

New Britain

INDIAN
OCEAN

Banjarmasin

rubber

Java
Sea

Banda
Sea

bauxite
1926 oil

Surabaya

rubber

Batavia

oil

Dutch East Indies
(Netherlands India)

**6**

Dili

rubber

Portuguese
Timor

New Guinea

Territory of Papua
to Australia

Port Moresby

Java

Timor

Arafura
Sea

Coral
Sea

AUSTRALIA

**1** In 1919 Gurkha troops under British command massacred almost 400 Hindus at Amritsar in an attempt to stem the rise of nationalism in India.

**2** Much of Tokyo was destroyed in an earthquake of 1923; subsequent rebuilding encouraged the trend of radical social and industrial modernization.

**3** A skirmish between the Japanese and the Chinese Nationalists at Marco Polo Bridge near Beijing is often considered the first engagement of World War II.

**4** A quarter of a million Chinese lost their lives in the looting and murder that followed the fall of Shanghai to the Japanese in December 1937.

**5** Mukden was the capital of Japanese-dominated Manzhouguo, where the last Qing emperor of China, Pu Yi, was installed as regent, then (1934) as emperor.

**6** The Dutch set up a Volksraad (People's Council) at Batavia in the Dutch East Indies. In 1937 it requested Dominion status for the colony.

See also 93 (19th-century Japan)
108 (World War II in Asia)

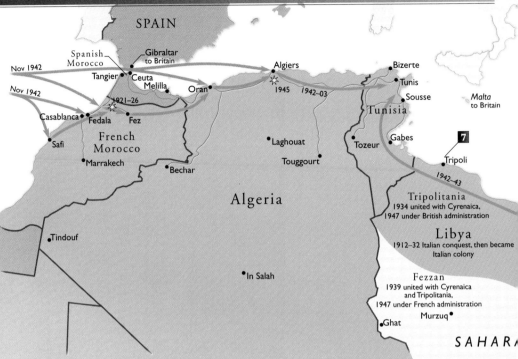

In 1914 the Allies decided to carry the war into every German colony in Africa. Military operations in Togoland, Cameroon and South-West Africa were completed by 1916; the campaigns in German East Africa (later Tanganyika) continued until 1918, a week after the armistice was signed on the Western Front. Turkey's alliance with Germany led to assaults on the Suez Canal and Basra, both repelled by Allied forces. The British supported the Arab revolts against the Turks: they took Jerusalem in 1917, and a more general assault on Turkish control of the Middle East followed as the British raced to occupy the Mesopotamian oilfields. Britain ensured its hold over the oilfields of southern Persia, too, claiming a *de facto* protectorate in 1918.

The Covenant of the League of Nations required the peacemakers to help underdeveloped peoples to cope with the "strenuous conditions of the modern world". The colonies of the defunct German and Turkish empires were administered under the mandate system. Some ex-colonies were scheduled for rapid independence: on this understanding Britain was awarded a mandate over Palestine, Iraq (formerly Mesopotamia) and Transjordan; France gained Syria and Lebanon. Less advanced areas could not expect independence in the near future; these included the Cameroons and Togoland, shared between Britain and France; Britain acquired Tanganyika, Belgium was awarded Ruanda-Urundi.

This redistribution of territory meant that the British and French colonial empires grew substantially; the indigenous peoples were not consulted about their aspirations for independence. The notable exception was in Palestine where, the British government declared in 1917, it favored the establishment of a national home for the Jews. This conflicted with an earlier promise to the Arabs that their

new lands would include Palestine, where the population was 90 percent Muslim. Jewish immigration to the area was limited through the 1920s, but grew substantially in the 1930s, when the British first proposed the division of Palestine into separate Jewish and Arab states. After World War II, with the world horrified by the Holocaust and the Jews and Arabs in Palestine engaged in civil war, the United Nations supported partition and approved the state of Israel which came into being in 1948.

Britain, by 1918 the dominant power in the region, held back from interfering in central Arabia, permitting the Saudi kingdom to emerge in 1932.

Britain's mandate in Iraq ended in 1932 but the right to protect oil and military interests was retained, notably by means of two airforce bases. A native Pahlavi dynasty seized control of Persia in 1925, renaming it Iran in 1935. By the outbreak of war, Iran produced more oil than the rest of the Middle East, and the shah's ties with Nazi Germany led the Allies to occupy the country again in 1941. The shah was forced to abdicate and his son Mohammed Reza Pahlavi installed in his place. The market for Middle Eastern oil grew in the interwar years, but the oilfields were not fully developed until the 1950s. French rule in Syria and Lebanon was benevolent, but was compromised by the fall of France in 1940; both countries were occupied during the war by Free French and British troops, and their independent status was recognized in 1946.

North and east Africa, too, were caught up in the conflicts of the European powers. The British confirmed Egyptian independence in 1922 but maintained the right to use Egypt's facilities in time of war, to defend the Suez Canal and maintain the Anglo-Egyptian joint rule in the Sudan. The British in Egypt and Italians in Libya began a conflict in 1940 which drew in the German army the following year; by 1943 the entire North Africa littoral was involved. Meanwhile indigenous independence movements were beginning to emerge, though most did not bear fruit until after World War II.

Ethiopia had retained its independence from colonial rule since defeating the Italians in 1896, and from 1935 was ruled by Haile Selassie (formerly Ras Tafari), who faced an invasion from Italy's Fascist dictator Mussolini. After using mustard gas on the Ethiopians, the Italians took Addis Ababa in 1936. A resistance movement continued to harry the Italians until World War II, when the British invaded and drove the Italians out once more, restoring Haile Selassie in 1941 and making Ethiopia the first African country to be liberated. Britain now took over the adminstration of the former Italian colonies of Eritrea and Somaliland.

French colonization of north Africa had failed to create a settler class comparable with the traditional peasantry of France. Settlers tended to be large farmers engaged in speculative agriculture for

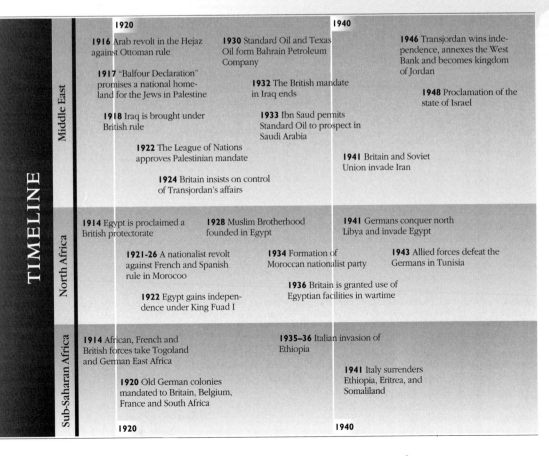

**TIMELINE**

**Middle East**

| 1920 | | 1940 | |
|---|---|---|---|
| **1916** Arab revolt in the Hejaz against Ottoman rule | **1930** Standard Oil and Texas Oil form Bahrain Petroleum Company | | **1946** Transjordan wins independence, annexes the West Bank and becomes kingdom of Jordan |
| **1917** "Balfour Declaration" promises a national homeland for the Jews in Palestine | **1932** The British mandate in Iraq ends | | **1948** Proclamation of the state of Israel |
| **1918** Iraq is brought under British rule | **1933** Ibn Saud permits Standard Oil to prospect in Saudi Arabia | | |
| **1922** The League of Nations approves Palestinian mandate | | **1941** Britain and Soviet Union invade Iran | |
| **1924** Britain insists on control of Transjordan's affairs | | | |

**North Africa**

| **1914** Egypt is proclaimed a British protectorate | **1928** Muslim Brotherhood founded in Egypt | **1941** Germans conquer north Libya and invade Egypt | |
|---|---|---|---|
| **1921-26** A nationalist revolt against French and Spanish rule in Morocco | **1934** Formation of Moroccan nationalist party | **1943** Allied forces defeat the Germans in Tunisia | |
| **1922** Egypt gains independence under King Fuad I | **1936** Britain is granted use of Egyptian facilities in wartime | | |

**Sub-Saharan Africa**

| **1914** African, French and British forces take Togoland and German East Africa | **1935–36** Italian invasion of Ethiopia | |
|---|---|---|
| **1920** Old German colonies mandated to Britain, Belgium, France and South Africa | **1941** Italy surrenders Ethiopia, Eritrea, and Somaliland | |
| 1920 | 1940 | |

GREECE

1918–23 · Istanbul

Ankara 1918–23

TURKEY
Ottoman empire until 1923

Kars
site of massacre, 1915

*Caspian
Sea*

Izmir
Athens 1918–23

1918–23 Konya
1918–23 Adana

1918–23 Ufra

1933

Mosul 1919, 1922–27, 1930–31

1931–32, 1935–36, 1943–44

Tabriz *Lake Urmia*

Tehran

IRAN
Persia until 1935,
1941–42 Allied occupation

*Lake
Van*

Nicosia
*Crete*
*Cyprus*

Aleppo 1920–21
1937–19

Latakia
1939

SYRIA
1920–41 French mandate,
1946 independent

Homs

Beirut 1936, 1943

LEBANON
1920–41 French mandate,
1946 independent

Damascus 1925–26, 1945

Kirkuk 1920

Baghdad 1920, 1935

Habbiniyah 1936, 1941

Kirkuk

IRAQ
1920–32 British mandate,
1932 independent

An Najaf Oct 1914–Nov 1918

Isfahan

Kerman

Hamadan

Shiraz

*Mediterranean Sea*

Benghazi Tobruk
1923–32
Cyrenaica
1934 united with
Tripolitania,
1947 under British
administration

1942

Alexandria

PALESTINE
1920–48 British mandate

Tel Aviv

Jerusalem 1920, 1936–39

Amman
1929

Aqaba

1925–27, 1937–39
Aug–Oct 1918

JORDAN
1920–46 British mandate,
Transjordan until independent 1946

Basra
Shaiba
Abadan

Kuwait
Kuwait

Bandar Abbas

*Persian Gulf*

Al Manamah Bahrain
Doha Qatar

Abu Dhabi

Muscat

Cairo Suez
Suez Canal
1919

EGYPT
1914 British protectorate,
1922 independent

El Kharga

Aswan

Medina

Jiddah Mecca

*Hejaz*
1916 independent,
1926 to Nejd

SAUDI ARABIA
1916–26 Nejd,
1926–32 Hejaz and Nejd

Riyadh

*Trucial Oman*

*Oman*

*DESERT*

Wadi Halfa

Port Sudan
Suakin

*Asir*
1917 independent,
1920 to Nejd

*Red Sea*

Jizan

YEMEN
1919 independent

Sana

Mukalla

*West Aden Protectorate*

Hadramaut
(East Aden
Protectorate)

*Socotra*

IBN SAUD with a representative
of ARAMCO (Arab-American oil
company) in 1939; from the
1930s oil took on a crucial role
in the region.

Anglo-Egyptian
Sudan

Omdurman
Khartoum

Kassala

Eritrea
1941 under British
administration

Asmera Massawa

Adowa

Gondar

Aden

Djibouti
French
Somaliland

Berbera

British Somaliland

*INDIAN
OCEAN*

El Obeid

Sennar

Adowa

Jan–Sep 1941

Oct 1935–May 1936

1941

Apr 1941

Mar–Apr 1941 Harar

Addis Ababa

Walwal
Apr–May 1936

*Shebelle*

ETHIOPIA
1936–41 to Italy,
1941 independence restored

*Italian Somaliland*
Italian protectorate until 1941,
1941 under British administration

**Legend:**
Ottoman empire, 1914

colonial powers, 1914
- France
- Italy
- Spain
- United Kingdom

mandate territory, 1920
- British mandate
- French mandate

independent Armenia, 1918–21
area under Greek control, 1922
border, 1948
oilfield
nationalist revolt or political disturbance
railroad
Allied campaign
Italian campaign

0 — 600 km
0 — 400 mi

---

export to France. Intensively farmed wheat, olives and vines required capital investment but between 1914 and 1935 these produced spectacular yields, strong exports and brought about the development of the north African workforce. In the same way control of mineral resources by French managers meant that virtually all the production of iron ore and phosphates, and the zinc, lead and cobalt deposits, went to France. The depression of the 1930s led to the collapse of much of this activity, and a rise in unemployment.

Libyan resistance to Italian colonization persisted until 1932. Italy's Fascist government encouraged large estates worked by Italian settlers, but there was little investment in infrastructure and barely 90,000 Italians had settled in Libya by 1939.

British policy toward Egypt and the Sudan was very different, with little or no settlement from

Britain. The British saw Egypt as a major source of cotton, and encouraged Egyptian financial institutions to support local industry and cotton-related projects in the Sudan. By 1939 Egypt was approaching self-sufficiency in a range of manufactured goods; production rose further during the war years.

**1** Masjed-Suleyman was the site of the first oil find in the Middle East, in 1908. Oil was found in Libya in the 1920s, and in Kuwait in 1932.

**2** Tel Aviv was founded in 1909 by Zionist idealists as a suburb of the ancient city of Jaffa; the Turks cleared the settlement in 1916–17, but it became the focus for Jewish immigration in the 1920s and 1930s.

**3** Aden, an important British coaling station on the route to India, was ruled from India until 1937 when it became a crown colony.

**4** Abdul Aziz Ibn Saud (r.1901–53) took Riyadh in 1901, consolidated his hold over Nejd by 1906 and Hejaz (1926) and set up the kingdom of Saudi Arabia in 1932. Oil reserves were found there in 1938.

**5** The Sennar Dam was completed in 1925, marking the beginning of a plan to irrigate the Sudan and develop the cotton industry for export.

**6** Italy's invasion of Ethiopia in October 1935 began with a land and air attack on Adowa, the scene of an Italian defeat in 1896.

**7** Tripoli was the center of Mussolini's Libyan industrial program: more than 700 factories were in operation there by 1939.

See also 115 (postwar Middle East);
118 (Africa)

The declaration of war on Germany by Britain and France in 1939 took Hitler by surprise; he was now forced to deal with the threat to Germany's western flank in order to avoid fighting the war on two fronts. His primary objective, though, remained the conquest of the Soviet Union.

Germany and the Soviet Union divided Poland between them as they had agreed in the Nazi–Soviet pact of 1939, both sides deporting large numbers of people. The USSR later absorbed the Baltic states with the exception of Finland, which preserved its independence in the "Winter War" of 1939–40. A "phoney war" ensued, the first break in the inactivity being the German invasion of Denmark and Norway in April 1940. The Allies had planned to seize Narvik to deny Germany access to the only port capable of handling the exports of vital Swedish iron ore; however, the rapid and well-planned German advance resulted in a hurried Allied withdrawal.

Soon after, Winston Churchill took over as British prime minister, but Allied resistance was ineffectual during the German attack on the Low Countries and France in May. France surrendered within six weeks. Germany occupied the north, while a collaborationist regime at Vichy controlled the south; Belgium and the Netherlands became satellites in the German industrial complex. Britain evacuated most of its forces from northern France, but in the Battle of Britain of 1940 (the first decisive battle to be fought in the air) stifled plans for a seaborne invasion by denying air superiority to the Luftwaffe (German air force). Italy chose this point to enter the war. The Mediterranean was closed to British shipping and fighting began in north and east Africa.

While the air offensive continued against Britain and escalated into the Blitz, Hitler turned his attention to the east. By the summer of 1940 he was planning the Barbarossa campaign – an invasion of the Soviet Union which he had planned for the mid-

1940s, but which was now brought forward by the success of the German war effort and the rapid rearmament of the other powers.

In April 1941 German, Bulgarian and Italian forces invaded Greece and Yugoslavia to secure their southern flank for Barbarossa. Italy had been defeated in Greece the previous year but now the Axis forces overran all opposition, driving British troops first to Crete and then to Egypt. German

success had been based on *blitzkrieg* or lightning war. With limited access to raw materials, Germany could not afford a long war. Tanks, dive-bombers and motorized infantry destroyed defenses before reserves could be mobilized or a war of attrition develop. Barbarossa was expected to last six weeks, but by November 1941 the campaign was bogged down by the weather. Hitler had ignored advice to seize Moscow, preferring to advance on all fronts. His forces were now dangerously stretched.

Stalin launched an offensive in the spring of 1942, but the Germans occupied more territory in the summer. It became clear, however, that they could not launch a knockout blow: the vast size of the

**Legend:**
- Germany, 1 Sep 1939
- territory gained by USSR, 1939–40
- western frontier of USSR, June 1941
- area of population and industry evacuated to Siberia, 1941–42
- borders, June 1942
- Axis power, June 1942
- ally of Axis power, June 1942
- under Axis occupation, June 1942
- Vichy territory, June 1942
- under Allied control, June 1942
- furthest Axis advance, 1941
- front lines, end Nov 1942
- Maginot line
- bombed city, 1940–42
- U-boat base
- siege
- atrocity or mass murder
- Lidice   reprisal killing
- death camp
- concentration camp
- Axis airborne operation
- British commando raid
- Allied withdrawal
- Axis offensive
- Allied offensive
- main convoy route, 1941–42

## TIMELINE

### East and north Europe

| 1940 | 1941 | 1942 |
|---|---|---|
| **1939 (Aug)** Nazi–Soviet non-aggression pact is signed | **1940 (Oct)** Italy invades Greece and Albania | **1941 (Nov)** Soviet counter-attack against the Germans |
| **1939 (Sep)** Germany and Soviet Union invade Poland | **1940 (Oct)** Germany and Italy invade Romania | **1942 (Jan)** Hitler adopts the "final solution" policy of exterminating Jews |
| **1939 (Nov)** The Soviet Union invades Finland | **1941 (Apr)** Germany invades Yugoslavia; Greece surrenders to the Germans | **1942 (Sep)** Beginning of the German siege of Stalingrad (to Jan 1943) |
| **1940 (Mar)** Finland and Soviet Union sign an armistice | **1941 (Jun)** Germany invades the Soviet Union (operation Barbarossa) | |
| **1940 (Apr)** Germany invades Denmark and Norway | **1941 (Sep)** Siege of Leningrad begins (to Jan 1944) | |
| **1940 (Jun)** USSR annexes Latvia, Estonia and Lithuania | | |

### Western Europe

| 1940 | 1941 | 1942 |
|---|---|---|
| **1939 (Sep)** France and Britain declare war on Germany | **1941 (Jul)** The Soviet Union and Britain sign a pact of mutual assistance | **1942 (Aug)** US bombing raids over Europe begin |
| **1940 (May)** Germany invades the Low Countries and France | **1941 (Aug)** Churchill and Roosevelt sign the Atlantic Charter (blueprint for the United Nations) | **1942 (Nov)** Germans occupy Vichy France following Allied successes in north Africa |
| **1940 (Jun)** Italy declares war on Britain and France | | |
| **1940 (Jun)** German troops enter Paris; fall of France | **1941 (Dec)** Germany declares war on the USA | |
| **1940 (Jul–Oct)** Battle of Britain over southern England | | |

**Map labels:** ICELAND, Reykjavik, from Canada and the United States, Faroe Islands to Denmark, winter route to Murmansk and Archangel, Shetland Islands to Britain, from Canada and the United States, Glasgow, Newcastl, Belfast, UNITED KINGDOM, IRELAND, Liverpool, Hull, Dublin, Manchester, Sheffield, Birmingham, Coventry, Cardiff, Bristol, London, Southampton, Dover, Plymouth, Dunkirk, Portsmouth, Dieppe, Le Hav, Brest, St Malo, Paris, Lorient, St Nazaire, Loire, FRANCE, ATLANTIC OCEAN, Vich, La Rochelle, Bordeaux, June 1940, occupied by Germany, Nov 1942, Bayonne, Toulou, Bilbao, ANDORRA, Ebro, Barcelona, Nov 1942, Douro, SPAIN, Madrid, PORTUGAL, Tagus, Guadiana, Valencia, Lisbon, Balearic Islands to Spain, Seville, Gibraltar to Britain, Algiers, Cádiz, July 1940, Nov 1942, Tangier, to Spain, Oran, Spanish Morocco, Algeria Vichy control until Nov 1942, Nov 1942, Fez, French Morocco Vichy control until Nov 1942, Fedala, Safi

See also 101 (Europe between the wars); 107 (World War II to 1945); 108 (World War II in Asia)

**1** London and other cities suffered aerial bombardment from September 1940 to May 1941. The "Blitz" failed to break British industry or civilian morale.

**2** A surprise amphibious attack in April 1940 allowed Germany to take Norway before British support could arrive. Only in Narvik did the plan falter temporarily.

**3** The defense of Greece in April 1941 was poorly coordinated and quickly overrun; the British forces were evacuated to Crete, and soon after to Alexandria.

**4** After the Soviet invasion of November 1939, the Finns caused heavy losses but sued for peace in March 1940. Though nominally neutral, Finland favored Germany against the USSR.

**5** Vichy, a spa town, was seat of the collaborationist French government from 1940 to November 1942.

**6** Britain's strategic naval base at Malta endured more than 1,200 air raids during World War II.

country and its population, and the safety of the industrial areas evacuated east of the Urals meant that the USSR had huge capacity. By the end of 1942, a turning point was approaching.

The United States had already been supplying Britain and the Soviet Union with materiel through the "lend–lease" scheme, and its entry into the war as a full belligerent in December 1941 gave the Allies a major boost. From then on Allied superiority in men and arms, and Hitler's lack of strategic vision were to lead to German defeat.

Disruption of the supply routes from America had become of central concern to the western Allies. The United States was anxious to invade western

Europe as quickly as possible, but U-boat attacks on convoys in the Atlantic hampered the transport of men and materiel. A minor invasion of north Africa, occupied by Italian and Vichy forces backed up by General Rommel's Afrika Korps, met with rapid success. If the Battle of the Atlantic could not be won, though, United States numerical and industrial power would count for little in the battle for Europe.

In eastern Europe the Germans undertook the enslavement and murder of the subject populations. Executions of civilians were commonplace in the invasion of Poland, and during Barbarossa mass murder was a tool of occupation policy. Hitler hoped to create a "new order" based on the Nazi idea of the

"historic conflict" between the Aryans (Germans) and the other "inferior races". Millions of Slavs and Gypsies were shot, deported, starved or enslaved to create a "living space" for Germans. In what was called the "final solution", mass shootings and gassings were used to exterminate the Jews. Death camps were built and by the end of 1942 almost the entire Jewish population of Poland, the Baltic states, and the USSR as far east as the Caucasus – about three million people – had been killed.

The international order which emerged from World War I failed to match the intentions of allowing for national self-determination for all, and left a deep resentment in Germany, which was made to carry the blame for the war. As a result, stability was not achieved, and the post-Versailles order was overturned by extremist powers which by 1942 dominated much of the globe. The Axis powers, Germany and Japan, exploited the political vacuum left by the withdrawal of the United States and Russia from world affairs after the war, and by the effects of the depression on Britain and France. However, although 1942 marked the zenith of Axis power, their attacks on the two nascent superpowers made their eventual victory unlikely.

Soviet Russia emerged from its civil war of the early 1920s and turned in on itself as Stalin tried to build "socialism in one country" (▷ 100). The attempt to entrench Soviet power and catch up with the west was partially successful but extremely costly, as Stalin unleashed famine and terror on the Soviet Union.

In Europe, economic recovery was built on American loans. The US stock market crash of 1929 precipitated the global economic collapse known as the Great Depression. Its effect was to increase the appeal of fascist or extreme rightwing schemes of national regeneration in countries dissatisfied with the outcome of the peace settlements of 1919–23 (notably Germany). Governments everywhere looked to protect their interests by erecting tariff barriers and closed trading blocs, which further depressed the world economy.

The United States became isolated from international affairs as it tried to resolve its internal problems, and Britain and France were left to try to contain fascist expansion. But, although the depression began to lift in the late 1930s, both countries were economically too weak and too preoccupied by their global commitments to act effectively (▷ 101). They feared the prospect of fighting on three fronts – against Germany in Europe, Italy in the Mediterranean, and Japan in Asia. Their empires were potentially unstable – especially British India, where the nationalist Congress Party was growing in strength (▷ 103) – as were their domestic economies and societies.

The League of Nations reacted weakly to a series of crises in the 1930s – an Italian invasion of Ethiopia and German invasions of the Rhineland, Austria, Czechoslovakia – and thereby lost its credibility. France and Britain tried but failed to preserve peace through negotiation, alliances

A.   Albania (Italy)
B.   Belgium
CR.  Croatia
D.   Denmark
DR.  Dominican Republic
H.   Hungary
L.   Luxembourg
M.   Montenegro
N.   Netherlands
PA.  Palestine (Britain)
PG.  Portuguese Guinea (Portugal)
SE.  Serbia
SR.  Southern Rhodesia (Britain)
S.   Switzerland
TO.  Trucial Oman
     (Britain)
YE.  Yemen

Alaska (United States)
CANADA
Newfoundland (Britain)
UNITED STATES
MEXICO
Hawaiian Islands (United States)
Bahamas (Britain)
British Honduras (Britain)
CUBA
HAITI
Puerto Rico (United States)
DR.
Barbados (Britain)
Jamaica (Britain)
GUATEMALA
EL SALVADOR
HONDURAS
NICARAGUA
COSTA RICA
Canal Zone (United States)
PANAMA
Trinidad (Britain)
British Guiana (Britain)
Dutch Guiana (Netherlands)
French Guiana (Free French)
VENEZUELA
COLOMBIA
ECUADOR
PERU
BRAZIL
BOLIVIA
French Polynesia (Free French)
PARAGUAY
CHILE
ARGENTINA
URUGUAY
Falkland Islands (Britain)

**1933** Adolf Hitler becomes German chancellor

**1932** US president F.D. Roosevelt initiates the "New Deal"

**1932** The kingdom of Saudi Arabia is founded

**1931** The Mukden incident: Japan occupies Manchuria

**1938** Munich crisis: Britain accepts German expansion in Czechoslovakia

**1937** Japan invades China; Sino-Japanese war begins

**1923** France occupies the Ruhr; hyperinflation results in Germany

**1923** Foundation of the modern republic of Turkey

**1921** The Russian civil war ends with a Bolshevik victory

**1929** Wall St Crash begins the Great Depression and world trading collapse

| TIMELINE | | 1920 | | 1930 | |
|---|---|---|---|---|---|
| The Americas | | | | | |
| Europe | | | | | |
| Middle East | | | | | |
| Africa | | | | | |
| Asia and Australasia | | | | | |

**1922** Mussolini marches on Rome, establishing the first Fascist government

**1922** Washington Naval Agreement limits Japanese naval power in the Pacific

**1925** Joseph Stalin comes to power in USSR

**1927** A Chinese Nationalist government is established under Jiang Jieshi

**1928** Russia's first Five Year Plan of industrialization is introduced

**1934** Chinese Communists undertake the "Long March" to Yan'an

**1935** Mussolini invades Ethiopia to set up an Italian empire

**1936** Civil war in Spain after a rightwing uprising against the government

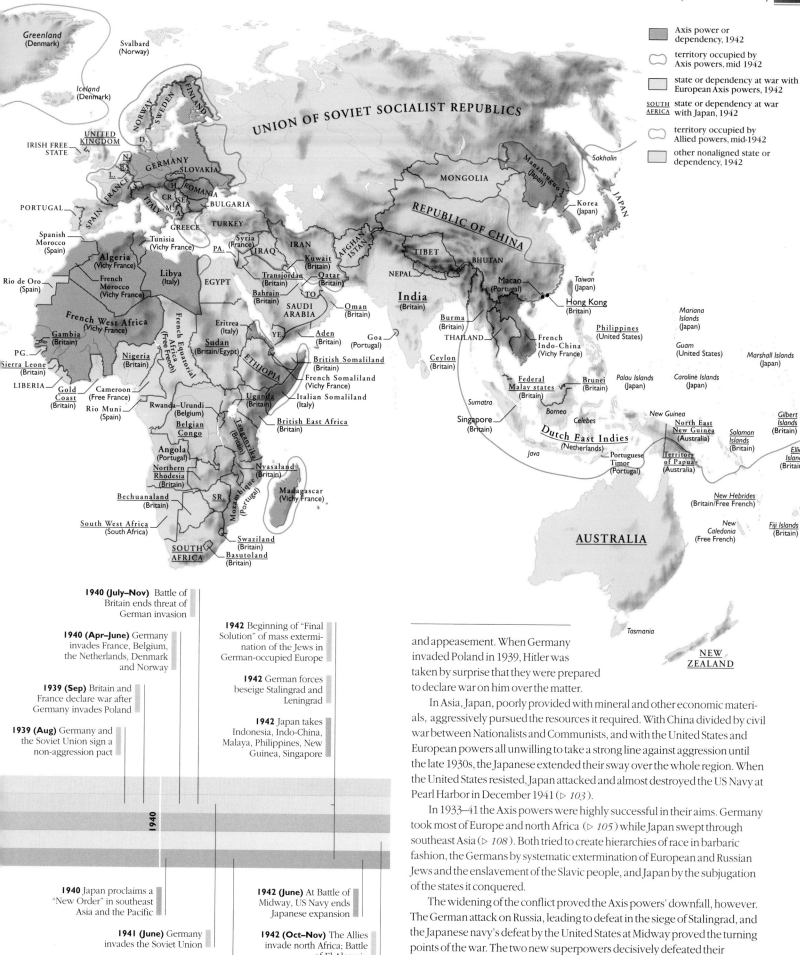

Axis power or dependency, 1942

territory occupied by Axis powers, mid 1942

state or dependency at war with European Axis powers, 1942

SOUTH AFRICA state or dependency at war with Japan, 1942

territory occupied by Allied powers, mid-1942

other nonaligned state or dependency, 1942

Greenland (Denmark)

Svalbard (Norway)

Iceland (Denmark)

UNITED KINGDOM

IRISH FREE STATE

NORWAY SWEDEN FINLAND

D.

UNION OF SOVIET SOCIALIST REPUBLICS

Sakhalin

GERMANY SLOVAKIA

N. B. L. FRANCE H. CR. SER. M. A. ROMANIA BULGARIA GREECE

Sakhalin

Manzhouguo (Japan)

MONGOLIA

Korea (Japan)

JAPAN

PORTUGAL

SPAIN

ITALY

TURKEY

Syria (France)

IRAQ

IRAN

AFGHANISTAN

REPUBLIC OF CHINA

Taiwan (Japan)

Spanish Morocco (Spain)

Tunisia (Vichy France)

PA.

Kuwait (Britain)

TIBET

Macao (Portugal)

Hong Kong (Britain)

Rio de Oro (Spain)

Algeria (Vichy France)

Libya (Italy)

EGYPT

Transjordan (Britain)

Qatar (Britain)

TO.

Bahrain (Britain)

SAUDI ARABIA

BHUTAN

NEPAL

Mariana Islands (Japan)

French Morocco (Vichy France)

Oman (Britain)

India (Britain)

Burma (Britain)

Philippines (United States)

French West Africa (Vichy France)

French Equatorial Africa (Free French)

Eritrea (Italy)

Aden (Britain)

Goa (Portugal)

THAILAND

French Indo-China (Vichy France)

Guam (United States)

Marshall Islands

PG.

Gambia (Britain)

Sudan (Britain/Egypt)

YE.

Ceylon (Britain)

Sierra Leone (Britain)

LIBERIA

Nigeria (Britain)

British Somaliland (Britain)

Federal Malay states (Britain)

Brunei (Japan)

Palau Islands (Japan)

Caroline Islands (Japan)

Gold Coast (Britain)

Cameroon (Free France)

ETHIOPIA

French Somaliland (Vichy France)

Italian Somaliland (Italy)

Sumatra

Singapore (Britain)

Borneo

Celebes

New Guinea

North East New Guinea (Australia)

Solomon Islands (Britain)

Gilbert Islands (Britain)

Rio Muni (Spain)

Rwanda–Urundi (Belgium)

Uganda (Britain)

Dutch East Indies (Netherlands)

Java

Portuguese Timor (Portugal)

Territory of Papua (Australia)

Ellice Islands (Britain)

Belgian Congo

Tanganyika (Britain)

British East Africa (Britain)

Angola (Portugal)

Northern Rhodesia (Britain)

Nyasaland (Britain)

Mozambique (Portugal)

Madagascar (Vichy France)

New Hebrides (Britain/Free French)

New Caledonia (Free French)

Fiji Islands (Britain)

Bechuanaland (Britain)

SR.

AUSTRALIA

South West Africa (South Africa)

SOUTH AFRICA

Swaziland (Britain)

Basutoland (Britain)

Tasmania

NEW ZEALAND

**1940 (July–Nov)** Battle of Britain ends threat of German invasion

**1940 (Apr–June)** Germany invades France, Belgium, the Netherlands, Denmark and Norway

**1939 (Sep)** Britain and France declare war after Germany invades Poland

**1939 (Aug)** Germany and the Soviet Union sign a non-aggression pact

**1942** Beginning of "Final Solution" of mass extermination of the Jews in German-occupied Europe

**1942** German forces beseige Stalingrad and Leningrad

**1942** Japan takes Indonesia, Indo-China, Malaya, Philippines, New Guinea, Singapore

1940

**1940** Japan proclaims a "New Order" in southeast Asia and the Pacific

**1941 (June)** Germany invades the Soviet Union

**1941 (Dec)** Japanese attack on Pearl Harbor leads USA to enter the war

**1942 (June)** At Battle of Midway, US Navy ends Japanese expansion

**1942 (Oct–Nov)** The Allies invade north Africa; Battle of El Alamein

and appeasement. When Germany invaded Poland in 1939, Hitler was taken by surprise that they were prepared to declare war on him over the matter.

In Asia, Japan, poorly provided with mineral and other economic materials, aggressively pursued the resources it required. With China divided by civil war between Nationalists and Communists, and with the United States and European powers all unwilling to take a strong line against aggression until the late 1930s, the Japanese extended their sway over the whole region. When the United States resisted, Japan attacked and almost destroyed the US Navy at Pearl Harbor in December 1941 (▷ 103).

In 1933–41 the Axis powers were highly successful in their aims. Germany took most of Europe and north Africa (▷ 105) while Japan swept through southeast Asia (▷ 108). Both tried to create hierarchies of race in barbaric fashion, the Germans by systematic extermination of European and Russian Jews and the enslavement of the Slavic people, and Japan by the subjugation of the states it conquered.

The widening of the conflict proved the Axis powers' downfall, however. The German attack on Russia, leading to defeat in the siege of Stalingrad, and the Japanese navy's defeat by the United States at Midway proved the turning points of the war. The two new superpowers decisively defeated their adversaries, and marshalled their greater array of resources to follow up their victories. In doing so they forged the shape of the postwar world ∎

The end of 1942 marked a turning point, but two more years of fighting were needed before the war in Europe ended. The German surrender at Stalingrad was a blow to Hitler, who was committed to holding the city and supplying it by air. In July the Soviet army repulsed the Germans at Kursk in the war's biggest land battle; the Red Army then drove westward, its next victory being at Kharkov.

In May 1943, the Germans capitulated in north Africa. By mid-1943 Germany had also lost the crucial Battle of the Atlantic, where the Allied use of long-range aircraft made Germany's submarine assault on transatlantic convoy routes less effective. The German war effort intensified with the announcement of total war (the complete mobilization of the economy). The Allies invaded Sicily, Mussolini was deposed and the Italians sued for peace. However Germany immediately occupied north and central Italy and made further Allied progress very difficult through the mountainous terrain.

The Allies' Italian campaign was a relatively minor response to success in north Africa, though it dragged on until the end of the war. The main action in the west – the "second front" that Stalin had long demanded – was to be the Allied landing in Normandy, as the Allied leaders had agreed at their meeting in Tehran in November 1943. Even before this was launched, however, Hitler had to withdraw troops from the east to strengthen the western defenses. Allied bombing increased in strength and effectiveness as the US joined the British in attacking German cities in force. The first 1,000-bomber raid took place against Cologne in 1943. The bombing campaign directed German resources from the other fronts and weakened the war economy.

When the Normandy landings finally came in June 1944, they met with stiff resistance. The Allies liberated France and Belgium before halting briefly. Meanwhile in east and southeast Europe the Red Army took advantage of the increased pressure on Germany in the west, and defeated both Romania and Bulgaria. Germany pulled out of Greece but Hungary was kept in the war by a Nazi coup after initially surrendering to the Soviet Union; fierce fighting broke out around Budapest.

Political as well as military considerations had held back United States president Roosevelt from supporting British prime minister Churchill's plan to invade southeast Europe. Unlike Roosevelt, Churchill had little faith in Stalin's postwar intentions, and

**Key:**
- borders, 1943
- Axis power or ally
- Axis occupied, Mar 1943
- Allied control, Mar 1943
- front line, Dec 1943
- front line, Aug 1944
- front line, Dec 1944
- front line, Apr 1945
- defensive line
- heavily bombed city
- siege
- area of partisan activity
- German reprisal killing
- death camp
- concentration camp
- Allied airborne operation
- conference of Allied leaders, with date
- London  V-weapon target zone
- 26 Aug 1944  date of capitulation
- Axis withdrawal
- Axis offensive
- Allied offensive
- Soviet deportation, 1944–45

CIVILIANS, including women, were universally important to the war effort by working in the factories. This poster was from Britain.

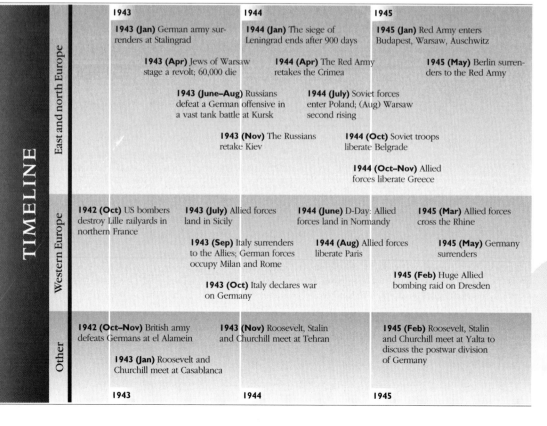

made an agreement with Stalin which stipulated the influence that Britain and the Soviet Union would each have in the region. Soviet action in Poland and elsewhere did not engender confidence. As the Red Army advanced toward Warsaw, a fullscale rising against the German forces occurred in the city. Despite surrounding the city, Stalin did not assist the rebels, and when the Germans eventually quashed the revolt, as many as 250,000 people were killed.

Across Europe guerrilla partisan forces fought the Axis powers. Many were divided on ethnic or political lines, and their activities provoked bloody reprisals. A revolt in Slovakia at the same time as the Warsaw rising was brutally put down, but in Yugoslavia the Communist-dominated partisans enjoyed

**TIMELINE**

**East and north Europe**

| 1943 | 1944 | 1945 |
|---|---|---|
| 1943 (Jan) German army surrenders at Stalingrad | 1944 (Jan) The siege of Leningrad ends after 900 days | 1945 (Jan) Red Army enters Budapest, Warsaw, Auschwitz |
| 1943 (Apr) Jews of Warsaw stage a revolt; 60,000 die | 1944 (Apr) The Red Army retakes the Crimea | 1945 (May) Berlin surrenders to the Red Army |
| 1943 (June–Aug) Russians defeat a German offensive in a vast tank battle at Kursk | 1944 (July) Soviet forces enter Poland; (Aug) Warsaw second rising | |
| 1943 (Nov) The Russians retake Kiev | 1944 (Oct) Soviet troops liberate Belgrade | |
| | 1944 (Oct–Nov) Allied forces liberate Greece | |

**Western Europe**

| 1943 | 1944 | 1945 |
|---|---|---|
| 1942 (Oct) US bombers destroy Lille railyards in northern France | 1943 (July) Allied forces land in Sicily | 1944 (June) D-Day: Allied forces land in Normandy | 1945 (Mar) Allied forces cross the Rhine |
| | 1943 (Sep) Italy surrenders to the Allies; German forces occupy Milan and Rome | 1944 (Aug) Allied forces liberate Paris | 1945 (May) Germany surrenders |
| | 1943 (Oct) Italy declares war on Germany | | 1945 (Feb) Huge Allied bombing raid on Dresden |

**Other**

| 1943 | 1944 | 1945 |
|---|---|---|
| 1942 (Oct–Nov) British army defeats Germans at el Alamein | 1943 (Nov) Roosevelt, Stalin and Churchill meet at Tehran | 1945 (Feb) Roosevelt, Stalin and Churchill meet at Yalta to discuss the postwar division of Germany |
| 1943 (Jan) Roosevelt and Churchill meet at Casablanca | | |

| 1943 | 1944 | 1945 |

**1** Hitler's attack on the Soviet defenses at Kursk (June 1943) led to a conflict between the Soviet light but nimble T-34 tanks, and the heavy German Tiger tanks. Despite huge losses, the Red Army broke through.

**2** Some 640 villagers, including 200 women and children, were burned to death in a church at the village of Oradour-sur Glane in June 1944.

**3** When the Germans retreated to their prewar defenses – the Siegfried Line – in September 1944, the Allies attacked via the Netherlands. The line was broken in February 1945.

**4** Peenemünde was the site of research into rocketry by the Germans under Werner von Braun. Allied intelligence knew of it from 1939.

**5** Auschwitz was the largest of the Nazi death camps, established in 1940. Well over a million Jews and Poles died there before liberation in January 1945.

**6** Churchill, Stalin and Roosevelt met at Yalta in February 1945 to coordinate strategy and agree to spheres of influence in postwar Europe.

considerable success and formed the basis of Tito's postwar government. In Prague, a popular rising helped the Soviet advance on the city. In Greece, the Communists, who dominated the rural resistance movement, defied the British who sought to reestablish the monarchy after the Germans had withdrawn in October 1944. The result was a civil war which ended only with the collapse of the Communists in 1949. Resistance in Poland and countries incorporated into the Soviet Union also continued after the war, but it was now directed against the USSR.

Hitler always believed that providence would save him. He tried to stop the Allied bomber assault on Germany by firing rocket-powered V-bombs at Britain, but the forces ranged against him were too

great. The last German offensive, through the Ardennes at the end of 1944, was a failure and after Hitler's suicide, Germany surrendered (8 May 1945).

The implementation of Nazi policies of genocide continued right up until the liberation of the death camps by Allied troops. As the Soviets marched westward, many inmates of camps in Poland were moved to Germany to join prisoners-of-war and other forced foreign labor. By 1944 there were almost eight million foreigners at work in Germany. Some Axis countries – Hungary, Bulgaria and Italy – refused to release many or all of their Jewish population to the Nazis, but the attempt to exterminate the Jews of Europe still proceeded. By the end of the war some six million had been killed, along with

millions of other nationalities including Ukrainians, Poles, Balts, Belorussians, Russians and Gypsies.

Of the 5.5 million Soviet soldiers captured by the Germans, 3.3 million had died; as the Red Army advanced it took its revenge. Ten million ethnic Germans were expelled from their homes in central and eastern Europe; perhaps two million died. The USSR deported five million of its subject nationalities for alleged collaboration; returning prisoners-of-war often faced exile or death. By 1945 much of Europe was destroyed, its peoples dead or homeless.

See also 105 (World War II to 1942);
108 (WorldWar II in Asia); 110 (postwar Europe)

In late 1941 the Japanese planned a series of synchronized attacks to secure control in the Pacific and Asia. Prime minister Hideki Tojo and Isoroko Yamamoto, head of the navy and mastermind behind the attack on the United States naval base of Pearl Harbor in Hawaii, sought to create a defense perimeter from the Kurils to the Dutch East Indies and containing all the oil, rubber and rice Japan would need for survival. Yamamoto promised a string of victories in the first six months.

The surprise attack on Pearl Harbor on 7 December 1941 destroyed the US Pacific fleet, but all the large aircraft carriers were at sea. Their survival was to be of crucial significance. By the spring of 1942 Japan had taken the Philippines (attacked the same day as Pearl Harbor), ejected the Dutch from the East Indies, driven the British from Hong Kong, Malaya (including the great naval base of Singapore) and most of Burma, and forced the Americans to surrender Guam, Wake Island, Attu and Kiska. At this point, Japan suffered a setback at the Battle of the Coral Sea as the Japanese attempted to take the Allied base at Port Moresby on New Guinea (thus isolating Australia). Further advances across the Pacific were decisively halted when their fleet was defeated by the US Navy at the Battle of Midway.

Allied strategy for the destruction of Japan's new empire depended upon the immense resources and manpower that the United States could bring to bear. The plan required the British, who had suffered during their long retreat in Burma, to block a Japanese invasion of India, undertake offensives in the Arakan and recapture Rangoon. They would have limited US assistance and cooperation from Chinese Nationalist armies from Yunnan. These forces came under a new southeast Asia command headed by Lord Louis Mountbatten. US forces in the south and southwest Pacific under General Douglas MacArthur

and Admiral William Halsey were planned to retake New Guinea and the Solomons. Admiral Nimitz would assemble fresh task forces at Pearl Harbor and attack Japanese-held islands in the central and north Pacific. Key bases would be established on the islands and in China for an air assault upon Japan.

In the north Pacific, US and Canadian troops attacked in the Aleutians and forced the Japanese back. In the central Pacific, US marines assaulted the tiny coral atoll of Tarawa, 5,000 kilometers (3,000 miles) from Japan. They wiped out its Japanese and Korean defenders, but only after three days of bitter fighting. After this experience, the Americans

decided to ignore unimportant islands and by-pass many Japanese bases. They fought and won the Battle of the Philippine Sea and then targeted Kwajalein and Eniwetok in the Marshalls. They went on to occupy Saipan, Guam and Tinian, the bases from which in 1944–45 US B-29 bombers undertook their raids on Japanese cities.

US forces returned to the Philippines and fought the Battle of Leyte Gulf, during which the Japanese navy was effectively destroyed. The Battle of Iwo Jima, the fiercest of the war, provided the Americans with a base for their fighter aircraft capable of escorting the bombers to Japan and back. About 500,000

| | borders, 7 Dec 1941 |
| --- | --- |
| | Japanese occupied territory, 7 Dec 1941 |
| | maximum extent of Japanese occupied territory, June 1942 |
| | intended eastern perimeter of Japanese territory |
| | Japanese occupied territory, 6 Aug 1945 |
| | Japanese occupied territory, Sep 1945 |
| | Allied territory, June 1942 |
| | Nationalist Chinese or warlord territory |
| | Communist Chinese territory, 1937 |
| → | Japanese advance, with date |
| → | Allied advance, with date |
| → | Russian advance, 9 Aug 1945 |
| | Japanese base, June 1942 |
| | Japanese air strike outside occupied territory |
| | US bombing raids on Japan, 1942–45 |
| | nuclear air strike, Aug 1945 |
| ⊗ | Japanese victory |
| ⊗ | Allied victory |
| *oil* | strategic resource vital to Japan |

0          1500 km
0          1200 mi

**1** The attack on Pearl Harbor was essential to Japan's plans to control the Pacific. Eight battleships were destroyed but dockyard facilities remained intact.

**2** Singapore was Britain's foremost and most recently equipped naval base in the region, but it fell to a surprise land attack in February 1942.

**3** The Bataan peninsula in the Philippines was the scene of an incident in April 1942, when the Japanese forced 35,000 men to march 100km (60 miles) in six days; more than 10,000 died.

**4** The Japanese invasion of the Dutch East Indies was welcomed by Ahmed Sukarno, leader of the Indonesian Nationalist Party (PNI).

**5** Darwin and other north Australian towns were bombed, and the east coast was blockaded by submarines in 1943; the country was a key base for US operations in the southwest Pacific.

**6** Saipan was a major air base, used by the US Air Force for bombing Japan from November 1944.

**7** Hiroshima suffered the world's first atomic bomb attack on 6 August 1945; 80,000 people died instantly.

## TIMELINE

### Japan

| 1943 | 1945 |
| --- | --- |
| **1941** Japan and the Soviet Union sign a neutrality pact | **1944 (July)** Prime minister Tojo resigns — **1945 (Aug)** Atomic attacks on Hiroshima and Nagasaki |
| **1942 (Apr)** B-25 bombers from USS *Hornet* raid Tokyo | **1945 (Sep)** Formal Japanese surrender |

### Pacific war

| | |
| --- | --- |
| **1941 (Dec)** Japan attacks Pearl Harbor and Philippines | **1943 (Nov)** Tarawa captured by US forces |
| **1942 (Feb)** Japanese troops win the Battle of Java Sea | **1944 (July)** US troops land on island of Leyte |
| **1942 (May)** Battle of the Coral Sea halts Japanese attack on Port Moresby | **1944 (Oct)** The Battle of Leyte Gulf ends Japanese naval power |
| **1942 (June)** Japanese carriers are destroyed at Midway | **1945 (Feb–Mar)** The Battle of Iwo Jima is followed by the invasion of Okinawa |
| **1942 (Aug)** US marines land on Guadalcanal | |

### Southeast Asia

| | | |
| --- | --- | --- |
| **1941 (Dec)** Japan attacks Hong Kong and Malaya | **1943** Nationalists stem the Japanese offensives in China | **1945 (May)** The Burma Road reopened and Rangoon recaptured |
| **1942 (Feb)** British forces in Singapore surrender to Japan | **1944** Japanese invasion of India; sieges of Imphal and Kohima (Mar–June) | **1945 (Aug)** The Soviet Union declares war and attacks in Manchuria and Korea |
| **1942 (Mar)** The Dutch surrender the East Indies | **1944** Chinese Communists and Japan stop fighting | |
| **1942** British retreat from Burma | | |

| 1943 | 1945 |
| --- | --- |

newly independent state, 1942-50

NATO member

Communist country and administrative area

Organization of American States member

Arab League founder member

CUBA United Nations founder member

other state or territory

Greenland (Denmark)

Svalbard (Norway)

ICELAND

SWEDEN

FINLAND

NORWAY

UNITED KINGDOM

D.

IRELAND

N.
L.
E.
W.G.
POLAND
C.
AU.
H.
YU.

UNION OF SOVIET SOCIALIST REPUBLICS

FRANCE

ITALY

ROMANIA

BULGARIA

PORTUGAL

SPAIN

GREECE

TURKEY

Sakhalin

MONGOLIA

NORTH KOREA

JAPAN (United States occupied)

SOUTH KOREA

PEOPLE'S REPUBLIC OF CHINA

Spanish Morocco (Spain)

Tunisia (France)

LEBANON

SYRIA

IRAQ

IRAN

AFGHAN ISTAN

Rio de Oro (Spain)

Algeria (France)

French Morocco (France)

Libya (Britain/France)

ISRAEL

EGYPT

JORDAN

Kuwait (Britain)

Qatar (Britain)

Bahrain (Britain)

TO.

SAUDI ARABIA

Oman (Britain)

PAKISTAN

NEPAL

BHUTAN

PAKISTAN

INDIA

BURMA

Macao (Portugal)

Hong Kong (Britain)

TAIWAN (Nationalist China)

Mariana Islands (United States)

French West Africa (France)

Gambia (Britain)

P.G.

erra Leone (Britain)

LIBERIA

Gold Coast (Britain)

Cameroon (France)

Rio Muni (Spain)

French Equatorial Africa (France)

Nigeria (Britain)

Sudan (Britain/Egypt)

Eritrea (Britain)

ETHIOPIA

YE.

Aden (Britain)

British Somaliland (Britain)

French Somaliland (France)

Italian Somaliland (Britain)

THAILAND

CEYLON

French Indo-China (France)

PHILIPPINES

Marshall Islands (United States)

Rwanda–Urundi (Belgium)

Uganda (Britain)

Belgian Congo (Belgium)

Tanganyika (Britain)

British East Africa (Britain)

Brunei (Britain)

Malaya (Britain)

Palau Islands (United States)

Caroline Islands (United States)

Celebes

Sumatra

Singapore (Britain)

Borneo

New Guinea

Dutch New Guinea (Netherlands)

Territory of Papua and New Guinea (Australia)

Solomon Islands (Britain)

Gilbert Islands (Britain)

Ellice Islands (Britain)

Angola (Portugal)

Northern Rhodesia (Britain)

Nyasaland (Britain)

Madagascar (France)

Mozambique (Portugal)

Java

INDONESIA

Portuguese Timor (Portugal)

New Hebrides (Britain/France)

New Caledonia (France)

Fiji Islands (Britain)

Bechuanaland (Britain)

SR.

South West Africa (South Africa)

Swaziland (Britain)

SOUTH AFRICA

Basutoland (Britain)

AUSTRALIA

Tasmania

NEW ZEALAND

**1949 (Oct)** East Germany (DDR) is created

**1949 (Oct)** The Communists under Mao Zedong complete a victory in Chinese civil war

**1948–49** The Allies airlift supplies into Berlin to counter a Soviet blockade

**1949 (Sep)** The Soviet Union explodes its first atomic bomb

1950

**1948 (May)** The state of Israel is founded, leading to war in the Middle East

**1948 (May)** National Party, committed to *apartheid*, wins power in South Africa

**1948 (June)** Yugoslavia is expelled from Cominform

**1949 (Apr)** The North Atlantic Treaty is signed, creating an anti-Soviet alliance

**1949 (Dec)** Indonesia gains its independence from the Dutch

**1950 (June)** The Korean War begins as Communist troops invade the south

The initial defeat of colonial forces by the Japanese had undermined respect for white authority, while the cost of maintaining overseas empires was heightened by the war.

Anticolonialism was also supported by the United States. A vital postwar loan to Britain was made dependent on Britain abandoning the idea of a closed imperial trading bloc. The decolonization of British territories began after 1945 and the independence of India moved rapidly ahead. In Indo-China, the French recognized Vietnam as an autonomous state in the French Union, but force was needed to keep the area under French rule. The Netherlands bowed to international pressure and granted independence to Indonesia. In Indo-China, Indonesia and Malaya, Communist activity was widespread but few people were yet concerned that American support for anticolonialism might contradict its opposition to Communism (▷ 113).

The global rivalry of the two superpowers escalated. In 1949 Americans were horrified as the Soviets acquired the atomic bomb and China turned Communist. Alliances such as the North Atlantic Treaty Organization (NATO) and the Organization of American States (OAS) marked a new commitment to worldwide opposition to the "Communist threat". West Germany and Japan, the states against which the Allies had fought, were now rehabilitated to fight for them in the new Cold War. Elsewhere, a Jewish homeland was finally created in the Middle East, provoking war (▷ 115). The region would grow ever more unstable as the value of its oil exports rose ■

The wartime cooperation of the Allies quickly broke down and two blocs emerged: the western democratic countries which were oriented toward the United States, and the eastern Communist countries dominated by the Soviet Union. Europe lived in the shadow of the superpowers.

Blame for the deterioration of international relations and the drawing of the "iron curtain" across Europe has been laid with both sides, and little is known of Soviet motives. It is clear, however, that US hopes of an "open" Europe were misplaced. Stalin never considered giving up the Soviet Union's new influence in eastern Europe and, though he probably did not envisage invading the west either, there was a real fear that the rest of the continent would succumb to Communism. As a result, with Europe devastated and trying to cope with millions of refugees, the United States produced a massive cash injection ("Marshall Plan") in 1947, becoming the counterweight to Soviet power in the east.

Crucial to the division of Europe was the partition of Germany. The economic and military powerbase of the continent was occupied jointly by the Allies, neither side being willing to risk losing overall control to the other. In 1948 the Soviets blockaded western-occupied West Berlin, and in 1949 the republics of West and East Germany were formally constituted. The same year the North Atlantic Treaty was signed, binding the western states and America in an anti-Soviet alliance (NATO). Comecon was formed to incorporate the east European countries in a system of Soviet-dominated interstate economic planning. In 1950 US troops returned to Europe as part of NATO after the outbreak of war in Korea; the Soviet-led Warsaw Pact was founded five years later.

Thereafter west and east Europe developed on different lines. The western countries soon recovered their prosperity, creating economic areas to increase trade. The Benelux Customs Union of 1948 was followed by the creation of the European Coal and Steel Community (ECSC), which laid the basis for the European Economic Community (EEC) in 1958. A looser affiliation, the European Free Trade Area (EFTA), also existed, but the EEC was the more important, later becoming the European Community (EC), aspiring to a political as well as economic role.

The EEC was intended to transcend national boundaries, prevent the strife that had characterized Europe's history and assist Europe to become an independent player on the world stage. The French president Charles de Gaulle twice vetoed Britain's application to join, on the grounds of Britain's "special relationship" with the United States. De Gaulle deplored US involvement in Europe, and withdrew France from NATO, yet the idea of an independent European Defense Community proved unworkable. The United States encouraged western European integration but American troops remained essential. Britain and France established independent nuclear capability; West German chancellor Willy Brandt negotiated cooperation agreements between West and East Germany. But given the Soviet Union's military might, Europe could not be independent until the iron curtain was raised.

In eastern Europe the influence of the Soviet Union was deeply resented. Eastern European countries did not enjoy the "economic miracle" seen in West Germany, and felt their national identities to be compromised by Soviet interference. Yugoslavia and Albania preserved their traditions of independent Communism as, to a lesser extent, did Romania. Hungary (1956) and Czechoslovakia (1968) tried more radical escapes from the Soviet bloc but were brought back into line by force.

Following the Helsinki agreement of 1975 under which the borders of the German Democratic Republic (East Germany) were recognized and the governments of eastern Europe accepted the principle of observing human rights, dissident activity grew more intense. In 1980 the Polish trade union Solidarity was set up and long-standing popular resentment (kept alive by the Catholic church and the accession of John Paul II as the first Polish pope) was manifested in widespread industrial disputes.

Protest in western Europe was directed both against the United States (over the Vietnam war or the presence of US-controlled nuclear missiles) or against individual governments. The Paris riots of 1968 were part of a general revolt of youth

## TIMELINE

### Western Europe

| 1950 | 1970 | 1990 |
|---|---|---|
| **1945** Potsdam conference of the great powers agrees the postwar position in Germany | **1966** France withdraws from NATO | **1986** Portugal and Spain join the EC |
| **1955** Allies end occupation of West Germany and Austria; West Germany joins NATO | **1974** Turkey invades northern Cyprus | |
| **1947** USA provides Marshall Aid to western Europe | **1967** French president de Gaulle vetoes UK entry to EEC for the second time | **1974** Portugal's rightwing government is overthrown |
| **1957** The Treaty of Rome sets up the European Economic Community (EEC), from Jan 1958 | **1968** Students riot in Paris and almost bring down the government; unrest is felt in West Germany and Britain | **1977** Spain's first postwar elections take place following the death of Franco in 1975 |
| **1948–49** The Berlin airlift follows a Soviet blockade of the city's western zone | | **1979** Conservative leader Margaret Thatcher is elected prime minister in Britain |
| **1949** North Atlantic Treaty is signed; NATO is set up | | |

### Eastern Europe

| 1950 | 1970 | 1990 |
|---|---|---|
| **1947–48** Sovietization of the governments of eastern Europe | **1968** Czechoslovak "Prague spring" ends with Warsaw Pact invasion | **1989** The Berlin Wall is taken down; regimes in Hungary, Poland, East Germany, Bulgaria, Czechoslovakia, Romania fall |
| **1956** An anti-Soviet revolt takes place in Hungary | **1975** Helsinki agreement on Germany's borders and human rights in east Europe | |
| **1949** Comecon is set up to integrate eastern Europe's economies | **1961** The Berlin Wall is built to prevent emigration from East to West Germany | **1970–72** *Ostpolitik* agreements for East and West German cooperation | **1980** Solidarity, Polish trade union, is founded |

## Map labels

NORWAY
Bergen
Oslo
SWEDEN
Gävle
Vasteras
Uppsala
Stockholm
Linköping
Vänern
Vättern
Göteborg

Pori
Tampere
FINLAND
Turku
Helsinki
Finns
Lake Ladoga
Leningrad

Rybinsk Reservoir
Volga

DENMARK
1973 EEC member
Århus
Copenhagen
Malmo
Odense

Tapa
Tallinn
Estonians
Kopu
Estonia
Estonians
Yedrovo
Pskov

Latvians
Riga
Latvia
Latvians
Liepaja
Latvians
Western Dvina
Vitebsk
Smolensk

Moscow

Russia

Hamburg
Bremen
GERMAN
DEMOCRATIC
REPUBLIC
1949
June 1953
Berlin
June 1953
June 1956
Poznan
Warsaw
Oct 1956
Belorussians
Derazhnaya
Kiev

Lithuania
Lithuanians
Kaliningrad
(Königsberg)
to Russia
Vilna
Minsk
BELORUSSIA
Poles

FEDERAL
REPUBLIC
OF
GERMANY
1945–61
Essen
Cologne
Bonn
Frankfurt
Vüscheim
xembourg
teckarsulm
Schwäbisch
Gmünd
Neu Ulm
Munich

June 1953
Leipzig
Dresden
Berhsdorf
Milovice
Krakow
Aug 1968
Prague
Temelin
Brno
Nuremberg
Linz
Vienna
Bratislava
CZECHOSLOVAKIA
1948
Aug 1968
Debrecen
Nov 1956

Szczecin
Poles
Lodz
Lublin
Poles
Lvov
POLAND
1947
1944–47
Vistula
Oder
Danube
Gdansk
(Danzig)

UNION OF SOVIET
SOCIALIST REPUBLICS

Ukrainians
Dnepropetrovsk
Pervomaysk
Ukraine
Dnieper

Jurassiens
Berne
SWITZERLAND
Germans
LIECHTENSTEIN
Salzburg
AUSTRIA
Graz
1956
Zagreb
Trieste
Milan
Venice
1954
Turin
Bologna
Florence
SAN MARINO
MONACO
Corsica to France
Corsicans
Ajaccio
ITALY
La Maddalena
ardinia to Italy
Cagliari
Rome
Gaeta
Naples
Palermo
Sicily
Catania
Comiso
Tunis
TUNISIA
1956 independent
Valletta
MALTA
1964 independent

HUNGARY
1947
1955 temporarily
leaves Warsaw Pact
Oct–Nov 1956
Budapest
Magyars
Iasi
Moldavia
Dniester
Kishinev
Odessa

ROMANIA
1945
Timisoara
Brasov
Ploiesti
Bucharest
Danube
Sevastopol

YUGOSLAVIA
1945
Belgrade
Sarajevo
Split
Dubrovnik
Albanians, since 1968
Skopje
Tiranë
ALBANIA
1945
1968 leaves
Warsaw Pact
GREECE
1952–74, 1982
NATO member
1981 EEC member
1944–1949
Patras
Athens
Heraklion
Crete

BULGARIA
1945
Sofia
Plovdiv
Varna
Burgas
Turks
Edirne
Istanbul
Bursa
Izmir
Konya
TURKEY
1952 NATO member
Adana
Gaziantep
Aleppo
Euphrates
SYRIA
Homs
Damascus
Beirut
LEBANON
1958
ISRAEL
1948 independent

Black Sea

Mediterranean Sea

Dodecanese
1947 to Greece
since 1974
Greeks & Turks
Nicosia
1974 1955–77
CYPRUS
1960 independent,
Northern Cyprus occupied by
Turks since 1974
TURKISH REPUBLIC OF
NORTHERN CYPRUS
since 1983

0 — 400 km
0 — 300 mi

Bari

## Legend

pre-war border of Poland

North Atlantic Treaty Organization
(NATO), established 1949

Warsaw Pact, established 1955

zones of occupation of Germany
and Austria, 1945–55,

American
British
French
Soviet

borders, 1989
NATO nuclear-capable base, 1980s
Warsaw Pact nuclear-capable base, 1980s
nationalist tension or violence, 1945–89
civil war, 1945–89
international dispute, 1945–89
attempted revolution, 1945–89
Soviet military intervention
movement of Germans 1945–50
movement of Russians 1945–50
other movement of peoples 1945–50
mass exodus of refugees, with date
ITALY   founding member of EEC, 1957
1945   date of Communist takeover

against authority, as was the Baader–Meinhof terrorist group in West Germany.

In the 1970s, the economic downturn caused by inflation, high public spending and the rise in oil prices led to unemployment and industrial militancy. British prime minster Margaret Thatcher's response to these problems after 1979 marked a radical departure from the consensus politics of the postwar period, which had stressed cooperation between employers, workers and the state. The introduction of free-market economics and revision of labor legislation brought a year-long miners' strike (1984–85). Elsewhere, terrorism and violence fueled by economic dislocation flared in areas of nationalist tension. Basque separatists mounted a bombing campaign in Spain (where the Catalans gained internal autonomy), and the British province of Ulster simmered on the brink of civil war.

In the late 1980s the disparity in living standards between east and west, and the moral and economic bankruptcy of Communism led the new Soviet leader, Mikhail Gorbachev, to slacken the ties binding eastern Europe in an effort to free up the east's economy. It was soon clear that he had unleashed forces beyond his control. Revolutions ensued, first in Poland and then East Germany, Hungary, Czechoslovakia, Bulgaria and Romania. The old order crumbled, as exhilaration mixed with apprehension at the new shape Europe would take.

**1** Divided Berlin was a focus for Cold War tension. In 1948–49 the western zone was supplied by air after Soviet forces surrounded the city; in 1961 the Berlin Wall was built to stop refugees from leaving the East.

**2** The Nuremberg war crimes trials of 1946 indicted many leading Nazis but lesser ones were unpunished; a strong West Germany was needed as a cornerstone of the rebuilding of western Europe.

**3** Hungary (1956) and Czechoslovakia (1968) looked to break away from the Communist bloc, but both were forced back into line by Warsaw Pact invasions.

**4** Yugoslavia remained neutral thanks to its tradition of independent Communism. Its unity was maintained to the 1980s by its Croat leader Tito.

**5** The Gdansk shipyards were the center of popular resistance in Poland, which led the way in the later opposition to Communism in eastern Europe.

**6** The Treaty of Rome – signed by France, Italy, West Germany, Belgium, the Netherlands and Luxembourg – in 1957 formed the basis for the integration of western Europe under the EEC (later EC and EU).

**7** The prolonged attempt by Nikolai Ceauçescu to collectivize the peasantry in Romania was one example of the introduction of Stalinism to eastern Europe, and met with great opposition.

**8** The "Forest Brethren" partisans in the Baltic states resisted incorporation into the USSR after 1945.

See also 107 (World War II);
119 (Europe in the 1990s)

The United States was the undoubted victor of World War II. It suffered only sporadic attacks on its territory, while its armed forces played a decisive role in theaters of war from east Asia to western Europe. Its economy was stimulated by the war; and with its unique access to the atomic bomb, the United States looked forward to dominating the postwar world, and to a spell of prosperity at home.

In many ways the domestic dream was realized. American families formed the largest property-owning democracy in the world. They moved in large numbers away from the drudgery of field and factory into the rewarding aerospace, automobile, information technology and service industries. Their ambitions led to continuous relocation in the United States itself, a pattern imitated by hopeful immigrants including Hispanics, Filipinos and east Asians. By 1960 almost 40 percent of American families were in the professional or skilled worker classes and prosperity grew faster than in any other industrialized country. Federal aid supported business, commerce and defense; consumer spending rose and strikes never obstructed production. Yet the United States failed to abolish the poverty that still touched a fifth of the population, to improve health care or to provide real educational opportunity for all. Poverty, especially among the blacks, was a major issue in the Civil Rights campaigns of the 1960s, and resurfaced in the 1980s and 1990s. Though sympathetic, the federal government tried to balance the undoubted needs of the poor with the demands of the United States' role as a superpower.

Nor was it unchallenged in that role, at least until the 1990s. With the start of the Cold War in the late 1940s, a nuclear arms race ensued that developed into the space race of the 1960s, culminating in putting men on the Moon in 1969. Meanwhile, the United States was drawn into costly conflicts across the globe. The Cold War affected Americans at home, too, with the McCarthy "witchhunts" against suspected Communists and sympathizers from 1950.

Latin America was a battleground of the Cold War; nowhere more so than Cuba, a virtual US client since 1898, but one overtaken by socialist–nationalist revolution in 1959. Soviet support for the new Castro regime led to a crisis in 1962, when the Soviet Union threatened to use the island as a base for nuclear missiles. The United States reasserted its dominance, though at the cost of increasing complaints at its heavy-handed involvement in the affairs of others.

The United States dominated even its northern neighbor, Canada, where economic and cultural life was increasingly dictated by the United States (most of the population lived within a few hundred kilometers of the border). Meanwhile Canada sought to build an independent Pacific role in the later 20th century. At the same time, Quebec's demands for independence grew louder.

South America too was a source of important United States commercial and political involvement, as the governments of the region – which ranged from the more or less democratic to out-and-out military dictatorships – wrestled with the problem of having such a rich and powerful neighbor. In Chile in 1973, an elected Marxist government was replaced, with United States instigation, by a rightwing dictatorship, whose practice of military rule characterized by brutal suppression of opposition was followed in many countries. Occasionally dictatorial methods were put to more constructive ends, notably in Brazil in the 1940s and 1950s. In the 1940s the charismatic Juan and Eva Perón were popular in Argentina until unemployment, strikes and inflation destroyed their appeal and brought the army to power. Argentina's military regime sought to revive its flagging popular appeal by invading the British Falkland Islands in 1982. Failure resulted in the civilian "Peronist" government of Carlos Menem, who sought to reduce inflation, privatize industry and introduce healthcare for workers.

The vested interests of the well-off, combined with the policies of the international banks to whom most countries were in debt, argued against drastic social change. As a result the environmental and social problems associated with a rapidly expanding population worsened (especially in Brazil, where São Paulo and Rio de Janiero were among the world's largest, fastest-growing cities). Indigenous peoples, like the rainforests that they inhabited, were treated as expendable in the face of land hunger and mineral-prospecting. Several countries, including Peru, endured long and violent revolutionary conflicts; others, such as Colombia, had their economies increasingly dominated by illegal drug trafficking.

Many countries entered into economic organizations: Venezuela and Ecuador were founder members of the Organization of Petroleum Exporting Countries (OPEC) in 1960; the Mercosur or Southern Cone Common Market (1991), Latin American Integration Association (1980) and Andean Pact (1969) were all attempts at economic cooperation. In 1992, to the dismay of many in the United States and Canada who feared the competition of Third World wages, the North American Free Trade Agreement was extended to include Mexico.

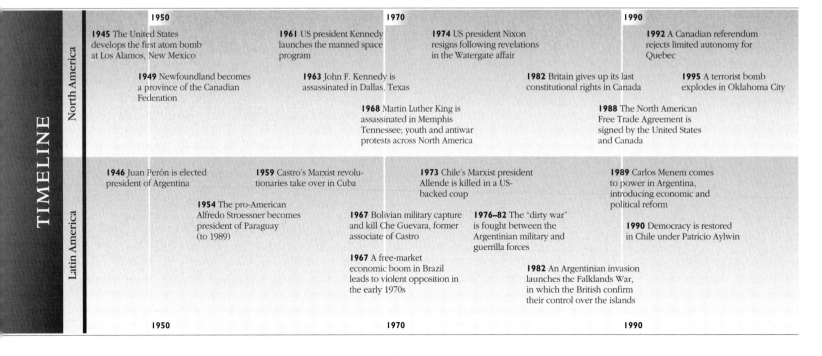

TIMELINE

North America

| 1950 | 1970 | 1990 |
|---|---|---|
| **1945** The United States develops the first atom bomb at Los Alamos, New Mexico | **1961** US president Kennedy launches the manned space program | **1974** US president Nixon resigns following revelations in the Watergate affair |
| | | **1992** A Canadian referendum rejects limited autonomy for Quebec |
| **1949** Newfoundland becomes a province of the Canadian Federation | **1963** John F. Kennedy is assassinated in Dallas, Texas | **1982** Britain gives up its last constitutional rights in Canada |
| | | **1995** A terrorist bomb explodes in Oklahoma City |
| | **1968** Martin Luther King is assassinated in Memphis Tennessee; youth and antiwar protests across North America | **1988** The North American Free Trade Agreement is signed by the United States and Canada |

Latin America

| 1950 | 1970 | 1990 |
|---|---|---|
| **1946** Juan Perón is elected president of Argentina | **1959** Castro's Marxist revolutionaries take over in Cuba | **1973** Chile's Marxist president Allende is killed in a US-backed coup |
| | | **1989** Carlos Menem comes to power in Argentina, introducing economic and political reform |
| **1954** The pro-American Alfredo Stroessner becomes president of Paraguay (to 1989) | **1967** Bolivian military capture and kill Che Guevara, former associate of Castro | **1976–82** The "dirty war" is fought between the Argentinian military and guerrilla forces |
| | | **1990** Democracy is restored in Chile under Patricio Aylwin |
| | **1967** A free-market economic boom in Brazil leads to violent opposition in the early 1970s | **1982** An Argentinian invasion launches the Falklands War, in which the British confirm their control over the islands |

1950                    1970                    1990

Map labels: Yukon, Mackenzie, Great Bear Lake, Great Slave Lake, Peace, Saskatchewan, Alaska to United States 1959 granted statehood, Gulf of Alaska, Edmonton, Calgary, Minot, Vancouver, from Asia, Seattle, Minneap, Malmstrom, Ellsworth, Portland, UNITED STATES, NORTH PACIFIC OCEAN, Salt Lake City, Colorado, Den, Ark, 4, Sacramento, Los Alamos, San Francisco, San José, from Asia, Los Angeles, Phoenix, San Diego, Tucson, El Paso, Rio Grande, 5, Tijuana, Davis-Monthan, Ciudad Juarez, Mexicali, Chihua, Torreón, MEXICO 1992 joins NA, León, Guadalaja

MARTIN LUTHER KING was at the heart of the Civil Rights movement for racial justice in the United States in the early 1960s.

**1** French president Charles de Gaulle visited Québec in 1967, and urged the cause of Québec separatism, a movement that grew in strength in the 1980s.

**2** Little Rock, Arkansas, was the focus for the campaign for education rights for African-Americans in the late 1950s.

**3** Cape Canaveral (Cape Kennedy 1963-73) was the base for the US space program from the early 1960s.

**4** The electronics industry brought new prosperity to California in the 1980s, with the Santa Clara Valley south of San Francisco known as "Silicon Valley".

**5** The Rio Grande was heavily guarded by the US immigration service to prevent floods of illegal immigrants from Mexico and the poorer countries of Central America.

**6** The Itaipú hydro-electric plant (built 1976-91) was the largest in the world, and allowed Paraguay to become the world's largest exporter of electricity.

**7** The Falklands War of 1982 was caused by an Argentinian invasion of the Falkland Islands which were claimed as a historic part of their nation.

**8** Uruguay, though one of the most advanced Latin American nations, was beset by Tupamaros urban guerrillas 1976-81.

Central American Common Market (CACM), established 1960

Andean Group, established 1969

Common Market of the Southern Cone (Mercosur), established 1991

North American Free Trade Association (NAFTA), established 1988

Caribbean Community (CARICOM), established 1973

Argentinian occupation, Apr-June 1982

the American Deep South, scene of economic revival in the 1990s

borders, 1997

Nunavut Territory, due to be implemented 1999

metropolitan area with a population over 1 million

other city

Soviet Intermediate Range Ballistic Missile (IRBM) base on Cuba, 1962

range of Cuban-based IRBMs, 1962

United States missile base

civil rights activity

country experiencing social revolution, with date

Cuban-inspired guerrilla movement, 1959-68

indigenous guerrilla movement

African-American migration within the United States

White American migration within the United States

other migration

rainforest

area of deforestation

0     1400 km
0     1000 mi

See also 102 (the Americas to 1945); 112 (Central America and Caribbean)

All the eight states of Central America, together with several islands of the Caribbean, have suffered from similar problems in the later 20th century. All had subsistence agriculture, unfair land distribution and a deprived native peasant class. Tax evasion by the wealthy was endemic, and labor-intensive industries were lacking. The states were too poor to fund welfare sufficiently to prevent political revolt, so political violence and state repression were commonplace. Aid (overwhelmingly from the United States) tended to prop up military leaders committed to anti-Communist policies despite frequent corruption and human rights abuses.

Before its revolution, Cuba was dominated by United States interests, with US marines stationed at their Guantánamo Bay base. Cubans who demanded political independence were treated as rebels, and any government that supported US interests was guaranteed a supply of dollars. Fidel Castro's successful revolution led to hostility from the United States and the International Monetary Fund (IMF). The Soviet Union gave Castro support, especially after the American-supported but abortive counter-coup at the Bay of Pigs in 1961. The following year, United States air surveillance revealed that Soviet intermediate range ballistic missiles (IRBMs) had been stationed on the island, and all of eastern and most of the southern United States lay within their 3,200-kilometer (2,000-mile) range. The US president Kennedy imposed a naval blockade on the islands and even considered invasion, a step that seemed inevitably to lead to nuclear war. When Soviet leader Khrushchev removed the missiles, the threat of invasion was lifted, but Castro became an enduring Soviet ally. He grew into the first Caribbean leader to have a marked impact on world affairs, sending trained guerrillas to spread Marxism–Leninism in Africa (including Angola and Ethiopia). The Soviet Union supported Cuba's economy and funded its welfare state, but Cuba went into decline after 1990 and faced severe American sanctions.

The United States believed Cuba to have fostered guerrilla revolts in Nicaragua, El Salvador, Guatemala and Honduras, and feared that these countries would come under Soviet control. Cuban guerrillas were active in El Salvador, training rebels and organizing protests. By 1976 they were fomenting strikes on coffee and cotton plantations. The army responded by taking over the government and thousands of civilian suspects were killed. A similar cycle of events occurred in Guatemala. In Nicaragua, which was ruled by the wealthy Samoza family, Sandinista guerrillas occupied Managua and set up a Marxist–Leninist state in 1979. This was, however, subverted by rightwing Contra guerrillas trained by the United States. In 1990, with more than three-quarters of the population still below the poverty line, the Sandinista leader Daniel Ortega was voted out of office in a general election.

Mexico, the richest country in the region thanks to its reserves of oil, opposed foreign intervention and defended the Sandinistas as a "stabilizing factor" entitled to transform the people's way of life through

TIMELINE

| | 1950 | 1970 | 1990 |
|---|---|---|---|
| **Central America** | **1948** Formation of the Organization of American States (OAS) to promote peace and security | **1964** Riots occur in the Canal Zone in Panama | **1988** US-backed Contra rebels from Nicaragua seek refuge in Honduras |
| | **1948** The Army of National Liberation forms a government in Costa Rica | **1969** The Honduran air force destroys the Acajutla oil refinery in the "football war" with El Salvador | **1990** The Sandanista government is voted out in Nicaragua |
| | **1957** The OAS settles a dispute between Nicaragua and Honduras | **1979–82** Guatemala systematically drives out native peoples | |
| **Caribbean** | **1941** A United States base is built on St Lucia under the 1940 Anglo-American "destroyers for bases" deal | **1968** The Caribbean Free Trade Association (CARIFTA) is formed | **1993** Puerto Rico votes to remain a United States "Commonwealth" |
| | **1958** Formation of the Federation of the British West Indies | **1973** CARIFTA members form the Caribbean Community via the Georgetown Accord | **1994** United States forces invade Haiti to overthrow the military regime |
| | **1959** Fidel Castro drives out the Cuban president Fulgencio Batista | **1983** United States forces invade Grenada following an attempted Marxist/Black Power coup led by Maurice Bishop | |
| | **1962** Cuban missile crisis; Cuba is expelled from the OAS | | |

Map labels:

Torréon, Monterrey, Rio Grande, San Luis Potosi, Aguascalientes, Tampico, León, Querétaro, Tuxpan, Lerma, Morelia, Toluca, Mexico City, Puebla, Balsas, MEXICO, Veracruz, Acapulco, Coatzacoalcos, Salina Cruz, Mérida, Chiapas, Usumacinta, Grijalba, Belize City, Belmopan, BELIZE (British Honduras) 1981 independent, border dispute to 1986, Puerto Cortes, 1954 1967–80, Puerto Barrios, Tela, La Ceiba, HONDURAS, Puerto Madero, Quetzaltenango, Champerico, Guatemala City, San José, 1979, Tegucigalpa, GUATEMALA 1954 US intervention, Acajutla, San Salvador, La Union, NICARAGUA, Esteli, EL SALVADOR 1979–91 US & Israeli aid to fight FMNLF guerrillas, Corinto, León, Managua, Lake Nicaragua, Los Chil, COSTA RICA, Caldera, San José, 1948, 1955, David, Puerto Armuel, from 1981 insurgency campaigns by US-backed Contras

Gulf of Mexico, PACIFIC OCEAN, to United States & Mexico

Legend:

- — — state borders
- ....... disputed border
- British territory, 1941
- Dutch territory, 1941
- French territory, 1941
- United States territory, 1941
- country experiencing intervention by the United States
- Organization for Petroleum Exporting Countries (OPEC)
- United States blockade of Cuba from 1962
- ✳ civil war
- ⊙ Contra base area
- ⊙ Sandinista base
- ✈ United States air base
- ⊗ United States naval base
- ⚙ Cuban missile site, 1962
- ⚓ principal port
- coalfield
- oilfield
- oil pipeline
- major migration since 1945

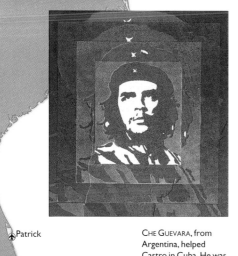

CHE GUEVARA, from Argentina, helped Castro in Cuba. He was an icon of revolution through the Americas.

**1** In 1977 the United States agreed that the Canal Zone, under US control since the beginning of the century, would be handed over to Panama in 2000.

**2** The population of Mexico City rose to more than 20 million in the mid-1990s. Many people lived on the streets or in squalid and dangerous conditions.

**3** The last Soviet advisors left Cuba in 1993, when a renewed United States blockade of the island took effect. Many Cubans attempted to reach the United States illegally; Miami became a popular destination for Cuban exiles.

**4** Costa Rica sought to avoid many of the political conflicts of Central America, and in 1987 its president Arias Sánchez won the Nobel Prize for his attempt to draw up a peace plan for the region.

**5** In 1969 war between Honduras and El Salvador broke out following a World Cup soccer match between the two countries.

**6** Barbados, which was a British colony until 1966, but which had enjoyed a degree of self-government since 1639, was used as a base for the United States invasion of Grenada in 1983.

revolution. The country had few law and order problems, although the population quadrupled from 1940 and a recession hit in 1984. A Zapatista revolt in Chiapas province was crushed ten years later.

The United States intervened in the internal affairs of several Caribbean islands, again prompted by fear of Communism. The Dominican Republic was invaded by paratroopers in 1965, Grenada in 1983, and Haiti in 1994. Another United States intervention was the arrest of the president of Panama, Manuel Noriega, in 1989, on drugs smuggling charges.

In 1958-62 an unsuccessful federation of West Indian states was tried, after which most sought independence (achieved peacefully for the most part) or chose to remain as British dependencies. In the 1950s, Britain actively sought immigrants from the West Indies, but curtailed this in 1962. Jamaica faced overpopulation, unemployment and racial tension, but its educational programs and tourist attractions improved job opportunities. Trinidad and Tobago, richly endowed with oil, natural gas and asphalt, suffered from a high birth rate, strikes and sabotage due to Black Power groups and embittered Asians working on the sugar plantations. Belize, a former British colony, was the last Central American country to gain its independence; it remained a firm supporter of United States policies.

See also 102 (early 20th-century America);
111 (the Americas from 1945)

The end of World War II left the United States dominant but the Soviet Union was also moving strongly into east Asia. The Chinese civil wars were soon to be resolved, while the European colonies had been decisively altered by the experience of Japanese occupation and US liberation.

In September 1945 US forces landed at Inchon on the former Japanese colony of Korea, in response to the presence of Soviet troops in north Korea. No formula could be found for unifying the country and the UN approved an American plan to hold elections in the south. Syngman Rhee's Republic of Korea (South Korea) emerged in 1948, followed shortly by Kim Il Sung's Communist Democratic Republic of Korea (North Korea). The Soviet Union and United States withdrew in 1948 and 1949 respectively, leaving Korea divided.

Many US troops withdrew to Japan, where America was responsible for its military occupation and the repatriation of three million Japanese servicemen. The United States and its Commonwealth Allies met with unexpected cooperation from Japanese police and local officials. Emperor Hirohito remained, though only as titular ruler, and real power was in the hands of General MacArthur, Supreme Commander of Allied Powers. MacArthur introduced a democratic constitution, ensured that the United States shipped in adequate food supplies and generally charmed the Japanese with his dignity and benevolence. The Japanese came to admire Americans and their way of life. By 1949 Japan was willingly drawn inside America's defense perimeter.

By 1950 Mao Zedong had succeeded in unifying China, partly by demonstrating that the PLA was no warlord army. Soldiers, workers, the Party hierarchy (cadres) and the government were united. Mao assured the people that China was no longer isolated: the Sino–Soviet Treaty (1950) guaranteed their membership of a international socialist brotherhood. He promised land reform and development plans, and protection for China's frontiers. His first move was to invade Tibet in the winter of 1950–51 to recover what China considered a historic province.

North Korea invaded South Korea in 1950. This provoked a major United Nations response and an army from sixteen nations, spearheaded by the Americans, was sent to Korea to resist the invaders. UN forces attacked across the 38th Parallel dividing North from South, and a few reached the border with China on the Yalu River. At this point the PLA entered the war and forced a UN retreat. A static war ensued, with both sides digging in. An armistice was agreed at Panmunjom in 1953 and five years later the PLA left Korea, although a UN presence remained. After the war, North Korea remained a Stalinist state, while the South began to rebuild its shattered economy. Heavy industry and infrastructure, as well as electronics and consumer industries, were all constructed from scratch as Korea, like Japan, used the opportunity of war to build a new prosperity.

Chinese armed forces were also involved in 1954 when PLA gunners shelled the two small islands of Quemoy and Matsu that were claimed by the Nationalist government based in Taiwan. PLA forces landed on other Nationalist islands and in 1958 resumed the shelling of Quemoy. America mobilized a massive fleet in the Taiwan Straits in support of Jiang Jieshi, who still claimed to be the legitimate ruler of the whole of mainland China. In 1962 PLA forces attempted to push across the Indian border and were poised to enter Assam. After brief fighting against ill-prepared Indian troops, the Chinese withdrew. Along the Ussuri River Chinese patrols clashed with Soviet troops in 1969.

In the 1950s and 1960s, Mao Zedong attempted to forge a Chinese version of Marxism, based on a drive toward establishing economic modernization (especially in the chaotic "Great Leap Forward" of 1958–60) and the collectivization of agriculture. From the mid-1960s he fomented "permanent revolution" by encouraging the youthful Red Guards to challenge all forms of authority, especially in education, administration, industry and the Party itself, and to send many intellectuals to work on communes. China was almost totally cut off from the outside world until after Mao's death in 1976.

1 Inchon was taken by US troops in September 1950 following a surprise amphibious attack.

2 The economy of postwar Japan was boosted by the presence of UN servicemen based there during the Korean War. After the destruction of 1944-45, Japan became the driving force in east Asia's economy.

3 The Hukbalahar revolt from 1945 in Luzon, a peasant uprising over land ownership, was crushed by the government in 1953-54.

4 In 1958 US president Eisenhower sent "the most powerful fighting force in history" to confront the Communist Chinese in the Taiwan Straits.

5 Tension between the Soviet Union and Maoist China on the Amur River border from 1969 emphasized the rift between these former allies.

6 Burma, which pursued a neutral foreign policy after independence under U Nu, was under a socialist military regime led by Ne Win from 1962.

7 East Timor, a Portuguese colony until the Portuguese revolution of 1975, was invaded by Indonesia the same year, and annexed in 1976.

Independence and unity arrived slowly for many east Asian nations. The Philippines became an independent republic in 1946; Burma in 1948; after the partition of India in 1947, East Pakistan became Bangladesh in 1971. But the former French Indo-Chinese colonies of Laos, Cambodia and Vietnam became embroiled in the longest war of the century. During World War II the French had accepted Japanese domination of the area; only the Communist Vietminh forces led by Ho Chi Minh resisted, and declared independence in 1945. The return of the French led to a long guerrilla war in which the French initially drove the Vietminh from the major cities, but in 1953–54 the Vietminh general Giap won a remarkable and decisive victory over the French at Dien Bien Phu.

Maoist China was the chief supporter of the insurgents in Indo-China, and also of the Communists in Malaya who inspired a long guerrilla campaign against the British; eventually independence was achieved by the anti-Communist, Malay-led nationalists in 1957. Indonesia, which claimed its independence after the war and won Dutch acceptance of the fact in 1949 after a bitter struggle, also suffered Communist, regionalist and Islamist activity. To a lesser extent, the Philippines (where United States' influence was still paramount), Burma and Thailand also saw Communist movements.

See also 108 (World War II in Asia); 114 (Vietnam War); 120 (the Pacific Rim after 1976)

Following the victories of Ho Chi Minh's Vietminh guerrilla forces in 1943–54, France withdrew from most of Indo-China. The subsequent Geneva Conference ruled that Vietnam would be divided between the North, ruled from Hanoi by the Vietminh, and the non-Communist South, with its capital in Saigon. Two neutral states, Laos and Cambodia, would also be formed and within two years the Vietnamese would hold free elections and be united under a government of their own choice.

The elections were never held. Vietnam stayed divided and weak: the North by being cut off from the rich rice-fields of the Mekong delta, and the South by the presence of the Vietminh. Land reform was a key issue in the Mekong delta where two million peasants were landless, with many more paying high rents to absentee landlords. Saigon was reluctant to redistribute the land, whereas the Vietminh soldiers gave land to the peasants and also handed over responsibility for food production and local government. The Communists thus began to win the hearts and minds of the people, who were alienated by the anti-Buddhist president Diem in Saigon. Coercion, too, was rife on the Communist side in intimidating or eliminating anti-Communists.

John Foster Dulles, US secretary of state from 1953, had never endorsed the Geneva agreements. He intended to save all of southeast Asia from Communism and to this end set up the South-East Asia Treaty Organization (SEATO) to prevent subversion within member states. When guerrilla uprisings began in Vietnam during 1955–56, the United States sent military advisers to train the ARVN (Army of the Republic of South Vietnam). Gradually the guerrillas, now termed the Viet Cong (Vietnamese Communists or VC), won control of half of Diem's provinces. Disillusioned ARVN officers killed him.

A succession of Saigon governments followed. For the United States, the war against North Vietnam (NVN) became "the great issue" of the 1960s. America's leaders accepted the "domino theory": if South Vietnam (SVN) succumbed to Communism, the same fate would in turn befall Laos, Cambodia, Thailand, Burma and Pakistan. After President

Kennedy's assassination in 1963, President Johnson left the conduct of the war in the hands of defense secretary Robert McNamara. More American troops arrived in the South as VCs and their supplies swarmed down the "Ho Chi Minh Trail". In an effort to halt the flow of war materiel from China and Russia via Hanoi, the US provoked the Tongking crisis in 1964: an attack on US destroyers became an excuse for bombing North Vietnam 1965–70.

Air attack failed to reduce VC activity. US soldiers (and others from Australasia and South Korea) were sent to fight an elusive enemy hiding in the hamlets, jungles and paddy fields. They had enormous firepower; but the fundamental issue – how to defeat well-armed, well-supplied nationalists operating in an agrarian economy – was never resolved. The Central Intelligence Agency (CIA) did not penetrate the VC high command; it did not warn of the Tet offensive of 1968 when Viet Cong battle-squads entered Saigon, Hue and other towns, and failed to reveal the buildup around the US base at Khe Sanh.

With antiwar sentiment growing in the United States, President Johnson authorized negotiations with North Vietnam in Paris. His successor Richard Nixon pledged to scale down US troop involvement and to "vietnamize" the war by boosting the ARVN military contribution. Even as US troops were quitting Vietnam, he backed the invasions of Cambodia and Laos plus Operation Linebacker II, a resumption of the air war designed to destroy the transportation systems of North Vietnam. US air power now proved irresistible, destroying bridges, truck factories and harbor installations. Linebacker II encouraged Le Duc Tho, the NVN delegation leader, to sign the Paris peace agreement with Henry Kissinger (US national security adviser). South Vietnam's President Thieu reluctantly agreed to the ceasefire, and the last American combat troops left Vietnam in 1973.

Nixon's subsequent resignation and the decline of US aid encouraged Le Duan (Ho Chi Minh's successor) to attempt the reunification of Vietnam. The Ho Chi Minh Trail now provided unhindered access to the south, and China and the Soviet Union had re-equipped the regular NVN Army so that it could put

infantry divisions, armored brigades and artillery regiments into the field. These advanced from the north and the west, fighting the kind of war that the Americans had always wanted them to fight. In 1975 SVN's president Thieu fled to Taiwan; American helicopters ferried their remaining personnel from the capital as NVN tanks entered Saigon. At the same time Laos and Cambodia, both destabilized by Viet Cong activity and by constant US air attack, also fell to the Communists: Pathet Lao guerrillas set up a People's Democratic Republic in Laos, while the Khmer Rouge captured Cambodia's capital, Phnom Penh. Vietnam was reunited as the Socialist Republic of Vietnam under the leadership of Le Duan.

**Legend:**
- border, 1954
- Communist control within Indo-China, 1954
- under Vietnamese Communist control, 1970
- Vietnamese Communist gains by Jan 1975
- Vietnamese Communist gains by Apr 1975
- Khmer Rouge control, 1975
- Pathet Lao control, 1975
- Communist guerrilla activity in Thailand, 1975
- US carrier fleet on permanent station
- US air base in South Vietnam and Thailand
- North Vietnamese air base
- Tet Offensive assault, Jan–Feb 1968
- major combat area
- interdiction by US Air Force
- VI A  zoned target area (Route Packages) of the US Air Force within North Vietnam
- border of zoned target area
- forbidden target for US air strikes until Operation Linebacker II, 1972
- Vinh  harbor mined by the US Navy
- Viet Cong supply route
- US and South Vietnamese offensive, 1970
- Vietnamese Communist advance, Jan–Apr 1975
- Vietnamese invasion of Cambodia, 1978–79
- Chinese invasion of Vietnam, 1979
- US evacuation, with date
- railroad

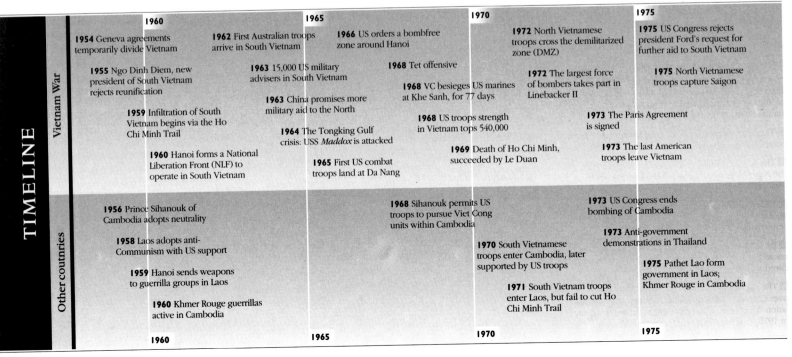

**TIMELINE**

**Vietnam War**

- **1954** Geneva agreements temporarily divide Vietnam
- **1955** Ngo Dinh Diem, new president of South Vietnam rejects reunification
- **1959** Infiltration of South Vietnam begins via the Ho Chi Minh Trail
- **1960** Hanoi forms a National Liberation Front (NLF) to operate in South Vietnam
- **1962** First Australian troops arrive in South Vietnam
- **1963** 15,000 US military advisers in South Vietnam
- **1963** China promises more military aid to the North
- **1964** The Tongking Gulf crisis; USS *Maddox* is attacked
- **1965** First US combat troops land at Da Nang
- **1966** US orders a bombfree zone around Hanoi
- **1968** Tet offensive
- **1968** VC besieges US marines at Khe Sanh, for 77 days
- **1968** US troops strength in Vietnam tops 540,000
- **1969** Death of Ho Chi Minh, succeeded by Le Duan
- **1972** North Vietnamese troops cross the demilitarized zone (DMZ)
- **1972** The largest force of bombers takes part in Linebacker II
- **1973** The Paris Agreement is signed
- **1973** The last American troops leave Vietnam
- **1975** US Congress rejects president Ford's request for further aid to South Vietnam
- **1975** North Vietnamese troops capture Saigon

**Other countries**

- **1956** Prince Sihanouk of Cambodia adopts neutrality
- **1958** Laos adopts anti-Communism with US support
- **1959** Hanoi sends weapons to guerrilla groups in Laos
- **1960** Khmer Rouge guerrillas active in Cambodia
- **1968** Sihanouk permits US troops to pursue Viet Cong units within Cambodia
- **1970** South Vietnamese troops enter Cambodia, later supported by US troops
- **1971** South Vietnam troops enter Laos, but fail to cut Ho Chi Minh Trail
- **1973** US Congress ends bombing of Cambodia
- **1973** Anti-government demonstrations in Thailand
- **1975** Pathet Lao form government in Laos; Khmer Rouge in Cambodia

1960    1965    1970    1975

Salween

PEOPLE'S REPUBLIC
OF CHINA

• Ha Giang
Cao Bang •

• Lao Cai
NORTH VIETNAM
1954 independent,
1976 united as Vietnam

Lai Chau •
Yen Bai •       VI A
Lang Son •
Thai Nguyen •
Mong Cai •

• Maomin

Zhanjiang •

Phong
Saly •
Dien Bien Phu •
Phu Tho •     • Kep
Viet Tri •  Phuc Yen •      VI B

V
Hoa Lac •   Gia Lam •  Hong Gai
Hanoi •      • Kien An   Haiphong •
Dong
Suong •

• Na Khang
Nam Dinh •
Thai Binh •

IV

Luang Prabang •
Bai
Thuong •     Thanh
Hoa •

Muang Suoy •
Xieng
Khouang •

III

Sayaboury •
• Quan
Lang

LAOS
1954 independent

Vinh •

• Chiang Mai

Gulf of
Tongking

Hainan

Na Pe Pass •

II

Vientiane •

Mu Gia Pass
Thakek •

I
• Dong Hoi

Yankee
Station

South
China
Sea

Udon Thani •

Nakhon Phanom •

2   17th Parallel,
demilitarized zone

THAILAND

Khon Kaen •

Savannakhet •

Khe
Sanh •   Quang Tri •

Nakhon Sawan •

3
Lang Vei •
A Shau •
Da Nang
Hoi An •

Ta Khli •

Hue •

Duy Xuyen •  Tam Ky •

Nakhon Ratchasima
(Khorat) •

Ubon Ratchathani •

Pakse •

Kham Duc •
Chu Lai
My Lai •
Quang Ngai •

5

4

• Nakhon Sawan

Dac To •

Tam Quam •
Bong Son •

• Don Muang
Bangkok •

Kon Tum •

Amphil •

Pleiku •
Qui Nhon •

Aranyaprathet •
Stung Treng •

SOUTH
VIETNAM
1954 independent,
1975 to North Vietnam,
1976 united as Vietnam

Siem Reap •
Lomphat •

Tuy An •
Tuy Hoa •

Battambang •
Tonle
Sap

U Tapao •
CAMBODIA
(KAMPUCHEA)
1954 independent   6

Ban Me Thuot •

Nha Trang •

US military
evacuation 1976

Pursat •
Kratie •

Cam Ranh Bay •

Kompong Chhnang •
Kompong
Cham •

Da Lat •

Bao Loc •

Phan Rang •

Fish
Hook
Loc Ninh •
An Loc •

Dixie
Station

Phnom Penh •

Parrot's
Beak
Tan Son Nhut
Bien Hoa

Svay
Rieng •
Sihanouk Trail
Saigon •
Tan An •

Xuan Loc •
Phan Thiet •

Kompong Som
(Sihanoukville) •
Chau Doc •

My Tho •  Vung Tau •

Kampot •

Long Xuyen •
Vinh
Long •  Ben Tre •

Dao Phu Quoc

Can Tho •

Gulf of
Thailand

Mekong
Delta

US military evacuation 1973, US embassy evacuation 1975

Quan Long •

Mekong
Nan
Yom
Ping
Chi
Mun
Kong
San
Srepok
Se San
Black
Red
Salween
Ho Chi Minh Trail
Kamphong Son •

1  Hanoi, the colonial capital of Indo-China and capital
of North Vietnam, was heavily bombed by the United
States in 1965, 1968 and 1972.

2  The Geneva agreements allowed for a demilitarized
zone (DMZ) between North and South Vietnam.

3  The US marine base at Khe Sanh was attacked by
the North Vietnamese Army (NVA) January–April
1968, prior to the Tet offensive.

4  US troops killed 109 South Vietnamese civilians at
My Lai in March 1968; the court-martial of the officer
responsible stimulated worldwide revulsion.

5  By 1970 the Ho Chi Minh Trail, once a series of
tracks for men and bicycles, was a road capable of
carrying heavy armor, despite continual US bombing.

6  The nationalist-Communist Khmer Rouge took
over Cambodia in 1975, killing a quarter of the population. Vietnam, with Soviet support, drove them out
in 1978–79; China then briefly invaded Vietnam.

0        250 km
0        200 mi

See also 113 (east Asia from World War II);
120 (southeast Asia after 1976)

Only a few hours after the proclamation of the independent state of Israel on 14 May 1948, the armies of Syria, Jordan, Egypt and Iraq invaded, expecting to crush the Jewish state and establish an Arab Palestine. The Jews drew on reserves of experienced soldiers from around the world, defeated the Arabs and conquered territory as far as West Jerusalem. When East Jerusalem and the West Bank of the Jordan became part of the territory of Jordan the following year, Palestine ceased to exist. No Arab state would recognize the permanence of the new frontiers, though they received *de facto* acceptance at armistice talks in 1949. Israel's victory meant that the new state attracted thousands of Jewish immigrants to a new homeland, while more than a million Palestinians became refugees in their own land – a potentially explosive force in the politics of the region and of Jordan in particular.

Defeat led to a nationalist revolt in Egypt in 1952, when the British-sponsored ruling family was expelled and a republic instituted by a group of army officers. Colonel Nasser, president from 1954, relied on American dollars to subsidize the massive Aswan Dam project, regarded as essential for Egypt's economic and industrial development. When the United States withdrew in response to Nasser's increasingly anti-western foreign policy, he nationalized the Suez Canal, long seen as a strategic key to the east by Britain and France. These two old colonial powers decided to invade. Israel's support was secretly secured and Israeli forces invaded Sinai in October 1956, with Anglo-French troops arriving a week later. American pressure brought about a withdrawal and a United Nations force was sent in, while Nasser blocked the canal with sunken ships.

Widespread condemnation of Britain and France was followed by increased superpower involvement in the region: Arab states turned to the Soviet Union for weaponry while the United States became Israel's arsenal. Nasser was convinced that Egypt, allied with Syria (the two were united as the United Arab Republic in 1958–61), would defeat Israel. He assembled an alliance of Arab states and provoked a crisis by closing the Gulf of Aqaba. Israel, however, launched the most effective pre-emptive strike in history, attacking all of Egypt's air bases in June 1967. Most Egyptian combat aircraft were destroyed; Syria and Jordan suffered similar devastation.

When a ceasefire was agreed six days later, Israeli forces had occupied Gaza and the entire Sinai east of Suez, Jordan surrendered East Jerusalem, Bethlehem and Hebron, and Syria lost the Golan Heights, an area dominating the north of Israel.

The United Nations, however, passed resolutions requiring Israel to evacuate the occupied territories, deploring the loss of Palestinian civil rights, and confirming the Palestinian right to selfdetermination. These pointed to the deep divisions within Israel, where the Palestinians were treated as second-class citizens, many of them – particularly in the areas recently occupied by Israel – condemned to a life in refugee camps. The Palestinian Liberation Organization (PLO) was founded in 1964, and by the early 1970s had won, through a combination of terrorist tactics and moral pressure, a powerful and independent voice in the politics of the region. Seeming to endanger the fragile stability of Jordan, the PLO was evicted from the kingdom in 1970 and settled in Lebanon. The growing numbers of refugees there, most with little to lose, proved destabilizing to that country as well and contributed to the outbreak of civil war in Beirut in 1975.

In October 1973 Egypt's new president Anwar Sadat broke through into Israeli-held territory without warning on the Jewish Day of Atonement (Yom Kippur). The Israelis concentrated on holding the Golan Heights against Syrian tanks, but three weeks later Israel had defeated both attacks comprehensively while the two superpowers refused to intervene actively to support the protagonists.

In response to the United States' supply of military materiel to the Israelis, Saudi Arabia (where oil

**1** Jerusalem, a holy city to Jews, Muslims and Christians, was divided after the failure of the Arab attack of 1948; the Israelis took the whole city in 1967, but disputes continued into the 1990s.

**2** In 1953 the CIA (US intelligence agency) backed a coup against Iranian prime minister Mohammed Moussadeq, who had tried to nationalize the oil industry in 1951. The exiled shah returned to power.

**3** Sharm el-Sheikh, a cove on the Sinai peninsula controlling entry to the Straits of Tiran, was captured by the Israelis in 1956 and controlled by the United Nations Emergency Force 1957-67.

**4** This neutral zone between Kuwait and Saudi Arabia was partitioned between the two countries in 1966.

**5** Israel bombed Palestinian bases in Jordan in 1968 and its troops defeated the Al Fatah (PLO military wing) guerrillas at the Battle of Karama.

**6** Jordan expelled the Al Fatah guerrillas in 1970; many established new bases in southern Lebanon.

**7** After ethnic conflict in Cyprus through the 1950s and UN intervention from 1964, a Turkish invasion in 1974 divided the island into Greek and Turkish zones.

revenues had grown dramatically since 1945 and which was the leading member of the Organization of Petroleum Exporting Countries, OPEC) imposed oil sanctions on the west, restricting OPEC exports and causing a sharp price rise. Despite this, the governments of Saudi Arabia and the Gulf states, including Iran (where the Allied occupation in World War II had left a legacy of popular bitterness toward "imperialists"), remained close to the United States and rejected the growing influence of the Soviet Union in the region. The main oil-producing states were reluctant to give military support to the anti-Israeli effort, and tensions developed between Saudi Arabia and Egypt over Egyptian policy in the southern Arabian peninsula. Syria and Iraq, however, were both under the control of the "anti-imperialist" and Arab nationalist Ba'ath Party, from 1963 and 1968 respectively. Libya too, another important oil producer, was in the control of a strongly anti-American regime inspired by the success of Nasser and led by Muammar Qadhafi from 1969.

Following the Yom Kippur War, Menachem Begin became prime minister of Israel, and realized that, like himself, Sadat was now interested in reducing Arab–Israeli tensions. Begin invited Sadat to Jerusalem, and a peace process was initiated which was formalized in the United States in 1979.

**TIMELINE**

**Arab-Israeli Wars**

**1948** Israel's foundation is followed by an Arab attack

**1949** One million Palestinians flee Israel

**1956** Nasser's nationalization of the Suez Canal leads to British, French and Israeli invasions of Egypt

**1958** Nationalist revolution in Iraq overthrows the monarchy

**1964** Palestinian Liberation Organization (PLO) is founded in Jerusalem

**1967** Six-Day War ends with Israeli control over Sinai

**1969** Yassir Arafat becomes PLO chairman

**1970** The PLO are driven out of Jordan and settle in Lebanon; terrorist hijacking of civilian aircraft begins

**1973** Sadat launches the fourth war against Israel

**1977** Egypt's president Sadat offers Israel peace in return for a Palestinian state

**Other developments**

**1951** Moussadeq becomes Iranian prime minister and nationalizes the oil industry

**1952** The Egyptian monarchy is overthrown

**1953** The CIA sponsor a coup in Iran and reinstate Reza Khan Pahlavi as shah

**1961** Kuwait gains its independence, though it is claimed by Iraq

**1965** Iran exiles Islamic leader Ayatollah Khomeini

**1968** Ba'ath leader Saddam Hussein takes power in Iraq

**1970** General Asad seizes power in Syria

**1973** OPEC countries raise the price of oil to exert political influence on the west

**1975** Civil war breaks out in Beirut

border, 1977
disputed border
member state of Arab League, 1945
member of NATO, 1967
member of Warsaw Pact, 1967
Israel, 1949
Israeli gains, 1967
area of Egyptian military presence, 1966
Arab airfield attacked, June 1973
Bar Lev line, 1973
Egyptian attack, 1973
Israeli counter attack, 1973

Turkish invasion, 1974
Cypriot ceasefire line, 1974
British base
Greek territory in Cyprus, 1977
Turkish territory in Cyprus, 1977
civil war
coup
PLO stronghold
oilfield
oil pipeline

Black Sea

Lake Van

Tabriz

Lake Urmia

Kurdish risings
1945–46,
1961–75

IRAN
2

Adana
Dörtyol
Gaziantep

TURKEY
1960, 1971

CYPRUS
1960 independent
Nicosia
Dhekelia
Akrotiri
1955–77
7

Aleppo

SYRIA
1946 independent,
1958–61 united with Egypt
as United Arab Republic
1949, 1961, 1963,
1966, 1970

Mosul
Arbil
Kirkuk

Kerman

Latakia
Hamah
Homs

Euphrates
Tigris
Diyala

Bahr al Tharthar

Baghdad

IRAQ
1958, 1963,
1968

Tripoli
1946 independent
Beirut
Sidon
1975–89
6
Dumeir
Damascus

Syrian Desert

Al Hillah
An Najaf

Basra

Haifa
GOLAN HEIGHTS
WEST BANK
Tel Aviv–Jaffa
ISRAEL
1948 independent
Jerusalem
Gaza
1
Hebron
Dead Sea
Karak
5
Mafraq
Amman

JORDAN
1946 independent
1970

KUWAIT
1961 independent
4
neutral zone

El Mansura
Alexandria
Inchas
Deversoir
Abu Sueir
Fayid
Kabrit
Cairo
Suez
Port Said
El Arish
Jebel Libni
Bir Gifgafa
Bir Thamada
Battle of Chinese Farm, 1973
Sudr
Aqaba

SAUDI ARABIA

Beni Sueif
Abu Rudeis
El Minya
Ras Gharib
Sharm el Sheikh

Eastern Desert
Hurghada

EGYPT
1958–61 united with Syria as
United Arab Republic
1952

Western Desert
Nile
Luxor

Aswan High Dam completed 1970
Aswan

Red Sea

Ras Banas

Lake Nasser

area disputed from 1958

SUDAN
1956 independent
1962–69      1958, 1969

Mediterranean Sea

from Cyprus
from Malta

LEBANON
Tyre
SYRIA
Haifa
Zefat
WEST BANK
Tel Aviv–Jaffa
Nablus
Amman
Jerusalem
Jericho
Bethlehem
GAZA STRIP
Gaza
Hebron
Beersheba
Dead Sea

Port Said
El Mansura
El Qantara
Romani
El Arish
Imailia
Suez Canal
Bir Hasana
Negev
JORDAN
EGYPT
Cairo
Suez
Bir Gifgafa
Mitla Pass  Oct 1956
El Kuntilla
Sudr
El Thamad
Eilat
Aqaba
SINAI
Abu Zenima
SAUDI ARABIA
Dahab
Nov 1956
El Tur
Gulf of Aqaba
3  Sharm el Sheikh

border, 1956
Israel, 1948
Israeli gains, 1948–49
Arab refugee camp, 1948
Israeli airborne attack, 1956
Israeli campaign, 1956
Anglo-French airborne and sea landing, 5–6 Nov 1956

0        200 km
0        150 mi

Jiddah
Mecca

See also 104 (Middle East between the wars);
118 (Middle East from 1977)

By 1974 rivalry between the Soviet Union and the United States still dominated international affairs. The USSR guarded its European satellite states jealously. When, in 1956, Hungary tried to break free from the Soviet-dominated Warsaw Pact, the Red Army crushed the revolution. In 1961 the Berlin Wall was erected to enforce Soviet control over East Germany. And in 1968, Warsaw Pact forces ended the Czech attempt to introduce a more liberal form of socialist government (▷ 110). Yet Yugoslavia, Albania and Romania all won some independence from Soviet control.

In western Europe, institutions were set up to integrate the economies of the main industrial nations. The European Economic Community (EEC) was seen as a step to political union and the creation of a European superstate, but most countries (France was the main exception) still relied on the United States membership of NATO for security from possible Soviet aggression.

It was in America's "backyard" that superpower rivalry was most apparent. The Cuban missile crisis of 1962 brought a real threat of nuclear war until the Soviet Union withdrew its missiles from within range of the American mainland (▷ 112). Anxiety for the spread of Communism also lay behind the United States involvement in southeast Asia. Fearing that neighboring countries would fall to Communism (the "domino effect"), the United States sent troops and dollars to prop up an unpopular regime in South Vietnam. It was another war by proxy but, unlike Korea, American withdrawal from Vietnam led to the collapse of South Vietnam and the descent of Cambodia into civil war (▷ 114).

Conflict between China and the Soviet Union, underlain by centuries of mutual suspicion, showed that America's opponents were not a unified bloc, however. The Chinese version of Communism was different from the Soviet, as China tried to develop a locally-based economy centered on communes, in contrast to the centralized bureaucracies of the Soviet Union. Chinese Communism was more applicable to non-industrial societies. Communist insurgents worldwide, especially in southeast Asia, where rapid decolonization was followed by political upheaval, turned to it for inspiration and support. Eventual American recognition of the Sino-Soviet split led in the early 1970s to an attempt to exploit the dispute and brought a new era of détente (▷ 113).

In Africa, opposition to imperial rule was the driving force. The Suez crisis of 1956 showed the weakness of the old imperial powers, and a wave of

Hawaii (United States)

French Polynesia (France)

| | |
|---|---|
| A. | Albania |
| AU. | Austria |
| B. | Belgium |
| CAR. | Central African Republic |
| C. | Czechoslovakia |
| D. | Denmark |
| DR. | Dominican Republic |
| DY. | People's Democratic Republic of Yemen |
| EG. | East Germany |
| H. | Hungary |
| LE. | Lebanon |
| L. | Luxembourg |

| | |
|---|---|
| N. | Netherlands |
| NV. | North Vietnam |
| S. | Switzerland |
| U. | United Arab Emirates |
| WG. | West Germany |
| YA. | Yemen Arab Republic |
| YU. | Yugoslavia |

Alaska (United States)

CANADA

UNITED STATES

MEXICO

BAHAMAS

British Honduras (Britain)

CUBA
HAITI
Puerto Rico (United States)

JAMAICA

DR.
GRENADA
PANAMA

GUATEMALA
EL SALVADOR
HONDURAS
NICARAGUA
COSTA RICA
Canal Zone (United States)

BARBADOS
TRINIDAD & TOBAGO
GUYANA
Dutch Guiana (Netherlands)
French Guiana (France)

VENEZUELA
COLOMBIA
ECUADOR

BRAZIL

PERU
BOLIVIA
PARAGUAY

CHILE
ARGENTINA

URUGUAY

Falkland Islands (Britain)

**TIMELINE**

The Americas
Europe
Middle East
Africa
Asia and Australasia

1955          1960          1965

**1956** Hungarian revolt is crushed by the Warsaw Pact

**1956** Egypt nationalizes the Suez Canal; Britain's invasion attempt fails

**1955** The Warsaw Pact is created as a Soviet-bloc opponent of NATO

**1962** Cuban missile crisis, as US president Kennedy insists on withdrawal of Soviet nuclear missiles

**1961** The Nonaligned Conference is founded; OPEC is founded

**1961** The Berlin Wall is built

**1965** US troops are sent to Vietnam, and open bombing of the North begins

**1965** India–Pakistan war

**1951** USA, Australia and New Zealand, sign a defense treaty

**1954** Algerian uprising begins against French rule

**1954** Laos, Cambodia, South and North Vietnam gain independence

**1957** The European Economic Community (EEC) is created

**1957** The Soviet Sputnik II, the first artificial satellite, is launched

**1958** Mao initiates the "Great Leap Forward" in China

**1960** Fifteen African countries gain their independence

**1962** US military advisors are sent to assist the South Vietnam regime

**1963** Sino–Soviet split as Mao and Khrushchev determine different paths

**1966-70** Mao Zedong leads the Cultural Revolution in China

**1967** Israel defeats Egypt and the other Arab nations in the Six Day War

**newly independent state,
1950–74**

**NATO member**

**Communist country and
administrative area**

**Warsaw Pact member**

**Arab League member**

GABON **OPEC member**

**other state or territory**

**1974** US president Nixon
resigns following the
Watergate scandal

**1972** US president Nixon
visits Beijing and Moscow

**1972** Arms Limitation
Treaty between the United
States and Soviet Union

**1971** East Pakistan secedes
to become Bangladesh

**1969** The US space agency
NASA puts the first men
on the Moon

1970

**1968** Student risings take
place in France, the United
States and other western
countries

**1968** "Prague Spring"
reforms in Czechoslovakia
are crushed by Warsaw
Pact forces

**1973** US-backed coup
against an elected Marxist
government in Chile

**1973** Arab states fail to
defeat Israel in the Yom
Kippur War

**1973** OPEC restricts flow
of oil to world markets

decolonization arose in the 1960s, as
Britain and France gave up their possessions. Instability frequently ensued, while
novice administrations tried to cope with mounting
problems in countries whose borders had often been arbitrarily defined by the
colonial powers themselves. Civil war was a feature of this era for many
African nations, the worst in the Congo (Zaire) and Nigeria. To some, Communism seemed to provide answers, but by 1974 only Ethiopia had an avow-
edly Marxist government (▷ *117*). Even the more experienced governments of
India and Pakistan faced difficulties in adjusting to decolonization.

The "nonaligned movement" was founded in 1961 by those countries that
did not wish to be superpower clients. The United Nations, too, had some
success in speaking for the world's newer countries. Another power center
emerged when the oil-producing nations – organized as OPEC – restricted oil
supplies and raised prices in response to western support for Israel. While the
Arab states had little success in using Soviet arms against Israel, this economic
weapon made them important players on the world stage (▷ *115*).

The oil crisis disrupted the developing countries most severely, as their
debt burden rose sharply. Its effects were also profound in Europe and the
United States, where the cost of providing welfare grew ever higher, while the
economies of the Soviet bloc were also under strain. In 1974, the United States
and the Soviet Union were unquestionably still the superpowers, but assumptions about national and international politics were being reviewed ■

**A**fricans played an active part in World War II, fighting on behalf of the Allies, and building roads, railroads, naval yards and fuel depots. They met whites of a type quite different from the traditional colonial administrators, discovered that imperial powers were not invincible, and identified with democratic freedom for which the Allies were fighting. The war meant that African independence could not long be denied.

No entrenched white community gave up without a fight. In British west Africa, though, where the white population was minimal, the transfer of power was relatively swift and peaceful. In the Gold Coast, the Convention People's Party leader Kwame Nkrumah worked closely with the British governor, and the idea of a unitary independent state was tested in an election in 1956. The Gold Coast became independent as Ghana, with Nkrumah as prime minister. Britain gave independence equally readily to Nigeria, Sierra Leone and the Gambia by 1965.

France had recruited a large number of Africans to its armies in both World Wars, and in French West Africa "colonies" were replaced by "overseas territories" with all Africans made citizens of the French republic itself. While many Africans accepted French control provided that they could keep economic links with France, Algeria began its fight for independence on the day that World War II ended in Europe. In 1958 the nationalist freedom fighters were confronted by settlers, causing a crisis that brought Charles de Gaulle back to the French presidency. He abandoned the policy of direct rule from Paris, and by 1960 most French colonies had been given their independence. In Algeria, though, de Gaulle committed half the army to maintain French rule, but this too was abandoned in 1962 after the loss of more than 10,000 French troops.

In Kenya, where white settlers controlled all the best farming regions, the Mau Mau movement terrorized and murdered 20,000 people, mostly Kikuyu sympathetic to their white masters. The British army and air force were sent in before independence was granted with Mau Mau leader Jomo Kenyatta as prime minister. In contrast, the independence movements in Uganda, Tanganyika, Nyasaland and Northern Rhodesia were relatively peaceful.

The ends of both the Belgian and Portuguese empires were violent. Belgium made no attempt to prepare the Congo for changes in government, and on independence the Congolese army mutinied and thousands of Belgian citizens became refugees. Belgian paratroopers went to their aid, and the copper-rich province of Katanga declared its own independence. Eventually, the Congolese general Mobutu crushed the Katangans and their mercenary supporters, creating a unified state which he renamed Zaire. Portugal was the last colonial power to leave Africa, and bitterly opposed the nationalists in Guinea, Angola and Mozambique. By 1975, though, when Portugal underwent its own political convulsions, the colonies became sovereign states.

Few African states found that independence brought stability or prosperity. Many faced ethnic conflict, a legacy of colonial borders that had little relevance to physical, social or economic realities. Most had impoverished, poorly educated and rapidly growing populations, and their economies proved vulnerable to multinational companies offering desperately needed investment to exploit the region's natural resources. Institutions of government were fragile, and arms manufacturers proved willing to supply weapons profligately. As a result, much of the continent experienced civil war, dictatorship and corruption, interrupted by humanitarian crises for which the world's aid agencies offered relief though they could never tackle the underlying problems.

The experience of Nigeria was typical: a civil war in the late 1960s brought on by a secessionist Igbo revolt led to widespread famine, and resulted in a cycle of weak civilian governments replaced by military strong men. Marxist forces, some with the support of the Soviet Union or Cuba, fought tenaciously in many countries including Mozambique and Angola, and won control of Ethiopia in 1974. Elsewhere, dictators such as Jean-Bédel Bokassa in the Central African Republic and Idi Amin in Uganda ruled by terror with few aims beyond personal aggrandizement. Environmental degradation, as the Sahara moved southward and the continent faced shortages of wood and fresh water, was matched in the 1980s by a demographic crisis as the AIDS virus swept through central and east Africa. Attempts to address such issues were made via the Organization of African Unity (OAU) and other regional groups, but these often foundered through lack of leadership and political will, and in the face of the overwhelming economic problems. The problems of Rwanda in the 1990s, where old ethnic rivalries overflowed into genocide in 1994, creating a flood of refugees (including many responsible for mass murder) into Zaire – itself suffering from civil war as insurgents attempted to throw off the long-standing Mobutu regime that finally fell in 1997 – seemed to sum up the intractable problems of the continent.

**1** Western Sahara was claimed by Morocco but was contested by Polisario guerrillas seeking to establish a Sahara Arab democratic republic.

**2** Eritrea was annexed by Ethiopia in 1952, but won its independence in 1993 following a bitter civil war.

**3** Zambia was ruled by Kenneth Kaunda from independence in 1964 until 1991; he became a leading figure in the Organization of African Unity.

**4** A 20,000-strong United Nations force intervened in the Congo in 1960 to assist in expelling the Belgians.

**5** Liberia was the only African country never to experience colonialism; but civil war broke out in 1985.

**6** Italian and British Somaliland were united as Somalia in 1960, but civil war broke out in the 1980s over the disputed Ogaden region.

## TIMELINE

### North & east Africa

**1944** French leader de Gaulle promises representative government to French colonies

**1954** Algerian National Liberation Front (FLN) declares war on French

**1974** Marxists oust emperor Haile Selassie in Ethiopia

**1984–85** Civil war in Eritrea leads to widespread famine in Ethiopia

**1946** Houphouet-Boigny of Liberia founds African Democratic Federation

**1962** End of war in Algeria against French rule

**1977–88** Somali forces clash with Ethiopia in a claim over the Ogaden area

**1992** Civil war in Algeria between Islamic fundamentalists and government

**1949** Mau Mau movement founded in Kenya

**1963** State of emergency ends in Kenya with independence

### West & central Africa

**1954** Gold Coast's National Liberation Movement begins

**1965** Southern Rhodesia's whites declare unilateral independence (UDI)

**1975** Civil war breaks out in Angola immediately after independence

**1994** Ethnic conflict in Rwanda results in mass slaughter and a refugee crisis

**1956** Representative government promised to Nigeria

**1967–70** Biafran war brings famine to eastern Nigeria

**1958** French colonies hold referenda on independence

**1961** Wars of liberation begin in Portuguese colonies

SPAIN

Tangier · Ceuta *to Spain* · Oran
Rabat · Fez · Melilla *to Spain*
≈ MOROCCO
1956 independent
Marrakech
☆1960

ITALY
GREECE
TURKEY

Annaba (Bone) · Tunis
Algiers · Sétif
Sousse
Gades · TUNISIA 1956 independent
Tripoli
Misurata

Malta
*Mediterranean Sea*
Crete

CYPRUS
SYRIA
LEBANON
ISRAEL
IRAQ
JORDAN

ALGERIA
1962 independent
☆1954–62
☆1992
☆1962

Benghazi · Derna · Tobruk

Alexandria
Cairo
Port Said ☆1956
Suez ☆1956

EGYPT
☆1974

OMAN

LIBYA
1947–51 under Anglo–French administration,
1951 independent

*HOGGAR MASSIF* SAHARA DESERT
*TIBESTI MASSIF*

JULIUS NYERERE, president of Tanzania 1964–85, attempted to introduce a uniquely African form of peasant socialism.

MALI
1960 independent
☞1971–74, 1983
(French West Africa)
Gao

*Niger* · Mopti

NIGER
1960 independent
Agadez ☞1971–74

Tahoua
Niamey
Zinder

BURKINA FASO
1960 independent
☞1971–75, 1977
Ouagadougou
·kasso

BENIN
1960 independent
NIGERIA
1960 independent

CHAD
1960 independent
☆from 1968
☞1971–74, 1983

Abéché

*Lake Chad*
Abéché
N'Djamena
Bongor

Administrative border
Political border

Port Sudan

*Red Sea*

ERITREA
1941–52 under British administration,
1952–91 to Ethiopia,
1993 independent
2 · Massawa
Asmara ☞1970–93

YEMEN

*Socotra to Yemen*

Omdurman · Khartoum
Wad Medani
El Obeid
SUDAN
1956 independent
☆1955–72
☆1973

Mekele
DJIBOUTI
(French Somaliland)
1977 independent
☞1983
Djibouti
Dese
Berbera
Burao
(British Somaliland)
1960 to Somalia

GHANA 1957 independent
TOGO 1960 independent
☞1971–74, 1977, 1983
Kumasi
IVORY COAST 1960 independent
☆1981
Yamoussoukro
Abidjan
Accra
Lomé
Porto Novo
Lagos
Ilorin
Oshogbo
Abuja
Kano

☆1967–69
☆1967–70, 1971–74

Sarh
Doba
CENTRAL AFRICAN REPUBLIC
1960 independent
☞1974
Bambari
Bossangoa
Bangui

*(French Equatorial Africa)*

Addis Ababa
ETHIOPIA
1936–41 to Italy,
1941 independence restored
☞from 1962
☞1973–79, from 1980

Harer
OGADEN
6
SOMALIA
(Italian Somaliland)
1960 independent
☆from 1963
☞1974–75, from 1980
Mogadishu
Marka

Port Harcourt
CAMEROON
1960 independent
Malabo · Yaoundé
Douala
*Bioko (Fernando Póo) to Equatorial Guinea*
EQUATORIAL GUINEA
(Spanish Guinea)
1968 independent
Bata
SÃO TOMÉ & PRÍNCIPE
1975 independent
São Tomé
GABON
1960 independent
Libreville
Port Gentil
Moanda

4 · *Congo*
DEMOCRATIC REPUBLIC OF CONGO
(Belgian Congo)
1960 independent,
Congo until 1971,
Zaire 1971–97
☞1960–61
☞1960–65, 1978–97

Kisangani

UGANDA
1962 independent
☆1980
RWANDA
1962 independent
☆1995–96
Kampala
Entebbe
☆1978–79
Kigali
☆1962–65, 1995–96
BURUNDI
1962 independent
Bujumbura
☆1972, 1995
☆1962–65

KENYA
(British East Africa)
1963 independent
☆Mau Mau, 1952–60
Mbale
Kisuma
Meru
Nairobi

Kisumu
*Lake Turkana*

Mombasa
*Pemba*
Malindi

*INDIAN OCEAN*

Victoria
SEYCHELLES
1976 independent

CONGO
1960 independent
☞1960–61
Brazzaville
Port Noire
Boma
Kinshasa (Leopoldville)
Cabinda *to Angola*

*ATLANTIC OCEAN*

Kananga
Mbuji Mayi
*Kasai*
*Lake Tanganyika*

TANZANIA
(Tanganyika)
1961 independent,
Republic of Tanganyika and Zanzibar until 1964
☞1983

Mwanza
*Lake Victoria*
Tanga
Pangani
Dodoma
Zanzibar 1963 to Tanzania
Dar es Salaam
Mbeya
*Lake Malawi*

Kismaayo

Luanda
Malange
ANGOLA
1975 independent
☆1961–75
☆1975–92
☞1971–74, 1983
Benguela · Lobito
Huambo
Namibe · Lubango

Lubumbashi
Mufulira
Chingola · Ndola
Luanshya
Kabwe
ZAMBIA
(Northern Rhodesia)
1964 independent
3 ☞1979, 1983
Lusaka
Livingstone

MALAWI
(Nyasaland)
1964 independent
Lilongwe

COMOROS
1975 independent
Moroni
*Mayotte to France*

Nacala
Nampula
Mozambique
Mahajanga

MOZAMBIQUE
1975 independent
Quelimane
Beira
☞1964–75
☞1971–74, 1983

NAMIBIA
(South-West Africa)
1949 to South Africa
1990 independent
☆1966–90
Swakopmund
Walvis Bay *to South Africa until 1994*
Windhoek

BOTSWANA
(Bechuanaland)
1966 independent
Francistown
Serowe
Mahalapye
Gaborone
Keetmanshoop

ZIMBABWE
(Southern Rhodesia)
1980 fully independent
Harare (Salisbury)
Bulawayo
☆1966–80
Mutare
☞1964–94
☆1983

MADAGASCAR
1960 independent
Toamasina
Antananarivo (Tananarive)
Toliara

MAURITIUS
1968 independent
*Réunion to France*

SOUTH AFRICA
1961 Republic
Johannesburg
Springs
Pretoria
Bloemfontein
Durban
East London
Cape Town
*Cape of Good Hope*
Port Elizabeth

SWAZILAND
1968 independent
☞1983
Mbabane
Lomba
Maputo

LESOTHO
1966 independent
☞1974, 1983
Maseru

*Vaal* · *Orange* · *Limpopo* · *Zambezi*

**Legend:**

prewar colonial powers
- Belgium
- France
- Italy
- Portugal
- Spain
- United Kingdom

territory placed under UN trusteeship, 1946

Federation of Rhodesia and Nyasaland, 1953–63

border, 1997

☆ anti-colonial war
☆ civil war
☆ interstate war
☞ famine or humanitarian crisis
area at risk of desertification, 1990s
desert
movement of refugees
migrant labor
oilfield
≈ hydroelectric power station

0 _____ 1000 km
0 _____ 800 mi

See also 89 (19th-century Africa);
104 (north Africa between the wars)

After Egypt's President Sadat visited Jerusalem in 1977, US President Carter arranged meetings between Sadat and Israeli Prime Minister Begin at Camp David which led to a treaty in 1979 between Israel and Egypt (the first Arab state to take such a step). This recognized the state of Israel, promised autonomy to the Palestinians in Gaza and the West Bank, and returned the Sinai to Egypt.

The Palestine Liberation Organization (PLO) now took on the main task of fighting Israel, through terrorist activities in Europe and from its Al Fatah bases in Lebanon, where civil war was raging between Christian Phalangist and Islamic forces and where, since 1976, Syria had provided the main authority. In 1978 Israel invaded and UN forces struggled to keep apart the armies of Israel, Syria and the Christian militia. Sadat was assassinated by Islamic activists in 1981 but his successor Hosni Mubarak continued his policies. Trying to restore stability to the region, the United States brokered an agreement that the PLO leave Beirut for Tunis, but Lebanon's civil war continued until Syria restored peace in the early 1990s; but Hizbollah fighters, funded by Iran, still used Lebanese bases for raids on Israel.

The political force of Islam had been dramatically seen in Iran, where the pro-western shah was overthrown in 1979 by street demonstrations in support of the Ayatollah Khomeini. As president of the new theocratic republic, Khomeini severed diplomatic relations with Israel, welcomed PLO leader Yassir Arafat to Tehran and defined the United States as the "main enemy of mankind". US embassy staff were taken hostage; 52 stayed in captivity for more than a year, despite a trade embargo and an abortive rescue mission that summed up the US failure to deal with this new force in regional politics.

Khomeini's resurgent Shiite Islam and apparent intentions of dominating the Middle East, led Saddam Hussein, Ba'athist leader of predominantly Sunni Iraq, to invade Iran in 1980. War between the two states continued for eight years, mainly in the oil-producing region around Abadan. Neither won a clear victory despite almost a million casualties and great damage to oil installations on both sides. After the ceasefire in 1988, Saddam revived an old Iraqi claim on the rich, pro-western emirate of Kuwait, and invaded in 1990. To his surprise, the United Nations condemned the move and imposed sanctions on Iraq. Saudi Arabia, fearing further Iraqi expansion, permitted its territory to be used as a base for an attack on Iraq. Despite Soviet support for Iraq, the United Nations agreed to the use of force, and war broke out in January 1991. Iraq tried to draw the entire region into the conflict by goading Israel with missile attacks, but the American-led UN coalition (including Egypt and Syria) managed to limit the scope of the conflict and won a quick victory by bombing followed by a devastating ground attack.

The postwar settlement proved less than straightforward. The coalition had no mandate to topple Saddam and did not wish to take power in Baghdad.

## Legend

| | |
|---|---|
| —— | border of Soviet Union to 1991 |
| ☐ | member of OPEC |
| ☐ | member of NATO |
| ☐ | Egypt, 1983 |
| ☐ | Israel, 1983 |
| ▨ | territory restored to Egypt, May 1979–Apr 1982 |
| ▨ | area occupied by Israel |
| ▨ | territory captured by Iraq, Sep–Dec 1980 |
| ▨ | territory captured by Iran, Oct 1984 |
| Qom | center of Islamic revolution in Iran, 1970s |
| ➤ | PLO diaspora, 1982 |
| 🔥 | Iran–Iraq war air strike, 1980–88 |
| ▢ | area of Shiite population, 1983 |
| ▢ | area claimed by Kurds as national homeland |
| ○ | Anti-Iraq coalition state, 1990–91 |
| ✚ | Coalition air base, 1990–91 |
| ➤ | Coalition offensive, 1991 |
| — | UN-imposed Iraqi "no-fly" zone |
| ▭ | UN peace-keeping force |
| ➤ | movement of refugees |
| — | migrant labor |
| — | border, 1997 |
| ▲ | oilfield |
| — | oil pipeline |
| ▢ | desert |

The attack ceased once Kuwait was liberated. Civil war broke out in Iraq as Shiites in the south and the Kurds in the north both sought to secede. Saddam remained in power, destroying the Shiite powerbase and forcing two million Kurds to seek asylum in Iran and Turkey, before the UN stepped in to enforce no-fly zones and safe havens from Iraqi attack. Devastating sanctions were imposed, but Saddam rebuilt his military base, including chemical weapons (forbidden by the postwar agreement); he also gradually restored his authority over the Kurdish areas.

Meanwhile, the Camp David agreements on Palestinian rights failed to materialize: Jewish settlers moved into the West Bank and built virtual fortresses there. In 1987 the Gaza and West Bank Palestinians began the *intifada* (uprising) against Israeli intransigence. Eventually a peace process was agreed, with phased Israeli withdrawals and recognition of a Palestinian National Authority under Arafat, initially only in Jericho but later intended to include Gaza and other areas. However, Israel faced a rightwing backlash and prime minister Rabin was murdered in 1995. Thereafter moves toward Palestinian self rule advanced slowly amid mutual suspicion.

## TIMELINE

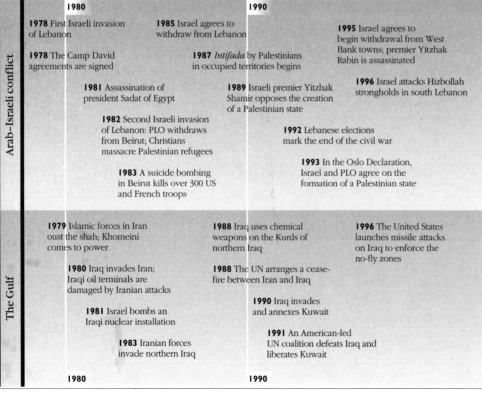

### Arab–Israeli conflict

**1978** First Israeli invasion of Lebanon

**1978** The Camp David agreements are signed

**1981** Assassination of president Sadat of Egypt

**1982** Second Israeli invasion of Lebanon: PLO withdraws from Beirut; Christians massacre Palestinian refugees

**1983** A suicide bombing in Beirut kills over 300 US and French troops

**1985** Israel agrees to withdraw from Lebanon

**1987** *Intifada* by Palestinians in occupied territories begins

**1989** Israeli premier Yitzhak Shamir opposes the creation of a Palestinian state

**1992** Lebanese elections mark the end of the civil war

**1993** In the Oslo Declaration, Israel and PLO agree on the formation of a Palestinian state

**1995** Israel agrees to begin withdrawal from West Bank towns; premier Yitzhak Rabin is assassinated

**1996** Israel attacks Hizbollah strongholds in south Lebanon

### The Gulf

**1979** Islamic forces in Iran oust the shah; Khomeini comes to power

**1980** Iraq invades Iran; Iraqi oil terminals are damaged by Iranian attacks

**1981** Israel bombs an Iraqi nuclear installation

**1983** Iranian forces invade northern Iraq

**1988** Iraq uses chemical weapons on the Kurds of northern Iraq

**1988** The UN arranges a cease-fire between Iran and Iraq

**1990** Iraq invades and annexes Kuwait

**1991** An American-led UN coalition defeats Iraq and liberates Kuwait

**1996** The United States launches missile attacks on Iraq to enforce the no-fly zones

ARMENIA

AZERBAIJAN

Baku

TURKMENISTAN

Yerevan

*Caspian
Sea*

to Azerbaijan

Mashhad
(Meshed)

Lake
Van

Tabriz

Lake
Urmia

Diyarbakir

Zakhu
Dahuk

KURDISTAN

Qazvin

Mosul
Arbil
southern limit
1991

Kirkuk
Sulamaniyah

Tehran

Baiji

Kifri
Qasr-e-Shirin

Hamadan

Qom

SYRIA

*Euphrates*

Bahr al
Tharthar

*Tigris*

Kerman

IRAN

**1**

*Diyala*

Ilam

Khorramabad

Isfahan

IRAQ

Baghdad

**5**
northern limit, 1996

Al Hillah

Al Kut

Dezful

Masjed Soleyman

An Najaf

northern limit, 1992

Ramhormoz

Bandar Khomeyni

Khorramshahr

Basra

Abadan

Al Faw

*Shatt
al-Arab*

from 1991

KUWAIT

Kharg Island

Shiraz

Kuwait

Bushire

Bandar Abbas

*Larak*

**4**

*Straits of Hormuz*

to Oman

Dhahran

Damman

BAHRAIN

Al Manamah

Al Ahsa

Doha

QATAR

Abu Dhabi

Muscat

*An Nafud*

Buraydah

UNITED ARAB EMIRATES

OMAN

from Bangladesh, India, Pakistan, Philippines and Sri Lanka

*Arabian
Sea*

Riyadh

Al Kharj

SAUDI ARABIA

Medina

Yanbu al Bahr

Jiddah

Mecca

**2**

Taif

*Rub al Khali*

Port Sudan

*Red
Sea*

Khamis Mushayt

PEOPLE'S
DEMOCRATIC
REPUBLIC OF
YEMEN
1967–1990

ERITREA

Asmera

YEMEN ARAB
REPUBLIC
1962–1990

YEMEN
united in 1990

Sana

Mukalla

Al Hudaydah

ETHIOPIA

DJIBOUTI

Ta'izz

Aden

SOMALIA

0      400 km
0      300 mi

---

**1** Khomeini's Shiite revolution in Iran led to a drastic reversal of pro-western and liberal ways of life, forcing many women back into *purdah*.

**2** For three days in 1979, militant Islamists seized Mecca's Grand Mosque, protesting against Saudi corruption.

**3** Beirut was devastated by the rival militias (including the Islamic Druze, two Shiite militias - Amal and Hizbollah - two Palestinian factions as well as the Christian Phalangists) in the civil war 1975–89.

**4** The Strait of Hormuz, one of the world's most important waterways, was mined and partially blocked by sunken ships during the First Gulf War, despite US Navy patrols.

**5** Baghdad was subjected to pinpoint missile attack during the coalition's assault early in 1991.

**6** In 1996-97, Arab–Israeli tensions focussed on building projects, including a Jewish tunnel under the temple mound, an underground mosque, and a Jewish housing project in East Jerusalem.

---

*Inset map legend:*

area occupied by Israel, 1967

territorial control, 1982
Christian militia
PLO and Muslim militia
Syria
United Nations

○ PLO base

→ Israeli advance June 1982

area occupied by Israel, Feb 1984

border, 1984

**3**

Beirut

Zahle

LEBANON

*Awwali*

*Litani*

Sidon

Jezzine

Qatana

Nabatea

Hasbaya

Marjayoun

Zrariye

Tyre

Qiryat
Shemona

SYRIA

El Quneitra

*Mediterranean
Sea*

*Jordan*

GOLAN
HEIGHTS

Nahariyya

Rafid

ISRAEL

Zefat

Tiberias

*Sea of
Galilee*

Fiq

Haifa

JORDAN

0      50 km
0      50 mi

See also 104 (Middle East between the wars);
115 (Arab–Israeli conflict to 1977)

When Communist control over eastern Europe collapsed in 1989, tension between the North Atlantic Treaty Organization (NATO) and the Warsaw Pact dissolved. However, many former Soviet satellite countries and, from 1991, the old Soviet republics, suffered problems of social restructuring, while the western countries faced disagreements over how to cooperate politically and economically.

The rapid reunification of Germany signaled the end of the bi-polar Europe and demonstrated many of the problems inherent in the creation of a new one. There were fears that a resurgent Germany at the geographical center of the continent would dominate Europe and create an instability similar to that which existed before 1914. In the short term, however, the price of German reunification was high. To achieve its political aims, the former West Germany was faced with a huge bill for taking over East Germany's backward economy. Germany's dominance in European finance meant that the costs of reunion were felt beyond its own borders. Interest rates rose across Europe, and in 1992 Britain and others were forced to leave the Exchange Rate Mechanism (ERM), which had been introduced to guarantee economic stability in the European Union (EU) and lead to eventual monetary union.

The failure to maintain the integrity of the ERM called into question the creation of more unified financial structures within the European Union (EU; formerly EC). This failure caused doubts to resurface in several member-states about the need for, and price of, a single European currency, planned for introduction in the late 1990s. Parallel with the debate about "deepening" the union was the question of "widening" it to include countries that had formerly chosen or been forced to stay outside. While many of the formerly Soviet-dominated countries were clamoring to join the Union, some countries (including Britain and Denmark) saw vociferous anti-EU campaigns, and a referendum on joining led to a "no" vote in Norway. As fears rose of migration, international terrorism and drug smuggling, doubts arose of the wisdom of the agreement to allow free movement of goods, people and services across the EU from 1992. In 1995 several countries abolished border controls between them, though others viewed this decision with disquiet.

Western Europe's division over such questions was heightened by instability in the east. The euphoria surrounding the demise of communism was soon replaced by uncertainty. The new governments of eastern Europe and the states of the former Soviet Union faced unprecedented difficulties in turning state-run "command economies" into market-driven ones. The nascent democracies often appeared fragile, not least in Russia itself where Boris Yeltsin, a president of authoritarian instincts but failing health, was faced with powerful forces both of reaction and radical reform, and problems of high unemployment and inflation, potent organized crime, alarming ethnic conflict and resurgent Russian nationalism.

Meanwhile, war was seen within Europe for the first time since 1945. Resurgent nationalism led to ethnic conflicts in Armenia and Azerbaijan, then engulfed Europe's heart as Yugoslavia tore itself apart. Here as elsewhere, different nationalities had been held together by the shackles of authoritarian

**Legend:**
- ⋯⋯ borders, 1997
- ☐ member state of EU, 1997
- ☐ associated state of EU
- ☐ member state of EFTA
- ☐ state with EU cooperation agreement
- **SPAIN** member state of NATO
- **1989** year of application for EU membership
- ── former boundary of Warsaw Pact
- ── implementation of "open frontier" Schengen agreement, 1995
- ☆ area of ethnic/nationalist tension

ethnic composition of Bosnia–Herzegovina, pre-1991
- ☐ more than 60 percent Croat
- ☐ more than 60 percent Muslim
- ☐ more than 60 percent Serb
- ☐ ethnically mixed area
- ◠ Bosnian–Croat Federation, 1995
- ◠ Bosnian Serb Republic, 1995
- ▨ Croatian territory under Serbian control, 1995
- ◉ UN-designated "safe havens"

0           800 km
0           600 mi

## TIMELINE

### Eastern Europe

| 1990 | 1992 | 1994 | 1996 |
|---|---|---|---|
| **1989** Fall of the Communist regimes in Poland, Hungary, Czechoslovakia, Bulgaria, East Germany, and Romania | **1991** A failed Communist coup leads to the breakup of the Soviet Union | **1993** Russia adopts a new constitution, giving the president increased powers | **1995** US president Clinton achieves agreement between the warring parties in Bosnia in Dayton Accord |
| **1989** Ethnic conflicts begin in Azerbaijan and Armenia | **1992** Bosnia-Herzegovina breaks away from Yugoslavia | **1994** Chechen nationalists are crushed by the Russian army at Grozny, southern Russia | **1996** Elections in Russia confirm Yeltsin's position |
| **1990** Slovenia breaks away from Yugoslavia | **1992** Siege of Sarajevo by the Bosnian Serbs begins | **1995** Croatia launches offensive against Serbs in Krajina and eastern Slavonia | |
| **1990** Croat-held Dubrovnik is shelled by Serb forces | **1993** Czechoslovakia splits into the Czech Republic and Slovakia | | |

### Western Europe

| 1990 | 1992 | 1994 | 1996 |
|---|---|---|---|
| **1990** The European Bank for Reconstruction and Development is founded | **1992** The EU single market comes into force | **1994** Norway rejects membership of the EU | **1996** Intergovernmental Conference (IGC) is held to explore the future of Europe |
| **1991** EU heads of government define a strategy for closer political and financial union at Maastricht | **1992** France and Germany found a joint army (Eurocorps) to strengthen the Western European Union | **1995** Austria, Sweden and Finland join the EU | **1997** NATO offers membership to Hungary, Poland and Czech Republic (from 1999) |
| | | **1995** Schengen agreement allows some open frontiers | |
| 1990 | 1992 | 1994 | 1996 |

communism. The country split into its constituent republics but – unlike in Czechoslovakia where a similar divorce occurred – this took no account of the ethnic complexity on the ground.

With the Serbs in the grip of a militant nationalist spirit, and with Bosnia's population divided culturally and religiously between Bosnians, Croats and Serbs, the conflict focused on Bosnia– Herzogovina and its capital Sarajevo, which had provided the stage for the outbreak of European war in 1914. The states of the former Yugoslavia – especially Bosnia and Croatia – experienced four years of bloody civil war, where atrocities and policies of "ethnic cleansing" forced hundreds of thousands of civilians to flee their homes. The war revealed the political and military impotence of the rest of Europe, which was unable to agree a common policy on the problem, preferring to leave the task of peace-keeping to the United Nations. Behind this failure lay a fear of the war spreading. For this reason, western Europe's economic and military ties with the east, particularly Russia, continued to grow in importance: foreign

policy cooperation agreements were signed while the EU assisted with trade and communication links.

The relationship between Europe and the United States was uncertain. The Western European Union (WEU), an alliance excluding the United States, was promoted as a alternative to the US-dominated NATO. In 1995, however, the United States succeeded where Europe had failed, and brokered a settlement in Bosnia. And in 1997 NATO and Russia signed an agreement that allowed for NATO's expansion and ended what remained of the Cold War.

**1** Berlin, symbol of the divided Europe from 1945, was quickly reunited and became capital of the new Germany in 1991.

**2** In 1991 at Maastricht the EU agreed to move to common economic and social conditions. Britain rejected Europe-wide provisions on social issues.

**3** In 1996, Venice was the focus of a movement, promoted by the separatist Northern League, for an independent "Padania", based on the Po valley.

**4** Prague, like many cities of eastern Europe, saw a boom in the early 1990s, with tourists and industrialists attracted by new opportunities and low costs.

**5** The mainly Muslim inhabitants of Sarajevo, capital of Bosnia, were besieged by Bosnian Serb forces from 1992 to 1995.

**6** Grozny, capital of the Chechens in their attempt to break away from the Russian Federation, was destroyed by the Russians in December 1994; elections in 1997 confirmed the desire for independence.

**7** A ceasefire from October 1994 to February 1996 interrupted 25 years of "troubles" in Northern Ireland, involving conflict between the Protestant majority, Catholic nationalists and the British government.

**8** Moscow and much of Russia suffered inflation, shortages, gangsterism and unemployment in the early 1990s in the rush to build a market economy.

See also 110 (Cold War Europe); 118 (Middle East)

The balance of world power was dramatically altered by the rise of the Asian economies in the last quarter of the 20th century; these were expected to be responsible for no less than half the world's growth by the year 2000. The region had plentiful supplies of cheap labor able to take on work of a highly technical nature. Infrastructural projects, heavy industry, textiles and high technology were developed in parallel to allow these countries – many of them, such as South Korea and China, devastated by political turmoil in mid-century – to emerge from poverty to compete on the world stage within a few decades.

The economic power driving this development was that of Japan, which trebled its investments in many of the east and southeast Asian countries after 1985 when a revaluation of the Yen made home-produced goods uncompetitive. By the late 1990s, the east and southeast Asian countries had overtaken the United States as Japan's main trading partner, with Malaysia, Hong Kong, Taiwan and, increasingly, China, as the main beneficiaries.

As the region developed, new countries opened up for development. Japan and Korea competed for a position in the Vietnam economy, especially after relations between Vietnam and the United States were normalized in 1995. Vietnam's transport and energy infrastructure was particularly weak following the destruction from the war that ended in 1975.

The tiger, or dragon, economies of Asia – South Korea, Hong Kong, Taiwan and Singapore – grew up alongside Japan. These newly industrializing economies (NIEs) had a number of characteristics in common. None had significant raw materials, so all had to export in order to grow. From the 1950s all nurtured their industries by government protection, and turned to export-oriented small light industries in the 1960s and 1970s. Like Japan, they had lost the advantage of low labor costs by the mid 1990s, and moved to invest in their neighbors with reserves of cheap labor, notably China.

By the 1980s South Korea had shifted its manufacturing base toward high technology, transport and heavy industry, and growth continued at a high rate. South Korean firms slowly opened trading links with the Communist regime in North Korea, but relationships between the two countries remained tense even after the death in 1994 of Kim Il Sung, ruler of North Korea since its foundation.

The foundations for Taiwan's economy were laid by Jiang Ching-kuo, the son of Chinese Nationalist leader Jiang Jieshi, from the late 1970s. He developed shipbuilding, petrochemicals and electronic industries, especially computers. By the mid-1990s this small island, remarkably, had the eighth largest trading power in the world. Mainland China, however, regarded Taiwan as a part of the People's Republic. Taiwan's democratic elections in 1987, and the election in 1996 of a leader more committed to an independent Taiwanese future, exacerbated tensions between the two. Hong Kong, China's small offshore island leased to Britain until 1997, moved toward trade and banking but retained its textile and other labor-intensive industries. Singapore, by contrast, pursued high-technology manufacture in conjunction with finance and business services.

In 1975, China had little or no foreign investment, no foreign loans and little direct trade with non-Communist states other than Japan. In 1978, vice-premier Deng Xiaoping embarked on economic and educational reforms, aiming to replace Mao Zedong's class struggle with the goal of economic modernization. Political reform, however, was not pursued and a prodemocracy movement that arose in the wake of economic reform was crushed in 1989. Despite worldwide condemnation of China's human rights record, China actively sought investment, trade and technology from overseas. South Korea located plant and machinery in China's special economic zones; but the tiger economies that did most in China were those with the strongest political or ethnic ties with the country – notably Singapore and Taiwan (even though trade between Taiwan and mainland China was officially illegal). From 1984 Hong Kong, many of whose inhabitants came from Guangdong province, increasingly shifted its production to nearby Chinese provinces to take advantage of lower labor costs. The return of Hong Kong to China in 1997 was a step toward further integration of the two economies.

Japan retained its status as economic superpower thanks to its technological superiority, even though its growth was slowing in the 1990s, and other Asian countries beside China were industrializing fast. Thailand, Malaysia and Indonesia – which has large reserves of oil and gas to finance the growth of heavy industries such as petrochemicals, shipbuilding and steel – were growing. The Philippines, too, opted in the mid-1990s for policies modeled on the successes of other economies of the region.

A few countries did not form part of the "Asian miracle": notably Cambodia and Myanmar (formerly Burma), where oppressive regimes deterred foreign

## Map legend

— border, 1997

■ original newly industrializing economies

emergent newly industrializing economies

Chinese special economic zone

little industrialization

Organization for Economic Cooperation and Development

⌒ ASEAN member state (Association of Southeast Asian Nations), 1967

▷ Japanese investment flow

■ population over 1,000,000

⚓ port

Manila industrial center

✳ Chinese prodemocracy demonstration

✵ separatist movement

— fiber-optic cable, 1996

source of major resource

◇ gold

◇ copper

✦ nickel

✦ tin

◇ other metal

⚱ oilfield

0 ————— 1200 km

0 ————— 800 mi

BHUTAN

NEPAL

BANGLADESH

INDIA

## TIMELINE

### East Asia

**1980**

**1975** In Taiwan, Jiang Ching-kuo plans for rapid growth

**1978** In China, Deng Xiaoping advocates economic reforms; China and Japan sign a trade agreement

**1979** China and the United States normalize relations

**1984** The NIEs begin to invest in China

**1984** Revaluation of the Yen leads Japanese countries to invest in southeast Asia

**1990**

**1987** Democratic elections are held in Taiwan, and martial law is lifted for the first time since 1949

**1989** Japan becomes the world's largest foreign aid donor and supplier of capital

**1989** In China, the prodemocracy movement led by students is crushed at Tiananmen Square, Beijing

**1993** Japan's Liberal Democratic Party loses power for the first time since 1955

**1994** Kim Il Sung, Stalinist president of North Korea, dies

**1997** Death of Deng Xiaoping; Hong Kong returns to Chinese rule

### Southeast Asia

**1975** The Khmer Rouge take over Cambodia, leading to mass killings

**1975** Collapse of South Vietnam and creation of a single Vietnamese state

**1976** Indonesia annexes Portuguese East Timor

**1977** The Communist regime in Laos signs a friendship treaty with Vietnam

**1978–79** Vietnam invades Cambodia to crush Khmer Rouge regime; China invades northern Vietnam

**1980**

**1986** Prodemocracy candidate Corazon Aquino takes over from Ferdinand Marcos after the Philippines presidential elections

**1986** Laos signs an economic development agreement with Thailand

**1987** Democratic elections are held in South Korea

**1988** A military junta seizes power in Burma

**1989** Australia initiates the Asia Pacific Economic Cooperation Forum

**1991** Burmese prodemocracy leader Aung San Suu Kyi is imprisoned by the military government

**1992** Vietnam opens a free-trade zone, funded by Taiwan

**1990**

**1** Taiwan's economic success was based on heavy investment in human resources: in 1995, four fifths of 18-year-olds were in higher education.

**2** Singapore's prosperity was built up by prime minister Lee Kuan Yew from 1959–90. His much-criticized authoritarian social policies were intended to ensure an orderly society.

**3** The gap between rich and poor was greater in Bangkok than in the other Asian NIEs, despite the efforts of the Thai government.

**4** In the late 1990s Japan endured ongoing recession for the first time since 1945, as the other east Asian economies competed in its traditional markets.

**5** Australia, which in the late 1990s was considering severing its last links with the British crown, was the most prominent supporter of the 1989 Asia Pacific Economic Cooperation Forum (APEC).

**6** Beijing's Tiananmen Square massacre of June 1989 was Deng Xiaoping's response to demands for democratic freedoms that would match the dramatic economic liberalization he had promoted.

investment, and Laos, which had poor infrastructure. Nevertheless the cheap pools of labor in these countries were expected to prove attractive to investors as wages elsewhere began to rise.

Politically, despite the intrusion of global market forces, the region saw the survival of Communism as the dominant ideology in China, Vietnam, North Korea and among some Filipino insurgents. Hong Kong witnessed belated democratic development after 1992 in an effort to protect the rights of its inhabitants after it was reincorporated into China in 1997. Profound changes in attitude toward the rising

Asian economies occurred among the older democracies – Canada, Australia and New Zealand as well as the United States – of the Pacific rim. Initially seeing themselves as investors and suppliers to the new economies, they rapidly became consumers of Asian goods. By the 1980s the Commonwealth countries had moved away from historic ties with Britain and accepted the arrival of Asian-owned companies, and radically changed their immigration laws to permit the settlement of Asian immigrants.

See also 111 (the Americas); 113 (east Asia to 1976); 114 (southeast Asia to 1976)

The years from 1975 saw seismic shifts in world politics. The end of the Cold War permitted longstanding problems in Europe, the Middle East and Africa to be addressed. Fears of imminent nuclear, environmental or demographic disaster, widely predicted in the preceding decades, calmed by the late 1990s, though the world's future political shape was still uncertain.

Central to these changes was the collapse of the Soviet Union. Under Leonid Brezhnev the country stagnated, and the *détente*, or cooling of the international tension, of the 1970s came to an end with a Soviet invasion of Afghanistan. The United States emerged from its post-Vietnam crisis of confidence under tough-talking president Ronald Reagan who changed the mood in the early 1980s. The soaring costs of arms production, combined with the Soviet Union's technological deficit, led the new leader Mikhail Gorbachev to try to improve superpower relations and liberalize the Soviet system. In doing so he unleashed disintegrative forces he could not control.

Gorbachev did not resist the demands for increased independence from many of the USSR's eastern European satellites. In 1989–90 the peoples of eastern Europe took the opportunity to overthrow their Communist govern- ments. In the Soviet Union itself, the separate republics seceded from the Union and formed the Commonwealth of Independent States. The old order was not so easily replaced in Yugoslavia, which was ripped apart by ethnic conflict (▷ 119 ).

Meanwhile, greater centralization was occurring in western Europe, where the European Community (later the European Union) expanded in size, abolished many border restrictions and initiated moves toward political and economic union.

The collapse of the Soviet Union led to change in Africa, where problems of decolonization and debt had been exacerbated by superpower conflict. South Africa's role in opposing the spread of Communism vanished, and as American support for the regime was withdrawn, the burden of upholding *apartheid* grew. South Africa ceased interfering in the politics of other countries of the region, and in 1994 achieved majority rule under the charismatic president Nelson Mandela (▷ 117 ).

In the Middle East, both the west and the Soviet Union felt vul- nerable to the threat posed by Islamist movements to oil supplies and the loyalty of the Muslim areas of the USSR. The Islamist takeover of Iran in 1979 complicated the politics of the Middle East: Iraq was supported in a long war

| A. | Albania |
| AR. | Armenia |
| AU. | Austria |
| AZ. | Azerbaijan |
| B. | Belgium |
| BO. | Bosnia–Herzegovina |
| CAR. | Central African Republic |
| CR. | Croatia |
| C. | Czech Republic |
| D. | Denmark |
| DR. | Dominican Republic |
| GE. | Georgia |
| GER. | Germany |
| H. | Hungary |
| LE. | Lebanon |
| L. | Luxembourg |
| M. | Macedonia (Former Yugoslav Republic of) |
| N. | Netherlands |

| RO. | Romania |
| S. | Switzerland |
| SK. | Saint Kitts–Nevis |
| SV. | Saint Vincent & the Grenadines |
| SL. | Slovakia |
| SLV. | Slovenia |
| U. | United Arab Emira |
| YU. | Yugoslavia |

Alaska (United States)

CANADA

UNITED STATES

MEXICO

Hawaii (United States)

BAHAMAS
HAITI
Puerto Rico (United States)
BELIZE   CUBA
JAMAICA
DR.
GUATEMALA
EL SALVADOR
HONDURAS
NICARAGUA
COSTA RICA
PANAMA
ANTIGUA & BARBUDA
DOMINICA
ST LUCIA
GRENADA
SK.
BARBADOS
SV.
TRINIDAD & TOBAGO
GUYANA
SURINAME
French Guiana (France)
VENEZUELA
COLOMBIA
ECUADOR
PERU
BRAZIL
BOLIVIA
PARAGUAY
CHILE
ARGENTINA
URUGUAY

French Polynesia (France)

Falkland Islands (Britain)

## TIMELINE

**1979** China and the United States establish diplomatic relations

**1979** Shiite Muslims lead an Islamic revolution in Iran

**1975** The Helsinki Agreement between the USA and USSR establishes an atmosphere of détente

**1979** The Soviet Union invades Afghanistan to support the Marxist regime

**1982** Falklands War between Britain and Argentina

**1987** The USA and USSR agree to limit intermediate nuclear weapons

**1985** Mikhail Gorbachev comes to power in the Soviet Union

The Americas
Europe
Middle East
Africa
Asia and Australasia

1975

1985

**1975** Angola and Mozambique gain independence

**1980** Zimbabwe wins independence under majority rule

**1986** A nuclear plant at Chernobyl, USSR, explodes, causing damage throughout northern Europe

**1975** The US-backed South Vietnam regime falls

**1984** Indian prime minister Indira Gandhi is assassin- ated by Sikh bodyguards

**1986** The United States bombs Libya

**1977** Egypt's president Sadat visits Israel, initiating the Middle Eastern peace process

**1988** Iran and Iraq end the First Gulf War (begun 1980)

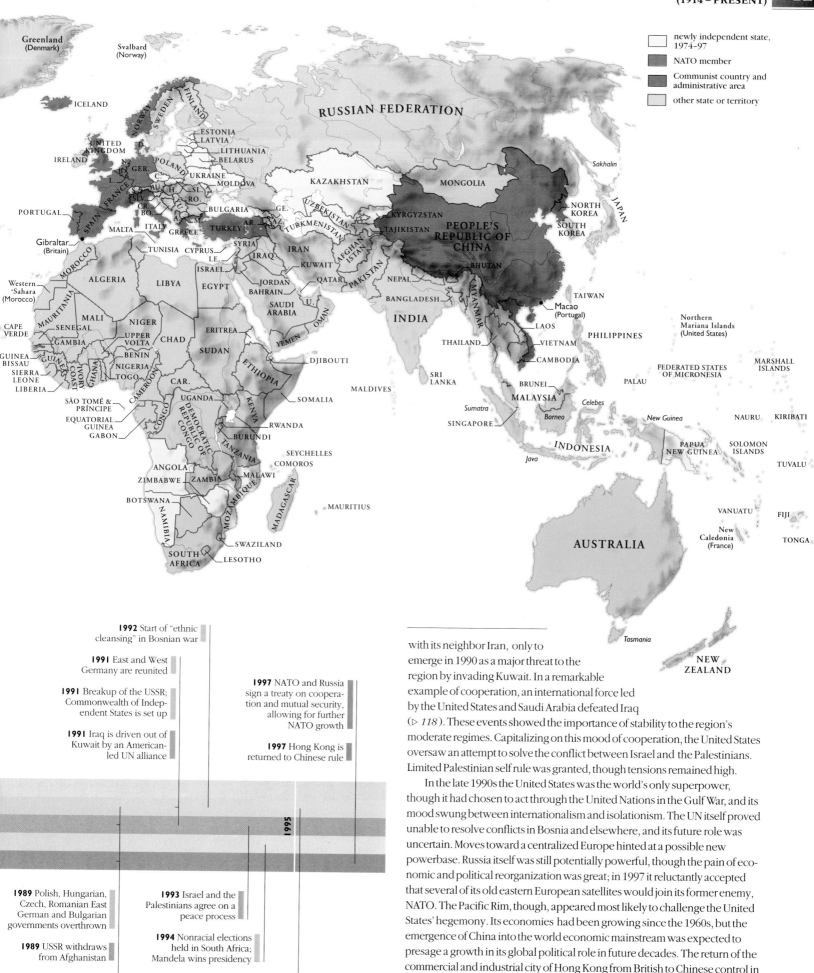

newly independent state, 1974-97

NATO member

Communist country and administrative area

other state or territory

Greenland
(Denmark)

Svalbard
(Norway)

ICELAND

RUSSIAN FEDERATION

NORWAY
SWEDEN
FINLAND

UNITED
KINGDOM
IRELAND

ESTONIA
LATVIA
LITHUANIA
BELARUS

D.

POLAND
GER.
UKRAINE
MOLDOVA

C.
AU.
L.
FRANCE
SLV.
H.
SL.
CR.
BO.
RO.
BULGARIA

KAZAKHSTAN

MONGOLIA

NORTH
KOREA
SOUTH
KOREA

Sakhalin

JAPAN

PORTUGAL
SPAIN
M.
ITALY
GREECE

MALTA

GE.
TURKEY
AR.
AZ.

UZBEKISTAN
TURKMENISTAN

KYRGYZSTAN
TAJIKISTAN

PEOPLE'S
REPUBLIC OF
CHINA

Gibraltar
(Britain)

TUNISIA
CYPRUS
SYRIA
LE.
IRAQ
IRAN

AFGHAN-
ISTAN

PAKISTAN

BHUTAN

TAIWAN

Western
'Sahara
(Morocco)

MOROCCO

ALGERIA
LIBYA
EGYPT

ISRAEL
JORDAN
BAHRAIN
KUWAIT
QATAR
U.
SAUDI
ARABIA
OMAN

NEPAL

INDIA

BANGLADESH

MYANMAR

Macao
(Portugal)

Northern
Mariana Islands
(United States)

CAPE
VERDE

MAURITANIA
MALI
SENEGAL
NIGER
UPPER
VOLTA
CHAD
SUDAN
ERITREA

DJIBOUTI

YEMEN

LAOS
THAILAND
VIETNAM
CAMBODIA

PHILIPPINES

FEDERATED STATES
OF MICRONESIA

MARSHALL
ISLANDS

GAMBIA
GUINEA
BISSAU
GUINEA
SIERRA
LEONE
LIBERIA
IVORY
COAST
GHANA
BENIN
TOGO
NIGERIA
CAMEROON
CAR.
ETHIOPIA
SOMALIA

SRI
LANKA

MALDIVES

BRUNEI
MALAYSIA
SINGAPORE

PALAU

SÃO TOMÉ &
PRÍNCIPE
EQUATORIAL
GUINEA
GABON
CONGO
DEMOCRATIC
REPUBLIC OF
CONGO
UGANDA
KENYA
RWANDA
BURUNDI
TANZANIA

SEYCHELLES
COMOROS

Sumatra
Borneo
Celebes
New Guinea
INDONESIA
Java
PAPUA
NEW GUINEA
SOLOMON
ISLANDS

NAURU
KIRIBATI

TUVALU

ANGOLA
ZIMBABWE
ZAMBIA
MALAWI
MOZAMBIQUE
MADAGASCAR
MAURITIUS

NAMIBIA
BOTSWANA
SWAZILAND
SOUTH
AFRICA
LESOTHO

AUSTRALIA

VANUATU
New
Caledonia
(France)

FIJI
TONGA

Tasmania

NEW
ZEALAND

**1992** Start of "ethnic cleansing" in Bosnian war

**1991** East and West Germany are reunited

**1991** Breakup of the USSR; Commonwealth of Independent States is set up

**1991** Iraq is driven out of Kuwait by an American-led UN alliance

**1997** NATO and Russia sign a treaty on cooperation and mutual security, allowing for further NATO growth

**1997** Hong Kong is returned to Chinese rule

1995

**1989** Polish, Hungarian, Czech, Romanian East German and Bulgarian governments overthrown

**1989** USSR withdraws from Afghanistan

**1989** Chinese pro-democracy demonstrations are crushed in Beijing

**1993** Israel and the Palestinians agree on a peace process

**1994** Nonracial elections held in South Africa; Mandela wins presidency

**1995** A US-brokered ceasefire is agreed in Bosnia–Herzegovina

with its neighbor Iran, only to emerge in 1990 as a major threat to the region by invading Kuwait. In a remarkable example of cooperation, an international force led by the United States and Saudi Arabia defeated Iraq (▷ 118). These events showed the importance of stability to the region's moderate regimes. Capitalizing on this mood of cooperation, the United States oversaw an attempt to solve the conflict between Israel and the Palestinians. Limited Palestinian self rule was granted, though tensions remained high.

In the late 1990s the United States was the world's only superpower, though it had chosen to act through the United Nations in the Gulf War, and its mood swung between internationalism and isolationism. The UN itself proved unable to resolve conflicts in Bosnia and elsewhere, and its future role was uncertain. Moves toward a centralized Europe hinted at a possible new powerbase. Russia itself was still potentially powerful, though the pain of economic and political reorganization was great; in 1997 it reluctantly accepted that several of its old eastern European satellites would join its former enemy, NATO. The Pacific Rim, though, appeared most likely to challenge the United States' hegemony. Its economies had been growing since the 1960s, but the emergence of China into the world economic mainstream was expected to presage a growth in its global political role in future decades. The return of the commercial and industrial city of Hong Kong from British to Chinese control in 1997 was an important step in this process (▷ 120) ∎

# Acknowledgments

## Text, timelines and maps

The authors and publishers readily acknowledge the work of a large number of scholars and published works, on which they have drawn in the preparation of this atlas. Many of these works remain in print, and can be used as reliable secondary reading on the many topics covered in this atlas. Among them are the following:

Adams, A.E., Matley, I.M. and McCagg, W.O. *An Atlas of Russian and East European History* (London 1967)

Ajayi, J.F.A. and Crowder, Michael (eds) *Historical Atlas of Africa* (Cambridge and New York 1985)

Allchin, B. and R. *The Birth of Indian Civilization: India and Pakistan before 500 BC* (2nd ed., London 1994)

Almond, M., Black, J. McKitterick, R., and Scarre, C. *The Times Atlas of European History* (London and New York 1994)

Ardagh, John with Jones, Colin *Cultural Atlas of France* (London and New York 1991)

Ashdown, P. *Caribbean History in Maps* (London and New York 1979)

Bagot Glubb, J. *The Great Arab Conquests* (London 1963)

Bahn, Paul G. (ed) *Cambridge Illustrated History of Archaeology* (Cambridge and New York 1996)

Baines, John and Malek, Jaromir *Atlas of Ancient Egypt* (Oxford and New York 1980)

Barraclough, G. (ed) *The Times Atlas of World History* (4th ed., London 1993 and New York 1994)

Bartlett, R. *The Making of Europe: Conquest, Colonisation and Cultural Change 950–1300* (London 1993)

Bayley, Christopher (ed) *Atlas of the British Empire* (London and New York 1989)

Black, C. and others *Cultural Atlas of the Renaissance* (London and New York 1993)

Black, Jeremy *The Cambridge Illustrated Atlas of Warfare: Renaissance to Revolution 1492–1792* (Cambridge and New York 1996)

Blunden, Caroline and Elvin, Mark *Cultural Atlas of China* (London and New York 1986)

Bolton, Geoffrey (ed) *The Oxford History of Australia* (Oxford and Melbourne 1994)

Braudel, Fernand *Civilization and Capitalism* (3 vols, revised ed., Princeton 1992)

Brown, Dee *The American West* (New York 1994)

Campbell, John (ed) *The Experience of World War II* (London and New York 1989)

Chadwick, Henry and Evans, Gillian R. (eds) *Atlas of the Christian Church* (London and New York 1987)

Champion, T., Gamble, C., Shennan, S. and Whittle, A. *Prehistoric Europe* (London 1984)

Chang, K.C. *The Archaeology of Ancient China* (Yale 1977)

Chard, C.S. *Northeast Asia in Prehistory* (Madison, USA 1974)

Coe, Michael, Snow, Dean and Benson, Elizabeth *Atlas of Ancient America* (London and New York 1986)

Coe, Michael *Mexico: from the Olmecs to the Aztecs* (4th ed., London and New York 1994)

Cohn-Sherbok, D. *Atlas of Jewish History* (London and New York 1994)

Collcutt, Martin, Jansen, Marius and Kumakura, Isao *Cultural Atlas of Japan* (London and New York 1988)

Connah, G. *African Civilizations: Precolonial cities and states in tropical Africa* (Cambridge and New York 1987)

Cook, J.M. *The Persian Empire* (London 1983)

Cornell, Tim and Matthews, John *Atlas of the Roman World* (London and New York 1982)

Cotterell, A. *East Asia* (London 1993, New York 1995)

Crawford, M. *The Roman Republic* (London 1978, Cambridge, Mass 1993)

Cunliffe, Barry (ed) *The Oxford Illustrated Prehistory of Europe* (Oxford and New York 1994)

Darby, H.C. and Fullard, Harold *The New Cambridge Modern History Atlas* (Cambrdge 1970)

Davies, R.H.C. *A History of Medieval Europe* (2nd ed., London and New York 1988)

Davis, Norman *Europe: a History* (Oxford and New York 1996)

Dear, I.C.B. and Foot, M.R.D. (eds) *The Oxford Companion to the Second World War* (Oxford and New York 1995)

de Lange, Nicholas *Atlas of the Jewish World* (London and New York 1984)

Elliott, J.H. (ed) *The Hispanic World* (London and New York 1991)

Fagan, Brian M. *The Journey from Eden: the Peopling of our World* (London and New York 1990)

Fagan, Brian M. *Ancient North America* (London and New York 1995)

Fage, J.D. and Oliver, R. (eds) *The Cambridge History of Africa* (Cambridge and New York 1975– )

Fernández-Armesto, Felipe (ed) *The Times Atlas of World Exploration* (London and New York 1991)

Fiedel, S.J. *Prehistory of the Americas* (2nd ed., Cambridge and New York 1992)

Freedman, Lawrence *Atlas of Global Strategy* (London and New York 1985)

Freeman-Grenville, G.S.P. *Historical Atlas of the Middle East* (New York 1993)

Frye, R.N. *The Heritage of Persia* (2nd ed., London 1976)

Gamble, C. *The Palaeolithic Settlement of Europe* (Cambridge 1986)

Gamble, C. *Timewalkers: the Prehistory of Global Colonization* (Stroud 1993, Cambridge, Mass. 1994)

Gaur, A. *A History of Writing* (London 1984, New York 1994)

Gilbert, Martin *The Atlas of Jewish History* (5th ed., London and New York 1996)

Graham Campbell, James (ed) *Cultural Atlas of the Viking World* (London and New York 1994)

Green, M.J. *The Celtic World* (London and New York 1995)

Griffiths, Ieuan L. *The Atlas of African Affairs* (London 1984)

*Grosser Historischer Weltatlas* (3 vols, Munich 1981)

Hall, D.G.E. *A History of South-east Asia* (4th ed., London 1981)

Handlin, O. *The History of the United States* (New York 1967)

Hartman, Tom *A World Atlas of Military History 1945–1984* (New York 1985)

Haywood, John *Historical Atlas of the Vikings* (London and New York 1995)

Haywood, John *Dark Age Naval Power* (London and New York 1991)

Holt, P.M., Lambeth, A.K.S. and Lewis, B. (eds) *The Cambridge History of Islam* (Cambridge 1970– )

Homberger, E. *Historical Atlas of North America* (London and New York 1995)

Hooper, Nicholas and Bennett, Matthew *The Cambridge Illustrated Atlas of Warfare: The Middle Ages 768–1487* (Cambridge and New York 1996)

Hosking, G. *A History of the Soviet Union* (London 1985)

Johnson, Gordon, Bayly, C. and Richards J.F. *The New Cambridge History of India* (Cambridge 1987– )

Johnson, Gordon *Cultural Atlas of India* (London 1995, New York 1996)

Kemp, B.J. *Ancient Egypt* (London 1989, New York 1992)

Kinder, H. and Hilgemann, W. *Atlas of World History* (2 vols, Munich, London and New York 1974)

King, P.D. *Charlemagne* (London 1986)

Kuhrt, A. *The Ancient Near East* (London and New York 1995)

Kulke, H. and Rothermund, D. *A History of India* (London 1990)

Langer, William L. *An Encyclopedia of World History* (5th ed., London and New York 1973)

Lee, K. *A New History of Korea* (Cambridge, Mass 1988)

Levi, Peter *Cultural Atlas of the Greek World* (London and New York 1984)

Lynch, J.H. *The Medieval Church* (Harlow 1992)

Mallory, J.P. *In Search of the Indo-Europeans* (London 1989, New York 1991)

Matthew, Donald *Atlas of Medieval Europe* (London and New York 1989)

McEvedy, Colin and Jones, Richard *Atlas of World Population History* (London 1978)

Milner, C.A., O'Connor, C.A. and Sandweiss, M. *The Oxford History of the American West* (Oxford and New York 1994)

Milner-Gulland, Robin with Dejevsky, Nikolai *Cultural Atlas of Russia and the Soviet Union* (London and New York 1989)

Moore, R.I. (ed) *The Hamlyn Historical Atlas* (London 1981)

Morgan, D. *The Mongols* (Oxford 1986, Cambridge, Mass 1990)

Moseley, M.E. *The Incas and their Ancestors* (London and New York 1993)

Murray, Oswyn *Early Greece* (2nd ed., London 1993)

Nile, R. and Clerk, C. *Cultural Atlas of Australia, New Zealand and the South Pacific* (London and New York 1995)

Ostrogorsky, G. *History of the Byzantine State* (revised ed., New Brunswick 1986)

Parker, W.H. *An Historical Geography of Russia* (London 1968)

Paxton, John *The Statesman's Yearbook Historical Companion* (London 1988)

Phillipson, D.W. *African Archaeology* (Cambridge 1993)

Pitcher, D.E. *An Historical Geography of the Ottoman Empire* (Leiden 1972)

Porter, A.N. (ed) *Atlas of British Overseas Expansion* (London 1991)

Pounds, Norman J.G. *An Historical Geography of Europe* (Cambridge 1990)

Reid, Anthony (ed) *Southeast Asia in the Early Modern Era: Trade, Power and Belief* (New York 1993)

Riasanovsky, N.V. *A History of Russia* (5th ed., Oxford and New York 1993)

Riley-Smith, Jonathon *The Atlas of the Crusades* (London and New York 1991)

Roaf, Michael and Postgate, Nicholas *Cultural Atlas of Mesopotamia* (London and New York 1990)

Roberts, J.M. *The Hutchinson History of the World* (London 1976)

Robinson, Francis *Atlas of the Islamic World since 1500* (London and New York, 1982)

Rogerson, John *Atlas of the Bible* (London and New York 1985)

Scammell, G.V. *The World Encompassed: the First European Maritime Empires c.800–1650* (London 1981)

Scarre, Dr Chris *Past Worlds: The Times Atlas of Archaeology* (London and New York 1988)

Schmidt, K.J. *An Atlas and Survey of South Asian History* (New York and London 1995)

Schwartzberg, Joseph E. (ed) *A Historical Atlas of South Asia* (revised ed., Chicago and London 1992)

Segal, Aaron *An Atlas of International Migration* (London and New Jersey 1993)

Sharer, R.J. *The Ancient Maya* (5th ed., Stanford Ca. 1994)

Shepherd, William R. *Shepherd's Historical Atlas* (9th ed., New York and London 1974)

Sinclair, Keith (ed) *The Oxford Illustrated History of New Zealand* (Oxford and Auckland 1990)

Sinor, D. (ed) *The Cambridge History of Early Inner Asia* (Cambridge 1990)

Smith, B.D. *The Emergence of Agriculture* (New York 1995)

Spence, J. *The Search for Modern China* (London and New York 1990)

Spence J.E. (ed) *The World Today* (London 1994)

Taylour, W. *The Mycenaeans* (2nd ed., London and New York 1990)

*The Times Atlas of the World* (8th ed., London and New York 1990)

Thornton, John K. *Africa and Africans in the Formation of the Atlantic World 1400-1680* (Cambridge and New York 1992)

Tindall, G. and Shi, D.E. *America, a Narrative History* (New York 1996)

Todd, M. *The Early Germans* (Oxford and Cambridge, Mass. 1992)

Twitchett, D. and Fairbank, J. (eds) *The Cambridge History of China* (15 vols, Cambridge and New York 1978–91 )

Vincent Mary and Stradling, R.A. *Cultural Atlas of Spain and Portugal* (London 1994, New York 1995)

Walbank F.W. *The Hellenistic World* (3rd ed., London 1992, Cambridge, Mass. 1993)

Wallace-Hadrill, J.M. *The Barbarian West 400–1000* (5th ed., Oxford and Cambridge, Mass. 1996)

Waller, Philip (ed) *Chronology of the 20th Century* (Oxford 1995)

*Webster's New Geographical Dictionary* (Springfield, Mass. 1984)

Whittle, A. *Neolithic Europe: a Survey* (Cambridge and New York 1985)

Winter, J.M. *The Experience of World War I* (London and New York 1988)

Wintle, J. *The Vietnam Wars* (London 1991)

## Photographs

Introductions: *Part 1:* Hutchison Library; *Part 2:* Images Colour Library; *Part 3:* Hutchison Library; *Part 4:* Images Colour Library; *Part 5:* Robert Harding Picture Library; *Part 6:* R. Ian Lloyd/Hutchison Library;

Maps: *104:* Saudi Aramco; *107:* ZEC/Dalkeith Poster Cards; *108:* Corbis-Bettmann/UPI; *111:* Popperfoto; *112:* Andromeda Oxford Limited; *117:* Hulton Getty.

Artwork references have been assembled from a wide variety of sources. Any individual or institution who can demonstrate that copyright may have been infringed is invited to contact Andromeda Oxford Ltd.

Figures refer to map numbers; **bold** type indicates major references.

# A

Aachen 38
Abbas I (the Great) 59, 64, 67
Abbasid caliphate 40–41, 43–45, 47, 51
  destruction of dynasty 49
Abelard, Peter 46
Abodrites 38, 41
Aboukir Bay, Battle of 78
Abrittus, Battle of 30
Abu Bakr, first caliph 37
Abushiri, Chief 89
Abyssinia see Ethiopia
Academy 34
Acadia 67, 71, 73. See also Nova Scotia
Acajutla 112
Acarnania 16, 20
Acaxee 70
Aceh 57, 60, 64, 67, 71, 95
Achaea, Achaeans 16, 20, 29
  Duchy of Achaea 52
  Principality of Achaea 48
  see also Mycenae, Mycenaean civilization
Achemenes 18
Achemenid empire 18, 19, 20, 22, 27
  Egypt 22, 35
  India 22
  Persian wars 22
Acheulian culture 1
Acre 48, 51
Actium, Battle of 24, 29
Adad-nirari II 14
Adal 57, 60, 72
Addis Ababa 104
Adelaide 82
Aden 64, 82, 97, 99, 104, 106
  East see Hadramaut
  see also Yemen
Adena 19, 22, 24, 28
Adil Shahis 61
Adowa 104
  Battle of 89, 97
Adrianople
  Battle of 33
  Ottoman capture 47
Adulis 35
Aegina 20
Aegyptus 28–29, 34. See also Egypt
Aeolia, Aeolian Greeks 16
Aeschylos 20
Aethelbald 38
Aetius 33
Afanasevo culture 9
Afghanistan, Afghans 47, 60–61, 64, 71, 76, 82–83, 86, 88, 97, 106, 109, 116
  Afghan Wars 82–83
  Soviet invasion 121
Africa 22, 28, **72**, **89**
  Anglo–Boer Wars 97
  Arab conquests 22
  Asante Wars 82, 86
  Berlin Conference 89, 97
  British colonies 79, 82, 86, 89, **89**
  Christian missionaries 62, 70, 72
  decolonization and nationalism 109, 116, **117**, 121
  Dutch colonies 71–72, 76, 79, 82, 86
  economic development 91
  European trade 57
  French colonies and trading bases 71–72, 82, 86, 89, 92
  German colonies 89
  hominid remains 1
  Iron Age 32, **35**, 36
  Italian colonies 92
  nomad invasions 32
  Ottoman empire 59–60, 71–72
  Portuguese colonies 64, 67, 71–72, 74, 76
  Roman province 29, 34
  scramble for Africa 86, **89**, 97
  single-origins theory 1–2
  slavery and the slave trade 62, 72, 74, 79, 82
  sub-Saharan **72**
  World War II 105–107, 109, 117
  see also individual states and peoples
African–Americans **85**, 92, 102, 111
African Democratic Federation 117
African Rift Valley 1
Afrikaners 82, 97
  Anglo–Boer Wars 97
Agadir crisis 89, 96
Agamemnon 11
Aghlabid emirate 40–41
Agincourt, Battle of 54
Agra 61, 83
Agricola (Georg Bauer) 66
agriculture 2, 4, 9, 19
  Africa 35–36
  Agricultural Revolution (18th-century) 66

Agricultural Revolution (Neolithic) see Neolithic
  Americas 4, 17, 39, 56, 91.
  See also North America below
  animal domestication 3–4, 7, 13, 17, 19, 22, 28, 35
  Bronze Age Europe 12
  Caribbean 28
  cereals 4, 7, 13, 17, 53
  chinampas 17, 55
  crop rotation 53
  and desertification 9
  east Asia 8
  Egypt 4, 6
  food plant cultivation 4, 7–8, 12, 17, 24, 36
  irrigation 4, 6, 17, 28, 42, 45
  legumes 7
  medieval Europe 53
  Mediterranean 11
  Mesoamerica 55
  Mughal India 61
  Neolithic and proto-Neolithic 3, 7
  North America 40, 42, 45, 57, 70, 73–75, 91–92
  pastoralism 13, 19
  pueblo farmers 42, 57
  slash-and-burn 17
Agri Decumates 29–30
Agrigentum, Battle of 23
Aguinaldo, Emileo 95
Ahab 15
Ah Cacau 39
Ah Canul 55
Ahmadnagar 61
Ahmad Shah Durrani 76
Ahmid Gran 60, 72
Ahmose 10
Ahoms 61, 69
Ahura Mazda 27
AIDS virus 117
'Ain Jalut, Battle of 47–49, 51
Ainu 40, 45, 50–51, 57, 79, 82
aircraft 99
Air, Kingdom of 44, 64, 67, 71–72, 76
Aix-la-Chapelle, Treaty of 76
Ajmer 61
Akamatsu 50
Akan 57, 60, 64, 67
Akbar 61, 64
Akhenaten 10
Akkad 5, 9
  Sargon the Great 5, 9
  see also Babylon, Babylonia
Akrotiri 11
Akshak 5
Alabama 73, 85
Alamo, Battle of 81
Alamut 47
Alans 28, 33–34, 36–37, 46, 48
Alaric 32–33, 36
Alashan Eleuth 69
Alaska 70, 76, 79, 84, 86, 88
Albania 54, 90, 96–97, 99, 101, 105–107, 109–110, 116, 119, 121
  World War II 105
Albazin (Yakesa) 69
Albert II, Duke of Austria 54
Albion see Britain
Albuquerque, Afonso de 60
Alcazarquivir, Battle of 59, 64
Alcock, John 99
alcohol 5, 7
Aleksinac, Battle of 96
Alemanni 30, 33
Aleppo 51
Alesia, Battle of 25, 29
Aleutian Islands 108
Aleuts 9, 13, 19, 22, 24, 28, 32, 36, 42, 70
Alexander VI, Pope 58
Alexander I, Czar 79, 82
Alexander II, Czar 86, 88
Alexander III, Czar 88
Alexander the Great 10, **21**, 22, 24
Alexander, King of Macedonia 101
Alexandria 21, 33, 35, 105
  Arab conquest 37
  Museum 21
Alexius I Comnenus, Emperor 48
Al Fatah 115, 118
Alfred the Great, King of Wessex 41
Al-Fustat 37
  Battle of 37
Algeciras conference 96
Algeria, Algiers 59–60, 71, 76, 82, 86, 89, 97, 99, 104–107, 109, 116–117, 121
  Algerian uprising 116–117
  civil war 117
  French control 82, 86
Algerian National Liberation Front (FLN) 117
Ali, Caliph 37, 44
Ali Pasha 59
Aljubarrota, Battle of 52
Allahabad 61
Allende Gossens, Salvador 111
Allia river, Battle of 25

Allied powers (World War I) 96, 98–101, 103
Allied powers (World War II) 102, 105–110, 117
Allobroges 25
Al-Maghrib 37
Almanza, Battle of 68
Almeida, Francisco de 61
Almohad caliphate 46, 48
alpaca 17
Alp Arslan 47
alphabets see writing
Al-Qadisiya, Battle of 37
al-Qasr al-Kabir see Alcazarquivir, Battle of
Alsace–Lorraine 65, 68, 80, 96
Altamira 3
Altan Khan 64
Alwa 27, 35–37, 40, 44–45, 51, 57
Amalasuntha, Queen 34
Amalekites 15
Amazonia 13, 19, 102
Amboina 67
Amenemhet I 10
Amenophis IV 10
American Revolution 62, 74, **75**, 76–77
Americas 19
  1914–1945 **102**
  1945–1997 **111–112**
  agriculture 4
  Amerindians 9
  Andean civilizations see Andean civilizations
  Archaic period 13
  British colonies 62, **70**, 71, 73, 75–76
  Canada see Canada
  discovery by Columbus 42, 54
  European colonization 41–42, 54
  European diseases 62, 70
  first civilizations **17**
  French colonies 62, 64, 67, 70–71, 73, 75–76
  Latin America see Latin America
  Mesoamerica see Mesoamerica
  Monroe Doctrine 81–82
  Native Americans see Native Americans
  Paleoindians 2, 42
  Portuguese empire 60, 62, **62**, 67, **70**, 74
  Russian America 70, 76, 79, 86, 88
  slavery 62, 71–72, 74–75
  Spanish empire 60, **62**, 64–65, 67, **70**, 71–72, 74, 76, 79, 82
  United States see United States of America
  World War I **102**
  World War II **102**
  see also individual states and peoples; New World
Amherst, Lord 94
Amiens, Treaty of 78
Amin, Idi 117
Ammon 15
Amorites 9, 14
amphictonies 16
Amsterdam 65–67, 71, 74
Amun, Oracle of 21
Amur 69, 71, 76, 88, 93–94
Anabaptists 58
anarchism 90
Anasazi culture 40, 42, 45, 51, 57
Anastasius 34
Anatolia 9, 13–14, 19, 25, 28–30, 33, 38, 41, 47–48, 59
  Alexander the Great 21
  Arab conquests 37
  Celts 25
  Crusades 48
  Ottoman Turk sultanate 57
  Palmyra 30
  Seleucids 24
  Seljuk Turks 47, 51
Anawrahta 51
Andaman Islands 95, 113
Andean civilizations 4, **17**, 19, 22, 24, 28, 32, 36, **56**
  Archaic period 13
  Early Horizon period 17
  Initial period 17
  Late Horizon Period 56
  Late Intermediate Period 56
  Middle Horizon Period 56
  Preceramic period 17
  Spanish conquest 60, **62**, 64
Andean Group 111
Andorra 52–54
Angevin dynasty 46
Angkor 45
Angles 33, 36
Anglican church 58
Anglo–American War 79
Anglo–Boer Wars 97
Anglo–Dutch Treaty 95
Anglo–Dutch wars 68, 71, 73
Anglo–Japanese Naval Alliance 93, 96
Anglo–Saxons 25, 27, 34, 36, 38, 40–41, 46. See also Saxons

Anglo–Siamese Treaty 95
Angola 64, 67, 71–72, 74, 76, 79, 82, 86, 89, 92, 97, 99, 106, 109, 112, 116–117, 121
  civil war 117
Anhalt 65
Anhui 69
animal domestication see agriculture
Anjou 46
Ankara, Battle of 47, 54, 57
Annam 43, 45, 49, 51, 57, 60, 64, 67, 71, 76, 79, 82–83, 86, 94–95, 103.
  See also Dai Viet; Vietnam
Anne, Queen of Britain 68
Ansbach 65
Anschluss 101
"ansei treaties" 93
Antietam, Battle of 85
Antigonos 21
Antigua and Barbuda 112, 121
Antioch, Antiochia 34
  Battle of Antioch 48
  Principality of Antioch 48
  sack 34
Antipater 21, 24
Antisuyu 56
Antonine dynasty 30
Antony, St 30
Antony, Mark 29
Antwerp 59, 64, 66
  sack 64, 66
Anxi 43
Anyang 8
Anzio landings 107
Aotearoa 45, 45. See also New Zealand
Apache 62, 70, 84
Apalachee 70
APEC see Asia Pacific Economic Cooperation Forum
Aqaba
  Battle of 98
  Gulf of 115
Aquileia 30, 41, 46
Aquino, Corazon 102
Aquitaine 38, 46, 52
Aquitania, Aquitaine 25, 29, 33
Arabia, Arabs 18–19, 22, 24, 28–29, 31–34, 36–37, 45–48, 59, 64, 71, 76, 79, 82
  Arab expansion and conquests 22, 34, **37**, 38, 40, 43, 46
  Arab–Israeli conflict see Arab–Israeli conflict
  Islam 37, 40
  nomadism 41, 45, 51, 57
  Roman province of Arabia 29
  Saba see Saba
  unity 37, 40, 45
Arabic language and script 37
Arab–Israeli conflict 109, **115**, 118, 121
  Camp David agreements 118
  Oslo Declaration 118
  peace process 121
  Six Day War 115–116
  Yom Kippur War 115–116
Arab league 109, 115–116
Arab revolt 99, 104
Arachosia 18, 21
Arachnukwu 72
Arafat, Yassir 115, 118
Aragon 41, 46, 51–54, 57–58
Arakan, Arakanese 61, 67, 71, 76, 79, 82–83, 95
Aramaic language and alphabet 13, 18
Aram, Aramaeans 13–15
Aram-Damascus 15
Aram-Zobah 15
Arapaho 70, 84
Araucanians 62
Arawak 57, 60, 62, 67
Arcadia 16, 20
Arcole, Battle of 77
Ardepithecus ramidus 1
Argentina 81–82, 86, 91–92, **92**, 97, 99, 102, 106, 109, 111, 116, 121
  "dirty war" 111
  Falklands War 111, 121
  independence 81–82
  Triple Alliance 81, 86
Argos 16
Aria 18
Arikamedu 31
Arikara 73
Aristagoras of Miletos 20
Aristotle 21
Arius 34
Arizona 84
Arkansas 84–85
Arkwright, Richard 66
Armada against England 64
Armada Española 64
Armagnac dynasty 54
Armenia, Armenians 18, 27, 29–30, 37, 45, 47–48, 52–53, 59, 100, 119, 121
  Satrapy of Armenia 21

Arms Limitation Treaty 116
Arochukwu 72
Arrapna 14
Arsuf, Battle of 48
Artemisium 20
Artois, Battle of 98
Arvad 15
Arverni 25
Aryans 13, 19, 27
Asad, Hafez al- 115
Asante 71–72, 76, 79, 82, 86
  Asante Wars 79, 82, 86, 89
Ascalon, Battle of 48
Asding Vandals 33
ASEAN see Association of Southeast Asian Nations
Ashikaga shogunate 50, 63
Ashkelon 15
Ashoka 24, 27
Ashur 13–14
Ashurbanipal 14, 18
Ashur-Dan II 14
Ashurnasirpal II 14
Asia (Roman province) 29
Asia Pacific Economic Cooperation Forum (APEC) 102
Asiana 30
Asir 104
Askia Mohammed 72
Aspern, Battle of 78
Aspero tradition 9, 17
Assam 83, 95. See also Sabeans
Assassins see Ismaili Nizari
Assiniboin 70, 73
Association of Southeast Asian Nations (ASEAN) 102
Assyrian empire 10, 13, **14**, 15, 18–19, 35
Astrakhan Tatars 60, 64
Asturias 38, 40–41
Astyages 18
Athens 11, 16, 18–19, **20**, 21–22, 54
  Academy 34
  Acropolis 16
  Delian league 20
  democracy 20–22
  Parthenon 20
  Peloponnesian War 20, 22
  Periclean 20
  Persian Wars **20**
Athos, Mount 20
Atiebates 25
Atlanta 85
Atlantic, Battle of the 105
Atlantic Charter 105
Atlas mountains 35
atomic energy 121
atomic weapons 102, 108–111, 116, 121
  arms limitation agreements 121
Atotonilco 55
Atropatene 21
Atsugashiyama, Battle of 50
Attalus I 25
Attica 16, 20
Attila 33, 36
Attu 108
Augsburg
  League of 68, 73
  Peace of 58
Augustodunum, Battle of 34
Augustulus, Romulus 33
Augustus, Gaius Julius Caesar Octavianus 25, 28–29, 32
Aung San Suu Kyi 102
Aurangabad 61
Aurangzeb, Emperor 61, 71, 74
Aurelian 30
Aurelius, Marcus 30
Aurignacian culture 3
Auschwitz 107
Austerlitz, Battle of 78–79
Australia 82, 86, 91–92, 95, 97, 99, 102–103, 106, 108–109, 116, 121
  British Commonwealth 102
  European discovery 67
  gold rush 86
  immigration 90, **92**
  Kaiser Wilhelmsland 99
  mandated territory 103
  penal colonies 79, 82, 92
  Vietnam War 114
  World War I 98–99, 103, 108
Australian Aboriginals 2, 9, 13, 19, 22, 24, 28, 32, 36, 40, 45, 60, 64, 67, 71, 76, 79
Australopithecus afarensis 1
Australopithecus africanus 1
Australopithecus robustus 1
Austrasia 38
Austria 46, 52, 54, 99, 101, 106, 109–110, 116, 119, 121
  Anschluss 101, 106
  see also Austria–Hungary; Austrian empire
Austria–Hungary 90, 92, 96–97
  collapse of empire 97

Congress of Berlin 96
Dreikaiserbund 96
Dual Alliance 96
Habsburg dynasty 101
Triple Alliance 96–97
World War I **96**, 98–99
Austrian empire 58, 65, 67–68, 71, 76–80, 82
  Austro–Prussian War 86
  French Revolutionary wars 77
  German Confederation 82
  Hungarian nationalist uprising 82
  Italy 80
  Napoleonic Wars 77–79
  Netherlands 77
  Schleswig–Holstein War 80
  Seven Weeks War 80
Austrian Succession, War of the 73, 76
Austro–Asiatic peoples 22, 24, 28
Austronesians 9, 13, 19, 22, 24, 28, 32, 35–36, 40
automobile 90–91, 97
Ava 67, 71
Avaris 10–11
Avar khanate 34, 36–38
Averröes see Ibn Rushd
Avignon papacy 44, 52, 54, 57
Awsa 64, 67, 71–72, 76
Axis powers 101, 105–107, 109
Axocopan 55
Axum, Axumites 27–28, 32, 35–37, 40, 45. See also Sabeans
Ayacucho, Battle of 81
Aylwin, Patricio 111
Aymara kingdoms 51, 56
Ayutthaya 57, 60, 64, 67, 71
Ayyubid sultanate 47, 49
Azcapotzalco 55
Azd 37
Azerbaijan 59, 67, 99–100, 119, 121
Azores 57
Azov 71
Aztec civilization 55, 57, 60, 62, 64
Azuchi-Momoyama period 63

# B

Ba 8
Baader–Meinhof group 110
Ba'athists 115, 118
Babi Yar 105
Babur, Emperor 60–61
Babwa 72
Babylon, Babylonia 13, **14**, 15, 18–19, 21
  Akkad see Akkad
  Alexander the Great 21
  Neo-Babylonian empire 14
  Persian conquest 18
Bacon, Roger 46
Bactria 18, 21, 24, 28, 31
Badajoz, Battle of 78
Badakhshan 61
Baden 80
Baerica 29
Baffin, William 70
Baghdad 40, 44–45, 47, 51, 67, 118
  Battle of 98
  Mongol capture 49
  Seljuk capture 47
Bagirmi 72
Bagyidaw 95
Bahamas 112, 116, 121
Bahawalpur 83
Bahia 62
Bahmani sultanate 57
Bahrain 104, 106, 109, 116, 118, 121
Bahrayn 37
Bailen, Battle of 78
Baipu 8
Bakhti movement 44
Balearic Islands 12, 23
Balfour Declaration 99, 104
Balistan 61
Balkans 33–34, 36, 52, 57
  Celts 25
  Ottoman rule 59, 71
Balkan Wars 96–97
Baltic 41, 46, 53
  Hanseatic league 53
Balts 19, 22, 24, 32–34, 36, 38, 40–41, 45–46, 107
Baluchistan 61, 82–83
Bambara 71–72
Bambata, Chief 89
Banat of Temesvar 68, 105, 107
Banda Oriental 62
Bandkeramik culture 4, 7
Bangkok 102
Bangladesh 113, 116, 121.
  See also East Pakistan; Pakistan
Bannockburn, Battle of 52
Bantam 67, 71, 74
Bantu 60, 64, 67
Bantu languages 19, 22, 24, 28, 32, 35–36, 45, 51, 57
Banu Hassan Arabs 72
Baol 72
Barbados 102, 112, 116, 121
barbarians 30, 33–34, 36
Barbarossa campaign 105

Barbary Coast 58–59, 79
Barbuda *see* Antigua and Barbuda
Barcelona 90–91
Barger–Oosterveld 12
Bar Lev line 115
barley 4
Barotseland, Barotse 86
Basketmaker culture 28, 32, 36
Basque Republic 101
Basques 33–34, 37–38
    Basque separatists 110
Basra 104
Bastar 83
Basutoland 82, 89, 97, 99, 106, 109.
    *See also* Lesotho
Bataan 108
Batavia 67, 74, 95
Batavian Republic 77
Batista, Fulgencio 112
Bauer, Georg *see* Agricola
Bautzen, Battle of 78
Bavaria 41, 46, 52, 65, 68, 77, 80, 90, 101
Bayeux Tapestry 46
Bay of Islands 79
Bay of Pigs 112
Bayreuth 65
Bechuanaland 89, 97, 99, 106, 109.
    *See also* Botswana
Becket, Thomas à 46
Bede, the Venerable 38
Bedouins 37
Bedr, Battle of 37
Begin, Menachem 115, 118
Beijing 49, 60, 69, 94, 116, 121
Beirut civil war 115, 118
Belarus 119, 121. *See also* Belorussia
Belgae 25
Belgian Congo (Congo Free State) 89, 92, 97, 99, 106, 109, 117.
    *See also* Congo; Zaire
Belgica 29
Belgium 80, 82, 86, 90, 96–97, 99, 101, 104, 106, 109–110, 116, 119, 121
    African colonies 89
    independence 80, 82
    revolt of Austrian Netherlands 77
    World War I 98
    World War II 105–107
Belgrade 60, 96, 107
    Battle of 47–48
Belisarius 34
Belize 67, 71, 76, 111–112, 121
Bella Bella 70
Bellini, Gentile 47
Belorussia 99–101, 107.
    *See also* Belarus
Belvoir 48
Benares. *See* Varanasi
Benedict, St 34
Benedictine order 34
Benelux Customs Union 110
Benevento 58–59, 65, 68, 80
    Duchy of 38, 41, 53–54
Beneventum 23
Bengal 57, 60–61, 64, 76, 83, 95, 103
Benin 51, 56–57, 64, 67, 72, 86, 117
Benkulen 95
Bentinck, Lord William Cavendish 83
Bentonville, Battle of 85
Benz, Karl 90
Beothuk 70
Berar 61
Berbers 9, 13, 19, 22–24, 28, 30, 32–38
Bergen 53
Bering, Vitus Jonassen 70
Bering Straits 2
Berlin 119
    Berlin Wall 110, 116
    blockade and airlift 109–110
    Congress of 86, 88, 96
    surrender to Red Army 107
    Treaty of 99
Berlin Conference 89, 97
Berlin Decrees 78–79
Berzem, Battle of 47
Bessarabia 78
Bessemer, Henry 90–91
Beth-horon 15
Bethlehem 15, 27, 44, 115
Beth-shean 15
Bhutan 69, 79, 82–83, 86, 97, 99, 113, 116, 121
Biafran war 117
Bialystok, Battle of 105
Bible
    *Book of Judges* 15
    Gospels 27
    *Gutenberg Bible* 54
    Old Testament 15
    Vulgate Latin translation 27
Bible lands **15**
Bidar 61
Bihar 61, 76
Bijapur 61, 67
Bilbao 90
Bindusara 24
Biscay squadron 65
Bishop, Maurice 112
Bishops' Wars 65
Bismarck, Prince Otto Edward Leopold von 90, 96
Bismarck Archipelago 13, 95
Bismarck Sea, Battle of 108

bison *see* buffalo
Bithynia 21, 29
Bituriges 25
Black Death 47, 52, 57
Blackfoot 70, 84
Black Hawk 84
Black Hills reservation 84
Blake, Admiral Robert 68
Blanco, Guzman 81
Blenheim, Battle of 68
*blitzkrieg* 105
Blücher, Gebbard Leberecht von, Prince of Wahlstadt 78
Bluefish Cave (Alaska) 2
boat-building 2, 6
    dug-out canoe 3
    outrigger canoe 13
    *see also* shipping
Bobangi 72
Boccaccio, Giovanni 52
Bocskay, Stephen 59
Bodh Gaya 44
Boeotia 16, 20
Boers *see* Afrikaners
Bogomils 59
Bogrib 70
Bohemia, Bohemians 38, 41, 46, 52, 54, 58, 65, 68, 77
    Hussites 48, 54
    *see also* Holy Roman empire
Bohemia–Moravia 101, 105
Bokassa, Jean-Bédel 117
Bolan Pass 83
Bolívar, Simón 81
Bolivia 81–82, 86, 97, 99, 102, 106, 109, 111, 116, 121
    Chaco War 102
Bolsheviks 98–100, 106
Bombay 61, 71, 83
Bonampak 39
Bonaparte, Joseph 78, 81
Bonaparte, Napoleon *see* Napoleon I
Bonin Islands 92, 103, 113
Bononia, Battle of 25
Booth, John Wilkes 85
Borgia family 58
Borneo 95
Bornu 67, 71, 76, 79
Borobudur 45
Borodino, Battle of 78
Bose, Subhas Chandra 103
Bosnia 47, 52, 54, 59, 68
Bosnia–Herzegovina 96
    anti-Turkish rebellion 96
    civil war 98, 119, 121
Bosporus 18, 20
    Kingdom of 21–22, 24, 30
Boston 75
    Tea Party 75
Bosworth Field, Battle of 54
Botswana 116–117, 121.
    *See also* Bechuanaland
Botticelli, Sandro 54
Boudicca 25
Bougainville, Louis Antoine de 76
Boulanger, Georges 96
Boulogne 78
Bourbon dynasty 58, 68, 80
Bouvines, Battle of 46, 51
bow and arrow 10, 24, 26, 42, 49
Bowl cultures 7
Boxer Uprising 93–94, 97
Boyacá, Battle of 81
*boyars*
Boyne, Battle of 68
Braganza dynasty 81
Brahmaputra river 83
Brahmins 27
Bramah, Joseph 90
Brandenburg 46, 52, 54, 58, 65, 68
Brandenburg–Prussia 77
Brandt, Willy 110
Brandywine, Battle of 75
Braun, Werner von 107
Brazil 64, 81, 86, 92, 94, 99, 102, 106, 109, 111, 116, 121
    Dutch 67
    empire 81
    independence 81–82
    Portuguese empire 60, 62, 67, 74, 76
    republic 81, 97
    slavery 62, 72, 79, 82
    Triple Alliance 81, 86
    Vice-Royalty of 79
    World War I 102
Breisach 67
Breitenfeld, Battle of 65
Bremen, Principality of 65
Bremen–Werden 65
Brest–Litovsk, Treaty of 98–100
Brétigny, Treaty of 52
Bretons 33–34, 38
Brezhnev, Leonid 121
Bridgewater canal 66
Brigantes 25
Brihuega, Battle of 68
Britain 13, 66, 68, 71, 76
    Act of Union (1800) 78
    Anglo–Dutch wars 68, 71, 73
    Anglo–Saxons 25, 33–34, 36, 38, 40, 46
    Battle of 105–106
    Belgic migrants 25
    Celts 25, 28, 36, 38, 40
    Christianity, introduction 27
    Commonwealth 65, 67–68

French Revolutionary Wars 77
    Glorious Revolution 68
    Hadrian's Wall 30
    Hanoverian dynasty 68
    Industrial Revolution 66
    Jacobites 68, 75
    Napoleonic Wars 77–79, 83, 95
    Norman conquest 46
    Peninsular War 78–79
    Romans 25, 28–30
    Saxon Shore 30
    Seven Years War 62, 73, 76
    slave trade 62, 71–72, 74
    Stuart dynasty 65, 68
    Vikings 41
    War of the Austrian Succession 73, 76
    *see also* British empire; England; Scotland; United Kingdom; Wales
Britanniae *see* Britain
British Columbia 84, 86
British East Africa 89, 92, 97, 99, 106, 109
British empire 60, 67, 75, 97, 101
    Africa 72, 79, 82, 86, **89**, 104, 116–117
    Americas 62, **70**, 71, 73, 75–76, 112
    Australia 79, 82, 92
    Canada 102, 111
    Caribbean 102, 112
    Ceylon 83
    Cyprus 104
    decolonization 109, 116
    Egypt 89, 97
    Falkland Islands 82
    Gurkhas 79, 82–83, 103
    Hong Kong 82, 94
    India 61, 71, 74, 76, 82, **83**, 86, 97, 103, 106, 109
    Iraq 104
    Jamaica 62, 71
    Java 95
    mandates 99, 101, 103–104
    Mediterranean bases 97
    Middle East 99, 104
    New Zealand 82, 86
    North America **70**, **73**
    Singapore 95
    slavery abolished 92
    southeast Asia **95**, 103, 113
    Straits Settlements 95
    Suez 86, 97
    Treaty of Utrecht 68, 73
    West Indies 62, 67, 71, 73–74
    World War I 102
British Guiana 79, 81–82, 86, 92, 97, 99, 102, 106, 112
British Honduras 79, 81–82, 86, 97, 99, 102, 106, 109, 112, 116
British New Guinea 95
British North Borneo 95, 103, 108
British Somaliland 89, 97, 99, 106, 109, 117
British West Africa 117
Britons 33
Brittany 25, 37, 41, 46, 52, 54, 58
Bronze Age 5, 7, 9, 13, 19
    Europe **12**
Bronze Age Europe 25
bronze working 4–5, 7–13, 19, 41
Brooke, James 95
Brown, Arthur 99
Brown, John 85
Bruges 53
Brunei 95, 102–103, 108, 121
Brunelleschi, Filippo 54
Brunswick 80
Brusilov offensive 98
Bruttians 23
bubonic plague 47, 52, 57, 67, 71
Buchanan, James 85
Buda, Battle of 68
Budapest 101, 107
Buddha (Siddhartha Gautama) 19, 22, 27
Buddhism 19, 24, 26–27, 31–32, 40, 44–45, 51, 57
    Ceylon 27
    Chan (Zen) 44, 50
    China 26–27, 43–44
    Gandhara 27
    India 24, 27, 31
    Iranian nomads 27
    Japan 50
    Lamaism 44
    Mahayana 27
    Mathura 31
    monasteries 27, 31
    Pacific and southeast Asia 27
    Pure Land 44, 50
    spread **27**, **44**
    Theravada 27
    Tibet 31
    Zen *see* Chan *above*
Buena Vista, Battle of 81
buffalo 19, 42, 57
Buganda 79, 82
Buhen 6
Bukhara 88
Bulgaria, Bulgars 34, 37–38, 40–41, 45–49, 53, 58–59, 86, 90, 96–99, 101, 105–107, 109–110, 116, 119, 121
    Bulgar khanate 38, 41, 45, 51
    independence 86

Ottoman empire 86
    Russian empire 88, 96
Bull Run, Battle of 85
Bülow, Bernard, Fürst von 89
Bundelas 61
Bundelkhand 83
Bunker Hill, Battle of 75
Bunyoro 79
Burgos, Battle of 78
Burgundy 30, 33–34, 58
    Duchy of 48, 52, 54
    Kingdom of 33–34, 41, 46, 54
    *see also* Holy Roman empire
Burkina Faso 117
Burma 60, 69, 76, 79, 82, 86, 94, 97, 99, 103, 106, 108–109, 113–114, 116
    British annexation 83, 94–95
    independence 113
    military regime 102
    *see also* Myanmar
Burma Road 103, 108
Burmese 13, 19, 24, 28, 32, 36, 40, 45, 51, 57
Burundi 79, 116–117, 121
Buryats 49
Busta Gallorum, Battle of 34
Buwayhids 45, 47
Byron, George Gordon, 6th Baron 80
Byzantium, Byzantine empire 30, **34**, 36, 38, 41, 44–46, 49, 51, 53–54, 57
    Arab conquests 37, 40, 47
    fall 44, 47, 54
    origins 34
    *see also* Constantinople

# C

Cabeço da Arrunda 3
Cabinda 117
Cabot, John 60, 70
Cabral, Pedro Alvares 60, 62
CACM *see* Central American Common Market
Caddoan 42
Cádiz 74. *See also* Gadez
Caen, Battle of 107
Caesar, Gaius Julius 25, 28–29
Cahokia 42
Cairo 37, 45, 47
Caizhou 43
Cakchiquel Maya 55
Calais 54, 58
Calakmul 39
Calcutta 71, 74
Caledonii 25
calendar
    Islamic 37, 40
    "long count" 17, 39
    Mayan 39
    Mesoamerica 28
Calicut 74
California 84–85, 91, 93, 97, 102, 111
caliphs 37
Callao, Battle of 81
Calmar, Union of 52, 54
Calvin, John 58
Calvinism 58, 65
Cambodia 57, 60, 64, 67, 71, 76, 79, 82, 95, 102, 113, **114**, 116, 121
    civil war 116
    independence 113
    Vietnamese invasion 102, 114
Cambrai, Battle of 98
Cambyses 18
Camden, Battle of 75
camel 4, 28, 35–36
Cameroon, Camaroons 35, 89, 97, 99, 104, 106, 109, 116–117
Camisards 68
Camp David agreements 118
Campo Formio, Treaty of 77
Canaan, Canaanites 13, 15
Canada 75–76, 79, 82, **84**, 86, 91–92, 97, 99, 102, 106, 109, 111, 116, 121
    British Colombia 86
    British rule 111
    Dominion of 86
    French 67, 73
    immigration **92**
    Quebec *see* Quebec
    unification 86
    United States border 82
    World War I 102
    World War II 102, 108
    *see also* North America
Canadian Pacific Railway 97
Canal d'Orleans 66
Canal du Midi 68
canal systems
    chamber lock 43
    China 43, 69
    Egypt 6
    European 66
    Kiel Canal 91
    Mesoamerica 17
    Nile to Red Sea 18
    Panama Canal *see* Panama Canal Zone
    Suez Canal *see* Suez Canal
Canary Islands 57
Cannae, Battle of 23
cannon 52
Cano, Juan Sebastián del 60
Canpech 55
Canton *see* Guangzhou
Cape Bojador 35

Cape Breton I *see* Ile Royale
Cape Canaveral (Cape Kennedy) 111
Cape Cod 67, 70
Cape Colony 72, 76, 79, 82, 86
    Great Trek 86
    Union of South Africa 97
Cape of Good Hope 32, 57, 79
Cape Matapan, Battle of 105
Cape St Vincent, Battle of 77
Capet, Hugh 41
Cape Town 71–72
Cape Verde 57, 62, 116–117, 121
capitalism **66**
Caporetto, Battle of 98
Cappadocia 18, 21–22, 29
Carabobo, Battle of 81
Caracas 81
Caraceni 23
Caracol 39
Caraja 62
Carbonari 80
Carchat 83
Carchemish 14
    Battle of 14–15
Cárdenas, Lázaro 102
Caria 18
Caribbean 28, 32, 57, 79, 102, **112**
    British colonies 62, 71
    French colonies 67
    Spanish colonies 60, 62, **62**, 71
    United States bases 102
    *see also* West Indies
Caribbean Community (CARICOM) 111–112
Caribbean Free Trade Association (CARIFTA) 112
caribou 42
Caribs 62
CARICOM *see* Caribbean Community
CARIFTA *see* Caribbean Free Trade Association
Carinthia 46, 52, 65, 68
Carloman 38
Carnac 7
Carnel, Battle of the 37
Carniola 65, 68
Carnutes 25
Carolinas 71
Caroline Islands 103, 116
Carolingian empire **38**, 40–41, 45
    break-up 41
    ecclesiastical centers 38
    feudalism 46
    Treaty of Verdun 41, 45
Carrhae, Battle of 29
Carron Iron Works 66
Cartagena 62
Carthage 19, 22–25, 28–29, 33, 35, 37, 40
    destruction 29
    Punic wars **23**, 24, 28–29, 35
Carthage ad Decimum, Battle of 34
Cartier, Jacques 64, 70
Cartwright, Edmund 90
Casablanca conference 107
Casa Grande 42
Casimir IV, King of Poland–Lithuania 54
Cassander 21
Castiglione, Battle of 77
Castile 46, 51–54, 57–58, 68
Castillon, Battle of 54
Castro, Fidel 111–112
Catacomb Grave cultures 9, 12
Catalan revolt 65
Catalaunian Plain, Battle of 33
Catalonia 68, 75, 78, 101, 110
Cateau–Cambrésis, Treaty of 58
Cathars 44, 48
Catherine II, Empress of Russia (the Great) 77, 88
Catholic league 65
Cattaro 68
cattle 4, 7, 13
Caucasus 19, 100
Caudine Forks 23
cave- and rock-art 2–3
Cavour, Camillo di 80, 86
Cawahie 62
Caxton, William 54
Cayenne 67, 71, 76
Cayuse 70
Ceaușescu, Nikolai 110
Ceh Pech 55
Celtiberians 13, 19, 22–25
Celtic language 25
Celts 19, 21–24, **25**, 28, 36, 38, 40, 45
    Christianity 38
Central African Republic 116–117, 121
Central American Common Market (CACM) 111
Central Pacific Forces 108
Central powers 96, 98–99
ceramics 5, 9, 19
    Americas 17
    Chinese 8, 43
    earliest 4
    Egyptian 6
    Greek 20
    Japanese 4
    kiln 4, 43
    Mayan 39
    Moche 28

Native American 42
Neolithic 4, 7, 9
porcelain 43
potter's wheel 4, 8, 25
Ceras 31
Cervantes, Miguel de 59
Ceuta 54, 57
Ceylon 27, 44, 106, 109
    British 83
    Dutch 61, 67, 71
    *see also* Saylan; Simhala; Sri Lanka
Chacabuco, Battle of 81
Chaco Canyon 42
Chaco War 102
Chad 72, 116–117, 121
Chagatai Khanate 44, 51, 57
Chahar 69
Chakan 55
Chalcedon, Council of 33
Chaldeans 14
Chaldiran, Battle of 59–60
Chalukyas 36
Chambord, château of 58
Champa 27, 32, 36, 40, 43, 45, 49, 51, 57. *See also* Viets
Champagne 53
Champlain, Samuel de 70
Champutun 55
Chams 22, 24, 28, 32
Chan (Zen) Buddhism 44, 50
Chancellorsville, Battle of 85
Chan Chan 56
Chandragupta I Maurya 22, 24, 31
Chandragupta II 31–32
Chang'an 36, 43–44
Changsa, Battles of 108
Chan Muan 39
Chaoxian *see* Korea
chariot 8, 10–11
Charles IV, Holy Roman emperor 52
Charles V, Holy Roman emperor 58–60
Charles I, King of England 65, 67–68
Charles II, King of England 68
Charles II, King of France (the Fat) 41, 45
Charles III, King of France (the Simple) 41
Charles IV, King of France 54
Charles VIII, King of France (the Affable) 54, 58
Charles X, King of France 80
Charles II, King of Spain 68
Charles III, King of Spain 74
Charles the Bold, Duke of Burgundy 54
Charles Martel 38
Charlemagne 38, 40–41, 45
Charleston 75
Charolais 58, 65, 68
Chartists 80
Chatal Huyuk 4
Chateau Thierry, Battle of 78
Châtelperronian culture 3
Chattanooga, Battle of 85
Chaucer, Geoffrey 52
Chavín de Huántar 17, 19, 24
Chechens, Chechnya 119
Chemins des Dames, Battle of 98
Chen 8
Chen-La 36, 40, 45
Chernigov, Principality of 46
Chernobyl accident 121
Cherokee 62, 70, 73, 84
Chesapeake Capes, Battle of 75
Chesowanja 1
Chetumal 55
Cheyenne 70, 73, 84
Chiang Kai-shek *see* Jiang Jieshi
Chiangs *see* Tibet, Tibetans; Xizang
Chiapas 12
Chibcha 62
Chichén Itzá 39, 55
Chichimeca 55
Chickamauga, Battle of 85
Chickasaw 73, 84
Chihuahua, Battle of 81
Chikinchel 55
Chile 81–82, 86, 91–92, 97, 99, 102, 106, 109, 111, 116, 121
Chimú empire 45, 51, 56–57
China 4, 8, **8**, 9, 13, 94–95, **102–103**, 108, **113**
    Boxer Uprising 93–94, 97
    canal systems 43, 69
    Chinese Revolution 97
    civil war 106, 109, 113
    communism 103, 106, 109, 113, 116
    Eastern Zhou 8
    emigration 81, **92**
    First Emperor 24, 26
    Five Dynasties 43, 45
    Former Han **26**
    Grand Canal (Da Yunhe) 43, 69
    Great Wall 26, 69
    Guomindang (Kuomintang; KMT) 94
    Hakka rebellion 82, 94
    Han dynasty *see* Han Dynasty
    International Protocol 94
    Iron Age 26
    Japanese invasion 103
    Jin dynasty *see* Jin dynasty
    Later Han **26**
    Long March 106

Longshan culture 8–9, 13
Manchu empire *see* Manchu empire
Maritime Edict 57
Miao rebellion 94
Ming empire *see* Ming empire
Mongol rule 49, 57
Nationalists 103, 106, 108–109, 113
Nian risings 94
Opium Wars 82, 86, 91, 94
Period of Disunion 43
population growth 69, 76
Qin dynasty 22, 24, **26**
Qing dynasty *see* Manchu empire republic 94, 97, 99
Revolution 94
Shang dynasty 8
Sino–Japanese War (1894–95) 93–94, 97
Sino–Japanese war (1937) 106
Song dynasty *see* Song dynasty
Springs and Autumns Period 8, 19
Sui dynasty 36, 40, **43**
Taiping rebellion 94
Taiwan 69, 71, 74
Tang dynasty *see* Tang dynasty
Ten Kingdoms 43
Three kingdoms **26**
Tibet 69, 76
Treaty of Nanjing 94
treaty ports 82, 94
unification **26**
Warring States period 8, 22, **26**
Western Zhou 8
White Lotus rebellion 94
Willow Palisade 69
World War II 103, 108
Xia dynasty 8
Yue kingdom 22
Zhou dynasty *see* Zhou dynasty
*see also* People's Republic of China
*chinampas* 55
Chinchasuyu 56
Chinchoros tradition 9, 13, 18–19
Chinese language and script 9
Chingis Khan (Temujin) 47, 49, 51, 57
Chioggia, Battle of 52
Chipewyan 70, 73
Chiribaya 56
Chiricahua 70
Chirikov, Aleksey 70
Chiripa culture 13, 17
Chittaurgarh 61
Battle of 61
Choctaw 62, 70, 73, 84
Choe dynasty 50
Cholas 45, 51
Chorasmia 18
Chorrera culture 13, 17, 19, 22
Choshu 93
Chosokabe 63
Chosroes I 36
Choxian *see* Korea
Christian IV, King of Denmark 65
Christianity 27, 30, 34
Africa 35–36, 57, 72
archbishoprics 38, 41
Arians 34
Armenia 27
Axum 36
Bible 27
Britain 27
China 43, 94
Counter-Reformation 59, 65
Crusades *See* Crusades
Franks 34
Gothic cathedrals 44
heresies 48, 52, 54
Iconoclast controversy 38, 44
India 83
Ireland 25, 38, 41
Japan 63
Magyars 41
military monastic orders 48
missionaries 62, 72, 95
monasteries 25, 27, 30, 34, 38, 41, 48
Nubia 35–36
patriarchates 34, 38
pilgrimage centers 44
Poland 41
Protestant Reformation **58**, 59–60, 67
Roman empire 27, 29–30, 32
Scandinavia 41, 44
spread **27**, 38, **44**
*see also individual sects*
Chu 8, 26
Chumash 70
Churchill, Winston 105, 107, 109
CIA *see* Central Intelligence Agency
Cihuatlan 55
Cilicia 14, 18, 21, 29
Cimmerians 13–14
Cisalpine Gaul 23, 25, 29
Cisalpine Republic 77
Civil Rights movement 111
Cixi, Empress 94
Clark, William 84
Claudius 29
Cleopatra 24, 28–29
Clermont, Council of 46, 48
climatic change 1–4, 67
Clinton, Bill 119
Clothar I 34
Clovis 34, 36
Clovis culture 2

Cluny, Cluniac order 41
Cnut 41
Coahuiltec 62, 70
Cobá 39
Cochimi 70
Cochin China 79, 82, 86, 103
Cochise 84
Cochuah 55
Cocom dynasty 55
Coffee Accords 102
coinage 16
Coixtlahuacan 55
Cokwe 82, 86
Colbert, Jean Baptiste 68
Colchis 18–22
Cold Harbor, Battle of 85
Cold War 109–111, 116, 121
Collasuyu 56
Colombia 81–82, 86, 97, 99, 102, 106, 109, 111, 116, 121
Colorado 84
Columbia 62, 81
Columbia river 84
Columbus, Christopher 42, 54, 57, 60, 62
Comanche 62, 84
Comecon 109–110
Cominform 109
Commagene *see* Kummukhu
Commodus 30
Common Market *see* European Economic Community
Common Market of the Southern Cone (Mercosur) 111
Commonwealth, English 65, 68
communism 90, 101, 116, 121
Africa 116
Albania 110
Chile 116
China 103, 106, 109, 113, **113**, 116
Cold War 109–111, 116, 121
Cuba 111–112
Czechoslovakia 109–110, 116
"domino effect" 114, 116
eastern Europe 107, 109–110, 116, 119, 121
Germany 101
Greece 107
Korean War 109, 113
North Korea 113
Sino–Soviet split 113, 116
southeast Asia 102–103, 109, 113, **114**
Union of Soviet Socialist Republics **100**, 116
Vietnam 103, 113–114
Warsaw Pact 116
Yugoslavia 110
Comoros 117, 121
Comunero revolt 58
concentration camps 105, 107
"Concert of Europe" congresses 80
Concho 70
Condé, Louis, Prince de 68
Confederate states **85**
Confederation of the Rhine 78–79
Confederation of the United Provinces 81
Confucianism 8, 26–27, 43–44, 50
Confucius 8, 19, 22, 27
Congo 44, 57, 60, 64, 67, 71–72, 76, 79, 116–117, 121. *See also* Belgian Congo; Zaire
Congo Free State *see* Belgian Congo
Congress Poland 88
Connecticut 73, 75, 84–85
conquistadors 55–56
Constance, Council of 54
Constantine the Great 27, 30, 32–33
Constantinian dynasty 30
Constantinople 30, 33–34, 36–37, 40, 54, 57, 59, 90
Ottoman conquest 44, 47, 59
sieges of 37, 47–48, 57
Theodosian walls 33
Topkapi palace 47
*see also* Byzantium, Byzantine empire
Continental System 78–79
Contras 112
Cook, James 70, 76
Copán 39
Copenhagen
Battle of (1801) 78
Battle of (1807) 78
copper working 4–7, 19
Coral Sea, Battle of 108
Corbie, Battle of 65
Córdoba 34, 38
Corfu 78
Corinth 11, 16, 20
Battle of 85
Corinthian league 21
Cornwallis, Charles, 1st Marquis 75, 83
Coronado, Francisco Vázquez de 62, 64, 70
Corregidor, Battle of 108
Corsica 12, 23–24, 29
Corte Real, Gaspar 70
Cortés, Hernán 55, 60, 62
Corvinus, Matthias 54
Cossacks 59, 100
Costa Rica 81–82, 86, 97, 99, 102, 106, 109, 111–112, 116, 121
Cotabambas 56
cotton 4, 17, 74, 84–85, 91

Counter-Reformation 59, 65
Courland 58, 68
Covadonga, Battle of 37–38
Covilhã, Pedro da 60
Cowpens, Battle of 75
Coyalapan 55
Cozumel, Isla de 55
Crazy Horse 84
Crécy, Battle of 52
Credit Mobilier 96
Cree 70, 73
Creek 70, 73, 84
Crete 7, 13, 16, 71, 96, 105
Minoan civilization 7, 9, 11, 13
Mycenaean civilization 11, 13
Crimea 52, 88
Crimean War 86, 88, 96
Khanate of 47, 59
World War II 107
Croatia, Croats 38, 41, 59, 80, 105–107, 119, 121
Croesus 18
Crompton, Samuel 66
Cromwell, Oliver 62, 65, 68
crossbow 26
Crow 70, 73, 84
Crown Point 73
Crusader States 47–49, 49.
*See also individual states*
Crusades 44, 46, **48**, 51
First 44, 46–48, 51
Second 46, 48
Third 48
Fourth 48
Cathars 44, 48
Nicopolis 52
Ctesiphon 30
Cuahtochco 55
Cuatlaxtlan 55
Cuba 57, 60, 81–82, 86, 92, 97, 99, 102, 106, 109, 111–112, 116–117, 121
Castro 111–112
Guantánamo Bay military base 102, 112
missile crisis 112, 116
Spanish colonization 60, 62
Cuetlaxtlan 55
Cultural Revolution 113, 116
Cumaná 62
Cumans 46, 48–49
Cumberland Road 84
cuneiform writing 5, 18
Cuntisuyu 56
Cupul 55
Curupayty, Battle of 81
Curzon Line 101
Custer, George Armstrong 84
Cuzco 56
Cynoscephalae, Battle of 28–29
Cyprus 11, 13, 18, 20–21, 29, 48, 52–53, 96, 104, 110, 115–116, 118–119, 121
division 115
Kingdom of 48
Turkish Republic of Northern 110, 115
Cyrenaica 29, 59, 89, 104
Cyrene 35
Cyrus II (the Great) 14–15, 18–19
Cythera 77–78
czars 59
Czech legion 100
Czechoslovakia 99, 101, 109–110, 116
communism 109, 119, 121
German invasion 101, 106
Prague Spring 110, 116
Sudetenland 101
Velvet Revolution 110, 119, 121
*see also* Czech Republic; Slovakia
Czech Republic 119, 121

## D

Dacia 25, 28–30
Dadu 49
Dagobert 38
Dagon 44
Dahomey 72, 76. *See also* Benin
Daimler, Gottlieb 90–91
Daito Islands 103, 113
Dai Viet 45
Chinese occupation 45
*see also* Annam; Vietnam
Dakar 89
Dakota 84
Dalai Lama 69, 83
Dalhousie, James Andrew Broun-Ramsay, Marquis of 83
Dali, Battle of 43
Dallas, Texas 111
Dalmatia 29, 33
Daman 61
Damascus 14–15, 37, 40
Battle of (1148) 48
Battle of (1918) 98
Damghan 21
Damietta 48
Dan 15
Da Nang *see* Tourane
Dandanqan, Battle of 47
Danegeld 41
Danelaw 41
Danes 33–34, 38, 46, 52
Vikings 41
Daniel, Prince of Moscow 52
Danishmend emirate 47
Danish Virgin Islands 102
Dannoura, Battle of 50

Dante Alighieri 52
Danube river 29–30, 41, 57
Danzig *see* Gdansk
*Dao De Jing* 27
Daoism 27, 44
Darby, Abraham 66
Dardanelles 98
Darfur 60, 64, 67, 71–72, 76
Darius I, King of Persia 20
Darius III, King of Persia 21
Darius 18
Datong, Battle of 26
Dauphiné 52
David 15
Davis, Jefferson 85
Davis, John 70
Dawes plan 101
Dayton Accord 119
Da Yunhe (Grand Canal) 69
D-Day 107, 109
DDR *see* German Democratic Republic
death camps 105, 107
Deccan 31, 61, 71, 83
Decembrist revolt 88
decimal system 31
Decius 30
*Declaration of the Rights of Man* 77
deforestation 111
de Gaulle, Charles 110–111, 117
Delagoa Bay 71–72, 76, 79
Delaware 75, 85
Delaware tribe 73, 84
Delhi 83
sack 76
sultanate 49, 51, 57, 61
Delian league 20
Delos 16, 20
Delphi 16, 20, 25
Democratic People's Republic of Korea *see* North Korea
Democratic Republic of the Congo *see* Zaire
Denain 68
Deng Xiaoping 102
Denmark 3, 41, 44–46, 51–54, 57, 78, 80, 82, 86, 90, 92, 96–99, 101, 106, 109–110, 116, 119, 121
Swedish, Norwegian and Danish crowns united 57
Thirty Years War 67
World War II 105–106
*see also* Danes
Denmark–Norway 58, 60, 64–65, 67–68, 71, 76–79
Der 14
Derevlians 38, 41
Dervishes 47
desertification 2, 4, 9, 117
Deshima Island 63
de Soto, Hernando (Fernando) 70
Detroit 102
*devaputra* 31
Dewey, George 95
Dhaka 83
Diadochi 21
Wars of the 21, 24
diamonds 91–92
Dias, Batholomew 57
Diaz, Porfirio 81
Diem, Ngo Dinh 114
Dien Bien Phu, Battle of 113
Diocletian 30, 32
Edict of 30
Diu 61, 64
divination 8, 16
Di-xin 8
Djerba, Battle of 59
Djibouti 117
Djoser 6
Dodecanese 96, 101
dog 4
Dogger Bank, Battle of 98
Doiran, Battle of 98
Dollfuss, Engelbert 101
Dominica 112, 121
Dominican Order 51
Dominican Republic 81–82, 86, 97, 99, 102, 106, 109, 112, 116, 121. *See also* Hispaniola; Santo Domingo
"domino effect" 114, 116
Donatello 54
Dongyi 8
Dorestad 41
Dorgun 69
Dorians 11, 16
Dorset Inuit 42
Dorylaeum, Battle of 48
Dost Muhammed 83
Drake, Francis 62, 64, 70
Drangiana 18, 21
Dravidians 9, 13, 19
*Dreikaiserbund* 96
Drepanum, Battle of 23
Dresden, Battle of 78
Dresden bombing 107
Druze militia 118
Dual Alliance 96
Dublin 41, 98
Dubrovnik 119
Du Fu 43
Duji 43
Dulles, John Foster 114
Dumnonii 25
Dunbar, Battle of 68
Dunkirk 65, 68
Dur-Kurigalzu 14
Dur-Sharrukin 14

Dushan, Stephen 52
Dutch East Indies 79, 82, 86, 95, 97, 99, 103, 106, 108, 113.
*See also* Netherlands trading bases and colonies
Dutch Guiana 81, 86, 92, 97, 99, 102, 106, 112, 116
Dutch New Guinea 95, 103, 109
Dvaravati 36, 40. *See also* Mons
Dyle, Battle of 41
Dyola 72
Dyukhtai tradition 2
Dzungaria 69, 94

## E

Eannatum of Kish 5
East Anglia 38, 52
East Bengal 83
Easter Island 32
Eastern Association 65
Eastern Cree 70, 73
Eastern Front (World War I) 98
Eastern Slavonia 119
Eastern Turk Khanate 36
eastern woodlands (North America) 13, 19, 22, 24, 28, 32, 36, 40, 42, 45
Eastern Zhou 8
Easter Rising 98
East Germany *see* German Democratic Republic (DDR)
East India companies 61, 63, 67, 71, 74, 76, 83
East Indies 66, 74, 76
Dutch 61, 64, 67, 71, 74
East Pakistan 113, 116.
*See also* Bangladesh; Pakistan
East Prussia 101
East Timor 102, 109, 113, 116
Ebersberg, Battle of 78
EC *see* European Community
Ecab 55
Ecbatana *see* Hamadan
Ecija, Battle of 37–38
Ecnomus, Battle of 23
ECSC *see* European Coal and Steel Community
Ecuador 81–82, 86, 97, 99, 102, 106, 109, 111–112, 116, 121
Eden Treaty 66
Edessa 29
Battle of (260) 30
Battle of (1144) 47–48
County of 48
Edgehill, Battle of 65
Edinburgh, Treaty of 52
Edington, Battle of 41
Edirne 47. *See also* Adrianople
Edo 63, 67, 93. *See also* Tokyo
Edom, Edomites 14–15
Edo period 63
education
Chinese examination system 43
Nizamayeh academy 47
Edward VII, King of Britain 96
Edward the Confessor 41
EEC *see* European Economic Community
EFTA *see* European Free Trade Association
Egypt 11–22, 27, 40, 45, 47, 59, 77, 86, 89, 97, 99, 104, 106, 109, 115–118, 121
Achemenid empire 22, 35
Alexander the Great 21
Arab–Israeli conflict **115**, **118**
British occupation 89, 97
Crusades 48
Fatimids 45, 47, 51
Greeks in 22
independence 104
Mamluke dynasty 60, 77
Muslim Brotherhood 104
Napoleonic Wars 77, 79
nationalist revolt 115
Nubian rule 35
Ottoman empire 82
Ptolemaic 21–22, 24, 28
Roman empire 28–29, 34
Six Day War 115–116
Suez crisis 104, 115–116
United Arab Republic 115
World War II 104–105, 107
*see also* Aegyptus; Egyptian civilization
Egyptian civilization 5, 13–15, 18
1st Dynasty 6
2nd Intermediate period 35
4th Dynasty 6
11th Dynasty 10
17th Dynasty 10
18th Dynasty 10
21st Dynasty 10
25th Dynasty 10
1st Intermediate period 6
2nd Intermediate period 10
3rd Intermediate period 10
agriculture 4
Assyrian conquest 10, 14
Babylonian campaign against 14
Early Dynastic period 6
foundation **6**, 9
invasion of Judah and Israel 15
Kushite rulers 19
Late period 10
Middle Kingdom 9, **10**, 13
Naqada period 6

New Kingdom **10**, 13, 35
Old Kingdom 6, 9
Persian conquest 10, 18–19
pyramids 6, 9–10
Sea Peoples 10, 13
Eion 20
Eire *see* Ireland
Eisenhower, Dwight David 113
El Alamein, Battle of 101, 105, 107
Elam, Elamites 5, 9, 13–14, 18
el-Amarna 10
Elba 78
El Baul 39
El Hierro 39
Elbe–Oder canal 66
El-Hasa 59
Elijah 15
Elis 16, 20
Elisha 15
Elizabeth I, Queen of England 58
Ellora 27
Elmina 72
El Mirador 39
El Paraiso tradition 13, 17
El Salvador 81–82, 86, 97, 99, 102, 106, 109, 111–112, 116, 121
"football war" 112
Elteken, Battle of 15
"Ems Telegram"
Engels, Friedrich 90
England 27, 41, 45–46, 51–54, 57–58, 60, 64–65, 67
Anglo–Dutch wars 68, 71, 73
Civil War 65
Glorious Revolution 68
Hundred Years War 47, 52, 54, 57
Norman conquest 46
Peasants Revolt 52
Protestant Reformation **58**, 67
Spanish Armada 64
Tudor dynasty 58
Wars of the Roses 54, 58
*see also* Britain; British empire; United Kingdom
English Guinea Company 72
English Newfoundland Company 73
Eniwetok, Battle of 108
Enlightenment 77
*Entente Cordiale* 89, 96–97
Ephesus 27
Ephthalite (White) Huns 31–32, 36
Epicuros 21
epidemics
Black Death 47, 52, 57
European diseases introduced to the Americas 55–56, 62, 70
plague 67–68, 71
syphilis 62
Epirus 16, 20–21, 23, 29
Despotate of 48
Equatorial Guinea 116–117, 121
Eran 31
Eridu 5
Erik the Red 41
Eritrea 89, 97, 99, 104, 106, 109, 117, 121
civil war 117
Erlitou culture 8
ERM *see* Exchange Rate Mechanism
Erzurum, Battle of 98
Esarhaddon 14
Eskisehir (Dorylaeum), Battle of 47
Essequibo 67
Estates-General 77
Estonia, Estonians 46, 58, 68, 98–101, 105, 109–110, 119, 121
Ethiopia 19, 28, 32, 35, 44–45, 51, 57, 64, 67, 71–72, 76, 79, 82, 86, 97, 99, 104, 106, 109, 112, 116–117, 121
Christians 72
Eritrean civil war 117
independence 97, 104
Italian invasion 89, 97, 101, 104, 106
*jihad* by Ahmad Gran 60, 72
Etruscans 19, 22–23, 25
EU *see* European Union
Euboea 20
Euboia 54
Eugene, Prince of Savoy 68
Euphrates river 5
Eurasian steppes 24
Euro-corps 119
Europe
alliance systems (1871–1914) **96**
alliance systems (1918–39) 101
*ancien régime* 77, 79
between the World Wars **101**
Bronze Age **12**, 25
Cold War 109–110, 116, 121
"Concert of Europe" congresses 80
Congress of Berlin 86, 88, 96
Congress of Vienna 78, 80, 82, 88
Counter-Reformation 59, 65
economy 52, **53**, 64–65, **66**, 67
Enlightenment 77
European colonies 54, 57
feudalism **46**
first Mediterranean civilizations **11**
Industrial Revolution **90**
Iron Age 25
migration 81, 90, **92**
Napoleonic Wars *see* Napoleonic Wars
nationalism 79, **80**, 82
Neolithic **7**
Ottoman advances 58–60, 64, 67–68, 71

## Europe (contd.)

Paleolithic **3**
post-World War II division **110**, 119
Reformation **58**, 59–60, 67
Renaissance **54**
states 45, 51
Treaty of Versailles 99, 101–102, 106
Viking Age **41**
Year of Revolutions (1848) 80, 82
*see also individual states and peoples*
European Bank for Reconstruction and Development 119
European Coal and Steel Community (ECSC) 110
European Community (EC) 110, 121
European Economic Community (EEC) 110, 116
European Free Trade Association (EFTA) 110
European Union (EU) 119, 121
Eutaw Springs, Battle of 75
Exchange Rate Mechanism (ERM) 119
exploration, explorers
Bougainville 76
Cabot 70
Cabral 62
Cartier 64, 70
Columbus 42, 54, 57, 60, 62, 70
Cook 70, 76
Coronado 62, 64
Cortés 55, 60, 62
da Covilhà 60
Drake 62, 64, 70
Fox 70
da Gama 54, 60–61, 74
Ibn Battuta 47
La Salle 70–71
New World 42, 54–55, 57
Pizarro, Francisco 56, 60, 62, 64
Polo 46, 49
Saavedra 62
Tasman 67
Vespucci 62
Zheng He 57
Eyck, Jan van 54
Eylau, Battle of 78
Ezana 35
Ezion-geber 15
Ezo 50

## F

Faiyum 6
Falaise, Battle of 107
Falkland Islands 81–82, 86, 99, 111
Falklands War 111, 121
Faraday, Michael 90
Far Eastern SSR 99–100
Faroe Islands 41
Fascism 101, 106
Fashoda crisis 89, 96
Fatehpur Sikri 61
Fatimid caliphate 45, 47–48, 51
Federal Republic of Germany (FRG) 109–110, 116, 119, 121
Fehrbellin, Battle of 68
Fenian Brotherhood 80
Fenland revolt 65
Ferdinand I, Holy Roman emperor 58–59
Ferdinand of Aragon 54, 58
Ferghana 37, 43, 60–61
Fertile Crescent 4
feudalism **46**, 50
Fezzan 89, 104
Fiji 92, 97, 102, 106, 116, 121
"Final Solution" 104–107
Finland 88, 98–101, 106–107, 109–110, 116, 119, 121
Winter War 100, 105
Finno–Ugrians 9, 13, 19, 22, 24, 28, 32
Finns 19, 22, 24, 28, 32, 36, 38, 40–41, 45–46
firearms 54, 63, 72
fire, earliest use 1
"Fire in the Fern"
First Coalition 77
First Emperor of China
*see* Shi Huangdi
"First of June", Battle of 77
fishing 3, 9, 17, 66, 73–74
Five Dynasties (China) 43, 45
Flagler Bay 42
Flanders 52–53, 65–66
Flat Head 84
Flavian dynasty 30
Fleurus, Battle of 68, 77
FLN *see* Algerian National Liberation Front
Flodden, Battle of 58
Flood, the 5
Florence 54
Florida 62, 64, 67, 70–71, 73, 75–76, 79, 81–82, 84–85, 112
Folsom culture 2
Fons 89
"football war" 112
Ford, Gerald R. 114
Ford, Henry 91
"Forest Brethren" 110
Former Han 26
Formigny, Battle of 54
Formosa 113.
*See also* Taiwan
Fort Ancient 42
Fort Caroline 70

Fort Dauphin 71
Fort Duquesne 73
Fort Sumter 85
Fort Zeelandia 69
Fourth Coalition 78
Fox, Luke 70
Fox tribe 84
France 41, 45–46, 48, 51, 54, 57–59, 64–65, 67–68, 71, 76–80, 82, 86, 90, 92, 96–99, 101, 106, 109–110, 116, 119, 121
*ancien régime* 77, 79
Bourbon dynasty 68, 80
Carolingians *see* Carolingian empire
colonies *see* French colonies and trading bases
Congress of Vienna 78, 80, 82
Crimean War 86, 88
*Entente Cordiale* 89, 96–97
Franco–Prussian War 80, 86, 96
Franco–Russian Alliance 96–97
Gaul *see* Gaul
Great Fear 77
Huguenots 64–66, 68
Hundred Years War 47, 52, 54, 57
intervention in Mexico 86
Italian Wars 54, 58
Jacquerie 52
July Revolution 80
Napoleonic *see* Napoleon I; Napoleonic Wars
National Assembly 77
Revolution **77**, 79
Revolutionary wars *see* French Revolutionary wars
second empire 86
Seven Years War 62, 73, 76
student risings 110, 116
Suez crisis 104, 115–116
Thirty Years War **65**, 67–68
Triple Entente 96
Vichy regime 105
War of the Austrian Succession 73, 76
War of the League of Augsburg 68, 73
Wars of Religion 67
World War I **96**, 98–99, 103
World War II 101, **105**, 106, **107**, 109
Franche-Comté 52, 54, 58, 65, 68
Francia, José 81
Francis I, King of France 58–59
Franco, Francisco 101, 110
Franconia 41, 46
Franco–Prussian War 80, 86, 96
Franco–Russian alliance 96–97
Frankish kingdom 37–38, 40–41
Franklin, Benjamin 75
Franks 30, 33–34, 36
Franz Ferdinand, Archduke 97–98
Frederick I, Holy Roman emperor (Frederick Barbarossa) 46
Frederick II, Holy Roman emperor 46, 48
Frederick II, King of Prussia 76
Fredericksburg, Battle of 85
Frederick William, "Great Elector" of Brandenburg 68
Fremont culture 42
French colonies and trading bases 74, 76, 101
Africa 71–72, 82, 86, 89, 92, 104, 116–117
Algeria 82, 86, 116–117
Americas 62, 64, 67, 70–71, 73, 75–76, 79, 112
Caribbean 67, 76, 112
India 61, 76
Indo–China 86, 92, 94, **95**, 97, 109
Louisiana Purchase 79, 84
mandates 99, 101, 104
Mauritius 76
Morocco 96, 104
southeast Asia **95**, 99, 103, 106, 108–109, 113
French Equatorial Africa 89, 97, 99, 106, 109
French Guiana 81–82, 86, 92, 97, 99, 102, 106, 111–112, 116, 121
French Guinea 89
French and Indian War 73
French Indo–China 86, 92, **95**, 97, 99, 103, 106, 108–109, 113
French Revolutionary wars **77**
Austerlitz 78–79
Egypt 79
Russians defeated at Friedland 79
French Somaliland 89, 97, 99, 106, 109, 116
French Sudan 89
French War of Devolution 68
French West Africa 89, 97, 99, 106, 109
FRG *see* Federal Republic of Germany
Friedland, Battle of 78–79
Friesland 52
Frisians 30, 33–34, 38
Fronde 68
Fuad I 104
Fugger bank 53
Fujian 69
Fuji, Mount 44
Fujiwara dynasty 50
Fulani empire 71–72, 79
Funan 27, 32, 36

Funj 57, 60, 64, 67, 71–72, 76
Futa-Jalon 72, 76, 86
Futa-Toro 72, 76, 86

## G

Gabon 82, 86, 89, 116–117, 121
Gabor, Bethlen 65
Gadsden Purchase 81, 84, 86
Gaixia, Battle of 26
Galapagos Islands 81, 86
Galatia 25, 29
Galerius 30
Galicia 38
Principality of 46
Galicia and Lodomeria 68, 77
Galla 60, 72
Gallaeci 25
Gallia, Galliae 30
Lugdunensis 29
Narbonensis 29
*see also* Gaul
Gallic empire 30
Gallipoli 52
Ottoman capture 47
Gallipoli campaign 98–99, 103
Gama, Cristoforo da 72
Gama, Vasco da 54, 60–61, 74
Gambia 82, 86, 89, 97, 99, 106, 109, 116–117, 121
Gandhara 18, 31
Gandhi, Indira 121
Gandhi, Mohandas "Mahatma" 103
Ganges plain 4, 13, 19
Ganges river 21, 44
Gangetic plain 22, 31
Gangotri 44
Gansu 69, 94
Gansu Corridor 26, 43
Gaoping, Battle of 26
Gaozong 43
Gaozu (Liu Bang) 24, 26, 28
Garibaldi, Giuseppe 80
Gascony 46, 52–54
Gaugamela, Battle of 21
Gaul 21, 25, 29–30, 33–34, 36
Aquitani 25
Belgae 25
Celts 23, 25
Cisalpine 23, 25, 29
Franks 36
German invasion 36
Roman empire 23, 25, 28–29, 34
*see also* Gallia, Galliae
Gauls *see* Celts; Gaul
Gaza 10, 15, 115, 118
Battle of 48
Gaza empire 82
Gdansk 101
Gempei war 50
Geneva 58
Geneva Conference 114
Genghis Khan *see* Chingis Khan
Geng Jingzhong 69
Genoa 46, 52–54, 64–68, 71
Geoffrey of Monmouth 46
George I, King of Britain 68
George V, King of Britain 83, 96
Georgetown Accord 112
Georgia 41–47, 49, 51–54, 57, 59, 67, 88, 99–100, 121
Georgia (USA) 73, 75, 84–85
Gepids 30, 33–34
German Confederation 80
Austro–Prussian War 86
Congress of Vienna 78, 80, 82
Franco–Prussian War 86
Seven Weeks War 80
German Democratic Republic (DDR) 109–110, 116, 119, 121
German East Africa 104.
*See also* Tanganyika; Tanzania
German empire 90, 92, 96, 98
Africa **89**
League of Nations mandates 99, 101, 103–104
Qingdao 94
southeast Asia 95, 103
World War I 99, 103, **104**
Germania 29
Germanic tribes 22, 24–25, 28–30, 32, 36
attacks on Roman empire 33–34, 36
German New Guinea 81, 95, 97, 103
German South-West Africa 89, 92, 97
Germans, proto- 19
Germany 38, 41, 45–46, 66, 71, 80, 86, 92, 97, 99, 101, 106, 119, 121
Carolingian rule ends 41
Carolingians *see* Carolingian empire
Communist revolutions 101
*Dreikaiserbund* 96
Dual Alliance 96
East *see* German Democratic Republic (DDR)
German–Polish non-aggression treaty 101
Habsburg dynasty *see* Habsburg dynasty
Hohenzollern dynasty 99, 101
Holy Roman empire *see* Holy Roman empire
hyperinflation 101, 106
Interregnum 46
Nazi party 101, 105, 107, 110

Nazi–Soviet pact 100–101, 105
*Ostpolitik* 110
Peasants' Wars 58
post-World War I reparations 101
post-World War II division 107, 110
Protestant Reformation **58**, 67
reunification 119, 121
Rome–Berlin Axis 101
Saxon dynasty 41
second empire 80, 86
Social Democratic party 90
Thirty Years War **65**, 67–68
Treaty of Brest–Litovsk 99–100
Treaty of Rapallo 100–101
Triple Alliance 96–97
West *see* Federal Republic of Germany (FRG)
World War I **96**, **98**, 99, **104**
World War II 100–101, **104–105**, 106, **107**, 109
*Zollverein* 80, 90–91
Geronimo (Goyathlay) 84
Gettysburg, Battle of 85
Gettysburg Address 85
Gezer 15
Ghana 40, 44–45, 117, 121
Gharra 60, 64, 67
Ghassan 37
Ghatafan 37
*ghazi* 47
Ghaznavid emirate 45, 47, 51
Ghent 53
Ghuzz Turks 45, 51
Giap, General 113
Gibraltar 106, 109, 116, 121
Gilboa, Battle of 15
Giotto di Bondone 52, 54
Girsu 5
Giza 6
Go-Daigo 50
Gokhale, Gopal 83
Golan Heights 115, 118
Golconda 61, 64, 67
gold 4, 7, 10–12, 31, 35, 39, 55–56, 82, 84, 91, 97
gold rushes 84, 86, 93, 97
Gold Coast 72, 82, 86, 89, 97, 99, 106, 109, 117
Golden Bull 52
Golden Horde, Khanate of the 44, 51–54, 57
Gómez, Juan Vicente 102
Gondwana 61
Gordian 14
Gordon, Charles 89
Gorbachev, Mikhail 110, 121
Gorlice-Tarnow, Battle of 98
Götar 33, 38, 41
Goths 30, 33–34, 36, 38, 41.
*See also* Ostrogoths; Visigoths
Gotland 41
Gracchus, Tiberius 29
Granada 46, 51–54, 58, 60
Christian reconquest 48
Gran Chaco 102
Gran Colombia 81–82
Granicus river 21
Grant, Ulysses 85
Grasse, François Joseph Paul, Marquis de Grasse-Tilly, Comte de 75
Gravettian culture 3
Gray, Robert 84
Great Depression 101–102, 106
Greater East Asian Co-Prosperity Sphere 103
Great Khanate 49, 51
"Great Leap Forward" 113, 116
Great Northern War 71
Great Plains 70, 102
Great Plains Indians 42, 45, 57
Great Poland 71
Great Schism 44, 47, 52, 54, 57
Great Seljuk sultanate 48
Great Trek 86
Great Wall of China 26, 69
Great Zimbabwe *see* Zimbabwe
Greece 82, 86, 90, 92, 96–99, 101, 104, 106, 109–110, 116, 119, 121
Balkan pact 101
civil war 109
War of Independence 80, 82
war with Turkey 101
World War II 105, 107
*see also* Greek civilization
Greek civilization 7, 9, 13, 18–19, 21, 23, 25
5th century BC **20**
aristocracy 16
Celts 25
city-states **16**, 18–19, 22
colonies 16
dark ages 11, 13, 16
Delian league 20
democracy 16, 18, 20–22
Hellenic league 22, 24
Hellenistic 28
Macedonian supremacy 24
monarchy 16
Mycenae *see* Mycenae, Mycenaean civilization
oligarchy 16
pan-Hellenic festivals 16

Peloponnesian War 20, 22
Persian Wars 20, **20**, 22
Roman rule 23, 28–29
Spartan league 20
trade 16
Trojan War 11
tyrants 16
Visigoth invasion 33
*see also* Athens; Bactria; Sparta
"Greek Fire"
Greek language 34
Greenland 38, 41–42, 45, 106
Greenville, Treaty of 84
Gregory the Great, Pope 34
Gregory of Tours 34
Grenada 58, 112, 116, 121
Grenadines *see* St Vincent and the Grenadines
Grenville, George 75
Gros Ventre 73
Grozny 119
Guadalcanal, Battle of 108
Guadalupe Hidalgo, Treaty of 81
Guahipo 62
Guam 97, 102–103, 108
Battle of 108
Guangdong 69, 102
Guangxi 69
Guangzhou 69, 94
Guannei 43
Guantánamo Bay 102
Guarani 62
Guatemala 39, 81–82, 86, 97, 99, 102, 106, 109, 111–112, 116, 121
Guernica 101
Battle of 101
Guetaria, Battle of 65
Guevara, Che 111–112
Guinea 64, 72, 116–117, 121
Guinea Bissau 116–117, 121
Guizhou 69, 94
Gujarat 61, 83
Gulf Wars
First (Iran–Iraq) **118**, 121
Second **118**, 121
gunpowder 43
Gunpowder Plot 65
Guomindang (Kuomintang; KMT) 94
Gupta empire **31**, 32
fall 31, 36
Gurjara-Pratiharas 37, 40, 43
Gurkhas 61, 79, 82–83, 103
Gurkha War 83
Gustavus I Vasa, King of Sweden 58
Gustavus II Adolphus, King of Sweden 65, 67
Gutenberg, Johannes 57
Gutians 5
Guyana 9, 71, 76, 111–112, 116, 121
Guyenne revolt 65
Gypsies 105, 107

## H

Habsburg dynasty 52, 54, 68, 99, 101
Austrian lands 58, 65
Charles V 58–60
Spanish lands 58, 65, 68
Thirty Years War **65**, 67–68
Treaty of Utrecht 68
*see also* Austrian empire; Holy Roman empire; Spain
Habsburg empire 77, 80, 86
French Revolutionary wars 77
Napoleonic Wars 77–78
Habuba Kabira 5
Hadar 1
Hadramaut 22, 24, 28, 35, 37, 45, 51, 57, 60, 64, 67, 104
Hadrian, Emperor 29–30
Hadrian's Wall 30
Hafrsfjord, Battle of 41
Hafsid caliphate 51, 57
Haile Selassie (Ras Tafari) 104, 117
Haiti 79, 81–82, 86, 97, 99, 102, 106, 109, 112, 112.
*See also* St Domingue, 116, 121
Hakataka Bay, Battle of 50
Hakka rebellion 94
Hakodate 93
halberd 12
Halifax (Nova Scotia) 73
Halikarnassos 21
Hallstatt culture 19, 25
Halsey, William 108
Hamadan 14, 18
Hamath 15
Hamazi 5
Hampton Roads, Battle of 85
Hamwih 38
Han 26, 28
Han Chinese 69
Han dynasty 24, **26**, 27–28, 32, 43
Hanifab 37
Hannibal 23–24
Hanoi 95, 114
Hanover 77, 80
Duchy of 68
Hanoverian dynasty 68
Hanseatic league 53, 66
Hao 8
Harald Bluetooth 41, 44
Harald Hadrada 51
Hara massacre 63
Hardwar 44
Harold II, King of England 46

Harpers Ferry Raid 85
Harran 14
Harsha 31, 37, 40
Hastings, Battle of 46
Hatakeyama 50
Hatshepsut 10
Hattin, Horns of, Battle of 46, 48
Hausaland 79
Hausa states 51, 57, 60, 64, 67, 71–72, 76
Havana 62, 73, 76
Hawaii 32, 86, 92
Hazor 15
Hebei 43
Hebrews 10, 13–15, 27
exile 15
*see also* Jews
Hebron 15, 115
Hecataeus 25
Hedong 43
Heian 40, 50
Heiji insurrection 50
Heilungjiang 69
Hein, Piet 62, 68
Hejaz 36–37, 59, 99, 104
Heje Kiakia 69
Heligoland (Helgoland) 78, 89, 96
Battle of 98
Hellenes 16
Hellenic league 22, 24
Hellenistic Greece 28
Hellespont 18, 20
Helsinki Agreement 110, 121
Helvetia 78–79
Helvetic Republic 77
Helvetii 25
Henan 43, 69, 94
henges 7, 9
Hennepin 70
Henry III, Holy Roman emperor 46
Henry IV, Holy Roman emperor 46
Henry V, Holy Roman emperor 46
Henry II, King of England 46
Henry IV, King of England 54
Henry V, King of England 54
Henry VII, King of England 54, 58
Henry VIII, King of England 58
Henry IV, King of France 65
Henry the Fowler, King of Germany 41
Henry the Lion, Duke of Saxony and Bavaria 46
Heraclea, Battle of 23
Heraclius 34, 36, 40
Herero 72, 89
heresies 48, 52, 54
hermits 27
Herodotos 20
Herzegovina 80
Hesse 65, 80
Hezekiah 15
Hidalgo, Father Miguel 79, 81
Hidetada 63
Hideyori 63
Hideyoshi Toyotomi 63–64
Hierakonpolis 6
*hijra* 36–37, 40, 44
hillforts 13
Himeji, White Heron Castle 50
Himyar 37
Himyarite kingdom 28, 32
Hinduism 19, 24, 27–28, 31–32, 36, 40, 45, 51, 57, 61
Bakhti movement 44
Brahmanic 27
and Buddhism 27
caste system 27
Dravidian 27
Indonesia 31
*karma* 27
*Mahabharata* 27, 31
Mathura 31
pilgrimage 44
*Ramayana* 27, 31
spread **27**, **44**
*Upanishads* 27
Vedas 27
Hindu Kush 31
Hippias 16
Hirado Island 63
Hirohito, Emperor 108, 113
Hiroshima bomb 108–109
Hirpini 23
Hispaniae 30
Hispaniola 57, 60, 62. *See also* Dominican Republic; Haiti; St Domingue; Santo Domingo
Hit 5
Hitler, Adolf 100–101, 105–107
Hittites 9–15
Neo-Hittites 14–15
Hizbollah 118
Hoababa 55
Ho Chi Minh 113–114
Ho Chi Minh Trail 114
Hogen insurrection 50
Hohenlinden, Battle of 77
Hohenstaufen dynasty 46
Hohenzollern dynasty 80, 99, 101
Hohokam culture 32, 36, 40, 42, 45, 51
Holland 52, 68, 77–78
Holstein 46, 54, 80
Holy Land 47, 51
Crusades *see* Crusades
Holy league 59
Holy Roman empire 41, 45–46,

48–49, 51–54, 57–60, 64–65, 67–68,
77–78
foundation 41, 45
Golden Bull 52
Habsburg emperors 54
Investiture Contest 46, 51
Peace of Augsburg 58
Protestant Reformation **58**
Thirty Years War **65**, 67–68
*see also* Germany
Homer 11, 16
hominoid apes 1
*Homo erectus* 1–2
*Homo habilis* 1
*Homo sapiens* 1–2
*Homo sapiens neanderthalensis* 1–2
*Homo sapiens sapiens* 1–2
Hondschoote, Battle of 77
Honduras 81–82, 86, 97, 99, 102, 106,
109, 111–112, 116, 121
"football war" 112
Hong Kong 94–95, 102, 106, 109, 113,
116
return to Chinese control 102, 121
World War II 108
Hong Xiuquan 94
Honorius 33
Honshu 32, 50
Hood, Samuel 75
Hopewell culture 28, 32, 36, 40
Hopi 70
Hormuz 67
horse 3–4, 7, 11–12, 19, 24, 26, 42
cavalry warfare 49, 52
Hoshea 15
Hosokawa 50
Hospital of St John, Order of the
(Hospitallers) 48, 52–54, 58–59
Houphouet-Boigny, Félix 117
Hova 72
Howe, Richard, Admiral Lord 75
Howe, William, 5th Viscount Howe
75
Hsien-pi 26
Hsiung-nu *see* Xiongnu
Huainan 43
Huanca 56
Huang Di 8
Huari empire 36, 40, 45, 56
Huáscar 56
Huaxtec 70
Huaxtepec 55
Huaymil 55
Huayna Capac 56, 60
Hubei 69
Hudson Bay 73
Hudson, Henry 70
Hudson river 73, 75
Hudson's Bay Company 70
Hué 114
Treaty of 95
Huerta, Victoriano 81
Huguenots 64–66, 68
Hui Muslims 69
Hukbalahar revolt 113
Hülegü
Humayun 61, 64
Hunac Ceel 55
Hunan 69
Hunas 31, 31. *See also* Ephthalite
Huns
Hundred Years War 47, 52, 54, 57
Hungary, Hungarians 41, 45–49,
51–54, 57–60, 65, 68, 80, 99, 101,
106, 109–110, 116, 119, 121
Habsburg empire 80
Hungarian revolt 110, 116
Kun regime 101
Russian empire 88
World War II 105, 107
*see also* Austria–Hungary
Huns 31–34, 36
Ephthalite (White) *see* Ephthalite
Huns
Hun confederation 36
hunter–gatherers 1–4, 7, 9, 13, 19, 22,
24, 28, 32, 36
Huron 70, 73
Hurrians 9
Husain 37, 44
Hus, Jan 54
Hussites 48, 54
Hydaspes river, Battle of 21
Hyderabad 83
Hyksos 10

# I

Iazygians 28
Ibadan empire 82, 86
Iberia, Iberians 25, 30
Ibn Battuta 47
Ibn Rushd (Averröes) 47
Ibn Saud, Abdul Aziz 104
Ibo 35
Ica 56
Ice Age 1–4, 10
Iceland 41, 45, 57, 99, 105, 109, 116,
119, 121
Icelandic sagas 46
"ice man" 7
Iceni 25
Iconium 47
Iconoclast controversy 44
Idaho 84
Idris III Aloma 64, 72
Idrisid caliphate 40–41
Ieyasu, Tokugawa 63, 93

121
Ifni 89
Ifriqiya 37
Ijebu 89
Ilerda, Battle of 29
Ile Royale (Cape Breton I) 73
Ile St Jean *see* Prince Edward Island
Ili Protectorate 69, 94
Ilkhanate 51, 53, 57
Illinois 84–85
Illyrian Provinces 78
Illyrians 13, 16, 19–20, 22–25
Ilopango, Lake 39
Imad Shahis 61
IMF *see* International Monetary Fund
Imphal, Battle of 108
Impressed Pottery cultures 7, 9, 12
Inca civilization **56**, 57, 60, 62, 64
Inchon 113
India 4, 19, 24, 27, 32, 72, 74, 79, 82,
86, 92, 97, 99, 103, 106, 108, 113,
116, 121
Achemenid empire 22
Aryan invasion 27
border dispute with China 113
British 71, 74, 76, 82, **83**, 86, 97,
103, 106, 109
caste system 27
Chola state 45
Congress party 106
Delhi sultanate 57
Dutch 67, 71
Ephthalites 31, 36
European exploration 54
French 61, 71, 76
Gupta empire *see* Gupta empire
Hunas 31
independence 109, 116
Indian Mutiny (First War of
Independence) 83, 86
Indo–Pakistan Wars 116
Kanauj (Harsha) empire 37, 40
Kushan empire **31**, 32
Magadha *see* Magadha
Marathas *see* Marathas
Maratha Wars 83
Mauryan empire *see* Mauryan
empire
Mughal empire *see* Mughal empire
National Congress 103
partition 113
Portuguese 59, 61, 74
religions 27, 44.
*See also* Buddhism; Hinduism;
Islam; Sikhism
Saka invasions 28
Satavahanihara 28, 31
Sur dynasty 61, 64
Vijayanagar 57
World War II 108
Indiana 84–85
Indian Ocean 4
Indian Territory 84–85
Indo–China **114**
French 99, 103, 106, 108–109, 113
Japanese control 103
Vietminh 103, 113–114
World War II 106
*see also individual countries*
Indo–Chinese Union *see* French
Indo–China
Indo–Iranian peoples 14
Indonesia 32, 36, 40, 57, 102–103,
109, 113, 116, 121
Austronesians 32
Hinduism 31
independence 109, 113
World War II 106, 108
Indus river 40
Industrial Revolution 66, **90**
Indus Valley civilization 9, 13
Ingalik 70
Innocent III, Pope 46, 48
Inquisition 44
Spanish 54
Insubres 25
internal combustion engine 99
International Monetary Fund (IMF)
109, 112
Inuit 42, 70, 73, 84
Investiture Contest 46, 51
Ionia, Ionian Greeks 16, 18, 20–21
Ionian Islands 77–78, 80
Iowa 84–85
Ipsus, Battle of 21
Iran 5, 13–14, 18–19, 45, 51, 104, 106,
109, 115–116, 118, 121
British and Soviet invasion 104
First Gulf (Iran–Iraq) War **118**, 121
Shiite revolution 118, 121
United State embassy hostages 118
United States restores shah to
power 115
*see also* Persia, Persians
Iranian nomads 24, 28. *See also* Parni
Iraq 99, 104–107, 109, 115–116, 118,
121
Ba'ath party 115
British mandate 104
British protectorate status 104
civil war 118
First Gulf (Iran–Iraq) War **118**, 121
Kurds 118
nationalist revolution 115
Second Gulf War **118**, 121
*see also* Mesopotamia
Ireland 12, 52, 54, 58, 65–66, 77,
79–80, 105, 107, 109–110, 116, 119,

121
Act of Union (1800) 78
Celts 25
Christianity 25, 38, 41
Easter Rising 98
Famine 80, 92
Irish kingdoms 38, 41, 46
Irish Republican Brotherhood
(Fenians) 80
Pale 54, 58
Scots 25
Ulster Protestants 65, 101
United Irishmen rebellion 77, 79
Vikings 41 -
*see also* Irish Free State; Northern
Ireland
Irian Jaya 113
Irish Free State 101, 106
civil war 101
Irish Rebellion 65
Irish Republican Brotherhood
(Fenians) 80
Iron Age 12, 16, 19
Africa 32, **35**, 36
China 26
Europe 19, 25
"iron curtain" 110
iron working 4, 8, 10, 12–13, 19, 22,
26, 32, 35–36
Iroquoian woodland farmers 51, 57,
60, 64, 67
Iroquois 42, 70, 73
irrigation 4, 6, 17
Isabella of Castile 54, 57–58
Isaiah 15
Isfahan 47
Isidore of Seville 38
Iskanderun 59
Islam 27, 36, 40–41, 45, 57–58
Africa 51, 71–72, 79
Arabs 37, 40
calendar 37, 40
caliphs 37
China 69, 94
*hijra* 36–37, 40, 44
India 51, **61**
*jihad* 47, 60, 72
*Koran* 37, 40, 44
Mughal empire **61**, 64
Ottoman empire **59**
renascent 117–118, 121
Shiite tradition 37, 44, 47, 118, 121
southeast Asia 57
Soviet Union 121
Spain 37–38, 40, 44–46, 48, 51
spread 37, **44**, 48
Sufism 44
Sunni tradition 37, 44, 47, 118
Ismail I 60
Ismaili Nizari (Assassins) 44, 47–48
Isonzo, Battles of the 98
Israel 2, 13–15, 19, 109, 115–116, 118,
121
Arab–Israeli conflict 109, **115**, 116,
**118**, 121
Assyrian conquest 14
Camp David agreements 118
Egyptian invasion 10, 15
foundation of modern state 104,
109, 115
Jewish settlement 15
Six Day War 115–116
split with Judah 15
Suez crisis 115
West Bank Jewish settlers 118
Yom Kippur War 115–116
Isshiki 50
Issus river, Battle of 21
Istanbul *see* Constantinople
Isthmus of Corinth 20
Itaipú hydro-electric plant 111
Italian Somaliland 89, 97, 99, 106,
109, 117
Italian Wars 54, 58
Italics 25
Italy 29–30, 41, 46, 52, 66, 78–79, 82,
86, 90, 92, 96–99, 101, 106,
109–110, 116, 119, 121
African colonies 89
Byzantine empire 38
Carbonari 80
Celts 22, 25
Etruscans *see* Etruscans
Fascism 101, 106
Greeks 23
Habsburg rule 58
invasion of Ethiopia 97, 101, 104,
106
Italian Wars 58
Lateran treaties 101
Lombard league 46
Lombards 30, 33–34, 36, 38
Napoleonic Wars 77
Normans 46
Northern League 119
Odoacer 33–34
Renaissance 54, 57–58
*Risorgimento* 80
Romans *see* Roman empire; Roman
republic; Rome
Rome–Berlin Axis 101
Triple Alliance 96–97
unification 80, 82, 86
Visigoths 33
World War I 96, 98–99
World War II 104, **107**, 109, **109**
Itsekiri resistance 89

Iturbide, Agustin 81
Itzcóatl 55, 57
Ivan III, (the Great) 54
ivory 35
Ivory Coast 82, 86, 116–117, 121
Iwo Jima, Battle of 108
Izmir 101

# J

Jackson, Andrew 84
Jackson, Thomas "Stonewall" 85
Jacobites 68, 75
Jacquerie 52
Jaffa 104
Jaguar Paw, King 39
Jahangir, Emperor 61
Jalalabad 83
Jamaica 62, 71, 99, 102, 106, 109, 112,
116, 121
James I, King of England (James VI,
King of Scotland) 65
James II, King of England 68
Jamestown 70
*janapadas*
Janissaries 47, 59
Jankau, Battle of 65
Japan 4, 40, 45, **50**, 51, 57, 60, **63**, 64,
67, 69, 71, 76, 79, 82, 86, 88, 92, **93**,
94, 97, 99–100, **102–103**, 106, **108**,
109, **113**, 116, 121
Anglo–Japanese Naval Alliance 93,
96
Ashikaga shogunate 50, 63
Azuchi-Momoyama period 63–64
Edo period 63
European trading bases 63–64, 67
first states 32
German Pacific colonies 99, 103
Heian period 40, 50
industrialization 93, 99, 102
invasion of China 103
Kamakura shogunate 50
Kuril Islands 86
medieval 50
Meiji restoration 86, 93
"New Order" 106
occupation of Manchuria and
Siberia 99, 106
Onin war 63
Russo–Japanese War 88, 93, 97,
103
Satsuma rebellion 93
Sino–Japanese War (1894–5)
93–94, 97
Sino–Japanese War (1937) 106
Tokugawa shogunate 63, 67, 86
United States military occupation
113
war with China 108
Washington Naval Agreement 106
world trade 86, 91
World War I 99, 103
World War II 103, 106, 108–109
Yayoi culture 24, 28, 32, 36
Jats 84
Java 45, 67, 74, 95
Java Sea, Battle of 108
Jazira 47
Jebel Barkal 35
Jebusites 15
Jedisan 58–59
Jefferson, Thomas 84
Jehol 103
Jehu 15
Jemappes 66
Battle of 77
Jemdet Nasr 5
Jena-Auerstädt, Battle of 78
Jend, Battle of 47
Jenne-jeno 35–36
Jerez de la Frontera, Battle of 37–38
Jericho 118
Jerome, St 22
Jerusalem 15, 27, 44, 115
Arab conquest 34, 37, 46–48, 51
Battle of (1917) 99
British occupation 99, 104
and Christianity 44, 48
Crusader conquest 44, 46–48, 51
division 115
Hebrew capture 15
Israeli occupation 115, 118
Kingdom of 48
patriarchal see 44
religious importance 15
sack 15
temple 15
Jesuit Order 58, 62, 69–70, 72
Jesus of Nazareth 27, 32
Jews 15, 27, 44, 101
Balfour Declaration 99, 104
Bible lands 15
Diaspora 15, 27
exile 15
expulsion from Spain 54
"Final Solution" 104–107
forcible conversion to Christianity
44, 54
Israel 104, 109
Jewish resettlement by
Nebuchadnezzar 14
Jewish state in Palestine 99, 104
massacres of 52
Old Testament 5, 15
Russian 88, 92
Warsaw revolt 107

Zionist movement 92, 104
*see also* Hebrews
Jiang Ching-kuo 102
Jiang Jieshi (Chiang Kai-shek) 102,
106, 113
Jiangnan-Dong 43
Jiangnan-Xi 43
Jiangsu 69
Jiangxi 69
Jiannan 43
Jin 8, 26, 32
Jin Chuans 69
Jin dynasty 26, 32, 49, 51, 69
Jingji 43
Jin Khan *see* Nurhachi
Jintian 94
Joan of Arc 54
João III, King of Portugal 60
Joao VI, King of Portugal 81–82
John II, Duke of Burgundy 52
John the Fearless, Duke of Burgundy
52, 54
John, King of England 46
John of Luxembourg, King of
Bohemia 52
John Paul II, Pope 110
Johnson, Lyndon Baines 114
Johore 95
Jomon 4, 13, 22
Joppa 15
Jordan 104, 109, 115–116, 118, 121
Arab–Israeli conflict 115
*see also* Transjordan
Jordan river 13
Joshua 15
Josiah 15
Juan-juan 32, 36
Judah 10, 14–15
Judaism *see* Jews
Judea 29
Juheina 37
Julian, Roman emperor 30
Julius II, Pope 58
July Revolution 80
Junagadh 31
Jürchen (Manchus) 45, 50, 57, 69
Jurjen 47
Justin 34
Justinian 34, 36
Jutes 33
Jutland, Battle of 98

# K

Kaarta 71–72, 76, 79, 82
Kabul 61, 83
Kadiri 51
Kaegyong 50
Kaesong 50
Battle of 63
Kaffa 52
Kagoshima 93
Kaifeng 49
Kailas, Mount 44
Kaintuck 73
*kaisara* 31
Kaiser Wilhelmsland 99
Kalb 37
Kalinga 24, 28
Kalka, Battle of 49
Kalhu 14
Kallias, peace of 20
Kalmar *see* Calmar
Kalmyks 60, 64, 67, 69, 71
Kamakura shogunate 50
Kamarupa 49
*Kamasutra* 31
Kamchatka 108
Kaminaljuyú 39
Kammu 40, 50
Kampuchea *see* Cambodia
Kan'ami Kiyotsugo 50
Kanauj (Harsha) empire 31, 36–37, 40
Kandahar 61
Kandy 79
Kanem-Bornu 51, 60, 64, 72, 79, 82,
86
Kanghwa 50
Kanishka 31
Kanpur 83
Kansas 62, 84–85
Kara-Khitai 49
Karakorum 49
Karama, Battle of 115
Karankawa 70
Karasuk culture 13
Karbala 37, 44
Battle of 37, 44
Karelia 105
Karkheh 14
Karlowitz, Treaty of 68
*karma* 27
Karnak 10
Kasanie 72
Kashgar, Khanate of 61
Kashmir 37, 43–44, 51, 61,
82–83
Kassites 5, 9
Kastri 11
Katanga 117
Kato Kiyomasa 63
Kaunda, Kenneth 117
Kay, John 66
Kazakhs 57, 88
Kazakhstan 121

Kazan Tatars 60, 64
Kazembe 79, 86
Kedah 95
Kelantan 95
Kelheim 12
Kelsey, Henry 70
Kellogg–Briand pact 101
Kennedy, John F. 111–112, 114, 116
Kentucky 70, 84–85
Kenya 116–117, 121
independence 117
Kenyatta, Jomo 117
Keraits 44–45, 49
Kerma 10, 35
Ket's rebellion 58
Keynes, J.M. 101
Khaireddin 59
Khairpur 83
Khalkas 57, 69, 71
Khalkin-Gol, Battle of 103
Khandesh 61
Khania 11
Kharga Oasis 18
Kharkov, Battle of 107
Khartoum 89
Khazar Khanate 41, 44
Khazars 36–37, 40, 45, 47
Khedive Ismail Pasha 89
Khendjer 10
Khephren 6
Khe Sanh 114
Khilakku 14
Khitans 40, 43, 45, 50
Khiva 88
Khmer 40, 45, 49, 51
Khmer Republic
*see* Cambodia
Khmer Rouge 102, 114
Khoisan 9, 13, 19, 24, 28, 32, 35–36,
40, 45, 51, 57, 60, 64, 67, 72, 76, 79,
82
Khomeini, Ayatollah 115, 118
Khorasan 37, 47
Khorchin 69
Khotan
Battle of 31
Khrushchev, Nikita 112, 116
Khubilai Khan 51
Khufu 6
Khwarizm shahdom 47, 49
Khyber Pass 83
Kiel Canal 91
Kiev 41, 107
Principality of 46
Kievan Rus 41, 45–46
Kikuyu 72
Killke 56
Kim Il Sung 102, 113
Kinda 37
Kingdom of the Two Sicilies 80
King, Martin Luther 111
"King Movement"
Kingsford-Smith, Charles 99
King's Mountain, Battle of 75
Kinkjikitele Ngwale 89
Kiowa 84
Kipchaks 49. *See also* Cumans
Kirghiz 36, 40, 45, 57, 60, 64, 67, 71
Kiribati 102, 121
Kirov, Sergey M. 100
Kish 5
Kiska 108
Kissinger, Henry 114
Kitchener, Horatio Herbert, Earl 89
Kleisthenes 16, 18, 20
Kleve 65
Klondike gold rush 97
KMT *see* Guomindang
Knossos 11
Kobayakawa 63
Koch 61
Koguryo 26, 28, 32, 36, 43, 50
Kohima, Battle of 108
Ko Hung 27
Kolchaks 100
Komchen 17
Konarak 44
Kong 76
Konishi Yukinaga 63
Kooorenay 70
*Koran* 37, 40, 44
Korea 4, 9, 13, 19, 24, 26, 28, 40, 43,
45, 49, 57, 60, 63–64, 67, 69, 71, 76,
79, 82, 86, 88, 92–94, 97, 99, 106
division 113
independence 93, 97
Japanese annexation 93, 97, 103
Koguryo *see* Koguryo
Korean War 109–110, 113
medieval 50
Mongol invasions 49–50
Silla *see* Silla
Tonghak revolt 93
World War II 108, 113
*see also* North Korea; South Korea
Koryo 43, 50
Kosala 31
Kosciuszko, Tadeusz 77
Kose Dagh, Battle of 47
Kosovo 52
Battle of 47, 52
Kotosh tradition 17
Koxinga
*see* Zheng Cheng–gong
Krajina 119
Kuba 72
Kujala Kadphises 31

### L

Kukulcán 55
Kulikovo, Battle of 52
Kumano 44
Kumanovo, Battle of 96
Kummukhu (Commagene) 14
Kun, Bela 101
Kunling 43
Kuomintang (KMT) see Guomindang
Kurdistan 59, 118
Kurds 47, 118
*kurgan*
Kuril Islands 86, 93, 108
Kurka 69
Kursk, Battle of 107, 109
Kush 10, 13, 19
Kushans 31–32, 35–36
Kut, Battle of 98
Kuwait 97, 99, 104, 106, 109, 115–116,
    118, 121
    independence 115
    Iraqi invasion 118, 121
Küyük 49
Kwajalein, Battle of 108
Kwangtung Territory 93–94
Kyakhta
    Treaty of 69
Kynouria 16
Kyogoku 50
Kyoto 40, 50, 63
Kyreskhata 18
Kyrgyzstan 121
Kythera 11, 16
Kyushu 63

## L

La Albuera, Battle of 78
Labrador 79, 82, 86, 97
Lachish 15
Laconia 16
Ladakh 51, 61, 69
Lagash 5
La Hogue, Battle of 68
Lahore 61
Laibach, Congress of 80
Laitoli 1
Lakhm 37
Lamaism 44
La Marche 58
Lambayeque 56
Lancastrian dynasty 54
Langson, Battle of 94
Languedoc revolt 65
Laos 57, 60, 64, 67, 69, 76, 79, 82, 86,
    95, 102, 113–114, 116, 121
Lao Zi (Lao Tsu) 27
Lapita culture 13, 19, 22
Lapland, Lapps 60
La Plata, Vice-Royalty of 79
Lapps 13, 19, 22, 24, 28, 32, 36, 40, 45,
    51, 57
Laramie, Treaty of 84
La Rochelle 65
Las Casas, Bartolomé de 62
Lascaux 3
Las Navas de Tolosa, Battle of 46
La Tène culture 22, 25
Lateran treaties 101
Latin America 81
    immigration 81, 92
    War of the Pacific 81, 86
    War of the Triple Alliance
        (Paraguayan War) 81, 86
Latin American Integration
    Association 111
Latin empire 47–48, 53
Latin language and alphabet 25, 34
Latins, Latium 23
Latvia 98–101, 105, 109–110, 119, 121
Laurion 20
La Vérendrye, Pierre Gaultier de 70
League of Augsburg, War of the 68,
    73
League of Nations 99–103, 106
    mandates 99, 101, 103–104
Lebanon 104–105, 107, 109, 115–116,
    118, 121
    Arab–Israeli conflict 115, 118
    civil war 115, 118
    French mandate 104
    Palestinian refugees 118
    World War II 104
Lechfeld, Battle of 41
Le Duan 114
Le Duc Tho 114
Lee Kuan Yew 102
Lee, Robert E. 85
Legnano 43
Legnica, Battle of 49
Leipzig, Battle of 78
Lend–Lease scheme 102, 105
Leningrad
    Siege of 105–107
    see also Petrograd; St Petersburg
Lenin, Vladimir Ilych 88, 100
Leo III, Pope 38
León 41, 45–46
Leonardo da Vinci 54
Leonidas of Sparta 20
Leopold II, King of the Belgians 89
Lepanto, Battle of 59, 64
Lepenski Vir 3
Leptis Magna 35
Lerida, Battle of 65
Lesotho 116–117, 121.
    See also Basutoland
Lesseps, Ferdinand de 81

Leubingen 12
Levant 10, 13–15, 28
    Aurignacian culture 3, 10
Levellers 65
Lewis, Meriwether 84
Lexington, Battle of 75
Leyte 108
    Battle of 108
Leyte Gulf, Battle of 108
Liao 45
Liaodong 69, 93
Liaoyang
    Battle of 93
Liberia 86, 89, 92, 97, 99, 106, 109,
    116–117, 121
    civil war 117
Licchavis 31
Liechtenstein 119
Liège, Battle of 98
Ligny, Battle of 78
Ligurian Republic 77
Ligurians 23
Li Hongzhang 94
Lille 107
Lilybaeum, Battle of 23–24
Lima 81
    Battle of 81
Limanowa, Battle of 98
Limerick 41
Lincoln, Abraham 85–86
Lindisfarne 38, 41
Linear A script 11
Linear B script 11
Linear Pottery culture
    see Bandkeramik culture
Linebacker II, Operation 114
linen (flax) 4
Lingjiu (Vulture Peak) 27
Lingnan 43
Lin Zexu 94
Li Po 43
Lirong 8
Lisbon 46, 48, 74
    Battle of 78
Lithuania 44, 46, 48, 51–54, 57–58,
    98–101, 105, 109–110, 119
    "Little Entente" 101
Little Poland 77
Little Rock, Arkansas 111
Liu Bang see Gaozu
Livonia 58, 68
Livs 46
Livy 29
Li Yuan 43
llama 17
Loango 72
Locarno, Treaties of 101
Lodi sultanate 60–61, 64
Lodz, Battle of 98
Lokris 20
Lollards 52
Lombard duchies 37
Lombard kingdom 37
Lombard league 46
Lombards 30, 33–34, 36, 38
Lombardy 80
London 53, 66, 105
    Great Plague 68, 71
longhouses 7
Long Island, Battle of 75
Long March 106
Longshan culture 8–9, 13
Long Wall of Wei 26
Long Wall of Yan 26
Long Wall of Zhao 26
Longyou 43
Lordship of the Isles 54
Lorraine 41, 46, 68, 90.
    See also Alsace–Lorraine
Los Alamos 111
lost-wax process 5
Lostwithiel, Battle of 65
Louis I, King of France (the Pious) 38,
    41
Louis IX, King of France (St Louis) 48
Louis XI, King of France 54, 58
Louis XIII, King of France 65
Louis XIV, King of France 67–68, 71,
    73
Louis XVI, King of France 77
Louis II, King of Hungary 58
Louis IV, Duke of Wittelsbach 52
Louisbourg 73
Louisiana 62, 71, 73, 84–85
    Louisiana Purchase 79, 84
Louis Napoleon see Napoleon III
Louis-Philippe, King of France 80
L'Ouverture, Toussaint 79
Louvois, François Michel le Tellier 68
Lozi 72, 79, 82, 86
Lu 8
Luanda 72, 74
Luang Prabang 71
Luba 60, 64, 67, 71–72, 76, 86
Lübeck 53
Lucanians 23
Lucca 78, 80
Lucknow 83
"Lucy" (*Australopithecus afarensis*) 1

Luddites 90
Ludendorff offensive 98
Luftwaffe 105
Lugalzagesi 5
Lugano 46
Lunda 60, 64, 67, 71–72, 76, 86
Luolang 26
Luoyang 8, 26, 43
Luristan 59
Lusatia 58
Lusitania, Lusitanians 23, 25, 29
*Lusitania*, SS 98
Lutheranism 58
Luther, Martin 58
Lutter, Battle of 65
Lützen, Battle of 65, 78
Luva 51
Luvians 13
Luxembourg 58, 68, 80, 90, 96, 98,
    101, 106, 110, 116, 119, 121
Luxembourg dynasty 52, 54
Luxeuil monastery 41
Lu Yu 43
Luzon 113
    Battle of 108
Lycia, Lycians 16, 29
Lydia, Lydians 16, 18, 20
Lysimachos 21

## M

Maan kingdom 24
Maastricht Treaty 119
Macao 64, 74, 95, 102, 106, 109, 113,
    116, 121
MacArthur, Douglas 108, 113
Macartney, Lord 94
Macchu Picchu 56
Macedonia (Former Yugoslav
    Republic of) 119, 121
Macedon, Macedonia 16, 18, 20–24,
    29, 97, 101
    Hellenic league 22, 24
    rise of 22
    see also Alexander the Great
McNamara, Robert 114
Madagascar 32, 35, 71–72, 79, 89, 97,
    99, 106, 109, 116, 117.
    See also Malagasy, 121
Madero, Francisco 81
Madras 76, 83
Madrid 68
    Treaty of 62
Madurai 61
Maeda 63
Magadha 19, 22, 24, 31, 44
    Seleucid invasion 24
    see also Mauryan empire
Magdalenian 3
Magdeburg, sack 65
Magellan, Ferdinand 60, 62
Magenta, Battle of 80
Maghrib 35
Maginot line 105
Magna Carta 46
Magna Mahumeria 48
Magnesia, Battle of 29
Magna Graecia 23
Magnitogorsk 100
Magyars 38, 40–41, 45
*Mahabharata* 27, 31
*maharaja* 31
Mahayana Buddhism 27
*Mahdi* 89
Mahmud of Ghazni 45
Mahra 60, 64, 67
Maine 73, 84–85
Mainz 54
maize 4, 9, 17, 28, 32, 36, 40, 42, 45
Maji-Maji rebellion 89
Makkura 27, 35–37, 40, 44–45, 51, 57
Makran 37
Malabar 61
Malacca 57, 60, 67, 74, 95
Malaga, Battle of 68
Malagasy 45, 51, 57, 60, 64, 67, 71–72,
    76. See also Madagascar
Malan, D.F.
Malawi 116–117, 121
Malaya 36, 91, 95, 109, 113
    World War II 106, 108
Malayo–Indonesians 36
Malays 57, 79, 82, 86, 95–95, 97, 99,
    103, 106
Malaysia 102, 113–113, 116, 121
Maldives 116
Mali 44–45, 51, 57, 60, 64, 67, 71, 89,
    116–117
Malik Shah 47
Mallet, P and P 70
Mallia 11
Mallorca 46, 53
Malta 48, 58–59, 77–78, 105, 107, 110,
    119
Malwa 61
Mamluke sultanate 47–49, 51–53, 57,
    59–61
    Napoleonic Wars 77–78
Mam Maya 55
Managua 112
Manaus 81
Man, Kingdom of 46
Manching 25
Manchu empire 67, 69, 71, 76, 79, 82,
    86, 88, 92–93, 103
    decline and overthrow 94, 97, 99,
    103

Manchuria 69, 88, 92–94, 103
    Japanese occupation 99, 103, 106
    Manzhouguo 103, 106, 108
    World War II 108
Manco Capac 56
Mandalay 108
Mandan 70, 73
Mandela, Nelson 117, 121
Manding 72
Mandinka 89
Manhattan Island 70, 73
Manichaeism 44–45
Manila 62, 95
Manila Bay, Battle of 95
Manipur 83, 95
Manitoba 84
Mannea 14
manorial system 53
Mansa Uli 51
Mansfeld, Count Ernst 65
Mansura, Battle of 48
Mantua 54, 65
Manzhouguo 103, 106, 108
Manzikert, Battle of 47, 51
Maoris 57, 60, 64, 67, 71, 76, 82
    Maori Wars 82, 86
Mao Zedong 102, 109, 113, 116
Maranhão 62
Marathas 61, 71, 76, 83
Marathon, Battle of 18, 20
"March to the Sea" 85
Marcomanni 30
Marco Polo Bridge incident 103
Marcos, Ferdinand 102
Marcus Island 103
Mardonios 20
Marduk (Babylonian god) 18
Mar, Earl of 68
Marengo, Battle of 77
Mari 5
Mariana Islands 103, 116
Marie Louise, Empress 78
Marignano, Battle of 58
Marinid caliphate 51
Maritime Edict 57
Marius, Gaius 29
Marj Dabiq, Battle of 59–60
Mark 65
Marlborough, John Churchill,
    1st Duke 68
Marne, Battle of 98
Marshall Aid 109–110
Marshall Islands 102, 108, 116, 121
Marsivan, Battle of 48
Marston Moor, Battle of 65
Marx, Karl 90
Mary I, Queen of England 58
Mary II, Queen of England 68
Maryland 70, 73, 75, 84–85
Masaccio 54
Masina 82
Masjed-Suleyman 104
Mason–Dixon line 85
Massachusetts 67, 73, 75, 84–85
Massawa 64
Massinissa 23
mastabas 6
Masulipatam 67
Masurian Lakes, Battle of 98
Matabeleland 76, 89.
    See also Ndebele
Matanzas 61
Mataram 40, 64, 67, 71
Mathura 31
Matsu 113
Matsukata, Masayoshi 93
Maudslay, Henry 90
Mau Mau 117
Mauretania 24, 29, 35
    Caesariensis 29
    Tingitana 29
Maurice 34
Mauritania 89, 116–117, 121
Mauritius 64, 76, 116, 121
Mauryan empire 21–22, 24, 28
Maximilian I, Emperor of Mexico 81
Maximilian I, Holy Roman emperor
    54, 58
Mayan civilization 17, 19, 22, 24, 28,
    32, 36, 39–40, 45, 51, 55, 57, 62
    Classic period 32
Mayapán 55
mayors of the palace 38
Mazarin, Jules, Cardinal 65, 68
Mazovia, Mazovians 38, 77
Mazzini, Giuseppe 80
Mbulya Mtelala see Mirambo
Mbundu 72
Meade, George Gordon 85
Mecca 36–37, 40, 44, 51, 61, 118
    *sharif* 59
Mecklenburg 65
Mecklenburg–Schwerin 78, 80
Medes 14, 18–19
Median empire 18
Medici, Cosimo de' 54
Medicis 53–54
Medina 35, 37, 40, 44
Mediterranean, first civilizations 11
Medway, Battle of 68
Meerut 83
megalithic monuments 7, 9, 12
Megiddo, Battle of 10, 15, 98
Mehmet II, Sultan 47, 59
Mehmet III, Sultan 59
Meiji dynasty 86, 93

Mekong 95
Melanesia 9, 13, 22
Melanesians 24, 28, 32, 36, 40, 45, 60,
    64, 67, 71, 76, 79
Memphis 6, 14, 18, 21, 35
Memphis, Tennessee 111
Mencius (Mengzi) 26
Menelik II 89
Menem, Carlos 111
Mengchi 43
Mengzi 43
menorah 27
Mentuhotpe II 10
Mercia 38
Mercosur see Common Market of the
    Southern Cone
Merina 79
Merkits 49
Meroë 18–19, 22, 24, 28, 32, 35
Meroitic script 35
Merovingian dynasty 38
Merv 37
Mesilim of Kish 5
Mesilla valley 81
Mesoamerica 22, 32, 36, 39, 42
    Archaic and Preclassic periods 4,
        13, 17, 19
    Classic period 32, 39–40, 45
    Early Postclassic period 39
    Late Preclassic period 39
    Middle Preclassic period 39
    Postclassic period 39, 45, 55
    Spanish conquest 60, 62
    see also individual cultures
Mesolithic 3–4, 7
Mesopotamia 4, 19, 21, 30, 37, 104
    Arab conquest 37
    Aramaeans 13
    Bronze Age
    earliest cities **5**
    Early Dynastic period 5
    Iron Age
    Roman empire 29, 34
    Seleucids 24
    Uruk period 5, 9
    World War I 99
    see also Abbasid caliphate; Akkad;
        Assyrian empire; Babylon,
        Babylonia; Chaldeans; Hittites;
        Iraq; Kassites; Ottoman empire;
        Sumeria
Messapians 23
Messenia 16
metal working
    blast furnace 66
    casting 8
    lost-wax process 5, 55
    smelting 4
    see also bronze working; copper
        working; gold; iron working;
        silver; tin
Metaurus river, Battle of 23
Metternich, Prince Clemens von 80
Metztitlan 55
Mexico 39, 81–82, 86, 92, 97, 102,
    106, 109, 111–112, 116, 121
    French war 86
    Gadsden Purchase 81, 84, 86
    land reform 102
    Mexican–American War 81–82, 85
    Mexican cession 84
    Revolution 79, 81
    Spanish conquest 60, 62
    Texan War of Independence 81
    War for Independence 79, 81
    see also Aztec civilization;
        Mesoamerica; Toltec civilization
Mexico City 55, 112
Mexico, valley of 22, 24
Mezhirich 3
Miami Wyandot 70, 73
Mian 69
Miao rebellion 94
Michigan 84–85
Michoacan, Tarascan kingdom of 55
Micmac 70
microlith tools 3
Micronesia, Federated States of 102,
    121
Micronesians 28, 32, 40, 45, 60, 64,
    67, 71, 76, 79
Midas 14
Middle East, Arab–Israeli conflict
    see Arab–Israeli conflict
Midway, Battle of 106, 108
migration, single-origins theory 1–2
Milan 65, 68, 107
    Edict of 30
Miletos 11, 20–21
millet 4, 8
Milvian Bridge, Battle of 30
Minamoto Yoritomo 50
Minamoto Yoshinaka 50
Minas Gerais 74, 102
Mindanao 95
Ming empire 57, 60, 63–64, 67, 69, 71,
    76
Minnesota 84–85
Minoan palace civilization 7, 9, 11, 13
Minorca 77
Minsk, Battle of 107
Minuit, Peter 70
Min-yue 24, 26, 28
Miocene epoch 1
Mirambo (Mbulya Mtelala) 86
Miskito 62
Mississippi 84–85

Mississippian temple-mound
    building cultures 40, 42, 45, 51, 57,
    60
Mississippi Company crash 66
Mississippi river 70–71, 73
Missolonghi 80
Missouri 84–85
Missouri compromise line 85
Missouri valley 32
Mitas (Midas) 14
Mithraism 27
Mithradates VI 29
Mitsubishi 93
Mitsui 93
Mittani 10
Miwok 70, 84
Mixtec civilization 51, 55, 57, 62
Mixu 8
Moab, Moabites 14–15
Mo Bei, Battle of 26
Mobutu, General 117
Moche state 28, 32, 36, 40
Moctezuma II 55
Modena 58, 65, 68, 80
Modoc 84
Moesia, Moesiae 30
    Inferior 29
    Superior 29
Mogami 50
Mogollon culture 32, 36, 40, 42, 45, 51
Mohács, Battle of 58–60, 68
Mohi, Battle of 49
Mojave 70, 84
Moldavia 47, 52, 54, 58–59, 78, 80, 88,
    110
Moldova 119, 121
Mombasa 71–72
Mondovi, Battle of 77
Möngke Khan 49
Mongolia, Mongols 13, 32, 40, 43–51,
    53, 57, 60–61, 64, 67, 69, 71, 88,
    93–94, 97, 99, 106, 109, 116
    Chagatai Khanate 44, 51, 57
    in China 49, 57
    Golden Horde 44, 51–54, 57
    Ilkhanate 48, 51, 53, 57
    see also Juan-juan;
        Turko–Mongols; Xiongnu
Monophysite Christians 37
Monroe Doctrine 81–82
Mons 27, 32, 36, 40, 45
Mons Graupius, Battle of 25
Mons Lactacius, Battle of 34
Montagnais 70, 73
Montana 84
Mont Bibracte, Battle of 25
Montcalm de Sainte-Vérain, Louis
    Joseph, Marquis de 73
Monté Albán 17, 22, 24, 28, 32, 36, 40,
    45, 55
Monte Cassino, Battle of 107
Montenegro 54, 58–59, 65, 68, 77, 96,
    98, 105–107, 119
Montjuich, Battle of 65
Montmirail and Vauchamps, Battle of
    78
Montréal 73, 75, 84
Moon landing 116
Moors 52–53
Moravia, Moravians 41, 58, 65, 68, 77
Morea 58–59, 80, 80. See also Greece
Morgan, Henry 62
Mori 63
Moriscos 66
Mormons 84
Morocco 40, 57, 59–60, 64, 71–72, 76,
    82, 86, 89, 92, 96–97, 99, 104–107,
    109, 116–117
    nationalist revolt 104
Moscow 97, 100, 116, 119
    Battle of (1812) 78
    Battle of (1941) 105
    Napoleonic occupation 79, 88
Moscow, Principality of 57
    territorial expansion 52
    see also Muscovy
Mosquito Coast 71, 76, 79, 81
Mossi 57, 60, 67, 71–72, 76, 79, 86
Mosul 47–48, 67
    Battle of 47
Mountbatten, Lord Louis 108
Moussadeq, Mohammed 115
Mousterian culture 1, 3
Mozambique 72, 89, 92, 97, 99, 106,
    109, 116–117, 121
Mpumbu 72
Muawiya, caliph 37, 40, 44
Mubarak, Hosni 118
Mughal empire 60–61, 64, 67, 71, 76
    fall
Muhammad 27, 36–37, 40, 44
Muhammad Ahmed 89
Mühlberg, Battle of 58
Mukden 103
    Battle of 93
Mukden incident 106
Multan 61
Munich agreement 101, 106
Münster 58
Murad I 47
Murad IV, Sultan 59, 67
Murasaki Shikibu 50
Murfreesboro, Battle of 85
Murmansk 93
Murom 52
Murom-Ryazan, Principality of 46
Muscat 51, 57, 59–60, 64

Muscovy 52, 54
territorial expansion 52
*see also* Moscow, Principality of
Muslim Brotherhood 104
Mussolini, Benito 101, 104, 106–107
Mu'tah, Battle of 37
Mwenemutapa 57, 60
Myanmar 102, 121. *See also* Burma
Mycale, Battle of 20
Mycenae, Mycenaean civilization
11–13
Mylae, Battle of 23
My Lai massacre 114
Myriocephalum, Battle of 47
Mysia 21
Mysore 61, 76, 83

N
Nabateans, Nabataean kingdom 21,
24
Nabonidus 14, 18
Nabopolassar 14
Nadir Shah 76
NAFTA *see* North American Free
Trade Association
Nagas 61, 69
Nagasaki 63
atomic bomb attack 108–109
Nagoya 108
Nahani 70
Naimans 44, 49
Naissus, Battle of 33
Nakbe 17
Nakum 39
Nalanda 31
Nama rebellions 89
Nambicuara 62
Namibia 117, 121. *See also* South-
West Africa
Nanak, Guru 44
Nan Chao 40, 43, 45, 49
Nanda dynasty 22, 24
Nanjing 60, 103
Treaty of 94
Nantes, Edict of 68
Nan-yue 26, 28
Napata 35
Naples 52–54, 58–59, 68, 75, 77–80
Napoleon I 77–81
Berlin Decrees 78–79
Continental System 78–79
defeat at Waterloo 78–79
Emperor 78–79
Napoleon III 80, 86, 95
Napoleonic Wars 77–78, 83, 95
Congress of Vienna 78, 80, 82
Continental System 78–79
Peninsular War 78–79
Naqada 6
Nara 50
Naranjo 39
Narmer 6
Narses 34
Narvik 105
NASA *see* National Aeronautics and
Space Administration
Naseby, Battle of 65
Nashville, Battle of 85
Naskapi 70, 73
Nasser, Gamal Abdel 115
Natal 82
Republic 82
Nataraja (Lord of the Dance) 44
National Aeronautics and Space
Administration (NASA) 116
Nations, Battle of the *see* Leipzig,
Battle of
Native American
Territory 75
Native Americans 42, 62, 70, 73,
84–85
"Five Civilized Tribes" 84
Indian Wars 84
Territory 84–85
"Trail of Tears" 84
*see also individual tribes*
NATO *see* North Atlantic Treaty
Organization
Natufian culture 4
Nauru 102, 121
Navajo 62, 70, 84
Navarino, Battle of 80
Navarre 41, 45–46, 52–54, 57–58
navigation
Austronesians 32
Polynesians 32
Portuguese 57
Naymlap 56
Nazca 24, 28, 32, 62
Nazi party 101, 105, 107, 110
Nazi–Soviet pact 100–101, 105, 107
Ndebele 82, 86, 89.
*See also* Matabeleland
Ndongo 72
Neanderthals 1–3
Nearchos 21
Nebraska 84
Nebuchadnezzar 14–15, 18, 27
Necho II 14
Nechtansmere, Battle of 38
Nedao, Battle of 33
Neerwinden, Battle of 77
Negora, Dipo 95
Negri Sembilan 95
Nehavend, Battle of 37
Nehru, Jawaharlal 103
Nejd 79, 99, 104

Nelson, Horatio, Lord 77
Neo-Babylonian empire 14
Neo-Hittites 14–15
Neolithic 3–5, 9, 19
east Asia 8
Europe **7**
neo-Platonism 30
Nepal 69, 76, 79, 82–83, 86, 97, 99,
106, 108–109, 113, 116
Nepala 31
Nepos, Julius 33
Nerchinsk, Treaty of 69, 71
Nestorian Christians 43–45
Netherlands 53–54, 58, 66–68, 71,
76–77, 80, 82, 86, 90, 96–97, 99,
101, 105–107, 109–110, 116, 119,
121
Anglo–Dutch wars 68, 71, 73
Austrian 77, 80
Batavian Republic 77
French Revolutionary wars 77
French wars against 68
independence 65
Napoleonic Wars 95
Protestant Reformation 58, 67
Spanish Netherlands 58, 64–65,
67–68
World War II 105–106
*see also* Holland; United Provinces
Netherlands trading bases and
colonies
Africa 71–72, 76, 79, 86
Americas 62, 67, 70–71, 73
Anglo–Dutch Treaty 95
Ceylon 61, 67, 71
Dutch Guiana 112
East Indies 61, 64, 67, 71, 74
Japan 63–64, 67
Mauritius 76
southeast Asia 95, 103, 108–109,
113
Straits Settlements 95
Taiwan 67, 71, 74
Neuilly, Treaty of 101
Neustria 38
Nevada 84
Neva river 46
Nevsky, Alexander 46
New Albion 70
New Amsterdam 67, 70–71, 73.
*See also* New York
New Brunswick 82, 84
New Caledonia 86, 97, 102, 116
Newcomen, Thomas 66
New Deal 102, 106
New East Prussia 77
New England 70, 73
Newfoundland 41, 70, 73, 79, 82, 84,
86, 97, 99, 102, 106, 111
New France 67, 71, 73, 76
New Granada, Vice-Royalty of 76, 79
New Guinea
*see* Papua New Guinea
New Hampshire 73, 75, 84–85
New Hebrides 97, 116
Ne Win 113
New Jersey 73, 75, 84–85
Newly Industrializing Economies
(NIEs) 102
New Mexico 70, 84–85, 102, 111
New Netherland 70, 73
New Orleans 71
New South Wales 79, 92
New Spain, Vice-Royalty of 64, 67, 71,
76, 79
New Sweden 70, 73
New World 42, 54–57
discovery by Columbus 54
Norse Greenlanders 41
New York 70, 73, 75, 84–85, 91.
*See also* New Amsterdam
New Zealand 45, 67, 82, 86, 92, 97,
99, 102, 106, 109, 116, 121
Maoris *see* Maoris
white settlers 79, 90, 92
World War I 99, 103
*see also* Aotearoa
Nez Percé 70, 84
Nguni 72
Nguyen Anh 95
Ngwato 86
Nian risings 94
Nicaea 47–48
Nicaragua 81–82, 86, 97, 99, 102, 106,
109, 111–112, 116, 121
civil war 102, 112
Nicholas I, Czar 82, 88
Nicholas II, Czar 88, 98, 100
Nicobar Islands 95
Nicomedia, Battle of 48
Nicopolis
Battle of (68 BC) 29
Battle of (1396) 47–48, 52
Crusade 48, 52
Niger 116–117, 121
Nigeria 89, 97, 99, 106, 109, 117, 121
Biafran war 117
civil war 116–117
Igbo revolt 117
independence 117
Niger-Kordofanian languages 35
Niger river 36, 56, 71–72, 89
Nile, Battle of the 77
Nile river 6, 35, 48
canal to Red Sea 18
Cataracts 6
Delta 6

Nimitz, Chester William 108
Nina 5
Nineveh 14
Battle of 34
sack 14, 18
Nishapur, Battle of 47
Nixon, Richard M. 111, 114, 116
Nizamayeh academy 47
Nizam Shahis 61
Nkore 79
Nkrumah, Kwame 117
Nobatia 27, 35–37
Nobunaga, Oda 63–64, 69
Nogai Tatars 64, 67, 71
Nok culture 35
nomadism 4, 9, 13, 19, 24, 26, 28,
31–32, 34, 36–37, 42
Nonaligned Conference 116
Nonoalca 55
Nootka 70
Nördlingen, Battle of 65
Nore mutiny 77
Noricum 29
Noriega, Manuel 112
Normandy 41, 46, 54
Normandy landings 107
Normans 46
Norsemen 38, 40–42, 45
North America 22, 24, 28, 32, 36
American Revolution 62, 74–75
Anglo–Dutch wars 68, 73
European exploration and
colonies *see* Americas
French and Indian War 73
immigration 75
King George's War 73
King Philip's War 73
King William's War 73
Pilgrim colonists 67, 70
Proclamation Line 75
Queen Anne's War 73
slavery 72, 74–75
*see also* Americas; Canada; United
States of America
North American Free Trade
Association (NAFTA) 111
North Atlantic Treaty Organization
(NATO) 109–110, 115–116, 119,
121
North Borneo 113
North Carolina 73, 75, 84–85
North Dakota 84
Northeast Frontier Agency 83
North East New Guinea 99, 106
Northern Circars 76, 83
Northern Frontier Province 83
Northern Ireland 101, 110, 119
Northern Mariana Islands 102
Northern Rhodesia 89, 92, 97, 99, 106,
109, 117. *See also* Zambia
Northern Shoshoni 70
North Korea 102, 109, 113, 116, 121
Korean War 109–110, 113
North Pacific Forces 108
Northumbria 38, 41
North Vietnam 113–114, 116
independence 116
Vietnam War 110, 113–114, 116
Northwest Ordinance 84
Norway 41, 45–46, 51–52, 54, 57, 80,
90, 92, 96–97, 99, 101, 106, 110, 119,
121
Denmark–Norway
*see* Denmark–Norway
Swedish, Norwegian and Danish
crowns united 57
World War II 105–107
Norway–Sweden 82, 86
Nova Scotia 71, 73, 75.
*See also* Acadia
Novgorod 41, 45–46, 51–54
Novgorod-Seversk, Principality of 46
Noviodunum, Battle of 34
Nubia 6, 9–10, 13, 15, 18–19, 32,
35–36, 72
nuclear energy *see* atomic energy
nuclear weapons *see* atomic weapons
Numantia 35
Battle of 25
Numidia 23–24, 35
"Nu-pieds" 65
*nuraghe* 12
Nur al-Din 47
Nuremberg trials 110
Nurhachi (Jin Khan) 67, 69
Nyasaland 89, 97, 99, 106, 109, 117
Nyerere, Julius 117
Nzinga Nkuwu 57

O
OAS *see* Organization of American
States
oats 4, 12
OAU *see* Organization of African
Unity
Oaxaca valley 17
obsidian 39
oca 17
Octavian *see* Augustus, Gaius Julius
Caesar Octavianus
Oda clan 63
Oda Nobunaga *see* Nobunaga
Odawara 63
Odenathus 30
Odoacer 33–34
Offa, King of Wessex 38
Offa's Dyke 38

Ogaden 117
Ogasawara *see* Bonin Islands
Ogedai Khan 49
O'Higgins, Bernardo 81
Ohio 32, 84–85
Ohio river 70, 73, 84
oil 90–91, 102, 104, 116, 121
Middle East 104, 115
Oirat Mongols 69
Oirats 57
Ojibwa 70, 73, 84
Okinawa 108
Oklahoma 84, 102, 111
Old Bering Sea Stage 42
Oldowan culture 1
Olduvai Gorge 1
Oleg 41
Oleneostravski 3
Olivares, Count 65
olive 11
Olmec civilization 13, 17, 19, 22, 24,
28, 39
Olympia 16
Temple of Zeus 20
Olympic Games 16
Oman, Omani 37, 47, 59, 67, 71–72,
76, 79, 82, 86, 97, 99, 104, 106, 109,
116, 118, 121
Omar Khayyam 47
Omdurman, Battle of 89
Omo 1
Omri 15
Oneota 42
Onguts 45, 49
Onin war 50, 63
OPEC *see* Organization of Petroleum
Exporting Countries
Opis, Battle of 18
Opium Wars
First 82, 91, 94
Second 86, 91, 94
*oppida* 25
Oradour-sur Glane 107
Oran 105
Orange Free State 86
Oregon 82, 84
Oregon Trail 84
Orellana, Francisco de 64
Organization of African Unity (OAU)
117
Organization of American States
(OAS) 109, 112
Organization of Petroleum Exporting
Countries (OPEC) 111, 115–116
Orhan 47
Oriens 30
Oriente 102
Orient Express 90
Oriskany, Battle of 75
Orissa 51, 60–61, 83
Orkney 7, 41, 46, 54
Orleans 46, 54
Oromo 60, 64, 67, 71–72, 76
Oronsay 3
Orrisa 7
Ortega, Daniel 112
Orthodox church 34, 41, 58
Iconoclast controversy 38, 44
Roman–Orthodox schism 38, 44
Osaka 93, 108
Battle of 63
Osaka castle 63
Osei Tutu 72
Oslo Declaration 118
Osman I 47, 57, 59
Ostland, Reichskommissariat 105,
107
*Ostpolitik* 110
Ostrogoths 33–34, 34. *See also* Goths
Otomo 50, 63
Otrar 49
Ottawa 73, 84
Otto I, Holy Roman emperor 41, 45
Ottoman dynasty 57
Ottoman empire 44, 47, 52, 54, 57–61,
64–65, 67–68, 71, 74, 76–77, 79–80,
82, 86, 88, 90, 96–98, 104
advances against Christian Europe
47, 58–60, 64, 67–68, 71
Africa 60, 64, 71–72
Arab revolt 99
Balkan Wars 96–97
Bulgaria 86
capture of Constantinople 44, 47
Congress of Berlin 86, 88, 96
Crimean War 86, 88
Crusades 48
decline and collapse 99, 104
Egypt 82
Greek War of Independence 80, 82
Safavid wars 59–60, 64, 67, 76
vassal states 47
World War I 98
*see also* Turkey; Turks
Otto, Nikolaus 90
Otztaler Alps 90
Ouagadougou 72
Ouchi 50
Oudenaarde 68
Oudh 61, 83
Ovambo 72
Ovid 29
Ovimbundu 72
Oxitipan 55
Oyo 57, 60, 64, 67, 71–72, 76, 79

P
Pacal 39
Pachacutec 56–57
Pacific Rim 102, 121
Pacific, War of the 81, 86
Pacific War (World War II) 108
Padania 119
Padua, Arena Chapel 52
Paekche 26, 32, 36, 50
Pagan 51
paganism 30
Pahang 95
Pahlavi dynasty 104, 115
Painted Ware cultures 7
Paiute 70
Pakistan 109, 113–114, 116, 121
East Pakistan secedes 113, 116
independence 109, 116
Indo–Pakistan Wars 116
*see also* Bangladesh; East Pakistan
Palatinate 59, 65, 68, 80
Palau 102
Pale (Irish) 54, 58
Palembang 51
Palenque 39
Paleoindians 2, 42
Paleolithic
Europe **3**
Lower 1
Mid 1–3
Upper 3
Palestine 11, 18, 21, 37, 45, 47, 51, 92,
99, 104–107
Arab conquest 40
Arab–Israeli conflict 109, 115–116,
118, 121
Balfour Declaration 99, 104
Camp David agreements 118
Christian principalities 47, 51
Crusader states 48
*intifada* 118
Jewish state 99, 104, 115
League of Nations mandate 104
limited selfrule 121
Oslo Declaration 118
Ottoman conquest 60
Palestinian National Authority 118
partition 104, 115
Roman empire 34
Zionist movement 92, 104
Palestine Liberation Organization
(PLO) 115, 118
Pallava dynasty 36, 40, 45
Palmyra 30
Palo Alto, Battle of 81
Pamphylia 29
Panama 60, 62, 81, 97, 99, 102, 106,
109, 111–112, 116, 121
Panama Canal Zone 81, 91, 97, 99,
102, 106, 109, 112, 116
Pan-American Congress 102
Panchala 31
Pandya state 40, 51
Panipat
Battle of (1526) 60–61
Battle of (1761) 76
Panmunjom 113
Pannoniae 25, 30, 41
Inferior 29
Superior 29
Papacy
Avignon 44, 52, 54, 57
Carolingian empire 38
Great Schism 44, 47, 52, 54, 57
Investiture Contest 46, 51
Jesuit Order *see* Jesuit Order
Lateran treaties 101
papal fiefs 46
Papal states 46, 51–54, 57–58, 60, 65,
68, 71, 76–78, 80, 82
Paphlagonia 21
Papua New Guinea 13, 22, 24, 28, 32,
36, 60, 64, 76, 79, 82, 86, 95, 97,
102–103, 106, 108–109, 113, 116,
121
Paracas culture 17, 19, 22, 24
Paraguay 79, 81–82, 86, 97, 99, 102,
106, 109, 111–112, 116, 121
Chaco War 102
War of the Triple Alliance 81
Pardo 70
Parhae 40, 50
Pariba 102
Paris 41, 46, 66, 90
Agreement (1973) 114
Allied liberation 107
Bastille stormed 77
German occupation 105
Ludendorff offensive 98
Treaty of (1763) 73
Treaty of (1783) 75, 77
Parisii 25
Parma 58, 65, 80
Parni 21. *See also* Iranian nomads
Parsees 18, 44
Parthenopean Republic 77
Parthia, Parthians 18, 21, 24, 27–30,
32
Parvan, Battle of 47
Pasargadae 18
Battle of 18
Passchendaele (Third Battle of Ypres)
98
Passy 66
pastoralism 4, 9, 13, 19, 22, 24, 28
Patagonia 2, 81
Patayan culture 42

Pathans 61, 83
Pathet Lao 114
patriarchs 34
Patrimony of St Peter 38, 41
Pattala 21
Paul I, Czar 88
*Paulistas* 62
Paul, St 27
Pavia
Battle of 58
sack 41
Pawnee 70
Pearl Harbor attack 102–103, 106, 108
Peasant "Croquants" 65
Peasants Revolt 52
Peasants' Wars 58
Pechenegs 41, 45
Pedro I, Emperor of Brazil 81
Pedro II, Emperor of Brazil 81
Peenemunde 107
Pegu 57, 60, 83
Peipus, Lake, Battle of 46
Peisistratus 16
Peking *see* Beijing
Pelagonia, Battle of 48
Peloponnese 9, 11, 16, 80
Peloponnesian War 20, 22
Pelusium 21
Battle of 18
Pemba 89
Penang 95
Penn, Admiral William 71
Penn, William 73
Pennsylvania 73, 75, 84–85, 91
Peñon d'Argel 59
Pentri 23
People's Republic of China 102, 109,
113–114, 116, 121
border dispute with India 113
border disputes with Soviet Union
113
collectivization 113
Cultural Revolution 113, 116
"Great Leap Forward" 113, 116
invasion of Vietnam 114
Korean War 113
pro-democracy movement 102,
121
Sino–Soviet split 113, 116
Sino–Soviet Treaty 113
special economic zones 102
Vietnam War 113–114
*see also* China
Pepin II of Herstal 38
Pepin III 38
Perak 95
Perdiccas 21
Pereyaslav, Principality of 46
Pergamon 25
Battle of 25
Roman empire 29
Pericles 20
Perlis 95
Perón, Eva 111
Perón, Juan 111
Perry, Matthew 86, 93
Persepolis 18
palace of Xerxes 21
sack 21
Persian Gates pass 21
Persian Wars 20, 22
Persia, Persians 10, 14, 16, 19, 21–22,
34, 44–45, 47, 76, 79, 82, 86, 88, 97,
104
Achaemenid empire *see* Achaemenid
empire
conquest of Egypt 35
Ilkhanate 51, 53, 57
Mongol invasion 49
Ottoman conquest of Baghdad 67
Parni *see* Parni
Parthians *see* Parthia, Parthians
Safavid empire *see* Safavid empire
Sasanian empire *see* Sasanian
empire
war with Roman empire 34
*see also* Iran
Perth (Australia) 82
Peru 4, 9, 13, 22, 24, 28, 32, 36, 81–82,
86, 92, 97, 99, 102, 106, 109, 111,
116, 121
Spanish conquest 60, 62, 64, 74
Vice-Royalty of 64, 67, 71, 76, 79
*see also* Inca civilization
Pescadores 93–94
Petén 39
Petén Maya 55
Peter I, Czar (the Great) 71
Petersburg, Battle of 85
Petrarch 52, 54
Petrograd 100, 100.
*See also* Leningrad; St Petersburg
Phaistos 11
Phalangists, Christian 118
pharaohs 10
Pharsalus, Battle of 29
Philadelphia 75
Philip II, King of France (Philip
Augustus) 46
Philip II, King of Macedon 21–22
Philip II, King of Spain 58, 62, 64
Philip V, King of Spain 68
Philip the Bold, Duke of Burgundy 52
Philip the Good, Duke of Burgundy
54
Philiphaugh, Battle of 65

Philippines 62, 74, 92, 95, 97, 99, 102, 106, 109, 113, 116, 121
  Hukbalahar revolt 113
  independence 109, 113
  United States control 103
  World War II 103, 106, 108
Philippine Sea, Battle of 108
Philistia 14–15
Philistines 15
Phocas 34
Phocis 20
Phocs 16
Phoenicia, Phoenicians 13–16, 19
  Alexander the Great 21
  trade and colonies 13–14
Phrygia, Phrygians 11, 13–14, 30
Piankashaw 84
Picardy 54, 58
Pickawillany 73
Pictones 25
Picts 30, 38
Piedmont 68, 80, 86
Pierpont Morgan, J.
Pieve di Cadore, Battle of 58
pig 4
pilgrimage 44, 441
  Christian 44, 441
  Crusades 48
  Hindu 441
  Inca solar cult 56
  Islamic 37, 61
Pilgrimage of Grace 58
Pilgrim colonists 67, 70
Pilsen 96
Pilsudski, Josef 101
Piombino 58, 65
Pisa 46, 54
Pisac 56
Pisidia 21
Pizarro, Francisco 56, 60, 62, 64
plague 47, 52, 67–68, 71
  Black Death 47, 52, 57
  Great Plague of London 68, 71
Plains of Abraham 73
Plains Cree 70, 73
Plains Gros Ventre 73
Plantagenet, Henry of Anjou
  see Henry II, King of England
Plaquemine Mississippian culture 42
Plassey, Battle of 76
Plataea, Battle of 18, 20, 22
Plautus 29
Pleistocene epoch 1–2
Pleven, Battle of 96
Pliocene epoch 1
PLO see Palestine Liberation Organization
Plotinus 30
plow 4, 7, 12, 53
Podolia 59
Poeni 23
Point Barrow 42
Poitiers
  Battle of (732) 37–38, 40
  Battle of (1356) 52
Pokomam Maya 55
Poland 45–46, 49, 51–54, 57–58, 67–68, 71, 76, 80, 90, 98–101, 105–107, 109–110, 116, 119, 121
  Congress 88
  General Government of 105, 107
  German–Polish non-aggression treaty 101
  German and Soviet invasions 100–101, 105, 107
  independence 99
  Jews 105, 107
  Kosciuszko rebellion 77
  Pilsudski government 101
  Russian empire 88
  Second Partition 77
  Solidarity 110
  Soviet domination 107, 110, 119
  Third Partition 77
  war with Soviet Union 101
  World War II 101, 105–107
Poland–Lithuania 54, 60
Polar ice caps 1
polis 16
Polisario guerrillas 117
Polish Corridor 101
Polo, Marco 46, 49
Polotsk, Principality of 46
Poltava, Battle of 71
Polynesia, Polynesians 13, 19, 22, 24, 28, 32, 36, 40, 45, 51, 60, 64, 67, 71, 76, 79
Pomerania, Pomeranians 38, 41, 65, 68, 78
Pompeii 29
Pompey 29
Ponce de Leon, Juan 62, 70
Pondicherry 71, 76
Pontiac's rebellion 73
Pontica 30
Pontus 29
population growth 4–5, 7, 86, 92
  Asia 64, 69, 76
  Europe 64, 66, 76, 86
  United States
Port Arthur 88, 93
  Battle of 93
Port Jackson see Sydney
Port Moresby 108
Porto Bello 62
Port Royal 73
Port Said 85

Portsmouth, Treaty of 93
Portugal 46, 51–54, 57–58, 60, 65–68, 71, 75–80, 82, 86, 90, 92, 96–99, 101, 103, 106–107, 109–110, 116, 119, 121
  Peninsular War 78–79
  Spanish rule 62, 64–65, 67
Portuguese East Africa 64, 67, 71–72, 76
Portuguese empire 54, 57, 60–61, 63–64, 67, 72
  Africa 64, 67, 71–72, 74, 76, 117
  Brazil 60, 62, 67, 70, 74
  Ceylon 71
  Dutch–Portuguese wars 62, 64, 67
  East Africa 79, 82, 86
  Guinea 82, 86, 89, 97
  India 59, 61, 74
  Latin America 81–82
  São Vicente 62
  slave trade 79
  Timor 95. See also East Timor
  wars of liberation 117
Portuguese Guinea 72, 99, 106, 109, 117
Port Wellesley 95
Porus 21
Postumus 30
potato 7
Potosí mines 62, 64, 74
Potsdam conference 110
Po valley 22
Poverty Point culture 13
Prague 52, 107, 119
Prague Spring 110, 116
Prayaga 31, 44
Prednosti 3
Preston, Battle of 65
Prevesa, Battle of 58–59
Prince Edward Island 73
Princeton, Battle of 75
printing 58
  Chinese block printing 43
  Gutenberg Bible 54
  moveable type 50, 57
  Renaissance Europe 54
Proclamation Line 75
Procopius 34
Promontory Point 84
Protestant Reformation 58–60, 67
Provence 41, 52, 54, 58, 65
Prus 41, 46, 48
Prussia 58, 65, 68, 76–80, 82
  Austro–Prussian War 86
  Franco–Prussian War 80, 86, 96
  German Confederation 82
  Napoleonic Wars 77–79
  Schleswig–Holstein War 80
  Seven Weeks War 80
  Third Partition of Poland 77
Przemysl, Battle of 98
Pskov 52, 58
Pteria 18
Ptolemaic Egypt 21–22, 24, 28
Ptolemy I 21–22
Ptolemy, Claudius 30
Pueblo farmers 42, 57, 60, 64, 67, 71
Puerto Rico 60, 62, 81, 97, 111–112, 121
Pukara culture 22, 24
Pundra 31
Punic Wars 23
  First 23–24
  Second 23–24, 28–29, 35
  Third 28–29
Punjab 28, 82–83
Pusan 63
Pusiamitras 31
Putney debates 65
Putún Maya 55
Pu Yi 94, 103
Pydna, Battle of 29
Pylos 11
pyramids
  Egyptian 6, 9–10
  Mayan 39
  Mesoamerican 17
  Nubian 35
  Teotihuacán 32
Pyramids, Battle of the 77
Pyrrhus 23
Pytheas of Massilia 21
Pyu 28, 32, 40, 43, 45

## Q
Qadesh 10
  Battle of 10
Qadhafi, Muammar 115
Qadisiya, Battle of 37
Qafzeh 2
Qarakhanids 47
Qarqar, Battle of 14–15
Qasr-i Shirin, Treaty of 59
Qataban 22, 24
Qatar 97, 99, 104, 106, 109, 116, 118, 121
Qi 8
Qianlong, Emperor 94
Qianzhong 43
Qin 8
Qin dynasty 22, 24, 26
Qingdao 93–94, 103
Qing dynasty see Manchu empire
Qinghai 69, 94
Quadi 30, 33

Quaternary period 1
Quebec 67, 73, 75–76, 79, 84, 102, 111
  American War of Independence 75
  Battle of 76
  Quebec separatists 111
Quechua language 56
Queen Anne's War 73
Queensland 95
Quemoy 113
Quentovic 38
Quetzalcóatl 55
Quiauhteopan 55
Quiberon Bay, Battle of 77
Quicab 55
Quiché Maya 55
quinua 17
Quirigua 39
Quraysh 37
Qutb Shahis 61

## R
Rabin, Yitzhak 118
Raetia 29
Raffles, Sir Stamford 95
Ragusa 52, 54, 77
railroads 83–84, 86, 88–92, 94, 97
rainforests 1
Rajastan 57
rajataraja 31
Rajput, Rajputana 60–61, 83
Raköczy, George 65, 68
Raleigh, Walter 70
Ramallah, Battle of 37
Ramayana 27, 31
Ramesses II (the Great) 10
Ramesses III 10
Ramillies, Battle of 68
Rangoon 95, 108
Rapallo, Treaty of 100–101
Rashtrakuta dynasty 40
Ras Tafari see Haile Selassie
Rathamhor 61
Rathors 61
Ratisbon, Battle of 78
Rauracian Republic 77
Ravenna 33–34
  Exarchate of 38
Ravensberg 65
Rayy, Battle of 47
Reagan, Ronald 121
Red Cliffs, Battle of 26
Red Guards 113
Red Russia 77, 100
Reformation see Protestant Reformation
Rehoboam 15
reindeer 3
Reinsurance Treaty 96
religion 5
  ancestor worship 27
  Counter-Reformation 59, 65
  medieval Europe
    paganism 30
  Paleolithic 3
  pilgrimage see pilgrimage
  Protestant Reformation 58
  spread of world religions 27, 44
  see also individual religions
Remi 25
Renaissance 54, 57–58
Republic of China see China; People's Republic of China
Republic of Korea see South Korea
Restitution, Edict of 65
Restoration of English monarchy 68
Reza Pahlavi, Mohammed 104, 115
Rhapta 35
Rhee, Syngman 113
Rhine, Confederation of the see Confederation of the Rhine
Rhineland 52
  German reoccupation 101, 106
Rhine river 3, 30, 33, 41
Rhode Island 75, 84–85
Rhodes 11
  Hospital of St John (Hospitallers) 48, 58–59
  Ottoman capture 75
Rhodesia 116, 117. See also Northern Rhodesia; Southern Rhodesia; Zambia; Zimbabwe
Riade, Battle of 41
Riben see Japan
Riblah 14
rice 4, 8, 24, 36
Richard I, King of England 48
Richelieu, Armand Jean du Plessis, Cardinal 65
Richmond 85
Riebeck, Jan van 72
Rio de Janeiro 62, 111
Rio de la Plata 62, 76
Rio de Oro 89, 92, 97, 99, 106, 109
Rio Grande 73, 102, 111
Rio Muni 97, 99, 106, 109
Risorgimento 80
Rivoli, Battle of 77
Rizan 57
road systems
  Inca marine 56
  Roman 23
Roanoke Island 70
Robespierre, Maximilien 77
Rochambeau 75
Rockefeller, John D.
Rocroi, Battle of 65

Rodney, George 75
Roman Catholic church
  Concordat with France 78
  Counter-Reformation 59, 65
  Edict of Restitution 65
  Great Schism 44, 47, 52, 54, 57
  Inquisition 44, 54
  Poland 101
  Roman–Orthodox schism 38, 44
  Spain 101
  "Time of Troubles" 67
  Treaty of Brest-Litovsk 98–100
  World War I 88, 96, 98–99
  see also Papacy
Roman empire 28–33, 36
  Africa 29, 34
  Antonine dynasty 30
  Arabia 29
  Armenia 29
  Asia 29
  barbarians 30, 33–34, 36
  Britain 25, 28–30
  Celts 25
  Christianity 27, 29–30, 32
  citizenship 23
  colonies 23, 29
  Constantinian dynasty 30
  Dacia 29
  dioceses 30
  division 32–33
  eastern 30, 32–34, 34. See also Byzantium, Byzantine empire, 36
  economy 30
  Egypt 28–29
  Flavian dynasty 30
  Galatia 29
  Gaul 25, 28–29, 34
  German and Slav tribes 29–30, 33, 36
  greatest extent of 32
  languages 34
  Macedon 29
  Mesopotamia 29, 34
  Mithraism 27
  paganism 30
  provinces 29
  Severan dynasty 30
  social organization 23, 34
  Spain 23, 29, 34
  trade 25, 29, 31–32, 35
  urbanization 30
  western 30, 32–33, 36
Romania 86, 88, 90, 92, 96–97, 99–101, 106, 109–110, 116, 119, 121
  Balkan pact 101
  independence 86
  World War I 98
  World War II 105, 107
Romanov dynasty 100–101
Roman republic 19, 22–23, 77
  Civil War 29–30
  collapse 28–29
  colonies 23, 29
  conquest of peninsular Italy 24
  domination of Greece 23, 28–29
  Punic wars 23–24, 28–29, 35
  Samnite wars 23
  Social war 29
  tribunes 23
  Twelve Tables 23
Rome 22–24, 44, 82, 107
  annexation by Italy 80
  as center of Christianity 34
  city walls 23
  Etruscans 23
  foundation 23
  patriarchal see 34
  sack (390 BC) 23, 25
  sack (410 AD) 32–33, 36
  sack (455 AD) 33
  sack (1527) 58
  as seat of Papacy 38
  Trajan's column 29
  Treaty of 107, 110
Rome–Berlin Axis 101
Rommel, Erwin 105
Romulus 23
Roncevalles, Battle of 38
Roosevelt, Franklin Delano 102, 105–107
Rosas, Juan Manuel 81
Rostov 52
Roussillon 65
Roxolani 28, 30
Rozwi 64, 67, 71–72
Ruad 48
rubber 81, 89, 91, 95
Rudna Glava 7
Rudraman 31
Rugians, Rugii 33
Ruhr 90, 101, 106
Rumelia 58–59
Rumi, Djelaleddin 47
Rum, sultanate of 47–48
Rupert's Land 71, 73, 75, 79, 82, 84
Russia 45, 58–60, 110, 121
  Bolshevik revolution 98–100, 103
  civil war 99–100, 106
  Congress of Berlin 88, 96
  Crimean War 86, 88, 96
  czars 54
  February revolution 100
  Franco–Russian Alliance 96–97
  Great Northern War 71
  Jews 88, 92
  Kievan 41, 45–46
  Mongol invasion 49
  Napoleonic Wars 77–79, 88
  post-Communist 119

Reinsurance Treaty 96
Revolution of 1905 88
Romanov dynasty 98, 100–101
Rus 41, 46
serfs emancipated 86, 88
Seven Years War 76
Soviet 99
"Time of Troubles" 67
Treaty of Brest-Litovsk 98–100
World War I 88, 96, 98–99
see also Russian empire; Union of Soviet Socialist Republics
Russian empire 77–79, 82–83, 86, 88, 90, 92–94, 96–97
  Afghan Wars 82–83
  Americas 70, 76, 79, 84, 86, 88
  Bulgaria 88
  Manchu China 69
  Manchurian railroad 94
  Poland 77
  Russo–Turkish wars 88, 96
  Sakhalin 86, 88, 93
  Siberia 64, 67, 74
  Trans-Siberian railroad 93–94, 97
  Treaty of San Stefano 96
Russian Federation 119, 121
Russian principalities 49, 51, 53–54, 57
Ruthenia 52
Ruzhen dynasty see Jin dynasty
Rwanda 79, 116–117, 121
  civil war 117
Rwanda–Urundi 99, 104, 106, 109
Ryazan 52, 54
Ryneveld and Brand 99
Ryukyu Islands 93–94, 113
Ryurik 45

## S
Saar 101
Saarwerden 77
Saavedra, Alvaro de 60, 62
Saba 13, 19, 22, 24, 35
Sabah 113
Sabeans 28, 35, 35. See also Axum, Axumites
Sabean script and language 35
Sabines 23
sachcs 39
Sacred Fire 27
Sadat, Anwar al- 115, 118, 121
Saddam Hussein 115, 118
Safavid empire 60, 64, 67, 71
  decline 67, 71, 76
  Ottoman wars 59–60, 64, 67
Safi 67
Sagartia 18
Saguntum 23
Sahara 2, 4, 9, 27–28, 35, 40, 47, 51
Sahel 40, 56, 72
Saigon 95, 114
  Treaty of 95
St Augustine 64
St Clair, General 84
St Denis-Albanel 70
St Domingue 71, 73, 76. See also Haiti
Saintes, The, Battle of 75
St-Germain 90
  Treaty of 101
St Helena 78
St Kitts and Nevis 75, 102, 112, 121
St Lawrence river 67, 70–71, 73
St Louis (Senegal) 72
St Lucia 102, 112, 121
St Petersburg 88, 88.
  See also Leningrad; Petrograd
St Vincent and the Grenadines 102, 112
Saipan 108
  Battle of 108
Sakarya River, Battle of 101
Sakas 18–19, 21–22, 24, 28, 31
  Northern 31
  Western 31
Sakhalin 86, 88, 93–94, 108, 113
Saladin 46–48, 51
Salamanca, Battle of 78
Salamis 20
  Battle of 16, 18, 20, 22
Salisbury, Lord 96
Salm 77
Saluzzo 58
Salzburg 65, 68
Samaria 15
Samarkand 40, 49, 57
Samnites 23
Samoa 13, 22
Samori empire 86
Samoyeds 22, 28, 32, 36, 40, 45, 51, 57
Samudragupta 31–32
samurai 93
San 40, 45, 51, 57, 60, 64, 67, 72, 76, 79, 82
Sánchez, Arias 112
Sand Creek 84
Sandinistas 112
San Francisco 70
San Ildefonso, Treaty of 62
San Jacinto River, Battle of 81
San Juan see Puerto Rico
San Lorenzo 17
San Martín, José de 81
San Stefano, Treaty of 96
Santa Anna, Antonio de 81
Santa Cruz Islands, Battle of 108
Santa Fe 70

Santiago see Jamaica
Santiago de Compostela 44
Santo Domingo see Dominican Republic; Hispaniola
Sanxingdui 8
São Paulo 62, 111
São Tomé and Principe 89, 117, 121
São Vicente 62
Saqqara 6, 9
Sarajevo 96–98, 119
Saratoga, Battle of 75
Sarawak 95, 103, 108, 113
Sardinia 12, 23–24, 29, 58–59, 65, 68, 77, 79–80
Sardinia–Piedmont 80
Sardis 18, 20
Sargon of Agade (the Great) 5, 9
Sargon II 14
Sarmatians 19, 24, 28
Sasa 63
Sasanian empire 27, 30–37
  dependencies 36
  fall 37, 40, 49
Saskatchewan 70, 73, 84
Satake 50
Satavahanihara 28, 31
Satnamis 61
Satsuma 93
Saudi Arabia 104, 106, 109, 115–116, 118, 121
  Arab–Israeli conflict 115
Saul 15
savanna 4
Savannah 75, 85
Savery, Thomas 66
Savoy 52, 54, 58, 65, 68
Saxon dynasty 41
Saxons 30, 33, 36, 38, 38.
  See also Anglo–Saxons
Saxon Shore 30
Saxony 41, 46, 52, 58, 65, 68, 78, 80
Saylan 60, 64
Sayyid Said 79
Scandinavia, Scandinavians 36, 38, 40, 44–45, 52
  Vikings see Vikings
Schengen agreement 119
Schleswig 80, 101
Schleswig–Holstein War 80
Schlieffen, Alfred von 96
Schlieffen plan 98
Schmalkaldic league 58
Scipio Africanus 23
Scordisci 25
Scotland 25, 30, 45–46, 51–54, 57–58, 60, 64–65, 68
  Act of Union 68
  Battle of Flodden 58
  Bishops' Wars 65
  Celtic tribes 25
  Covenanters 65
  see also Britain; British empire; United Kingdom
Scythians 18–19, 24–25, 28
  Black Sea 18
  Caspian 18
  pointed-hat 18
Sea Peoples 10–11, 13
SEATO see South-East Asia Treaty Organization
Sebastian I, King of Portugal 64
Segoyuela, Battle of 37–38
Segu 71–72, 76, 82
Seistan 37, 47
Sekani 70
Sekigahara, Battle of 63
Selangor 95
Seleucid kingdom 21, 24, 28
Seleucos 21, 24
Selim I (the Grim), Sultan 59
Selim II, Sultan 59
Seljuk sultanate, Great 47–48
Seljuk sultanate of Rum 47–48
Seljuk Turks 47–49, 51
Seminole Wars 84
Semites 9
Senegal 72, 76, 79, 82, 86, 116–117, 121
Senegambian states 60, 64
Sennacherib 14–15
Sennar Dam 104
Senones 25
Sentinum, Battle of 23
Senwosret III 10
Seoul 50
  Battle of 63
Seqenenre II 10
Sequani 25
Sequeira, Diego Lopez de 60
Serbia, Serbs 38, 41, 47–48, 51–54, 59, 66, 80, 86, 88, 90, 96–98, 105–107, 119
  independence 80, 86
  Ottoman defeat 47
  World War I 97–98
Serbs, Croats and Slovenes, Kingdom of 101, 101.
  See also Yugoslavia
serfdom 52–53, 86, 88
Seri 70
Seringapatam, Battle of 83
Serrano 62
Sethos I 10
Setsen 69
Seven Weeks War 80
Seven Years War 62, 73, 76
Severus, Septimus 30

Seville 62, 66, 74
Seychelles 121
Shaanxi 69
Shabaka 35
Shah Jahan 61, 67
Shahjahanabad 61
Shaka 82
Shalmaneser III 14
Shalmaneser V 14–15
shamanism 44
Shamir, Yitzhak 118
Shanan-Dong 43
Shanan-Xi 43
Shandong 69, 94, 97, 103
Shang dynasty 8, 13
Shanghai 94, 103
Shang Yang 26
Shang Zhixin 69
Shankara 44
Shans 60–61, 71
Shanxi 69, 94, 97
Shapur I 31
Sharm el-Sheikh 115
Shaskanka 44
Shatt al-Arab 118
Shawnee 70, 73, 84
Shechem 15
sheep 4, 7, 11, 35
Sherman, William 85
Sher Shah 61
Shetland 41, 54
Shiba 50
Shi Huangdi (First Emperor) 24, 26, 43
Shiite Muslims 37, 44, 47, 118, 121
Shiloh, Battle of 85
Shimabara, Battle of 63
Shimazu 50
Shimoda 93
Shimonoseki, Treaty of 93
Shintoism 50
shipping 91
  clipper 91
  cogs 53
  Dreadnought class 96–97
  European trade routes 53
  refrigeration 81, 91
  steamship 91
  see also boat-building
Shirvan 59
Shiva (Hindu deity) 44
Shivaji 61
Shoa 51
Shona 86
Shoni 50
Shoshenq I 10, 15
Shotoku 50
Shunzhi 69
Shushenskoye 88
Shuswap 70
Sialkot 31
Siam, Siamese 57, 69, 76, 79, 82, 86, 92, 95, 97, 99, 103. See also Thailand, Thais
Siberia 22, 24, 28, 32, 36, 60, 64, 67, 69, 74, 88, 94, 97
  Japanese occupation 99–100, 103
Siberians 45, 51, 57
Sibir, Khanate of 57, 60
Sicán state 56
Sichuan 69
Sicily 16, 19, 23–24, 29, 34, 46, 51–54, 58–59, 65, 68, 75, 77, 79–80, 107
  Norman kindom 48
Siddhartha Gautama see Buddha
Sidon 15
Siegfried Line 107
Siemens-Martin 90
Sierra Leone 79, 82, 86, 89, 97, 99, 106, 109, 116–117, 121
Sihanouk, Prince 114
Sihanouk Trail 114
Sikhism 44, 61, 83, 121
Sikkim 69, 83
Silesia 52, 58, 65, 68, 76–77
"Silicon Valley" 111
Siling Vandals 33
Silistria 59
Silk Route 19, 27, 49, 52, 74
Silla 26, 32, 36, 40, 43, 50
silver 20, 62, 74
Sima Qian 26
Simhala 28, 32, 36
Simonstown 79
Sinai 6, 115
Sind 18, 37, 82–83
Singapore 95, 102, 113, 116, 121
  British military presence ended 113
  World War II 106, 108
Singidunum 34
Sinhalese 40, 51, 57
Sino–Japanese War (1894–5) 93–94, 97
Sino–Japanese war (1937) 106
Sino–Soviet split 113, 116
Sino–Soviet Treaty 113
Sioux 70, 73, 84
Siraj ud-Daulah 76
Sisodiyas 61
Sitting Bull 84
Siwa 18, 21
Six Day War 115–116
Skandagupta 31
Skoda Works 96
Skudra 18
Slankamen, Battle of 68

slavery 5
  Africa 35, 62, 72, 74, 79, 82
  Americas 62, 71–72, 74–75, 79, 86
  Asiento Treaty 71, 74
  Aztecs 55
  Brazil 82
  Caribbean 79
  colonies for freed slaves 79, 89, 92
  early Mediterranean civilizations 11
  Europe 41
  Greek civilization 16, 20
  Paulistas 62
  Romans 29
  slave trade 71–72, 74, 79, 82
  Toussaint L'Ouverture revolt 79
  United States 79, 84–86, 92
  West Indies 72
Slave tribe 70
Slavic languages 96
Slavonia 119
Slavs 19, 22, 24, 32–34, 37–38, 40–41, 45–46, 48, 51, 105
Slovakia, Slovaks 41, 101, 105–107, 119, 119. See also Czechoslovakia, 121
Slovenia, Slovenes 38, 119, 121
Sluys, Battle of 52
smallpox 55–56
Smerdis 18
Smith, R. and K. 99
Smolensk 52
  Principality of 46
Snaketown 42
Snofru 6
socialism 90, 100, 106
Social War 29
Socotra 72
Socrates 22
Sogdiana 18, 21, 43
Soghd 37, 43, 47
Soissons, Battle of 34
Sokoto caliphate 82, 86, 89
Solferino, Battle of 80
Solidarity 110
Solomon 15
Solomon Islands 2, 97, 102, 108, 116, 121
Solon 16
Solutrean culture 3
Somalia, Somali 72, 79, 116–117
Somaliland 104, 117
Somme, Battle of the 98–99
Song dynasty 8, 26, 45, 49, 51
Songhai 45, 57, 60, 64, 67, 71–72, 76
Sonni Ali 72
Sorbs 38
Sotho 72
Sotuta 55
South Africa 89, 91–92, 97, 99, 104, 106, 109, 116–117, 121
  Anglo–Boer Wars 97
  immigration 92
  multiparty democracy 121
South Appalachian Mississippian 42
South Carolina 73, 75, 84–85
South Dakota 84
Southeast Asian Forces 108
South-East Asia Treaty Organization (SEATO) 114
Southern Cult 42
Southern Rhodesia 89, 97, 99, 106, 109, 117. See also Zimbabwe
South Georgia 111
South Korea 102, 109, 113, 116, 121
  democratic elections 102
  Korean War 109–110, 113
  Vietnam War 114
South Sea Bubble 66
South Vietnam 102, 113–114, 116, 121
  Vietnam War 110, 113–114, 116
South-West Africa 97, 104, 106, 109, 116. See also Namibia
Southwest Pacific Forces 108
Southwold Bay, Battle of 68
Soviet Russia 99
Soviet Union see Union of Soviet Socialist Republics
space exploration 111, 116
Spain 33, 59–60, 64–65, 67, 71, 76–80, 82, 86, 90, 92, 96–99, 101, 105–107, 109–110, 116, 119, 121
  Armada against England 64
  Bourbon dynasty 68
  Byzantine empire 38
  Celtiberians 25
  Christian reconquest 38, 44, 46, 48, 54, 58, 60
  civil war 101, 106
  elected government 110
  Ferdinand and Isabella 58
  feudal states 46
  Franco 101, 110
  French Revolutionary wars 77
  Habsburg dynasty 58, 68
  Islamic 37–38, 40, 44–46, 48, 51
  Italian Wars 58
  Jews in Spain 44, 54
  Moriscoes 66
  Morocco 104
  Napoleonic Wars 78–79, 81–82
  Peninsular War 78–79
  Republican election victory 101
  Roman empire 23, 29, 34
  Seven Years War 62, 73, 76
  Spanish Inquisition 54
  Thirty Years War 65, 67–68

Treaty of Utrecht 68
  Visigoths 36–37
  War of the Spanish Succession 62, 68, 71, 73
Spanish–American War 95, 97
Spanish empire 55–58, 60, 65–67, 71–72, 74
  Africa 64, 89
  Americas 60, 62, 64–65, 70–74, 76, 79, 81–82, 84
  Argentina 82
  Cuba 60, 62, 76
  Florida 62, 64, 70, 75
  King Philip's War 73
  Mexican Revolution 79, 81
  Mosquito Coast 71
  Netherlands 58, 64–65, 67–68
  Philippines 95
  Portugal 62, 64
  Puerto Rico 60, 62
  Santiago (Jamaica) 62, 71
  slavery 71, 74
  southeast Asia 95
  Texas 62
Spanish Guinea 89
Spanish Morocco 89, 97, 99, 101, 105–107, 109
Spanish Sahara 89
Spanish Succession, War of the 62, 68, 71, 73
Sparta 16, 20, 22
  constitution 20
  helot revolt 20
  Peloponnesian war 20, 22
Spartan league 20
Spinola, Ambrogio 65
Spithead mutiny 77
Spoleto, Duchy of 38
Spotsylvania, Battle of 85
Springs and Autumns period 8, 19
Sputnik II 116
squash 17
Sri Lanka 116, 121. See also Ceylon
Srivijaya empire 40, 45, 51
Sron-btsan-sgampo 43
Stalingrad, Battle of 105–107, 109
Stalin, Joseph 88, 100–101, 105–108
Stamford Bridge, Battle of 46, 51
Stanley, H.M.
Staraja Ladoga 38
Starcevo 7
Stato dei Presidii 68
steam engine 66
steelmaking 90
  Bessemer process 90–91
stelae 39
steppe nomads 24, 36, 45, 51
steppe pastoralist cultures 9
steppes 2–4, 9, 13, 19, 36
  Caspian 36
  European 36
Step Pyramid 6
Stilicho 33
Stockton and Darlington Railway 90
Stoics 21, 30
Stolypin, Pyotr 88
Stone Age see Mesolithic; Neolithic; Paleolithic
Stonehenge 7, 9
Stone's River, Battle of 85
Stormy Sky, King 39
Straits of Hormuz 118
Straits Settlements 95
Strasbourg 68
Strathclyde 38, 41
Stresemann, Gustav 101
Stroessner, Alfredo 111
Stuart dynasty 65, 68
stupas 27
Styria 46, 52, 65, 68
Sucre, Antonio José de 81
Sudan 89, 96–97, 99, 104, 106, 109, 116–117, 121
Sudetenland 101
Suevi 33–34
Suez Canal 86, 89, 91, 97, 104, 115
Suez crisis 104, 115–116
Sufism 44
sugar 91
Sui dynasty 36, 40, 43
Sui Wendi (Yang Jian) 36
Sukarno, Ahmed 103
Sukhothai 51, 57
Sulaym 37
Suleiman I (the Magnificent) 59–60
Sumatra 95
Sumeria 5, 9, 13
  Early Dynastic period 5
  King List 5
  trade 5
Sumitomo 93
Sun Diata Keita 51
Sunni Muslims 37, 44, 47, 118
Sun Tzu 26
Sun Yixian (Sun Yat-sen) 94
Surat 61, 74
Sur dynasty 61, 64
Suren 28
Suri 61
Surinam, Suriname 67, 111–112, 121
Susa 5, 14, 18, 21
Svear 38, 41
Svein Forkbeard 41
Svein Forkbeard 41
Svenskund, Battles of 77
Swabia 41, 46
Swahili 89
Swartkrans 1

Swaziland 82, 86, 89, 97, 99, 106, 109, 116–117, 121
Sweden, Swedes 41, 45–46, 51–54, 57–58, 60, 64–65, 67–68, 71, 76, 78–80, 90, 92, 96–97, 99, 101, 105–106, 109–110, 116, 119, 121
  colonies 70, 73
  Great Northern War 71
  Napoleonic Wars 78
  Swedish, Norwegian and Danish crowns united 57
  Thirty Years War 65, 67–68
  Vasa dynasty 58
Swiss Confederation 52, 54, 58, 65, 68, 77
  Calvinism 58
Switzerland 80, 82, 86, 90, 96–99, 101, 105–107, 109–110, 116, 119, 121
sword 11–12
Syagrius 33–34
Sydney 79
Syphax 23
syphilis 62
Syracuse 62
Syria 4, 14, 18, 21, 29, 37, 45, 47, 51, 59–60, 99, 104–107, 109, 115–116, 118, 121
  Arab–Israeli conflict 115
  Ba'ath party 115
  Crusader states 48
  French mandate 104
  Lebanese civil war 118
  Palmyra 30
  Roman empire 34
  United Arab Republic 115
  World War II 104
  Zangid emirate 47

T
Tabaristan 37
Tabasco 55
Tacitus 29
Tadmor 15
Tahiti 24
taiga 9
Taiho laws 50
Taiping rebellion 94
Taira clan 50
Taiwan 69, 79, 93–94, 97, 102–103, 106, 113, 116, 121
  Chinese control 69, 71, 74
  democratic elections 102
  Dutch bases 67, 71, 74
  see also Formosa
Taiyuan 43
Taizu, Song 43
Tajikistan 121
Takamori, Saigo 93
Takeda 50, 63
Takrur 45
Talas river, Battle of 40, 43
Talwandi 44
Tamar 15
Tambo Colorado 56
Tambov 100
Tampico 81
Tanegashima 63–64
Tanganyika 99, 104, 106, 109, 117. See also German East Africa; Tanzania
Tang dynasty 36–37, 40, 43–45, 57
Tangier 37
Tangier crisis 96
Tanguts 45
Tannenberg, Battle of 54, 88, 98
Tannu Tuva 94
Tanzania 116–117, 121. See also Tanganyika; Zanzibar
Tara, Battle of 25
Tarawa, Battle of 108
Tarentum 23
Tarim basin 43
Tarraco 30
Tarraconensis 29
Tartaria 7
Tartars see Tatars
Tartessos, Tartessians 25
Taruga 35
Tarxien 7
Tases 55
Tashkent 43, 88
Tasman, Abel 67
Tasmania 9, 13, 19, 22, 24, 28, 32, 60, 64, 67, 71, 76. See also Van Diemen's Land
Tatar-Kalmuks 67
Tatars 45, 49, 54, 57, 60–61, 64, 71
Taurus mountains 37
Tayasal 55
Tayyichi'ut 49
Tectosages 25
Tehran conference 107
Tejas 70
Teke 72, 86
Tekrur 44, 67, 71
Telamon, Battle of 25
Tel Aviv 104
telegraph 86, 91
Temujin see Chingis Khan
Tenasserim 82–83
Teng 8
Ten Kingdoms (China) 43
Tennessee 70, 84–85, 102
Tenochtitlán 55
Teotihuacán 24, 28, 32, 36, 39–40, 45
  Classic period 32
Teotitlán 55
Tepeacac 55

Tepecuacuilco 55
Tepe Yahya 5
Terra Amata 1
Tertiary period 1
Tet Offensive 114
Teutoburgerwald, Battle of 29
Teutonic Knights 46, 48, 51–54, 57
Tevr 52
Texas 62, 70, 73, 81–82, 84–85, 102
  United States annexation 81, 84
  War of Independence 81
Texcoco 55
Texel, Battle of 68
textiles 4–5, 74
  cotton 4, 17, 74, 84–85, 91
  European production 53
  India 61, 74
  industrialization 66, 84, 90, 93
  linen 4
  silk 4, 19
  spinning 4
  weaving 4–5
  wool 4, 11, 91
Tezcatlipoca (Toltec and Aztec deity) 55
Tezozomoc 55
Thailand, Thais 9, 13, 19, 24, 28, 32, 36, 40, 43, 45, 57, 102–103, 108–109, 113–114, 116, 121. See also Siam, Siamese
Thai language 26
Thames river 3
Thaneswar 44
Thasos 20
Thatcher, Margaret 110
Thatta 61
Thebes 6, 10, 14, 18, 35
Themistocles 20
Theodoric 34
Theodosian dynasty 33
Theodosius I 30, 33
Thera 11, 16
Theravada Buddhism 27
Thermopylae, Battle of 20
Thessalonica
  Battle of 98
  Kingdom of 48
Thessaly 16, 20
Thieu Nguyen Van 114
Third Coalition 78
Thirty Years War 65, 67–68
tholos 11
Thrace, Thracians 13, 16, 18–22, 24–25, 29–30, 33, 47
Three Emperors, league of (Dreikaiserbund) 96
Three Feudatories" 69
Three Kingdoms (China) 26
Three Kingdoms (Korea) 50
Thule Inuit 42
Thuringia, Thuringians 34, 46
Tiahuanaco empire 17, 28, 32, 36, 40, 45, 56
Tiananmen Square massacre 102
Tiberius 29, 32
Tibet, Tibetans 13, 19, 24, 26, 31–32, 36, 43–45, 49, 51, 57, 60–61, 64, 67, 71, 83, 94, 97, 99, 106, 113
  Chinese occupation 113
  Manchu Chinese control 69, 76, 97
  see also Xizang
Ticinus river, Battle of 23
Ticonderoga, Battle of 73
Tidore 67
tiger (dragon) economies 102
Tiglath-pileser III 14–15
Tigris river 5
Tikal 39
Tilly, Count 65
Tilsit, Treaty of 78–79
Timbira 62
Timbuktu 51, 72
Timor 67, 95, 97
Timurid emirates 57
Timur the Lame 47, 57
tin 5, 8, 12
Tingzhou, Battle of 43
Tinian 108
  Battle of 108
Tipu Sultan 83
Tiran, Straits of 115
Titicaca, Lake 17, 32
Tito, Josip Broz 107, 110
Tlachco 55
Tlacopan 55
Tlapan 55
Tlatlauhquitepec 55
Tlaxcallan 55
tobacco 74–75
Tobago 112, 116, 121
Toba Wei 32, 36
Tochtepec 55
Toghril Beg 47
Togo, Heihachiro 93
Togo, Togoland 89, 97, 104, 116–117
Tojo, Hideki 108
Toki 50
Tokugawa Ieyasu see Ieyasu, Tokugawa
Tokugawa shogunate 63, 67, 86
Tokyo 63, 93, 108
  earthquake (1923) 103
  see also Edo
Toledo, Francisco 62
Tolistobogii Trocmi 25

Toltec civilization 39–40, 45, 51, 55
Tondibi, Battle of 64
Tone, Wolf 77, 79
Tonga 13, 22, 116, 121
Tonghak revolt 93
Tongking 69, 94–95, 103
Tongking crisis 114
Toninia 39
toolmaking cultures 1, 3–4, 7
Topiltzin-Quetzalcóatl 55
Tordesillas, Treaty of 60, 62
Torres Vedras, Battle of 78
Totila 34
Toulon 68
Toulouse 46
  Battle of 78
Toungou 61, 64
Tourane (Da Nang) 95, 114
Toure, Samori 89
Trabzon, Battle of 98
trade 20, 74, 91, 110
  Africa 35–36, 40, 45, 51, 72
  Arabs 37
  Baltic 41
  Britain 79, 82
  Bronze Age 12
  caravan routes 59–60
  Carolingian empire 38
  China 43, 57, 60, 64, 69, 74, 79, 82, 94
  Continental System 78–79
  Crusades and the Holy Land 48
  Dutch 61–64, 67, 70–73
  early Mediterranean civilizations 11
  East India companies 61, 63, 67, 71, 74, 76
  Egyptian civilization 6, 10
  European economic development 66
  European trade fairs 53
  fur trade 74
  Great Depression 101–102, 106
  Greek civilization 16, 20
  guilds 53
  Hanseatic league 53, 66
  Hudson's Bay Company 70
  India 31, 60–61, 69, 72, 74
  Industrial Revolution 90
  Iron Age Africa 35
  Japan 63–64, 67, 86, 93
  Mayan 39
  medieval Europe 53
  Mycenaean 12
  North American colonies 70, 73, 75
  northern Europe 38
  Olmecs 17
  Ottoman empire 59, 74
  Phoenicians 13–14
  Portuguese empire 59–61, 63–64, 67, 72
  Roman empire 25, 29, 31–32, 35
  Russia 67
  Sahara 40, 51
  Silk Route 19, 27, 52, 74
  slave trade 71–72, 74
  southeast Asia 95
  Spanish empire 74
  spice trade 67
  Sumerians 5
  trading colonies 13, 19
  Venice 52
  Vikings 41
  Zollverein 80, 90–91
trade unionism 90, 93, 102, 110
Trafalgar, Battle of 78
"Trail of Tears" 84
Trajan 29–30
Transcaucasia 76, 100
transhumance 13, 19, 22, 24, 28
Transjordan 99, 104–106, 107. See also Jordan
Transnistria 107
transport
  wheeled vehicles 4, 7, 12
  see also boat-building; canal systems; road systems; shipping
Trans-Siberian railroad 93–94, 97
Transvaal 86, 89, 97
Transylvania 58–59, 65, 68, 101, 105, 107
Trasimenus, Lake, Battle of 23
Travancore 83
Trebia river, Battle of 23
Trebizond 51, 54
  empire of 48
  see also Trabzon
Trengganu 95
Trent, Council of 58
Trento, Battle of 98
Trenton, Battle of 75
Tres Zapotes 17
Trianon, Treaty of 101
Tricameron, Battle of 34
Trinidad 112, 116, 121
Triple Alliance (Brazil, Argentina, Uruguay) 81, 86
Triple Alliance (Germany, Austria–Hungary, Italy) 96–97
Triple Alliance (Mesoamerica) 55
Triple Entente 96
Tripoli, County of 48
Tripoli, Tripolitania 59–60, 89, 104
  see also Libya
Tripolye-Cucuteni culture 7
Tripura 83
Troppau, Congress of 80

Trotsky, Leon 88
Trouillas, Battle of 77
Troy 11
    Trojan War 11
Trucial Oman 86, 97, 99, 104, 106, 109
"Truman Doctrine" 109
Truman, Harry S. 108–109
Trundholm 12
Tsunayoshi 63
Tsushima 50
Tsushima Straits 88, 93
Tudor dynasty 54, 58
Tughluk, Muhammad ibn 57
Tukulor caliphate 86, 89
Tula 51, 55
Tulucan 55
Tulunid emirate 45
tundra 2, 4
Tung Cho 26
Tung-nu 24, 28
Tungusic tribes 40, 45, 51, 57, 69
Tunis, Tunisia 40, 45, 59–60, 71, 86,
    89, 92, 97, 99, 104–107, 116–118,
    121
    siege of Tunis 48
    World War II 104
Tupac Yupanqui 56
Tupamaros guerillas 111
Tupi-Guarani 60, 67, 71
Tupinamba 62
Turenne, Henri de la Tour
    d'Auvergne 68
Turfan, Khanate of 61
Turkestan 69, 88, 100
Turkey 4, 101, 104–107, 109–110,
    115–116, 118–119, 121
    Anatolia see Anatolia
    Balkan pact 101
    invasion of Cyprus 110
    Ottoman empire see Ottoman
    empire
    republic 106
    World War I 99, 104
Turkish emirates 52, 54
Turkish khanates 36
Turkmenistan 121
Turkomans 60, 64, 67, 71
Turko–Mongols 13, 22, 24, 28.
    See also Xiongnu
Turks 36, 40, 45, 47, 49, 51, 57, 76
    conversion to Islam 44
    Ghuzz 45, 51
    Kirghiz see Kirghiz
    Mamluke 47, 51–53, 57
    Ottoman see Ottoman empire
    Seljuk see Seljuk Turks
    Uighur 43–45
    White Sheep 57
Turks and Caicos Islands 112
Turnham Green, Battle of 65
Turov–Pinsk, Principality of 46
Tuscany 52, 65, 68, 77, 80
Tuscarora 73, 75
Tushiyetu 69
Tushki, Battle of 89
Tutankhamun 10
Tuthmosis I 10
Tuthmosis III 10
Tutul Xiuh 55
Tuvalu 102, 121
Tü-yü-hun 32, 36
Twelve Tables 23
Tyre 14–15
Tyrol 54, 58, 65, 68, 80
Tyrone's rebellion 65
Tziccoac 55

U

Uaxactun 39
Ubangi Shari 89
Uesugi 50
Uganda 89, 92, 97, 99, 106, 109,
    116–117, 121
Uhud, Mount, Battle of 37
Uighurs 40, 43–45, 49
Uitlanders
Ukraine 58–59, 98–101, 107, 110, 119,
    121
    Reichskommissariat 105, 107
Ulan Bator, Battle of 69
Ulfilas, Bishop 30
ullucu 17
Ulm, Battle of 78
Ulm, Charles 99
Ulster 65, 65. See also Northern
    Ireland
Ulu Burun shipwreck 11
Umar, Caliph 37, 40
Umayyad caliphate 37–38, 40, 44–45
    collapse 41
Umbrians 23
Umma 5
Unetice culture 9, 12
Union of South Africa see South Africa
Union of Soviet Socialist Republics
    99–101, 103, 106, 108–110, 113,
    116–117
    Arms Limitation Treaty 116
    Baltic states 100, 105, 109–110
    border disputes with China 113
    Cold War 109–111, 116, 121

collectivization 100
Cuban missile crisis 112, 116
decline 119, 121
eastern European satellites 107,
    109–110, 116, 119, 121
Five Year Plans 100, 106
formation 100
German invasion 105
gulags 100
Helsinki Agreement 121
invasion of Afghanistan 121
Nazi–Soviet pact 100–101, 105
new economic policy (NEP) 100
Sino–Soviet split 116
Sino–Soviet Treaty 113
Treaty of Rapallo 100–101
Vietnam War 114
Warsaw Pact 116
World War II 100–101, 105–109
see also Russia
USA see United States of America
Usman dan Fodio 79
USSR see Union of Soviet Socialist
    Republics
Ussuri 93
Utah 84–85
Ute 62, 70
Uthman, third caliph 37
Utrecht
    Treaty of 68, 73
Uzbegs 57, 60–61, 64, 67, 71
Uzbekistan 121

V

Vaal river 82
Vakataka 31–32
Valabhi 37
Valdivia tradition 9, 17
Valens 30, 33
Valentinian III 33
Valerian 30
Valley Forge 75
Valley of the Kings 10
Valley of Mexico 55
Vallon Pont d'Arc 3
Valmy, Battle of 77
Valparaiso, Battle of 81
Valtelline 65
Vancouver 79
Vandals 30, 33–34, 36
Van Diemen's Land 79.
    See also Tasmania
Vangiones, Battle of 33
Van Lang 19, 24
Vanuatu 13, 102, 121
Varanasi 31, 44
Vargas, Getúlio 102
Varna, Battle of 47–48, 54
Vasa dynasty 58
Vatican 101
    sack 41
Vatsayara 31
Vauban, Sébastien le Prestre de 68
Vedas 27
Vedic Aryans 13, 19
Veii 23
Venables, Robert 71
Venaissin 77
Vendée 77
Veneti 25
Venetia 97. See also Venice
Venezuela 79, 81–82, 86, 97, 99, 102,
    106, 109, 111–112, 116, 121
Venice 23, 46, 48, 52–54, 57, 59–60,
    64–68, 71, 76, 119
    Holy league 59
    Italian Wars 58
    Napoleonic Wars 77
    Republic of 59
Veracruz 32, 36, 62, 81
Vercingetorix 25
Verdun
    Battle of 98–99
    Treaty of 41, 45
Verkholensk 88
Vermont 84–85
Vernet, Battle of 77
Verona, Congress of 80
Verrazano, Giovanni da 70
Versailles 68, 86
    Treaty of 99, 101–103, 106
Vespucci, Amerigo 60, 62
Viatchians 41
Vichy France 105
Vicksburg 85
Victor Emmanuel II, King of Sardinia
    80
Victoria, Lake 89
Victoria, Queen of Britain, Empress
    of India 82–83, 86, 89, 96
Vien Chan 71
Vienna 65
    Congress of 78, 80, 82, 88
    siege (1529) 58–60
    siege (1683) 68, 71
Viennensis 30
Viet Cong 113–114
Vietminh 103, 113–114
Vietnam 95, 102, 109, 113–114, 121
    Chinese invasion 102, 114
    division 113–114
    invasion of Cambodia 102, 114

Ur 5, 9, 14
Uraga 93
Urartu, Urartians 13–14
Urban II, Pope 46, 48
urbanization 5, 9, 54
    and agriculture 4–5, 9
    Americas 42, 55
    China 8, 43
    Mediterranean civilizations 11
    medieval Europe 53
    Roman empire 30, 53
Urbino 54
Urmia, Lake, Battle of 14
Uruguay 81–82, 86, 92, 97, 99, 102,
    106, 109, 111, 116, 121
Uruk 5, 9
Urukagina 5
USA see United States of America
Usman dan Fodio 79
USSR see Union of Soviet Socialist
    Republics

reunification 102, 113
see also Annam; Dai Viet; North
    Vietnam; South Vietnam
Vietnam War 110, 113–114, 116
Viets 26. See also Annam; Champa
Vijayanagara 57, 60–61
Vikings 38, 40–41, 45, 51
    raids, trade and colonization routes
    40–41
Villa, Pancho 81
Villars, Claude Louis Hector, Duc de
    68
Villaviciosa, Battle of 68
Villavicosa, Battle of 68
Vima Kadphises 31
Vindelici 25
Virgil 29
Virginia 67, 70, 73, 75, 84–85
Visby, Battle of 52
Visigoths 30, 32–34, 36, 38, 40
    Spain 37
    see also Goths
Vitoria, Battle of 78
Vitruvius Pollio, Marcus 29
Vittorio Veneto, Battle of 98
Vlacs 38
Vladimir-Suzdal 52
Vladivostok 88, 93–94, 97
Vojvodina 119
Volcae 25
Volcano Islands 103, 113
Volga river 41
Volhynia, Principality of 38, 46
Volturno, Battle of 80
Votadini 25
Vouillé, Battle of 34
V-weapons 107

W

Wadai 60, 64, 67, 71–72, 76
Wagram, Battle of 78
Waitangi, Treaty of 82
Wake Island 108
Wakhan 88
Wales 54. See also Britain; British
    empire; United Kingdom
Wallachia 47, 52, 54, 58–59, 78, 80, 88
Wallenstein, Albrecht von 65
Wall St Crash 102, 106
Walo 72
Walvis Bay 89
Wang Kon 50
Wang Mang 26
Warring States period 8, 22, 26
warrior class 9
Warsaw 77, 107
    Battle of (1914) 98
    Grand Duchy of 78–79
    Jewish revolt 107
    second rising 107
Warsaw Pact 115–116, 119
Wars of the Roses 54, 58
Washington 84
Washington, George 75, 84
Washington Naval Agreement 106
Waterford 41
Watergate scandal 111, 116
Waterloo, Battle of 78–79
Wattasid caliphate 57
Wattignies, Battle of 77
Waywaka 17
weaving 4–5
Wei 8, 26
Weihaiwei 93
Welf dynasty 46
Wellington, Arthur Wellesley,
    1st Duke 78
Welsh principalities 38, 41, 46
Wen 43
Wends 46, 48
Werden 65
Wessex 38, 41
Wessex culture 13
West Aden 104
West Bank 104, 115, 118
Western European Union (WEU) 119
Western Front (World War I) 98–99,
    104
Western Ghats 61
Western revolt 65
Western Sahara 116–117, 121
Western Turk Khanate 36–37
Western Woods Cree 70, 73
Western Zhou 8
West Francia 41
West Galicia 77
West Germany see Federal Republic
    of Germany (FRG)
West Indies 57
    American revolution 75–76
    Battle of the Saintes 75
    British colonies 62, 67, 71, 73–74,
    76
    Federation of the British 112
    French colonies 67
    Indian laborers 92
    slavery 72
    Spanish colonies 62, 67, 71
    see also Caribbean
Westphalia 65
    Treaty of 65, 67

West Virginia 84–85
WEU see Western European Union
Wewak, Battle of 108
Wexford 41, 77
Weyden, Rogier van der 54
whaling 66
wheat 4, 7, 11
wheel 4–5, 7–8, 12
Whitby, Synod of 38
White Huns see Ephthalite Huns
White Lotus rebellion 94
White Mountain, Battle of 65
White Plains, Battle of 75
White Russia 100
White Sheep Turks
    emirate of 57
Wichita 62, 70, 84
Wilderness, Battle of 85
Wilhelm I, Kaiser 86
Wilhelm II, Kaiser 96–98
Willendorf, Venus of 3
Willow Palisade 69
William III, King of England (William
    of Orange) 68
William the Conqueror, Duke of
    Normandy 46
Willow Palisade 69
Wilson, Woodrow 81, 98–99,
    101–102
Wiltzites 38
Winnebago 70, 73
Winnipeg, Lake 73
Winter War 105
Wisconsin 84–85
Wissembourg, Battle of 77
Witbooi, Hendrik 89
Witoto 62
Witte, Count Sergei 88
Wittelsbach dynasty 52
Wittenberg 58
Wixot 70
Woina, Battle of 72
Wolfe, James 73, 76
wool 4, 11, 91
Worcester, Battle of 65
World War I 88, 91–92, 95–99,
    102–104, 111
    Arab revolt 99, 104
World War II 100–109, 117
Wounded Knee 84
Wovoka 84
writing 5, 7, 9
    Aramaic alphabet 13, 18
    cuneiform 5, 18
    Greek alphabet 16
    hieroglyphs 6, 11, 17, 19, 39, 55
    Latin alphabet 25, 34
    Linear A script 11
    Linear B script 11
    Meroitic script 35
    parchment 18
    Phoenician alphabet 13, 16
    phonetic alphabet 13
    pictographs 5, 8
    Sabean script 35
    Sanskrit 31
Wu 8
Wuhan 94
Württemberg 80
Wu Sangui 69
Wu-su 26
Wu-Sun 28
Wuzhong 8
Wyatt's rebellion 58
Wyoming 84

X

Xerxes I 14, 18, 20–22
Xhosa 72, 79
Xia dynasty 8
Xiamen 69
Xiang Yu 26
Xianyang 26
    Terracotta army 26
Xianyun 8
Xianzong 43
Xiao 26
Xilotepec 55
Xinjiang 69, 79, 94
Xiongnu 24, 26, 28, 32
Xixia 45, 49
Xizang 69, 113. See also Tibet,
    Tibetans
Xoconochco 55

Y

Yahua Huyacac 56
Yaka 86
Yakesa see Albazin
Yakut 40, 45, 51, 57
Yalta conference 107
Yalu river 93
Yamamoto, Isoroko 108
Yamana 50
Yamassee 73
Yamato period 32, 36, 50
Yan 8
Yan'an 106
Yang 43
Yang Jian 43
Yang Jian see Sui Wendi; Wen
Yangshao culture 8

Yangtze river 43
Yangtze valley 4, 8
Yaqui 70
Yarmuk River, Battle of 37
Yasuda 93
Yaxchilán 39
Yaxuná 39
Yaya-Mama religious traditions 17, 19
Yayoi culture 24, 28, 32, 36
Year of Four Emperors 29
Year of Revolutions (1848) 80, 82
Yeha 35
Yellowknife 70, 73
Yellow river 8
Yellow Sea, Battle of 93
Yeltsin, Boris 119
Yemen 35–37, 45, 51, 57, 59–60, 64,
    67, 71–72, 76, 99, 104, 106, 109,
    118, 121
    People's Democratic Republic of
    116, 118
    see also Aden
Yemen Arab Republic 116, 118
Yezdegird III 37
Yi dynasty 50
Yi Songgye 50
Yoaltepec 55
Yokohama 93
Yom Kippur War 115–116
Yong 8
Yopitzinco 55
York 41, 46
Yorktown, Battle of 75–76
Yoruba states 35, 72, 76, 89
Younghusband, Colonel 83
Young Italy movement 80
Ypres, Battles of 98
Yuan Shikai 94
Yucatán 17, 39, 45, 55, 81
Yue 8, 22
Yuenan (Annam) 69
Yue Qi 19, 22, 24, 26, 28, 31–32
Yugoslavia 99, 101, 109–110, 116,
    119, 121
    Balkan pact 101
    civil war 119, 121
    Tito 107, 110
    World War II 105, 107
Yu the Great 8
Yukon 84, 97
Yuma 70
Yunnan 43, 69, 94
Yurok 70
Yuxian 8

Z

Zacatec 62, 70
Zacharias, Pope 38
Zagros mountains 4
Zaire 116–117
    civil war 116–117
    see also Belgian Congo; Congo
Zama, Battle of 23–24
Zambia 116–117, 121. See also
    Northern Rhodesia; Rhodesia
Zangid emirate 47–48, 51
Zanzibar 89, 96
    Sultanate of 71–72, 82, 86
    see also Tanzania
Zapata, Emiliano 81
Zapatistas 112
Zapotec civilization 17, 19, 22, 24, 32,
    39–40, 45, 51, 55
Zayyanid caliphate 51
Zedekiah 15
Zeebrugge, Battle of 98
Zen Buddhism see Chan Buddhism
Zeno 21, 33–34
Zenobia 30
Zenta, Battle of 68
Zhanjiang 94
Zhao 26
Zhejiang 69
Zheng 8
Zheng Cheng-gong (Koxinga) 69, 71
Zheng (First Emperor) see Shi
    Huangdi
Zheng He 57
Zheng Jing 69
Zhili 69
Zhou dynasty 8, 13, 19, 22, 26
Zimbabwe 51, 117, 121
    Great 51
    independence 121
    see also Rhodesia; Southern
    Rhodesia
Zionist movement 92, 104
Zobah 15
Zoroaster 18, 27
Zoroastrianism 27, 44
Zulu, Zululand 82, 86, 89
    empire 79, 82
    mfecane 82
Zuni 62, 70
Zurich, Battle of 77